MW01089803

TAIWAN UNDER JAPANESE COLONIAL RULE, 1895–1945

TAIWAN UNDER JAPANESE COLONIAL RULE
1895–1945

History, Culture, Memory

EDITED BY

LIAO PING-HUI AND DAVID DER-WEI WANG

Columbia University Press
New York

CUP wishes to express its appreciation for assistance given by the Council
for Cultural Affairs, Taiwan, ROC, and the Chiang Ching-kuo Foundation for
International Scholarly Exchange toward the cost of publishing this book.

Columbia University Press
Publishers Since 1893
New York Chichester, West Sussex
Copyright © 2006 Columbia University Press

Library of Congress Cataloging-in-Publication Data
Taiwan under Japanese colonial rule, 1895–1945 : history, culture, memory /
edited by Liao Ping-hui and David Der-wei Wang.
p.   cm.
Includes bibliographical references and index.
ISBN 0–231–13798–2 (cloth)
1. Taiwan—Civilization—20th century. 2. Taiwan—Civilization—Japanese influences.
I. Liao, Binghui. II. Wang, Dewei.
DS799.712.T38   2006
951.24′904—dc22
2005051798
∞

Columbia University Press books are printed on permanent
and durable acid-free paper.

This book was printed on paper with recycled content.
Printed in the United States of America
c 10 9 8 7 6 5 4 3 2

This book is dedicated to the memory of Huang Wu-chung (1949–2005),
writer, editor, collector, scholar, teacher, and pioneer
in Taiwan's New Literature movement fieldwork.

CONTENTS

FIGURES

TABLES

PREFACE

This volume brings together essays by leading scholars in the field to offer comparative perspectives concerning Taiwan under Japanese colonial rule. While much has been written about the European and American empires, scholars tend to pay less attention to the development of colonialism and modernity in East Asia. As editors, we hope to fill in these gaps as we focus on Japan's first and also its last colony — Taiwan — concentrating on such issues as language and ethnic identity, colonial policy and cultural hegemony, art and literature, historical memory, and postcolonial aftermaths, among others.

This volume originated in a conference held at Columbia University in March 2001 on the topic of history, culture, and memory; the event was sponsored by Taiwan's National Science Council, with additional generous support from the East Asian Languages and Cultures Department and the Chiang Ching-kuo Foundation at our host institution. Over the years we have tried to expand on the scope of the original conference by inviting submissions from experts in related fields; during the course of the relatively long editorial process we have also benefited from reader feedback. The publication project was made possible largely through an endowment from Taiwan's Cultural Affairs Council.

In addition to thanking these institutions and friends, we wish to express our gratitude to a number of people. Jennifer Crewe, editorial director of Columbia University Press, was most congenial and patient in arranging the publication of this volume. Robert Christensen read through most of the papers and offered indispensable comments, but Kerri Sullivan went even further in rendering them more readable and coherent. Attia Miller, Juree Sondker, and Philip Leventhal were helpful in facilitating the publication process of the book. Several of Ping-hui Liao's research assistants at Taiwan's National Tsinghua University not only carried on voluminous correspondence with contributors but also undertook the difficult task of reformatting the papers; in this regard, Yi-yun Liu, Phaedra Wang, Yu-wei Lin, Ching-huan Lin, Po-kai Hsu, and Tsai-ling Hsu deserve special mention.

Finally, we would like to dedicate the book to the fond memory of the late Huang Wu-chung, a true friend and colleague in Taiwan studies, who supported our project from the start in his capacity as director of cultural commission but regrettably passed away prematurely at the age of fifty-seven on April 7, 2005.

— Liao Ping-hui and David Der-wei Wang

TAIWAN UNDER JAPANESE COLONIAL RULE, 1895–1945: HISTORY, CULTURE, MEMORY

LIAO PING-HUI

This volume represents a first attempt to discuss colonialism and modernity in East Asia from the perspective of subjects very different from those that continue to occupy the attention of postcolonial scholars—with the probable exceptions of Gayatri Spivak and of Prasenjit Duara, who have recently begun to map territories that did not attract European imperial forces.[1] For many reasons Taiwan should regularly be featured in comparative colonial and postcolonial studies, but, re-grettably, it has managed only to catch the eye of social scientists, who have considered Taiwan alternately as a window on China, a cold war bastion of freedom and modernization against communism, a minidragon of an economic miracle, a "state without nationhood," the first Asian country to hold a general election, and a cosmopolitan albeit marginal Chinese polity whose "renegade province" status has been renegotiated in terms of "one state, two systems" since the hand-over of Hong Kong in 1997.

Occasionally there are book chapters and even entire books in English or other Western languages devoted to contemporary Taiwan arts and literature, but they are written in a third-world context or try to respond to global-local cultural dialectics within the framework of modernism, nativism, and Asian popular or visual culture. They tend to bypass the historical period most consequential to the formation of the complex identity of the island: Taiwan under Japanese rule, from 1895 to 1945.

Together with Pescadores, Taiwan was ceded to Japan in perpetuity on May 8, 1895, by the Qing in the Treaty of Shimonoseki 馬關條約, which marked the defeat of the Manchu empire in the first Sino-Japanese War. For the fifty years that followed, Taiwan was considered a second son and a younger brother of Okinawa, thus holding a special place in the heart of the emperor in Tokyo.

As a Japanese colony Taiwan is arguably distinct in several ways. First of all, Taiwan was the first and also the last of Japan's colonies. It underwent at least four stages of colonialism under Japanese rule: assimilation as the main policy from 1895 to 1919, integration from 1919 to 1930, differential incorporation and coercion from 1930 to 1937, and the subjugation (kōminka 皇民化, literally meaning "Japanization" or "imperial subjectification") and mobilization of "imperial subjects" to participate in the "holy" war in Asia from 1937 to 1945.[2]

Taiwan was considered an extension of Japan, and shared a common script and race. Taiwan may not have been unlike other colonies when viewed at the turn of the last century from the comparative perspective adapted by Benedict Anderson.[3] However, the destinies of individuals and collectives rendered Japanese colonialism in Taiwan relatively unique. It is to address the complexities of this colonial experience and legacy that essays by leading scholars in Taiwan, Japan, and the United States have been collected here.

Between 1895 and 1945 China was in the hands of warlords, while Japan was beginning its modernization processes and launching its Greater East Asia Co-Prosperity Sphere 大東亞共榮圈 colonial project. When Taiwan was cut away from China and handed over to Japan, Taiwanese intellectuals formed a strategic identity to forge strong ties with China, developing cultural as well as economic relationships that resisted Japanese domination. This dual structure of affiliating with both China and Japan, an imaginary fatherland and a new colonial power, was made more complex by the fact that Japan had been influenced by Chinese culture since the Tang dynasty. Unlike the French in Indochina or the Dutch or British in south Asia, who discriminated against the natives because of race, color, religion, and so on, Japanese colonizers in Taiwan often invoked their common cultural roots, highlighting the fact that the Japanese and the Taiwanese shared the same language and ethnicity. As a result, not only did Taiwanese identities—cultural, ethnic, and national—waver between Chinese and Japanese (and in so doing continue to puzzle scholars like Leo Ching 荆子蓉 and Melissa Brown, among others),[4] but the mixed reactions to the Japanese colonial legacy continue to be evident in local politics as well as in cultural production, with opinions ranging from former president Lee Tenghui 李登輝's open hailing of Japan as a benevolent "motherland" to the totally different views of Taiwan's colonial and postcolonial histories expressed by filmmakers such as Hou Hsiao-hsien 侯孝賢 or Wu Nien-chen 吳念真.

A few critics have examined the Japanese colonial empire in comparison to its Western counterparts. Lewis H. Gann, for example, noted that Japan resembled Wilhelmian Germany in its modernization strategies and the recruitment of military and civil officers from among colonial elites, but lacked the evangelical or romantic inspirations that informed British and French missionaries.[5]

Over the years several books have appeared that address the economic development, educational system, and social movements that characterized Japanese colonialism in East Asia. While seminally revealing, they have seldom discussed colonialism and modernity in the region from a transnational perspective and have focused instead on Japan's southward advance or on Taiwan as the site in which Japan forged its colonial and orientalist scholarship. In fact, Taiwan presents an interesting if not unique case in the comparative study of colonial modernity, especially when juxtaposed with the situations of Korea, Manchuria, Hong Kong, and Shanghai.

Taiwan was a Japanese colony for fifty (or in some accounts fifty-one) years, while Korea was a Japanese colony for only thirty-five—1910–1945 (or 1905–1945, if we take into consideration the fact that Korea was made a protectorate of Japan in 1905). The major difference between the typical Taiwanese and Korean reactions to the Japanese colonizers has been succinctly summed up by E. Patricia Tsurumi: "By the end of the Japanese period, Taiwanese of all classes had become enthusiasts for the sports and games introduced along with Japanese education," whereas in Korea "to be educated was to be anti-Japanese."[6] To this day, the Korean intellectual scene remains dominated by the attempted purge of Japanese influences.

In the case of Manchuria 滿州國, the Japanese occupation was ultimately the result of prior international control of the territory gained through negotiations with China over the transfer of Russian rights and through entanglements with diplomatic ties with United States and other European countries. Manchuria's primal role in the Qing empire as a sacred place of origin and its transnational borderline stance were issues that Japanese rulers tried to appropriate, while Taiwan, in contrast, had been a Qing settlement frontier and an island populated by a "barbaric" race and illiterate fishermen. The ways in which Japanese colonial officers promoted "aboriginality" functioned in different directions in the two colonies: in Manchuria, aboriginality was associated with authority and authenticity (see the work of Prasenjit Duara mentioned above), while in Taiwan it was related to backwardness and mobility. In the case of Shanghai, Japan was one of a dozen foreign forces occupying parts of the city, making it a semi-colony and a contested site for a transnational capital with hybrid albeit cosmopolitan lifestyles being imported.

TAIWAN AT THE EDGE OF EMPIRES

The differences between the experience of Taiwan and that of other Japanese colonies owe a great deal to place, history, and material culture; to elucidate them let us briefly review the history of the island. Traditionally, the Han Chinese considered Taiwan to be a barren island in the east occupied by savages and pirates.[7] One origin for the term *Taiwan* is reported to be the derogatory *dong-fan* 東番 ("eastern barbarians"); an earlier and more reliable literary source indicates that it might have been derived from *dai-yuan* 大員 ("big circle" or "big shelter").

When Taiwan was taken by the Qing dynasty from the hand of Koxinga 國姓爺's grandson in 1683, Emperor Kangxi 康熙 was at first quite opposed to making Taiwan a part of his empire, because neither gain nor loss was at issue. Some two hundred years later, the Qing government finally recognized the crucial role of Taiwan in its battles with British and French forces.

Between 1885 and 1892, under the leadership of Liu Ming-chuan 劉銘傳, who followed Shen Bao-jen 沈葆楨 as governor, the island underwent its initial modernization. In those seven years, public education systems and light industries were introduced, a railroad was constructed on the west coast between Keelung and Hsinchu, and telegram and postal services were established. During the Japanese occupation (1895–1945), the infrastructure was further developed, and political stability and economic growth accelerated the modernization processes.

Before the name *Ilha Formosa* was suggested by the Portuguese sailors in 1544, Taiwan had received practically no geographical recognition in the region except for being occasionally misidentified as the Ryukyus or labeled Little Ryukyus 小琉球. This geographic marginality, however, has proven both disabling and enabling in the formation of Taiwan's modernity and identity. Kept separate by the Taiwan Strait and physically detached from the mainland, Taiwan has on the one hand been capable of maintaining its own cultural autonomy, while on the other hand it started its modernization process relatively late, and partly as a response to European and Japanese imperialisms. In fact, Taiwan has gone through several colonial stages—Dutch conquest (1622–1661), Chinese settlement (1661–1895), Japanese occupation (1895–1945), and Nationalist "recovery" (after 1945).

Various ethnic groups came to the island at different times and brought with them diverse racial and cultural heritages. Taiwan's different communities and their historical experiences have been made more complex by this hybrid ethnic and genealogical mixture. The predominantly Malayo-Polynesian aboriginal population, for instance, suffered the most: they were first forced to change religious beliefs, then pushed into the mountains, made to serve the Japanese as soldiers, compelled to adopt and use the official language, Mandarin, and finally driven by poverty to come down from the mountains to eke out a living through cheap labor or prostitution. Other groups, among them the southern Fukienese, Hakka, and mainlanders, underwent differing experiences of subjectification, depending largely on the relative dates of their immigration to the island. These differences complicated the accessibility or applicability of symbolic or cultural capitals, since some were more informed and powerful than others, while in terms of the fluidity or multiplicity of layers of everyday life, each group seemed to have its own distinctive ways of achieving maximum instrumentality and efficacy when exposed to possible entanglements with the practices of others.

When negotiating from the margin and with multiple heritages, Taiwanese intellectuals under Japanese rule often became *bricoleurs* in mixing transnational codes and forces to their own advantage, especially in the case of overseas students in Tokyo between 1915 and 1935, who seemed to have no difficulty in accepting both the Chinese and the Japanese modernization experiences. From the late 1910s onward, hundreds of students went to study in Japan each year. According to *Taiwan Sōtokufu gakuji nenpō* 台灣總督府學事年報, these overseas students came from three major counties: for 1926 (see vol. 25: 50–51), Taipei 129, Taichung 326, Tainan 184; and for 1928 (see vol. 28: 46), Taipei 184, Taichung 499, and Tainan 371.

Inspired by the 1911 revolution in China and the liberal spirit of the 1912–1925 Taishō 大正 era, Taiwanese students in Tokyo formed the *Qifahui* 啟發會 ("the Society of Enlightenment") in 1918 and began to publish the first Chinese-language journal, *Shin minpō* 新民報, in 1920, at which time the society was renamed the New People's. In addition to inviting important Chinese intellectuals, among them Dr. Sun Yat-sen and Liang Qichao 梁啟超, to visit Taiwan and to speak on the subject of a new China, members of the society tried to appropriate what they had learned from Japan about the social constructs of its emerging alternative modernity, such as the concept of *tōyōshi* 東洋史 (Oriental history), new science, cultural difference, socialism, and so on.

In many ways, Chinese and Japanese modernity projects were able to leave their semantic traces on modern Taiwanese public culture, particularly in the print media, art movements, lifestyles, social thought, and political institutions. Taiwanese intellectuals of the period often used Japanese as a means to acquire skills and knowledge for modernization, while at the same time cultivating their Chinese identities in order to resist Japanese influences. Sometimes the partial hybridization of the two modernity projects ended up producing morally ambivalent sentiments in the colonizers as well as in the colonized, as in the cases of many artists discussed in this volume.

In order to highlight the complexity of using material culture in considering the colonial or transnational agencies of art education and exhibition, we can consider some specific incidents that might have contributed to the shifting of public and private lives in terms of historical contingency, irony, and moral luck.

Rather than highlighting "hybridity," "catachresis," "conviviality," etc., with the focus on critical acts of cultural appropriation on the part of postcolonial subjects, we may be better off looking at the ways in which individuals, as moral and political agents, are affected by their experiences traveling across national borders, and are constituted by and constitutive of the cultural institution of a specific historical moment. The dynamics of travel and cultural translation is not necessarily played out in the form of an ambivalent chronotopical lag between metropole and colony, of tensions between the often polarized discursive positions of dwelling and traveling (or, to follow Edward W. Said's terminology, of the "potentate" and the "traveler"). A useful example of such individual experience involves the life and work of Ishikawa Kinichirō 石川欽一郎 (1871–1945) in the Japanese period.

COMPARATIVE STUDY IN NATURE AND CULTURE: TAIWAN VERSUS JAPAN

According to legend, the place is hell, but once one sees it, it becomes heaven. This was my first impression of Taiwan. It is an island of very beautiful forms and colors, and it is pleasing.

Thus wrote Ishikawa Kinichirō in a piece for *Taiwan jihō* 台灣時報.[8] Ishikawa was at the time back in Tokyo, recalling fondly (though on many other occasions quite ambivalently) his encounter with the island and his experiences there as a colonial officer and, later, as an art teacher at the Taipei Middle School.

Within months of his arrival in Taipei, Ishikawa published an essay in a leading newspaper, *Taiwan nichinichi shinpō* 台灣日日新報 (January 23–24, 1908), entitled "Watercolor painting and Taiwan landscape," in which he commented:

Some twelve years after the Occupation, most Japanese still have very vague ideas of Taiwan. I wish I could at least let these unfortunate folks know a little bit about Taiwan landscape which is to be rated Japan's No. 1. Perhaps people may regard my view of Taiwan as Japan's No. 1 landscape to be an overstatement, but I deeply believe so and I am sure my friends and colleagues in Tokyo would come to the same opinion if they should have the chance to see the landscape here. If we compare Taipei with any Japanese city, Kyōto seems to bear the closest resemblance. Tamshui River is equivalent to the Kamogawa, while Mounts Datun and Guanyin surrounding Taipei city are very commensurable to Mounts Hiei and Atago. Yuanshan evokes an image of Yoshida and Shirakawa. Luchou is very much like the neighborhood of Sagano. The Gutin district of southern Taipei reminds me of Fushimi of southern Kyōto. So many similarities are revealed that it is difficult not to form analogues and allusions. However, Taipei's colors appear more beautiful, with red roofs, orange walls, and green bamboos, contrasting strongly against the viridescent tree leaves. Can we imagine such serene and solemn scenery of sublimity in Japan? Under the blue sky Taiwan shines even more brightly.[9]

In 1926, eighteen years later, however, Ishikawa said this of the same subject: "Bright as it is, the Taiwan landscape lacks nuances and doesn't present subtle details to a second look."[10]

Though much touched by Taiwan's sublime landscape, he felt somehow discontented with its insufficient mystery, its melancholic beauty: its lights and colors were simply too focused and sharp, with little shade, tone, spirit, enigma, or puzzling detail. In sum, it was too boisterous and exorbitant to be generic or profound.[11] By no means systemic or even serious, Ishikawa's comments on the landscape varied over the years of his Taiwan sojourn, as detailed by Yen Chuan-ying 顏娟英's comprehensive and nuanced account in this volume. During his life there, from 1907 to 1933, Ishikawa witnessed changes in the history of colonial policy as well as in cultural identity and memory in relation to the Japanese colonial legacy, and his personal experiences here encapsulate Taiwan's historical changes, cultural identity formations, personal emotions, and memory under Japanese rule.

Ishikawa Kinichirō was a teacher of Japanese at the Taipei Middle School (part-time from 1907 to 1916,) and Taipei Normal School (full-time from 1923 to 1933). Self-taught and dedicated to Japanese nationalism, Ishikawa was at an early stage strongly influenced by modernism, particularly English impressionistic and realistic landscape watercolors. In his home country he was not very active and was thought to be a conservative artist belonging to the rather popular school of naturalism of the Meiji 明治 period of the 1910s. In the Japanese imperial army, however, Ishikawa was better known as an officer and an interpreter who bravely engaged the Chinese (1900) and the Russian armies (1904–1905) in battles for the Japanese rule of Manchuria.

In October 1907 Ishikawa was made an interpreter for the colonial governor-general in Taiwan. He moved to the island and became a part-time art and language teacher at Taipei Middle School. During those nine years in Taiwan, he was in many ways an ambivalent teacher and colonizer. In some of the watercolors done in the period, he glorified the conquest of the native in colonial encounters. He toured the island widely, in order to be able to recall in realistic detail his exotic memories of aborigine peoples and objects, but he was also involved in the founding of the Lan-tin Tea Klatch to promote cultural exchange and to get other Japanese artists and officers interested in Chinese and Taiwanese art and literature. He even organized a 1914 public exhibition of his artworks, one of the first in Taiwan art history.

Despite his accomplishments as an artist who made use of impressive local knowledge, Ishikawa was still primarily an officer and a colonizer, as manifested not only by his watercolors but by the appearance of the colonial governor-general at the exhibit. Of course, for Ishikawa, a product of—and participant in—the Japanese imperial era, art was an ideal agency of domination and redemption. In those days, the governor-generals and their staff were mostly high-ranking military officers who supported the policy of suppressing and of eventually assimilating local people.

The situation had changed, however, when Ishikawa made his second visit to Taiwan. In September 1923 Ishikawa's Tokyo home was destroyed by a major earthquake. A one-time colleague, then principal of the Taipei Normal School, sent him a telegram saying that he would be welcome to return to Taipei to undertake a full-time teaching position. Now without a family, Ishikawa decided to accept and thereafter spent another nine years in Taiwan.

The intellectual milieu in 1923 was different from that of the previous decade. The colonial policy had changed when civilians—rather than admirals or generals—like Hara Kei 原敬 and Den Kenjirō 田健治郎 assumed power as prime minister or cabinet members. In fact, the death of the seventh governor-general, Lieutenant-General Akashi Motojirō 明石元二郎, in October 1919 gave Prime Minister Hara Kei the opportunity to make the reforms in both Taiwan's and Korea's governing structures that he had long favored. The reforms were easier to carry out after the administration of Gotō Shimpei 後藤新平, who had directed colonial policy toward localization and incorporation. Hara Kei was then able to appoint Den Kenjirō as Taiwan's first civilian governor-general (1919–1923) to implant his reform programs in the colony.[12] These men managed to survive political struggles first by doing remarkably well in the colonies—particularly in Taiwan—and then by overcoming their domestic opponents when the latter made mistakes in their responses to riots in the colonies. Under the edict of integration and equality designed to make the colonized useful subjects to the Japanese emperor, the arts and humanities were increasingly emphasized as a means to tame the Taiwanese. Prince Hirohito of Japan visited Taiwan in 1923 and openly expressed his satisfaction with the relatively localized art education.

Just before the earthquake that destroyed his former home, Ishikawa had returned from a tour to Europe, where he had been deeply impressed by the salons, art exhibits, and art institutions of Paris. When he returned to Taipei in 1923, Ishikawa found himself in a different ambiance; his approach to art education switched from British and Japanese ways to a more French orientation and greater emphasis was put on outdoor interactions with the environment. To facilitate his teaching, he translated Japanese art textbooks into Chinese and supplied local equivalents wherever necessary.

As Taipei Normal School was a major college for future teachers, Ishikawa's influence on local artists was strong, even though his ties with Japanese politicians were undercut by his work as a civilian and a teacher. Like other Japanese artists—Shiotzuki Tōhō 塩月桃甫, for example—Ishikawa tried to protect his Taiwanese friends and students from political persecution. His students often depicted him as participating in, if not leading the way for, a collective effort to improve the quality of modern Taiwan art. Together with Taiwanese and Japanese friends, he founded various art associations, among them the "Taiwan Watercolors" (1927), the "Graduate Institute of Western Painting" (1929), and "Studies in Taiwan Art" (1930). Several students—such as Lan Yin-ting 藍蔭鼎 (1903–1979) and Hung Rui-lin 洪瑞麟 (1912–1997)—later became outstanding watercolorists.

Ishikawa might not have been as active or even have had a significant impact on modern Japanese art—especially the so-called local-color souvenir painting—if he had stayed in his home country. However, because of his early-twentieth-century travels and translations, he was able to be part of an alternative modernism that was being developed in a transnational pan-Asian and global-local cultural dialectics. The timing of his return to Taipei was crucial. If he had returned earlier, he would still have been a colonizer and a painter in the naturalist tradition, instead of an advocate of the new French art and a friend to local artists. Several transnational factors contributed to Ishikawa's ambivalent and benevolent roles in those years. The unexpected earthquake that shook his house and his livelihood; his recent tour around Europe and his exposure to contemporary French painting; the warm welcome he received from his friends in Taiwan and his position as a civilian and an art teacher; the emergence of Taiwanese artists and a cultural elite that began to win recognition in Japan; new developments in Korea and Manchuria that forced Japan to readjust its colonial policies—all these factors helped shape his new identity.

Since 1910, the landed gentry, especially those from Taichung county in Taiwan, had eagerly sent their children to Japan to acquire modernization skills and knowledge. In 1915 they helped establish in Taichung the first middle school for Taiwanese. One year before Ishikawa returned to Taipei, the "Association for Culture" 文化協會 was founded in Taichung to introduce ideas that would blend both Japanese and Chinese modernity projects. Each season in the cities and countryside, members of the association gave a variety of lectures, seminars, concerts, and plays before huge audiences. At first the association represented a moderate political and cultural opposition by the elite against the colonial regime. Gradually, with an increasing number of students returning from Japan, new trends in socialism and democracy were vigorously advocated and embraced by farmers and the working class, until the association was forced to go underground in 1930.

Unfortunately, 1930 also saw the disastrous Musha aboriginal uprising and the unprecedented violent suppression carried out by the Japanese colonial government, with the Japanese military and police—numbering up to 1,306—supported by 1,048 Han Taiwanese and 331 other aborigines in cracking down on the "rebel" Mona Rudao 莫那魯道 and his followers. It was reported that during the battles 87 aborigines were decapitated, while 85 were shot, 171 died in bombings, and

296 hanged themselves to avoid humiliation. The tragic incident and its outcome shocked politicians and intellectuals in both the colony and in Japan. Harsh criticism in the local newspapers pushed the colonial government to reinstate coercive administrative measures that forced the alternative media to go underground, thereby replacing its prior peaceful albeit differential incorporation policy with that of strategic suppression and relocation.[13]

The material culture that Ishikawa consequently confronted in 1923 and thereafter was different from that of 1907. Even Ishikawa himself was a different person after the earthquake and his grand tour of Europe. We can see this in several of his paintings—for instance, his portrait of the famous tower built by Koxinga after he had defeated the Dutch. Whereas had he earlier tended to be a distant observer, he was now more engaged. He picked particular settings and asked his students to accompany him in portraying the landscape as if it were part of the self. As a result, he left behind numerous pictures of local subjects and some scholars claimed he had become an integral part of modern Taiwan art.

TAIWAN UNDER JAPANESE RULE

Ishikawa's diaspora experience in Taiwan transformed in many ways his art career and his cultural affiliation. With many people like Ishikawa traveling back and forth between the metropolis and the colony during this formative period, the relationships of Taiwan with Japan and China became more complicated. As Wu Chuo-liu 吳濁流 has noted in his novel *Asia's Orphan*, the Taiwanese were having difficulty developing a distinctive sense of cultural belonging, of defining themselves as either Chinese or Japanese. The ambivalent cultural as well as ethnic identification thus fractured Taiwanese imaginations of comradeship and citizenship in relation to Japan and China, and was made worse by the disastrous tragedy of the February 28 Incident in 1947 when the KMT government used force against the local people after taking over the island.

The lingering effect of the Japanese colonial legacy, among other complications, has left a great number of Taiwanese unwilling to come to terms with the "one nation, two systems" proposed by the PRC, and Taiwan has become, in the words of Melissa Brown, "a global hot pot" of transnational conflicts and a divisive issue involving China, the United States, Japan, and indeed many other Asian countries.[14] It is imperative, therefore, to consider the construction of Taiwan's national and ethnic identity from a trans-Asian perspective, and to reexamine Taiwan's most consequential period under Japanese rule.

This volume is divided into four sections: historical and theoretical case studies on colonialism and modernity; colonial policies and cultural change; visual culture and literary expressions; and postcolonial reflections and their aftermath.

On the problems of rethinking postwar Asian political and intellectual history, Wakabayashi Masahiro 若林正丈 leads us expertly through the minefield of Taiwan studies in contemporary Japan. He opens with the comment that until recently "the Japanese colonial period received relatively little academic attention," while Yao Jen-to 姚人多 then follows him by elaborating on the Taiwanese colonial period as a unique case that complicates our understanding of postcolonial theory. Wakabayashi singles out the structures of limitation in postwar–East Asian historiography and suggests ways to bridge national historical approaches and new area studies in considering Japanese imperialism/colonialism in Taiwan and the modern history of Taiwan. He challenges traditional conceptions of political institutions and of class structure by pointing out ways in which a Taiwanese cultural elite composed of landlords and educated gentry helped advance the Japanese colonial project while the impact of modernization on the local majority was limited.

Employing a Foucauldian conceptual framework, Yao then directs attention to land surveys and census issues. In contradistinction to the dominant postcolonial practice, which emphasizes discursive struggle and resistance, he highlights the roles of numerology in Japanese colonial policy in terms of land measurement and management. According to Yao, statistics, census, and numbers in fact constituted the core of Japanese governmentality over the Taiwanese subjects and lands.

Fujii Shōzō 藤井省三 gives an overview of the long history of colonialism in Taiwan, with missionaries, settlers, and occupants ranging from the Dutch to the Japanese. Against the background of a wide variety of colonial experience, Taiwanese intellectuals and writers managed to find their cultural expressions and to voice their internal strife. Fujii thus deepens our understanding of such critical notions as "domination" and "resistance" by examining the assimilative policies of the Japanese colonial government and their impact on the formation of Taiwanese identity. Drawing on work by Benedict Anderson and Jürgen Habermas, Fujii argues that because of the Japanese national language system during Japanese rule, the percentages of school attendance and knowledge of the Japanese language reached a high level in the colony. By the 1930s, literacy in colonial Taiwan had been achieved by three million two hundred thousand people, thereby paving the way for Taiwanese cultural nationalism.

Liao Ping-hui 廖炳惠 also refers to Anderson's seminal work on print capitalism in tracing the development of media culture in Taiwan after the Japanese colonial government decided to introduce newspapers and periodicals in 1896. For Liao, what started as official colonial policy could have become, in the process of reception and reproduction, a politically useful tool for local cultural criticism and resistance against the regime. His essay singles out the transnational, anamorphic, and cosmopolitan character of the news media in the constitution of a public sphere from 1896 to 1945.

In part 2, Ts'ai Hui-yu Caroline 蔡慧玉 discusses the issue of modernity and colonial subjectivity by employing Foucault's notion of governmentality to ask: How did the Japanese manage their administrative work? Tsai points out that the number of bureaucrats in colonial Taiwan at any one time was relatively small. The Japanese colonial administration was made possible by turning the civil bureaucracy into a disciplinary and modernizing institution.

Kawahara Isao 河原功 examines the effect of censorship on Taiwan literature by discussing the material in *Taiwan Shuppan keisatsuhō* 台灣出版法, considered the most reliable source available regarding permission to publish books in the colony. When social movements in Taiwan reached a peak in 1930, the Japanese authorities built up vigilant defenses not only against literary and nonliterary activities in the colony but also against proletarian literature in Japan. As a consequence, bookstores in Taiwan learned to avoid stocking books that were likely to be banned, and they imported only the cheapest, salable books; they maintained their monopoly on imported books by signing special contracts with schools, and shunning competition with rivals. Censorship thus distorted and misled the literary movements of the period.

Fong Shiaw-Chian 方孝謙 presents a distinctive picture of Japanese colonial administration and of censorship, with the interesting observation that the Japanese rulers achieved a weak hegemony by polarizing ordinary Taiwanese as "Chinese" and Taiwanese elites as "moderns." As a result, the subaltern Taiwanese had a residual folk culture that helped keep them from being totally assimilated, while cultural elites were preoccupied with "Japanization." Drawing on valuable documents and information of the period, Fong complicates our understanding of the ways in which hegemony operated in Taiwan's colonial experience. He challenges conventional notions of censorship and domination by drawing attention to the nuanced processes of identity and modernity formation.

Four papers on literature and the arts are found in the third section. Using a framework of repressed modernity, Huang Mei-er 黃美娥 argues that Taiwanese traditional writers managed to develop canonical revision and cultural criticism at a time when the old literature was supposedly in decline and being replaced by modern expressive cultures. But "old" literature was still very influential and debates between the old and the new modes of expression lasted for two decades—from the 1920s to the 1940s. In 1937, for example, when the Japanese colonial government banned the use of Chinese in newspapers, traditional writers still had no difficulty exercising their rights of expression. Even writers who normally thought of themselves as representatives of new literary movements, among them Lai Ho 賴和 and Yang Shouyu 楊守愚, chose to organize poetry clubs to compose classical poems to articulate their ideas and thoughts.

Of writers belonging to the so-called new literary movements, Peng Hsiao-yen 彭小妍 singles out Yang Kui 楊逵 and Liu Na'ou 劉吶鷗 as a contrastive pair who produced critical responses to colonialism and the predicament of identity. Both writers were born in Tainan in 1905—and that might be the only thing they had in common. They came from two distinct classes—one a laborer's son and the other the son of a rich landlord—and they eventually moved in different paths: the former became a proleterianist and the latter a neo-sensationist. Both writers were indebted to the realist movement of the time, but it was their junior colleague Lu Heruo 呂赫若 who became involved in the famous "*kuso*-realism debate" with the Japanese author Nishikawa Mitsuru 西川滿. Chie Tarumi 垂水千惠 reads these two authors against each other to reveal differences in their conceptual framework, literary style, and impact. Interestingly, both writers used *fūsui* 風水 (fengshui) as a general theme, and it was a subject with which such landscape painters as Ishikawa Kinichirō were preoccupied.

Yen Chuan-ying describes the transformation of landscape aesthetics by this important art educator and traces his indebtedness to both contemporary Japanese art theory and comparative geography.

In the final section, five scholars trace the transition from the colonial to the postcolonial period; they raise questions concerning the politics of cultural representation, the demands of redeeming the Other, and reinventing tradition. The playwright Wu Man-sha 吳漫沙 is discussed in the first essay by Shimomura Sakujirō 下村作次郎; the subject is the production, edification, and circulation of different versions involving a Taiwanese aboriginal girl's tragic story. Shimomura studies the formation and reception of the tale that arose during the *kōminka* movement, first told by the Japanese writer Murakami Genzō 村上元三, and later elaborated by the Chinese artist Wu Man-sha. The tale then traveled back and forth between the metropolis and the colony along a circuitous route. Nishikawa Mitsuru's quasi-ethnographic discourse is a most revealing case in mapping the two-way traffic between Japan and Taiwan.

Faye Yuan Kleeman 阮斐娜 closely reads Nishikawa's work to identify the ways in which colonial encounters generated the need to produce and possess the knowledge of others. In Kleeman's view, Nishikawa interwove authentic cultural information with more personal observations that are focused on Taiwanese women and are colored by the author's background as a Romantic poet. In the final analysis, the resulting eroticization of the exotic served the interests of colonial ideology: it feminized the colonized culture.

Three essays in this final section examine the recovery of Taiwan by the ROC Nationalist government in 1945. It was commonly held that the Taiwanese were to be re-sinicized after fifty years of Japanization. Huang Ying-che 黃英哲 gives a nuanced and sensible account of the relocation of culture, while Douglas Fix details the difficult transition in terms of rebels and riots. When Taiwan was handed over to the ROC, Chen Yi 陳儀 took on the responsibility for decolonizing the minds of the Taiwanese people. The re-sinification process, however, had begun much earlier with the emergence of Chinese columns in popular newspapers like *Fenggyuebao* 風月報(Wind and moon news). They were administered by an intermediate figure and a disciple of Lu Xun 魯迅, Xu Shoushang 許壽裳, who had been better known as a Lu Xun expert in Japan and who later worked in the KMT regime to promote literacy in modern Chinese. Even Governor Chen Yi himself had been trained in Japan in his early years. The relocation of cultural identity was thus more complex than usually assumed, and the bias against the Taiwanese as the colonized inferior Other was constantly challenged not only by local people but by those who came from China to take over the island.

According to Fix, some three hundred incidents of assault and theft were reported by the colonial police bureau between the announcement of Japan's surrender to the Allied Forces and the formal takeover of Taiwan in the fall of 1945. Fix rigorously analyzes the quantitative and qualitative data, and reevaluates demands for various kinds of restitution and reimbursement as partial responses to Japanese colonial rule and, soon, to Chen Yi and his government made up mostly by the newcomers from China.

Finally, Wu Micha 吳密察 singles out two instances of colonial and postcolonial Japanese ethnology to discuss the construction of Greater East Asia Co-Prosperity Sphere discourse as associated with the journal *Minzoku Taiwan* 民族台灣. Wu raises the question of the local perspectives in such a presumably autonomous and comparative study in pan-Asian societies and cultures.

Between 1945 and 1947, Taiwanese intellectuals openly criticized corruption in the KMT government, and tensions finally exploded in the February 28 Incident of 1947, which marked a turning point in the historical transformation of Taiwan's national and ethnic identity. Since then, the Japanese colonial legacy has been ambivalently reevaluated in postcolonial revisions, and it is within this complex psycho-social structure of identification that a political leader such as Lee Tenghui has questioned whether Taiwan should be considered to be Chinese. The essays collected here offer nuanced and sensible accounts that reveal intricate intertwined histories and tortured memories. They certainly shed new light on postcolonial and transcultural studies.

NOTES

1. Gayatri Spivak highlights the complexity of East Asian colonial modernity and postcolonial histories in her book *Other Asias* (Blackwell, 2003), while Prasenjit Duara examines the transnational trajectories of Manchukuo and the East Asian modern in *Sovereignty and Authenticity: Manchukuo and the East Asian Modern* (New York: Rowman and Littlefield, 2004).

2. *Kōminka* refers to the Japanization or imperial subjectification project launched in the 1930s to turn Taiwanese into colonial subjects loyal to the Japanese emperor; throughout the book the term is rendered in different ways to reflect its significance and impacts.

3. Benedict Anderson, "Empire/Taiwan," paper presented at the international conference "Reimagining Taiwan: Nation, Ethnicity, Narrative," Taipei, December 20–21, 2003.

4. See Leo T. S. Ching, *Becoming Japanese: Colonial Taiwan and the Politics of Identity Formation* (Berkeley: University of California Press, 2001); Melissa Brown, *Is Taiwan Chinese?* (Berkeley: University of California Press, 2004).

5. Lewis H. Gann, "Western and Japanese Colonialism: Some Preliminary Comparisons," in *The Japanese Colonial Empire, 1895–1945*, ed. Ramon H. Myers and Mark R. Peattie (Princeton: Princeton University Press, 1984), 497–525.

6. E. Patricia Tsurumi, "Colonial Education in Korea and Taiwan," in *The Japanese Colonial Empire, 1895–1945*, ed. Ramon H. Myers and Mark R. Peattie (Princeton: Princeton University Press, 1984), 293–294.

7. See Emma Jinhua Teng, *Taiwan's Imagined Geography: Chinese Colonial Travel Writing and Pictures, 1683–1895* (Cambridge, Mass.: Harvard University Press, 2004), 60–68.

8. Ishikawa Kinichirō, "Taiwan fengguang de huixiang [Reflections on Taiwan's landscape]," *Taiwan shibao* [Taiwan Times] (June 1935), 53; translated in Chuen-yin Yen, ed., *Landscape and Inscape: Anthology of Modern Taiwan Art Documents (Fengjing xinjing: Taiwan xiandai meishu wenxian daodu)*, 2 vols. (Taipei: Xiongshi, 2001), 1:54–56.

9. Translated in Yen, *Landscape and Inscape*, 1:30.

10. Translated in Yen, *Landscape and Inscape*, 1:34.

11. Yen, *Landscape and Inscape*, 1:41.

12. Peter Duus et al., *The Japanese Wartime Empire, 1931–1945* (Princeton: Princeton University Press, 1996); and especially in Tsurumi, "Colonial Education," 289.

13. Leo Ching, "The Musha Rebellion As Unthinkable," paper presented at Japan's Fifth Annual Taiwan Studies Conference, Kansei University, Japan, May 10, 2003.

14. Brown, *Is Taiwan Chinese?*, 1–2. Also see my review essay entitled "Envisioning a Nation," *Tsinghua Journal of Chinese Studies* (summer 2005).

PART 1

Rethinking Colonialism and Modernity

————————————————

HISTORICAL AND THEORETICAL CASE STUDIES

[1]

A PERSPECTIVE ON STUDIES OF TAIWANESE POLITICAL HISTORY

Reconsidering the Postwar Japanese Historiography of Japanese Colonial Rule in Taiwan

WAKABAYASHI MASAHIRO

It is well known that in the 1980s, when Taiwan underwent significant political changes, Taiwanese history suddenly began to generate a great deal of domestic and international academic interest. Particularly in Taiwan considerable time and material resources have been invested in this field of study.

It is worth noting that prior to this, however, the Japanese colonial period received relatively little academic attention (Chang 1983:15–16). This was the result of both historical and political factors. Most historians of the subject have hurriedly explored merely the frequent shifts of political rulers and have come to the premature conclusion that Taiwanese history is but "the process of development of peoples of various ethnic origins coming from outside" (Wu 1994:229–230). Such historical evaluations of Taiwan actually privilege the viewpoint and the values not of the ruled but of the ruling class. Given this historiographical trend, we can say that Taiwanese history in the period of Japanese colonization has been "doubly exploited" (Wu 1994:230), in that "Taiwan" in the period of Japanese colonization was forced into a passive position and identified as merely a stage in the "Empire's South Advance" (*teikoku nanshin* 帝國南進). In the postwar period, Taiwan's assigned passive position was taken for granted and depreciated as such in historical reviews. As a result, scholarly inquiry into this period was hindered.

Studies on the history of Taiwan in the colonial period were undertaken primarily by Japanese academics in the postwar period. Although there sometimes are expressed in Japan's mass media certain opinions that retrieve the past from the viewpoint of the colonizer, only a few such discourses exist, and these among academics. More common, however, are scholars who have tried hard to over- come such viewpoints and historical perspectives. These studies, however, are far from being proof that "Taiwanese history" has itself become a recognized aca- demic subfield in history. This is because the previous scholarship constitutes, in practice, the study not of the modern history "of Taiwan itself," but of "Japa- nese imperialism/colonialism in Taiwan"; that is, Taiwan in this period *is* only insofar as it is a part of the modern history of "Japan." To be sure, studies regard- ing Japanese imperialism/colonialism in Taiwan are not without significance. In- deed, they form a necessary element in the designation of modern Taiwanese history as a legitimate field of study. However, the currently received approach cannot be considered a comprehensive history of modern Taiwan: several Tai- wanese scholars have made these observations (Wu 1983:18; Ka 1983:25). What then is the study of modern Taiwanese history? What kind of relationship should operate between the history of modern Taiwan and the history of Japanese im- perialism/colonialism in Taiwan?

I begin this paper with a critical revisit to my previous work and attempt to evaluate what analytic mode such a historical approach might have and to what extent a constructive relationship could be bridged between the two approaches mentioned above. The resource materials for the establishment of my working hypothesis are mainly my own works; thus, this paper has to be subtitled "recon- sidering the postwar Japanese historiography of Japanese colonial rule in Taiwan."

POLITICAL DYNAMISM IN THE TRANSFORMATION OF COLONIAL POLICIES: HARUYAMA MEITETSU'S "MODERN JAPANESE COLONIAL RULE AND HARA TAKASHI"

I have addressed the necessity of having a research perspective on the political history of Japanese colonialism in a co-authored book, *The Political Development of Japanese Colonialism*, published in 1980 (Wakabayashi and Haruyama 1980). This perspective was fully developed in Haruyama's article "Modern Japanese Colonial Rule and Hara Takashi 原敬 [also known as Hara Kei]" therein. Here I would like to review Haruyama's work in order to determine in what ways this perspective might be useful to the current study.

Before we wrote *The Political Development of Japanese Colonialism*, studies of colonial politics focused mostly on individual cases of resistance or on the nation- alist movement in history. Perhaps we can put the issue in bolder, if not too reduc- tionist, terms: these previous studies adopted an analytic framework that, based on a theory of binary oppositions, pitted "Japanese imperialism" against "the colo- nized people." This focus on opposition generated two noteworthy results. First, these studies equate Japanese imperialism with the on-site colonial authority (the colonial authority that encounters, first hand, the resistance and opposition of the colonized). Second, these studies, mostly based on Marx's theory of class, have identified the colonized people with different class categories and have treated these classes' interactions with the on-site colonial authority. In so doing, these studies amount to a history of oppression and resistance that, as diagrammed in figure 1.1 below, is based on an old analytic mode: the problem consciousness as it relates to studies of the political history of Japanese colonialism.

a. Japanese imperialism = the on-site power, the immediate colonial government

⇩ ⇧

b. the colonized people = the comprador, the national bourgeoisie, the peasants, industrial labor

FIGURE 1.1 Old mode: The problem consciousness in studies of the political history of Japanese colonialism

Haruyama has deviated from this old analytic mode. In previous studies based on the old mode, "although each individual colonial institution was mentioned respectively," wrote Haruyama, "studies of the entire system of Japanese colonial rule are still lacking." Thus, Haruyama continued, "this lack hinders our understanding of what political position the on-site colonial rule occupied within the entire Japanese state system," and "it seems as though there is no relation between the development of Japan's mainland political structure and its colonial rule" (Haruyama 1980:1). In order then to clarify the dynamic relations between the political history of Japan proper and the wider history of imperial Japan, Haruyama focused on a political leader, Hara Takashi, who played a significant role in the development both of mainland Japan's political history and of imperial Japan's colonial history. Haruyama's resulting findings are diagrammed in figure 1.2.

A longtime leader of the political party Rikken Seiyukai 立憲政友會 (in existence since the late Meiji period), Hara Takashi transformed modern Japan's political system from an oligarchy to a party-based democracy (see level *a* in fig. 1.2). He skillfully managed to play the politics of compromise and resistance with the existing oligarchy and helped install party-politics in the accepted political system. Through his efforts, Japan witnessed the successful establishment not only of the Imperial Diet (*teikoku gikai* 帝國議會) as a state institution in which political parties functioned, but also of a party-based system that played a key role in the

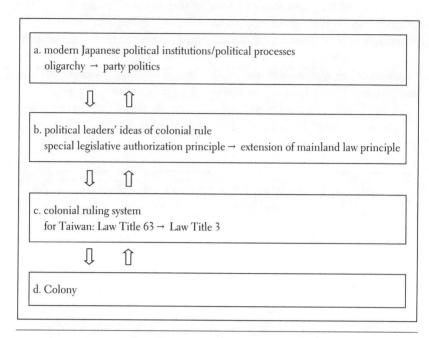

FIGURE 1.2 New mode: The problem consciousness in studies of the political history of Japanese colonialism

entire state system. In the midst of the Taisho period, Hara Takashi became prime minister of the first civil, party-organized cabinet in Japanese modern history. Immediately after he organized his Seiyukai cabinet, the First World War ended, and half a year later the March 1 Independence movement took place in Korea. Japan's colonial ruling system experienced the profound effects of these events.

In his article, Haruyama traced the development of Hara Takashi's beliefs and political career and found that, long before becoming a politician, he had developed a model for Japanese colonial rule that was later to be called "the principle of the extension of mainland law" (*naichienchoshugi* 内地延長主義). Haruyama also discovered that Hara Takashi stood firmly by this idea when he engaged in debates over colonial policymaking within the Meiji government.[1] On the difficulties surrounding the policy of the special authorization of colonial jurisdiction (the "Problem of Law Title 63," *rokusan mondai* 六三問題—that is, the controversy over the special legislative authority assigned to the governor-general of Taiwan), and on the problem concerning colonial administrative institutions (whether the military or the civil governor should be in charge of the colonial administration), Hara Takashi, with his party's support, used political means to reduce the degree of legal exceptions (for example, authorization of the governor-general's special legislative authority) and of political exceptions (for example, the appointment of a military governor-general) in the already oligarchized colonial administration. In short, Hara embraced colonial administration insofar as it operated within the domain of the mainland's party-politics. After becoming prime minister, he put an end to the appointment of the military governor-general and reduced the scope of the legislative authority that had found its way to the governor-general (as seen in the enactment of Law Title 3).

Through this case study of political leader Hara Takashi's ideas and career (the *b* level of fig. 1.2), Haruyama was able to clarify the dynamic relation between the political system of modern Japan and the colonial ruling system (the *c* level of fig. 1.2). In other words, the new analytical framework that Haruyama adopted (fig. 1.2) identified the existence of specific political dynamics in the formation of colonial policy in modern Japanese history — an insight exceptionally lacking in the previous framework (see fig. 1.1), which was based on binary oppositions. Hence, Haruyama has helped create a new conceptual space for studies of modern Japanese colonialism, a space in which the history of the mother country's politics becomes closely tied up with the history of modern Taiwan.[2]

There is, however, no doubt that such research belongs to "the field of modern Japanese history, not the field of Taiwanese history" (Wu 1993:18). As mentioned above, Haruyama's intent was to overcome the received notions — the unexamined assumptions — of the old research mode, which he did, but he has not explored the new research mode in detail. For this reason, we can say that Haruyama's work has contributed mostly to a modification of the exterior environment and thus of the historical context that informs studies of Taiwanese political history during Japanese colonial rule.

PRACTICING A CONTROL SYSTEM THROUGH EXCHANGE AND MEDIATION: A WORKING HYPOTHESIS REGARDING THE "TAIWANESE NATIVE LANDED BOURGEOISIE"

In the light of the discussion in the previous section, I would like here to explore further the *d* level in figure 1.2, that is, questions concerning the local structure of colonial politics in Taiwan. I articulated a working hypothesis regarding "Taiwanese native landed bourgeoisie" (*Taiwan dōchaku jinushi shisan kaikyū* 臺灣土著地主資產階級) in two case studies: "The Colonial State and Taiwanese Native Landed Bourgeoisie: Questions Surrounding the Establishment of the Taichung Middle School, 1912–1915" (Wakabayashi 1983b) and "Taisho Democracy and the Petition for the Establishment of a Taiwan Parliament: Japanese Colonial Politics and the Taiwanese Anti-colonial Movement" (Wakabayashi 1983a).

The former is an examination of why the local apparatus of the Japanese empire (that is, Japan's governor-general government in Taiwan), after violently suppressing riots that had spread over the entire island and after establishing the administration in the early stages of colonization, had no choice but then to negotiate with the Taiwanese upper classes in order to maintain power. The colonial government regarded the Taiwanese upper classes, which I conceptualized as the "native landed bourgeoisie," as an important target of its political policies.

In exploring this working hypothesis about the existence of Taiwan's "native landed bourgeoisie" to better depict the nature of colonial politics, I looked at Taiwanese educational demands as seen in the movement to establish the Taichung Middle School, which lasted four years, from 1912 to 1915, and which was once described by Yanaihara Tadao as "the first shot of the Taiwanese Nationalist movement" (Yanaihara 1988:190). In order to draw out the contours of the political process surrounding the establishment of the Taichung Middle School in 1915, I highlighted Governor-General Sakuma Samata's decision to accept the Taiwanese upper classes' petition for "the establishment of a middle school in Taiwan on the same level as middle schools in domestic Japan." It is interesting to note that, in the end, this educational petition was only partially realized after negotiations with Tokyo.

The second case study listed above incorporated both Haruyama's research findings and the idea of a "native landed bourgeoisie" in Taiwan and is an exploration of the political process underlying requests to mainland Japan for the establishment of a Taiwan parliament (1921–1934). This movement for home rule was in fact a civil rights movement launched by Taiwanese intellectuals on Japan's domestic central political stage in a period called the *Taisho Democracy*, which spanned from the mid-Taisho period to the early Showa period.

Before we look at the case studies in detail, let us consider what is meant in this working hypothesis by the designation *native landed bourgeoisie*. The term refers to those members of Taiwan's social upper classes (including property owners like local strongmen, gentry, landlords, and wealthy businessmen) who could trace their roots to the former late Qing period and who were historically transformed "during the process whereby Japan consolidated its colonial domination—that is, a process whereby Japanese political power and capital imposingly launched a top-down colonialist modernization project" (Wakabayashi 1983b:6). There were two historically significant conditions for the emergence of this "class": the uneasy securing of public safety in the seventh year of Japanese rule and the land survey commission's goal of clearing up the complicated landed property relationships that characterized regulation of the island's cultivated land.

In securing the public safety, the native militias, which were privately patronized under the local strongmen, were either destroyed by superior Japanese military and police forces or disarmed. Those gentry who had received higher honor-titles in the Qing civil examinations, and who felt a deep commitment to the Chinese dynastic order, had mostly returned to China in the moment of territo-rial transition in 1895. Those local gentry who stayed in Taiwan lost the political influence that had been guaranteed by the Qing authority in local societies.

The land survey commission eliminated the existing custom of shared land-ownership (the one-land, two-owners issue, *ichiden ryōshū* 一田兩主) by rescind-ing the patent (*ta-tsu* 大租) rights, by ensuring that land ownership would go to the actual proprietors (*hsiao-tsu* holders 小租戶), and by protecting their right to collect land rents. Although the Japanese colonial government through these policies, along with setting up an official monopoly, determined the colonial reve-nue, the actual landowners, who were natives of the island, received legal pro-tection of their landed property from the new regime (the Japanese colonial gov-ernment) and were thus allowed to keep collecting high rents from their peasant tenants.

This confluence of policies and practices allowed Taiwan's upper classes from the late Qing period to become the people who "had fame and property" in the early period of Japanese colonization; in other words, their economic bases were protected by the new regime, and to some extent their social influences were also maintained accordingly (Wakabayashi 1983b:7–8).

What kind of relationship did this native landed bourgeoisie cultivate with the Japanese colonial government? In the first place, the Japanese authority stripped the old Taiwanese leading stratum of their ostensible power and authority. How-ever, the Japanese authority was unable to root out the existing economic bases of these Taiwanese and even paradoxically protected their interests by means of modern law and public safety. Furthermore, the Japanese colonial authority in Taiwan also took advantage of these people who possessed "fame and property" by using their social influence to smooth Japan's domination of the island. This means that the colonial authority, when deciding where in the hierarchy to as-sign individual Taiwanese, judged them in relation to their property, fame, and degree of willingness to collaborate. These criteria were used to assign Taiwanese to the specific positions, for example, of village head, local district administrative assistant, and *hokō* leader, each of which was designed to assist the local police station. Even more prestigious was the position of district consultant in the local administration, the holders of which would be invited as honored participants to official banquets and nominated as receivers of the "gentry certificate" (*shinshō* 紳章) or other honors.

By so doing, the new Japanese colonial authority successfully took the place of the old Qing mandarins in redistributing the resources of power and authority. It was of course a prerequisite that these men of "fame and property," as receivers of the privileges and honors authorized and distributed by the Japanese, must pose no threat to Japanese rule. However, to maintain their influence in local society,

these men also had to accommodate local interests and sentiments. This adjustment to local interests took place in the context of colonization and might turn,
at certain moments, into a source of opposition to Japanese rule. Moreover, in
their adjustment to the modernization that took place under colonial rule, some
of these privileged Taiwanese learned afresh the essence of colonial constraints on
their sociopolitical potential and, in response, gradually accumulated economic
power by collecting higher rents from their tenants and by investing in their children's education.

No matter how the colonial authority constantly created conditions of dependency—perhaps best exemplified in the nature of the "collaborationist gentry"
(gōyō shinshi 御用紳士)—we can still see the possibility of resistance, as a force
emerged from within this upper social stratum to limit the growth of the native bourgeoisie itself and even to oppose Japanese domination (Wakabayashi
1983b:9).

This research hypothesis, depicting the nature of the native landed bourgeoisie, thus formed the basis for the two case studies mentioned above. In the first
(1983b), my investigation of the establishment of Taichung Middle School, I
looked up board members, donators, and honor-title holders in the *Taiwan retsu-
shin den* (臺灣列紳傳, a collective biographic dictionary of people who received
gentry titles from the colonial government), and discovered that the majority of
petitioners involved in the movement to establish the school were basically native
landed bourgeoisie. The colonial archive and *Taiwan nichinichi shinpō* (臺灣日
日新報, Taiwan daily news) provided resource materials to show the decision-
making process underlying the establishment of the school. I argue that Taiwan's
governor-general, Sakuma Samata, was at that time commencing what he considered to be the most significant task within his purview, the "Five-Year Project for
the Pacification of the Savage Territory" (which became, in fact, a series of wars
of conquest waged against the indigenous tribes in northern Taiwan's mountainous regions). Sakuma was critically in need of assistance from the native landed
bourgeoisie because of the difficulties arising from fiscal problems and the mobilization of military aid. In return for their assistance, Sakuma promised to establish a middle school "on the same level as middle schools in domestic Japan."

In my other study (1983a), dealing with the petitionary movements for the
establishment of a Taiwan parliament, I examined this movement's strategy: that
is, how the colonized people sent their petition to the mother country's parliament, and how their demand for civil rights and home rule was dealt with in
the domestic politics of the Taisho Democracy period. This is indeed a research
perspective echoing the above-mentioned "politics of Japanese colonialism." In

addition, this paper deals with the hypothesis concerning the native landed bourgeoisie in order to analyze the movement's participants and their relationship to Japanese colonial power. By rigorously investigating the petitioners' social backgrounds and the leaders' activities (preserved in the files on this petition movement in the colonial police's archive), I proved that Taiwanese "new intellectuals"—who were the first generation of modern intellectuals, Han Taiwanese, and alumni of Japanese colonial education—had teamed up with some native landed bourgeoisie to make possible this petitioning movement (Wakabayashi 1983a:24–35).

Through these analyses, I was able to extract from the history of this movement insights into the colonial politics on the island and pointed out that "such historical phenomena (the coalition between the new intellectuals and some native landed bourgeoisie) tell us that, under the conditions of (a) the further development of Japanese monopoly capitalism, (b) modern ideologies' influences over the offspring of native landed bourgeoisie, and (c) a growing nationalistic consciousness, the native landed bourgeoisie, who had earlier played the role of political and economic mediators in the context of Japanese colonization, disintegrated; some became new emerging compradors and some Nationalists" (Wakabayashi 1983a:38–39). Thus, "the Japanese authority had encountered an important two-fold political problem in its effort to strengthen Japan's relationship to its colony in the post–First World War era: (a) how, given time constraints, to handle the oppositional force that emerged in the petitionary movement for the establishment of a Taiwan parliament and (b) how to reorganize the colonial ruling structure in which these oppositionists were still made to play the mediating role for colonial rule. This was a crucial political problem that, in the post–First World War era, plagued the on-site colonial authority as it attempted to restructure the unity of Japan and its colony. This problem surfaced because the colonized representatives directly petitioned the Japanese central government, demanding that a Taiwan parliament should be established in the colony to meet the best interest of the colonized. Consequently, this problem did not concern merely the colonial government in Taiwan" (Wakabayashi 1983a:38).

My two papers led then to findings on two different levels. On the first level, there exist some relationships of political exchange between, on the one hand, the governor-general government that constituted the on-site representative of Japanese colonialism in Taiwan and, on the other hand, native Taiwanese men of "fame and property" in Taiwanese society. One can see this exchange relationship operate in the establishment of Taichung Middle School, for which the colonial government had answered Taiwanese educational demands in exchange for fiscal and manpower assistance at a time when the Japanese colonizers were commencing a war of conquest against the mountainous indigenous tribes. This was surely an uneven exchange. When the school was eventually established, the Taiwanese had to raise funds by themselves, and what they got from the colonial government in return for their assistance during the war was merely a validating piece of paper. (Even the promise that Taiwanese middle schools would be "on the same level as middle schools in domestic Japan" was not kept.) What the colonial government offered according to this give-and-take condition was but a *rent* in the form of pronouncements naming these Taiwanese franchisees in the colonial monopolistic businesses.[3]

In addition, the exploration of the petitioning movement for the establishment of a Taiwanese parliament reveals that this movement was made possible through a coalition between the new intellectuals and some native landed bourgeoisie. The explanation of this historical phenomenon hinges on the fact that Taiwanese elites as men of "fame and property" were not satisfied with their exchange relation with the colonial authority. There were thus some native elites who rejected this exchange relationship, which had been defining the nature of their own power, and who took a stand that aligned them with Taiwan's social masses. This stand in turn facilitated the emergence of Taiwanese anticolonial nationalism.

I suggest that these findings can contribute to the development of a working hypothesis concerning the politics of Japanese colonialism in Taiwan. That is, a ruling mechanism exists at the receiving end of the exchange relationship between the Taiwanese colonial government as the on-site manifestation of Japanese imperial power and the native Taiwanese men of "fame and property" in Taiwanese society. This mechanism and its relation to a number of component elements in Taiwanese society constituted the primary content of politics in colonial Taiwan. It goes without saying that what the Japanese authority required was not solely money from those men of "fame and property" but also—and of greater importance—their attitude of collaboration. The colonial authority hoped that, through collaboration among these Taiwanese, enacted in certain exchanges, Taiwanese elites' social credits could be used to influence the common people.

The aim set by the colonial authority was to transform this collaboration into a force that would render the common colonized people more obedient. And if this aim were not easily achieved, their collaboration would at least render the Taiwanese silent subordinates. In short, the colonial government intended to use the exchange as a way to effectively impose the prestige of the colonial power throughout Taiwanese society. The mediating mechanism of exchange must also have functioned well in Japan's use of the Hoko system to facilitate the establishment of a full-scale police force network. It can be thought of as a mechanism that controls through exchange and mediation.

On the second level, men of "fame and property" who embraced, or were compelled under pressure to embrace, this control mechanism of exchange and mediation were native landed bourgeoisie. To be sure, I have some reservations over the use of this conception, and regard it only as a working hypothesis. Whether these people's real conditions of existence can be correctly described by a category such as *native landed bourgeoisie* requires more empirical research.

However, there are some points still to be emphasized here. First, the Japanese authority wanted to incorporate some people who possessed resources of various sorts into the control mechanism of exchange and mediation; whether these people truly wished to participate in that relationship is another issue. The situation in fact differed greatly from case to case. Some of those who possessed "fame and property" did not get involved, whereas some who were in the process of accumulating fortunes collaborated extensively with the Japanese. This is an easily overlooked problem if approached from only the perspective of the Japanese ruler, as found in the existing formulation of "Japanese colonialism *in* Taiwan," but is nonetheless a necessary consideration in studies of Taiwanese modern political history. The choices for the elites were many: to be involved or not, to be a volunteer or to be forced, to quit or to stay, to silently reject this exchange and mediation mechanism or to openly attack it—all these choices and their accumulation constituted, quite precisely, the politics of the Taiwanese people in the colonial context.[4] To explain the process in which specific people made their own "fortune" and "fame" under colonial rule is to study a set of circumstances from the perspective of political economics or political science, while to inquire into the real conditions of existence as they are revealed in the accumulation of these individual choices is to study the politics of colonialism from the perspective of historical studies (say, studies in political history). These two perspectives stand in relation to each other but are not identical.

A second point is that the definition of what were considered "useful" resources to be managed in the control mechanism of exchange and mediation changed over time, as Japanese colonization progressed. For example, people involved in the exchange mechanism used the social resources that they had acquired through tradition as a tool with which to effect colonial education reform; and their children, possessing new cultural resources that they had received from this new colonial education, encountered this already politicized exchange mechanism and actively contended with it—and what had been regarded as exchangeable in the give-and-take relation of their fathers' period was no longer current.

Both I (Wakabayashi 1983c) and Wu Wen-shin (1992) have pointed out that it is exactly this changing set of terms that well explains why, from the 1920s onward, the Taiwanese new intellectuals heavily criticized personnel problems in the local administration. As the content of useful resources changed over time, the choices Taiwanese people made in the exchange and mediation mechanism changed accordingly. In 1935 the colonial government put a limited local election into practice and, by co-opting native elites through this election system, restructured local politics. This development also reflects the changes taking place in the conditions of exchange between the colonial authority and the native society.

As Taiwan's economic development continued and more people received a formal education, the population involved in the exchange mechanism became larger in number. As more and more Taiwanese people who possessed certain resources became candidates in this one-to-many exchange relation that was managed by the colonial government as a means of social control, the give-and-take mechanism eventually faltered. As a result, another mechanism—by control through participation and incorporation—featuring more objective standards by which to filter its targets was later introduced. And, indeed, when this "later time" met the moment in which the colonial government had to mobilize people on behalf of the war effort, this mechanism came to operate at an unprecedented level (Mitani Taichirō 1993).

PRACTICING THE CONTROL SYSTEM THROUGH DISCIPLINING AND TRAINING: WAKABAYASHI MASHAHIRO'S "THE IMPERIAL VISIT OF THE CROWN PRINCE TO TAIWAN IN 1923" (1992A)

The state form that, in prewar Japan, governed colonial Taiwan was a constitutional monarchy, that is, an emperor-system state (*tennōsei kokka* 天皇制國家), in which the emperor himself represented the mighty sovereign. Throughout the history of this emperor-state's rule over colonial Taiwan, the emperor never visited (*gyoko* 行幸) the island. Only the crown prince (*tōgū* 東宮), the Taishō emperor's prince Hirohito (later the Showa Emperor), had visited (*gyokei* 行啓) his colonies of Taiwan and Karafuto. Because the residents of Karafuto were in fact early Japanese immigrants, Crown Prince Hirohito's Taiwan visit (*Taiwan gyōkei*, 臺灣 行啟) in April 1923 can be seen as the only instance in which a member of the imperial royalty visited the colony. Crown Prince Hirohito was in fact a prince regent, because the Taisho emperor was ill at the time, and this situation had made Hirohito the *de facto* superior human symbol of the emperor-system. His imperial visit thus became the most important political event in the ruling of a foreign people at the time (Wakabayashi 1992a:87–88).

The imperial visit conducted by the crown prince as the human symbol of the emperor-system was composed of a series of imperial rituals and ceremonies (*Tennō gishiki* 天皇儀式). This consisted of rituals of mutual presence, performance, and even demonstration between the imperial human symbol and his subjects. In "The Crown Prince's Taiwan Visit of 1923 and the 'Principle of the Extension of Mainland Law' (Naichigenchoshugi)" (1992a), I tried to decipher the symbolic structure of Crown Prince Hirohito's 1923 Taiwan visit by depicting the interaction in rituals and ceremonies between the emperor and his subjects as a scene of demonstration in which the emperor-system state exercised its symbolic power over the colony.

According to my research, this performance by the emperor, rarely seen in the history of Japanese colonialism, can be divided into three components: (1) a display of the ordering—the "authorization sealing" in which the "sacred stamp" is appended to the existing order; (2) a display of the civilizing—the "symbolic moral" of the human symbol of the emperor-system in which the emperor and the imperial family are seen as "the very foundation of civilization, the mighty origins of institution and learning," enhancing the desirable Japanese process of modernization (that is, the emperor's tour will provide the resources for imposing the civilizing mission on his subjects); and (3) a display of the mystifying—the crown prince's official visit to the Taiwan shrine at which he worshiped an imperial kinsman, Prince *Kitashirakawanomiya Yoshihisa*, who had commanded, and died in, the war to conquer Taiwan in 1895; he also granted an gracious imperial remission to the prisoners of the Hsilai An incident (*Seiraian jiken* 西來庵事件). Each one of these invoked a corresponding set of symbolic actions, known as *the rites of passage, the rites of conquering,* and *the rites of reconciliation.*

Among these three symbolic ritual actions, the rites of reconciliation were more about the colonizer's unilateral self-deception as a way to legitimize the past history of colonization; the rites of passage and the rites of conquering referred to the techniques used to directly connect the colonial society to the imperial political order. For example, for the rites of passage, when the crown prince visited an administrative institution, the hierarchical order that already existed in that institution would inevitably be emphasized in the spatial formation of the participants. The human symbol of the emperor-system presented himself in front of the display and appended his sacred seal to this order.

For the sacred seal to be granted in this way, however, the would-be approved display had to be indisputably in order. Thus, members of that institution were required to be kept in a state of high morale, and, by relying upon the suppressive force of police and public safety organizations, any undesirable action in the scenario of the display of the ordering had to be prevented in advance. Here one sees that the emperor, as the symbolic leader, and his visit functioned to approve the already well-regulated order. Some of the local Taiwanese leaders who possessed "fame and property" participated, or were forced to participate, in the system of *control through exchange and mediation,* as the previous section detailed, and were then relegated to subordinate positions in the display's hierarchical spatial formation. Indeed, these participants stood still, waiting to "welcome" (*hōgei* 奉迎) the coming of the crown prince (Wakabayashi 1992a:102).

In the rites of conquering in the "display of the civilizing," the crown prince—who embodied "the very foundation of civilization, the mighty origins of institution and learning"—was displayed in front of the masses (*minshū* 民眾); at the same time, the masses were gathered together and subjected to the powerful gaze of the crown prince (as the human symbol of the imperial sovereignty). Because the prince's gaze could be downwardly conferred, the masses were also exposed to the gaze of many "middle instructors"; playing the role of the so-called little emperor (*shotennō* 小天皇), they were components in the hierarchy of the state apparatus who presented and re-presented the emperor's gaze on every level. In order to be displayed before the gaze of the sovereign, the masses had to faithfully embody the empire's "loyal and virtuous subjects" (*shūryōshinmin* 忠良臣民). The body of the masses was not a physical body as such but a culturally defined body, always wearing certain exterior garments and participating in certain rituals and ceremonies; the middle instructors worked to discipline and to train them. In the ritual of the display of the civilizing, schoolchildren and students were purposefully and systematically made to be present under the disciplining and training gaze of the crown prince (Wakabayashi 1992a:103–107).

My article about the crown prince's colonial visit discusses the ways in which in the moment of 1923, through the crown prince's imperial visit, the Japanese emperor-system state symbolically recolonized Taiwan (see also Fujutani 1994: 57). By including a sectional drawing of this visit's power mechanism, I was able to demonstrate the existence of the *control system through exchange and mediation.* At the same time, there was another form of control mechanism. This mechanism, not aimed primarily at the resourced elites but at all the inhabitants of the island (yet strategically targeting schoolchildren and students), made itself effective through the disciplining and training gaze delivered by the emperor and his agents (as the middle instructors) in a hierarchical top-down register. I call this the *control system through disciplining and training.*

Takashi Fujitani has demonstrated that the imperial-Nationalistic rituals and ceremonies — of which the emperor played the prime protagonist — designed and promoted by the Meiji leaders constituted a form of *domination of the gazing.* Two ways of visualization can be found in this domination of gazing: "the emperor of modern Japan becomes the transcendental subject by receiving the centripetal gaze from all his subjects to whom the existing internal differences was surmounted; on the reversing gaze, all national subjects in the empire, without considering their differences in places or classes, become visible under the sole, dominant and suffusing gaze of the emperor." And, "if such attempt of *visualization* accomplished, the modern national subjects as being constantly self-positioned as the monitored objects would consciously emerge from the interior" (Fujitani 1992:141).

What we have called the *control system through disciplining and training* is the extension to the colony of what Fujitani calls *the domination of the gazing in modern Japan.* How this extension was made possible is of course an issue in modern Japanese history. How the modern national subjects emerged, or did not emerge, over the course of this extension is a historical question of significance in both modern Japanese history and modern Taiwanese history. Under the operation of this control system through disciplining and training, to what extent, if any, was the Taiwanese people's "body" transformed into "Japanese subjects"?

Did the differences revealed in the colonial transformation have something to do with inhabitants' cultural and social differences (such as different ethnic backgrounds)? Can the interaction between the native cultures and this control system have successfully brought about the formation of the "Taiwanese identity"? If so, to what extent did it create modern Nationalistic subjects? All these questions should be investigated from the perspective of the modern political history of the Taiwanese people.[5]

CONCLUSION

The above review of Haruyama's work has enabled us to locate the difference between studies of political history that concern Japanese colonialism in Taiwan and studies of political history that concern modern Taiwanese political history. In a reexamination of two of my earlier articles I explored the mechanism by which ruling power was exercised in colonial Taiwan, identifying two forms of control: *exchange and mediation* and *disciplining and training*. Nevertheless, I am well aware that, in the study of modern Taiwanese political history, more than a few questions have yet to be answered satisfactorily.

To be sure, the mechanism of colonial control had more than these two forms; indeed, one other form of the control mechanism is clearly identifiable: the colonial authority's monopoly on violence, wherein punishment was exercised to keep the public order, and where the possibility of punishment was made visible and manifest. This control mechanism can be called *control through the mechanism of punishment and threat*. This is a necessary and intrinsic mechanism within the modern state's exercise of power and accordingly guarantees the effectiveness of the two forms of control mechanism reviewed above. Therefore, questions concerning the historical process according to which the Japanese monopoly on violence in colonial Taiwan took root, collapsed, and finally yielded to another political regime—in short, questions concerning the military history of the Japanese colonization of Taiwan—should be embraced as a subfield in modern Taiwanese political history.

The discussion above can be summarized in the table below.

If the viewpoints stated above can be used to effectively analyze Taiwan's political history under Japanese colonial rule, we should extend our analysis to the historical periods before and after the period discussed in this paper. That is, we should ask whether these three control mechanisms from the colonial period also existed in the late Qing period or in the postwar period. If not, was there any other mechanism that facilitated political control in these periods? When encountering such a control mechanism, what kind of resources did Taiwanese people use to negotiate with it? How did these negotiations then trigger a qualitative transformation of the control mechanism?

TABLE 1.1 Control Mechanisms in Colonial Taiwan

Control mechanism	Target	Institutions/ Means	Purpose
Exchange and mediation	Elites	Local administration, consulting institution, economic monopoly policy, etc./ Rent, distribution of authority	Manipulation of elite's collaboration, acquisition of nonelite's obedience, and silent subordination through elite's collaborationist mediation
Disciplining and training	All inhabitants (strategic focus on schoolchildren and students)	School education, Hoko system, etc./ Royal family's imperial visit, rituals, ceremonies, athletic gatherings, etc.	Creating the body of the imperial subject (*shinmin*) and disciplining its obedience
Punishment and threat	All inhabitants	Military force, police, prison system, etc./ Enacting penalty	Maintaining the public order

By asking questions like these, we may be able to achieve a proper understanding of historical continuity and discontinuity in Taiwanese political history. For example, we have asked how the economic transformation regarding foreign trade in Taiwan that took place during the rapid growth of the late Qing period changed the accepted power structure of society. Is there any difference between the dual clientism (Wakabayashi 1992b: chapter 3) or the dual structure of factional politics (Chen 1995: chapter 4) in postwar Taiwan under the Kuomingtang's party-state regime and *the control mechanism through exchange and mediation* in the Japanese colonial period? Such reflections on other periods could deepen our understanding of the nature of Taiwanese politics under Japanese colonial rule.

NOTES

*Translated from the Japanese text by Chen Wei-chi.

1. Immediately after Japan took over Taiwan in 1895, the Japanese government set up a new provisional organization within the cabinet, the "Bureau of Taiwanese Affairs." The bureau was under the direct control of the prime minister, Ito Hirobumi, and was aimed at setting some foundational principles for the rule of the colony. Hara Takashi, who then was vice-minister of foreign affairs, participated in this organization. He already had ideas on the project of Japanese colonial rule in Taiwan that were different from the principles already then in effect. He stated, "[We] should not treat Taiwan as a colony, even when there is some variety between Taiwan and Japan proper" and "The administrative institution in Taiwan

should be as close as possible to the mainland's, even to the point that there is no difference between them" (Haruyama 1980:23).

2. Wu Mi-cha has offered a concise introduction similar to Haruyama's to the historical studies that followed (Wu 1993).

3. One interpretation of the function of such rent posits that "the state apparatus can use all kinds of policy tools to create contrived rents, including state monopoly, charter policy, import quota, government's selective purchase, selective wealth redistribution, credit and foreign exchange preference, and so on; that is, the state apparatus can adopt selectively limitative or punitive legal regulations in order to enable a few producers to take advantage of markets and further expand their profits" (Chu 1989:139 140).

4. Wu Wen-shin's study of "social leadership" (1992) and the "family history studies" recently current in Taiwan—such as Chen 1992, Hsu 1992, and Huang 1995—give important insight concerning the issue of Taiwanese politics under Japanese colonization.

5. Both Fujitani's arguments (1994) and the findings of Taki Koji (1988)—on which I rely (1992a) for my understanding of "the gazing of disciplining and training" launched by the Tenno—are based on the theories of Michel Foucault.

REFERENCES

Chang Yen-hsien. 1983. "Introduction." Special forum on the review and prospect of the studies of the Japanese colonial period in Taiwan history: *Newsletter of Taiwan History Field Research* 26.

Chen Tsu-yu. 1992. "The Yen Family of Keelung and Taiwan's Coal Mining Industry Under Japanese Rule." In *Family Process and Political Process in Modern Chinese History* 2. Taipei: Institute of Modern History, Academia Sinica.

Chu Yun-han. 1989. "Monopoly Economics and Authoritarian Political System." In Taiwan Research Foundation, ed., *Monopoly and Exploitation*. Taipei: Taiwan Research Foundation.

Fujitani, T., trans. 1994. *Tennō Pageant: Toward a Historical Ethnography of Modern Japan*, by Yoneyama Lisa. Tokyo: NHK.

Haruyama Meitetsu. 1980. "Modern Japanese Colonial Rule and Hara Takashi." In Haruyama Meitetsu and Wakabayashi Mashahiro, eds., *The Political Development of Japanese Colonialism, 1895–1934: Its Ruling Institutions and the Taiwanese National Movement.* Tokyo: Japan Association for Asian Studies.

Haruyama Meitetsu and Wakabayashi Mashahiro. 1980. *The Political Development of Japanese Colonialism, 1895–1934: Its Ruling Institutions and the Taiwanese National Movement.* Tokyo: Japan Association for Asian Studies.

Hsu Hsueh-chi. 1992. "The Lin of Banqiao in the Japanese Colonial Period—A Study of Family History and Its Political Relation." In *Family Process and Political Process in Modern Chinese History* 2. Taipei: Institute of Modern History, Academia Sinica.

Huang Fu-san. 1995. "A Study on the Characters and Fates of Two Taiwanese Big Families: The Lin of Panchiau and the Lin of Wufong." Paper presented at the one hundredth seminar on Taiwan Studies, Lin Benyuan Chinese Cultural Foundation.

Ka Chi-ming. 1983. "Colonial Economics." Special forum on the review and prospect of the studies of the Japanese colonial period in Taiwan history: *Newsletter of Taiwan History Field Research* 26.

Lin Man-hung. 1988. "Trade and Social Economic Changes in the Late Qing Taiwan (1860–1895)." In Chang Yen-hsien, ed., *History, Culture, and Taiwan — Fifty Seminars on Taiwan Studies*. Banqiao: Taiwan Folkway Magazine Society.

Mitani Taiichirō. 1993. "Wartime System and Postwar System." In *Iwanami Seminar Modern Japan and Colony 8: Cold War in Asia and the Decolonization*. Tokyo: Iwanami Shoten.

Taki Kōji. 1988. *The Emperor's Portrait*. Tokyo: Iwanami Shoten.

Wakabayashi Masahiro. 1980. "Taishō Democracy and the Petition for the Establishment of a Taiwan Parliament." In Haruyama Meitetsu and Wakabayashi Mashahiro, eds., *The Political Development of Japanese Colonialism, 1895–1934: Its Ruling Institutions and the Taiwanese National Movement*. Tokyo: Japan Association for Asian Studies.

———. 1983a. "Taisho Democracy and the Petition for the Establishment of a Taiwan Parliament: Japanese Colonial Politics and the Taiwanese Anti-colonial Movement." In *A Historical Study of the Taiwanese Anti-colonial Movement*. Tokyo: Kenbun Shupan.

———. 1983b. "The Colonial State and Taiwanese Native Landed Bourgeoisie: Questions Surrounding the Establishment of the Taichung Middle School, 1912–1915." *Ajia Kenkyu* 29.4.

———. 1983c. "The Meaning of Mr. Huang Cheng-chung's 'Waiting the Opportunity.'" In *A Historical Study of the Taiwanese Anti-Colonial Movement*. Tokyo: Kenbun Shupan.

———. 1984. "The Situational Context of the Crown Prince's Visit to Taiwan in 1923." *Kyoyo Gakka Kiyo* 16:21–32.

———. 1992a. "The Crown Prince's Taiwan Visit of 1923 and the 'Principle of Extension of Mainland Law (Naichigenchoshugi)." In *Iwanami Seminar Modern Japan and Colony 2: Structure of Imperial Rule*. Tokyo: Iwanami Shoten.

———. 1992b. *Taiwan: Democratization in a Divided Country*. Tokyo: University of Tokyo Press.

Wu Micha. 1993. "Colonial Policy." Special forum on the review and prospect of the studies of the Japanese colonial period in Taiwan history: *Newsletter of Taiwan History Field Research* 26.

———. 1994. "The Acceptance and the Task of the Study of Taiwanese History." In Mizoguchi Yuzo, Hamashita Takeshi, Hiraishi Naoaki, and Miyajima Hiroshi, eds., *Series Asian Perspectives 3: The Periphery in Asian Studies*. Tokyo: University of Tokyo Press.

———. 1995. "Afterword." In Taiwan Research Foundation, ed., *One Hundred Years of Taiwan*. Taipei: Qianwei.

Wu Wen-hsing. 1992. *A Study of Taiwanese Social Leadership Under Japanese Rule*. Taipei: Zhengzhong.

Yanaihara Tadao. 1988 (1928). *Taiwan Under Imperialism*. Tokyo: Iwanami Shoten.

[2]

THE JAPANESE COLONIAL STATE AND ITS FORM
OF KNOWLEDGE IN TAIWAN

YAO JEN-TO

*The fact that societies can become the object of scientific observation, that human
behaviour became, from a certain point on, a problem to be analysed and resolved,
all that is bound up, I believe, with mechanisms of power.*
— *Michel Foucault*

As alien rulers who hardly knew anything about Taiwan before they landed on
the island at the end of the nineteenth century, the members of the Japanese
colonial government inevitably encountered two fundamental difficulties, which
can be encapsulated in the universal questions posed by Bruno Latour in another context: "how to be familiar with things, people and events which are distant," and, in turn, "how to act at a distance on unfamiliar events, places, and
people" (Latour 1987:220, 223). Latour's answer to these questions is, of course,
already well known: by appealing to "some mobile, stable and combinable means
to bring home these events, places and people" (Latour 1987:223). This essay is
an attempt to investigate the specific knowledge made possible by those "mobile, stable and combinable means" which from the end of the nineteenth century began to "bring home" everything about the faraway colony to the Japanese
rulers.

One of my concerns here is with the form of colonial knowledge in Taiwan.
"Colonial knowledge" involves two types of question: first, "who represents
whom," or "who is represented at the expense of whom" (i.e., the question of
imagination or representation); second, and important, questions regarding what
tool is used to understand and describe the colonized, what exactly the technique
of the representation is, and what the relationship, if any, is between the specific
technique and the colonial administration.

Mainly because of the great success and influence of Edward Said's *Orientalism* (1978), which is almost exclusively focused on the former type of question, there has been relatively little attempt among scholars to explore the latter aspect of colonial knowledge. That is to say, colonial knowledge is now conceived of by most postcolonial theorists purely as a matter of discourse and representation. Moreover, these theorists overwhelmingly prefer the question of "what has been mis-represented" to the question of "what has been represented." This is a serious theoretical inadequacy and bias. I am not suggesting, of course, that the "discursive approach" of Said and his followers is totally wrong. What is being suggested here is rather that, as far as colonial knowledge is concerned, we need to begin to see things from a governmentality approach. To do so, we must pay attention less to the "effect" of (mis)representation and more to those "humble and mundane mechanisms which appear to make it possible to govern" (Miller and Rose 1990:8). Again, to borrow Latour's wisdom, "what is called 'knowledge' cannot be defined without understanding what *gaining* knowledge means" (Latour 1987:220; italics in the original).

Two general types of source material will be discussed here: maps and numbers. Both are mobile, stable, and combinable means, as suggested by Latour. Of course, I am not the first person to draw attention to those "humble and mundane mechanisms" in the colonial contexts. Matthew Edney's *Mapping an Empire* (1997), for example, offers an excellent explanation of the link between cartography and British colonialism in India. As far as numbers are concerned, Arjun Appadurai's essay "Number in the Colonial Imagination" investigates the agrarian surveys and censuses in colonial India, and relates them to the formation of Indian nationalism and the discipline of the colonized. Appadurai's discussion is particularly useful and interesting for the current purpose, for he points out that Said's *Orientalism* "does not specify how exactly the orientalist knowledge project and the colonial project of domination and extraction were connected" (Appadurai 1997:115). In fact, what is missing in Said's *Orientalism* is exactly the driving force of this article. As in colonial India, the precise and distinctive links between enumeration and government in colonial Taiwan have not yet been specified. This is indeed a perilous oversight, because if we overlook those tools employed by the colonial state to know, understand, study, scrutinize, and investigate the subjected people, we must inevitably give an incorrect interpretation of the way in which the colonized are governed and controlled.

From this perspective, we are in a position to consider an important question posed by Appadurai: "Is there any special force to the systematic counting of bodies under colonial states in India, Africa, and Southeast Asia?" (Appadurai 1997:114). That is, do colonialism and colonization contain some exceptional elements of quantification that cannot be found in other forms of controlling or governing? In other words, is there any difference here between governing the citizen and governing the colonized? Appadurai answers these questions in the affirmative. "I believe that the British colonial state employed quantification in its rule of the Indian subcontinent in a way that was different from its domestic counterpart in the eighteenth century and from its predecessor states in India" (115). Appadurai himself fails to tell his readers exactly what this difference is; nevertheless, such difference can be identified in the study of colonial Taiwan.

Unlike Appadurai, I will link the censuses and agrarian surveys in colonial Taiwan not so much to the development of nationalism, but to political rationalities and governmental technologies. In what follows, I will first demonstrate the colonial government's infatuation with numbers and statistics. Second, I will discuss Gotō Shimpei's "biological politics." In doing so, I will reveal the political rationality behind the government's effort to know and to govern the colonized. Finally, I will discuss land surveys and censuses launched by the colonial government. They were the key means by which the alien government was able to "make visible domains of life that were once invisible" (Murdoch and Ward 1997:308).

COLONIAL STATE

Before we discuss the Japanese colonial state's obsession with numbers, let me give a quick review of the nature of the colonial state itself. Anne Phillips calls the colonial state a "facsimile of a state" (1989:11). J. C. Heesterman, a Dutch colonial historian, argues that the public domain of the colonial state "had been taken out and set apart from society" (1987:54). Partha Chatterjee, in *The Nation and Its Fragments*, therefore asks an important question: "Does it serve any useful analytical purpose to make a distinction between the colonial state and the forms of the modern state?" (1993:14). His answer is affirmative, although he does not have a lot to say in his book about the difference between the colonial state and the modern state. Addressing the same question, Jurgen Osterhammel, a German colonial historian, argues that "the colonial state was no simple extension of the metropolitan political system to overseas possessions, but a political form in and of itself" (Osterhammel 1997:57). As to "why" and "how," however, Osterhammel, like Chatterjee, has very little to say, except this: "The liberal achievements of Europe did not usually extend to the colonized" (57).

In the introduction to their *Tensions of Empire: Colonial Cultures in a Bourgeois World*, Ann Laura Stoler and Frederick Cooper (1997) provide a comprehensive review of existing (post)colonial studies. The piece covers more than fifty pages, but one thing is conspicuous by its absence: discussions of the difference between governing a metropole and governing a colony.[1] As far as colonial states and political economy are concerned, they seem to call for a rethinking of Paul Rabinow's statement (1986:259): "We need a more complex understanding of power in the colonies. The state is something we need to know a lot more about" (Stoler and Copper 1997:20). Ironically, then, given its title, "Between Metropole and Colony" also offers us no research agenda for finding the difference in governmentality between metropole and colony.

Lastly, John Comaroff, an American anthropologist, claims that the difference between metropolitan and colonial governance is that "one depended, for its existence, on the ideological work of manufacturing sameness, of engendering a horizontal sense of fraternity; the other ... was concerned with the practical management of difference" (1997:16). This is true. But on closer inspection, his theorization of the colonial state, in fact, adds only more abstract elements to the conventional framework.

A paradox: everyone (whether Dutch, German, British, American) agrees that the colonial state, colonial government, or colonial regime is special, but few find it necessary to push their arguments further. Matthew G. Hannah (2000) is an exception, though. In his *Governmentality and the Mastery of Territory in Nineteenth-Century America* he gives useful clues to thinking about the particulars of colonial government in concrete terms. He concludes that colonial regimes differ from metropolitan governments in three ways: first, "imperial state officials have frequently assumed greater freedom to experiment abroad than at home"; second, "they have also benefited from the relative weakness (at a national scale) of a Western-style civil society among colonized peoples"; and third, "colonial states have often been more bureaucratised and less tolerant of popular resistance" (Hannah 2000:114). He summarizes: "In principle, the kind of governmental thinking characterised by a more careful and solicitous approach to social control has been less prominent in imperial regimes" (114). To caricature somewhat, colonial governments seem good at only two things: unchecked rule by violence and endless bureaucratization.

Hannah's summary is only a different—more polite and less explicit—way of expressing Abdullahi Ali Ibrahim's point: "the colonial state ... retreated into a governmental 'infantile disorder' in which the art of government had still to be invented" (1997:14). For Ibrahim, "a colonial administration could never have been other than a pre-government institution qualified to run a piece of land not a population" (28). His judgment is wholly inapplicable to Taiwan, however. It is clear that we are not in the habit of seeing the colonial state as a "bio-political" government that takes charge of colonized lives.

What is, then, the form of knowledge accompanying the colonial state that "retreated into a governmental infantile disorder"? A passage by Albert Memmi will help clarify. He says, in his *The Colonizer and the Colonized*, that "the point is that the colonized means little to the colonizer. Far from wanting to understand him as he really is, the colonizer is preoccupied with making him undergo this urgent change" (1965:149). Similarly, D.K. Fieldhouse, one of the most famous colonial scholars in the English-speaking world, observes that as long as colonies provided advantages (strategic bases, raw materials, perhaps merely the satisfaction of imperial ownership), "few cared anything about what happened to them or their inhabitants" (Fieldhouse 1981:44). What emerges from Memmi and Field-house's descriptions is a deep-seated indifference in the colonizer's mind, or, to be more precise, inside European colonial governmentality: the colonizer is not interested in knowing and understanding the colonized in any great detail or with any great accuracy.

Yet the Japanese in Taiwan were in fact different. In his *Colonial Development and Population in Taiwan*, George W. Barclay observes of Japanese's peculiar way of governing the colonized:

> While under Japanese rule Taiwan probably had the distinction of being the most thoroughly inventoried colonial area in the world. Huge compilations of statistics and numerous special surveys were made from year to year. The economy, the terrain, the aboriginal tribes, the mineral wealth, the agricultural output, the industrial production and the foreign trade have all been studied and restudied until there is little to be added to this knowledge unless new evidence is uncovered that is not now available. (Barclay 1954:x)

Of course, having been "the most thoroughly inventoried colonial area in the world" was hardly a matter of pride for the Taiwanese. Why did the Japanese colonizer need such a wealth of knowledge when a more typical attitude was a certain degree of indifference to what was really happening in the colony? This is not the place to judge the arguments of Memmi and Fieldhouse, but to note that, whether or not their arguments hold in the cases of European colonization, they are hardly applicable to the Japanese colonization of Taiwan. Not only did the Japanese show great curiosity and enthusiasm about their new colony, but throughout the colonial period they were determined to know everything about the colonized as scientifically as possible. In short, the Japanese did not suffer from what might be called "the starvation of knowledge" of European colonialists. In fact, no other colonial power in the world invested more energy in knowing the colonized and, in turn, on contemplating and producing an "ideal" colonized—obedient, loyal, productive, diligent, healthy, and useful—than the Japanese. The Japanese colonial empire was indeed an "anomaly," not only because of its lack of expansive capital, as Jon Halliday suggested (1975), but also because of its peculiar ways of *governing the colonized*.

COLONIAL NUMBERS

Among all the efforts made by the colonial government to understand its newly gained territory and people, the compilation of statistics was the most important. It must be noted that, according to Stuart Woolf, "the umbilical cord between statistics and modern state in the West was historically not always the case." For instance, "the earliest mathematically sophisticated utilisation of statistics ... was developed in England as a direct by-product of the insurance trade" (1989:588). Mary Poovey, in her *A History of the Modern Fact* (1998), claimed that the supremacy of statistics was a historically contingent phenomenon.

The situation in colonial Taiwan, however, was different because statistics were at the heart of colonial statecraft from the very beginning. This was mainly due to Japan's "advantage" of being the "latecomer" among colonial powers. By the time the Japanese occupied the island, "the link between number, fact and good government" (Rose 1999:218) had already become commonplace, and it partly explained why there was hardly any debate in Japan about applying statistics to the governing of Taiwan. According to Ian Hacking, Western society between 1820 and 1840 witnessed a period of what he calls "the avalanche of printed numbers" (Hacking 1982:281). In Taiwan the period of "the avalanche of printed numbers" came much later than in the West. It was the Japanese colonial government that raised the curtain on "the era of enthusiasm for statistical data-collection" in Taiwan (Hacking 1982:281); or, to borrow a phrase from Mitchell Dean (1995), statistics were the *episteme* of colonial government.

This contention is best verified by *The Statistical Summaries of Taiwan Province in the Past Fifty-One Years*. This huge book, published in December 1946 by the Chinese Nationalist government after they took over the island at the end of the Second World War, contains more than 1,400 pages and 540 chronological statistical tables. For example, we can find in its table 245 the total number of cows in Taiwan's farms from 1900 to 1945, while in its table 480 we can find the total number of books in Taiwan's libraries from 1901 to 1942. The time spans covered by these tables are different, depending upon topic, purpose, availability, and government preference. For instance, numbers on colonial population were not available until after the first census was taken in 1905. The earliest statistics collected, accumulated, and systematically analyzed by the colonial government date back to 1897, two years after the Japanese landed on the island. These were statistics of public health, including the numbers of doctors, hospitals, and epidemic mortality. In this respect Taiwan resembles the European cases, especially that of France, where, according to Theodore Porter, the statistical initiative was taken chiefly by advocates of public health (Porter 1986:28). Yet in Taiwan these statistics were, in fact, an early sign of a special colonial governmentality that from the beginning of the twentieth century began to take the health of the colonized as one of its most important political agendas.

It is crucial to realize that all the numerical data in *Statistical Summaries of Taiwan Province* were collected by the Japanese colonial government. What the Chinese officials did was simply to compile, translate, and publish them in Chinese. The reaction of the Chinese Nationalist government is worth mentioning. They were stunned by the massive ocean of numbers accumulated by their Japanese predecessors. In the preface to the book there is an interesting statement by the Chinese official responsible for the compilation and translation.

> We all know that the Japanese in Taiwan, in order to strengthen their colonial administration, maintained statistics every year; their accomplishment in this respect is even better than in Japan itself. When we came here to take over, we saw that they had a very well organized statistical department, a great number of books and documents, a fine legal record, an immense scope of scientific enterprise, and a proliferation of publications. All of the above can be taken as an indication that the Japanese had great respect for the statistics business. *By maintaining rigid and correct statistical data, the Japanese then fulfilled their oppression plot.* (iii; emphasis added)

Two major themes dominate the above remarks: (colonial) knowledge and (colonial) power. As the official said, numbers and statistics were nothing other than a colonial weapon. Unlike the other rulers prior to them, the Japanese governmentality was a number-, knowledge-, and truth-producing machine. Seen from this perspective, the historical moment of colonial occupation was thus not only a political rupture, but an epistemological rupture. What was involved in colonialism in Taiwan was, in other words, not only a change of rulers but a change of *episteme*. The numbers, facts, and knowledge all together generated a wealth of administrative records, which in turn created a sense of certainty and control in the colonial office. It is here that we can understand most clearly the argument of Jonathan Murdoch and Neil Ward that "an archetypal form of governmentality is statistics" (1997:313). Not only are statistics an archetypal form of governmentality, but they are also an archetypal form of *colonial* governmentality.

Yet why did numbers and numerical representation appeal to a colonial government in particular? Because, first of all, statistics are a mobile, stable, and combinable means of "government at a distance." They are a means of representation by which Taiwan could be brought back to Japan with minimal dispute. As Poovey puts it, "Quantification was different from qualitative descriptions *in being less subject to controversy or dispute*" (Poovey 1998:122; italics in the original). Second, statistics are particularly suitable for those who must find a quick and convenient way of "studying mass phenomena profitably without first having to attain detailed knowledge of the constituent individuals" (Porter 1986:6). Confronted by a different race, culture, and language in the colony, the Japanese colonial government obviously faced this task. Third, statistics can ensure that the "confusion of politics could be replaced by an orderly reign of facts" (Porter 1986:27). The harsh colonial encounter in Taiwan created political confusion and tension that could be resolved only by certainty produced at a different level, namely, the statistical.

It takes only a glance at the categorization in the first few pages of *Statistical Summaries of Taiwan Province* to understand the increasingly "profitable dialectic of information and control" (Said 1978:36) in the colony. The 540 tables have been divided into 24 categories: calendar and weather, land, population, administration organization, justice, agriculture, forestry, marine products, animal husbandry, mineral resources, industry, labor, business, finance, monopoly, monetary, postal and cable service, rail, highway, shipping administration, education, hygiene, philanthropy and religion, and police. As a result, multifarious colonial phenomena ranging from the sunrise times to the total number of sheep; from the forest area to exact colonial population levels; from the total number of factory workers to the number of postal packages sent by the colonial people; from the total number of prostitutes examined by hospitals to the number of temples, monks, nuns, and religious followers—all are documented in the book. In short, every aspect of colonial society was counted. The Japanese showed remarkable and consistent energy, passion, and patience in their effort to keep all sorts of colonial phenomena under tabs. Those astonishingly all-embracing statistical tables represented the fact-hunting nature of the colonial state, and indicate that the colonized in Taiwan were observed, recorded, analyzed, and then governed in every way and on every side. "Nothing was left untouched by the statisticians" (Hacking 1982:280).

The purposes of the colonial state's determination to numeralize everything in the colony were probably several: some had a utilitarian and pragmatic purpose, such as public health measures, crime prevention, food distribution, taxation, and natural disease prediction. In addition, the Japanese may simply have wished to show off to the West the results of their successful colonial administration. The important point here is that, whatever the purpose, all were tools of colonial government. If nothing escaped the eyes of Japanese colonial statistical analysis, then nothing would be able to escape from the colonial administration. Here I take a view opposite that of Appadurai. In the essay mentioned earlier Appadurai argues:

> Although early colonial policies of quantification were utilitarian in design, I would suggest that numbers gradually became more importantly part of the *illusion* of bureaucratic control and a key to a colonial imaginary in which countable abstractions, of people and resources at every imaginable level and for every conceivable purpose, created the sense of a controllable indigenous reality. (Appadurai 1997:117; italics added)

I have a problem with Appadurai's word "illusion." Numbers are of greatest use to colonial social control in terms of their administration rather than their imagination. It is here that we see Said's great influence on Appadurai (although he leaves a strong anti-Saidian impression). A technique as pragmatic as statistics is predominantly conceived of by Appadurai as part of the general framework of colonial fabrication, illusion, and imagination. That is, Appadurai, like many of Said's followers, draws too heavily on a conception of number as a *cultural* product rather than a *governmental* technology. This is not the place to judge whether Appadurai's argument on the "illusion of bureaucratic control" is sociologically or historically correct, but I want to point out that, judging from the scope and behavior of the colonial administration, what was created by number in colonial Taiwan was not an illusion but a sufficient authority; not a controllable indigenous reality but a *controlled* indigenous reality.

BIOLOGICAL POLITICS

What then was the politics, if any, accompanying the proliferation of scientific colonial knowledge? The answer: biological politics. For Gotō Shimpei 後藤新平, the main advocate of the idea, "colonisation policy was biology" (Tsurumi 1967:107). And "government of a colony cannot go beyond biological laws" (Takekoshi 1907:97). But what are "biological laws"? Gotō gives a first definition in his famous *Emergent Proposal for Governing Taiwan*, which he offered to the authorities in Japan before he took his position in Taiwan's government-general in 1898:

> Any scheme of colonial administration, given the present advances in science, should be based on principles of Biology. What are these principles? They are to promote science, and to develop agriculture, industry, sanitation, education, communications and police force. If these are satisfactorily accomplished, we will be able to preserve in the struggle for survival and win the struggle for the "survival of the fittest." Animals survive by overcoming heat and cold, and by enduring thirst and hunger. This is possible for them because they adapt to their environment. Thus depending upon time and space, we too should adopt suitable measures and try to overcome the various difficulties that confront us. (Gotō, cited in Chang and Myers 1963:438)

These principles could be seen as the epitome of the political rationality of colonial government. The entire colonial question for Gotō came down to this: in what way could the Japanese adapt to the harsh and hostile colonial environment? Gotō's primary solution was to promote science, namely, knowledge. A "regime of truth" was quickly established in the colony, and its task was to forge a link that could not otherwise have been made: mutual enforcement between a disciplinary colonial power and scientific investigation. Successful adaptation to the harsh colonial environment "could be achieved only after careful study of the colony" (Chang and Myers 1963:439). "More than anything else, this meant obtaining sound and relevant information on which to base policy, information to be derived from careful research" (Peattie 1984:84). In short, biological politics for Gotō was a politics of knowledge, of know-how. "Each individual problem demanded a separate investigation" (Tsurumi 1967:108). Gotō insisted that colonial policy had to be "based on thorough research," so he "promoted extensive research in many fields" (108).

If taken at face value, there is hardly any similarity, save the etymological, between Gotō's "biological politics" and Foucault's idea of "bio-politics." The former is largely based on social Darwinism while the latter designates a special historical period in which bio-power "brought life and its mechanisms into a realm of explicit calculations and made knowledge-power an agent of transformation of human life" (Foucault 1979b:143). However, on closer inspection, these two terms—invented by different people, in different parts of the world, in different periods of history, and for different reasons—are in fact highly congruent. The secret of this unlikely congruence lies in its relation of power and knowledge. Just as demography found its *raison d'être* in the era of bio-politics, as Foucault suggests, so too a variety of colonial knowledge came to be formed and institutionalized in the Taiwanese colonial era of "biological politics." In both cases, we witness an explosion of knowledge and techniques, including reports about inhabitants and resources, and numbers and tables analyzing trends. Such knowledge-producing activities, such techniques of numbers, classifications, and measurement, were by no means outside the colonial power relation. They were rather at the heart of colonial governmentality.

The second meaning of Gotō's "biological politics" concerns the moral justifications for particular ways of exercising racial politics in the colony, as evidenced in the following statement:

> In governing Taiwan, first of all we must investigate scientifically the local customs and institutions, and not adopt any policy that provokes the locals. If we transplant what we have in Japan to Taiwan without any careful investigation beforehand, it is no different from the naive idea of transforming the eyes of flatfish to the eyes of scup. It would be a typical behavior only from someone who does not understand the true meaning of politics. (Gotō, cited in Chen Yen-hong 1986:48)

Like the previous quotation, this is an important statement of the political rationality of colonial government. Not only does Gotō explain to his countrymen how to govern Taiwan—investigate before action—but he also points out the limits of governing the colonized—the eyes of flatfish cannot be transformed to the scup's. On Japan's own peculiar "fishery" scale, the scup is far more expensive than the flatfish, so when Gotō said that it would be naive to transform one kind of fish to another, he was actually indicating an insurmountable racial hierarchy, that is, a gap between Japanese and Taiwanese, colonizer and colonized, ruler and ruled, civilized and uncivilized. In short, "biological politics" was a racial politics. It served simultaneously as a political rationality and as a moral discourse in order to make sense of and/or justify the colonizer's particular ways of *governing the colonized.*

THE LAND SURVEY

Driven by the principle of "biological politics," in September 1898 the colonial government established the "Temporary Land Survey Bureau" in order to carry out a thorough land survey of colonial Taiwan. There had been some cadastral surveys conducted by the Qing government; according to John Shepherd, the first could be dated back to 1728 (1993:138). But the colonial government's land survey was special in that it was the first undertaken by any ruler on the island seeking to understand Taiwan and its inhabitants *scientifically*, and can therefore be seen as the beginning of the singular colonial power/knowledge. The duties of the land survey bureau were "to survey the whole island, to estimate the produce, to make maps, ledgers, and land registers" (Takekoshi 1907:126). It was written in the "Cadastral Regulations in Taiwan," enacted in 1901, that "apart from rail and sewage, each and every piece of land must be given a number, and thus be registered" (Chen Chao-ming 2000:47).

This massive survey was divided into three parts: land registration, trigonometrical surveys, and topographical surveys. It was the aim of the colonial government that each and every inch of land in the colony be investigated and thus registered.[2] It took the Japanese seven years in total (1898–1905) to complete this survey, during which more than 5,225,000 yen were spent and more than 1,670,000 personnel were mobilized and involved (Tu 1981:37). The colonial government investigated a total of 777,850 *chia* of land, produced 37,869 maps of villages and cities, compiled up to 9,610 cadasters, and accumulated 5,624 volumes of land rent registration (Chen Yen-hong 1986:73). The massive expenditure and mobilization were deemed by the colonial government to be justified by the increased understanding of, and the correspondingly increased control over, the land and its inhabitants.

Much has been written about the contribution of the land surveys to Japanese colonial rule in Taiwan. Takekoshi, for instance, observed: "The whole area of Formosa has now been accurately measured, its hills and valleys carefully surveyed, and its productive capacity ascertained. This is of untold value to the military and civil administration" (Takekoshi 1907:129). And: "The land survey business had played a decisive role in helping the government-general in Taiwan to control the Han people as well as consolidate its foundation for governing" (Fujii 1997:140).

Yanaihara Tadao 矢内原忠雄's understanding of land survey is the most comprehensive. The land survey in Taiwan served at least three major purposes, he said: "to promote security and peace by clarifying the topographical situation, to increase the land-tax revenues by finding unregistered or 'hidden' lands and simplifying land-ownership, and to make transactions of land safe and secure by ascertaining and simplifying land-ownership" (Yanaihara 1985:17; see also Tsurumi 1967:112). In short, the land survey served a threefold purpose: first, to ascertain and understand the topography of the colony; second, to clarify land ownership, and thus to build up a clear and official relation between the land and its inhabitants, as well as increase land revenues from taxation; third, to pave the way for the later expropriation in which the state's capital investment (mainly in sugar factories) could claim monopoly status over the land of the colonized.

Yanaihara's points are worth dwelling on for a moment. According to him, the first purpose of the land survey was to "promote security and peace." This had been achieved simply by "clarifying the topographical situation." During their first few years of colonization, the Japanese had been deeply frustrated by rebellious Taiwanese bandits and guerrillas who had been forced to take refuge in rural villages, where the Japanese had real difficulties in finding them, let alone in enforcing the peace. But after the survey, the guerrillas could run but they couldn't hide. The colonial government, in the process of investigation, had drawn numerous maps on which the tribes, villages, rivers, and mountains were all clearly depicted. This was exactly the moment, to put it in Latour's phrase, when "the *implicit* geography of the native is made *explicit* by geographers; ... the fuzzy, approximate and ungrounded *beliefs* of the locals are turned into a precise, certain and justified *knowledge*" (Latour 1987:216; italics in the original). His implication is clear enough: if everything was shown on maps, then nothing was escaping the colonial government. Of course, the pacification of the Taiwanese guerrilla depended largely on the superior military force of the Japanese colonizer, but the land survey performed a role that guns and tanks alone could not.

So, beyond Said, what is at issue here is by no means a question of "imaginative geography and its representation" (Said 1978:49). It is instead a practical question of obtaining a "real" geography. The land survey gives us a clear example of the coincidence and mutually enforcing relationship among geography, mapping, knowledge, and government. On this point, just consider Takekoshi's personal experience during his visit to Taiwan. Due to its importance, I quote his description at some length below:

When I inspected the different maps and ledgers in the Bureau of Surveys, and had the pleasure of seeing the officials at work, I could not but admire the vastness of the undertaking, and the scientific way in which it was being carried through. There is no town or village on the island the exact position of which has not been determined, no field or plantation, however small, which will not be found upon one or other of the prepared maps; in short, precise information is at once obtainable as the size, etc., of any piece of ground down to the smallest rice field. When we arrived at the *godown* reserved for ledgers, Baron Gotō asked one of the officials to show me the map of a certain village. The officials referred to the index, and speedily spread a map out before us. ... On the village map we saw rice fields, tea plantations, brooks, hills, and woods, all drawn with a precision trigonometrical survey alone can secure. ... With one of these maps and a pencil it was easy at once to ascertain the size of each village. In that *godown* it would be almost as easy to examine the physical contour and geographical features of Formosa as it is to study the palm of one's own hand. (Takekoshi 1907:128–129)

Notwithstanding Takekoshi's exaggeration and overconfidence about Japanese colonial rule, the accomplishment of the land survey offered the alien government the opportunity to know the territory and its productivity without overlooking any detail; and, more important, the opportunity to exercise its governing power at minimal cost: a map and a pencil. Takekoshi's confidence perhaps sounds bizarre, but it is telling. It underlines the fundamental determination of a colonial government obsessed with complicated enumeration and detailed accuracy in measurement. The result: the colonizers were able to examine the colony as easily "as it is to study the palm of one's own hand." This is what Shih Tien-Fu 施添福 has described as "govern the land by maps, and people by land" (Shih 2000:13; 2001:4).

Timothy Mitchell comments in *Colonising Egypt* that "colonial power required the country to become readable, like a book" (1988:33). The Japanese set for themselves a "higher" standard; in a similar context, Edney's argument in *Mapping an Empire* is intriguing. In defining the scope and nature of his study of the surveys and maps in British India, Edney remarks:

It is a study of how the British represented their India. I say "their India" because they did not map the "real" India. They mapped the India that they perceived and that they governed. ... India could never be entirely and perfectly known. The British deluded themselves that their science enabled them to know the "real" India. But what they did map, what they did create, was a *British* India. (Edney 1997:14–15; italics in the original)

Inevitably, an important question has to be raised: what then is the "real" India? Edney does not offer us the answer. My aim here is, of course, not to judge whether Edney's interpretation of British colonialism is correct. Nor is it my aim to squabble with the postcolonial theorists over the meaning of the "real." My concern is with whether maps can achieve their governmental ends. Takekoshi and perhaps most of the administrators in Taiwan would have been sure that they could. When compared with Edney's phrase "India could never be entirely and perfectly known," Takekoshi's metaphor seems highly significant. In the eyes of the colonial government Taiwan was by no means an imaginary objectification.

In fact, throughout the whole colonial period the colonial government hardly invented or created an *imaginary* Taiwan in order to "override" the *real* Taiwan. Quite the contrary: the whole purpose of this colonial "cadastral politics" was to replace the imaginary colonial contours with the real things, to replace inaccurate numbers with the correct ones.

Apart from its contribution to ensuring peace, the land survey also fulfilled a financial function in the colony. It was an effort to ascertain the relation between the inhabitants and their land: Who owns it? Who is responsible for paying taxes on it? A passage from George Kerr in his *Formosa: Licensed Revolution and the Home Rule Movement, 1895–1945* gives us a clear description of this function:

> The inaccuracies of nineteenth-century Chinese official records were now revealed in their true dimensions. According to the Chinese land registers surrendered to the Japanese, a total of 867,000 acres were yielding revenue, whereas Gotō's men discovered that the figure should have been 1,866,000 acres. This means that when the new records were complete, tens of thousands of Formosan landholders were compelled to pay taxes on land never before taxed. (Kerr 1974:86)

Attention should first be paid to Kerr's statement that the numbers, records, and registration of land under the Qing government were inaccurate, and that these inaccuracies were not modified and corrected until the Japanese colonial government launched its massive land survey. The Qing government in Taiwan, in other words, failed to understand what is now seen as one of the most taken-for-granted motifs of political rationality: to govern territories, one must know them. Table 2.1 gives a rough idea of the improved cadastral enumeration and classification system introduced in Taiwan by the Japanese colonial government.

It is here that we can see most clearly the operation of "governing by numbers" (Rose 1991). What changed, of course, was not the actual area of the land itself, but the techniques of measurement and, more important and fundamental, the governmentality of the ruler. Or, in the words of Bernard Cohn, "they [the colonizer] ... invaded and conquered not only a territory but an epistemological space as well" (Cohn 1996:4). In fact, as the Taiwanese case demonstrates, the colonial territory actually became "bigger" as a result of the change in the epistemological space.

The huge changes illustrated in the above table were a consequence of the general project of colonial enumeration and classification. The Japanese "discovered" that the revenue-yielding area was much larger than had been thought before, and after the survey many more Taiwanese people were forced to pay taxes on their land. Revenue greatly increased, which helped ease the financial difficulties facing the colonial government. According to Tu, total land revenue in 1903 was about 920,000 yen, but in 1905 the figure surged to 2,980,000 yen (Tu

TABLE 2.1 Results of the Japanese Land Survey of Taiwan

	Total Recorded Area Before Survey*	Total Recorded Area After Survey	Difference
Paddy field	214,734	313,693	98,959
Dry farmland	146,713	305,594	158,881
Building	—	36,395	36,395
Other	—	122,168	122,168
Total	361,447	777,850	416,403

*Measured in *chia*, a Taiwanese unit equal to approximately 0.97 hectare.

Source: adapted from Chen Yen-hong 1986:72.

1991:39). However, to suggest that the sole purpose of levying more land taxes was to increase the colonial state's revenue is to misunderstand the essence of the land survey and, more generally, the whole project of colonial enumeration and classification. The land survey project was not so much a method of finding new sources of land revenue as it was a method of overcoming and controlling potential threats to the colonial government: lack of knowledge about the colony (its size, shape, fertility, productivity), uncertainty over the land's relation to its inhabitants, and a resulting interstice between the colonial power and its people. In short, what was created by the land survey was not an illusion (as suggested by Appadurai concerning the Indian colonial situation) but a certainty, a controlled cadastral reality.

Yanaihara's third purpose of the land survey—simplifying land ownership—is perhaps the most complex. There is no room to discuss this issue in great detail here. The landholding system in Taiwan before Japanese colonization was indeed very complicated.[3] This was mainly the result of the intriguing triangular relationship among plains aborigines, Chinese settlers, and the state under the Qing's frontier policy (see Shepherd 1993). The multitiered land right in Taiwan can be described in the following way: "The tenant worked the land and paid an annual fixed rent in grain called *shosō* 小租 (small rent) to a holder who possessed the right to the *shosō*. The holder in turn paid an annual grain rent to the holder of *taisō* 大租 (great rent), who had originally received the land in trust from the government, an aborigine, or an aborigine tribe. The *taisō*-holder was the acknowledged 'owner,' insofar as ownership could be said to have existed" (Tsurumi 1967:113). In short, the majority of taxes in the agricultural sector were not paid directly from actual landowners to the colonial government. As far as the colonial administration was concerned, this was something that had to be changed.

According to Tu's research on land ownership in Taiwan, the class structure of the agricultural population in 1905 was as follows: 38,000 *taiso*-holders, 300,000 *shoso*-holders, and 750,000 tenants who actually worked the land. In 1904 the colonial government abolished the right of the *taiso*-holder, and gave to the *shoso*-holder the formal and legal right to the land. The *taiso*-holders were compensated with government loan bonds. Thereafter, the new landholding system in Taiwan was established: the *shoso*-holders paid their taxes directly to the government-general without the intermediation of *taiso*-holders. Once the question of ownership was legally clarified, the purchase of land was legally protected and the way was paved for the massive investment of Japanese capital and the establishment of its monopoly. The Japanese capitalists began to realize that all of the colony's land was now at their disposal. This is why Yanaihara claims that "the land survey became the necessary precondition and basic foundation for Taiwan's capitalization" (Yanaihara 1985:18).

In terms of landholding relations, then, the old order had been destroyed in Taiwan. (The right of the *taiso*-holders had been annulled, and in place of them now were just the *shoso*-holders, more numerous but each with much less land.) With no real delay the old order had been replaced by the new. This new order was established via a regime of cartography and statistics. But, whatever the form of ownership, for the vast majority of farmers in Taiwan throughout the colonial period the general conditions remained the same. The only difference was that they now found themselves governed by a far more scientific, efficient, and complicated system of domination since their land had been completely and inexorably scrutinized by the foreign ruler.

THE CENSUS

The colonial government in Taiwan spared no expense or energy in finding out everything it possibly could about the colonial territory. It also spared no expense or energy in finding out everything about its subjects—namely, the population of the colony. In contrast to the Qing government, which governed Taiwan for more than two and a half centuries without taking a census and therefore without knowing exactly how many people lived under the its regime, the Japanese colonial government was very quick to understand a "common sense" dictum of twentieth-century political rationality: "the people should be counted" (Hacking 1982:290).

Like the land survey, the census represented another aspect of the general project of colonial enumeration and classification. It was therefore a genuinely political calculation and political measure. According to Barclay, among all the statistics collected by the colonial government, "the numerical data relating to the population are the best of all, since their collection was most directly linked to the very effective system of control imposed by the Japanese" (Barclay 1954:x). Thanks to the census, for the first time in Taiwanese history the inhabitants of the island had been transformed into a governable population. Afterward, the natives became identifiable, classifiable, and describable by government. Cohn has noted that "the taking of the census was based on administrative necessity" (Cohn 1987:242). And he is absolutely correct in saying that "the history of the Indian census must be seen in the total context of the efforts of the British colonial government to collect systematic information about many aspects of Indian society and economy" (231). Quite clearly, although Taiwan was colonized by a different colonizer, the reason for the census-taking in the colony was no different from that in India.

In his *Colonial Development and Population in Taiwan*, George Barclay points out that:

> Taiwan is the *only* place where it is possible to study the processes of change of a Chinese population over a substantial period of time on the basis of excellent data. … Under Japanese rule an *unusually accurate* statistical record was maintained in Taiwan from 1905 to 1943, providing an unbroken series of data that is longer, and in some respects richer, than that for Japan proper. (Barclay 1954:v; emphasis added)

In using the words "unusually accurate," he appears to imply that there is no reason for any given colonizer to extract such a great deal of accurate information from its colonized. Hidden in Barclay's argument is a long-term stereotype about colonization and colonialism—that there is no need to know the colonized people—but this need not concern us here. Here I focus on why the Japanese colonizers, against the norm, were so keen on knowing the colonial population. This is partly explained by Barclay's subsequent sentence, suggesting that the data on the colony is "in some respects richer than that for Japan proper." Such an assertion may seem surprising at first, but if we consider that the earliest census was actually taken in the colonial context (Hacking 1990:17), then it is more plausible. As Rose points out, "by and large the first to be enumerated were the most dominated—the inhabitants of the colonies" (Rose 1999:215). It would be wrong to infer that the same infatuation with censuses in Japan did not exist. Because the colonized are more difficult to tame and to govern, richer data and greater knowledge are inevitably required by the colonizer.

After three years of preparation the first census in Taiwan was taken in October 1905 (ten years earlier than the first census in Japan itself), involving 842 supervisory staff, 1,339 assistants, and 5,224 census-takers (or "enumerators") (Tsurumi 1967:113). These numbers have little meaning, though, until we consider that the population to enumerator ratio in this census was as low as 582 (3,039,751÷ 5,224). Each enumerator in Taiwan was responsible for counting 582 people on average. Compare this to the situation in nineteenth-century America in which, according to Hannah, "enumeration districts could engross as many as 20,000 people" (Hannah 2000:118). Clearly, the ratio in colonial Taiwan was very low, and this is highly significant. While the land survey was a starting point of the special colonial power/knowledge, the first census was no doubt the starting point in Taiwan of what has been called by Foucault "the governmentalisation of state" (Foucault 1979a:20) in Taiwan. It was, in other words, a historical moment, when the government's knowledge of the population was transformed from estimation and imagination to calculation and classification.

In 1915 the colonial government organized the second census in Taiwan, and one took place every five years thereafter until 1940. During the fifty years of colonization, people in Taiwan were counted *seven* times by the alien government! The census, which in turn led to a new kind of calculating rationality in colonial Taiwan, made it possible to know the number, identity, sex, occupation, age, marital status, language, birthplace, education, wealth, and production of the colonized. This series of censuses, described by Barclay as a "complete monument to their [i.e., the colonizers'] enumerative capacities," comprises "the only trustworthy information that we have about the numbers and kinds of people in Taiwan at any time" (Barclay 1954:10). Again, as he remarks, the Taiwanese censuses

> all maintained uniformly high standards in the completeness of reporting, in the consistency of defining ethnic classes, and in the accuracy of information such as age reporting. In these respects they often ranked in quality well above the more advanced censuses of the Western world. The first two censuses, in 1905 and 1915, were carried out before a genuine enumerative census was ever conducted in Japan Proper. (Barclay 1954:10)

In order to highlight the extraordinary effort of the colonial government and the satisfactory results of the census, it might be helpful here to take the colonial census in India as a comparison. Cohn notices that the Indian censuses of 1871–1872 were not satisfactory and that "such imperfections, both in administration and in conception, developed that not much reliance was put in the census at the time" (Cohn 1987:238). In contrast to the Indian census organized by the British, the Taiwanese ones—right from the first—were highly accurate. According to Cohn, one of the main reasons for the inaccuracy of the Indian census was that the British colonial state had no correct knowledge and information about the colonial territory. Cohn says, "for twenty years starting with the census of 1871–2, there were difficulties in Bengal in getting an accurate list of villages or, for that matter, even defining what a village was" (239).

Yet thanks to the land survey completed in 1905 (not coincidentally, the year of the first census-taking), the Japanese colonial state in Taiwan was free of the uncertainty that afflicted the British census-taker in India. Perhaps nothing could be more remote from the ethos of the Japanese colonial governmentality than to imagine that a colonial ruler, after governing the colony for more than a century, still lacked knowledge about the subject territory. Not only did they know what a village was, but in most cases there was a map at their disposal. According to Hannah, the land survey was a prerequisite for census-taking: "It is impossible to undertake an accurate census unless there is some geographical framework on which to define and precisely locate enumeration districts which exhaust the territory without any overlap" (Hannah 2000:118). Perhaps it is now impossible to identify the exact person in the colonial government responsible for making the decision to organize the land survey prior to the census, but what is clear is that, at the turn of the century, the colonial government began, perhaps only gradually, to build up a power/knowledge network in which the scientific knowledge obtained by different institutions for different purposes was nevertheless highly complementary.

Of course, such high-quality data collection in the census was not a result simply of the curiosity of the colonizer; it stemmed rather from the need for registration, administration, and an effective system of control. One of the most important purposes of these censuses was to make a register of the population under the colonizer's control. And "this was undertaken for purposes of regulation, and not to satisfy disinterested curiosity about the inhabitants" (Barclay 1954:10). Everyone in the colony had to be clearly identified, by name, age, sex, family, marriage, address, ethnicity, occupation, and so on. This was another act of the colonizer aimed at eliminating uncertainty in the colonial situation. All of the colonized could fit into one of the categories (male/female; Taiwanese/Chinese, etc.) on the census form. On this point, Benedict Anderson notes something important for us. In his second edition of *Imagined Communities* he writes:

> One notices ... the census-makers' passion for completeness and unambiguity. Hence their intolerance of multiple, politically "transvestite," blurred, or changing identifications. Hence the weird subcategory, under each racial group, of "Other" —who, nonetheless, are absolutely not to be confused with other "Others." The fiction of the census is that everyone is in it, and that everyone has one—and only one—extremely clear place. No fractions. (Anderson 1991:166–167)

What is described here by Anderson is an important aspect of the colonial subject, an aspect that disappointingly is more often than not neglected by contemporary (post)colonial theorists. When we are considering the keywords used by Anderson—"completeness," "unambiguity," "extremely clear place," and "no fractions"—we see how different they are from (post)colonial jargon such as "mimicry," "ambivalence," or "hybridity." The image of the colonized in the census is indeed in conflict with that drawn from other colonial discourses such as novels. The census represents a colonial governmentality, whereas other discourses perhaps represent colonial hybridity. But what is important is that, confronted by such a power-knowledge combination as the census, nothing in the colony was ambiguous, and nobody in the colony had the privilege of remaining anonymous. Given this, one would wonder where the idea of "ambivalence" or "the mark of the plural" (Memmi 1990:151) comes from, or how it is that "mimicry emerges as one of the most elusive and effective strategies of colonial power and knowledge" (Bhabha 1994:85). To what extent can it be true that "both coloniser and colonised are in a process of miscognition" (Bhabha 1994:97)? In what sense is it that "the colonial authority is best understood and resisted through its ambivalence" (110)? And how can the colonized be "a chaotic, disorganized, and anonymous collectivity" (Hartsock 1990:160)?

One minor episode from 1915 can best describe the impact of the census-taking and thereby the whole power/knowledge complex in the colony. On October 1, 1915, when the second census was due to be taken, all trains before midnight were jammed with panicking Taiwanese passengers: they desperately wanted to rush back to the places where they had originally registered before the census started. At that time, there was a rumour spreading widely among the natives: if they failed to show up at home to answer the census-taker's questions, they would be deemed and classified as anticolonial "bandits," with consequences that are not difficult to imagine. So people tried everything that they could to rush home. Those jammed trains were a sign of a certain form of governmentality. And those panicking nocturnal travelers were nothing but objects of knowledge who were determined to meet this singular "regime of truth" punctually, and thus subjected themselves to the successful administration of colonial power/knowledge.

One commentator in Taiwan observes, "When these people were rushing on their way home in the night, they had unwittingly entered a brand new world of time" (Lu 1998:56). Lu is right to point out the temporal dimension of colonial discipline, but it makes more sense to say that the people rushing home had unwittingly entered a new world of colonial governmentality in which knowledge had become an effective technique of power, and power became increasingly reliant on accurate systems of knowledge. As Rose and Miller point out, "making people write things down and count them—register births, report incomes, fill in censuses—is itself a kind of government of them, an incitement to individuals to construe their lives according to such norms" (Rose and Miller 1992:187).

In 1901 the Japanese colonial government organized the "Temporary Bureau for Investigation of Traditional Customs," which was arguably "the first investigation institution of human sciences in Taiwan" (Tu 1991:34). The results of its investigations, according to some commentators, were the *first* organized books about the tradition and customs of the Han people (Chen Chi-liu 1980:7). In 1905 (when the land survey was completed), ten years after the Japanese colonizer occupied Taiwan, the *first* accurate, complete, and detailed map of Taiwan was drawn up by the colonial government. Also in 1905, the Japanese colonial government held the *first* census in Taiwan and estimated the total population in Taiwan to be 3,039,751 (Taiwanese: 2,973,280; others: 66,471). There were on average 6.2 people per household; the ratio of men to women was 112.7:100; and there were 85 people per square kilometer (Chen Yen-hong 1986:75). For the first time, the island's rulers knew the exact numbers of its population. "The Manchu [Qing] government did not even know the number of its subjects, far less their behaviour with respect to births and deaths. The colonial regime founded by the Japanese started a thorough system of vital statistics only after a decade of control" (Barclay 1954:145). In 1908 the Japanese colonial government began its study of the aborigine people in Taiwan. It found nine main groups: *Taiyal, Saisett, Ami, Bunun, Tsuou, Piyuma, Tsarisen, Paiwan,* and *Yami*. For the *first* time in Taiwan's history the aborigine people on the island had all been put under scientific study and clearly identified. And, in 1911, some Japanese botanists published a book entitled *The Dictionary of Vegetation in Taiwan*, in which for the *first* time in Taiwanese history the plants of the island—which have no direct governmental meaning—were clearly identified, described, and categorized in print. More examples could be given.

So what kind of conclusion can be drawn from these "firsts"? Seen individually, these events are no more than five minor episodes drawn from a long colonial history, but if seen from a panoramic point of view, these separate events have a previously unseen feature. They all demonstrate the close relation between power and knowledge, between political rationality and governmental technologies; more precisely, they are all products of a certain form of colonial "governmentalization of the state."

Yet the peculiarity of the Japanese form of colonial knowledge should not be exaggerated. The Japanese were by no means the only colonizer that launched massive colonial surveys, nor had the Japanese "invented" the link between science and colonial administration. "Knowing the colonized" is also an essential element of other colonial governments. Zaheer Baber, for instance, claims that "British India proved to be a good testing ground for a number of experiments in the application of science and technology by the colonial state. What followed in nineteenth-century India was one of the largest state-sponsored scientific research and development activities undertaken in modern time" (Baber 1996: 185–186). I do not claim that the Japanese had the most "accurate" colonial knowledge in the world. Nor do I deny entirely the "scientific" knowledge of the European colonial powers. What is proposed here is a rather simple theoretical point: the form of colonial knowledge—whether knowledge is imaginary, and whether colonial knowledge entails an imaginary governance—is not an epistemological question; it is above all a governmental question. In fact, it is those concrete governmental technologies—police and hokō system, for example—that determine the scope, nature, and "usefulness" of colonial knowledge.[4]

In 1978 Edward Said asked a famous question in his *Orientalism:* can there be a true representation of anything? Said answered in the negative, at least as far as Islam was concerned. He asserted that "a representation is *eo ipso* implicated, intertwined, embedded, interwoven with a great many other things besides the 'truth,' which is itself a representation" (1978:22). I agree. Thanks to Said, we now understand that every form of colonial representation is bound up with the colonial power itself. However, Said's disillusionment has ironically created a new illusion: after *Orientalism,* colonial knowledge and colonial discourse in general became asymmetrically conceived of as a matter of imagination and mis-representation, as if the whole scope and purpose of colonial knowledge and colonial discourse were simply to distort the colonized. In the words of David Ludden, "the particulars that connect histories of imperialism and knowledge are missing" (Ludden 1993:250). This is an inadequate interpretation of colonial knowledge. I am not denying, of course, Said's contribution, nor am I suggesting that colonial discourse contains no element of mis-representation and distortion. What I am suggesting, rather, is that we should stop naively equating a colonial government's "regime of truth" with an enterprise of distortion. To say that colonial power is always based on imagination and illusions, and always attempts to distort and mis-represent the colonized, is to conceal the most subtle technologies and techniques of colonial government.

The land survey and census discussed in this article both had their importance for the colonial governmentality. In the land survey, the colonizer showed its thirst for knowledge of its newly gained territory. Maps and numbers were produced to represent what was to be governed. Similarly, in the census we witness one of the most accomplished feats of data-collection from any population, at any given time, anywhere in the world. After being carefully counted, not only were the natives construed to be a governable entity but they began to enter a sphere of governmental calculation.

So, can there ever be a true representation of anything? As far as governmentality is concerned, Said obviously asked the wrong question and then searched for his answer in the wrong places: novels, operas, and so on. To understand the way in which the colonized were actually governed, we have to answer the question posed by Dean: what forms of thought, knowledge, expertise, strategies, means of calculation, or rationality are employed in practices of governing? (Dean 1999:31). We should talk less about how representations of colonial subjects have been distorted, and more about how the alien government came to be able to know the colonized and their colony as well as they knew the palms of their own hands.

NOTES

1. Another significant omission is Japanese colonialism. Japan as a colonial power is not mentioned in this introduction.

2. The land survey focused only on the west side of Taiwan, and left the east coast and the mountain area untouched. It was not until the forest survey started in 1910 that the entire island was thoroughly investigated.

3. For a discussion of this point, see Ka 1995.

4. For a detailed discussion on the relation between knowledge and governmental technologies in colonial Taiwan, see Yao 2002.

REFERENCES

Anderson, Benedict. 1991. *Imagined Communities: Reflections on the Origin and Spread of Nationalism.* London: Verso.

Appadurai, Arjun. 1997. "Number in the Colonial Imagination." In *Modernity at Large: Cultural Dimensions of Globalization.* Minneapolis: University of Minnesota Press.

Baber, Zaheer, 1996. *The Science of Empire: Scientific Knowledge, Civilization, and Colonial Rule in India.* New York: State University of New York Press.

Barclay, George. 1954. *Colonial Development and Population in Taiwan.* Port Washington: Kennikat Press.

Bhabha, Homi. 1994. *The Location of Culture.* London: Routledge.

Chang Han-yu and Ramon Myers. 1963. "Japanese Colonial Development Policy in Taiwan, 1895–1906: A Case of Bureaucratic Entrepreneurship." *Journal of Asian Studies* 22.2.

Chatterjee, Partha. 1993. *The Nation and Its Fragments: Colonial and Postcolonial Histories.* Princeton: Princeton University Press.

Chen Chao-ming 陳昭銘. 2000. "淺釋日據時期台灣土地調查. [Some preliminary accounts of Taiwan's land survey under Japanese rule]." 現代地政 [Modern land administration] 228.

Chen Chi-liu 陳奇祿. 1980. "台灣的人類學研究 [Anthropological studies in Taiwan]." *Chinese Cultural Renaissance Monthly* 11.6.

Chen Yen-hong 陳豔紅. 1986. "後藤新平的治台政策 [Gotō Shimpei's colonial policies in Taiwan]." M.A. thesis, Japanese Research Centre, Dan-Chiang University.

Cohn, Bernard. 1987. "The Census, Social Structure, and Objectification in South Asia." In *An Anthropologist Among the Historians, and Other Essays.* Delhi: Oxford University Press.

———. 1996. *Colonialism and Its Forms of Knowledge: The British in India.* Princeton: Princeton University Press.

Comaroff, John. 1997. "Reflections on the Colonial State, in South Africa and Elsewhere: Factions, Fragments, Facts, and Fictions." *Bulletin of the Institute of Ethnology, Academia Sinica* 83:1–50.

Dean, Mitchell. 1995. "Governing the Unemployed Self in an Active Society." *Economy and Society* 24.4:559–583.

———. 1999. *Governmentality: Power and Rule in Modern Society.* London: Sage.

Edney, Matthew. 1997. *Mapping an Empire: The Geographical Construction of British India, 1765–1843.* Chicago: University of Chicago Press.

Fieldhouse, D.K. 1981. *Colonialism, 1870–1945: An Introduction.* London: Macmillan.

Foucault, Michel. 1979a. "On Governmentality." *Ideology and Consciousness* 6:5–22.

———. 1979b. *The History of Sexuality: An Introduction.* London: Allen Lane.

Fujii, Shizue 藤井志津枝. 1997. 理蕃: 日本治理台灣的計策 (1895–1915) [The aborigine policy of the Taiwan government-general in the period of Japanese dominance, 1895–1915]. Taipei: Wen-Yin-Tong.

Hacking, Ian. 1982. "Biopower and the Avalanche of Printed Numbers." *Humanities in Society* 5:279–295.

———. 1990. *The Taming of Chance.* Cambridge: Cambridge University Press.

———. 1991. "How Should We Do the History of Statistics?" In Graham Burchell, Colin Gordon, and Peter Miller, eds., *Foucault Effect: Studies in Governmentality.* Chicago: University of Chicago Press.

Halliday, Jon. 1975. *A Political History of Japanese Capitalism.* New York: Pantheon.

Hannah, Matthew. 2000. *Governmentality and the Mastery of Territory in Nineteenth-Century America.* Cambridge: Cambridge University Press.

Hartsock, Nancy. 1990. "Foucault on Power: A Theory for Women?" In Linda Nicholson, ed., *Feminism/Postmodernism.* London: Routledge.

Heesterman, J.C. 1978. "Was There an Indian Reaction? Western Expansion in Indian Perspective." In H.L. Wesseling, ed., *Expansion and Reaction: Essays on European Expansion and Reaction in Asia and Africa.* Leiden: Leiden University Press.

Ibrahim, Abdullahi Ali. 1997. "Tales of Two Sudanese Courts: Colonial Governmentality Revisited." *African Studies Review* 40.1:13–33.

Ka Chih-ming. 1995. *Japanese Colonialism in Taiwan: Land Tenure, Development, and Dependency, 1895–1945.* Boulder, Co.: Westview Press.

Kerr, George. 1974. *Formosa: Licensed Revolution and the Home Rule Movement, 1895–1945.* Honolulu: University Press of Hawaii.

Latour, Bruno. 1987. *Science in Action.* Cambridge: Cambridge University Press.

Lu Shao-li 呂紹理. 1998. 水螺響起 [Whistle from the sugarcane factory: The transition of time cognition and rhythms of social life in Taiwan under Japanese rule, 1895–1945]. Taipei: Yuong-Liu Publications.

Ludden, David. 1993. "Orientalist Empiricism: Transformations of Colonial Knowledge." In C.A. Breckenridge and P. Van Der Veer, eds., *Orientalism and the Postcolonial Predicament: Perspectives on South Asia.* Philadelphia: University of Pennsylvania Press.

Memmi, Albert. 1965 [1990]. *The Colonizer and the Colonized.* London: Earthscan.

Miller, Peter, and Nikolas Rose. 1990. "Governing Economic Life." *Economy and Society* 19.1:1–31.

Mitchell, Timothy. 1988. *Colonising Egypt.* Berkeley: University of California Press.

Murdoch, Jonathan, and Neil Ward. 1997. "Governmentality and Territoriality: The Statistical Manufacture of Britain's 'National Farm.'" *Political Geography* 16.4:307–324.

Osterhammel, Jurgen. 1997. *Colonialism: A Theoretical Overview.* Trans. Shelley L. Frisch. Princeton: Markus Wiener Publishers.

Peattie, Mark. 1984. "Japanese Attitude Towards Colonialism, 1895–1945." In R. Myers and M. Peattie, eds., *The Japanese Colonial Empire, 1985–1945.* Princeton: Princeton University Press.

Poovey, Mary. 1998. A *History of the Modern Fact: Problems of Knowledge in the Science of Wealth and Society.* Chicago: University of Chicago Press.

Porter, Theodore. 1986. *The Rise of Statistical Thinking, 1820–1900.* Princeton: Princeton University Press.

Rabinow, Paul. "Representations Are Social Facts: Modernity and Post-Modernity in Anthropology." In J. Clifford and G. Marcus, eds., *Writing Culture: The Poetics and Politics of Ethnography.* Berkeley: University of California Press.

Rose, Nikolas. 1991. "Governing by Numbers: Figuring Out Democracy." *Accounting Organizations and Society* 16.7:673–692.

———. 1999. *Powers of Freedom: Reframing Political Thought.* Cambridge: Cambridge University Press.

Rose, Nikolas, and Peter Miller. 1992. "Political Power Beyond the State: Problematic of Government." *British Journal of Sociology* 43:173–205.

Said, Edward. 1978 [1991]. *Orientalism: Western Conceptions of the Orient.* London: Penguin.

Shepherd, John Robert. 1993. *Statecraft and Political Economy on the Taiwan Frontier, 1600–1800.* Stanford: Stanford University Press.

Shih, Tien-fu 施添福. 2000. "台灣傳統聚落的血緣構成: 以研究方法為中心 [The lineage constitution of traditional settlement in Taiwan: A research method]." 宜蘭文獻 [The Yilan journal of history] 47:3–47.

———. 2001. "日治時代台灣地域社會的空間結構及其發展機制: 以民雄為例 [Spatial structure and the development mechanism of Taiwan's territorial society during the Japanese era: The case of Ming-hsiung]." 台灣史 研究 [Taiwan historical research] 8.1:1–39.

Stoler, Ann Laura, and Frederick Cooper. 1997. "Between Metropole and Colony: Rethinking a Research Agenda." In L. A. Stoler and F. Cooper, eds., *Tensions of Empire: Colonial Cultures in a Bourgeois World.* Berkeley: University of California Press.

Statistical Office of Taiwan's Administrative Bureau 台灣省行政長官公署統計室. 1946. 台灣省五十一年來統計提要 [Statistical summaries of Taiwan province in the past fifty-one years]. Taipei.

Takekoshi, Yosaburo. 1907. *Japanese Rule in Formosa.* Trans. George Braithwaite. London: Longmans, Green and Co.

Tsurumi, Patricia. 1967. "Taiwan Under Kodama Gentaro and Goto Shimpei." In Albert Craig, ed., *Papers on Japan* 4. Harvard East Asian Research Center, Cambridge, Mass.

Tu Zhaoyan 涂照彥. 1991. 日本帝國主義的台灣 [Taiwan under Japanese imperialism]. Taipei: Jen Chian Publications.

Woolf, Stuart. 1989. "Statistics and the Modern State." *Comparative Studies of Society and History* 31.1:588–604.

Yanaihara Tadao 矢內原忠雄. 1985. 帝國主義下之台灣 [Taiwan under imperialism]. Trans. S. W Cho. Taipei: Pamier Books.

Yao Jen-to. 2002. "Governing the Colonised: Governmentality in the Japanese Colonisation of Taiwan." Ph.D. diss., University of Essex.

[3]

THE FORMATION OF TAIWANESE IDENTITY AND THE CULTURAL POLICY OF VARIOUS OUTSIDE REGIMES

FUJII SHŌZŌ*

TWO HISTORICAL VIEWS: "OPPRESSION AND RESISTANCE" AND "INTENTIONAL ASSIMILATION"

In a dialogue with the Japanese writer Shiba Ryōtarō 司馬遼太郎 published in May 1994, Lee Tenghui 李登輝 noted that "up until today, those who have held power over Taiwan were all foreign regimes." In the same dialogue, he also talked about the sadness of being "born as a Taiwanese who cannot do anything for Taiwan."[1]

A year before this dialogue took place, Japanese political scientist of East Asia Itō Kiyoshi 伊藤潔 published *Taiwan: Four Hundred Years of History and Its Outlook* (Chūkō shinsho series). There Itō describes his mother, Liu Zhu, who lives in Taiwan and is part of the generation of Taiwanese that was educated in the Japanese language. Summarizing Taiwanese history since 1624, the author points out that the four hundred years of Taiwanese history, from the Dutch rule during the age of mercantilism (大航海時代) to now, is a chronicle of oppression by foreign regimes and the resistance of its inhabitants. The foreign regimes have included the Dutch (and Spanish), Zheng Chenggong 鄭成功's reign, the Qing (清) dynasty, Japan, and later the KMT.[2] More specifically, Itō locates the first birth of "Taiwanese consciousness" in the resistance that occurred during the early days of Japanese rule, and its further maturation in the struggle for Taiwanese independence that arose out of the February 28 Incident in the early days of KMT rule.[3]

There is no doubt that repressive foreign regimes had a great impact on the Taiwanese people. During the fifty years of Japanese rule, the population of Han ethnicity increased 135 percent, from roughly two and a half million people to six million, an indication that even though it was "under a repressive foreign regime," the society nevertheless transformed significantly. Just as the official languages of these foreign regimes shifted—from the literary Chinese of the Qing dynasty, to Japanese language during the Japanese colonial period, and then to Mandarin Chinese (modern Chinese vernacular)—the dominant ideology and media also changed considerably. Moreover, even the Taiwanese language itself has changed quite a bit under the rule of the Japanese and the KMT, becoming a dialect with distinctive characteristics that differentiate it from Minnan Fujianese (or Fukienese 閩南福建話).

How does a later regime deal with the cultural policies and cultural legacy of the previous regime? What kind of impact did the turmoil in cultural history caused by the frequent shifts of political power have on the identity of the Taiwanese people? In November 1994 the first international conference on Taiwanese literature during the colonial period was held at Tsinghua 清華 University in Hsinchu 新竹, Taiwan. At the conference I presented a paper entitled "The Establishment and Maturing of the Reading Market in Taiwan During the 'Great East Asian War': From the Imperial Subject Movement to Taiwanese Nationalism." Applying Jürgen Habermas's theory of the public sphere and Benedict Anderson's ideas about the "imagined community," I traced the formation of Taiwanese nationalism. When the outbreak of the Sino-Japanese War (1937–1945) and the Pacific War (1941–1945) led to a total mobilization, combining industrialization and the "imperial subject movement," the Taiwanese were put in the position of collaborating with the war. On the other hand, the enrollment in public schools (*kōgakkō* 公學校, elementary schools for the Taiwanese) and the number of people who were competent in Japanese language increased dramatically, providing a rapidly maturing reading market. This gave birth to numerous literary journals, and for the first time many native writers were able to express their wartime experience, which they shared with the six million Taiwanese.[4] What developed under Japanese rule was not a simple relationship of oppressive subjugator and the resisting subjugated, but rather a struggle by the Taiwanese people to form a Taiwanese identity while intentionally assimilating the Japanese ideology imposed upon them. What I proposed was a view of history focusing on "intentional assimilation" rather than a simplistic view of "oppression and resistance."

My paper here examines the process of the formation of Taiwanese identity under Japanese rule; I employ the methodology of social history to examine how it adapted to foreign regimes through the ages. Moreover, through a revision of my previous article on the occupation period, I intend to reconstruct a history of the formation of Taiwanese identity that links all three regimes. In any case, I would like to note that the following hypothesis was formulated within a limited amount of time based on the sources and previous studies available to me in Tokyo.

DUTCH RULE AND ZHENG RULE

Taiwan had been inhabited by Austronesian aborigines since ancient times. Han Chinese migrated from the Fujian 福建 and Guangdong 廣東 provinces beginning in the sixteenth century. In 1624 the Dutch East India Company established organizations to rule and trade in Tainan and ruled the island for thirty-eight years as its first foreign ruler. According to Chen Shaoxin 陳紹馨, the population of Han Chinese was about 10,000 when the Dutch first occupied the island; by 1661, it had increased to 34,000.[5] The Dutch set up churches and missionary schools for the purpose of proselytization. In 1638 there were 400 students from four villages registered in these schools, learning church doctrine via an alphabetically represented indigenous language called *Xinkang* 新港. Further, in 1657 a seminary was set up to educate thirty indigenous seminarians. They were also taught the Dutch language. In 1656, of 10,109 members of the aboriginal population, 6,078 understood Christian teachings, and 2,784 of them understood more than simple prayers.[6] The Dutch missionary education and its rule came to an end in 1661 when Zheng Chenggong (also known as Koxinga 國姓爺) attacked with 25,000 soldiers.

Zheng Chenggong plotted to use Taiwan as a base to eradicate the Qing, a conquest dynasty of Manchurians, and to reestablish the Ming dynasty. He encouraged the immigration of Han Chinese, and it is estimated that by 1680 the population had reached two hundred thousand.[7] Scholarly opinion on this period is divided, with some claiming that "the educational system was well established through the pyramid structure of *shexue* 社學, *fuxue* 府學, and *xueyuan* 學院,"[8] while others maintain that "political and economic stability and military expansion superceded concerns for education."[9] In any case, the three generations of Zheng rule lasted twenty-two years, and in 1683 Taiwan was officially incorporated into Qing territory.

Though the missionary educational system and the examination-centered education institutions were instituted under Dutch rule and the Zheng regime, their impact on the formation of Taiwanese identity was less than that of three later foreign rulers, the Qing, Japan, and KMT, because of the short duration of their power.

QING RULE AND THE EXAMINATION CULTURAL APPARATUS

Qing rule ushered in a period of rapid population growth. According to the estimates of Chen Shaoxing, the Han ethnic population increased by 1.8 million, reaching 2 million, during the period from 1680 to 1810. However, during the last eight decades of Qing rule leading up to 1890, there was an increase of only half a million, with the rate of expansion decreasing from 1.8 to 0.3 percent.[10] In response to rebellions in the interior of Taiwan and to the advance of foreign countries into the island during the late nineteenth century, the Qing government expanded administrative institutions, so that by 1885, when it became an independent province, the one prefecture and three districts initially established in southwest Taiwan had grown into a network—of three prefectures, eleven districts, three subprefectures, and one directly administered department—that covered the entire island.

Further, during the nineteenth century Han immigrants began to worship in their ancestral temples not the clan founders from mainland China (*tangshanzu* 唐山祖) but rather those who had first established their consanguineous lineages in Taiwan (*kaishanzu* 開山祖). The "armed fights among various regional groups" (*fenlei xiedou* 分類械鬥) of the early period gradually developed into conflicts between clan groups, an indication that groups from the mainland had reconstituted themselves and matured as a local Han society settled in Taiwan. Chen Chi-nan 陳其南 identifies 1860 as the turning point for the establishment of a governing system and the nativization of the Han immigrants.[11]

In an article published last year that focused on the local administrator and traditional educational institutions, the Japanese researcher Nakama Kazuhiro 中間和洋 discussed the relationship of the formation of the Han elite class to the process of maturation of local Tainan 台南 society. He notes: "The economic and social development of the Taiwanese local community was clearly reflected in the establishment of educational institutions, the number of students enrolled, and in the number of local gentry and intellectuals who were produced."[12] One might venture to say that the examination system and the educational institutions that supported the system were the major cultural policies during the period of Qing rule. Nakama quotes from the *Tainan City Gazetteer:* "The Qing education system followed that of the Ming dynasty in focusing on the examination system as a way to gather talented individuals and consolidate the foundation for the regime."[13] However, Nakama failed to consult the most significant study on the Taiwanese examination system, namely, Yin Chang-yi 尹章義's "Taiwan, Fujian, and the capital: The impact of examination groups (*keju shequn* 科舉社群) on the development of Taiwan and on Taiwan's relationship with the mainland."[14] I would like to analyze the examination system during the period of Qing rule on the basis of Yin's article.

According to Yin, from 1686 to 1725 schools were established one after another in the one prefecture and three districts, with a total enrollment of sixty-four. Many groups associated with the examination entered, including individuals who, having residency on the mainland but being unable to get into schools there, counterfeited Taiwanese registration documents and crossed over to Taiwan in hopes of attending the newly founded schools there. Paralleling economic growth, population increase, and the elaboration of the administrative infrastructure, by 1890 there were thirteen prefecture and district schools with an enrollment of 155 students. During the Jiaqing 嘉慶 period (late eighteenth century), a reverse phenomenon occurred when some Taiwanese students counterfeited mainland registry to get into schools on the mainland.[15]

On the other hand, the central government worked hard to strengthen the relationship between Taiwan and the center by adjusting the quota of students who would pass. Beginning in 1687, Taiwan was allowed one provincial graduate (ju-ren 舉人) among those from the Fujian province examination, on the model of remote regions such as Gansu 甘肅 and Ningxia 寧夏. The quota for Taiwan gradually expanded. Between 1854 to 1858, when Taiwanese gentry donated a great amount of money toward the military expenses incurred in suppressing the Taiping 太平天國 Rebellion, the number of Taiwanese juren was increased to seven. In 1739 a quota of one in ten Taiwanese examinees was allowed the finalist status of jinshi 進士 and, in 1757, the first Taiwanese jinshi was awarded. Later, around 1850, the quota of Taiwanese juren 舉人 was expanded and as a consequence, from 1823 to 1894, twenty-six Taiwanese jinshi were produced.[16]

While the examination system and the immigration of groups involved in examination society advanced the sinicization and confucianization of Taiwan, the nativizing examination-society groups made great contributions to the opening up of agricultural land through contracts with aboriginal people based on the Qing legal system, which had as its goal the preservation of aboriginal land rights. Further, they assisted in providing funds and lodging for Taiwanese students to participate in local and national examinations. The lengthy "pilgrimage" for the examination not only promoted interactions between various elite groups around the island, it also strengthened the ties between the center and the periphery.[17] Finally, Yin Zhangyi finds in the political, social, cultural, and economic conditions that facilitated the examinations the reason why Taiwan developed differently from the Philippines, Indonesia, and Singapore, all areas to which Chinese were immigrating at this time.

Tracing the history of how the prefectural and district schools established at the beginning of Qing rule developed into a vast examination system that formed the backbone of Taiwanese society, Yin estimates that by the Guangxu 光緒 period (1875–1895), Taiwanese exam-takers numbered around 7,000.[18] However, considering that the Han population had by this time reached two and a half million, and that the examinees ranged from teenagers to men in their sixties, seven thousand examinees cannot be considered numerous; rather, they represented the elite minority of Taiwanese society.

Moreover, as scholars such as Li Yuanhui 李園會 and Wang Zhiting 汪知亭 have pointed out, the prefectural and district schools did not offer classes on a daily basis. They conducted rituals and ceremonies at the Confucian temple and offered poetry instruction once or twice every month.[19] Similar to these schools were the private academies (*shuyuan* 書院). Distinct from these, there were also actual educational entities such as *yixue* 義學 (charity schools), *minxue* 民學 (schools for commoners), and *shufang* 書房 (private schools) that taught reading and writing in literary Chinese and the abacus. It was in these schools that students were instructed in the classics in preparation for the examination. The educational language used was not Mandarin Chinese but Taiwanese.

Shufang continued under Japanese rule. In 1898, a few years after the colonization, there were 1,707 *shufang* schools with an equal number of teachers, and the number of students amounted to 29,876. Numbers decreased for the following three years, and though they rebounded in 1903, they immediately began to decline again. In 1904 the number of students dwindled to 21,000 and was surpassed by the public schools (*kōgakkō* 公学校) set up by the colonial government; by 1919, 302 schools remained, with less than 11,000 students; by 1941, there were only 7 schools with 254 students.[20] From these numerical data, we can surmise that there were about 30,000 students studying in *shufang* schools and the best of those who graduated constituted the 7,000 examinees.

In 1941, near the end of Japanese colonial rule, the population of Taiwan numbered 5,680,000, of whom 57 percent understood the Japanese language. 744,000 students were enrolled in primary schools for Taiwanese (1942 statistic: see Zhong Qinghan 鍾清漢, p. 177). On top of that, there were middle school students (5,895), girls' high school students (3,354), agricultural and forestry school students (1,854), industrial school students (998), business school students (1,675), vocational school students (9,141), and teachers' college students (479). The students enrolled in secondary education were 23,354, compared with a late Qing literacy rate of less than 10 percent. Although in late Qing Taiwan there was a cultural circle with the group participating in examination society at its core, individuals who participated in this society were a very small minority.

What sort of media environment, then, was constructed by this small elite group? According to the M.A. thesis of an assistant professor at Cheng Kung University, Taiwan, Li Cheng-chi 李承機, even though the technology of woodblock printing was brought into Taiwan during the Zheng's reign, movable-type printing of Chinese was never introduced into Taiwan, even at the very end of Qing rule. Liu Mingchuan 劉銘傳's official newspaper *Dichao* 邸抄 in 1886 was printed by woodblock print. After Taiwan opened its ports in 1860, the commodity economy prospered and there was most likely a hunger for news, yet neither newspapers nor magazines were published.[21]

On mainland China, on the other hand, British missionaries had been publishing Chinese language journals such as *Xiaer guanzhen* 遐邇貫珍 (Hong Kong, 1853) and *Liuhe congtan* 六合叢談 (Shanghai, 1857). In 1872 the British merchant Major funded the first Chinese language newspaper, *Shenbao* 申報. Protesting *Shenbao's* biased editorials, Rong Hong 容閎 (1828–1912) countered with his own *Huibao* 匯報, which was funded by Chinese capital. *Shenbao* published only 600 copies initially, but by 1919 the circulation had reached 30,000. In 1909 Xi Yufu 席裕福 bought the newspaper,[22] thus returning it to Chinese management. Incidentally, Japan published its first newspaper, the *Yokohama Daily* 横浜每日新聞, in 1870.

For this period the literacy rate in both Taiwan and the mainland has been estimated as 10 percent. The population of Shanghai in 1865 was already 690,000,[23] the Chinese population of Hong Kong in 1872 was around 100,000,[24] but the population of Taipei 台北 even in 1896 was only 47,000. We can conclude from all this that the resident population had a great influence on the appearance of newspapers.

The infrastructure for transportation in Taiwan was not well developed. Even by the end of Qing rule, narrow roads only thirty centimeters wide connected the cities with neighboring villages. For travel most people relied on walking or single-wheeled *rinrikisha* 人力車, or sedan chairs. Seaports on the west side of the island traded with Quanzhou and Zhangzhou in Fujian province by boat and modern means of transportation were unheard of. As a consequence, commodity prices varied greatly. For example, in Taipei one *koku* 石 (bushel) of rice cost 5 yen 圓 36 sen 錢, but it would have cost only 3 yen 20 sen in the southern part of the island; in Jiayi one hundred kilograms of coal cost one yen, but in Taipei would have only cost 34 sen.[25] Although the island has an area only the size of Massachusetts and Connecticut combined, an island-wide market had not yet been formed.

With its low literacy rate, absence of modern publishing media, and nonexistent public transportation network, Taiwanese society was a long way from Habermas's idea of a "public sphere." The cultural apparatus built upon the examination system, though effective during Qing rule, had become an obstacle to the self-determination of the Taiwanese people. I shall now look back at the "Taiwanese Democratic Nation" established at the point when the Qing ceded Taiwan to Japan in 1895.

According to a study done by Huang Zhaotang 黃昭堂, when it was decided in the Shimonoseki 馬關 Treaty of 1895 that Taiwan would be ceded, native elites joined with the bureaucrats appointed by the Qing court to protect their own rights, and to persuade the Three Nations that not only should they focus their attentions on the Liaodong 遼東 Peninsula, but they should also intervene to overturn Japanese rule in Taiwan.[26] As stated in their declaration of independence: "All national affairs should be conducted by officials who were chosen by citizens through public elections,"[27] the first evidence of a decisive action being taken toward the concept of treating Taiwan as a national territory. Qiu Fengjia 邱逢甲, who became the vice president of the Taiwanese Democratic Nation, said: "Taiwan belongs to us Taiwanese. How can it be given and taken by others? The Qing court abandoned us, but how can we abandon ourselves?" For some intellectuals, a Taiwanese consciousness that took Taiwan as its boundary had already sprouted.[28]

However, the Qing soldiers who were stationed in Taiwan were Cantonese; they disbanded before ever fighting the Japanese army and eventually turned into a gang of bandits. As a result, city dwellers awaited the arrival of Japanese soldiers to restore order. There was no national army to fight for the newly established democracy. Not only were the soldiers Cantonese, but Tang Jingsong 唐景崧, who was made president over his own protests, was also a Cantonese who probably could not communicate with the Taiwanese inhabitants. He fled back to the mainland only ten days after the proclamation of independence. On the other hand, though the declaration of independence proclaimed loudly the ideal of a democratic nation, there was no movable-type printing to print it, no newspaper to publish it. Several hundred copies were printed through woodblock printing, but the only railway that could distribute them was a hundred-kilometer stretch linking Keelung 基隆 and Hsinchu 新竹, and even if the declaration could be delivered by foot or by boat, only one in ten could have read it.

Local organizations drawn from the inhabitants did fight the Japanese for six months. Huang Zhaotang identifies this resistance as "the genesis of Taiwanese consciousness,"[29] but he notes:

> Resistance arose spontaneously in response to the Japanese invasion, but in organizational terms, it was mostly immature small groups. Their reasons for joining with the Taiwanese democratic government in opposing them were primarily their traditional contempt toward Japan and their disgust at the behavior of the Japanese soldiers; they were not necessarily fighting under the command of the Democratic Nation. Even though there were those who resisted the Japanese with great gusto, there were also many who did not care about the war and even some who cooperated with Japanese soldiers.[30]

Qing rule lasted about two hundred and ten years; the intention from the beginning was to set up the cultural institution of the examinations. But it was only during the last thirty years of Qing rule, the Tongzhi 同治 (1862–1874) and Guangxu 光緒 (1875–1895) periods, when twelve presented scholars were graduated, that it resulted in a shared Chinese communal identity and a Taiwanese identity among the literati. In the nineteenth century, the nativized descendants of the early immigrants created their own ruling examination elite groups by actively assimilating the examination culture bestowed by the Qing court. However, this was still a long way from forming a modern Taiwanese identity that could enable the creation of the Taiwanese Democratic Nation when faced with the crisis of cession to Japan.

JAPANESE RULE AND THE JAPANESE NATIONAL LANGUAGE APPARATUS

Under Japanese colonial rule, there were those Taiwanese intellectuals who opposed the colonial system and even some who sympathized with revolutionary movements to create a nation-state after the May Fourth cultural movement that began in the latter half of the 1910s. But the Mandarin that formed the foundation of the continental vernacular movement was clearly differentiated from the Taiwan regional language in terms of both pronunciation and vocabulary. For the Taiwanese, isolated from the continent and its emerging citizen market, assimilation of the mainland's vernacular culture was impossible.

On the other hand, colonial Taiwan was slowly but surely being incorporated into the Japanese economic sphere. On top of that, the colonial government implemented assimilation policies to popularize Japanese language education. In 1933, 37 percent of children were enrolled in elementary schools and one-quarter of the population understood Japanese. Creative endeavors in Japanese also started formally when Yang Kui 楊逵's (1905–1985) "Newspaper boy" and Long Yingzong 龍瑛宗's (1910–1999) "The town with papaya" were both awarded prizes by *Kaizō* 改造, the representative general interest journal of that time.

The outbreak of the Sino-Japanese War in 1937 and the Pacific War in 1941 prompted Japan to intensify its advance to the south. To mobilize Taiwanese as the vanguard of its southern advance, the colonial government promoted the "imperial subject movement," an assimilation campaign that sought to Japanize everyday customs (weddings, funerals, and festivals, etc.) and to draft the natives into the Japanese military forces. As a result, enrollment in the elementary schools and Japanese literacy doubled in less than ten years. The reading market for Japanese language materials increased rapidly to 3.2 million. It was under these circumstances that the colonial government concocted the "Imperial Subject literature" to promote the campaign. Other than the cultural campaign, there was a planned economic campaign called "controlled economy," with an aim to expand military-related industries. In 1939, industrial output for the first time outpaced agricultural output, thus propelling Taiwan into the industrial age. From 1940 to 1941, various literary journals with circulations totally around 3,000 were created in Taipei and a fierce competition ensued for shares of the cultural marketplace. In other words, "the public sphere"[31] as conceived by Habermas had finally made its way to the colony.

Zhang Wenhuan 張文環 (1909–1978), Lu Heruo 呂赫若 (1914–1947), Wang Changxiong 王昶雄 (1916–2000), and Zhou Jinbo 周金波 (1920–1996) were all active during this period. The usual critical assessment of Zhou Jinbo as an Imperial Subject writer "toeing the collaborator's line" (Ye Shitao 葉石濤, *Taiwan wenxueshi* 台灣文學史綱, Kaohsiung 高雄: Wenxue zazhishe 文學雜誌社) has been revised recently and he is now seen as someone who "expresses the suffering of an identity that is torn apart."[32]

Taiwan's Imperial Subject literature can be said to depict the logic and sentiment of a Taiwanese people who, though not Japanese, claimed equality with the Japanese and asserted their superiority toward the inhabitants of Japan's newly acquired colonies. These sentiments and rationales were mediated through literary journals, which circulated in the reading market, and through a cyclic process of production, consumption, and reproduction entailing reading → critique → new creation → reading, they became the shared cultural experience of the Taiwanese masses. We can say that the Taiwanese masses, through their reading, came to sympathize with this argument and sentiment and to imagine that they belonged to a single community.

In discussing the formation of nationalism, Benedict Anderson maintains that "national citizens are an imagined political community depicted as a mental image."[33] We are justified in thinking that Taiwanese citizens during the war had formed, or were on the verge of forming, a nationalism, with Imperial Subject literature at its core.

When Japan launched the Great East Asia War, its proclaimed purpose was to construct a Greater East Asia Co-Prosperity Sphere. In reality, the so-called Greater East Asia Co-Prosperity Sphere was not intended to liberate various East Asian ethnic groups but rather to transform the Euro-American colonies into Japanese colonies by invading China. Nevertheless, in Taiwan the masses that emerged together with the ongoing war actively fashioned a Taiwanese nationalism.

Attention must be paid to the recent study of the educational system by Chen Peifeng. In his book Chen points out that:

> As for language education under colonial rule, Taiwanese realized the significance of assimilating civilization and enthusiastically pursued the goal of "assimilation leading to civilization" that was embedded in the Japanese language education system. In a sense, their acceptance of the language education because of their desire for modern civilization subverted Gotō Shimpei 後藤新平's theory that "assimilation equals discrimination" and functioned to advance the evolution of civilization toward equality. In other words, deconstruction by popularization. It was the Taiwanese position of "acceptance as resistance" that gave rise to this possibility.[34]

The Japanese language apparatus matured in the mid-1930s, roughly the last third of the colonial period, with 1933's Japanese literacy rate of 24.5 percent as its turning point. One example is the inaugural edition, in September 1934, of *Taiwan bungei* 台灣文藝, a literary journal published half in Japanese and half in Chinese, though in reality most of the submissions were in Japanese. In the editor's postface (in Japanese) to the April 1935 issue, he remarks, "We were accused of limiting the number of articles in Mandarin, but nothing could be further from the truth. We were always worrying about the small number of submissions [in Mandarin]."[35]

The examination system under Qing rule focused on the literary language, or "poetic language" (*shiwen* 詩文). Literary Chinese was pronounced throughout the island in a variety of local dialects. During the Japanese period the national language system was focused on modern Japanese, a language that took shape through the *genbun itchi* 言文一致 movement (unity of spoken and written languages) after the Meiji 明治 Restoration. Though Japanese, like literary Chinese and Mandarin Chinese, did not accord with the native spoken language, with the advances in literacy it nevertheless was able to function as an official language. A yawning gulf separated the language of the examination cultural system, with its roots in the traditional literary language, and the Japanese national language system, which was based upon the modern colloquial language, but there were also some points of continuity, such as the poetry societies, or *shishe* 詩社, which functioned as a transitional mechanism from the end of the Qing dynasty to the mid-1930s and early 1940s.

Zhang Wojun 張我軍 pointed out in 1924 that "perhaps this was true throughout history, but there is no Taiwanese literature other than poetry."[36] Neither prose fiction nor drama was produced during the period of Qing rule. Perhaps because of the limited literary market and frequent trade with the mainland, all classical popular literature was imported from Fujian province across the straits.

The ideologies of the examination social groups were created amid the poetic exchanges at banquets for government officials and landowners. Gradually this type of poetic exchange was institutionalized in the poetry society. Although it is often said that the first poetry society, the *Dongyinshe* 東吟社,[37] was created by Shen Guanwen 沈光文 during Zheng Chenggong's time, according to Huang Meiling 黃美玲, it was not until the end of Qing rule, when Tang Jingsong and Qiu Fengjia created the Peony Poetry Society (*Mudanshe* 牡丹社), that poetry societies appeared.[38] They appeared only when the examination system had reached maturity.

Poetry societies were in vogue during the early days of Japanese rule. Lian Yatang 連雅堂 wrote in the preface to his *Collection of Taiwanese Poems* (*Taiwan shihui* 臺灣詩薈) in 1924: "After the storm and fire, they first used the joy of chanting poetry to dispel the feelings of depression. When one voice sang lead, a hundred harmonized, and north and south vied to compete in establishing poetry societies so that now there are almost seventy."[39] By 1934 the number of poetry societies had reached 98.[40] Why did poetry societies, relics of the Qing examination cultural apparatus, prosper under Japanese rule?

The first reason may be the many Japanese language newspapers set up by the Japanese throughout the island. For example, when the *Taiwan Daily News* (*Taiwan nichinichi shinpō* 台湾日日新報) was founded in 1898, a Chinese section was inaugurated and a column called "The forest of letters and the garden of literature" published poems in Chinese (*kanshi* 漢詩) by both Japanese and Taiwanese authors. It is estimated that at the beginning of the twentieth century Taiwan had two to three hundred readers of literature,[41] and after 1899 representative figures like Lian Yatang often served as editor for the Chinese section.[42]

The representative modern Japanese writer Satō Haruo 佐藤春夫 visited Taiwan in 1920. Five years later, based on his experiences, he wrote "Jokaisen kidan 女誡扇綺譚" (Strange tale of the fan with women's precepts), which was not only a representative work of modern Japanese literature at that time, but also became a primary source for the prewar Japanese language literature of Taiwan.[43] The protagonist, a Japanese reporter for a newspaper in Tainan, becomes the close friend of a Taiwanese man named Segaimin 世外民 when he publishes in his newspaper Chinese-style poems opposing the Japanese.

In contrast to the examination cultural system, under which only a small number of wealthy literati had the opportunity to publish a few volumes of poetry, the newspaper, which relied on the new technology of movable-type printing, was able to publish several, or even ten-odd, poems that had been composed only a few days before, presenting them every day to an audience that had numbered several hundred at the beginning of Japanese rule but had grown to several thousand or several tens of thousands of readers by the 1920s. The old examination social groups were pleasantly surprised by this and produced large numbers of poems to express their thoughts and feelings, including anti-Japanese ones. Through the newspaper, they were able to gather many poets from a large area.

Ye Shitao has highlighted the conciliatory approach adopted by the colonial authority: "Many of the Japanese officials and staff members who came to Taiwan were familiar with literary Chinese. Promoting Chinese poetry became part of the policy of administering the island, and poetry societies were encouraged."[44] In 1900 Governor-General Kodama Gentarō 兒玉源太郎 and his number two man, the governor for civil affairs, Gotō Shimpei, sponsored a poetry group called the *Yōbunkai* 揚文會 (Gathering to promote literature) and Gotō promoted the idea of "study of the daily new affairs and the virtues of civilization." 151 invitations were sent out, and 72 people attended. The headquarters was established in Taipei, with branch offices in Taipei, Taichung 台中, Tainan, Yilan 宜蘭, and Penghu 澎湖. The headquarters held a grand meeting once every three years and the branch offices held a smaller meeting every fall. The governor-general served as the president of the society and was also in charge of setting the poetic theme.[45]

The 151 invitees were no doubt drawn from the poets who had published in the Chinese poetry sections of the newspapers. Almost half of them resided in Taipei; they were able to plan regular grand and branch meetings because of Governor for Civil Affairs Gotō's plans for a network of roads and a trans-island railway. In the eight years from 1898 to 1906, Gotō built 5,600 kilometers of roads 6 feet wide, 2,900 kilometers of roads wider than 6 feet, 800 kilometers of roads 18 feet wide, and 80 kilometers of roads that were wider that 24 feet. In 1899 he began to repair the old rail lines and build new ones, so that by the time the project was finished in 1908, he had created a 395 kilometer–long trans-island railway connecting Keelung and Kaohsiung.[46]

Yōbunkai almost stopped its activities, but in 1902 the poetry society *Rekisha* 櫟社 was founded in Taichung, then in 1909 *Eisha* 瀛社 was founded in Taipei and *Nansha* 南社 in Tainan. In 1921 *Eisha* held an island-wide gathering attended by more than one hundred poets.[47] Thus the classical poetry that was a remnant of the Qing examination culture, supported by the Chinese sections in Japanese newspapers all over Taiwan as well as the network of railways and roads, reached its apex during the first half of the Japanese colonial period. With the consolidation of the Japanese national language system, the younger generation abandoned Chinese poetry and began to write in Japanese. After the 1920s Chinese-style poetry declined precipitously.

OLD KMT RULE AND MANDARIN NATIONAL LANGUAGE APPARATUS

As I come to the end of my paper, I would like to end with a brief overview of the period of KMT rule.

Just as there was a major break between the Qing period, with its examination cultural system based on literary Chinese, and the Japanese colonial period, with its national language system based on Japanese, there was also a major shift between the Japanese colonial period and the period of KMT rule, arising from the transition to a system that took Mandarin as the national language.[48] The KMT fully exploited the Japanese educational system, which had achieved a level of secondary education so high that it almost qualified as compulsory education. They took control of all educational institutions, from primary school through university, and all organs of mass communication, including newspapers, magazines, and broadcasting, in order to move in a short period of time to a system based on Mandarin as the national language.

Whereas forty years after the inception of Japanese rule, literary Chinese was still being used in mass media, the KMT language policy was much stricter: little more than a year after occupying Taiwan, they had prohibited the use of Japanese in newspapers and magazines. This was no doubt because Japanese was six times more widely used as a common language than literary Chinese had been, but the KMT in promoting Mandarin made full use of the educational system and mass communication industry that the previous regime had thought essential to the dissemination of the Japanese language. Here again we see a transfer between foreign powers of a cultural inheritance.

Li Ang 李昂, a young amateur Taiwanese writer who had been educated under the new language system, debuted in the 1960s, some fifteen years after the end of the war. In 1982 she published *The Butcher's Wife (Shafu* 殺夫). At the time of the unveiling of the German translation in 1987, it was also translated into the national languages of America, France, Japan, Sweden, and Holland, and won praise around the world. This was very similar to the early 1930s, when native Japanese-language writers first published in local coterie magazines but soon appeared one after another on Japan's central literary scene.

In the two hundred and ten years of Qing rule, the last thirty years can be seen as the period when the examination system achieved maturity, and it was during the last ten-odd years of the half-century of Japanese rule that the Japanese national language system reached maturity. The latter half of the three-plus decades of pre-democratic KMT rule saw the maturation of the system taking Mandarin as the national language. By actively assimilating the cultural policies imported by foreign regimes, the Taiwanese people under each regime fostered the development of a Taiwanese identity and in the 1990s finally achieved a democratic nation-state. The question then is: How will the national language transform itself after a citizenry has taken shaped based on a Taiwanese identity and how will this change of linguistic consciousness affect the development of an already highly hybrid Taiwanese literature?

NOTES

*Translated by Faye Yuan Kleeman.

1. Shiba Ryōtarō, *Kaidō o yuku 40 Taiwan kikō* (Tokyo: Asahi shinbunsha, 1994), 495–498.

2. Itō Kiyoshi, *Taiwan: 400 nen no rekishi to tenbō* (Tokyo: Chūōkōronsha, 1993), 241–235.

3. Itō, *Taiwan*, 76 and 160.

4. Fujii Shōzō, "'Daitōa sensō'ki ni okeru Taiwan kōmin bungaku—dokusho shijō no sci-juku to Taiwan nashonarizumu no keisei," in *Taiwan bungaku kono hyakunen* (Tokyo: Tōhō shoten, 1998), 25–67.

5. Chen Shaoxing, *Tawian de renkou bienqien yu shehui bienqien* (Taipei: Liangjing chubanshe, 1979), 18 and 25.

6. Taiwan wenxian weiyuanhui, *Chongxiu Taiwansheng tongzhi v.6 wenjiaozhi xuexing jiaoyu pien* (Taiwan: Taiwansheng wenxian weiyuanhui, 1993), 3–17.

7. Chen Shaoxing, *Tawian de renkou bienqien yu shehui bienqien*, 18.

8. Zhiting Wang, *Taiwan jiaoyushiliao xinbien* (Taipei: Taiwan shangwu yinshuguan, 1978), 8.

9. Yuanhui Li, *Nihon tōjika ni okeru Taiwan shotō kyōiku no kenkyū* (Taichung: Taiwan shengli Taichung shifan zhuangke xuexiao, 1981), 3.

10. Chen Shaoxing, *Tawian de renkou bienqien yu shehui bienqien*, 19–20.

11. Chen Qinan, *Taiwan de chuantong zhongguo shehui* (Taiwan: Yunchen wenhua shiye, 1987), 25.

12. Nakama Kazuhiro, "Shindai Tainan chihō ni okeru kanzoku eriito no keiseikatei ni tsuite," *Shigaku* 3.4 (2001): 41.

13. Tainan shizhengfu, *Tainanshi zhi v.5 jiaoyuzhi (shang) jiaoyu sheshi pien* (Tainan: Tainan shizhenfu, 1979), 3.

14. Yin Zhangyi, "Taiwan ←→ Fujien ←→ jingshi: 'Kejushecun' duiyu Taiwan kaifa yiji Taiwan yu dalu guanxi zhi yingxiang," in *Taiwan kaifashi yenjiu* (Taiwan: Liangjing chuban shiye, 1989).

15. Yin Zhangyi, *Taiwan kaifashi yenjiu*, 535–552.

16. Yin Zhangyi, *Taiwan kaifashi yenjiu*, 567–573.

17. Yin Zhangyi, *Taiwan kaifashi yenjiu*, 573–579.

18. Yin Zhangyi, *Taiwan kaifashi yenjiu*, 552.

19. Li Yuanhui, *Nihon tōjika ni okeru Taiwan shotō kyōiku no kenkyū* (Taichung: Taiwan shengli Taichung shifan zhuangke xuexiao, 1981): 15. Wang Zhiting, *Taiwan jiaoyushiliao xinbien* (Taipei: Taiwan shangwu yinshuguan, 1978) 14.

20. Taiwan kyōikukai, ed., *Taiwan kyōiku enkakushi* (1939) (reprint Tokyo: Seishisha, 1982): 984. Zhong Qinghan, *Nihon shokuminchika ni okeru Taiwan kyōikushi* (Tokyo: Taga shuppan, 1993), 121.

21. Information derived from Li Chengchi's unpublished M.A. thesis. I would like to express my thanks to Mr. Li. Also, there were late Qing intellectuals such as Li Chunsheng who advocated creating newspapers. See Huan Junjie, *Li Chunsheng de sixiang yu shidai* (Taiwan: Zhengzhong shuju, 1995), 154–158.

22. Liu Huiwu, ed., *Shanghai jindaishi shang xia* (Shanghai: Huadong shifan daxue chubanshe, 1985), 218 and 260.

23. Zou Yiren, *Jiu Shanghai renkou biencien de yenjiu* (Shanghai: Shanghai renmin chubanshe, 1980), 90.

24. Norman Miners, *Hong Kong Under Imperial Rule, 1912–1941* (Oxford: Oxford University Press, 1987), 191.

25. Tsurumi Yūsuke, *Gotō shimpei*, 4 vols. (Tokyo: Kinsō shobo, 1965–1967), 338.

26. Huan Zhaotang, *Taiwan minshūkoku no kenkyū Taiwan dokuritsu undōshi no ichidanshō* (Tokyo: Tokyo University Press, 1970), 3.

27. Huan Zhaotang, *Taiwan minshūkoku no kenky*, 60.

28. Huan Zhaotang, *Taiwan minshūkoku no kenkyū*, 125.

29. Huan Zhaotang, *Taiwan minshūkoku no kenkyū*, 246.

30. Huan Zhaotang, *Taiwan minshūkoku no kenkyū*, 3.

31. Jürgen Habermas, *The Structural Transformation of the Public Sphere: An Inquiry Into a Category of Bourgeois Society*, trans. Hosotani Sadao (Tokyo: Miraisha, 1973).

32. Tarumi Chie, *Taiwan no nihongo bungaku* (Tokyo: Goryū shoin, 1995)67.

33. Benedict Anderson, *Imagined Communities: Reflections on the Origin and Spread of Nationalism*, trans. Shiraishi Takashi and Shiraishi Saya (Tokyo: Libroport, 1987), 17.

34. Chen Peifong, *Dōka no dōsōyimu: Nihon tōchika Taiwan no kokugo kyōikushi saikō* (Tokyo: Sangensha, 2001), 236.

35. Fujii Shōzō, *Taiwan bungaku kono hyakunen* (Tokyo: Tōhō shoten, 1998), 38.

36. Zhang Wojun, "Zaogao de Taiwan wenxuejie," in *Zhang Wojun pinglunji* (Taipei: Taipei xienli wenhua zhongxin, 1993), 6. Also, Huan Meiling, *Liang Yatang de wenxue yenjiu* (Taipei: Wenjin chuban, 2000), 69.

37. Ye Shitao, *Taiwan bungakushi*, trans. Nakajima Toshio and Sawai Noriyuki (Tokyo: Gcnbun shuppan, 2000), 3.

38. Huan Meiling, *Liang Yatang de wenxue yenjiu* (Taipei: Wenjin chuban, 2000), 70.

39. Huan, *Liang Yatang de wenxue yenjiu*, 70.

40. Ye Shitao, *Taiwan bungakushi*, 193 n.

41. Shimada Kinji, "Taiwan no bungakuteki kagenzai," in *Bengei Taiwan* 8 (May 1941). Also included in Shimada Kinji, *Kareitō bengakushi* (Tokyo: Meiji shoin, 1995).

42. Huan, *Liang Yatang de wenxue yenjiu*, 398–401.

43. For Satō Haruo's trip to Taiwan, see "Satō Haruo *Shokuminchi no tabi* no shinsō," in Kawahara Isao, *Taiwan shinbungaku undō no tenkai: Nihonbungaku to no setten* (Tokyo: Genbun shuppan, 1997), 3–23. For discussion of "Jokaisen kidan," see "Taishō bungaku to shokuminchi Taiwan: Satō Haruo 'Jokaisen kidan,'" in Fujii Shōzō, *Taiwan bungaku kono hyakunen*, 79–103.

44. Ye Shitao, *Taiwan bungakushi*, 20.

45. Wenlan, "Cong 'Yangwenhui' tandao 'Shinxue yenjiuhui,'" in *Taipei wenwu jikan* 28 (January 1960): 40.

46. Kitaoka Shin'ichi, *Gotō Shimpei: Gaikō to bijon* (Tokyo: Chūōkōronsha, 1988)50.

47. Ye Shitao, *Taiwan bungakushi*, 193.

48. For details, see Huan Yingche, *Taiwan bunka saikōchiku 1945–1947 no hikari to kage* (Tokyo: Sōtosha, 1999).

[4]

PRINT CULTURE AND THE EMERGENT PUBLIC SPHERE IN COLONIAL TAIWAN, 1895–1945*

LIAO PING-HUI

*[F]or a true collector the whole background of an item adds up to a magic encyclo-
pedia whose quintessence is the fate of his object. ... [C]ollectors are the physiogno-
mists of the world of things—turn into interpreters of fate.*
— *Walter Benjamin,* "Unpacking My Library"

*[N]ewspapers everywhere take "this world of mankind" as their domain no matter
how partially they read it.*
— *Benedict Anderson,* The Spectre of Comparisons

THE TANAKA COLLECTION AND THE "ANGEL OF [POST]COLONIAL HISTORY"

On March 6, 1929, the renowned German botanist Otto Penzig (1856–1929) died in Genoa, Italy, leaving behind him a rich collection of old books and periodicals on citrus fruits and other related subjects that contained studies dating from antiquity up to the era of Carolus Linnaeus (1707–1778). Among the 2,446 titles and 3,326 volumes,[1] four are especially valuable, as they were printed between 1480 and 1499, only a few decades after the Gutenberg Bible (1456): *Regimen sanitatis salernitanum* (Venice, 1480) by Arnaldi de Villanova (1240–1311); *Il Libro della agricultura* (Vicenza, 1490) by Pietro de Crescenzi; *Etymologiarum et De summo bono* (Venice, 1493) by Isidorus Hispalensis (560–636); and *De virtutibus herbarum* (Venice, 1499) by S. Avicenna (980–1037).

Penzig's private collection was auctioned upon his death and soon sold through an agent to Tanaka Tyozaburō 田中長三郎 (1885–1976), then professor in the agriculture division of Taipei Imperial University (the forerunner of the National Taiwan University, hereafter abbreviated as TIU). Tanaka had just been appointed the first university librarian (1929–1934) and was charged with starting to build the university's collection. An eminent Japanese orchard horticulturalist, Tanaka came from a very wealthy family—his father, Tanaka Tashichirō 田中太七郎,

was the founder of Kobe Bank—and used US$100,000 of the inheritance from his father to purchase the Penzig Collection in 1930 (figs. 4.1 and 4.2).

In his capacity as librarian, Tanaka arranged the purchase of several precious collections, among them the Inō 伊能, Huart, U-shih-shan-fang 烏石山房, Ueta 上田, Momoki 桃木, and Nagasawa 長澤 collections,[2] thereby making the TIU library one of the best in East Asia. The Inō Collection, for one, is the most comprehensive collection of materials concerning the Pacific Asia region under the South Advance Project launched by the Japanese government in its attempt to expand Japanese imperial forces before the Second World War to include the Philippines and Solomon Islands. To this day, the materials in the Inō Collection are most useful for the study of the aborigines in Taiwan.

The Penzig Collection, however, held a special place in Tanaka's heart. Not only did he place bookplates in memory of his father in each of the books, but he carried on the unfinished project of classifying and naming species by updating this material in the manuscripts. Tanaka, a notable agronomist himself, drew and catalogued trees and crops that he discovered in Taiwan and elsewhere during field trips, mostly by adding real-sized portraits of specimens to the volumes. The accumulated pictures detailed the process of Taiwanese oranges recovering from various types of termite bites and worm attacks; they helped establish Tanaka's reputation in his field. When the Japanese emperor acknowledged defeat and gave up sovereignty over Taiwan in 1945, Tanaka left his collection and manuscripts behind as the Kuomingtang (KMT) government declared them the property of National Taiwan University. In the 1960s Tanaka returned to Taipei to claim the Penzig Collection and his manuscripts. He was told that the collection belonged to NTU and that his drawings had been mistaken for useless cardboard. They had been cut up and distributed to schoolchildren for use during their art lessons at a time when the supply of good-quality sketch paper was deficient. Tanaka gave up his claims, although he found the results difficult to accept. He never visited Taiwan again and died in 1976.

Several elements are synecdochically revealing about the historical trajectories in which Taiwanese print culture became more developed under the Japanese colonial regime. First of all, small if historically contingent incidents like the death of Otto Penzig and Tanaka's inheritance helped make the Penzig purchase possible and contributed to the enrichment of the TIU library collection. 1929 was a crucial year, in which Tanaka became university librarian and had both the chance and the desire to purchase more books.

Second, in this exceptional case of colonialism and modernity, the ambivalent roles of colonizer and benefactor, of librarian and collector, played out in sev-

FIGURE 4.1 Tanaka Special Collection: the fifteenth-century incunabula.

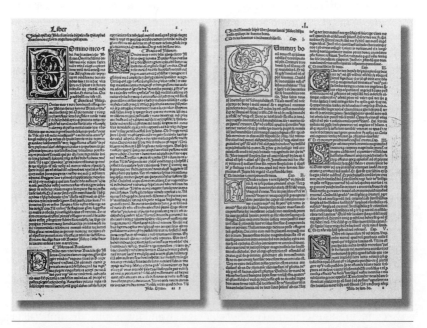

FIGURE 4.2 *Regimen sanitatis salernitanum* (1480), by Arnaldi de Villanova (1240–1311).

eral diverse arenas, among them public/private resources, personal/transnational predicaments, colonial and postcolonial situations. Like Penzig, Tanaka kept the collection personal even though he used the TIU library space and staff to catalogue his new possessions. He apparently didn't intend the books to be public property or part of the library collection. However, the semiofficial and problematic status of the Penzig Collection in the library put Tanaka in an awkward position when he tried to reclaim what had originally been purchased under his name. The question was further complicated by Japan's defeat, which left Tanaka a victim of transnational deals. These personal and historical mishaps ironically made Tanaka a contributor—albeit unwillingly—to the NTU library collection.

Librarians such as Tanaka thus helped build both valuable and comprehensive collections of material on modern social and technological issues, slowly albeit unconsciously paving the way for Taiwanese students to develop cultural literacy. Three major libraries in the Japanese period were instrumental in this regard: the archival material of the colonial government library, the special collections and modern library of TIU, and books on various subjects in the Taichung public library. Together with newspapers and journals, these libraries made texts in Japanese, Chinese, and a rich diversity of European languages available to Taiwanese scholars as well as the general public.[3] Motivated by the colonial assimilation policy, newspapers were published in bilingual forms from the time they were launched in 1896, with approximately eight pages in Japanese and two to three pages in Chinese translation (and one page designated for advertisements or public announcements). Common readers thus gained access to global and local news or information, and acquired modern cultural knowledge and skills. And because higher education was promoted, especially with the establishment of normal colleges and of TIU, private and public libraries were filled with books from Japan and Europe. In this regard, then, Tanaka's library project went hand in hand with the introduction of print culture and literacy at the time.

Third, the Tanaka incident is also a representative case of colonialism and modernity. Tanaka came to TIU largely because of the interests, power, and prestige that the colonial regime provided. His stipend at TIU was 60 percent more than he had drawn at Kyushu Imperial University, not to mention other subsidies and benefits.[4] The relatively "marginal" location of Taiwan gave him more freedom to collect research materials and books that would otherwise have been beyond his reach. It was colonial policy that TIU should have a library collection equivalent to what Tokyo Imperial University was purchasing at the time. This explains why NTU now has many good editions and rare books on European literature and philosophy in its special collections section, such as *Naturalis Historiae* (Venice, 1479) by Caius Secundus or the limited corrected version of Heidegger's *Sein und Zeit*. This is of course a legacy of the assimilation policy introduced by Izawa Shuji 伊澤修二, the first minister of academic affairs under the Taiwan governor-general, and realized in July 1898, when the "Regulations concerning Taiwan public schools" were promulgated to familiarize the Taiwanese with the "national" Japanese language and culture, and when three systems of schooling were adopted—Japanese, Taiwanese, and aborigine—to reinforce racial differences.[5]

Founded in 1928, TIU followed the colonial government's educational policy by employing a majority of Japanese professors to more "effectively" advance learning even though Taiwan was held to be an "extended" part of Japan, a part of the "interior." In 1928, when Tanaka joined TIU, only 6 Taiwanese were enrolled, while 49 Japanese formed the main student body. It is against this background of racial inequality and discrimination that Tanaka taught his disciples agronomy and built his public as well as private collections. The situation changed when his home country was defeated and the university was handed over to the KMT government from China. His private collection was then declared to be public property. Because of anti-Japanese sentiments, the Tanaka, Inō, and other collections were actually left abandoned in the basements of the general and research libraries for almost half a century. It was not until Lee Tenghui 李登輝 became president and launched a "Taiwanization" movement that the collections, by then heavily deteriorated and in deplorable conditions, drew attention again. History thus plays another traitorous and naughty trick on the collector, making narration of the colonial and postcolonial histories increasingly difficult.

The Tanaka case shows Walter Benjamin to have been correct when he associated history with an "automaton constructed in such a way that it could respond to every move by a chess player with a countermove that would ensure the winning of the game" or with a "hunchbacked dwarf—a master at chess—[who] sat inside and guided the puppet's hand by means of strings."[6] The relationship between colonialism and modernity is a "no-win game." Taiwan print culture, our more immediate concern here, has a more complex story to tell than simply a victim's tale or a celebration of moral good luck.

If we were to rewrite Benjamin's story of the "Angel of History" in a postcolonial hindsight, this is how one could picture the angel and the collector. His face turns away from the past. Where we perceive a chain reaction of events, he sees catastrophes—among them the February 28 Incident—which keep piling wreckage upon wreckage and hurling them in front of his feet. The angel would like to move, awaken the dead, and make use of what has been collected. But a storm is blowing, propelling the angel into the future, to which his back is turned, while the pile of debris and ruins grows underneath him.

THE DEVELOPMENT OF PRINT CAPITALISM IN COLONIAL TAIWAN

Print culture—"a new way of linking fraternity, power, and time meaningfully together ... which made it possible for rapidly growing numbers of people to think about themselves, and to relate themselves to others"—includes newspapers, books, and any form of printed material that helps promote literacy and a sense of an imagined community.[7]

Chinese books were brought to Taiwan when Ming loyalists such as Shen Guanwen 沈光文 followed Koxinga 國姓爺 there. Shen and twelve other exiled literati formed a literary society called *Dongyin* 東吟 (Reciting in the East) and saw to the distribution of their poems. In fact, even before the Chinese immigrants and exiles came to the island, Dutch missionaries had introduced the aborigines to the Bible and provided a translation of the New Testament in one of the local languages. The style of printing indicates that the printers may have come from the Fukien province of southern China.

However, it was only in 1895, when the Japanese colonial government took command and began its rule, that colonial officials on the island proposed printing a Japanese newspaper. On June 17, 1896, the first anniversary of the "initiation" of Japanese rule, *Taiwan shinpō* 台灣新報 (Taiwan News) was launched. One of its goals was to satisfy the needs of the Japanese in Taiwan who had developed newspaper-reading habits back in Japan. It also aimed to report important events as they occurred. The Meiji era is famous for its modernization project to "popularize" Western knowledge and national news.[8] *Taiwan shinpō* was inspired by just such a spirit, and in order to succeed it had to import everything from Japan to Taiwan—machinery, printers, and even paper were shipped directly from the homeland.[9]

According to Li Cheng-chi 李承機, between 1898 and 1900, Taiwan newspaper and media culture underwent a second structural transformation by going public. As sanctioned by the governor-general, Kodama Gentarō 兒玉源太郎, and civil officer Gotō Shimpei 後藤新平 (1857–1929), the right to operate newspapers was handed over to Japanese commoners in Taiwan, who collected capital and ran their businesses according to market logic. Public opinion was galvanized for the first time to criticize the colonial regime in Taiwan, and interest shifted to local issues in order to attract the attention of readers and consumers located in three cities—Taipei, Tainan, and later Taichung. From 1898 onward, local newspapers in Japanese had a much wider circulation in Taiwan than in Japan (see tables 4.1 and 4.2 for durations and circulations).

Even though the newspapers and weeklies or periodicals were in Japanese, anticolonial sentiments and cultural criticism prevailed in their pages, and corruption in the colonial government was exposed and satirized in political cartoons. Of course, from 1898 to 1945 the colonial government continued prepublication censorship and banned any printed material (and from 1930, films as well) that appeared to conflict with the interests of the colonial regime or of the Japanese emperor. Documents show that police stations were piled with censored books and news articles.[10] Together with censoring and banning the import of dangerous items from Japan, the colonial government resorted to all sorts of means

TABLE 4.1 Histories of Major Newspapers in Colonial Taiwan

Newspaper Title	Place of Issue	First Issue Date	Last Issue Date	Alterations
Taiwan shinpō (daily)	Taipei	6/1896	5/1898	Combined with Taiwan nippō into nichinichi shinpō.
Taiwan nippō (daily)	Taipei	3/1897	5/1898	Combined with Taiwan shinpō into Taiwan nichinichi shinpō.
Taiwan nichinichi shinpō (daily); ※	Taipei	5/1898	3/1944	1944: combined with five other newspapers into Taiwan shinpō.
Taipon shinpō (daily); ※ (Tainan shinpō)	Tainan	6/1899	3/1944	1900: renamed Tainan shinpō. 1937: renamed Taiwan nippō. 1944: combined with five other newspapers into Taiwan shinpō.
Taiwan minpō (daily); ○	Taipei	8/1900	3/1904	Publication permit revoked.
Taichu mainichi shinbun (daily); ※ (Taiwan shinpō)	Taichung	5/1901	3/1944	1903: renamed Central Taiwan nippō. 1907: renamed Taiwan shinbun. 1944: combined with other 5 newspapers into Taiwan shinpō.
Tainan mainichi shinbun (periodical, every 2 days); ○ (Taiwan Daily Times)	Tainan	3/1903	7/1909	1906: renamed Zentai nippō (Taiwan Daily Times). 1908: publication transferred to Taipei.
Kanbun Taiwan nichinichi shinpō (daily [in Chinese])	Taipei	7/1905	11/1911	Separated from the Chinese column in Taiwan nichinichi shinpō. 1911: resubordinated to Taiwan nichinichi shinpō.
Jitsugyo no Taiwan (Taiwan Industry) (monthly); ○◎	Taipei	9/1909	6/1942	1916: newspaper publication permitted. 1926: renamed Minami nippon (Southern Japan), published every 10 days. 1928: renamed Minami nippon shinpō (Southern Japan News), published weekly. 1938: renamed Honan jiho (Southern Times).
Taiwan puck (monthly); ○	Taipei	1/1911	1937?	1915 publication permit revoked. 1916 publication transferred to Kobe, Japan. 1918 import license permitted. Published until 1937.

TABLE 4.1 *(continued)*

Newspaper Title	Place of Issue	First Issue Date	Last Issue Date	Alterations
New Taiwan (monthly); ○	Tokyo	12/1914	5/1921	1915 publication transferred to Kobe, Japan. 1918 import license permitted. 1921 publication permitted in Taiwan, but ceased publication in the same year.
Higashi Taiwan shinpō (daily)	Hualien Harbor	9/1916	3/1944	Published with irregular schedule at first. 1924: published daily. 1944: combined with five other newspapers into Taiwan shinpō.
Takasago puck (monthly); ○◎	Keelung	1/1916	3/1938	1922: renamed Taisei shinpō (Taiwan Politics Report). 1924: renamed Niitaka shinpō. 1928: published every 10 days. 1930: published weekly.
Taiwan Business News (weekly); ○◎	Taipei	7/1916	12/1937	1918: renamed Taiwan keisei shinpō (Taiwan Government News), published weekly.
Tai oan chheng lian (monthly)	Tokyo	7/1920	5/1924	8/1920: import license permitted. 4/1922: renamed Taiwan.
Taiwan minpō (fortnightly)	Tokyo	4/1923	3/1944	5/1923: import license permitted. 10/1923: published in every 10 days. 7/1925: published weekly. 8/1927: publication in Taiwan permitted. 3/1930: renamed Taiwan shin minpō. 4/1932: published daily. 1944: combined with five other newspapers into Taiwan shinpō.
Nanei shinpō ○◎	Taipei	3/1928	8/1937	Publication permit revoked.
Showa shinpō (weekly); ◎	Taipei	11/1928	6/1942	1938: renamed Nanpō shinbun.
Taiwan Economic Times (weekly); ○◎	Taipci	6/1932	1937	
Takao shinpō	Kaohsiung	10/1934	3/1944	Published weekly twice. 1937: published daily. 1944: combined with five other papers into Taiwan shinpō.

※ = One of three newspapers for Imperial use in Taiwan
○ = One of the nonofficial newspapers funded by the Japanese living in Taiwan
◎ = One of the "yellow" newspapers in the 1930s (notorious for reporting on violence, murders, rapes)
Table provided with the assistance of Li Cheng-chi.

TABLE 4.2 Average Publication of Major Newspapers in Colonial Taiwan

		1898	1899	1900	1901	1902	1903	1904	1905	1906	1907	1908
Taiwan nichinichi shinpō (Taiwan Daily News) (daily)	Taiwan	1,444,651	746,929	1,214,782	1,383,471	1,420,292	1,587,534	2,171,220	1,599,611	1,986,863	1,667,156	2,590,697
	Japan	182,116	64,586	27,569	21,727	58,756	80,745	128,247	65,750	235,550	60,852	62,037
	Total	1,626,767	812,227	1,243,791	1,407,145	1,481,749	1,672,758	2,307,272	1,681,377	2,855,613	1,741,488	2,680,134
	(Average)	(5,198)	(2,595)	(3,974)	(4,496)	(4,735)	(5,345)	(7,371)	(5,372)	(9,123)	(5,564)	(8,563)
Taiwan minpō (Taiwan People's News) (daily)	Taiwan			135,415	831,692	1,107,307	884,146					
	Japan			72,893	361,770	379,630	116,470					
	Total			208,308	1,211,688	1,505,777	1,462,936					
	(Average)			(2,395)	(3,872)	(4,811)	(4,674)					
Taiwan shohō (Taiwan Business News) (weekly)	Taiwan	2,100	19,273	20,325								
	Japan	3,350	1,637	6,776								
	Total	5,450	20,952	27,101								
	(Average)	(838)	(655)	(554)								
Taihō (Taiwan Report) (every 5 days)	Taiwan				70,810	26,600						
	Japan				26,489	3,674						
	Total				101,682	31,504						
	(Average)				(2,034)	(2,626)						

Publication	Metric									
Kōzan koku (High Mt. Nation) (monthly)	Taiwan	2,586	8,683							
	Japan	732	5,621							
	Total	3,318	15,277							
	(Average)	(1,659)	(2,183)							
Tainan shinpō (Tainan News Report) (daily)	Taiwan	620,232	524,400	300,800	295,500	886,400	1,812,695	1,279,612	1,380,206	1,466,188
	Japan	93,059	69,000	45,000	42,000	17,664	66,402	176,416	137,088	200,767
	Total	723,138	609,900	356,000	345,300	907,245	1,895,897	1,480,762	1,530,716	1,687,724
	(Average)	(2,311)	(1,949)	(1,138)	(1,104)	(2,899)	(6,058)	(4,731)	(4,891)	(5,393)
Tainan mainichi shinbun (Tainan Daily News) (daily) (renamed *Taiwan Daily* Sept. 1906 onward)	Taiwan	182,574	335,735	373,800	496,766	644,867	517,634			
	Japan	18,630	17,690	22,500	24,138	26,509	18,404			
	Total	204,516	356,475	401,400	538,188	676,582	539,968			
	(Average)	N/A	(820)	(1,283)	(1,720)	(2,162)	(1,726)			
Kanbun Taiwan nichinichi shinpō (Taiwan Daily News) (daily; in Chinese)	Taiwan	1,349,528	859,700	1,183,460	1,254,725					
	Japan	12,298	23,100	29,688	13,102					
	Total	1,366,116	944,300	1,219,548	1,278,489					
	(Average)	(4,365)	(3,017)	(3,897)	(4,085)					

(average) : Average Publication (by year)

both to promote news media that supported the regime and to repress the public sphere.

It has often been assumed that the colonial government had *Taiwan nichinichi shinpō* 台灣日日新報 (Taiwan Daily News) on its side, countered by *Tai oan chheng lian* 台灣青年 (Taiwan Youth, 1920) and *Taiwan shin minpō* 台灣 (新) 民報 (Taiwan People's News, 1923), which were introduced by Taiwanese intellectuals. However, a detailed analysis of the content of the newspapers and journals shows that ideology might not have been an important motivation. In early issues of the so-called official newspaper *Taiwan nichinichi shinpō*, several Taiwanese publically demanded the right to challenge or correct "untruthful reports," and by 1910 half of the advertising sections were devoted to Taiwanese goods. Apparently long before 1910, the public sphere had come into being even within the news media controlled by the colonial government. We may well describe this institution of public opinion and anticolonial discourse as "anamorphosis" (as defined by Jacques Lacan) or "unbound seriality" (which Benedict Anderson found to be ubiquitous in tracing the development of nationalism and cosmopolitanism in media dialectics at home and in the world).

Drawing on Baltrusaitis' book on Hans Holbein's intriguing *The Ambassadors*, Lacan suggests that the distorted fetus-like shape in the foreground of this painting is not simply a skull or even the dread of death but "a trap for the gaze,"[11] a gaze "imagined by me in the field of the Other,"[12] the illusion of "seeing itself seeing itself" in the "inside-out structure of the gaze."[13] The phenomenon that he calls "anamorphosis" involves the projection of one's fears and anxieties (of annihilation and of castration) onto an "oblique" surface to produce a "figure enlarged and distorted according to the lines of what may be called a perspective."[14]

In the case of Japanese newspapers in Taiwan and their discursive practice of doing cultural critique from the inside out, of exposing corruption from a transnational perspective, the anamorphic vision was constructed around power struggles at home between Tokyo imperialists who supported the occupation of Taiwan and Kyoto radicals who were in favor of giving up Taiwan or even of trading Taiwan to China or any foreign nation for a billion yuan to avoid further budgetary deficits.[15] Fiscally, the 1896 tax income from Taiwan amounted to two and a half million yuan (2,710,000) while keeping the colonial government running required almost seven million yuan (6,940,275). During the following two years, aid from the Japanese government also neared six and four million yuan, respectively.[16]

Printed in Taiwan and circulated in Taiwan and Japan, newspapers like *Taiwan nichinichi shinpō* criticized the colonial government in Taiwan in rather harsh terms. Two political cartoons, for example, satirized the colonial officials' grand narratives of their accomplishments in the colony, and laid bare the corrupt official strategies of containment by using a pretty-looking jar to store rotten fish (see figs. 4.3 and 4.4).

FIGURE 4.3 Political cartoon: "Rotten fish stored in a pretty-looking jar." From *Kōzan Koku*, extra-vendor no. 3, February 17, 1899, 15. 即使蓋上它臭味也還漏出，不會 (閉口) 再用這個蓋上去吧 高山国. "Even if covered up it still stinks; it just won't shup up." "Try to cover it up with one more piece of paper." [The paper is aptly entitled "peace and prosperity."]

On the basis of newspaper circulation numbers, it appears that more Taiwanese were reading such newspapers and learning from the anamorphic visions of Japanese politicians and intellectuals in order to cultivate both their own literacy and their consciousness of an incubating civil society. Entries in an 1899 diary by Zhang Lijun 張麗俊, a town clerk at Fengyuan in Taichung county, show that he was a dedicated subscriber to and an avid reader of both the *Taiwan nichinichi shinpō* and the *Taiwan shinbun* 台灣新聞 (Taiwan News) from as early as 1900.

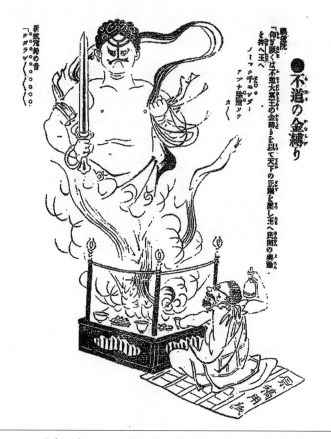

FIGURE 4.4 Political cartoon: "Evoking the false deity to fend off criticism." From *Kōzan Koku*, extra-vendor no. 5, October 28, 1899, 10.

不正道的魔咒 誤道 (諧音後藤) 院. Hudō Daimeiō (punning on Gotō): "While evoking the false deity to fend off criticism, Gotō heard the voice from above: 'Thou Shalt Not.'" 不許可.

After his retirement from a small office job, Zhang kept his newspaper-reading habit.[17]

According to Anderson, a newspaper or periodical makes national as well as world news available to its readers and performs an everyday institutional modeling by not only reporting news stories that are quotidian universals but also by translating events as they happen elsewhere into comprehensible and relevant codes or discourses for local readers.[18] Early Japanese language newspapers and periodicals allowed Japanese subscribers to see themselves via anamorphic visions while at the same time opening up possibilities for Taiwanese readers to connect with the outside world and to acquire a standardized modern vocabulary.

It is small wonder that by 1920 news media such as the *Taiwan shin minbō* (Taiwan People's News) very openly published Taiwanese views and critical opinions, and when the newspaper was issued daily it published many popular and imaginative fictional works representing social realities in addition to providing news reports and commentaries. Schools and public places were major sites where new newspaper literary works circulated. In several recent collections of oral narratives, public school teachers are said to have used newspapers articles in their classrooms. Together with the newspaper distributors, school libraries, hospitals, and other communal public facilities provided billboards for common readers.

As the news media rapidly expanded and evolved, more Taiwanese became subscribers to daily newspapers than to weekly periodicals. Statistics show that the print media on the island grew at such an accelerated speed that by 1937 there was practically one newspaper sale or subscription for every 34.41 Taiwanese. In the same year the total annual sale of newspapers imported from the metropolitan territory of Japan amounted to fifteen million copies, with Taiwanese newspapers taking up to 42.9%.

It is estimated that in Asia the literacy rate in Taiwan in 1930 was second only to that of Japan.[19] Though censorship and discrimination kept local Taiwanese from receiving a higher education, rich businessmen and the cultural elites sent their children to high schools and colleges in Japan. A checklist of publications by Taipei county writers between 1920 and 1945 catalogued thousands of poetic and fictional works that appeared in literary magazines and were made available by publishing houses.[20] It is apparent that during this period magazines, books, and the news media were becoming commonplace in Taiwanese people's daily experience.

ANAMORPHIC VISION AND COSMOPOLITANISM

Newspapers and the media had since 1895 become the domestic battleground for Japanese wars fought on distant fields—Taiwan, Manchuria, Korea, and even Okinawa. Officials and statesmen survived political struggles first by doing remarkably well in the colonies—particularly in Taiwan, as in the case of Gotō Shimpei, who modernized the systems of census, public health, and infrastructure, among other things—and then by overturning their opponents at home when the latter made wrong judgments or moves about riots in the colonies. The transnational or transcolonial character of the news media thus brought about anamorphic visions of seeing colonizers seeing themselves and of envisioning the colonized seeing their "masters" exposed by their colleagues from afar.

Often the rivalries and tensions between the military and the civilian officials in the metropolis were acted out in and displaced and distorted onto the colony. In spite of Gotō's achievements in modernizing Taiwan, he was faulted for failing to realize his colonial policy regarding localization and incorporation. Because of such criticisms launched against him from home, Gotō was recalled. Although he was later cleared of accusations, he was not able to form his cabinet in spite of his popularity as minister of transportation.[21]

In October 1919, with the death of the seventh governor-general, Lieutenant-General Akashi Motojirō 明石元二郎, Prime Minister Hara Kei 原敬 was finally able to appoint Den Kenjirō 田健治郎 (1919–1923) as Taiwan's first civilian governor-general to bring into effect his reforms in the colony. Hara Kei's rise to power greatly depended on using Taiwanese news media to expose corruption and violence in the colony.

The second feature of Taiwan's news media between 1895 and 1945 is the "unself-conscious" modernization process it brought about in modeling readers and citizens to follow national and international news in serialization, and in standardizing new vocabulary in such areas as the economy, technology, cultural literacy, and political representation. In addition to channeling the anamorphic vision back and forth between the metropolitan center and the colonial peripheries, the news media of the time also reported local and foreign events, thus providing the Taiwanese a cosmopolitan knowledge of the modern world.

As advanced by Anderson, newspapers embody two interconnected principles of coherence: worldliness and universality.[22] No matter how partially readers may be able to decode messages in the media, "newspapers everywhere take 'this world of mankind' as their domain" and override formal boundaries. "In Misbach's era, Peru, Austro-Hungary, Japan, the Ottoman Empire—no matter how vast the real differences between the populations, languages, beliefs, and conditions of life within them—," Anderson suggests, "were reported on in a profoundly homogenized manner." "Tenno there might be inside Japan, but he would appear in newspapers everywhere else as (an) Emperor. Gandhi might be the Mahatma in Bombay, but elsewhere he would be described as 'a' Nationalist, 'an' agitator, 'a' [Hindu] leader. St. Petersburg, Caracas, and Addis Ababa—all capitals. Jamaica, Cambodia, Angola—all colonies."[23]

This kind of "unself-conscious" modeling character of the media brings us back to the "unself-conscious" albeit "unwilling" contribution of Tanaka to NTU's library collection. In fact, when Tanaka tried to catalogue his Penzig Collection using research assistants—two of them were Taiwanese students—and library space, he was already engaging in the standardized labeling of new possessions and in offering privately purchased materials for public use.

Armed with new worldviews and with anamorphic visions, Taiwanese intellectuals in the Japanese period were bricoleurs in mixing transnational codes and cultural goods to their own advantages. This was especially true in the case of those overseas students in Tokyo between 1915 and 1935, who seemed to have no difficulty acquiring the Chinese and Japanese modernization experiences. Inspired by the revolution in China (1911) and the liberal spirit of the Taisho 大正

era (1912–1925), Taiwanese students in Tokyo formed the *Qifahui* 啟發會 (the Enlightenment Society) in 1918 and began to publish the first Chinese and Japanese bilingual monthly journal *Tai oan chheng lian* (Taiwan Youth) in 1920 when the society was renamed New People's 新民. It has been often pointed out that Taiwan print culture began its modernization with this locally produced journal.[24] However, our study suggests that modernization had taken root from as early as 1896, and that news media of the time already exhibited a transnational, anamorphic, and cosmopolitan (albeit discrepant or uneven) character.

NOTES

*An early version of this paper was presented at the Books in Number Conference, October 17–16, 2003, at Harvard University, in commemoration of the seventy-fifth anniversary of the Harvard-Yenching Library. Yingche Huang of Aichi University, Japan, and Chengji Li of Tokyo University, Japan, contributed substantially to the arguments of this paper, to such an extent that they may well be considered coauthors. I would like to take the opportunity to thank them and to express my gratitude to the organizers and participants in the conference: James Cheng, Wilt Idema, Jessica Eykholt, Rudolph Wagner, and Patrick Hanan, among many others.

Epigraphs: Walter Benjamin, "Unpacking My Library," *Selected Writings, 1927–1934* (Cambridge: Harvard University Press, 1999), 127.

Benedict Anderson, *The Spectre of Comparisons: Nationalism, Southeast Asia, and the World* (New York: Verso, 1998), 33.

1. Tanaka continued to add his own books to the Penzig Collection, making it difficult to tell what comprised the original acquisition. The number is given on the basis of the initial count. All references to the titles, publication data, and names (including Tanaa) are to the catalogue as compiled by National Taiwan University Library.

2. The collections are named either for the scholars who headed research projects on Taiwan aborigines (such as Inō) or in referrence to special collections of rare books originally owned by individuals (such as Ueta and U-shih-shan-fan).

3. See Huang Ying-che 黃英哲, preface to 記憶する台湾 [Remembering Taiwan], ed. Wu Mi-cha 吳密察 et al., Tokyo University Press, 2005, 9–27; also, Li Cheng-chi 李承機, 一九三〇年代台湾における「読者大眾」の出現—新聞市の場競爭化から考える植民地のモダニテイ [The emergence of the reading public in 1930s Taiwan], 245–279.

4. Wu Mingde 吳明德 and Cai Pingli 蔡平里, eds., *Guoli taiwan daxue tushuguan tian zhong wenku cangshu mulu* 國立臺灣大學圖書館田中文庫藏書目錄 (Taipei: Guoli taiwan daxue tushuguan, 1998), 18.

5. Wu Wenhsing 吳文星, *Riju shidai Taiwan shifanjiaoyu zhi yanjiu* 日據時代台灣師範教育之研究 (Taipei: Guoli taiwan shifan daxue lishi yanjiusuo zhuankan, 1983), 12–13.

6. Walter Benjamin, *Selected Writings*, vol. 4 (1938–1940), trans. Edmund Jephcott et al. (Cambridge: Harvard University Press, 1996–2003), 389.

7. Benedict Anderson, *Imagined Communities: Reflections on the Origin and Spread of Nationalism*, rev. ed. (New York: Verso, 1991), 36.

8. Yamamoto Taketoshi 山本武利, *Jindai riben di xinwen duzheceng* 近代日本的新聞讀者層 (Tokyo: Fazheng daxue chubanshe, 1981), 180–181.

9. Ishihara Kōsaku 石原幸作, *Taiwan Nichinichi sanshinian shi* 台灣日日三十年史 (Taipei: Taiwan ririxin baoshe, 1928), 9.

10. Kawahara Isao 河原功, "The State of the Taiwanese Culture and Taiwanese New Literature in 1937: Issues on Banning Chinese Newspaper Sections and Abolishing Chinese Writings," in this volume.

11. Jacques Lacan, *The Four Fundamental Concepts of Psychoanalysis*, trans. Alan Sheridan (New York: Norton, 1978), 89.

12. Lacan, *Four Fundamental Concepts*, 84.

13. Lacan, *Four Fundamental Concepts*, 82.

14. Lacan, *Four Fundamental Concepts*, 85.

15. See Tadao Yanaihara 矢内原忠雄, *Shi nei yuan zhong xiong quanji* 矢内原忠雄全集, vol. 2 (Tokyo: Yanbo shudian, 1963), 196.

16. Takekoshi Yosaburo 竹越與三郎, *Japanese Rule in Formosa* (London: Longmans, 1907), 134.

17. Hsu Hsueh-chi 許雪姬 et al., eds., Shui zhu ju zhuren riji 水竹居主人日記, 6 vols. (Taipei: Academia Sinica, 2000–2002).

18. Anderson, *Spectre of Comparisons*, 32–33.

19. Wu Wen-hsing 吳文星, *Riju shidai taiwan jiaoyu zhi yanjiu* 日據時代台灣師範教育之研究 (Taipei: Guoli taiwan shifan daxue lishi yanjiusuo zhuankan, 1983).

20. Huang Meier 黃美娥, *Ruzhi shiqi taipei diqu wenxue zuopin mulu* 日治時期台北地區文學作品目錄 (Taipei: Taipeishi wenxian weiyuanhui, 2003), 49–60.

21. Yang Bichuan 楊碧川, *Hou teng xin ping zhuan: taiwan xiandaihua dianjizhe* 後藤新平傳: 臺灣現代化奠基者 (Taipei: Yiqiao chubanshe, 1996).

22. Anderson, *Spectre of Comparisons*, 33.

23. Anderson, *Spectre of Comparisons*, 33.

24. Wu Sanlian 吳三連, Cai Peihuo 蔡培火, Ye Rongzhong 葉榮鐘, Chen Fengyuan 陳逢源, and Lin Boshou 林柏壽, *Taiwan minzu yundongshi* 台灣民族運動史 (Taipei: Zili wanbao chubanshe, 1971).

PART 2

Colonial Policy and Cultural Change

[5]

SHAPING ADMINISTRATION IN COLONIAL TAIWAN, 1895–1945

TS'AI HUI-YU CAROLINE

This paper examines how the colonial administration was shaped in the specific context of Taiwan under Japanese rule. From the beginning of Japanese rule in Taiwan, the colonial government mapped, reworked, and created a series of organizations based on natural villages, and actively sought to integrate these colonial spaces, themselves structured and overlapping, into the hierarchy of the colonial administrative mechanism. The Japanese colonial bureaucracy imposed a discipline of order on Taiwan, and by the 1930s wartime concerns reshaped this order, thus turning Taiwan into not only a disciplined but also a disciplinary society.

To decipher the operational network of the bureaucracy in the government-general of Taiwan (*Taiwan sōtokufu* 臺灣總督府), I rely heavily on legal sources. My major source materials include various compilations of laws, ordinances, and archives concerning Taiwan. I begin with the statement that the administration of Taiwan paralleled that of modern Japan—with major and minor revisions adapted to local conditions. The crux of my interpretation lies in the techniques of governance and the art of political and social "grafting," a process which I tentatively term "colonial engineering." I conclude that this governance technique worked thanks to the creation of a hierarchically orchestrated network based on bounded spatiality.

By 1902 a centralized police system had been put in place, the *hokō* system had been built into it, and state and society were beginning to meet at the county level where the police system interacted with the administrative hierarchy. By 1920, when the colonial administration of Taiwan delegated part of its power to local governments—following Tokyo's "extension of policies in Japan proper to colonies" (*naichi enchō* 内地延長)—this process of structural integration by and large had been completed. Structural integration, however, did not necessarily result in social integration. It took the two decades of the interwar period, according to my ongoing research, for the colonial administration to appropriate Taiwanese society for its use. In the 1930s the Moral Suasion movement, which came to be called "village revival" (*minfū sakkō* 民風作興) in Taiwan, was key to this process of social grafting.[1] Wartime concerns reshaped this order, turning Taiwan into a disciplinary society.

The examination of Japan's colonial administration in Taiwan points to the need to understand the informal bureaucracy; here the basic point is that the informal bureaucratic setup contributed to the "creation" of the "local." For analytical purposes, this inevitably raises the embedded issues of colonial governmentality[2] and, to a limited extent, also identity politics. Japan's colonial administrative initiatives in Taiwan illustrate the growing importance of colonial governmentality.

THE COLONIAL BUREAUCRACY

The administration of colonial Taiwan paralleled that of modern Japan itself—with major and minor revisions adapted to local conditions from time to time. As Japan's first colony, Taiwan was also a laboratory of Japanese empire-building, so to speak. It has become generally accepted that the bureaucrats who were recruited into Taiwan followed an established order of official ranking, which determined salary as well as the package of career benefits and outlook. Much of this experimentation was taken to Korea after 1910; after 1932, it found its way to Manchukuo, then drifted even further into the "Greater East Asia Co-Prosperity Sphere" (*Dai-Tōa kyōeiken* 大東亞共榮圈) during the Pacific War (Yamamuro 1998). This was the same source for the bureaucracy that the Taiwan government-general tapped into to run the colonial administration for half a century—with remarkable stability and efficiency.

In colonial Taiwan, as in Japan's other colonies, the bureaucratic system relied greatly on native leadership and local initiatives for control and mobilization. And yet the number of bureaucrats in Taiwan at any time during the fifty years of Japanese rule remained very small. The key to the mechanism of Japanese colonial administration in Taiwan, as I will argue, lay not in the formal structure but in the extra-bureaucratic setup. This argument is not new, but previous scholars have neglected the nature of this "extra-bureaucracy"[3] in a total empire of which Japan was the dominating part.

The modern Japanese bureaucratic system, like all bureaucratic organizations, was rigid in structure, and the law-making process could be painfully slow. Thus the tendency was for the bureaucracy to encourage central intervention at times, while making little room for local improvisation (Rueschemeyer and Evans 1985: 50–52). In Japan, the years between 1885 and 1900 witnessed the implementation of a series of reforms that ushered in a new civil bureaucracy (Silberman 1966 and 1974; Hata 1983). But from the beginning (1896–1912) of the Meiji period, an informal bureaucratic system had been created to help recruit personnel outside the formal bureaucratic structure (Yamanaka 1990; Ishikawa 1993 [1987]). In colonial Taiwan, as in Japan proper, the extra-bureaucrats and functionaries thus recruited were responding to the practical calls of the early colonial administration, and naturally fell into three major categories: technical support, administrative assistance, and the police force. Significantly, extra-bureaucratic personnel (such as *shokutaku* 囑託, *koin* 雇員, and *junsa* 巡査) were eligible to become officials after the turn of the twentieth century, thus entitling them to enter into the formal bureaucracy.

After 1920, the extra-bureaucratic system continued to grow in variety and to expand in scale, as witnessed in the institutionalization of the system of the "temporary staff" of the Taiwan government-general. Meanwhile, the extra-bureaucracy was extended to local administration, as seen in the installation of the "local official-treatment staff" (*chihō taigū shokuin* 地方待遇職員), which became a permanent feature internalized into, and yet remaining outside of, the formal bureaucracy. Equally important, it was later maximized to convert to Japan's war efforts with remarkable efficiency (Ts'ai 2001).

THE POLICE IN LOCAL ADMINISTRATION

Japanese rule in Taiwan was characterized by a large police role in the colonial administration. It has often been claimed that the Japanese succeeded in penetrating one step deeper into hamlets in colonial Taiwan than had Qing China, thanks to the Japanese employment of the police force. But how exactly was this institutionalization of the village administration accomplished? The process can be identified in three stages, as witnessed in the 1901, 1909, and 1920 local reforms. By 1920, the village administration had been fully integrated into the colonial administration, a bureaucratic structure with which we are familiar from oral sources. It was upon this structure that war mobilization was later built, and it was by and large this structure that the Nationalist government took over in 1945 (Ts'ai 2000).

On the whole, the police force, with the aid of the *hokō* 保甲, was key to local administration. It was the 1901 bureaucratic reform that institutionalized the role of the police in the administration of local affairs. The bureaucratic system in prewar Japan operated primarily via civilian officials in the order of command, thus involving the authorization of power. A "local" reform had to be initiated by, and meanwhile was accompanied by, a change in the bureaucratic system ("local" is here defined as "prefectures and below") in the administrative hierarchy; the term "bureaucratic" here is sometimes interchangeable with "local" or "administrative," depending on the context.

How could this happen in a colony that was closely administered by a group of bureaucrats who jealously guarded the system? The answer can be found in the 1901 revision of the "bureaucratic system of the government-general of Taiwan" (*Taiwan sōtokufu kansei*). According to article 22 of the revision, "the commander-in-chief of police inspectors (*keishi sōchō* 警視總長) was to be supervised by both the governor-general and the chief of civil administration (*minsei chōkan* 民政長官) and, in case of emergency, was to be empowered to direct prefectural heads within the jurisdiction of his authorization [i.e., the police administration]."[4] In this way, the police force was not only internalized into, but also placed above, the civil administration.

Also, the police force was institutionalized in local administration. Significantly, the general board of the police (*keisatsu honsho* 警察本署) was independent of the bureau of civil administration (*minseibu* 民政部), and this was to be a key feature of the Japanese rule in Taiwan. According to Article 17 of the partial revision of the draft for the 1901 bureaucratic system, the general bureau of the police was established within the bureau of civil administration—along with five other boards.[5] Suffice it to say that the board of interior affairs (*naimukyoku* 內務局) once challenged the installation of commander-in-chief of police inspectors, but the latter had the right to command prefectural chiefs, thus acting independently from both governor-general and chief of civil administration. The objection, however, was overruled.[6] Thus lay, despite later administrative reforms, the legal foundation for the police involvement in local administration. In 1910 an administrative law was enacted in Japan authorizing the police force to assist local administrators in cases of emergency. The 1920 administrative reform of Taiwan upheld this principle, and secured the role of the police in local affairs.[7]

Specifically, a mechanism had to be constructed so that the expansion of senior police officers was comparable to that of senior local officials. The 1901 local reforms witnessed the increase in the number of prefectures from seven (including four sub-prefectures) to twenty (*chō* 廳, or prefectures). In this way the door for prefectural chiefs was opened for both incumbent senior civilian officials and junior officials who had served in their positions since the beginning of Japanese rule. This was achieved by means of a "special appointment order of local staff of the government-general of Taiwan 臺灣總督府地方職員特別任用令," thus making way for qualified senior officials and for junior officials with a minimum of five years' service to be nominated as prefectural chiefs (*chōchō* 廳長). A similar device was applicable via the "special appointment order of police inspectors (*keishi* 警視)" to qualified senior police officers and junior officers with at least five years' service to become police inspectors; the number of police inspectors was then increased from one to three.[8] Both junior police officers and junior local officials had to be at the rank of level two (and up) of *hanninkan* 判任官 who also met the qualification of having served for five years or more. *Hanninkan* were the lowest-ranking officials, the other three being—in descending order—*shinnin* 親任, *chokunin* 任, and *sōnin* 奏任. A police inspector had the rank of *sōninkan* 奏任官, which was categorized as a higher-ranking official (*kōdōkan* 高等官). Also ranked as *sōninkan* were *keibuchō* (heads of *keibu*), whereas senior police officers (*keibu* 警部) were *hanninkan*, lower-ranking officials. The commander-in-chief of police inspectors was ranked either as *chokunin* or *sōnin*.[9]

So far it seems that police officers followed different recruitment and promotion paths from administrative officials. The level of observation here, however, is not the government-general of Taiwan or prefectures, but sub-prefectures. In accordance with Article 17 of the finalized version of the "1901 Bureaucratic System," a sub-prefecture chief was to be appointed from three sources, including senior police officers (*keibu*); the other two sources were *zoku* 屬 and *gite* 技手; *zoku* were junior civilian officials in general administration and *gite*, assistant engineers.[10] The "special appointment order of local staff" mentioned above was also applicable to *hanninkan* incumbents (except for *gite* and *tsūyaku* 通譯, that is, interpreters) to be promoted to the rank of *zoku*.[11] The appointment of police officers to head sub-prefectures was an institutional invention carried on from the earlier period of *bemmusho* (1897–1907, a predecessor of the county system). The 1898 administrative reform, for example, also made officials of general affairs (*shoki* 書記) and of assistant engineers (*gite*) candidates for offices of sub-*bemmusho* 辨務分屬; the third source, of course, was again senior police officers (*keibu*).[12] The 1901 bureaucratic reform, however, institutionalized the practice, thus making it difficult in later years to separate the police administration from the general administration.

There were twenty prefectures (*chō* or *ting*) between 1901 and 1909, but the number was reduced to twelve during the period 1909–1920. Special channels for promotion for senior administrative officials and police officers remained opened in the 1909 bureaucratic reform.[13] However, although the 1901 reform authorized the commander-in-chief of police inspectors to intervene in general administration only in emergencies, in the 1909 reform it was legalized as a general rule. According to the revised "1909 bureaucratic system," the commander-in-chief of police inspectors was to "direct and supervise" prefectural chiefs and police officers in matters related to police affairs. This development to unify the police administration with the general administration was further enforced by the fact that the commander-in-chief of police inspectors was also to serve as the chief of civil administration. This was the case even when the general board of the police was abolished during the two years from 1909 to 1911.[14]

In the light of the dominant role played by the police force in local administration, it is understandable why the 1920 administrative reform did not go so far as to challenge the established practice of so-called "unification of the police administration with the general administration" (*keisei gōichi* 警政合一). Rather, an alternative was offered so that qualified police officers could be appointed as *hannin* 判任 officials,[15] thereby completing the integration of the police system into the bureaucracy.

The county system that was formally institutionalized in 1920 was, in geospatial and administrative terms, based on the sub-prefectural (*bunchō*; or Ch. *fenting* 分廳) system established in 1901. The sub-prefectural system had made it possible for police officers to be nominated to the position of sub-prefectural chiefs, hence imposing the police system upon the administrative system by legitimizing police involvement in local administration. Not surprisingly, after 1920 county seats housed the local police headquarters, supervising dispatched offices (or police boxes) within the jurisdiction of the county. As such, instead of being abolished in 1920, they were further institutionalized into an intermediary level of administrative hierarchy for coordination, although by legal definition it was only coordinative in nature. In this way, the county system helped shape local society in an unexpected way.

The police system thus constructed was a centralized one, independent of (and also superior to, when necessary) local administration. This was to characterize Japanese colonial rule first in Taiwan and later in many parts of the Japanese empire, Korea in particular. Shih Tien-fu 施添福, a geo-historian, recently proposed a three-division geo-spatial (Ch. *kongjian* 空間) framework in an attempt to reinterpret Japanese rule in Taiwan. In Shih's model, local society in colonial Taiwan can be conceived of as being composed of three levels of communities. By and large following the local administrative hierarchy, the model refers to: (1) police officers (Ch. *jingchaguan* 警察官), corresponding to the county (*gun*) level; people of towns and villages (*gaishōmin* 街庄民), equivalent to the *gaishō* level; and "hamlet people" (*burakumin* 部落民), at the hamlet or natural-village level.[16] Shih's reconstruction of this local society in effect reconfirms the importance of the police in county administration.

Even granted that Shih's geo-spatial framework is valid when referring to the early part of Japanese rule, however, it is also important to point out that from the perspective of the bureaucratic system, these three spaces were developed in three distinctive stages, shaped in 1901, 1909, and 1920. The 1901 local reforms set the framework for the police involvement in county administration. However, it was not until 1909 that the *hokō* (built upon natural villages) system was made to assist in the "sub-county" (*ku* 區) administration, making the *hokō* an integral part of formal administration.

The 1920 local reforms completed the process of the institutionalization by converting big-wards into administrative villages (*gai* 街 or *shō* 庄), making *gaishō* the lowest administrative hierarchy of the colonial bureaucracy. The 1935 local reforms did not change this setup, except for some minor alterations of legal defi-

TABLE 5.1 Ratios of County Policemen to Prefecture-Level Policemen (1942)

Prefecture-Level Names	County Policemen	Prefectural Policemen	Ratios (%)
Taipei	739	1407	52.6
Hsinchu	895	1020	87.8
Taichung	960	1197	80.2
Tainan	839	1129	74.3
Kaohsiung	714	993	71.9
Taitung	410	445	92.1
Hualien-kang	400	528	75.8

Sources: "Shūchō ni okeru junsa no teiin" (April 1942; *Kunrei* no. 43) and "Taiwan Sōtokufu chihōkan kansei dai sanjūsan jō dai roku kō no kitei ni yori gun ni haichi subeki junsa no teiin" (June 1942; *Kunrei* no. 74), *Taiwan Sōtokufu oyobi shoshoku kansho shokuinroku (1942)*, 56, 58.

nitions; for example, *gaishō* for the first time was recognized as a legal body. Essentially, the 1920 administrative structure lasted until the end of Japanese rule.

The county (*gun* 郡) did not in itself function as a full-fledged local system, as it had no authority over local finance. The county government as created in the 1920 local reforms was composed of only two divisions: general affairs (*shomuka* 庶務課) and police (*keisatsuka* 警察課). It was by nature coordinative, thus emerging as a lower center of administration for local coordination. In Taiwan, as in Korea, the county system was kept throughout the colonial period. By contrast, Japan itself abolished the county system in 1921, and in 1926 county heads also came to an end. Thereafter, the term "county" existed only as a geo-spatial denomination in Japan.

In Taiwan after 1920, the county was once again employed as the operational boundary for the local police force, very much in line with the tradition of sub-prefectures in which the police played a dominant role in local administration. According to Article 33 of the "local bureaucratic system" of 1920, "the governor-general of Taiwan was able to distribute to the county police inspectors (*keishi*), senior police officers (*keibu*), and assistant senior police officers (*keibuho* 警部補), as well as policemen (*junsa*)."[17] In 1942, for example, in accordance with the above-mentioned Article 33, roughly three-fourths to four-fifths of policemen in each prefecture or sub-prefecture were dispatched to the county level, except for Taipei prefecture, where a greater police force was concentrated at the prefectural level. The ratios of county policemen to prefectural (or sub-prefectural) policemen can be seen in table 5.1.

Not surprisingly, the county formed the highest level in the local command of police power. Police bureaus (in cities) and boxes (in rural areas) were only dispatched units within the jurisdiction of the county. The model of Shih's three-division framework serves to highlight the local command of the police order. The *burakumin* simply refers to "*hokōmin*" 保甲民, which literally means the "supporting force to the police system." And the *gaishōmin* is a referential term, normally referring to a group of people who came to share an enlarged identity within the border of an administrative village. As such, Shih argues that the county embodied the integration of local administration with the police system.

By upholding the county as the pinnacle of his three-graded "imaginary communities," however, Shih in essence suggests that the county exerted a visible imprint on local society. This argument needs qualification, I contend, especially for the period before the war. There were certainly signs of growth and extension in terms of the expansion of social boundaries to the county level, but the centrality of social life remained focused on towns and villages.

CREATING THE "LOCAL"

I will now turn to the examination of the way the "local" was created. By making the point that the "local" was "created" in colonial Taiwan, I aim to test the idea of the "local" as an invented identity. I argue that the Japanese attempted to build a modern system in the colony out of a traditional one by "collapsing the temporal with the spatial." The geo-administrative system for administrative purposes was an institutional innovation developed over time in Japan's colonial rule. The "ward" (*ku*) system is a good example of this process.

The term "ward" was a sub-village unit used for administrative purposes. Much of the administrative system in colonial Taiwan was patterned after that of Japan proper, and the ward system was no exception—with historical variations and local adaptations. The ward system in Japan evolved from the *ōaza* 大字, or *mura* 村 after the turn of the century, and its counterpart in Taiwan was largely built upon the *hokō* (or hamlets) after 1920. Three major revisions took place over the course of the institutionalization of the ward system. Just as the implementation of the *ōaza* in Japan was antedated by a "big ward" system prior to the 1889 local administrative reforms, the ward system in Taiwan too was proceeded by a "big ward" system effective from 1909 to 1920. The 1920 local administrative reforms witnessed the creation of a "small ward" system, with ward representatives (*ku-sōdai* 區總代) in 1935 renamed ward committee members (*ku-iin* 區委員). Moreover, the history of the ward reflects both the evolution of Taiwan's local administration in general and changes in local settlements in particular (Ts'ai 2001).

More importantly, while the creation of the ward system in modern Japan was administrative and oriented toward state-building, it also provided links of social instrumentality for regional identity and local reformation built along geo-spatial boundaries. The local administrative system, such as the ward, worked not only because it was a fully integrated state mechanism, but also because the mechanism tapped into local sources (historical roots, social needs, and romanticization of "natural community"), which offered a vital means for organization. In this way "local" identities were bridged, although it remains to be seen to what extent such an enlarged regional identity was shaped over time. Moreover, the ward system was less normative in Taiwan than in Japan proper, and the *hokō* system in Taiwan worked both to regulate and to complement the ward system in a way unique in the Japanese empire.

In Taiwan, a "big ward" (*ku*) system was carried out between 1909 and 1920, as opposed to a "small ward" (also named *ku*) system for the second half of Japanese rule. A "big ward" of pre-1920 consisted of several hamlets and was equivalent to an administrative village of post-1920. A post-1920 "small-ward" was subdivided from an administrative village, but the system should not be confused with an earlier small-ward system implemented in the early years of Japanese rule. For a period from 1897 to 1905, small-wards (hamlets, adopting same name of *ku*) under the "big-district" (*gai-shō-sha* 街庄社; that is, sub-county) system were enumerated. The year 1897 witnessed the implementation of the "three-division" (plains, mountains, and in-between areas) administrative suppression strategies initiated by Governor-General Nogi Maresuke 乃木希典 (1849–1912), and 1905 was the year when the island-wide land survey was completed except for mountainous areas. The early small-ward system was carried out at a time when anti-Japanese movements threatened the colonial administration and when land and population surveys were still in flux. Accordingly, the enumerated small-ward system preceded a well-surveyed land and population as well as a stable social and political order.

The first period of the small-ward system survived the "three-division" system to the end of the Kodama (Gentarō 兒玉源太郎)–Gotō (Shimpei 後藤新平) administration (1898–1906). By 1915, these small-wards had come to be named in principle after one of the leading settlements, and the system paralleled much of the big-ward system. By 1920, the local system had been by and large institutionalized, and for the next quarter century until 1945 the "wards" were recognized as sub-village (towns included) administrative units under the *gaishō* (towns and villages), coexisting with the *hokō*, which was revived by the Kodama-Gotō administration in 1898. Both post-1920 small-wards and the *hokō* shared same bounded units of natural settlements. In this way, the "local" was created and the sub-village networks were both bound and bounded. As Mary Douglas notes from the perspective of institution-making,

> To recognize a class of things is to polarize and to exclude. It involves drawing
> boundaries, a very different activity from grading. To move from recognizing de-

grees of difference to creating a similarity class is a big jump. The one activity can never of itself lead toward the other, any more than institutions can evolve toward a complete organizing of information by beginning from spontaneous self-policing conventions. (Douglas 1986:60)

The creation of the "neighborhood" was another example. The prevailing view of neighborhood organization stresses the role of the state, in terms of control and mobilization, thus placing "neighborhood" in the service of Japan's "mobilization machine." An alternative view, adopted originally by a few Japanese anthropologists and geo-historians, approaches neighborhood organization from a geo-spatial perspective and zeroes in on the study of "spheres of worship." A revisionist argument, as I contend, is that "neighborhood" is a mediating paradigm that accommodates the two perspectives and provides a comparative framework of analysis.

The crux of my operational analysis of neighborhood lies in the "nexus" where the state met society. The "nexus-of-operation" approach highlights structural similarities, and it also underscores functional variations. In Japan, the development from *buraku* (or hamlets) to *burakukai* (部落會, wartime sub-village units organized along the line of "*buraku*"),[18] for example, exemplified constant tensions built up within the structure of Japanese-style bureaucratic rule with overlapping, but often also conflicting, norms and values. As such, the concept of *buraku* (and for that matter, also *kyōdōtai* 共同體) needs to be contextualized in its historicity.

In Shōwa Japan, *buraku* was generally employed as an equivalent of *ōaza* (*son* 村) or *ku* (sub-village divisions),[19] and the watershed occurred in 1889 when Meiji law provided for the system of towns and villages. As a discourse, postwar Japanese scholarship on hamlets has been impressively rich and well articulated (for example, Ōishi and Nishida 1994 [1991]; Ōshima 1980 [1977]). It will suffice to borrow the following generalization from John Embree's work:

> Before the Meiji Restoration there were about seventy thousand mura in Japan, whereas today there are less than ten thousand. For administrative purposes many groups of two or three mura were consolidated, and, as the mura now became in part self-governing and self-supporting, it was often necessary to have a larger geographical unit with greater economic resources. When this occurred, the old mura, as included in the new larger political units, were called ōaza. Naturally such a mura covers a comparatively large area. ... Each ōaza continued to function as a mura, much as it did before the consolidation. (Embree 1964 [1939]:22–23)

Ku and *buraku*, referring to settlements of people within a village, are not strictly geographical terms. In Suye village, where John Embree conducted fieldwork in

Japan in the 1930s, there were seventeen *buraku*, "natural communities of about twenty households each," and many *kumi* 組, "groups of three to five houses."

> Historically the social and economic unit is this *buraku*. It has its own head (nushi-dōri) and takes care of its own affairs, such as funerals, festivals, roads, and bridges, on a co-operative basis. … While for official elections involving governmental matters all men over twenty-five vote, in all local affairs each house has but one vote, a household being the political unit in the *buraku*. Life in the *buraku* is notable for its lack of bosses, and the nushidōri is not so much a chief as a caretaker of buraku affairs. Formerly *nushidōri* also supervised agricultural matters. During the last ten years, with the formation of the Agricultural Co-operative Association (*sangyō kumiai* [産業組合]) in each buraku, these functions of the nushidōri have been greatly reduced. Rivalry exists between the buraku. … Formerly buraku rivalry was more manifest than it is today. Buraku lines are to a certain extent giving way to social class lines. (Embree 1964 [1939]:26–29)[20]

A geographical sub-*buraku* unit for administrative purposes was *aza* 字, a basic division in geo-administration and household administration. Some *buraku* consisted of but one *aza*, but most *buraku* included several *aza*. Many *aza* were forest or paddy fields with no houses, thus often uninhabited. Like *buraku*, each *aza* had its own name. Another geographical division came to be called *shikona* 醜名 (an equivalent of what we call *tumi* 土名, that is, local names, in Chinese), which was not recorded on any official maps or geo-administrative registers. As small areas, *shikona* usually included only very few houses, although many of them had popular names. The words *mura*, *aza*, and *buraku* were often used synonymously, but *mura* was the most commonly used term (Embree, 1964 [1939]:24–26).

Briefly, *mura*, *ku*, *buraku*, and *kumi* were social and political divisions; *ōaza*, *aza*, and *shikona* were geographical terms. Both *mura* and *son* share the same Chinese character, which literally means "village"; hence a "hamlet" (*mura*) refers to a "natural village," while a "village" (*son*) points to an "administrative village." Thus, in modern Japan *buraku* in geo-administrative structure equals *ōaza*, which, in turn, also means *mura*, that is, "natural villages" (Torigoe 1985:74–75).

Tonarigumi (neighborhood organization 鄰組) was an economic, as well as a social, system dating back to the days of the Tokugawa period. Once Japan's "old standby," the *tonarigumi* was revived to cope with wartime mobilization at home, and the employment of the *tonarigumi* enabled Japan to maintain an effective national front. In wartime Japan, *tonarigumi* functioned not only to maintain neighborly harmony and daily needs, but also performed wartime duties such as neighborhood air defense, fire-fighting, and first-aid training. The basic problems that confronted a nation at war—food, clothing, fuel, shelter, and its bureaucratic continuity—had a vital bearing on the maintenance of daily life in Japan proper.

In operation, the neighborhood association was really a simple affair. Circulating bulletins (*kairanban* 回覽板) passed around from one household to the next served as *tonarigumi*'s voice and its only medium of control. In addition, monthly meetings of *tonarigumi* provided member households a place to air complaints over privations. Significantly, *tonarigumi* were mostly run by women, as men were engaged in other war-defense related work (Satō 1944:779–787).

Buraku, like such terms as *hokō* of colonial Taiwan, served as basic units for administration in imperial Japan. Until the 1920s, *buraku* was a derogatory term, an abbreviation for special *buraku*, meaning people who were by profession involved in socially contemptible careers (such as leather-making). In the 1930s, however, along with the unfolding of the rural revival movement, the term *buraku* was increasingly employed to refer to natural settlements, invoking the image of hamlets. It was based on this conception of *buraku* as natural settlements that hamlet associations (*burakukai*) were later to be created in the 1940 "new polity" (*shintaisei* 新體制) movement in Japan. Specifically, it was upon this structural basis of administrative unification that the movement of Imperial Subjects for Patriotic Services (*kōmin hōkō* 皇民奉公, hereafter ISPS), an umbrella organization for wartime mobilization, was launched in 1941 in Taiwan (Nakai 1996 [1945]).

A further step down, and at the bottom of the administrative hierarchy, was the neighborhood organization. Broadly defined, the term "neighborhood," in accordance with the change of time and place, has been conceived as a settlement (*shūraku*), a natural village (*sonraku* 村落), a *buraku*, a section of an administrative village (*ōaza*), a tithing structure of households (*hokō*), or a neighborhood unit of ten to twenty households (*tonarigumi*); in popular terminology both *ōaza* and *buraku* were often called *mura* (Embree 1964 [1939]:23). Narrowly conceived, it refers to the Japanese term *tonarigumi*, a tithing organization of ten to twenty households in pre-1945 Japan.[21] As a tithing structure, *tonarigumi* had a well-defined geographical boundary.

In Taiwan, the *tonarigumi* was structurally an equivalent of the *kō* 甲 of the *hokō*. Thus, the evolving transformation of the functional *hokō* made possible an alternative conceptualization of "neighborhood." For colonial Taiwan, however, the term *buraku* is not so clearly identified. As a term, *buraku* did not begin to sink into popular consciousness until the early 1920s, as social reform movements began. This does not mean that *buraku* was not introduced to the island earlier, but it does mean that it was a borrowed term, imported directly from Taishō Japan and later tailored to the tastes, problems, and therefore commands of Shōwa Japan.

In practice, due to the implementation of the *hokō*, the Japanese version of the age-old Chinese system for social control, the geo-administrative structure of *buraku* or *ōaza* was much more complicated than in Japan proper. The *hokō* had evolved on the geographical boundaries of "natural villages" that had existed long before the Japanese takeover of 1895, despite the fact that many "natural villages" were merged or redefined over time. It is perhaps not an exaggeration to claim that in colonial Taiwan the *hokō* mediated between state and society by constantly modifying the boundaries of natural settlements.[22] More often than not, a *hokō* merged with other *hokō* units to form a *buraku*, although in remote areas it also existed as a single-*hokō buraku*. In Taiwan, many *buraku* formed in this way were re-merged into the boundary of *ōaza* after 1920, when the *ōaza* began to take on a definitive shape as a synonym for the divisions of "administrative villages."[23] Thus, a *hokō* was almost always smaller in size than an *ōaza*, and a *buraku* in colonial Taiwan could be a *hokō* or an *ōaza*, but more likely it was something in between (Ts'ai 1998:82).

FORGING AN "ADMINISTRATIVE FRONT"

This picture began to change quickly after the war began.[24] A closer look at Taiwan and Korea reveals that mobilization in the form of social reform began earlier and more intensively in the colonies than in Japan proper, suggesting that the centralized police system in the colonies served as a backup force. The 1920s in both colonies witnessed campaigns for acculturation and the promotion of the Japanese language in the name of social reform. By the mid-1930s campaigns for social reform had been institutionalized, and the campaigns were translated into movements.

The key to the transformation in imperial Japan has to be found both in the Great Depression and in the escalation of war with China. The Great Depression of 1929 led in 1932 to an empire-wide movement of economic regeneration centered on Japan. It was against the background of this "movement of rural revival" (*nōsan gyōson keizai kōsei undō* 農山漁村經濟更生運動) that the "campaign for spiritual mobilization" (*kokumin seishin sōdōin* 國民精神總動員) was launched in 1937. Meanwhile, the escalation of war with China in 1931 was followed by the creation of the "Nation of Manchuria" in 1932, and eventually total war with China in 1937.

In Japan proper, in view of the outbreak of the Sino-Japanese War, the local bureau (*chihōkyoku* 地方局) of the Ministry of Interior Affairs (*naimushō* 內務省) set up in August 1937 a "survey committee of local system" in an attempt to reform the local system. Following the initiative of the local bureau, the Konoe (Fumimaro 近衛文麿, 1891–1945) cabinet enacted a "revised outline of village self-rule system" on June 30, 1938. The revised outline made villages and towns (*chōson* 町村) all-inclusive in terms of local mediation, and—among other things—turned *buraku* into cell units in the ward administration. The Ministry of Interior Affairs managed to limit the functions of *chōson* councils and strengthen central control over them, in order to imitate the movement of rural revival of 1932 and the "purification movement of elections" of 1935. It was hoped that by doing this, the ministry would be able, first, to integrate the administration of towns and villages, making it possible to control local economy; second, to expand the reach of town and village administration, with *buraku* as bases; and third, to facilitate local administration by strengthening the power of town and village heads. The purpose of all these attempts was to enhance local efficiency and finance.

The range of reform proposed in the outline was so wide that it in effect suggested the overhaul of Japan's local system. Not surprisingly, this plan provoked strong reactions, in particular protests from *chōson* councils as well as agricultural and industrial cooperatives. Meanwhile, the integration of local agricultural groups into the governments of towns and villages also involved the restructuring of agricultural administration, which remained under the jurisdiction of the Ministry of Agriculture and Forest, which in turn opposed the plan. A compromise was reached so that the local reform was moderated, and the emphasis was now on coordination rather than integration. For the first time, *buraku* were to be institutionalized into local administration. On the one hand, the legal acknowledgment of *buraku* as sub-village units necessitated a redefinition of *buraku* previously taken as natural settlements, thus involving the mapping of geo-spatial boundaries among *buraku*, administrative wards, *ōaza*, natural settlements, and agricultural cooperative groups. On the other hand, it facilitated the efficiency of the integration, after the merging of towns and villages. However, opposition continued to grow, causing the entire plan finally to be abandoned.[25]

In 1940, the Imperial Rule Assistance Association (*taisei yokusankai* 大政翼贊會, hereafter IRAA) was created in Japan, aimed at direct participation of all imperial subjects for national mobilization. After the war with China erupted in 1937, Japan began to claim that it was creating a "New Order in East Asia (*Dōa shin-chikujō* 東亞新秩序)." This slogan was later modified into a "New Order of Greater East Asia 大東亞新秩序." On August 1, 1940, the term "Greater East Asia Co-Prosperity Sphere" was officially used at a press conference for the first time. Meanwhile, all political parties were dissolved. The IRAA was an umbrella organization built along the all-embracing networks of the administrative system. At the substructure of the IRAA were auxiliary bodies of gender-specific or age-specific organizations such as women's associations (*fujinkai* 婦人會), youth corps (*seinendan* 青年團), and vigilance corps (*keibōdan* 警保團, and the like). In this way, the entire population was regimented into bounded networks and merged into the administrative hierarchy. Neighborhood associations turned out to be at the smallest and lowest, all-inclusive, multifunctional level of the Japanese administrative machinery. Apart from being a social organization, they played a crucial role in the controlled economy of wartime Japan, channeling the rationing of daily necessaries.[26]

More importantly, the *ōaza* (or *buraku*) began to serve as the connecting nexus of power in the hierarchical transmission of wartime administration. A directive issued on September 11, 1940, by the Ministry of Interior Affairs in response to the

IRAA movement for the first time acknowledged hamlets (*chōkai* 町會 and *bu-rakukai*) as auxiliary administrative units; meanwhile, it further subdivided *chō-kai* and *burakukai* into *tonarigumi* and *rinpo* 鄰保 (neighborhood associations).[27] From a geo-administrative unit of pre-1940, the *ōaza* was turned after 1940 into a crucial part of Japan's wartime mobilization machine.[28] As Gregory J. Kasza maintains (1988:281), the "New Order" movement of 1940–1941 brought about a "structural revolution of administration" comparable to the Meiji Restoration and the postwar Allied Occupation of Japan.

The 1943 local reforms legally defined *chōnaikai* 町內會 and *burakukai* as cell organizations for lower-level local administration (namely, cities, towns, and villages). In the meantime, the authorization of power relegated from the central government to higher-level local administration (that is, prefectures of *fu* 府 and *ken* 縣) was greatly expanded. The new local system was aimed at simplifying the administrative process in the face of total war. The idea was to streamline and centralize the bureaucratic system in an attempt to establish an effective administrative hierarchy. Compared with the revised outline of 1938, the 1943 system all the more favored the bureaucratic rule. In this way, the local system was restructured in wartime in a way Fujita Takao aptly terms "a process of bureaucratic rationalization" (1944b and 1944c).

In Taiwan, by comparison, the *hokō* constituted a *viable* bounded network. It was fundamental to the Japanese control and consolidation of power over rural areas. Conventional wisdom has it that it worked because of the threat of authority and sometimes also violence. From a control system in the employ of the police, the *hokō* evolved during peacetime into the basic infrastructure of colonial local administration and after 1932, but particularly after 1937, was quickly transformed into a vehicle for Japan's wartime mobilization (Ts'ai 1990). This picture began to change quickly after the war set in.[29]

So far as Taiwan was concerned, it was the 1936 movement to "remake local customs" that laid the foundation for the movement for general mobilization in 1938. The 1936 customs-reform movement in Taiwan began in 1933 with initiatives taken by prefectural governments for economic regeneration (the five-year economic plan of industry). The implementation of the plan in 1936 culminated in a social reform program. Thus, a key to the 1936 movement was the examination of hamlet-level agricultural units (*nōgyō jikkō kumiai* 農業實行組合, or agricultural implementation associations), which involved both corporate bodies and individuals.

At the hamlet level in Taiwan in the mid-1930s, the movement for social reform took the form of *buraku shinkōkai* (部落振興會, sub-village revival associations). It is commonly assumed that the sub-village revival associations were organized along the lines of the *hokō*. While this observation remains largely valid, a closer look reveals that the picture was somewhat more complex. Briefly, *ōaza*, along with *hokō*, are two key concepts for conceptualizing the spatial structure of the sub-village level administration in rural Taiwan during the latter part (1920–1945) of Japanese colonial rule—depending on regional variations. In principle, the 1936 movement was organized—as were many other movements within the Japanese empire—along the administrative hierarchy of prefecture (*shū* 州), county (*gun*), and towns or villages (*gai* or *shō*); in addition, *buraku shinkōkai* were set up at the *ōaza* or *hokō* level. In reality, the implementation varied in accordance with locality.

In this way, various agricultural groups were brought under the unified supervision of *buraku shinkōkai*, most of which were newly created. However, where the majority of agricultural implementation associations were created before the *buraku shinkōkai*, such as in Kaohsiung prefecture, agricultural implementation associations rather than the *buraku shinkōkai* played the key role in the movement. The case of Taichung prefecture, by and large as a result of compromise, suggests another form the movement took. And implementation in eastern Taiwan was only loosely observed. Significantly, the *buraku shinkōkai* was created partially to reinforce—not replace—the coordination of existing local groups; thus transportation, social order, and sanitation, traditionally under the police administration, remained the responsibility of the *hokō*. As such, the 1936 movement was designed mainly to improve local "enlightenment," despite its intention of being all-inclusive (Ts'ai 1998).

NANSHIN, TOTAL WAR, AND *ICHIGENKA*

In the wake of Pearl Harbor, the notion of abolishing Japan's "overseas territories" was first seriously voiced in terms of the incorporation of Japan's direct colonies, mainly Taiwan, Korea, and Karafuto. *Ichigenka* 一元化 as engineered by the government-general in Taiwan, for example, was a movement that had a clearly identifiable pattern of development, each stage corresponding to Japan's overall military condition in the war. The first stage, "administrative incorporation" (*nai-gaichi gyōsei ichigenka* 內外地行政一元化), in 1942, aimed at the administrative integration between *gaichi* and *naichi*. The second stage, "administrative speedup" (*fusei minsokuka*), in 1943, concerned the question of bureaucratic modernity geared toward "decisive battle." And the third stage, "improved treatment" (*shogū kaizen* 待遇改善) of the colonized, in 1944, rested on the assumption of a binary framework with "cultural integration" posted against "national integration," as Komagome Takeshi (1996) has argued. On March 26, 1945, use of the term "overseas territory" (*gaichi* 外地) finally ended.

Events in Taiwan cannot be understood without reference to events in Japan proper and other colonies and territories. The outbreak of full-scale war in 1937 changed the situation and brought Japanese plans for total war into reality. The "law of air raids" came into force as early as November 1937, and soon Taiwan became a "stepping-stone" for Japan's "Southward Advance" (*nanshin* 南進).[30] The government-general of Taiwan took upon itself the mission of "becoming the south-bound advance base of the empire," providing technology, talent, and materiel for administration, industry, finance, and propaganda. Its "cooperation" region covered Indo-China, Thailand, the Malay regions, the East Indonesian archipelago, and Burma; that is, what was identified by the Japanese as "the South of the Greater East Asia Co-prosperity Sphere" (*Nanpō kyōeiken* 南方共榮圈).

In June 1941, Germany entered into war with Russia. Later in the same month, the Japanese cabinet passed a resolution to enhance the role of Taiwan in terms of policy implementation in Southeast Asia. Taiwan was given the mission of providing military supplies by stepping up military-related industrialization, chemicals in particular, and by quickly expanding or constructing air bases. From a "stepping-stone," Taiwan was now poised to become an "unsinkable aircraft carrier." The Pearl Harbor incident (December 8, 1941, Pacific time) led to war between the United States and Japan. Total war diminished useful manpower and precious resources, and the crisis Japan faced demanded an overhaul of an imperial government that valued efficiency by means of centralized control. It was against this background that a major administrative reform began in 1942. Given the fact that this reform was empire-wide, it inevitably posed the question of how the colonies were bureaucratically linked to Tokyo. It also illuminates the dilemma Japan faced in redefining where its colonies should be located in the wartime empire.

Taiwan, for example, became a focal point of competition between the colonial government and the central government of Japan. To embrace trade with "the South," the government-general had to restructure Taiwan. On the one hand, to pursue the goal of total-war mobilization, the unification of administration had to be maximized, or rationalized, thus making Taiwan a potential part of Japan proper. This was clear from the decision to shift the supervision of the government-general of Taiwan from the minister of the colonial affairs to the minister of interior affairs in 1942. On the other hand, Taiwan had traditionally been an "exterior" (*gaichi*), outside of Japan proper, thus practices, practical considerations, and ethnic prejudices all worked to dictate that Taiwan remain an "exterior" of Japan. It was against this background that the issue of the abolition of the *hokō* system, among other things, reemerged in the final years of Japanese rule in Taiwan.[31] Meanwhile, the *hokō* remained under the jurisdiction of the police system, thus staying outside the realm of the 1942 and later administrative reforms.[32]

There is also the issue of colonial engineering in terms of wartime mobilization. The county system began to take on an increasingly important role during wartime, especially after the ISPS movement was launched. This development was both an embodiment and an endorsement of a contemporary political slogan, "general mobilization within the county" (*gunka sōdōin* 郡下總動員).[33] Furthermore, the enhanced role of the county government imposed a permanent imprint on the structural formation of postwar Taiwan, whereby the prefecture was abolished in 1945 and the county has survived in a modified form.

Once Japan turned down the road toward the Pacific War in 1941, the scale of mobilization was quickly enlarged. The "army special volunteer system of Taiwan" was instituted in April 1942, and the "navy special volunteer system of Taiwan" in August 1943. As Japan's losses mounted, the Koiso [Kuniaki, 1880–1950] cabinet began taking "improved treatment" of the colonized seriously in 1944. Indeed, the fundamental point is that, so far as modes of colonial power were concerned, military laborers were chiefly mobilized without any great changes to existing colonial political and social structures. In Taiwan, this was made possible partly by indoctrination: mass media were key in shaping an image of loyal subjects in such a way that being a military laborer was praiseworthy. Wartime-labor mobilization was also enhanced by a shift from requisition or recruitment to both "volunteerism" and organized local groups. Volunteers came to be called "glorious military laborers" (*homere no gunpu* 褒めれの軍夫). With the populations of Korea and Taiwan together constituting one-fourth of the empire, Tokyo was well aware that positive inducements were necessary.

After June 1942 Japan's war strategy began to turn from offense to defense, and by the fall of 1943 Tokyo turned to the policy of the "sphere of absolute national defense" to defend the main islands from Allied attacks. In Taiwan, the colonial government instituted a "policy for strengthening the decisive battle of Taiwan" on October 19, 1943. Its goal was to rapidly expand materiel and food for military use, as well as providing supply. In March 1944, expecting that the Allies would land on Taiwan, the government-general promulgated the "outline for implementing extraordinary measures in decisive war." At this point Taiwan entered the final defense stage: in January 1945, to expand the "volunteer" system as Japan was clearly losing the war, conscription was carried out in Taiwan. By 1945, therefore, Taiwan was not only a disciplined society—it was a disciplinary one (Ts'ai 2005).

THE EXTRA-BUREAUCRACY

As of September 1, 1945, in the wake of Japan's defeat, the size of the staff serving in the government-general of Taiwan was 117,231. Of them, 110 (0.1%) were *chokuninkan*; 2,070, *sōninkan* (1.8%, or 1.9% if including the equivalents); 20,909, *hanninkan* (17.8%, or 27.1% if including the equivalents). The rest were support staff, totaling 83,100, or 70.9%. Race was no doubt a significant factor in bureaucratic employment. Broken down by race, then only 1 Taiwanese (Tu Ts'ung-ming 杜聰明) served as *chokuninkan* (or 0.9% of the rank); 27 Taiwanese as *sōninkan* (1.3% of the rank), or 51 (15.4%) if including the equivalents. Even at the lowest official rank where the overwhelming majority of Taiwanese held their official posts, only 3,673 Taiwanese served as *hanninkan*, or 17.6% of the rank; if another 5,177 Taiwanese *taigūsha* 待遇者 who served at the equivalent level are added, then the ratio rises to 47.6%. Simply put, the majority of the Taiwanese worked as the supporting clerks.[34]

The Japanese "created" the "local" as a colonial space and, after 1920, further institutionalized it, thus integrating the local into the bureaucratic structure. This bureaucratic structure was deeply rooted in the bounded and overlapping networks of natural villages, which were built into semi-official local organizations. From this aspect, the formation of a dual bureaucratic structure in colonial Taiwan was not much different from its Japanese counterpart. What distinguished the colonial model from the mother country was mainly that in Taiwan, the county—rather than *ōaza* (sub-village administrative units), towns, or villages— was created as a colonial space parallel to the police system, thus forming a solid boundary of sociopolitical space for local Taiwanese.

The development of this colonial dual structure also enabled Japan to tap into Taiwan's manpower and natural sources outside of its formal bureaucratic structure, set up initially to serve as an intervention mechanism for the colonial government. The integration of the local into the colonial administrative structure after 1920 along the colonial space, for example, significantly improved the coordination between the colonizer and the colonized, but the continued existence of such a dual-structured colonial space in local administration could also complicate coordination problems in unexpected ways, especially during wartime. The integration problem of the *hokō* into the umbrella organization of the ISPS provides only one such example during the war years.

For all its harshness and racial discrimination, the *hokō* now symbolizes in an idealized measure the "good old days" of order, discipline, and community identity. This reconstruction of a Japanese rule of order and discipline was shaped over the course of fifty years of Japanese rule. Moreover, it was reinforced by the civil war–cum–cold war political structure in East Asia in which Taiwan has been struggling to search for a self-identity. Thanks to the *hokō*'s tie to the police system, the *gaishō* heads did not become the targets of resentment, either before or after the war. Rather, resentment was directed at the police system and, to some extent, the *hokō* system.[35] The *hokō* was not improvised by the Japanese as a makeshift wartime measure—it was rooted in traditional Han Chinese society and evolved over four decades, from a policing system for social control to an all-embracing cell organization for local administration and wartime mobilization (Ts'ai 1990).

The extra-bureaucracy of the Japanese colonial administration allowed the government-general of Taiwan to respond promptly to Japan's wartime demands with minimal bureaucratic red tape. This may help explain, if only partly, why wartime mobilization was carried out earlier and more effectively in Japan's colonies than in Japan proper. The Japanese made their administration of Taiwan work, in essence, by turning the civil bureaucracy into a disciplinary institution for effective administration. Colonial governance also worked to shape the colonial administration into a disciplined tool for social control.

NOTES

*I would like to thank Dr. Peter Zarrow of the Institute of Modern History, Academia Sinica (Taiwan) and Edmund Fung of the University of West Sydney (Australia), for their critical remarks and editorial help in this and earlier versions of this paper.

1. By social "grafting," I mean a certain mixing of Taiwanese and Japanese, such as the revived *hokō* (*baojia* 保甲, a tithing organization of households for social control) system in colonial Taiwan.

2. "Governmentality," referring to "techniques of government," is a neologism created by Michel Foucault; see his article on "governmentality" (1991). The term is employed in this essay to "pose the question of the epistemological and technical conditions of existence of the political, to analyse the historical *a priori* by which we construct politics as a domain of thought and action, and to analyse the instrumentation, vocabulary and forms of reason by which this is done," see Dean 1999:47.

3. The term "extra-bureaucracy," rather than "informal bureaucracy," is employed here with a broader definition, which not only embraces the informal bureaucracy but also extends to a gray area, of which semibureaucratic organizations such as the Youth Corps and the *hokō* were important components. It is important to note that while in the study of modern Japan the term "extra-bureaucracy"often applies to political parties, there was no such mechanism in colonial Taiwan.

4. "Taiwan sōtokufu kansei chū kaisei" (November 9, 1901), *Chokurei* no. 201, *Kōbun ruishū* [Hōseikyoku, ed.] file no. 25 (1901), vol. 4.

5. The five boards are, respectively, board of general affairs (*sōmukyoku*), board of finance (*zaimukyoku*), board of communication (*tsūshinkyoku*), board of industry (*shokusankyoku*), and board of public works (*dobokukyoku*).

6. "Naimu daishin seigi Taiwan sōtokufu kansei chū kaisei" (October 1, 1901; *Naikō* no. 204), and *Kōbun ruishū* file no. 25 (1901), vol. 4.

7. "Keisatsu kanri shokumu ōen ni kansuru ken" (November 9, 1910; *Chokurei* no. 427 of Japan) and same law (November 26, 1920; *Chokurei* no. 553 of Taiwan), *Kōbun ruishū* file no. 44 (1920), vol. 10.

8. "Qualified senior officials" here refers to incumbent high-ranking administrative officials (*kōdō gyōseikan* 高等行政官) at the time of the 1901 reform, and "qualified senior police officers," to *keibuchō* (警部長), chief *keibu* of a prefecture or a sub-prefecture (*benmusho* 辨務署, a dispatched unit of a prefecture). Article one of "Taiwan sōtokufu chihō shokuin tokubetsu ninyōrei" (November 1901; *Chokurei* no. 214), and "Taiwan sōtokufu keishi tokubetsu ninyōrei" (November 1901; *Chokurei* no. 212), see *Kōbun ruishū* file no. 25 (1901), vol. 4.

9. Articles 7 and 8 of "Taiwan sōtokufu chihōkan kansei" (March 1896; *Chokurei* no. 91), *Kōbun ruishū* file no. 21 (1897), vol. 11; article 19 of "Taiwan sōtokufu kansei chū kaisei" (November 9, 1901; *Chokurei* no. 201), *Kanpō* no. 5508 (November 11, 1901), 209.

10. "Taiwan sōtokufu chihōkan kansei" (November 9, 1901; *Chokurei* no. 202), *Kanpō* no. 5508 (November 11, 1901), 210.

11. Article two of "Taiwan sōtokufu chihō shokuin tokubetsu ninyōrei" (November 1901; *Chokurei* no. 214), *Kōbun ruishū* file no. 25 (1901), vol. 4.

12. Article 38 of "Taiwan sōtokufu chihōkan kansei" (June 1898; *Chokurei* no. 108), *Kōbun ruishū* file no. 25 (1901), vol. 4.

13. "Taiwan sōtokufu chō jimukan oyobi chō keishi tokubetsu ninyōrei" (October 25, 1909; *Chokurei* no. 287), *Taiwan hōrei shūran* (1918), part I, 129.

14. "Taiwan sōtokufu kansei," *Taiwan sōtokufu shokuinroku (1910)*, 2. Incidentally, the chief of civil administration was to head the bureau of civil administration from 1901 through 1919. And, from 1920 till the end of Japanese rule, it was renamed *sōmu chōkan* (chief of the bureau of general affairs), while the board of general affairs (*sōmukyoku*) came to be abolished. See the revised bureaucratic system of 1919, *Taiwan sōtokufu shokuinroku (1920)*, 23.

15. "Hannin bunkan tokubetsu ninyōrei" (August 20, 1920; *Chokurei* no. 357), *Kōbun ruishū* file no. 44 (1920), vol. 10.

16. Shih 2001. This case study, however, refers only to the last two decades of Japanese rule.

17. "Taiwan sōtokufu chihōkan kansei" (July 27, 1920; *Chokurei* no. 218), *Taiwan hōrei shūran* (1918), part I, 47.

18. *Buraku* as a term in Japanese history means both natural settlements (*shūraku*) and special *buraku* (*tokubetsu buraku*). *Buraku* (a hamlet or natural village) was a term popularly used in both prewar and postwar Taiwan. While it remains to be examined, this term seems to have first been used by the Japanese, consciously or unconsciously, to identify natural settlements in "undeveloped" regions, in contrast with regions well "developed" in terms of modernity. It was reified by anthropologists working in Taiwan in the early twentieth century, and since then has been taken for granted by the academy until today.

19. Torigoe 1985:72–74. *Buraku* also refers to the meaning of "outcastes" or "the lowly" in modern Japan, but it is the geo-historical, and not the social, implication that concerns us here.

20. As of 1936, there were 9,724 *mura*, 1,693 towns (*machi*), and 129 cities (*shi*) in Japan (Embree 1964 [1939]:35).

21. In practice, moreover, it referred to neighborhood associations in cities and urban areas only, as neighborhood associations were called *rinpo* when applied to rural Japan. Nevertheless, "neighborhood associations" in English generally refer to both *tonarigumi* and *rinpo*, as well as similar organizations such as *hokō*.

22. For excellent research on the theoretical formulation of traditional Taiwanese settlements, see Shih 1996.

23. Again, this does not mean that prior to 1920 the concept of *aza* and *ōaza* was not introduced to Taiwan—it was. However, the pair of vocabulary items existed only in a geographical sense whereby a variety of colonial administrative purposes (such as investigations of land and population, and thus household registrations and taxation systems, as well as social controls) were made possible.

24. In this paper, the "war era" refers to the period from 1931 through 1945; that is, the "Fifteen Years' War."

25. Fujita 1944a. Fujita Takeo headed the survey section of the "survey committee of metropolitan Tōkyō administration" at the time of the writing.

26. Ralph Braibanti, however, pointed out the fact that the distribution of rationed commodities in Japan did not actually begin until October 29, 1942, some two years after the implementation of the *tonarigumi* system, and he thus cautioned against remarks made in some recent studies that "the *tonarigumi* was reorganized for the purpose of distributing rations" (1948:150).

27. For *chōnaikai*, see also *Taisei yokusankai chōsakai daikyū iinkai* 1943.

28. Nakatsuka 1978 and 1983. Nakatsuka Akira is one of very few Japanese scholars today who treat the *ōaza* seriously in terms of its role in Japan's war mobilization.

29. "Southward Advance," as opposed to "Northward Advance" (*hokushin* 北進), was not formally endorsed as Japan's national policy until 1936. In Taiwan, this policy was further elaborated, three years later, and put into a slogan: "Japanization, industrialization, and Southward Advance" (*kōminka* 皇民化, *kōgyōka* 工業化, and *nanshinka* 南進化).

30. The abolition issue of the *hokō* was once raised in the self-rule movement of the 1920s. For details, see Ts'ai 1995.

31. Since the *hokō* system was racially directed against the Han Taiwanese, one wonders if the *hokō* agents (*hosei* or *baozheng* in particular) ever became a source of resentment after the colonial rule came to an end. This, however, does not seem to have been the case in the immediate period of postwar Taiwan. The surveys I conducted as a form of oral history in the early 1990s revealed that the elders who had lived through the two regimes indeed embraced mixed feelings toward the *hokō* system (Ts'ai 1994).

32. It is intriguing to note that the county (*gun*) system in Japan was abolished in 1921, followed by the abolition of county chiefs in 1926. In this way, *gun* was abolished as a political division, thus placing *mura* directly under the prefectural government. The county remained, however, a geographical and social unit, as people continued to be conscious of their identity with a particular county, and many agricultural and business organizations were built upon a county-wide basis (Embree, 1964 [1939]:22). Debates over whether the county system should be abolished included attacks on its ineffectiveness and financial insufficiency, as well as on county heads who had supported anti-establishment movements, and so forth. Yet such debates may help explain why at roughly the same time the county system was re-enforced in Taiwan.

33. Taiwan sōtokufu 1945:8; Kondō 1996:432. The term "employees for both government offices and public organizations" (*kankōga shokuin*) refers not only to civilian officials of four formal ranks of statute (*shinninkan, chokuninkan, sōninkan,* and *hanninkan*) and their equivalents, *taigūsha,* but also all support staff who worked as clerks (*riin*), commissioned (part-time) employees (*shokutaku*), daily-waged employees (*yatoi*) and office runners (*jimu yatoi*), and the like.

34. In the comparison between Taiwan and Indonesia, the former under Japanese colonial rule and the latter under Japanese wartime occupation, historical contingency matters. In Indonesia under Japanese rule, for instance, the peasants' hatred was directed immediately at the village and hamlet heads and other lower-level administrators, mainly because of the latter's identification with the strict conscription of labor and food (rice in particular) (Kurasawa 1981).

REFERENCES

Braibanti, Ralph J.D. 1948. "Neighborhood Associations in Japan and Their Democratic Potentialities." *Far Eastern Quarterly* 7.2:136–164.

Burchell, Graham, Colin Gordon, and Peter Miller, eds. 1991. *The Foucault Effect: Studies in Governmentality.* Chicago: University of Chicago Press.

Dean, Mitchell. 1999. *Governmentality: Power and Rule in Modern Society.* London: Sage Publications.

Douglas, Mary. 1986. *How Institutions Think.* Syracuse: Syracuse University Press.

Duus, Peter, and Hideo Kobayashi, eds. 1998. *Teikoku to iu gensō: "Dai-Tōa Kyōeiken" no shisō to genjitsu* [The illusion of empire: Ideology and practice in Greater East Asia]. Tokyo: Aoki Shoten.

Embree, John F. 1964 [1939]. *Suye Mura: A Japanese Village.* Chicago: University of Chicago Press.

Evans, Peter B., Dietrich Rueschemeyer, and Theda Skocpol, eds. 1985. *Bringing the State Back In.* Cambridge: Cambridge University Press.

Foucault, Michel. 1991. "Governmentality." In *The Foucault Effect*, ed. Burchell, Gordon, and Miller, pp. 87–104.

Fujita, Takeo. 1944a. "Chihō seido no kakkiteki tenkai (1): chōsonsei kaisei mondai no shinten [The epoch-making development of the local system (1)]." *Toshi mondai* [Urban problems] 38.5:25–44.

———. 1944b. "Chihō seido no kakkiteki tenkai (4): Chihō seido no kakkiteki kaikaku no jitsugen (2) [The epoch-making development of the local system (4)]." *Toshi mondai* [Urban problems] 39.2:29–39.

———. 1944c. "Chihō seido no kakkiteki tenkai (5): Chihō seido no kakkiteki kaikaku no jitsugen (3) [The epoch-making development of the local system (5)]." *Toshi mondai* [Urban problems] 39.3:32–54.

[Hōseikyoku]. 1882–1945. *Kōbun ruishū* [Categorized archives of government documents]. Tokyo: Kokuritsu Kobunshokan.

Hata, Ikuhiko, ed. 1983. *Kanryō no kenkyū: fumetsu no pa-wa (1868–1983)* [A study of bureaucrats: The immortality of power]. Tokyo: Kōdansha.

Ishikawa, Hisao. 1993 [1987]. *Kindai Nihon no meibōka to jichi* [Men of high repute and self-rule in modern Japan]. Tokyo: Bokutakusha.

Kasza, Gregory J. 1988. *The State and the Mass Media in Japan, 1918–1945.* Berkeley: University of California Press.

Komagome, Takeshi, 1996. *Shokuminchi teikoku Nihon no bunka tōgō* [The cultural integration of Japan's colonial empire]. Tokyo: Iwanami Bookstore.

Kondō, Masami. 1996. *Sōryokusen to Taiwan: Nihon shokuminchi hōkai no kenkyū* [Total war and Taiwan: A study of the collapse of Japan's colonies]. Tokyo: Tōshui shoten.

Kratoska, H. Paul, ed. 2005. *Asian Labor in the Wartime Japanese Empire: Unknown Histories.* New York: M. E. Sharpe.

Kurasawa, Aiko. 1981. "Ja-wa no sonraku ni okeru shakai henyō no ichi kōsatsu: Nihon gunseika no momi kyōshutsu seido to sono eikyō [A survey of the social changes in the villages of Java: The supply system of unhulled rice and its influence under Japan's military administration]." *Tōnan A-ji-a kenkyū* [Journal of Southeast Asian studies] 19.1:77–105.

Nakai, Atsushi. 1996 [1945]. "Hōmin hōkō undō no shinden [The development of the movement of imperial subjects for public services]. In *Taiwan keizai nenpō, 1944* [The yearly news on the Taiwan economy, 1944], vol. 4, pp. 251–310. Taipei: Nan-t'ien, 1996; originally published in 1945 by Taiwan shuppan bunka kabushiki kaisha, Taihoku, 4 vols (1941–1945).

Nakatsuka, Akira. 1978. "Aru 'mura' no Taiheiyō sensō [The Pacific War as seen from a "natural village"]." *Kenkyū nenpō* [Annual report of studies in humanities and social sciences, Nara Women's University] 22:69–86.

———. 1983. "Aru ōaza ni miru tennōsei shihai no tenkai [The development of the domination of the emperor system as seen from an ōaza]." In *Kindai Nihon kokka no hō kōzō* [The legal construction of the state of modern Japan], ed. Yamanaka, pp. 11–36.

Ōishi Kaichirō and Nishida Yoshiaki, eds. 1994 [1991]. *Kindai Nihon no gyōseison: Nagao-ken Hanishina-gun Goka-son no kenkyū* [Administrative villages in modern Japan: A case study of Goka village, Hanishina county, Nagano prefecture]. Tokyo: Nihon Keizai Hyōronsha.

[Ōkurashō kanpōka, ed.] 1885–1945. *Kanpō* [Official gazette]. [Tokyo: Ōkurashō Kanpōka].

Ōshima, Mitsuko. 1980 [1977]. *Meiji no Mura* [Natural villages in the Meiji period]. Tokyo: Kabushiki Kaisha Kyōikusha.

Rueschemeyer, Dietrich, and Peter B. Evans. 1985. "The State and Economic Transformation: Toward an Analysis of the Conditions Underlying Effective Intervention." In *Bringing the State Back In*, ed. Peter B. Evans, Dietrich Rueschemeyer, and Theda Skocpol, 44–77 (Cambridge: Cambridge University Press).

Sato [Satō] Kennosuke. 1944. "How the Tonari-Gumi Operates." *Contemporary Japan: A Review of East Asiatic Affairs* 13.7–9:779–787.

Shih, T'ien-fu. 1996. *Lanyang pingyuan de chuantong juluo: lilun jiagou yü jiben ziliao* [The traditional settlements of the Lanyang plain: Theoretical constructs and the basic archival material], vol. 1. Yilan: Yilan Xianli Wenhua Zhongxin.

———. 2001. "Rizhi shidai Taiwan diyu shehui de kongjian jiegou jiqi fazhan jizhi—yi Minxiong difang weili [Spatial structure and the developmental mechanism of Taiwan's territorial society during the Japanese era: The case of Ming-hsiung]." *Taiwanshi yanjiu* [Taiwan historical research] 8.1:1–39.

Taisei yokusankai chōsakai daikyū iinkai, ed. 1943. *Chōnaikai, tonarigumi no seibi kyōka ni kansuru chōsa* [A survey of the enforced preparation (for war) of urban and rural neighorhood organizations]. [Tōkyō]: Taisei Yokusankai Chōsakai.

Taiwan shifan daxue, lishixue xisuo. 1995. *Jiawu zhanzheng yibai zhounian jinian xueshu yantaohui lunwenji* [Conference volume in memory of the centenary of the Sino-Japanese War, 1894–1895]. Taipei: Department of History, National Taiwan Normal University.

Taiwan sōtokufu, comp. 1910. *Taiwan Sōtokufu shokuinroku (1910)* [A directory of government officials and the staff of the government-general of Taiwan, 1910]. Taihoku: Kabushiki kaisha Taiwan nichi nichi shinpōsha.

———. 1918. *Taiwan hōrei shūran [1918]* [A directory of government officials and the staff of the government-general of Taiwan, 1918]. Tōkyō: Teikoku chihō gyōsei gakkai.

———. 1920. *Taiwan sōtokufu shokuinroku (1920)* [A directory of government officials and the staff of the government-general of Taiwan, 1920]. Taihoku: Kabushiki kaisha Taiwan nichi nichi shinpōsha.

———. 1945. *Taiwan tōchi gaiyō* [An outline of (Japan's) rule in Taiwan]. Taihoku: Taiwan sōtokufu.

Taiwan sōtokufu nai Taiwan jihō hakkōjo, comp. 1942. *Taiwan sōtokufu oyobi shoshoku kan-sho shokuinroku (1942)* [A directory of government officials and the staff of the government-general of Taiwan and its attached offices and burueas, 1942]. Taihoku: Taiwan nichinichi shinpōsha.

Torigoe, Hiroyuki. 1985. *Ie to mura no shakaigaku* [The sociology of the family system and natural villages]. Tokyo: Sekai shisōsha.

Ts'ai Hui-yu Caroline. 1990. "One Kind of Control: The *Hokō* System in Taiwan Under Japanese Rule, 1895–1945" (Ph.D. diss., Columbia University, New York City).

———. 1994. "Japanese Rule in Taiwan as Oral History: Findings of Hokō Questionnaire Investigations [sic], 1992–1993." *Xingda Lishi Xuebao* [Chung-hsing journal of history] 4:121–144.

———. 1995. "Baojia zhidu chefei lun: Cong 'yu zizhi yu chefei' dao 'yu chefei yu zizhi.' [On the abolition of the hokō system: From "promoting self-rule by means of advancing the abolition of the hokō system" to "advancing the abolition of the hokō system by means of promoting self-rule]" In the conference volume of *Jiawu zhanzheng yibai zhounian jinian xueshu yantaohui lunwenji*, ed. Taiwan Shifan Daxue, 617–639.

———. 1998. "1930 niandai Taiwan jiceng xingzheng de kongjian jiegou fenxi: yi 'nong-shi shixing zuhe' weili [A spatial analysis of the administrative foundation in Taiwan in the 1930s: A case study of "agricultural implementation associations"]" *Taiwanshi yanjiu* 5.2:55–100.

———. 2000. "Rizhi Taiwan jiezhuang xingzheng (1920–1945) de bianzhi yu yunzuo: jie-zhuang xingzheng xiangguan mingci zhi tantao [Township administration in Taiwan un-der Japanese rule (1920–1945): A study of related terms]," in *Taiwan falüshi yanjiu de fangfa*, ed. Wang, 95–159; originally published in *Taiwanshi yanjiu* 3.2 (1996 [1998]): 93–141.

———. 2001. "Rizhi Taiwan zhiguan bianzhi de faling jichu: jianlun lianghua de mixi [The legal construction of the bureaucratic system in Taiwan under Japanese rule: Notes on quantitative methodology]," Research Seminar of Thematic Projects Sponsored by the National Science Council, Nankang, Taipei, Academia Sinica, June 28.

———. 2004. "Total War, Labor Drafts, and Colonial Administration: Wartime Mobiliza-tion in Taiwan (1936–1945)." In *Asian Labor in the Wartime Japanese Empire*, ed. Paul H. Kratoska, 106–126, 365–372 (New York: M.E. Sharpe).

Wang T'ai-sheng, ed. 2000. *Taiwan falüshi yanjiu de fangfa* [Approaches to the study of the legal history of Taiwan]. Taipei: Xuelin Wenhua, 2000.

Yamamuro Shin'ichi. 1998. "Shokumin teikoku, Nihon no kōsei to Manshūkoku: Tōchi yō-shiki no sen'i to tōchi jinsai no shūryū [The colonial empire, the construction of Japan, and the nation of Manchuria: Shifting modes of rule and the circulation of people with special talent or skills]." In *Teikoku to iu gensō*, ed. Duus and Kobayashi, 155–202.

Yamanaka Einosuke, ed. 1983. *Kindai Nihon kokka no hō kōzō* [The legal construction of the state of modern Japan]. Tokyo: Bokutakusha.

———. 1990. *Kindai Nihon no chihō seido to meibōka* [The local system and men of high repute in modern Japan]. Tokyo: Kōbundō.

[6]

THE STATE OF TAIWANESE CULTURE AND TAIWANESE NEW LITERATURE IN 1937

Issues on Banning Chinese Newspaper Sections and Abolishing Chinese Writings

KAWAHARA ISAO

ABOLISHING THE CHINESE-LANGUAGE SECTION IN ALL DAILY NEWSPAPERS

On March 1, 1937, the second page of the *Taiwan Daily News* printed the following announcement:

> The following four newspapers jointly announce that due to the current state of affairs we have decided to abolish the Chinese section. It has been over forty years since Japan took over Taiwan. In the light of the thoroughness of imperialization and the flourishing of cultural activities, we believe there is no hindrance to the complete abolition of the Chinese section. Beginning on April 1, the *Taiwan News*, *Tainan News*, and *Taiwan Daily News* will drop their Chinese sections; *Taiwan shinminpō* 台灣新民報 will cut its Chinese section to half of its current four pages on April 1 and abolish it completely on the first of June. In place of the Chinese section, we are determined to double our efforts in our mission as news organizations to strengthen our content. We sincerely hope you, our readers, will understand this change.

In accordance with this notice, the Chinese language disappeared from the three listed daily newspapers on April 1, 1937. The only newspaper that was run by the Taiwanese, *Taiwan New Civil News*, reduced its Chinese sections from four pages to two pages on April 1, and then abolished it completely on June 1 to accommodate its mostly native readership.

Though the abolishment of Chinese language was framed as an agreement negotiated by the four newspaper organizations, it was implemented at a time when only one-third of the population was considered proficient in Japanese. In other words, though there were about one and half million natives who understood some level of Japanese, their capability was still rather limited, and about three and a half million people still had no knowledge of the Japanese language. The banning of the Chinese section newspaper definitely would have had a great impact on the business of the news organizations.[1]

Further, it seems rather unlikely that all daily newspapers, considering they competed with each other for readership, all voluntarily took the same action. Rather, it might be more appropriate for us to suppose that they were under some sort of pressure or order from the office of the governor-general to take up this action. Here I will examine the process and methods through which the office of the governor-general forced the newspaper organizations to ban all Chinese in the news media.

THE INQUIRY AT THE LOWER HOUSE BUDGET COMMITTEE

Before the above statement was issued by the four newspaper organizations, Matsuda Takechiyo 松田竹千代, representative of the Minsei 民政 Party, made inquiries into the issue of abolishing the Chinese section in newspapers in the Lower House Budget Committee at the general assembly on February 25. Mention of the inquiry appeared as a brief item in the newspaper in Japan the next day, stating only that "Matsuda inquired about the abolition of the Chinese section in newspapers and magazines but the government did not reply to the inquiry."[2] Further, the morning edition of the *Taiwan Daily News* dated February 26, 1937, recorded that the minister of colonial affairs, Yūki Toyotarō 結城豊太郎, literally cut off Representative Matsuda Takechiyo's inquiry into the motivation for abolishment of all Chinese in newspapers and magazines by delaying his reply and submitting the matter to further investigation.

Either way, the issue did not garner much attention in the Lower House Budget Committee at the general assembly. However, the February 25 assembly record shows the inquiry made by Representative Matsuda:

> This is something that occurred in Taiwan, with the military advisor at the center of the matter. It is said that due to the wishes of the military, as of this April 1, the Chinese language will be forced to disappear from all newspapers and magazines, including the *Taiwan Daily News*, *Taiwan News*, and *Tainan News*, and only the

Taiwan New Civil News will maintain one page of Chinese. I would like to have government officials from the Ministry of Colonial Affairs elaborate on the truth of this matter.

Representative Matsuda's inquiry is significant in that it indicates that the initiative for the abolishment of the Chinese language in newspapers and magazines did not come from the news media organizations themselves. The abolishment of the Chinese language was imposed upon them by the military. Further, though the joint public announcement of the policy was published on March 1, Matsuda knew of it beforehand and brought it up during the February 25 assembly inquiry.

Morioka Jirō 森岡二郎, the head of general affairs in the governor-general's office of Taiwan, replied to Matsuda's inquiry as follows:

> Let me answer the question which Mr. Matsuda raised a while ago. The Chinese section in newspapers will be abolished soon in Taiwan. As everyone knows, we have been trying very hard to promote the National Language [i.e., Japanese] in Taiwan. All the newspapers echo our effort, realizing that Chinese language is an impediment to the popularization of Japanese. They also understand that at this day and time, abolishing the Chinese paper section will not cause inconveniences to their readers, so they all came to the agreement to do it in unison. I count on your understanding of this matter. (Quoted in *Taiwan Daily News*, March 2, 1937, morning edition)

Representative Matsuda wanted to continue his inquiry, but was interrupted by the head of the committee, Koyama Matsutoshi, who moved the Chinese language issue to the first subcommittee for the budget committee. However, the discussion that ensued in the subcommittee was not reported in the Japanese news media at all and even *Taiwan Daily News* gave it scant attention.[3] Because of the lack of publicity in the mass media, researchers of Taiwan have never looked into the subcommittee record. Fortunately, it is well preserved and we can get a clear picture of the heated debate at the time.

On March 2, Representative Matsuda Takechiyo continued his inquiry at the first subcommittee for the budget committee. Deputy Minister of Colonial Affairs Irie Kaihei 入江海平 replied to his question that since the Japanese language had been widely popularized, all major news media organizations determined that there was no longer a need for Chinese language sections. Upon consultations held among all the newspapers, it was decided that Chinese would be abolished as of April 1.

Representative Matsuda pushed for the truth, dubious that the newspaper media would abolish Chinese language voluntarily. He continued his quest, stating: "This does not accord with information we have learned. Rather, we think it is the result of Chief of Staff of the Army Ogisu's forceful persuasion and pressure on the news media since last year. The news media is incapable of resistance and thus reluctantly agreed to do so. I would like you to elaborate on this speculation."

Representative Nakamura Hirotoshi 中村浩利 (Seiyūkai 政友会 faction) also chimed in with the following inquiry: "I understand that in order to teach the Taiwanese people Japanese, Taiwanese papers were not allowed to be published. ... However, it seems to me rather drastic to make all the newspapers published in nothing but Japanese. I am afraid that it may cause resentment (from the native population)."

Again, to this concern, Morioka Jirō pointed to the fact that the policy had been discussed by the "Committee for Promoting Good Citizenship" during the time of the previous governor-general, Nakagawa Kenzō 中川憲造, in July two years before. He indicated that although the chief of staff of the military had emphasized the need for banning Chinese, he was only one of many who held the same opinion. Also, as for the date for implementing the banning policy—originally it was to be January first, but after several extensions, but now had settled into two different starting dates: April 1 and June 1.

Representative Matsuda, rebutting Morioka's response, pointed to the news media's powerlessness in resisting Chief of Staff Ogisu's pressure on the banning policy: "I would simply like you to acknowledge the fact that the military played a potent role in fostering this measure in order to thoroughly elevate the spirit of the citizen by promoting National Language." Matsuda continued: "There are five million ethnic Han and only about two hundred thousand Japanese in Taiwan. I do not understand how you can talk about elevating the spirit of the citizen on one hand and on the other suddenly abolish the Chinese section in news media." Matsuda pushed on: "I think it is outrageous to try to abolish the Chinese language, a language of another ethnic group, the most stubborn Han ethnic group, a majority group."

To his outrage, Morioka retorted: "It is certainly not an easy task to completely erase the native language of the islanders. However, it is a matter of course to compel them to use Japanese since they are the subjects of Japan. I would not say so of all island inhabitants, but there are some that still regard Chinese as their mother tongue. One way to rid them of this idea is to get rid of their own national language. Making them use the Japanese language will be one way to make them realize that Japan is the only motherland they have." Morioka insisted that since the Taiwanese had now become Japanese, it was their duty to learn the "national language" and it was all but natural to eliminate Hanwen 漢文 (i.e., Chinese).

The debate went on for a long time. However, perhaps because of pressure from the office of the governor-general and also because Representative Matsuda did not have sufficient evidence to prove his point, he was not able to get a very satisfactory explanation. Nevertheless, from the record we can safely conclude that banning the Chinese newspaper section was the result of Ogisu's strong-arm tactics forced upon a news media that was too weak to resist. It reveals a deeply rooted, complicit scheme by the military, the governor-general, and the news media.

THE COUNCIL FOR PROMOTING GOOD CITIZENSHIP

I will now focus on the "Committee for Promoting Good Citizenship" mentioned by Morioka. The correct title for the organization should be "council" rather than "committee" (*Minfu sakko kyogikai*). A council meeting that included the military, bureaucracy, and powerful civilians had been called by Governor-General Nakagawa on July 25, with its purpose being "to emphasize our concerns for the promotion of good citizenship in order to achieve a comprehensive assimilation and to elevate the national spirit of the people on the island during this urgent time." Those who attended included chiefs of bureaus under the governor-general's office, heads of the states, administrators, the mayor of Taipei City, President Shidehara Hiroshi 幣原坦 of Taipei Imperial University, Supreme Court Judge Saitō, Chief Prosecutor Tomono, Chief of Staff for the Military Ogisu, Security Chief Iwamatsu, Captain Satō, Head of the Military Police Oki, naval officer Sakai, principals of public schools, powerful civilians, and section chiefs from all ministries—in all, about one hundred and twenty people.[4]

The meeting began with Governor-General Nakagawa reading the "Imperial Edict for Promoting National Spirit," followed by Chief of General Affairs Hiratsuka's 平塚 welcoming remarks. After Culture and Education Minister Fukagawa's 深川 address, the meeting started its deliberations. The morning was a free discussion session, and Miyamoto Ichigaku 宮本一學 (president of *Tainan News*) moved to organize a committee to submit a formal report. The motion was passed and twelve members and one chair were appointed.

Even though Miyamoto was the one who made the motion for organizing the committee, it is difficult to ascertain whether he did this of his own volition. Another attendee, civilian Miyoshi Tokusaburō 三好德三郎, later stated in his book that it seemed that the Culture and Education Ministry asked him to make the motion.[5] Of the committee members, seven were Japanese and five were Taiwanese, and the majority of them were well-known industrialists and socially prominent members of society. The fact that some of the most important figures of the Taiwanese news media, such as Ōsawa Teikichi 大澤貞吉 (chief editor of *Taiwan Daily News*), Matsuoka Tomio 松岡富雄 (owner of *Taiwan News*), and Miyamoto Ichigaku (president of *Tainan News*), were serving on the committee implies that the office of the governor-general had played a role in determining its composition. On the other hand, it is also rather suspicious that the only daily newspaper that did not fully comply with the ban, *Taiwan shin minpō*, was not included in the committee. The twelve members of the committee were able to come back later that day with a full report, indicating that it had been prepared by the Culture and Education Ministry beforehand.

In the afternoon session of the meeting some proposals were made to amend the report, and a final version could not be agreed upon immediately. Again, according to Miyoshi's book, the military took a hard line on the issue and there was some tension. Ōsawa, Matsuoka, and Miyamoto all agreed on banning the Chinese language. Also, Abbot Takabayashi 高林 expressed his wish to include religious groups in the final report.

The hard-line position taken by the military included two amendments made by naval officer Sakai. One replaced "In order to promote good citizenship, all governmental offices, schools, companies, banks, and other civil organizations should take the lead in implementing appropriate policies" with "In order to thoroughly carry out the movement of promoting good citizenship, all governmental offices, schools, companies, banks, civil organizations, *religious groups, and news media* should take the lead in implementing appropriate policies."

The statement "In order to popularize the national language, all everyday speech should be in Japanese to reinforce the consciousness of nationhood" was replaced with "In order to thoroughly popularize the national language, all everyday speech, *newspapers, and magazines* should be in Japanese to reinforce the consciousness of nationhood. *In the light of the nation's state of emergency, the creed of national defense should be fully implemented.*"

In other words, the core proposal of the military's tough position was that "all newspapers and magazines should get rid of the Chinese sections and be unified in using the Japanese language only." To this proposal, three newspapers (*Taiwan Daily News, Taiwan News, Tainan News*) that catered to the government's favor agreed with the military's proposal while the *Shinminpō* indicated disagreement with the policy, though there was no record of what kind of protest they made. There were some oppositional comments, but the situation seemed to be moving toward one side. The next day, the *Taiwan Daily News* reported on the meeting:

> Mr. Tanimoto [principal of Taipei High School Tanimoto Seishin 谷本清心] stood up and said that it's all well and fine to abolish the Chinese language but he worried what old people who relied solely on Chinese sources to get their information would do. To his comment, Chief of Staff of the Military Ogisu responded strongly, and there was a lively debate.

The meeting was able to proceed according to the wishes of the office of the governor-general and the military, and the two amendments made by the military were accepted and passed unanimously. In other words, the decision to ban the Chinese language in newspapers and magazines was forced upon the committee by Ogisu and passed by the floor.

For the office of the governor-general to "promote complete and thorough use of Japanese," it was felt necessary to ban Chinese from newspaper and magazines. As for the military, Chinese in newspapers and magazines was an obstacle to its goal of "fully implementing the creed of national defense." So in a sense, the office of the governor-general and the military apparatus shared the same interest in banning Chinese. Knowing that no one could resist the will of the military, the office of the governor-general assigned the three major newspapers to draft the final report, indicating that everyone present should agree to the proposal. The first charge of the "imperial subject movement" (kōmin undō 皇民運動) was to "promote complete and thorough use of Japanese," and the council meeting achieved this goal—all that was left was to find the right timing for implementing the policy, and the office had only to put more pressure on the newspapers to come up with a date of execution.

However, banning Chinese was not a decision made out of the blue at the council meeting. Several days before, on July 22 and 23, a conference for local governors throughout the whole island was held in the same conference room. Governors of five prefectures (Taipei, Hsinchu, Taichung, Tainan, Kaohsiung) plus district administrators from the three districts (Hualian, Taidong, Penghu), together with all bureau chiefs and section heads of the office, were gathered to hear the call by Hiratsuka "to see progress in the popularization of the Japanese language and the expansion of language facilities, to promote everyday use of the language. I wish wholeheartedly that you will all do your best to realize the ideal of one single unified national language."

No matter how each newspaper might have resisted the idea, then, it is apparent that the office of the governor-general had already determined the direction of the matter. This political position of "promoting everyday use of the language" and "realizing the ideal of one single unified national language" was passed on by Hiratsuka to his successor, Morioka Jirō, without alteration. Both accepted that the Chinese language was an obstacle to the spread of Japanese, and both strongly felt that in order to unify the national language, banning Chinese was a necessary strategy.

According to the record of the general assembly and of the Lower House Budget Committee, despite Representative Matsuda's repeated inquiries, neither the office of the governor-general nor the minister of colonial affairs was willing to admit to putting any pressure on the news media. As for the military, it did not even seem aware that it had applied pressure at all. However, from the announcement by Hiratsuka at the conference for the local governors of the island and the proclaimed report in the Council for Promoting Good Citizenship one may conclude that the office of the governor-general had been carefully laying the foundation for implementation of a policy that the news media could only go along with. The banning of Chinese language was based on the will of both the government and the military, and certainly not voluntarily taken up by the news media themselves. Yet in the joint statement issued by the newspapers it was portrayed as a voluntary act.

THE POLICY OF GOVERNOR-GENERAL KOBAYASHI SEIZŌ

In 1937, when the Chinese-language ban was issued, the governor-general of Taiwan was Kobayashi Seizō 小林躋造 (1896–1962). He was born in Hiroshima. After he graduated with honors from the naval academy, his military career went smoothly. He became deputy naval officer in 1930, and in 1931 he was commissioned as Commander in Chief for the First Naval Battalion and the Joint Battalions. In 1933 he was promoted to admiral and was seen as the next minister of the navy. His position regarding reduction of naval force was at odds with the navy, however, and he thus lost his chance to serve as minister and was assigned to the reserves in March 1936, right after the February 26 Incident. Most people thought that was the end of his professional career, but six months later, on September 2, he was appointed governor-general of Taiwan. He served for four years, until he was removed from the position on November 27, 1940.

The appointment of Kobayashi signaled the end of nine consecutive terms of civilian rule that had begun in 1919 when the Seiyūkai 政友會 faction of Hara Takashi 原敬's cabinet appointed Yamada Kenjirō to replace the previous governor-general, who came from the military. The other notable feature of Kobayashi's appointment is that he came from the navy despite the fact that the army had a dominant position in Taiwan. In any case, Taiwan entered into its second period of rule by governors-general with military backgrounds.

During the period when civilians occupied the position of governor-general of Taiwan there were frequent changes in the position, whenever the cabinet went through any change. It is understandable that the position needed to reflect the cabinet's colonial policy. For example, neither Hamaguchi Osachi 浜口雄幸's (Minsei Party) cabinet in July 1929 nor Kawamura Takeji 川村竹治's (Seiyūkai) cabinet lasted more than a year. In December of 1931 the Inukai Tsuyoshi (Seiyūkai) cabinet was established. During the January 13 cabinet meeting of the following year, without consulting the governor-general of Taiwan, Ota Masahiro 太田政弘 (Minsei Party), it was decided to terminate the chief of general affairs, Kinoshita Shinsaburō 竹上新三郎. Again, in the cabinet meeting on January 29, it was also determined that the head of the police, Inoue Ei, would be terminated. Ota resigned in protest of the direct interference by the cabinet.

Domestic politics had a great impact on Taiwan. Whenever a new governor-general was appointed, the position of chief of general affairs also underwent a change. At the same time, when a new governor-general arrived, new rules and regulations would be put in place to replace the old ones, causing confusion among the bureaucrats and the Taiwanese people. Therefore, the islanders did not trust the civilian administrators. In some cases, "in order to expand the influence of the political party the governor belonged to and to raise funds for the party, the governor's office established special relationships with sugar companies or other special interest companies. They spent most of their time receiving and socializing with visitors from Japan."⁶ Therefore, Kobayashi Seizō's appointment garnered a lot of attention. Once Kobayashi arrived in Taiwan, he proclaimed his wish to implement the imperial subjugation of the Taiwanese people, the industrialization of Taiwan, and also the transformation of Taiwan into a base for the southern advance in Japan's military expansion to the South. Kobayashi stated in his memoir *My Abridged History* (*Hisha no ryakureki* ひしゃの略歴):

> I think the Japanese and the Taiwanese are all the children of the emperor. There is no great difference between their abilities. And since there is a whole string of islands connecting the two places, certainly I think all discriminative policies making distinctions between the Japanese and the islanders should be removed. I will make "Japan and Taiwan as one" (*naitai itchi*) as my basic strategy. Because of that we should promote education, strengthen the compulsory education system, creating new organs for formulating autonomous local rules, and making an effort to make them our equals in the spiritual and intellectual dimensions.

In other words, Kobayashi's basic strategy was "Japan and Taiwan as one" and making the Taiwanese into Japanese. For that purpose, promoting the national language (Japanese) was essential. Therefore, he sought to remove Chinese from the school system and also from all newspapers and magazines. Other than the language issue, to press forward with "reverence to *kami* 敬神思想" he also enforced obligatory worship at Shinto shrines, the reorganization of traditional temples, and the prohibition of long-established local religious activities and festivals as well as native theatrical performances in order to rid Taiwanese of their native consciousness and to promote the "imperial subject movement."

CRITICISM OF GOVERNOR-GENERAL
KOBAYASHI SEIZŌ

Kobayashi was a pioneer in implementing the imperial subject movement and was very aggressive in promoting the Japanese language in order to graft the Japanese spirit onto the Taiwanese. There is powerful evidence that he put pressure on the news media. In his *My Humble Opinion on the Taiwanese News Media Under the Japanese Colonial Rule* (*Nihon tōchi jidai no Taiwan shinbunkai kan-*

ken 日本統治時代の台湾新聞界管見) Mutsu Kojō was critical of Kobayashi, but particularly harsh toward the chief of general affairs, Morioka.[7]

> The planning stage to rein in the Taiwanese news media was undertaken by the military, the bureaucrats, and some of the civilians. The execution of the plan was carried out by Navy General Governor Kobayashi, Chief of General Affairs Morioka Jirō, head of the police Futami Naozō 二見直三, Secretary-General Suzuki, and military police section chief Hashitsume Kiyoto 橋爪清人. Kobayashi came from the military and did not know much about politics. Morioka had served as the head of the police and security bureau at the interior ministry and was also a protégée of Mori Itaru at the Seiyūkai faction. It is no wonder that Morioka chose two Seiyūkai faction members—Futami and Hashitsume—whereas Suzuki was a high-ranking bureaucrat who did not show a particular political tinge but often went along with the flow. Morioka was a hardcore Seiyūkai member, and he found out before he arrived in Taiwan the political affiliations of the bureaucrats who would be working under him. He was a suspicious, difficult person who guarded vigilantly against anyone affiliated with the Minsei Party and made personnel changes accordingly. Therefore, it is no surprise that the bureaucracy in Taiwan began to take on a Seiyūkai tinge. Next, he proceeded to politicize the news media. … Morioka viewed Kobayashi as a hindrance and acted arrogantly toward him. Morioka's first and foremost enemy was the Minsei Party. He used the excuse that the news media was dominated by Minsei Party loyalists, which hindered the governor-general's political goals, to crack down, without any warning, on news media that reported the progress of the war.[8] It was Morioka and Hashitsume who conspired to implement these acts of media control. We can also view the three civilians who concurred with the act as co-conspirators. … It was the military and a few powerful civilians who put the Taiwanese news media in dire straits.[9]
>
> The consolidation of Taiwanese news media into one started with the Sino-Japanese War in 1937 by Kobayashi Seizō, Morioka Jirō, and Hashitsume Kiyoto. We should never forget that these three are the founding fathers of the suppression of the Taiwanese news media. Besides Kawamura Tōoru 川村徹 and Miyoshi Tokusaburō, two civilians who were involved in the issue, it was these three who were responsible for censoring newspapers.[10]

What Mutsu Kojō refers to as "censoring newspapers" did not include the abolition of the Chinese-language section. However, from this record we can clearly see that the Kobayashi regime put a lot of pressure on the news media, thereby limiting freedom of speech, and that Morioka, Futami, and Hashitsume were the ones who carried out the policy.

In April 1937 the Chinese-language sections in newspapers were banned. At the same time, all writing and publication in Chinese was also forbidden. Kobayashi was also the one who got rid of the Chinese course in the public schools for natives, and the one who initiated the policy on unifying and managing the temples. His four-year reign is comparatively long, but he initiated many unpopular policies and so was not a very popular governor.[11]

THE CHINESE ERADICATION POLICY OF THE OFFICE OF THE GOVERNOR-GENERAL

In April 1937, when the Chinese-language sections in newspapers were banned, Chinese courses in all the public schools were also removed from the curriculum. Up until that time, Chinese had been available as an elective course. However, in February 1937, an amendment to the "Rules and Regulations for Public Schools" was made to remove the section that said "Chinese can be added as an elective course." In other words, Chinese was eliminated from the public schools in order to achieve the goal of "cultivating virtue, meritorious actions, and civic spirit through the promotion of the National Language, which is our fundamental charge in the education of this island." In fact, only 37 schools (13 in Taipei county, 24 in Taichung county) in the entire island offered Chinese as an elective course, a mere 6 percent out of the total 625 schools on the island.[12] As there was no urgent reason to change the rule, one may see reflected in this change the emphasis that the governor-general placed on the eradication of Chinese. The abolition of the Chinese sections in the newspapers and the elimination of the Chinese courses in school worked in tandem with each other.

On April 1, 1937, the first day the eradication policy were put into place, the *Taiwan Daily News* carried a conversation with Kobayashi, as well as celebratory notes from Hata Shunroku 鈿俊六, the commander in chief of the military, acting Chief of General Affairs Tabata, and the chief of the bureau of culture and education, Shimada Shōsei.

Kobayashi first stated that "from my own standpoint in ruling this island, which is to make Taiwan to fully become part of Japan, this occasion is indeed worth celebrating." He expressed his gratitude to the news media: "I am sure you have encountered numerous difficulties in pursuing this policy. I would like to convey my appreciation for your courage and sacrifice for the greater cause of assimilating Taiwan into Japan." He further elaborated: "For the convenience of our readers we were not able to completely eliminate Chinese before this. But it was only a matter of time; no one questioned that we would one day have to do this," and concluded, "Basically, promoting spoken and written Japanese is a long-established policy of the Office of Governor-General. We firmly believe that only in this way [eradicating Chinese] can we achieve true assimilation and can bring happiness to the islanders, both materially and spiritually. With the banning of Chinese from the news media, we are hoping to hasten the adoption of Japanese.

The office of the governor-general not only urges all government organizations to use Japanese on a daily basis, but also asks the public to cooperate in this matter."

The office of the governor-general issued an order, signed by Morioka, to all local administrators, enforcing total daily use of Japanese language, an unprecedented order that cast a wide net. Thus, on April 1, 1937, Chinese disappeared completely from all daily newspapers.

At the same time, the "Alliance for the Acculturation of Taiwan" (*Taiwan kyōka rengōkai* 台灣教化連合会) mobilized all cultural and civic groups throughout the colony to promote guidelines regarding the use of Japanese at home, the promotion of Japanese in the countryside, the advocation of Japanese in cities and townships, the organization of various Japanese language groups, etc.

Because of these campaigns, the popularization of the Japanese language accelerated rapidly. The movement became established throughout the island with the recognition of "Japanese language families" (*kokugo jōyō katei* 国語常用家庭) and the provision of many actual material benefits to families using Japanese daily. For example, in Taipei the benefits for the privileged families were clearly stated: enrollment in the elementary schools reserved for the Japanese only (*shōgakkō* 小学校); priority consideration for middle school admission; employment at all levels of public offices; commissions to honorary positions in social organizations; eligibility for business permits and assistance; and permission to visit Japan on business trips.[13]

In actuality, Chinese was purged from elementary schools for natives (*kōgakkō* 公学校), newspapers were only in Japanese, and both in the workplace and at home Japanese was the compulsory language. The attempt was to compel those who used Taiwanese not only to feel uneasy but to have a guilty conscience. As of April 1937, creative writing in Chinese, the traditional language of the Taiwanese people, was essentially eliminated through its banning in all elementary schools for natives and the prohibition on Chinese-language sections in all newspapers and magazines. In its place, people were coerced into using Japanese.

REACTIONS AND THE AFTERMATH OF CHINESE ERADICATION POLICY

The prohibition on use of the Chinese language in Taiwanese news media does not seem to have received any attention inside Japan. There was no report in either the Osaka *Mainichi News* 毎日新聞 or the Tokyo *Asahi News* 朝日新聞. The people of Japan appear to have regarded the prohibition on Chinese in Taiwan as a matter of course, a matter that had no news value. The issue did not merit a single line in the *Great Taiwanese Chronicle* published by the *Taiwan keisei shinpō* (Taiwan Printing, Inc., December 1938, 4th ed.). Even in the realm of Taiwanese public opinion, then, the issue was not a big one.

On the other hand, an article in *Nihon gakugei shinbun* 日本学芸新聞 (no. 82: April 20, 1937), most likely written by Yang Kui 楊逵, satirized the news media's complicity in this matter as a way to ingratiate themselves with the authorities:

Four Taiwanese daily newspapers and more than ten weekly publications eliminated their Chinese language section in unison (only *Shin minpō* 新民報 cut its Chinese language section to half and will formally ban it on the first of June) on April 1 in order to curry favor with the authorities. For this reason, the eyes of those Taiwanese who want to learn about what happens in the world but know only the Chinese language will be veiled. There was a report that an old man in his seventies began to learn Japanese. Some carping chaps ridiculed him saying "Learning a, i, u, e, o (Japanese vowels) in your seventies, perhaps by the time you are about to go into your tomb you will be able to read the newspaper." In any case, the constant slander in the news reported by the current newspapers is probably fit for those in the grave to read.

In his book, *Tōa no ko kaku omou* (東亜の子かく思ふ, The child of East Asia thinks thus; Iwanami shoten, July, 1937), Cai Peihuo 蔡培火 spoke frankly about his views on this issue:

Starting this April 1, throughout the island of Taiwan Chinese language was purged from the newspapers. Because of this, many elderly islanders, who know no Japanese and always get their information through the Chinese language alone, were suddenly thrust into a world of darkness and remain there now. This is a serious matter that not only inconvenienced many common folks, but also is problematic as a national policy of the Japanese empire, in view of the absolute necessity to maintain friendly relations with China and keep communications between the two countries smooth. This acceleration of the prohibition on the Chinese language is something I sincerely hope that both the government and general populace of the Japanese empire, which aspires to be the leader of peace in East Asia, should reflect upon. Though the authorities wish to assimilate (the natives) completely, and to be looked upon as the benevolent elders whose merit is to be admired by all nations, is it not the case that too much pressure was applied to the common folks, inconveniencing their lives? Besides, I do not think those old folks, who were forced to rid themselves of the Chinese language, can turn around and pick up Japanese right away and become acculturated, as those governmental officials expect. Although this type of act demonstrates the government's authority, it also indicates a failure of benevolent rule. As a policy, I suspect that it will not succeed and that practical benefits will be miniscule. I do not say this on behalf of the humble folks of my island; I speak for the greater plan of our East Asia and the future of my Japan. (pp. 178–179)

FROM THE ERADICATION OF CHINESE
IN NEWSPAPERS TO BANNING
WRITINGS IN CHINESE

The office of the governor-general also issued a prohibition that banned the use of Chinese in all bilingual literary journals. The biggest victim of this act was Yang Kui's journal *New Taiwanese Literature* (*Taiwan Shinbungaku* 台湾新文学). Its December 1936 issue (1:10) had announced an upcoming special issue on "Chinese literature": "People have been lamenting the decline of Chinese literature, and we are trying to show (through this journal) the skill and the passion for breaking the silence and come back with will be deployed by many writers who have not been writing for a while." Unfortunately, censors banned this special issue, as mentioned in the next "Editor's note," (2:1), which stated: "For no obvious reason, we somehow touched a nerve with the authorities and the issue was banned." Since the office of the governor-general was aggressively promoting policies such as "Taiwan and Japan are one" and "Imperial Subject Movement" and the Council for Promoting Good Citizenship had decided in July 1936 that "all newspapers and journals are to be published in Japanese," the authorities could not permit the special Chinese issue, which seemed in contravention of official policy.

Since Li Xianzhang 李獻璋's *A Collection of Taiwanese Folk Literature* (台灣民間文學集; published by *Taiwan bungei kyōkai* 台湾文芸協会, June 1936) was published just before the government hardened its policy, we may conclude that the aggressive enforcement was put in place after the meeting of the Council for Promoting Good Citizenship in July 1936. In other words, the foundations for the policy had already been laid in July.

In the "Editor's note" to one issue of *New Taiwanese Literature* (2:4; May 1937) Yang Kui noted: "In response to current tendencies, Chinese publication in this journal is decreasing and in no time it will face the fate of being completely expunged. For those who only write in Chinese and for those readers who read only Chinese, I beg your understanding and forgiveness. Let's all start again by learning a, i, u, e, o." Thus magazines were also forced to take the same measures as the newspapers concerning their Chinese sections. Moreover, in the next issue of *New Taiwanese Literature* (2:5; June 1937) the editor lamented: "As of this issue, the Chinese section has been terminated. Not only is it sad for those who write and read only in Chinese, all of us feel a great sense of loss." Even *Taiwan Shinminpō*, which had until June to do away with its Chinese section, had already eliminated all Chinese; there was no way that *New Taiwanese Literature* could have published anything in Chinese.

In a sense, the act signified the end of the journal *New Taiwanese Literature*. Though the main reason for the elimination of the journal was financial, it is hard to deny the role governmental censorship and the ban on Chinese played in its demise. For the security division of the police department, which was directly in charge of censorship, the *Edict for Taiwanese Newspapers* (*Taiwan shinbun rei* 台湾新聞令) was applicable to all newspapers and journals, and *New Taiwanese Literature* was no exception. In the end, banning the Chinese sections in newspapers amounted to banning all Chinese creative writing.

On the surface, there was no official order issued to ban publication in Chinese. Rather, it was a decision agreed upon through negotiations among all news media organizations. However, it was only window dressing. As we have seen from Representative Matsuda's inquiry in the budget committee, the office of the governor-general and the military applied certain "forceful persuasions" (though he did not go into the exact content of the "forceful persuasions") to the heads of the four major papers. So we can come to the conclusion that the four, at the urging of the authority and the military, caved in to their demands.

The censorship system in Taiwan[14] involved a censor's inspection of pre-publication offprints. If he determined that there were any inappropriate expressions, he would notify the publisher to erase the sections and forbid their publication in the future. This was the so-called eradication decision or warning decision, an ad hoc judgment that was different from an administrative penalty for violating the *Edict for Taiwanese Newspapers*. Further, according to the content, there were three types of rejection: a "notification" was issued when an article was banned upon its publication; a "warning" was issued when a ban might be issued if social conditions changed; "dialogue" meant no ban had been issued but that the authorities relied on the discretion of the newspaper to refrain from publishing the said article. The so-called dialogue rejection really did not allow the newspaper to assert anything that was against the will of the authority. The same principles applied to magazines as well.

The four major newspapers that came to agree upon banning Chinese must have received "dialogue" messages prior to their decision, and once the daily newspapers had banned the language, other weekly news outlets were bound to follow suit. Clear orders were issued to the magazines requesting them to also eliminate Chinese sections, threatening them that anything contravening the ban would result in a ban on that particular issue. Since magazines were not that numerous and pre-publication censorship was in place, it was not too difficult for the government to totally prevent publication in Chinese. Because this was censorship, it fell under the jurisdiction of the security section of the police department.

SPECIAL PERMISSIONS FOR SOME CHINESE MAGAZINES AND WRITING IN CHINESE

The ban on Chinese sections in the newspapers literally resulted in there being no creative literary works being published in newspapers thereafter. Li Xianzhang's

A *Collection of Taiwanese Fiction* (*Taiwan shōsetsu sen* 台湾小説選, originally scheduled to come out in January 1940) was an attempt to collect together fictional works written during the period of the Taiwanese New Literature Movement. However, it failed to pass the censor's inspection and its publication was prohibited.

On the other hand, there was a Chinese literary magazine named *Fengguebao* 風月報 (Wind and moon) and a Chinese-Japanese art journal called *Taiwan yishu* 台灣藝術 (Taiwan art). Many Chinese novels were also published, such as Wu Mansha's 吳漫沙 *Shayang zhi zhong* 莎秧之鐘 (*The Bell of Sayang*). How do we take into account this seemingly contradictory situation, with the banning of Chinese in the newspaper and forbidding the use of Chinese and the reality of these Chinese language publications? This is our second question.

The predecessor of the Chinese literary magazine *Fengguebao* was the Chinese newspaper *Fengyue* 風月, which was founded on May 9, 1935. It published on days ending in -3, -6, or -9 and was distributed to members who knew Chinese. However, the content was crude and it did not last long. It folded on February 8, 1936, after putting out its forty-fourth issue. On July 20, 1937, it reappeared in a new format and published its forty-fifth issue under the new name *Fengguebao*. From July 1, 1941 (the 133th issue), it was renamed *Nanfang* 南方 (The south). Later, due to the shortage of paper, its name was again changed to *Nanfang shiji* 南方詩集 (Southern poetry) on February 25, 1944; and finally, on March 25 of the same year, after 190 issues, the magazine folded for good. At one point, the magazine arranged to have Zhang Wenhuan 張文環 start a Japanese language section, but throughout its publication, it remained a Chinese magazine with lasting support from its Chinese readers.[15]

The Chinese-Japanese art journal *Taiwan yishu* was founded by Huang Zongque in March 1940. It was a private commercial magazine, and was therefore allowed to serialize Chinese language novels. All the staff, from editorial to management, was native Taiwanese. With a circulation of 40,000, it was published as an entertaining, popular magazine, selling in train station kiosks, and was also sent to the battlefield for the soldiers. Beginning in the mid-1940s, the Chinese pages disappeared, but the magazine was able to continue for a long time. In December 1944, beginning with volume 5, issue 12, it was forced to change its name to *Xindazhong* 新大眾 (New masses), but it somehow escape the consolidation of magazines in 1944 and was able to continue to publish until October 1945, right after the war.[16]

In the end, banning the Chinese section in the newspapers or forbidding writing in Chinese was not a direct result of any law or ordinance. The governor-general's office would not risk carrying out an ordinance that would have been criticized by the international world for trying to impede freedom of speech. Since there was no law created to ban Chinese, they had a certain leeway for "forbidding" and "permitting." Censorship could be conducted behind closed doors through the *Edict on Taiwanese Newspapers* and the *Rules and Regulations for Publications in Taiwan*.

In addition, banning Chinese section in the newspapers or forbidding writing in Chinese was part of the strategy to popularize the "National Language," Japanese. On the other hand, the fact that the Chinese-language magazine *Fengguebao* was allowed to survive indicates that the authorities indeed understood the importance of mollifying those who knew only Chinese. As for the bilingual *Taiwan yishu*, it was deemed necessary as a forum connecting both languages that would advance the Imperial Subject Movement. The publishing permits were issued by the security section of the police department, which was in charge of the censorship, therefore they were at liberty to allow *Fengyuepō* and *Taiwan yishu* to continue to publish. Also, by allowing these two journals to continue in print, the authorities were able to claim that the banning of the Chinese section in newspapers was something initiated by the news media themselves and not forced upon them by the authorities.

In April 1937, with the banning of Chinese sections in the newspapers and the prohibition of writings in Chinese language, those who knew only Chinese were literally shut off from the media. The readership that had subscribed to the newspaper for its Chinese-language section decreased significantly. *New Taiwanese Literature* lost a lot of subscribers who read the journal for its Chinese language writings, and many Taiwanese natives who provided financial support to the journal also withdrew support. There was no place for Chinese language writers to publish. Many writers who were active in the New Taiwanese Literary Movement, writing in both Chinese and Japanese, were totally discouraged and left the movement. The movement came to an end before it matured. In this sense, the 1937 banning episode was a symbolic event.

After the Chinese sections were banned, the *Taiwan Daily News* dated April 1 stated:

> As we notified you before, as of April 1 the Chinese language section has been abolished. The last page of the morning and evening news will be filled with novels, sports, entertainment reports, market reports, Chinese poetry, and news in *kana* 仮名. We are eager to improve and enrich the content of the whole newspaper, and fulfill our mission as an organ of public opinion.

After getting rid of the Chinese language section, *Taiwan Daily News* beefed up its literary, non-news section. Other papers also followed suit. *Osaka Asahi News* added a section called "South Island Literary Arts" and *Taiwan News* added "Monday Literary Forum." The increase of the literary arts sections (in place of the Chinese-language sections) was a benefit to the promotion of Japanese-language literature.

The Taiwanese literary movement again gained momentum in 1940 when the Taiwan Writers' Association was founded with its own journal, *Bungei Taiwan* 文芸台湾. The next year, 1941, Zhang Wenhuan's quarterly magazine *Taiwan Bungaku* 台湾文学 was born. Because of the emergence of these two journals, Taiwanese colonial literature entered a flourishing period. Due to the abolishing of the Chinese section in the newspaper, literary arts sections had been set up in its place, which in turn fostered literature written in Japanese. Three years after the elimination of the Chinese-language section in the newspaper, Taiwanese writers, having abandoned Chinese, began engaging in the creation of the Japanese language literature. Though the period from 1937 to 1940 is often considered a blank period in Taiwanese literary history, it can nevertheless be seen as the period of incubation for a new kind of Taiwanese literature. In order to truly comprehend the Taiwanese literature of the 1940s, further research on this incubation period is needed.

NOTES

1. The office of the governor-general (*sōtokufu* 總督府) asserted that promoting Japanese language would "not only improve the cultural and spiritual education of the citizens but also enhance the benefit of the islanders. Therefore, it is the most fundamental and basic aspect of managing the island." In December 1931, a decision was made to establish national language schools and elementary national language schools. The national language school was for those between the ages of twelve and twenty-five who did not know Japanese; it had a mandate to teach at least one hundred days a year of basic education with Japanese language education at its core. The elementary national language school provided night classes in basic Japanese to farmers during the less busy agricultural season (three–six months per semester). Further, in 1933 a "Ten-Year Plan for Popularization of the National Language" was set up with the goal to achieve a Japanese literacy rate of 50 percent in ten years. In 1932 the literacy rate was 22.7%; 1933, 24.5%; 1934, 27%; 1935, 29.7%; in 1936 the rate finally reached one-third of the population at 32.9%, and by 1937 it had reached 37.8% (data from *Taiwan jihō* 台湾事情, 1939 edition, published by Taiwan Jihō Publications, December 1934?).

2. Other major Tokyo newspapers, such as *Tokyo Asahi News* and *Tokyo Daily News*, did not even report the inquiry by Matsuda Takechiyo.

3. Two major new papers in the Tokyo area, *Tokyo Asahi News* and *Tokyo Daily News*, did not report this exchange about abolishing the Chinese language at all.

4. *Taiwan Daily News*, July 26, 1936.

5. Miyoshi Tokusaburō, *The Gleans of Mountain Recluse Miyoshi Chakurai* (Namigata Shōichi, ed., *Miyoshi Tokusaburō to Tsujiri Chaho* [Tokyo: Nihon tosho center, August 2002], 239).

6. Itō Kinjirō, *Taiwan azamukazaru no ki* 台湾欺かざるの気 (Meirinkan, March 1948), 66.

7. Ito Takashi and Nomura Minoru, eds., *Kaigun taishō Kobayashi Seizō oboegaki* 海軍大将小林躋造覺書 (Yamakawa shuppansha 山川出版社, 1981), 200–201.

8. I refere here to the July 1937 crackdown on Izumi Furō's weekly, *Nanei shinpō*.

9. Mutsu Kojō, *Nihon tōchi jidai no Taiwan shinbunkai kanken* <3> (Taiwan dōmei tsūshin 28, January 1957).

10. Mutsu Kojō, *Nihon tōchi jidai no Taiwan shinbunkai kanken* <9> (Taiwan dōmei tsūshin 39, December 1957).

11. On the reorganization of temples, Itō Kinjirō in his book, *Taiwan azamukazaru no ki* (68–69) criticized Kobayashi in this way: "After the July 7 incident, Kobayashi hastened his pace in propagating the Imperial Subject movement. He was the pioneer in bringing an intellectual dimension to the movement. However, since he was anxious to see the results of the Imperial Subject movement, and also due to Morioka's fervency in making the movement a success, they reorganized and banished the traditional temples swiftly, and as a consequence they lost the trust of the people. Everyone knows that Chenghuang temples 城隍廟 (City God Temple) and Mazu temples 媽祖廟 are the sacred sites where the Han people worshiped from ancient times. It is a feature of the Han people, who had the greatest reverence for their temples and tombs. Seeing the Japanese abruptly getting rid of these temples, erasing the native traditions, and rejecting their beliefs, trampling on their customs—it is no wonder that Kobayashi's plan caused a lot of discontent among the people."

12. *Taiwan Daily News*, April 1, 1937.

13. *Taiwan shibao* 台灣時報 211 (June 1937), 143–148.

14. Publication of newspapers and magazines was regulated by the *Edict for Taiwanese Newspapers* (*Taiwan shinbun rei*) while other publications fell under the *Rules and Regulations for Publications in Taiwan* (*Taiwan shuppan kisoku*). Compared to regulations in Japan, the rules in Taiwan were obviously much more strict. Further, cases that were not specified in the law were subject to ad hoc decisions. As a result, censor officials had a lot of flexibility in their pre-publication assessment. For details, see Kawahara Isao, "Kaisetsu," in *Taiwan shuppan keisatsu hō* 台湾出版警察法 (Fuji shuppan 富士出版, 2001). Also see, Nakajima Toshio's "Nihon tōchiki Taiwan kenkyū no mondaitenTaiwan sōtokufu ni yoru kanbun kinshi to Nihon tōchi makki no Taiwango kinshi o rei to shite" (*Gifu shōtoku gakuen daigaku gaikokugo gakubu chūgokugo gakka kiyō* 5: March 2002), which deals with the banning of the Chinese language from a different angle.

15. For details, see Kawahara Isao, ed., *Fengyue, Fengyuepō, Nanfang, Nanfang shiji zongmulu zhuanlun zhuzhe suoyin* 風月, 風月報, 南方, 南方詩集總目錄, 專論, 著者索引 (Taipei: Nantian shuju, 2001).

16. For details see Kawahara Isao, "Zasshi 'Taiwan yishu' to Jiang Xiaomei Taiwan yishu Xindazhong Yihua zonmuci" (*Seikei ronsō* 39 [March 2002]).

[7]

COLONIAL MODERNITY FOR AN ELITE TAIWANESE, LIM BO-SENG

The Labyrinth of Cosmopolitanism

KOMAGOME TAKESHI

THE QUESTION OF COLONIAL MODERNITY

In the context of Taiwanese history it is important to analyze the concept of colonial modernity, understanding both the attraction and the oppression of modernity, without regarding it simply as evidence of historical progress. Like so many other fashionable terms, however, the term "colonial modernity" is ambiguous: its meaning depends on each writer. Before we proceed we must first make clear what is meant by the term here.

As Leo Ching has pointed out, one of the intended effects of the term "colonial modernity" is to draw attention to structural similarities between Western imperialism and Japanese imperialism, and to emphasize "the interrelationship and interdependency of the specific Japanese case, with, and within, the generality of global capitalist colonialism."[1] I would like to discuss a perspective here that investigates colonial modernity as generally as possible, while focusing mainly on Japan's rule in Taiwan.

Colonial rule in the nineteenth and twentieth century was different from earlier colonial rule in that it was closely connected with modernization in various fields, such as politics, economic development, and the use of military power. Not only were the new rulers superior militarily, but they carried prestige as representatives of Western civilization. The notion of "civilization" involved a variety of elements, such as a political system based on parliamentarism, the capitalist mode of production, scientific technology, and Christianity. Imperial powers situated people in a racial hierarchy, according to the degree to which they were "civilized," and created a system that would allow and even justify the unjust treatment of those who were categorized as "barbarian." Even those under imperial rule came to share in the desire to elevate themselves within the hierarchy of "civilization." Modern colonial rule, while rooted in absolute military superiority, engendered a desire for civilization and maintained hegemony by addressing that desire.

Of course, creating an interest in modern Western civilization was not the same as actually introducing modern institutions and technologies. What was crucial for colonial modernity was that among the components of modern Western civilization there be a great gap between what was actually spread and what was prevented from being spread. It is this gap that characterizes colonial modernity. In the colony those who ruled economically were still mercilessly ensnared by a global capitalism that subordinated them to a political system that was far from democratic. Between the promotion of modernization as capitalization and the prevention of modernization as democratization is an ambiguous area that could be called a cultural stage.

New media, such as newspaper, movies, and radio—which were sometimes a means of propaganda used by power and other times a means of resistance used by the subordinated people—eventually established an urban and popular culture. Schools basically functioned as apparati facilitating political control, but they also served as both the producers and the consumers of new culture and technologies. As Gi-wook Shin and Michael Robinson have pointed out, "modernity can both assist and endanger a prevailing hegemony."[2] Contrary to the general image of them as "the bearers of civilization," the rulers were not necessarily active in spreading new cultures and technologies. Even when they tried to spread new initiatives, they did not want to give up the ability to determine the direction of the development.

In this situation, the ruled, the male elites of the native class in particular, often participated in the ruling structure; by supporting the spread of such modern institutions as schools and hospitals, they became the agent that extended the hegemony of colonial rule to the bottom of society. The position of the native elite, however, was always unstable. While they were attracted to the modern Western civilization that the rulers had brought, and tried to accept it in full, they nevertheless faced racial discrimination from the rulers and discovered in the midst of their disappointment "their nation" as a subordinate entity capable of resistance. Importantly, between the moment when they faced the rulers from outside and the moment when they recognized "their nation,", there was a time gap. Nationalistic descriptions of history tend to assume that such a time gap should not exist. But we should remember that even Gandhi, before he took to his spinning wheel in simple, traditional clothes, had walked around the city of London in Western dress. When trying to understand experience of colonial modernity, it is important not to read into the past the nationalism later discovered, but to focus on the aspirations and disappointments engendered by this time delay.

Here we must be sure that these conditions can be applied not only to Western imperialism but also to Japanese imperialism. The Japanese also flaunted their nation as the bearer of "the mission of civilization" to those both within its boundaries and beyond. The infrastructure construction that was promoted vigorously in the early stage of the occupation of Taiwan—including the construction of railways and harbors, for example—demonstrates that this intention as professed by the Japanese was not a mere pose. And there were Taiwanese elites who joined with the Japanese colonial system in trying to diffuse modern Western civilization.

Of course, there were differences between Western imperialism and Japanese imperialism. No matter how much the Japanese boasted of themselves as the bearers of the "mission of civilization," it was obvious that their civilization was one that the Japanese had hastened to learn only after the Meiji Restoration. Not only outside the Japanese colonial empire but also within the empire, there were many Westerners, such as councilors, merchants, and missionaries, who were regarded as more "authentic" bears of civilization. The "civilization" that the Japanese intended to spread did not include Christianity.

From the Western perspective the Japanese were not qualified to call themselves the bears of the "mission of civilization." The British missionary Thomas Barclay, working in Taiwan from the 1870s, witnessed the Japanese occupation of Taiwan in 1895 and reported to his mission headquarters: "one cannot but sympathise with the people, dissociated without their consent being asked from the ancient Empire of China, with all its tradition, of which they are so proud, and handed over to form part of a despised Empire."[3] There was not even the superficial respect shown at least to the Chinese empire; Japan was nothing but "a despised empire." Nevertheless, Barclay also wrote,

> In the meantime, there seem to be some advantages to be hoped for. The change will improve the conditions of life for the missionaries, and the greater facilities of communication will greatly help our work. The destruction of the Mandarinate, and perhaps still more of the literacy class as a body, involving the discrediting of Confucianism, will remove many obstacles out of our way.[4]

Barclay expected Japanese colonial rule to promote modernization, and to dismantle the literacy class, which was seen as an obstacle to the propagation of Christianity. The interdependent relationship between British missionaries and the Japanese colonists was mediated through the realism that "the enemy of my enemy is my friend."

When the Taiwanese, under the rule of the "despised empire," accepted Christianity through contact with British missionaries, what was the relationship among the Japanese, the Taiwanese, and British missionaries? This complicated relationship can be traced in the footprints of Lim Bo-seng 林茂生 (1887–1947), the subject of this article.

Lim Bo-seng was born in the city of Tainan in 1887. His father, Lim Ian-sin, a member of the literacy class, was converted to Christianity after he came in contact with British missionaries as a teacher of Taiwanese language and later was ordained as a pastor. Baptized as a young boy under his father's influence, Lim Bo-seng studied at the Tainan Presbyterian Middle School, established by missionaries, and after graduation went to Japan proper to study. He graduated from Tokyo Imperial University in 1916, and after returning to Taiwan gained a position as head teacher at the middle school from which he had graduated, as well as a position at a government school. In 1927 he went to Columbia University as a researcher under the auspices of the government-general, and there obtained his Ph.D. In 1930 he went back to Taiwan and assumed the directorship of the board of managers of the Tainan Presbyterian Middle School.

In Taiwan today Lim Bo-seng is famous as a martyr of the February 28 Incident, but he has not received much attention in the context of history of the anti-Japanese movement.[5] In the prewar era, through he was considered a representative intellectual and educator of Taiwan, he was also criticized for his "pro-Japanese" statements, and for having worked in a government school. I do not want here, however, to answer this criticism by listing his "anti-Japanese" speeches and actions. Instead, I want to ask what his experience of colonial modernity was. In what sense did he think it important to spread modern education in Taiwan? How did his encounter with British missionaries and his experience of studying in the United States influence his evaluation of education under Japanese colonial rule? Did he consider the Japanese to propagate modernity? Or did he dismiss Japanese rule as a deviation from modernity? If so, by internalizing the values of an "authentic" modernity, could he discover a way to escape imperialism? The answers to these questions are not simple.

I will here examine the contents of his dissertation, titled "Public Education in Formosa Under Japanese Administration: A Historical and Analytical Study of the Development and the Cultural Problems" (New York, 1929).[6] There is an excellent study by E. Patricia Tsurumi (1977) on the history of colonial education in Taiwan under Japan, but the task of this paper is not to describe that history "objectively." Rather, it is to read his paper as a historical narration written from within that history, that is, to read it as an academic narration of history and at the same time as a testimony of that history. Then I will consider the significance of his dissertation as a part of the world of knowledge around 1930. Since I have already discussed elsewhere his activities with the Tainan Presbyterian Middle School and their failure,[7] I will make minimal reference to these issues here.

COLONIAL/MODERN EDUCATION

The narration of history is a space of power/knowledge contestations; one need not quote the theory of postcolonialism to support this statement. Lim Bo-seng was aware of this, too. In the introduction to his dissertation, he pointed out that books written by those related to the colonial authorities are often "biased, partial, and misleading." Furthermore, although the government-general's records were precise, they constituted propaganda because the government-general selected their contents with "preconceived viewpoints" (Lim 1929:7). He makes his own position clear while explaining his methodology: "personal observation has been carried on by the author for more than ten years as an educator serving government and private schools in Formosa, and also as a leader of the cultural movement of the intellectual class" (7). His writing style is appropriate for an academic research paper, and he does not mention his own personal experience directly, but both his choice of objects of study and his way of evaluating them do reflect his experiences, and the position from which he evaluates history may oscillate slightly between the objective and the subjective.

I will examine the contents of his dissertation in the following rough division of time: around 1900, the 1910s, and the 1920s.

Around 1900

At the beginning of his main argument, Lim Bo-seng sees the political and economic conditions in Taiwan as a special case, in which "the governor-general still retains considerable arbitrary power in legislation and administration" (21). Any order by the governor-general of Taiwan had legal effect. Although the governor-general's power began to be restricted by the central government in the 1920s, a Taiwanese parliament was never established and the governor-general continued to possess arbitrary power.

The Japanese occupied a superior position economically as well, and Lim argues as follows:

> Generally speaking, we find in Formosa agricultural and laboring population made up almost entirely of Formosan natives, with the Japanese in charge of most of the large commercial and industrial undertakings. (23)

Because the Taiwan natives, deprived of political rights, were confined to agricultural and industrial labor, and the nonnative rulers held political and economic power, Taiwan was unambiguously only a colony. And, like his contemporaries in the Taiwanese elite, Lim Bo-seng held critical attitudes toward the discriminatory institutions of colonial rule. When it came to education, however, the tone of his argument was different. He focuses his attention here on the words of Kodama Gentarō 兒玉源太郎, the governor-general in 1898:

Education is urgently needed on this island, but the ill effects of an education which wantonly introduced a superficial civilization which led people to discuss right and duty at random should be widely avoided. Therefore, great care should be taken in fixing our educational principles. (37)

As this statement illustrates, those on the side of the rulers showed reluctance to spread education. Lim Bo-seng critically examines this response using the expression "negative educational policy," and seeks to pin responsibility for it in part on the conservative attitude of the Taiwanese themselves. He says:

The Formosan people, for reasons of their own, failed to appreciate the new type of culture that the Japanese were introducing. Their conservative attitude and strict adherence to their old culture reacted on the government and led the government to assume this negative educational policy (38).

Lim Bo-seng was trying to find a positive significance in "the new type of culture" that the Japanese had introduced to the island. His evaluation might reflect his own experience. When he was eleven, his father was converted to Christianity and he entered a Japanese-language school founded by a Buddhist association from Japan. After graduating from that school, he ran errands at a local post office using his newly acquired Japanese abilities.[8] Armed uprisings against the alien rulers continued in various places, and the father and son were in the minority in the choices they made. To them what was important was whether they should accept the new type of culture, rather than whether they were pro-Japan or anti-Japan. Lim Bo-seng regarded those who rejected this new type of culture as conservative, and he did not change his idea between 1898 and 1929, when he wrote his dissertation.

He used the term "new type of culture" as almost the equivalent of "Japanese culture," but they were not exactly synonymous. A "new type of culture" had been introduced by the British missionaries. He wrote also the mission schools of Qing dynasty:

The most modernized and systematic educational work during the Chinese regime was carried on by the English and Canadian Presbyterian Missions, operating in the southern and northern halves of the island, respectively. The former began by merely training young men for the ministry, but in 1885 a middle school was opened in Tainan, with instruction in Chinese, history, geography, arithmetic, astronomy, and Scriptures. (27)

The middle school was the Tainan Presbyterian Middle School, where he had studied. Christianity was taught there, along with such subjects as geography and arithmetic. He considered this "the most modernized and systematic education work," and concluded that the Japanese language schools and missionary schools had played a similar role in initiating the new type of culture.

In another part of the dissertation, he strongly criticized education under the contemporary government-general. His high evaluation of the Japanese as bearers of a new type of culture leaves a rather strange impression, but we should probably think of this as the strangeness that characterizes historical descriptions written from within that history. Further, as his dissertation dealt with different time periods, his own stance underwent changes and a slight blurring.

The 1910s

In discussing the post–Russo-Japanese War period, Lim Bo-seng emphasized that the Taiwanese began to recognize what seemed to be universal values in Japanese culture and education, which he calls "modern education." He pointed to the increasing number of students at public schools established for the primary-level education of the natives, and to an increase in the number who went to Japan proper to study.

At the same time as the demand for modern education was rising among the Taiwanese, he came to realize that it was not enough to criticize only the conservative attitudes of the Taiwanese who did not accept the new culture, but that the discriminative practices of the colonial rulers in regard to post–primary-level education should also be questioned. On the one hand, the government-general organized secondary schools that would prepare students for entrance to universities in Japan proper, for the Japanese residing in Taiwan. On the other hand, however, the government-general did not prepare systematic educational institutions for the Taiwanese, but rather founded only a national language school for learning Japanese and a medical school.

In the 1910s, local Taiwanese elite society, dissatisfied with the policies of the government-general, initiated a movement to found a middle school for the Taiwanese. Lim Bo-seng discusses this movement in detail. He praised those people who donated a great amount of money for a school as "public-spirited Formosan Chinese." He also mentioned the unsatisfactory result of the movement; contrary to the expectation of those "public-spirited Formosan Chinese," the Taichu Public Middle School was founded by the government-general only as a lower-level institution than comparable schools in Japan. The curriculum of the school was one year shorter than that in schools in Japan proper and English was optional, while it was required in Japan proper (58–60).

The Taichu Middle School provided a turning point at which Lim Bo-seng's historical understanding could become conscious of criticism of the educational policy of the government-general. Though we do not know whether he was aware of it, there arise from his dissertation multiple implications of "public." There was a serious discrepancy between the founding of a middle school for which public-spirited Formosan Chinese donated money, and the Taichu Public Middle School, which the government-general founded. While the former "public" means the collectivity of spontaneous will shared by each Taiwanese, the latter "public" means subordination to the government-general's control. They contradict each other. In his dissertation, however, he does not highlight this dual conception of "public." The meaning of "public education," which he uses in the title of his dissertation, is not clear. This does not necessarily indicate a theoretical lack on his part, but is probably an expression of the ambiguous duality of the phrase "public sphere" under colonial rule.

Lim Bo-seng was not necessarily opposed to education sponsored by the government-general. The problem was that the government-general did not build schools in response to Taiwanese demands for education.

The 1920s

For the period of the 1920s, when he wrote his dissertation, the stance of his writing changes drastically. He first emphasizes the "awakening of national consciousness among the Formosan people" (73) in the 1920s. After World War I, those who studied in either Japan or mainland China came back to Taiwan with a new democratic spirit: "they were free, outspoken, critical" (74). "They" perhaps included Lim Bo-seng himself. He mentions the growth of an anti-Japanese movement, including the establishment of the Taiwan Cultural Association in 1921. Although he worked as a summer school lecturer for the association, we cannot find any further connection between him and the group. While he shared in the "awakening of national consciousness" with those who devoted themselves to the anti-Japanese movement, he probably found his own role in the reform of education and culture, rather than in political movements per se. In any case, a young man who entered a Japanese-language school in the late nineteenth century while anti-Japanese armed uprisings were still occurring found himself a nationalist by the 1920s.

He now criticized the government-general for making its educational policy more culturally assimilatory in exchange for the equalization of educational institutions. He assumed this cultural assimilation policy was a reactionary response to the growth of Taiwanese national consciousness. He argued:

> With the growth of this liberal attitude on the part of people, the result was restraining force on the part of the government and consequently stricter assimilation. This is why in the year 1922 those Formosans were now merged and consolidated so as to mold the Formosan people more closely to the Japanese pattern and extend the principle of assimilation. (93)

The government-general greatly revised its "negative" educational policy through the 1922 reform mentioned above. It created a way for some Taiwan-

ese to go to elementary school, and established the principle of coeducation between the Taiwanese and the Japanese beyond secondary schools. In addition, it
founded Taipei Imperial University in 1928. Den Kenjirō, the governor-general,
praised himself, saying that he had abolished educational discrimination and
brought about complete equality.

Lim Bo-seng, however, paid more attention to the question of cultural assimilation as being to some degree the price of the equalization. In the last half of his
dissertation, he discusses the question intensively, focusing on the proper use of
the Japanese language and of coeducation between the two ethnicities.

He does not deny the value of the Japanese as the official language for education, but he questions whether it would be acceptable for the native language to
be extinguished:

> To solve this problem it is important to understand the status of the "Formosan
> language." There are two dialects of Chinese spoken in Formosa, and the written
> language in both dialects, as in all dialects throughout China, is exactly the same.
> Of these two spoken languages, the Fukienese is dominant and spoken widely even
> among the Cantonese districts. (116)

Furthermore, no matter how broadly Japanese spread, the importance of the
mother tongue would not disappear: "This language is not in a decadent state but
[still] alive, growing, changing, and expressing the thoughts and sentiments of the
Formosan people" (117–118). He manifests a typically nationalist way of thinking.

He intensively discussed questions of "our language" and "our culture," which
he had omitted from the first half of his dissertation, where he talked about the
importance of the new type of culture being introduced by the Japanese. The
meanings of his terms however, were not self-evident, as he had to explain what
the "Formosan language" was. He charged, for example, that "the curriculum
was so designed that it left out entirely any consideration of the old Formosan
culture—Chinese." "Old Formosan culture" is here equivalent to "Chinese culture." But it was unclear what a "new Formosan culture," different from "Chinese
culture," would be. Besides, the expression seldom appeared in his dissertation.
He uses the adjective "Chinese" for culture, but "Formosan" for language, a telling dichotomy.

In this way, neither "our language" nor "our culture" was self-evident. But he
stressed their importance: it was obvious that ignorance of these terms put Taiwanese children and youth at a disadvantage. The fact that Japanese was the
language used in the middle school entrance exam was a severe impediment to
the Taiwanese. Although in principle there was to be coeducation for the two
ethnicities, some schools were mostly for the Japanese and others were mostly
for the Taiwanese. The former had "an unwritten law" that allowed Taiwanese to comprise no more than ten percent of the total number of students. He
maintains:

If this actual, though not on the surface apparent, racial discrimination is maintained as it is now, it is not only an injustice to those who apply for admission, but also to these ten percent admitted to enter, for they are in the minority, so that no individual differences are provided for in actual teaching, and these students consequently cannot appear to the best advantage. (139)

Before coming to New York to study, Lim Bo-seng had gone, with the title of professor, to Tainan Commercial College. Because there were only two Taiwanese professors at universities and colleges at the time he enjoyed rare social status. He was in a position to recognize implicit but institutionalized racial discrimination. Because of this, his opinions carried weight. He probably also knew through experience that young Taiwanese entering as minorities a school designed for Japanese would be exposed to the pressures of cultural assimilation.

When discussing the situation of around 1900, he expected much of Japan as the introducer of new type of culture, and he criticized the Taiwanese for their conservativism. But his hopes for the Japanese were being betrayed by their racial discrimination. The next passage indicates that he was becoming aware of this:

Modern education aims to develop the individual from within, not impose a development from without for fear that it would spoil the creative power on the part of the child. Assimilation sets out to impose standards for its own from without which are not desired, for the need is neither imperative nor recognized. (125)

In this passage, he supposes that for the Taiwanese children "native culture" should be respected, according to the principle of individual development "from within." His point of view, from which he identified modernity in the new type of culture introduced by the Japanese, enabled him to criticize the "negative" educational policy, but not the cultural assimilation policy. This is because the positioning of native culture in human formation had to be negative in principle. In this dilemma, he reconstructed his own perspective, asking first of all what modern education was at a basic level. What is worth noting here is that when reconstructing his own perspective, he referred to the thought of John Dewey, then professor at Columbia University. For example, in the paragraph that follows the passage above, he cites Dewey's expression "modern life means modern democracy; democracy means freeing intelligence for independence effectiveness [cited from Dewey, *Elementary School Teachers* (1903), 125]." Dewey's thought was well known in Japanese education, and so his citing of Dewey itself is not especially novel. What is important is that Lim Bo-seng appropriates Dewey's thoughts in the context of criticizing assimilation policy in the colony. By placing his thoughts in this context, he discovers the actuality of Dewey's thought in the contemporary imperialistic global order, which was perhaps beyond Dewey's own intentions.

However, the appropriation of Dewey's thought introduces a kind of split into Lim Bo-seng's position. The theoretical ground from which he criticizes cultural assimilation is the principle that individuals' creative power should not be undermined. "The loss of one's culture is ominous, for it forebodes the crumbling of personality and the undermining of one's very existence, especially when it is forced from outside" (123). His focus is "personality." Both "individuals' creative power" and "personality" are notions conceptualized by a psychology aimed at individuals. A cosmopolitanism based on individuality is opposed to a nationalism that emphasizes "our language" and "our culture." And there is also the conflict over whether nationalism should be Formosa-based or Chinese-based. Individuality and "our language" and "our culture" are barely connected here in the context of criticizing cultural assimilation, but there is a danger that they might be dismantled outside this context. This is an inherent theme of colonial modernity in Taiwan.

Furthermore, no matter how much he criticized cultural assimilation, Lim Bo-seng did not totally criticize education in Taiwan as colonial education. He did not surrender the possibility that modern education, apart from cultural assimilation, could be realized under Japanese colonial rule. He proposed that Taiwanese be used as a complementary educational language and that middle schools be built, some exclusively for the Japanese and others exclusively for the Taiwanese, separately in big cities. These are at best proposals for improvement within the framework of colonial rule. Moreover, in the final part of his dissertation, he points out as an important consideration for the future of Taiwan "the use of power wisely directed to the guiding of the destiny of colonial people by seeking for the source of misunderstanding and, through careful application of modern education, by establishing a spiritual unity that goes beyond the barriers of ethnicity." Although he began to experience nationalistic feelings after he faced Japanese racial discrimination, at the base of his thinking he was still cosmopolitan.

THE CONSTELLATION OF KNOWLEDGE IN THE IMPERIALISTIC WORLD

Could the hope that Lim Bo-seng derived from cosmopolitanism have been realized in Taiwan under colonial rule? Subsequent history shows that his vision was too optimistic. In the mid-1930s, the Taiwanese language was completely erased from the school curriculum, just the opposite of his proposed solution. Harsh attacks from the Japanese led to his banishment from Tainan Presbyterian Middle School. British missionaries now began to collaborate with the Japanese, and betrayed him (Komagome 2001). Rather than review these events in detail, I would like to consider the significance of his dissertation for the imperialistic global order.

Lim Bo-seng's dissertation was not published in Japan or in Taiwan. Even if he had intended to publish it, it would have been impossible. For example, Yanaihara Tadao 矢内原忠雄's article "Taiwan Under Imperialism (Teikoku shugika no Taiwan 帝国主義下の台湾)," which Lim Bo-seng cites in his dissertation of 1929, was banned in 1930 in Taiwan. It was a time when even a book written by a professor at Tokyo Imperial University was banned; there was virtually no chance that Lim Bo-seng's dissertation could be published. We cannot find a direct response to his dissertation, but one article does provide an indirect clue: Abe Shigetaka 阿部重孝's "Education in Formosa and Korea," which was published in the *Educational Yearbook, 1931* edited by I. L. Kandel, a professor at Columbia University. The ideas in Lim Bo-seng's dissertation are in contrast with Abe's experience.

In 1923 an international research institute was founded at Columbia University with a donation from the Rockefeller Foundation, and Kandel was named a researcher there. The institute began to publish its *Educational Yearbook* in 1924, with Kandel as editor. Special theme issues from 1929 to 1933 were:

1929: The philosophy underlying national systems of education
1930: The expansion of secondary education
1931: Education in the colonial dependencies
1932: The relation of state to religious education
1933: Missionary education

Since missionary activities were pursued mainly in the colonies, the 1933 theme is closely related to the 1931 and 1932 themes. Colonial education became an important topic in the early 1930s, as international tension was increasing after the Great Depression in 1929. The Columbia University institute conducted research on the Philippines and Puerto Rico under U.S. colonial rule and published its reports. For instance, in *Twenty-Five Years of American Education* (New York, 1924), edited by Kandel, one chapter was devoted to education in the Philippines.

In the introduction to his dissertation, Lim Bo-seng expressed "his deep gratitude to Professors Paul Monroe, I. L. Kandel, and L. M. Wilson for their valuable suggestions and criticisms and their friendly interest during the preparation of this work" (iv). He also cites a statement by Kandel regarding education in the Philippines as compared to Taiwan:

> The 3,500,000 Formosans, or 95 percent of the total population, do not feel that they lack a common languages as is the situation in the Philippines, where English is a coordinating factor to bring together eight dialects which otherwise can only be barriers and obstruction to progress. (116)

He also cites Kandel's book in his notes concerning educational conditions in the Philippines. Kandel argued that English played a role in removing obstructions to progress. But Lim Bo-seng stressed a difference between Taiwan and the Philippines. We can sense that he feared that if he did not stress this difference, the ground upon which he criticized the government-general's policy of excluding the Taiwanese would be undermined.

Abe Shigetaka, author of the article about education in Taiwan and Korea, graduated from the College of Literature of Tokyo Imperial University in 1913. It was three years before Lim Bo-seng's graduation from the same college, and, if we consider that both majored in philosophy, we might suppose that they had known each other there. After 1915, Abe was in charge of investigating educational conditions all over the world after World War I, as a contract researcher for the ministry of education. He became an assistant professor in the Department of Literature at Tokyo Imperial University in 1922, and he went to the United States the next year to study as a research worker from the ministry of education. In Japan at that time, where a type of pedagogy influenced by German philosophical education was predominant, he became well known as a person who insisted on the establishment of educational science through incorporating empirical research methods from the United States.[9]

Abe conducted research on education in Taiwan from 1925 to 1926. Lim Bo-seng mentioned this research in his dissertation: he says that "in 1926, Prof. Abe from Tokyo Imperial University came to Formosa to give intelligence tests at the leading schools," but as far as the author knew the result had not yet been published (137). According to Tokiomi Kaigo, who was one of Abe's students, Abe conducted the research entrusted to him by the government-general of Taiwan, but "the results were not published out of concern for colonial rule because the intelligence and the scholarly attainment of the Japanese, Chinese, and Taiwan natives residing in Taiwan became obvious."[10] Although the results were not published, it seemed the research threatened Lim Bo-seng, as did the statement in Kandel's book about the Philippines. If by any chance the result had revealed that the Taiwanese were intellectually inferior, it would have given a "scientific" ground to the government-general's discriminatory educational policy.

How, then, doe Abe discuss "education in Taiwan and Korea"? He first states that "the educational system of Formosa and Korea differ somewhat from education in colonial dependencies because their fundamental aims are exactly the same as those of Japan proper," and he differentiates the position of Taiwan and Korea toward Japan from that of colonies toward Western nations. In his opinion, educational institutions in Taiwan and Korea are "extensions of the educational system of the homeland, and are expected to carry out the same ideals as were common to Japan proper." At the root of his opinions was the idea that Japan's colonial education was based on equality while colonial education under Western nations was discriminatory; however, he is not explicit about this, since he wrote his piece for readers in English-speaking countries.

After insisting on the principle of commonality between education in Japan proper and the colony, he says:

A slight variation, however, has been found necessary in Formosa and Korea, because of their different languages, customs, and manners, and the level of their culture which is much lower in general than that of the Japanese people at home. Nevertheless, it must not be assumed that education in these parts of the Empire is controlled with any sense of discrimination. The ultimate aims of their education are to cultivate the newly annexed peoples in order to raise their social and economic, as well as political, positions to the standard of those of the Japanese, and to realize the principle of "give and take." [11]

Abe is arguing that the Japanese, with their high level of culture, were educating the Taiwanese and Koreans, with their lower level of culture, in order to raise their standards. This rhetoric is often employed to justify colonial rule. At the time when Japanese education was received as the new type of culture, this rhetoric might have been accepted. But at the time when a national consciousness had emerged among the ruled, and the government-general's cultural assimilation policy was being questioned, Abe's rhetoric was out of date. He was not able to realize that inequality could be reproduced by means of culture.

To borrow a bitter expression from Lim Bo-seng, Abe's article was propaganda. Why, then, did Kandel place this "propaganda" in the *Education Yearbook*, which he himself had edited? He had supervised Lim Bo-seng during the writing of his dissertation—didn't he then question the content of Abe's article? It is hard to answer these questions. There is no source that suggests concretely the ways in which Kandel was involved in the editing of the *Educational Yearbook*. But it is worth clarifying here how he discusses colonial education in the introduction of this book.

Kandel defines as "assimilation in education" the policy that transplants the education system of the metropole directly to the colony, and argues that this kind of educational policy is failing. For example, he charges that "the educational unrest in India, although closely interwoven with the nationalist movement, is equally a manifestation of the failure of the attempt to transplant the educational system of one country to another." [12] He argues that American education in the Philippines and Puerto Rico had failed, even if it was carried out as "the most advanced experiment in democratic spirit." As evidence, he pointed out that study that required the reading of materials based on "alien culture and environments" may have "resulted in psittacism, and external polish, which was of no value in itself and only resulted in rendering the learner unhappy in his own environment."

Lim Bo-seng and Kandel seem to agree with each other in that both criticize assimilation policy. For instance, when Lim Bo-seng says that through assimilation, "the freedom of action and effectiveness of independent intelligence will be subordinated to the mere imitating habit" (125), he follows on Kandel's discussion of "an external polish." This is a perspective that Abe lacks. More detailed observation, however, forces us to recognize that Kandel and Lim Bo-seng differ importantly from each other on why they disagree with assimilation policy. For example, Kandel argues as follows:

> The premium placed on book learning and the neglect of any other type of education weaned the native away from his everyday work; the man who could read and write felt it beneath his dignity to engage in manual occupations. The rudiments of an elementary education were just as disinteresting among backward peoples as the expansion of secondary education among advanced peoples is so far as they led to aspirations for "white collar" jobs. That considerable mischief has already been done by the assimilation policy can be abundantly proved.[13]

Kandel criticizes assimilation policy and insists on the necessity of "adaptation to social and economic needs" because, as the passage above indicates, he is afraid of backward people's aspiration for "white collar" jobs. Doesn't this opinion tend to indicate a return to negative educational policy? At least, Kandel does not suggest any reason to refute this. We should notice that whereas he discusses native people's social and economic needs, he does not mention political rights. In a context in which respect for native culture could not be considered together with the expansion of their political rights, he seems almost to be saying that natives should be engaged in manual occupations. Although both Kandel and Lim Bo-seng criticize assimilation policy, their theoretical grounds are clearly different.

While Dewey's article provides Lim Bo-seng with a critical perspective, Kandel's writing has implications that imprison him once again within the cage called imperialism. Where does this difference come from? Kandel was critical of the movement that called for progressive education, promoted mainly by Dewey. But we cannot reduce the different meanings that these two people's arguments had for Lim Bo-seng simply to the difference between these two positions. Rather, it seems to stem from the fact that while Dewey's argument is a theoretical principle, which it is possible to appropriate, Kandel's is more related to the reality of colonial education. That is to say, modern education essentially contains these dual characteristics.

Modern scholarship and the space of the university not only granted Lim Bo-seng an academic career, but also made him recognize the importance of "the freedom of intelligence," to borrow Dewey's expression. He probably regarded it as the origin of all cultural values. But modern scholarship and the university had another aspect which oppressed him, as a member of the elite from the colony. This aspect is suggested by the fact that Kandel placed Abe's out-of-date article in the *Educational Yearbook*. Of course, it is possible that Kandel did not know about the content of Abe's article and that he entrusted the writing of an article to him only because Abe was a professor at Tokyo Imperial University. If so, we will have to ask whether there was any way for member of the elite from colonial

Taiwan also to become a professor at Tokyo Imperial University. Although there was a very little chance, that does not mean that there was none. According to his son's recollections, although Lim Bo-seng was asked to take a professor's post at Taipei Imperial University by the government-general when he came back from New York, he turned down that offer, believing that the purpose of this university was to bring up manpower in order to promote Japan's southward expansion policy.[14] Imperial universities, as the names suggest, were organs for training high-class bureaucrats for the colonial empire of Japan. The universities were by no means free from the cage of imperialism. The article by Abe that was included in the *Educational Yearbook* edited by Kandel was already predicting the catastrophe that Lim Bo-seng would face in the 1930s.

CONCLUSION

Gi-wook Shin and Michael Robinson have made the following comments about Korean colonial modernity.

> Koreans participated directly and indirectly in the construction of a unique colonial modernity—a modernity that produced cosmopolitanism (a sense of shared universals) without political emancipation. Colonial modernity possessed liberating forces and a raw, transformative power, and it affected more nuanced forms of domination and repression in the colony. Its sheer complexity must be recognized.[15]

These comments could be applied to Lim Bo-seng as well. He was not simply a recipient of modern Western civilization: he actively participated in the construction of colonial modernity in Taiwan. In his writing, such key terms such as "liberalism," "freedom of action," and "independent intelligence" occupied important positions. As such phrases make clear, he believed in the liberating forces of modernity. It is probable that he was much influenced by Christianity. Lim saw continuity between British missionaries and the Japanese, the new rulers from outside who would bring a new type of culture to Taiwan. And he criticized as conservative those Taiwanese who rejected this new culture.

At the turn of the century, a person like Lim Bo-seng belonged in the minority. But in the 1910s, the demand for modern education among the Taiwanese grew greatly, and at the same time, the problems with the government-general's negative education policy became obvious. In the 1920s the government-general enhanced the trend of cultural assimilation in the educational curriculum, as a reactionary response to the growth of national consciousness among the Taiwanese. At this point, Lim Bo-seng could not help becoming aware that education by the Japanese contradicted the liberating forces of Taiwanese modernity. When racial discrimination, which he himself must have experienced, reinforced this perception, he voiced the opinion that cultural assimilation was opposed to the principles of modern education, but even at this point, however, he did not reject imperialistic colonial rule per se. The expression "cosmopolitanism without political emancipation" explains well his thinking. Eventually, in the 1930s, even the plans for improvement that he had suggested came to nothing.

We must conclude that his political vision was overly optimistic, although it is easy for us to say that from today's point of view. The important thing, however, is that belief in the liberating forces of modernity deeply captured the elite Taiwanese Lim Bo-seng, and that this belief led him into a dead end.

Gi-wook Shin and Michael Robinson's statement suggests that what I have presented on Lim Bo-seng here can be observed quite generally, whether in Taiwan or in Korea. But Taiwan, no more than a peripheral part of the Qing Dynasty, offered a clearer cosmopolitanism in its longing for modernity. But even if they intended to resist cultural assimilation by mobilizing native culture, it was not clear what should be considered "our language" and "our culture"; a gap developed such that the adjective "Formosan" was used for "language," and "Chinese" for "culture." Also, it may have been influential that the occupation of Taiwan by Japan took place at a stage when reforms for modernization in Taiwan were just beginning. Though it was obvious that Japanese culture was not identical to modern culture, it was even harder to find a way of reaching the latter without going through the former.

In this circumstance, the example of mission schools and the experience of studying in the United States could become footholds from which to relativize the modernity that the Japanese brought. Utilizing fully these opportunities, Lim Bo-seng tried to seek an alternative education in mission schools. Also, by appropriating Dewey's thoughts, he criticized Japan's policy from a perspective that asked what education was in its original sense. But while the British empire and the United States overtly respected institutions based on modern values such as freedom, equality, and democracy, the expansion of colonies and of areas of influence that they promoted abroad was based on national interests, and often contradictory to modern values. Therefore, it was not easy to inspire Westerners to sympathize and collaborate with the colonized. In fact, Kandel, one of Lim Bo-seng's advisors, discussed colonial education from the point of view of the imperialistic ruler. In the deep recesses of modernity, which produced the attractive catchphrase "cosmopolitanism," racism was waiting. The experience of colonial modernity for Lim Bo-seng was to wander in that labyrinth.

In 1939, as a birthday gift to his son Lin Tsung-yi 林宗義, who had decided to major in psychiatry at Tokyo Imperial University, Lim Bo-seng gave a calligraphic rendering of the following poem by Wang Yang-ming 王陽明:

Where is utopia?
The deepest place in the mountains of the west
It is not necessary to ask a fisherman
Walking along the valley, stepping on flowers, and leaving[16]

One cannot find utopia even when one visits the deepest place in the mountains of the west. It is not necessary to ask fishermen who say that they have found utopia. The path of the valley can be dangerous, but flowers are blooming. ... Or, though this might be an extreme interpretation, the expression "the deepest place in the mountains of the west" could refer to his own experience of seeking the possibility of modernity as its deepest point by an experience of the West that brought him to the United States to study. And, when we interpret the poem in this way, his intention rises to the surface: even while running toward the dead end of "colonial modernity," he had intended to go beyond.

NOTES

1. Ching Leo T. S., *Becoming Japanese: "Colonial" Taiwan and the Politics of Identity Formation* (Berkeley: University of California Press, 2001), 20.

2. Shin Gi-wook and Michael Robinson, *Colonial Modernity in Korea* (Cambridge Mass.: Harvard University Press, 1994), 12.

3. Thomas Barclay, *The Church in Formosa in 1895: The War, Mission Work, the Outlook* (London: Publication Committee, 1895), 3, Presbyterian Church of England Archives, School of Orient and Africa Studies, University of London, microfiche no. 153.

4. Ibid.

5. Regarding the February 28 Incident, see Tsung-yi Lin, ed., *An Introduction to 2–28 Tragedy in Taiwan: For World Citizens* (Taipei: Taiwan Renaissance Foundation, 1998). The editor of the book, Tsung-yi Lin, is the son of Lim Bo-seng.

6. Lim Bo-seng's original dissertation is deposited in the Columbia University library; in 2000, the Taiwan Renaissance Foundation published a Chinese translation as well as an English version of the dissertation. Although in the course of research I consulted the original text in the special collection of the Department of Education, Columbia University, pagination here refers to the English version published by the Taiwan Renaissance Foundation.

7. Takeshi Komagome, "Japanese Colonial Rule and Modernity: Successive Layers of Violence," *Traces* 2 (2001).

8. Li Xiao-feng, *Lim Bo-seng Chen Jin he tamen de shidai* [Lim Bo-seng, Chen Jin, and their times] (Taipei: Yushan chubansha, 1996), 23.

9. Yasushi Yamanouchi, J. Victor Koschmann, and Ryuichi Narita, eds., *Total War and "Modernization"* (Ithaca, N.Y.: East Asia Program, Cornell University, 1998).

10. Tokiomi Kaigo, *Kaigo Tokiomi Chosakushu* [Collected works of Tokiomi Kaigo], vol. 1 (Tokyo: Tokyo-Shoseki, 1981), 307–308.

11. Abe Shigetaka, "Education in Formosa and Korea," in I. L. Kandel, ed., *Educational*

Yearbook of the International Institute of Teachers College, Columbia University, 1931 (New York, 1932), 681.

12. I. L. Kandel, "The Education of Indigenous Peoples," in I. L. Kandel, ed., *Educational Yearbook of the International Institute of Teachers College, Columbia University, 1931* (New York, 1932), xi.

13. Kandel, "Education of Indigenous Peoples," xii.

14. Li Xiao-feng, *Lim Bo-seng*, 109.

15. Shin and Robinson, *Colonial Modernity in Korea*, 11.

16. Lin Shu-fen, *Catalog of Calligraphy by Lim Bo-seng* (Taipei: Taiwan Renaissance Foundation, 2002), 130.

[8]

HEGEMONY AND IDENTITY IN THE COLONIAL EXPERIENCE OF TAIWAN, 1895–1945

FONG SHIAW-CHIAN

Prior to the 1990s, the story of colonial Taiwan under Japanese rule was rarely heard in the English-speaking world; it also lacked an audience in Taiwan itself. With its democratization, which also removed pan-Chinese ideology, people on the island began to show interest in their own history. A space was thus created in which colonial experience could be researched and its stories told. However, since the time for intensive research has been relatively short thus far, the stories of both the colonizer and the colonized, particularly in regard to cultural domains, remain rudimentary, and not entirely precise in many details. At best, it may be more like an outline than a narrative; it may be a study based on two organizing concepts, hegemony on the colonizer's side and identity on the side of the colonized.

After a short discussion of the template—hegemony and identity—in terms of which the stories will be told, my essay will focus on the discourses of both colonizers and colonized in three specific periods, the 1910s, the 1920s and 1931–1945. The three periods roughly correspond to the three stages of the colonial viceroyship, in which the military viceroys dominated the first and the third stages, and the civilian the second period. Because of these shifts in power base, either from the military to bureaucracy or vice versa, we also witness the shifts of the source of coercion from soldiers to the police and then back to the soldiers and hence the shift of social atmosphere from tension to relaxation and back to tension. This rhythm also affected the spaces in which cultural activities, including discourses of ideologies, could be initiated.

By focusing on discourses from both sides of colonialism, we raise the issue of how the Japanese colonizers achieved a "weak hegemony" by polarizing the Taiwanese into two types and ascribing onto them different memberships—a traditional Chinese identity for the masses and a "modern" identity for the elites. (Compared with the Japanese, the Taiwanese elites were tacitly recognized as second-class though almost as equally modern.)

THE SCHEME OF HEGEMONY
AND COUNTERHEGEMONY

"The intellectuals," Antonio Gramsci suggests (1971:12), "are the dominant group's 'deputies' exercising the subaltern functions of social hegemony and political government." He refers to the indoctrinating and coercive work done by fellow Italian intellectuals of rural background. Gramsci highlights the intellectuals' role in the noncoercive state influence in civil society in terms of "moral leadership" or "social hegemony"; however, such a role worked to support the hegemonic regime in a colonial context where the Japanese ruled over the Han-Taiwanese. Gramsci's notion of hegemony serves as an ideal starting point for us to tackle the identity problem of the Taiwanese under Japanese rule. But first we need to elaborate it with the help of other notions, such as counterhegemony (Williams 1980), narrative (Ricoeur 1992 and White 1987), and a typology of compliance (Etzioni 1975).

Hegemony, as Gramsci (1971:334) views it, denotes an intellectual unity theory and practice. For an intellectual to support the state's noncoercive hegemonic control what she says must be consistent both with what the rulers intended and with what the ruled actually felt. Her consistent discourse, especially when put in a narrative form, then amounts to a constant patchwork that gauges and reflects developments in state-society relations. Here Etzioni's "exhaustive" classification of power and compliance is helpful; for he asserts that the rulers always have coercive, remunerative, and normative powers in stock and the ruled have the choice of alienative, calculative, or moral compliance in response. Not only does he thus unintentionally capture a nuance of hegemony by specifying both the practice (coercion and normalization) and the response (alienation and moralization) of the two dimensions of power, but he also adds the power of remuneration, or simply bribery in a power relation, which is certainly a time-honored tactic to induce popular compliance (Lukes 1974). But in order to render the Japanese rule and the Taiwanese submission intelligible, we must examine the constituents of both "normative" power and "moral" compliance. It is at this juncture that the notion of narrative discourse becomes helpful.

In a colonial context, the ruling regime, with the help of intellectuals, "talks" the colonized into compliance by weaving stories about them. These stories sanction the colonized both negatively, by describing how rebels will be punished, and positively, by exhorting the merits of being loyal colonial subjects. The stories can of course always be told with a mixture of coercive and remunerative powers available to the regime. They can on their own be effective only by inducing compliance. Their effectiveness is due to two mechanisms specified by Ricoeur and White.

For Ricoeur (1992), the mechanism of narrative identity functions in the context of story communication. In that context, every listener comes to the story with her distinctive personality traits and life commitments, all molded by dominant social values. The same set of values is represented first in the characters and in their personal involvement in the events that make up "episodes." When a storyteller edits the episodes into a causal sequence, a "causal employment" (Somers 1994:616), she contrives a story to be told. Social values are often the criteria for turning episodes into plots and stories. The value-molded listener can thus identify herself with the character tailored by the story in accord with the same set of values. This moment of identification is the moment of coming to pass of a narrative identity with which she grows and thus changes her perception of her "real" self.

For White (1980), it is the mechanism of a secondary referent that makes a reader recognize the figurative truths of a narrative, whether in fiction or in history. Every narrative possesses a primary referent that is the literal reflection of the objective world; it gives the reader a sense of realism. But the story also provides a secondary referent, which, parallel to Ricoeur's expanding units of episode, plot, and story, is made of motifs, themes, and plot structure. It is the secondary referent that induces emotional and attitudinal changes in the reader by sending her to the allegorical world immanent in the story. White wisely comments that the effectiveness of the secondary referent depends on the repertoire of literary genres available in a culture. A secondary referent embedded in an alien genre may thus suffer from a lack of familiarity among its readers and thus a diminishment of its persuasiveness.

With the mechanisms of the narrative identity and the secondary referent, a hegemon's stories about its subjects are arguably capable of entrapping the latter's loyalty, provided that the subjects do not possess either "residual" or "emergent" culture that can tell them alternative stories. These two types of counterhegemonic culture signify, for Williams (1977), resources for the subjects to imagine stories about themselves (also with the help of the notions of narrative identity and secondary referent) other than what the hegemon imposes upon them by means of education or mass media. Tradition and conventions constitute the residual resources that have always been ingredients of the subjects' lifestyle and that the hegemon seeks to transform, if not destroy. Emergent resources, on the other hand, lie in the future when industrialization gives rise to a working class that is conscious of both resisting and altering the industrial status quo. The two countercultures thus situate the subjects, including the colonized, in a temporal sequence—they have at their disposal cultural resources either from past or from future to fight back their hegemon's attempts at indoctrination. In that sense, a ruler's hegemonic control is never complete; as we have mentioned, it is a patchwork that requires constant attention to countercultures in order to outwit them.

This scheme of hegemony and counterhegemony therefore focuses on the stories of the identities of the colonized. On the one hand, the colonizers construct the narratives of their subjects by means of narrative identity and secondary referent. Their purpose is to induce the subjects' moral compliance. But when the normative attempt fails, they can always switch back to coercion or bribery for remedy. On the other hand, facing growing hegemonic pressures, the colonized still have the residual and/or the emergent symbolic resources with them. Their posture may be on the whole resistant but they appear to be most vulnerable when the old type of resource is dwindling but the new type is not forthcoming. This is the juncture where "weak hegemony," a situation where a portion of the colonized is brainwashed into loyal subjects, comes to existence, as we shall describe in what follows.

THE THREE PHASES
OF THE TAIWANESE COLONIAL STORY

The Seiraian 西來庵 Incident of 1915

As the Taiwan government-general (*sōtokufu* 總督府) celebrated its twenty-year rod-of-iron rule on June 17, 1915, with a "custom improvement movement,"[1] the largest millenarian rebellion the Japanese had ever seen in Taiwan erupted to chill their celebratory mood. Its participants, mostly illiterate peasants, were drawn to a surrogate "godly master" (*shenzhu* 神主), called Yu Qingfang 余清芳, who promised to build a "state of immense brightness and benevolence" (*daming cibei guo* 大明慈悲國) here and now, and because it was "pre-political" (Hobsbawm 1959:57–59), with the leader stratum being extremely vague about how to bring the chiliastic state to pass, let alone any articulation of the relationship between the godly state and the nation-states in the rest of the world. The Japanese government, on its part, treated the rebellion as but another incident of banditry, although of a significant magnitude, and believed its superstitious participants deserved nothing short of hanging. The official discourse on colonized banditry was well set before the incident.

The notion of banditry presupposes an interruption of the established social order of whatever nature. It implies more than a nuisance from the ruler's point of view; it implies an undesirable reading of the colonized that, without distinction, should be eliminated. "Bandit" was a term invented under the colonial context, as a famous historian of contemporary police affairs, Washizu Atsushiya 鷲巢敦

哉, candidly admitted: "The so-called bandit, or local villain, was not used in traditional Taiwan. It gained currency after Taiwan was ceded to Japan" (*TSKE* 1938, 2:267).

After "bandit" came into vogue, the officials used it to designate three types of rebels: Qing soldiers who stayed in Taiwan after 1895 and who were committed to toppling the Japanese colonial government, indigenous gangsters who controlled fixed turfs, and common-folks-turned-rebels whose family members were mistakenly killed by the Japanese military or who themselves were maliciously accused of being bandits.[2] Washizu wasted no time in pointing out that the government could apply means of redress most effectively to the last group. The exact number of "bandits" was not available, but from the 8,258 cases of banditry reported to police stations in the period 1897–1900, Washizu estimated that, by 1903, the Japanese had killed or arrested well over ten thousand bandits on the island of some three million Han-Taiwanese (*TSKE* 1938, 2:268–269). This official classification of "bandits" (to be lumped together as "patriots" after the 1945 change of regime) met the *sōtokufu* 's control expediency. The government coined the publicly degrading term "bandit" for the Taiwanese to use in refer to their rebellious compatriots. The term pressured the majority of the Taiwanese, by focusing punishment on the "bandit" groups, to do what the colonizers desired, and it divided its potential threat onto the three groups that could be subjected to different counterstrategies.[3]

Why were there so many rebellions in Taiwan not only under Japanese rule but also in the earlier Qing period (1644–1911)?[4] Implicitly comparing it to the unbroken Japanese emperorship,[5] Washizu specifically pointed out the notion of "replaceable emperorship" (*TSKE* 1938, 2:265; 1939, 3:3), which, as a few contemporary Japanese colonizers asserted, was based on the Chinese cosmo-political view of the "mandate of heaven." According to this view, an emperor would be dethroned if he did not follow heaven's will by being "virtuous" (Shibata 1923:208). His loss of virtue was best indicated by his subjects' complaints. A virtuous person, of whatever social level, would be mandated by heaven to lead the disgruntled people to oust the old emperor. This essentially Confucian political view became a folk belief with a twist—not only would heaven protect the people who followed the virtuous leader with his godly soldiers, but the people themselves would also become such soldiers by drinking holy water or by carrying paper charms (*shenfu* 神符; Shibata 1923:211–216; Igeda 1981:196). This notion of "heavenly generals and godly soldiers" (*tianjiang shenbing* 天將神兵) loomed large in the Seiraian incident and was the core element of its millenarianism.

In the colonial context, rebels who believed in the heavenly mandate had spiritually sinned against the irreplaceable Japanese emperor, and their treasonous behavior could be redeemed only by the death penalty. In 1898 Viceroy Kodama Gentarō 玉源太郎 proclaimed an extremely harsh order for punishing bandits, with the first article reading:

Those bandits who gather themselves to coerce or threaten others, no matter what their purposes are, are subject to punishment according to the following criteria:

1. The leaders and instigators are sentenced to death.
2. Those who participate in the decision-making or commanding are sentenced to death.
3. The mere participants or those who provide services are subject to imprisonment for a definite term and to harsh corvée. (*TSKE* 1938, 2:282)

By the time of the Seiraian incident in 1915, the *sōtokufu* had already defined who the rebels were, why they were motivated, and how they were to be treated by the government. The last and the largest pre-modern millenarial violence in Taiwan was to be framed by the mundane bureaucratic discourse on banditry, a discourse couched heavily on the coercive power at the *sōtokufu*'s disposal.

What, however, did the Seiraian rebels think of themselves? The answer could not be as "bandits," and the question could not be answered directly. It is from their religion and its morality books (*shanshu* 善書) that we might hope to look into their moral universe. The stories in these books can tell us both the narrative identities as imagined in the rebels' reading (or more precisely, listening, since most of them were illiterate peasants), and the secondary referents that set the tone for their emotions and attitudes. These morality books may be divided into two parts: wartime literature used by leaders such as Yu Qingfang to agitate their believers, and a peacetime narrative that was preached as a daily routine. Nonetheless, stories in both parts focused on the need for the male believers fearing Buddhist-type retribution (*baoying* 報應), to respect both gods and parents, and to avoid at all costs greed and lust.

In his wartime literature, Yu Qingfang declares war against Japanese (Chen 1977:149):

Now it is May of 1915. Japanese thieves have been in Taiwan for two decades and their rulership has come to an end. ... Our State of Immense Brightness and Benevolence has just been set up. I, the Marshal, have received the heavenly mandate to fight with the thieves. ... Wherever our heavenly soldiers go, the enemies will surrender.

Before this declaration, the morality books of the Seiraian Temple, the stronghold of the rebels, had prepared the believers to accept a coming Second Advent. One such morality book, *The Book of Five Masters*, described the coming calamity: "The heaven and earth are immensely dark ... humans are beheaded and ghosts' feet are cut off. There is no justice; there is no hierarchy" (Anonymous 1862:5). Behind this picture of living hell was the traditional Buddhist notion of retribution: "If you sow this melon seed, you inevitably get this melon," a famous

Buddhist allegory explains. The living hell was to be caused by nonbelievers, especially by Japanese: "You the commoners should behave yourselves, otherwise evils will fall upon you. Do not obtain unjust wealth, lest your descendants should not live long. Respect the gods and parents, and you should prosper" (Anonymous 1862:5). In Seiraian's wartime literature, what was to have been learned were the moral teachings that believers should have absorbed—be careful with money and respect both gods and parents. However, it was in peacetime morality books that believers were to be gendered: in addition to prudence and respect, male converts should abstain from lust.

The only book written by Seiraian priests, with Yu Qingfang as a coauthor, *The Book of the Alert Heart* (*Jingxinpian* 警心篇), tells two stories. One is about a rich man who married a widow by force and forsook her son. His wealth was exhausted in two years due to thefts and fire and he thus died of anxiety. The son, on the other hand, did well and married a merchant's daughter. Later, he married a concubine who happened to be a former concubine of his stepfather. The other story is about two sisters-in-law who spoke ill of the other brother to each other's husband. They caused the two brothers to divide their family properties. The morals of the stories are clearly encapsulated in the Seiraian morality books: "Sons who do not pay their parents piety will be struck to death by thunder, and who are addictive to lust ... will be imposed upon disasters from heaven. Proper and just behavior is a must and one should respect all agnate and cognate hierarchies" (Anonymous 7).

From both wartime and peacetime Seiraian literature, therefore, there emerged an ideal model, a gentleman who believed in the Buddhist teaching of retribution and who thus respected both gods and parents, abstained from womanizing, and earned a just income. This narrative identity was the goal striven for by Seiraian believers lest they, as indicated by the secondary referent in the stories, should be exposed to violent death in living hell. In their imaginations, they were not bandits with superstitious beliefs in heavenly generals and godly soldiers, as the Japanese colonizers would have imagined.

In regard to the underclass of Han-Taiwanese involved in the Seiraian incident, the identity stories from themselves and from the colonizers simply crossed each other. This also indicated that, except by resorting to coercion, twenty years after their occupation of Taiwan Japanese were still far away from hegemonizing the moral universe of the Han-Taiwanese who came from a lower-class background.

The Discourses of Assimilation and Nationalism in the 1920s

The 1920s were a transitional period in the social history of Taiwan. Epidemics no longer threatened. Malaria had been effectively controlled. Physicians trained in Western medicine outnumbered Chinese herbal doctors. Even rinderpest had been eliminated. ... Education had become popular. Conservative peasants also actively

adopted new species and new technology. Productivity increased. Mobility of the
population also increased. Bicycles, cars, and trucks became popular. Life had thus
been improved. [Modern social movements occurred precisely at this juncture.]
(Chen Shaoxin 1979:127)[6]

With these words, Chen Shaoxin 陳紹馨, a Taiwanese sociologist trained during
the colonial period (1906–1966), described a society just entering on the thresh-
old of modernity, which was being imposed by a colonial regime.[7] It is against this
technology-based background that we should probe the contrasting discourses
between assimilationism on the rulers' side and the nationalist ideology of Taiwanese modern social movements on the side of the ruled. Under the colonizers'
modernizing and assimilating assault, the nationalism that Taiwanese intellectuals had learned from their Japanese professors was fundamentally ambiguous. It
referred to a nationalist "I" that could be Taiwanese, or Chinese, or Japanese, or
all of them. In other words, this nationalist discourse indicated the beginning of
hegemonic control, especially of Taiwanese intellectuals.

Out of the public discourses on assimilationism in the early 1920s, *Taiwan
dōkasaku ron* (On the assimilative policy in Taiwan 台灣同化策論) by Shibata
Sunao 柴田廉 (1923)[8] probably stood out as the most systematic and articulate account of the new 1920 policy of "gradual assimilation."[9] Together with Nakanishi
中西牛郎's *Dōkaron* (On assimilation 同化論, 1914),[10] the two texts set the tone
and themes that would resonate among the Japanese assimilationists throughout
the 1920s.

Assimilation as a policy, Shibata contended, was to be framed in cultural terms.
It aimed to bring the Taiwanese "national ethos," or simply nationality, in line
with its Japanese counterpart—which he, incidentally, never specified in the text.
This cultural policy required a long time to become effective and, when it did,
it would show in changes of "social phenomena" in Taiwan (1923:6–8). After almost three decades of Japanese rule, Taiwan society had reached a "humdrum"
moment (53) of boredom caused by tensions between constant and variable
thoughts that together comprised the configuration of the Taiwanese nationality.
The variable thoughts informed by reason and knowledge had been "rationalized" (26) by an advanced culture, Japan, in an effort to improve the socioeconomic infrastructure of Taiwan over the previous three decades. Thus the rationalizing process disconnected the variable thoughts from the constant thoughts,
which remained centered on the "heavenly mandate" and "ancestry worship"
(30–40). Out of this discord between the rational and the traditional sprang
the general Taiwanese public boredom; they were ready for a movement of
enlightenment:[11]

When the constant thoughts, which serve as the guidance of national spirit, cannot accord with the variable thoughts ... which respond to environmental stimu-

lus, this is a time when people wake up from their past life and feel puzzled about leading their future life. In cultural history, this is called a time of enlightenment. (Shibata 1923:53)

For Shibata, these constant thoughts could serve as a buffer against the "radical thoughts" of socialism and anarchism in the name of "enlightenment" (65). But assimilation would, in the long run, erode these traditional thoughts.

He thus suggested that the government should heed three fundamental policies in order to promote assimilation. Regarding religion, if the governmental authority was to change its hitherto free-handed policy, it should avoid encroaching on the functions Taiwanese folk beliefs, or what Shibata calls "imperial pantheism," had performed—a highly tolerant attitude toward other religions, a substitute for an set of ethical criteria for good and evil, and the only entertainment for the rank and file (75–81). In education, the authority should promote the study of Confucianism and Chinese learning, for—contrary to his predecessor, Nakanishi—Shibata insisted that the ideals of Confucianism had been incorporated into the Japanese "national essence" (*kokutai* 國體) and that their promotion would contribute to assimilation (82–66)—a point to which I shall return shortly. Finally, in social education, he suggested that a new office should be created in the government-general to coordinate the efforts of several civilian associations to change old customs (mainly queue-wearing and foot-binding) and to promote the learning of the Japanese language (98–102).

The overall tone of this scheme was, as Shibata himself admitted (61), "conservative." In fact, other than the creation of an office of social education, he was suggesting that the colonial government refrain from interfering in either religion or education. He seemed to be optimistic about the inevitable coming of assimilation over the long run. This optimism in part arose from Shibata's eccentric view of the congruent national ethos of the Japanese and Chinese peoples, as can be seen in the following comparison.

If we turn to the relationship between Shibata and Nakanishi's books, we immediately notice their opposing interpretation of the connection between "national essence" and assimilation in the famous "Rescript on Education," always the supreme official source for justifying the assimilative policy.

Nakanishi's 1914 text distinguished two main categories in the rescript. One was about "universal ethics": filial piety, affection, harmony, truthfulness, modesty, and benevolence (2). These were essentially what traditional Confucian scholars in both China and Japan would subsume under the term "the five virtuous categories" (*gorin* 五倫), with the single omission of loyalty from the 1914 text. The other category concerned the special national essence of Japan: the loyalty of the subjects for "the prosperity of our Imperial Throne coeval with heaven and earth" (2, 30):[12] "As [the rescript describes,] our empire was founded on a broad and everlasting basis ... and our people united in loyalty and filial piety ..., these are unique in Japan and can be seen nowhere else. These are therefore called

Japan's *kokutai*" (Nakanishi 1914:2). Hence the national ethos of the Japanese people: "be loyal to the Emperor and be patriotic to the state" (*chūkun aikoku* 忠君愛國), with the catch that the Emperor *was* the state (5). Thus, for Nakanishi, to assimilate the Taiwanese required the transplantation into their consciousness of the Japanese ethos of *chūkun aikoku*.

But for Shibata, it was precisely the Confucian *gorin*, what Nakanishi called "the universal ethics," that could help achieve a viable assimilative policy (1923: 85). Shibata claimed that the Chinese were culturally distinguished from the Japanese by the former's collective notions of heavenly mandate and ancestry worship, and the only way to influence these constant thoughts was by gradually rationalizing variable thoughts of mundane life until the Chinese self-consciously changed their fundamental ideas. With this concern, Shibata could only see *gorin* as a godsend, an extra help that might speed the assimilative process, but the important thing was to continue the rationalizing policies in the socioeconomic domains while keeping Taiwanese religion, education, and socialization intact.

In retrospect, the importance of Shibata's work lies not so much in his offering guidance for policy-making, although an office of social education (*shakaika* 社會局) at the *sōtokufu* level was established in 1926 (Ajiken 1973:227), as in his systemizing Japanese themes of assimilation in the period after Nakanishi's pioneering work and in directing discussion thereafter. Hence, in terms of the importance of education, Shibata redirected the focus on equal educational opportunities for both Japanese and Taiwanese students (TY 1.1 [1920]: 16; 2.1 [1921]: 20; 3.4 [1921]: 27) to respect for Confucian learning. He thus foreshadowed what Yanaihara, a famous Japanese scholar of imperialism, would later attack as Japan's capitalistic substitution of the premodern Confucian schools, *shobō* 書房 (1984:148–151). In respect to religion, he contrasted what Yamoto (TY 2.5 [1921]: 28–31; 3.1 [1921]:15–20) proposed in basing colonial domination on Buddhism and asked that the functions of Taiwanese folk beliefs be taken seriously. Finally, regarding nationality, he clarified the previously vague discussions of the differences in national ethos (TY 1.1 [1920]: 27; 2.1 [1921]: 21–22; 3.4 [1921]: 21–33) and talked instead about "constant thoughts," ideas which would later be echoed in, for example, Ihara's elaboration of the Japanese nationality—*chūkunaikoku* and, incidentally, in ancestry worship (1926:222–249).

Therefore, in the Japanese discourse on assimilationism, there emerged a prototheory and practice. The theory dictated that the national essence of the Taiwanese could be assimilated into the Japanese *chūkunaikoku* only by long-term socioeconomic policies that rationalized first the form and then, very gradually, the content of Taiwanese culture. In practice, the dominant assimilative discourse suggested a restrained attitude toward upsetting the cultural life of the Taiwanese in the domains of religion, education, and social education.

Turning now to the indigenous nationalism on the Taiwanese' side, Dr. Jiang Weishui 蔣渭水 (1891–1931), a Japanese-trained physician who founded both the Taiwan Cultural Society (1921) and later, the Taiwan Populist Party (1927), stood out as a middle-of-the-road advocate.[13] Together with his long-term comrade, Xie Chunmu 謝春木 (1902–1969), and his comrade-turned-foe, Cai Peihuo 蔡培火 (1889–1983), he shared a discourse of nationalism that was not only willing to compromise but fundamentally ambiguous. When Jiang became determined to set up the Populist Party, he had to convince the Japanese authorities that his party would serve as "a medium to promote good will between Japan and China." His justification was as follows:

> Eighty percent of the Taiwanese came from Fujian [福建] and twenty percent from Guangdong [廣東]. The aborigines of these two provinces were assimilated into Chinese culture in the Han Dynasty [202 B.C.–A.D. 220]. This was also the era when Japan imported culture from China. ... [Therefore] the three groups of aborigines had certainly married with the Han people and absorbed the latter's culture. (Jiang 1998:127)

Since the people of Fujian and Guangdong had been incorporated into China, their descendants in Taiwan understood Chinese better than the Japanese did and could work to improve Sino-Japanese relationships. Note that in this justification, it was *the* people of Fujian and *the* people of Guangdong who were the real ancestors of the Taiwanese and who could therefore be distinguished from the Han people. Written in early 1927, the tone of this piece is different from that of Jiang's earlier text of 1924. There he defined "people," or more precisely "nation," as "an anthropological fact": "no matter how the Taiwanese changed into Japanese citizens, they did not thereby become members of the Japanese nation. It cannot be denied as fact that the Taiwanese are Chinese, belonging to the Han people" (Jiang 1998:27). When talking about being a medium between China and Japan, his justification in 1924 was that because the "Taiwanese have both Chinese origins and Japanese citizenship," they can naturally play the role well (1998:30). Jiang's idea of Taiwanese identity subsequently evolved further into "Taiwanese *in toto*." In mid-1927, when the authority publicly criticized this special usage of Jiang's and demanded that it be changed into "this-islanders (*hontōjin* 本島人)," he responded,

> "This-islanders" refers only to the traditional Han people, so they can only mean the Han people in Taiwan, excluding Japanese and aboriginal tribes. ... "Taiwanese" is a name based on living quarters. Therefore, broadly defined, "Taiwanese *in toto*" can include anyone residing in Taiwan. It is more adequate than "this-islanders," which is especially for the Han people. (1998:212–213)

With the invention of Taiwanese *in toto*, Jiang seemed to have reached the end of his abilities in imagining national identity. Heavily involved in his Populist Party before his untimely death, he grew ever more sympathetic with socialism.

The collective identity that concerned him now was no longer nation, but class (Jiang 1998:244, 302).

Therefore, in the 1920s and against a modernizing and assimilative background, Jiang Weishui's imagination of Taiwanese national identity rapidly changed from that of Han origin to that of Fujian and Guangdong aborigines and, finally, to that of Taiwanese *in toto*. But his changing the collective name is just like changing the subject in a sentence: inevitably the predicate that describes the subject will have to change in order to maintain the sentence's consistency both grammatically and substantively. Jiang's discourse of national identity kept changing its subject, thus rendering his discourse totally ambiguous in regard to what he really thought of the issue. In this he was not alone in his quest of a proper definition of national identity, as our study of his contemporaries, Xie Chunmu and Cai Peihuo, will show.

For Xie, a journalist and a key cadre in Jiang's party, the ambiguity of his sense of national identity was seen when asked whether he himself was a member of the "Chinese nation" or the "Han people in Taiwan." From May to June 1929, Xie traveled extensively in Japan and China, where he reported on Dr. Sun Yat-sen's national funeral held in Nanking, then the capital of China. In his travelogue, he reports that when he landed in Shanghai, he saw Indians serving as "loyal doormen of imperialism." He could not help but compare the status of Indians to that of Chinese: "We Chinese people are trotting the same miserable route as they are … [and] we Taiwanese are not just slaves, we are slaves who have lost their nation" (*Taiwan minpō* 274 [1929]: 11). But this slave felt very much at home in Nanking, because individual Chinese were together again. Xie had heard that Chinese people were "persistent, enduring, and strong. . . As a member of this people, I hope all these qualities are true" (*Taiwan minpō* 276 [1929]: 12). He fully agreed with his fellow Taipeinese' comment, "As an overseas Chinese, we should try our best to contribute to our ancestral place, the new republic" (Xie 1999:184).

However, by the time of his writing Taiwan had been separated from China for over three decades. Senses of difference had inevitably grown on both sides. Xie says, for example, "The most inconvenient thing in traveling in China is the Chinese' lack of efficiency." This kind of judgment frequently deteriorated into a "we Chinese, you Japanese" kind of quarrel. Worse still, Taiwanese working in China were accused of being "the running dogs of Japanese. … And if they want to change their nationality to that of Chinese, what are they going to do with their wives, kids, and especially, the ancestral graves in Taiwan?" (Xie 1999:295–296). Caught between the non-clear-cut identities of the Chinese nation and the Han people in Taiwan, he asked himself, "Which system is better for the inhabitants: a colony or a semi-colony?" (Xie 1999:259).[14] Colonial subjects (Taiwanese) served one metropolis without any sense of autonomy, but semicolonial subjects (Chinese) served several metropolises with their own autonomy. In Xie's view, Taiwanese as colonial subjects had only two options: bowing to their fate or rising up to fight. It took another three years after the death of Jiang Weishui for him to reach his decision; he opted for fighting and joined the Chinese army against Japan. Xie's ambiguity regarding his national identity was real but short.

Finally, we come to Cai Peihuo, a brilliant social reformer in the early 1920s who, after Jiang Weishui founded the Populist Party, denounced the party and leaned toward a conservative, assimilative mode. The point of Cai's social reform was to set up a special Taiwan council within the jurisdiction of the Japanese constitution in order that it could overview the budget and laws raised by the sō-tokufu. In 1928 he put his ideas into a Japanese book, called *Nihon honkokumin ni ataeru* (To Japanese compatriots 日本本國民に與ふ), in which he explained his understanding of national identity.

He called the Japanese his "compatriots" because, although they belonged to different "nations," they "not only shared the same passport status but were comrades in terms of sharing a common humanity and a love of peace and freedom" (Cai 1928:29). The concept of "compatriots with different nationalities" was the ambiguity underlying Cai's imagination of his national identity. Because they were compatriots, he demanded that Taiwanese be treated equally in political and economic affairs; but because they were of different "nations"—referring to "different languages, habits, and lifestyles" (1928:108–110)—the Japanese in Taiwan had both a sense of superiority to the Taiwanese and exploitative policies toward them. This was the reason why, in the 1920s, there arose a national consciousness in the minds of the Taiwanese (1928:43). Cai proposed a Taiwan council composed of local residents to help bridge the widening gap of national differences.

Furthermore, Cai criticized Japanese officials who tended to reject the possibility of Han people becoming His Majesty's loyal subjects, because they thought that Han-Taiwanese did not possess Japanese nationality. It was "common humanity," not "nationality," that should be the criterion for compatriotship. "Nationality is subsumed in humanity" (1928:144). Since Confucianism had indoctrinated nothing but decent humanity in both Japanese and Taiwanese people, there was no reason why Han-Taiwanese could not become Japanese who were "loyal to the Emperor and patriotic to the state" (*chūkun aikoku*).

Once granted the Taiwan council by the Japanese Diet, Cai contended, the Taiwanese would not, and could not, pursue independence. There were four conditions that could then prevent the movement from succeeding: Japan continued its imperialist policy; Japan could not maintain its current power; the Taiwanese abandoned Confucianism and became a warlike people; and a strong nation came to Taiwan's help in fighting with Japan (1928:181–182). None of these was acceptable to Cai, and he was determined to pursue limited Taiwanese' autonomy under the Japanese empire's tutelage.

In the thought of Cai Peihuo, compatriotship and nation were different but bridgeable; they required a common humanity, molded by the same Confucian learning, and an institutional innovation to convert one to the other. Unless the Japanese yielded to the demands of the Taiwan council, the "Han-ness" of the Taiwanese would be preserved precisely because of the Japanese colonizers' superior sense of national identity.

In the discourses of Taiwanese nationalism, it was Cai whose thought most showed the influence of assimilationism. Pursuit of limited autonomy, inclination to *chūkun aikoku*, and the notion of the malleability of nationality all underlined his vagueness over the issue of national identity. This ambiguity also applied to Jiang Weishui and Xie Chunmu. There was the rapid change in the subject of nationalism, from that of Han origin to that of Fujian and Guangdong aborigines and to that of Taiwanese *in toto* on Jiang's part. On Xie's part, there was his hesitation between the Chinese nation and the Han people in Taiwan. The ambiguity inherent in the incipient Taiwanese nationalism came, we suggest, from the fact that, because of the Taiwanese nationalists' complete Japanese education, their residual Han-culture could no longer be a resource for identity formation. Furthermore, the emergence of socialism was not yet strong enough to guide this nationalism. Finally, this ambiguity indicated the beginning of hegemonic control of Taiwanese intellectuals against the modernizing and assimilative background of the 1920s.

POLARIZED IDENTITY IN THE PERIOD OF HIGH JAPANIZATION (1931–1945)

On the periphery of the Japanese empire in the 1920s, Taiwan began to be upgraded to a "semi-periphery" by metropolitan politicians in the early 1930s. This was due to the military expansionism adopted by Japan. Especially after the Marco Polo Bridge incident in mid-1937, Taiwan served as a bridgehead to push Japan's "Southbound" policy, that is, the military inroad upon both South China and Southeast Asia. Taiwan's changed military status is important if we are to understand why the government-general relentlessly enforced the comprehensive cultural policy *kōminka* 皇民化 (literally, to Japanize) during the last period (1931–1945) of its rule. It needed both loyal soldiers and resources to refuel Japan's war machine.

With each major military advance, notably the Marco Polo Bridge incident and the Pearl Harbor attack (1941), the *sōtokufu* redirected *kōminka*, under different names,[15] to cope with the new reality. Over time we see a pattern of enhanced assimilating efforts, which reached a climax around 1940 and then diminished afterward, apparently due to a trade-off for extraction of wartime materiel. In the main, *kōminka* involved four cultural practices in regard to Taiwanese daily life: changing to Japanese-style names, teaching Japanese language, imposing upon families the worship of the Japanese sun goddess, Amaterasu 天照大御神,[16] and

TABLE 8.1 Statistics Supporting Weak Hegemony

	Name Change (household) %		Japanese Learning (person) %		Parlor Improvement (household) %		Temple Management (temple)
	T**	K	T	K	Tab	Shrine	
1935			29.7	8.8	2.1		
1936			32.3	9.8	36.6		100 (3,649)
1937			37.8	11.0	59.6		
1938			41.9	12.4	64.1		
1939			45.6	13.9	66.0	73.8	
1940	0.0 (289)	80.0	51.0	15.6	67.8	74.3	
1941	0.2		57.0	16.6	68.8	81.3	
1942			58.0	19.9	(76.0)		70 (2,551)
1943	(7.3)			22.2			
1944			(71.0)				

* Unit of percentage
** T = Taiwan
K = Korea
Tab = Paper tablet of the Sun Goddess
Shrine = Small Shinto-shrine to house the paper tablet
Numbers in parentheses are taken from sources whose statistical bases are different from those without parentheses or else unknown.

Source: Cai 1990:319, 322; Ihara 1988:359; Uesuki 1987:156; Chen 1987:75, 78; Wu 1987, 37.4:71; Yokomori 1982:215–220.

abolishing both local temples and the idols they housed. Table 8.1 shows how effective these practices had been.

From table 8.1, it is easy to infer that, except for the change in name, Taiwanese on the whole were very responsive to the new cultural policies of the *sōtokufu*. Their enthusiasm showed particularly in the learning and use of Japanese language. With over 70 percent of Taiwanese able to communicate in Japanese by 1944, it is no wonder that the short stories and novels regarding identity confusion that Taiwanese authors wrote were in Japanese.

But before discussing this identity issue, let us first say a word about the name-changing movement. Contrary to the commonly held opinion that name-changing was one of the most significant *kōminka* movements in the early 1940s

(Ko 1981:167; Uesuki 1987:169) and that its poor result showed Taiwanese "lack of interest" or plain "resistance" (Ko 1981:168; Chen 1984:50; Chen 1987:78), we suggest that the Taiwan *sōtokufu* lacked the enthusiasm to promote the movement. Elsewhere we have documented that, in implementing the policy, the *sōtokufu* had bypassed the powerful neighbor-watching system (*hokō* 保甲) for help, imposed no deadline for application, and especially insisted that only the Japanese-speaking family could apply (Fong 1993). All this suggests that by 1940 the *sōtokufu* was reluctant to commit itself to this metropolitan-imposed policy of name-changing. If this interpretation is acceptable, then not *all kōminka* cultural policies were resisted by the Taiwanese, a further indication that Japanese hegemonic control was, by then, effective. However, it was a "weak hegemony" because only the educated upper Taiwanese class identified with *kōminka*. The rest of the population remained marginalized, outside hegemonic control. It is this polarized Taiwanese identity that is revealed in contemporary short stories and novels.

Taiwanese fiction during the *kōminka* period may be classified into two genres: that of the masses and that of the intellectuals. The mass genre underlined the socioeconomic predicaments of minority groups—mainly the poor and women who were tradition bound, while the intellectual genre constituted a grand narrative of the elite immersion into Japanese identity.

The situation of poverty, as described in the mass genre, was best symbolized by the image of the "public steelyard." In "Overload" (Zhang 1935), a mother carrying a baby and a load of bananas (which weigh 36 kilograms) walks 6 kilometers to the market with her twelve-year-old son, who carries another load of 12 kilograms. She sells all the bananas for 48 *qian* 錢 but is responsible for paying the use of the public steelyard (3 *qian*) and sales tax (8 *qian* for 48 kilograms). She pleas for mercy with the policeman in charge of collecting the money. After being humiliated, she still has to pay all 11 *qian*.

In "A Steelyard" (Lai 1926), Chin sells vegetables in the market. A policeman wants to take the produce for free. Chin does not agree to this and is fined on the pretext of using an imprecise private steelyard. Next day, the Chinese Lunar New Year's Eve, the cop shows up again and this time puts Chin in jail for three days, presumably because he did not use the steelyard at all and thus broke the law. Bailed out by his wife, Chin kills the cop that night and commits suicide.

In addition to Japanese police brutality, women's predicaments were often explored in the mass genre. Not only were they depicted as their husbands' scapegoats, they were often trapped on a dead-end road, becoming first concubines and then prostitutes. In his short story of 1935, Lu Heruo 呂赫若 first describes how the modern highway replaced trails and caused the drivers of oxcarts to become unemployed. One such unfortunate driver, Young, thus asks his wife to sleep with his creditors. Lu also tells the story of a tenant who could only keep his farmland by letting his wife become the landlord's mistress. Worse, because of poverty and male chauvinism, Taiwanese families often sent their baby girls to be adopted by the rich. The fate of these girls was miserable. In one story (Zhang 1941), a fourteen-year-old Caiyun was sent to keep a sixty-year-old man company for three days because her adopted mother had received a thousand *yan* and a golden bracelet from him. She was then sent to become a *geisha*. In another (Lu 1936), a dancing girl, Shuangmei, was forsaken by her boyfriend after six years of cohabitation. In order raise their daughter, she decides both to become a prostitute and to train the daughter to follow in her steps for revenge.

Lu Heruo's artistic talent and his concern for the underclass in Taiwanese tradition reached its peak in the early 1940s. In order to expose the contradictions within traditional families, he created an evil character, Zhou Wenhai, in "Wealth, Sons, and Longevity" (1942). Zhou, as the elder son and, hence, householder, causes every kind of misery for other family members. His brother's family is expelled from the ancestral house under his charge. He rapes his maid, who then competes with his wife for his favor. His wife subsequently goes crazy. His ancestral house is called the Hall of Happiness and Longevity, an ironic name that contrasted with what Zhou does to betray it.

However, the real gem of Lu's achievement is his "Pomegranate" (1943). Here he tells the story of two orphaned brothers, Jinsheng and Muhuo. Jinsheng married into his wife's house and became less than a man in the Taiwanese value system, while Muhuo was adopted by a clansman. One day Muhuo, who was single, went mad and accidentally died without a son; he thus could not be worshiped by his offspring and become an ancestor. To solve this lineage problem, Jinsheng, being poor, seeks to combine two rituals—one to put Muhuo's name on the wooden ancestral tablet that Jinsheng, as an elder son, had to keep, the other to let Jinsheng's son be adopted by Muhuo in order for them to worship him—together. The description of how the rituals were held at night and away from the family of Jinsheng's wife are meticulous and filled with such folk knowledge that the story moves its readers.

In its depiction of police brutality (as symbolized in the steelyard), the unequal status of women, and the Han-tradition, which perpetuated minority groups' miseries, the mass genre in fact kept the underclass away from the Japanese hegemon. Being exploited and humiliated, the weak were reminded in their daily life that they were insignificant and marginal, an enduring experience that effectively served as an antidote against Japanization indoctrination. Their immunization was further reinforced by residual Taiwanese culture, as seen in Jinsheng's performance of the rituals of ancestral worship and son adoption. It was doubtful whether people like Jinsheng really understood the meaning of these rituals. But by enacting the form of the rituals to address their daily concerns, they were empowering the tradition to reaffirm their Taiwanese identity. The residual culture, however, could not serve the same purpose for the Japanese-educated Taiwanese upper class; they actively responded to the calling of *kōminka* and sought from the bottom of their hearts to Japanize themselves. Their experience, as captured in fiction, constituted the intellectual's genre.

Taiwanese elites' change of heart was first set forth in the short story "The Little Town with Papaya Trees" (Long 1937). After graduating from high school, Chen cannot find a job for five years. Finally he becomes an accounting assistant in a township government through civil examination. As a clerk, he decides he must either pass the exam for an accountant certificate or marry a Japanese girl and become a Japanese himself (then he would get a 60 percent raise in his salary). Frustrated in both attempts, he gradually adopts the lifestyle of his Taiwanese associates—lustful, alcoholic, and greedy.

If Chen's degeneration was largely caused by the colonial environment, this was plainly not the case in the 1941 story of Zhang Minggui, Chen Qingnan, or Itō. In "Voluntary Soldiers" (Zhou 1998), Minggui, a college student just returned from Japan, gets into an argument with his friend, Gao Jinliu, over how to become a Japanese. Gao's method is "mysterious": he thinks that only by obeying strictly the Shintō ritual of *kashiwade* 柏手 (clapping hands) can one's Taiwanese soul be cleansed and become Japanese. Minggui's solution, however, is essentially based on self-recognition: "Born in Japan, raised up in the Japanese language, knowing nothing but Japanese *kana*, I have to be a Japanese to survive" (Zhou 1998:35). It was this recognition of forced Japanization that revealed Taiwanese intellectuals' understanding that, at best, they could strive to be second-class Japanese. This sub-Japanese complex was reincarnated in Itō, while Gao's Shintō way toward becoming Japanese is embodied in Chen Qingnan.

In the story of "The Way" (Chen 1943), Qingnan puzzles over the transformation of "Taiwanese I" into "Japanized I." He first seeks inspiration from his Japanese colleagues but soon realizes that it is only being born with Japanese blood that would make one Japanese. This means training oneself to possess the Japanese spirit, which boils down to being loyal to the emperor and being patriotic to the state. To have this spirit, Qingnan tries to marry a Japanese girl (which fails), to worship the Sun Goddess, and finally to become a voluntary Japanese soldier. "To be loyal to the emperor amounts to death": these were Qingnan's last words and belief.

The sub-Japanese issue reappears in "Torrent" (Wang 1943). Itō Cunsheng wants to become Japanese so badly that he changes his Taiwanese surname, marries a Japanese, and lives in his wife's house so that he speaks nothing but Japanese. Even at his father's funeral, he refuses to practice the Chinese ritual of kneeling down before the coffin. The narrator reveals that, in his early thirties and desperate to become Japanese, Itō has already turned his hair gray.

Itō's choices are contrasted with those of his cousin and student, Lin Bonian, in the same story. Lin is on bad terms with Itō because he did not care about his own mother, Lin's aunt. Lin is good at the Japanese art of sword play and won the championship over his Japanese schoolmates. Subsequently, Lin, against his parents' wish but with Itō's financial help, goes to Japan to study the art of the sword. He writes a letter, asserting that "to be an honorable Japanese I have to be an honorable Taiwanese first." However, one wonders if Lin is too young to say this. Who knows what he would become, given that he would spend years studying in Japan?

In the intellectual genre, the key issue was not Taiwanese identity at all. It was about the means to become a fully Japanese, which involved both mysterious (Shintō 神道) and rational paths. Particularly in the rational path, the identity-seekers knew perfectly well that they were imitating the Japanese way and that the best they could hope to achieve was a second-class Japanese nationality. Contrasting this genre with the mass genre, we suggest the Han-Taiwanese in the early 1940s had effectively been polarized into two identity groups: the educated elites who imagined themselves to be sub-Japanese and the underclass majority who had not yet forgotten their Han-ness. We attribute this polarizing effect to the hegemonic attempts of the Japanese colonizers, what might be called the success of the "weak hegemony."

CONCLUSION

In the cultural domain of the Japanese colonial project, coercion and remuneration were administrative practices constantly at the rulers' disposal. Hence, in the Seiraian incident, it was the sheer brutality of the military strength that suppressed the Taiwanese rebels. The death penalties for the captives, 866 altogether, were soon reduced to life imprisonment due to the rescript of amnesty issued in celebration of the enthronement of Emperor Taishō 大正 in 1915. It was a substantive favor that reinforced the coercive power of the colonial government. Furthermore, in the agitation of nationalism in the 1920s, countless arrests of Taiwanese advocates and the banning orders of their gatherings and public speeches all testified to the power of the Japanese police, whose atrocities also had a salient presence in the mass genre of Taiwanese fiction.

During this decade, higher education became the sōtokufu's tool for buying off the Taiwanese elite families. To study in the metropolis they would need special permission from the administration; family business in wines, tobacco, salt, and rice all required the sōtokufu's licenses. Finally, during the Pacific War, military power and martial laws again replaced the police in keeping peace on Taiwan island. Material quotas were set up, but those who adopted Japanese names and spoke Japanese were given double or triple shares. Coercive and remunerative powers were always present to enhance the colonizer's indoctrination attempts.

However, from the discourse of bandits, to that of assimilation, and finally to kōminka, the effect of the sōtokufu's moral appeal was on the whole limited. Not only was the banditry discourse countered by the religious imagination of the Seiraian rebels' ideal self, the discourse of assimilation was also seriously circumscribed by Taiwanese nationalism. The changing subjects in the incipient ideology of nationalism also revealed the ambiguity in the Taiwanese elites' imagination of national identity, the first sign of the effectiveness of the hegemonic control. It was in the period of high Japanization and among the cultural practices (of name-changing, the enhancement of Japanese literacy, parlor improvement, and temple management) that the polarizing effect of hegemonic discourse was seen. Since the effect only brainwashed some Taiwanese intellectuals into believing they possessed the Japanese spirit (tacitly understood as a second-class spirit), what Japanese had achieved must be judged to be a weak hegemony.

To the underclass of Taiwanese colonial subjects, their discourses in Seiraian and, later, in the mass genre of fiction consistently suggest that it was the residual culture from their precolonial life that was the fundamental source of their collective identity. We can distinguish this identity as a traditional one, which, up to the 1910s, still was free of any contamination from the colonial project, and a proto-national one, molded in the daily experience of being humiliated and exploited under the regime. In either case, the Taiwanese underclass was immune to the Japanese hegemon.

It was Taiwanese intellectuals who were fully immersed in Japanese education and who eventually became the fifth column of the Japanese colonizers. In the short stories told about them during *kōminka*, they were portrayed as enthusiasts for becoming Japanese, often by way of rational or irrational means. It is not surprising, given that the colonial project was also a modern project, that one could not be addicted to the latter (as indicated by Chen Shaoxin's description) without being trapped in the former at the same time. They had contributed to the success of the weak hegemony.

One wonders, however, what would have become of this colonial project had there been no Pacific War. Most likely the hegemonic success would have spread and the Taiwanese would have become no different from the people of Okinawa, for four centuries an independent nation under the name of Ryukyu but now a periphery of Japan and suffering continuing discrimination from the metropolis.

NOTES

1. This customs movement included cutting Han-Taiwanese' queues, unbinding Han-women's feet, and stopping opium-smoking (*TSKE* 1938, 2:741–752).

2. Viceroy Kodama, who made his career in suppressing the "bandits," had his own classification of seven types, based on why they had become bandits: (1) because, in the process of an army expedition, they had suffered either from scouts' mistranslation or from improper killings; (2) because they had lost their jobs due to the law "regulation of the mining industries"; (3) because they had lost their jobs due to the new system of recruiting guards against aborigines; (4) because they were coerced by other bandits; (5) because they believed other bandits' rumors and lies; (6) because they had committed crimes in Qing China and fled to

Taiwan; (7) for revenge against the Japanese army and police who had killed their parents or siblings (this is the largest category) (Tsurumi 1944, 2:1356).

3. For example, the former Qing soldiers, once caught, would be sent back to mainland China; the gangsters would be sentenced to death; and common-folks-turned-rebels would be given a second chance to lead a normal life.

4. In the 268-year reign of the Qing Dynasty, there occurred 148 riots waged by Han-Taiwanese immigrants from mainland China. Of these riots, 85 were classified as rebellions against the Qing government and 63 as clan struggles (Weng 1986:44).

5. This was one of the most fundamental tenets of Japanese fascism before and during World War II.

6. The last sentence, in brackets, was taken from the site of an ellipsis in the citation.

7. In one sociological account, "modernity has operated with the rationality/irrationality distinction as its core organizing code" (Albrow 1996:56). Hence the expansion of technological rationality into the fields of health, agriculture, and transportation, as indicated in Chen's words, certainly serves as a criterion for distinguishing the modern from the premodern.

8. Shibata Sunao was a social scientist who was responsible for the first and the only official religious survey (1915–1917) in the Taihoku area (Masuda 1939:234). He had lived in Taiwan for eleven years before he published the book. His book was apparently well received, and went into a second printing in less than six months. The second printing drew favorable reviews from major newspapers and magazines in both Taiwan and Japan.

9. An editorial in *Taiwan Minpō* (1925, 3.6:1) summarized Viceroy Den's gradual assimilative policy of interior extensionism: "[T]he policy is first implemented in the easily done aspect—substituting local Taiwanese names with Japanese ones. It then gradually eliminates the written Chinese language (*hanwen*) and replaces it with Japanese for daily use. It subsequently transplants the Japanese legal system to Taiwan."

10. Nakanishi Ushio was a key supporter of Itagaki Taisuke 板垣退助's assimilation society, which was established in Taipei in January 1915 but banned two months later. In fact, he wrote *Dōkaron*, in *classical Chinese*, both to advocate Itagaki's idea—namely, Taiwan should be assimilated into Japan so that the Taiwanese could bridge the relationship between Japan and China in fighting against the white race—and to impress traditional Taiwanese Confucians (see Ye 1971:15).

11. It may be inferred that Shibata here was pointing to what the young Taiwanese intelligentsia had been doing in Tokyo (publishing *Taiwan Youth* and petitioning for a Taiwan legislature) and in Taiwan (opening up island-wide cultural associations, which served as the initial institutional base for the fourteen-year "petitionary movement for establishing a Taiwan legislature").

12. Nakanishi used synonyms and parallel phases to express this rescript phase, but I shall stick to the official English translation. After the Manchuria incident in 1931, the phase was changed to "the unbroken imperial line" (*banseiikkei*). This new phase suggests that Nakanishi's view on the Japanese national essence was a widely accepted one.

13. Jiang Weishui was sympathetic to the Taiwanese Communist Party (founded in Shanghai in 1928), and became more so toward the end of his life. However, he firmly directed his new party away from both radical socialism and pro-Japanese conservatism.

14. "Semi-colony" was a term made famous by Dr. Sun Yat-sen, who used it to refer to the status of China when it conceded enclaves to several imperial powers, including Great Britain, France, and Japan, in the early 1920s.

15. At the end of 1935, the Bureau of Culture and Education of *Sōtokufu* promoted "the movement for exalting civilian customs" (*minpū sakkō undō* 民風作興運動), which was restructured as "the general movement for mobilizing the national spirit" (*kokumin seishin sōdōin undō* 國民精神總動員運動) in 1937, an event modeled after the same movement, with different emphases, in Japan proper. In mid-1941, before Pearl Harbor but after Japan's alliance with Germany and Italy, the movement was retitled and restructured as "the movement for the devotion of the Emperor's subjects to the national course" (*kōmin hōkō undō* 皇民奉公運動; *Taiwan jihō* [Taiwan times] 11 [1937]: 10; 6 [1941]: 37).

16. This practice was called the "parlor improvement" movement, because every family had to set up a small shrine to contain a sacred paper tablet, the symbol of Amaterasu, in its parlor, or living room.

REFERENCES

Ajiken (Ajia keizai kenkyusho), ed. 1973. *Union Catalogue of Publications by Former Colonial Institutions—Taiwan.* Tokyo: Institute of Developing Economics.

Albrow, Martin. 1996. *The Global Age: State and Society Beyond Modernity.* Stanford: Stanford University Press.

Ang Kaim. 1986. *Taiwan hanren wuzhuang kanrishi yanjiu (1895–1902)* [Taiwanese armed resistance under early Japanese rule (1895–1902)]. Taipei: Taiwan National University.

Anonymous. *Dadongjing* [The book of the immense cave]. Tainan: Songyunxuan.

———. 1912–1915. *Jingxinpian* [The book of the alert heart]. Tainan: Seiraian.

———. 1862. *Wugongjing* [The book of five masters]. Tainan: Songyunxuan.

Cai Jintang. 1990. "Riju shiqi de taiwan zongjiao zhengche yanjiu: Fengsi 'shengong dama' ji faxing *shengong li* [A study of the religious policy in Taiwan under Japanese rule: The worship of the paper tablet and the circulation of the calendar from the Sun Goddess' shrine]." In Zheng Liangsheng, ed., *Dierjie zhongguo zhengjiao guanxi guoji xueshu yantaohui lunwenji* [The second international symposium on politico-religious relations in China]. Taipei: Department of History, Danjiang University.

Cai Peihuo. 1928. *Nihon honkokumin ni ataeru* [To Japanese compatriots]. Tokyo: Taiwan mondai kenkyūkai.

Chen Huoquan. 1943. "Dō [The way]." *Bungei Taiwan* [Literature and art of Taiwan] 6.3:87–141.

Chen Jinzhong. 1977. "Xilaian kangri shijian zhi xingzhi quantan—jiu qishi 'yugaowei' fenxi [A preliminary study of the nature of the Seiraian anti-Japanese incident: An analysis of its "Declaration of War"]. *Donghai daxue lishi xuebao* (Donghai University: Journal of history) 1:147–158.

Chen Renkui. 1984. "Riju meqi taibao dizhi 'huangminhua' yundong zhi tantao [A discussion of Taiwanese' resistance to the *kōminka* movement at the end of Japanese occupation]." *Taiwan wen hsien* [Archival materials of Taiwan] 35.1:45–52.

Chen Shaoxin. 1979. *Taiwan de renkou bianqian yu shehui bianqian* [Population and social change in Taiwan]. Taipei: Lianjing.

Chen Xiaochong. 1987. "1937–1945 nian Taiwan huangminhua yundong shulun [A discussion of the *kōminka* movement in Taiwan from 1937 to 1945]." *Taiwan yanjiu jikan* [Taiwan research quarterly] 18:72–81.

Etzioni, Amitai. 1975. *A Comparative Analysis of Complex Organization*. Rev. and enlarged ed. New York: Free Press.

Fong Shiaw-Chian. 1993. "Achieving Weak Hegemony: Taiwanese Cultural Experience Under Japanese Rule, 1895–1945." Ph.D. diss., Chicago: University of Chicago.

Gramsci, Antonio. 1971. *Selections from the Prison Notebooks of Antonio Gramsci*. New York: International Publishers.

Hobsbawm, Eric J. 1959. *Primitive Rebels*. New York: Norton.

Igeda Toshio. 1981. "Yanagita Kunio yu Taiwan—Seiraian shijian de chaqu [Yanagita Kunio and Taiwan: An episode of the Seiraian incident]." Trans. Cheng Daxue. *Taiwan wen hsien* 32.3:180–202.

Ihara Kichinoshke. 1988. "Taiwan no kominka undo—shōwa junendai no taiwan (2) [The *kōminka* movement in Taiwan: Taiwan in the second decade of Shōwa (2)]." In Nakamura Koshi, ed., *Nihon no nanpo kanyo to taiwan*, 271–386. Nara: Tenrikyo doyusha.

Jiang Weishui. 1998. *Jiang Weishui quanji* [The complete works of Jiang Weishui]. Ed. Wang Xiaobo. Taipei: Haixia xueshu chubanshe.

Ko Shodo. 1981. *Taiwan sōtokufu* [The government-general of Taiwan]. Tokyo: Kyoikusha.

Lai Ho. 1926. "Yigan chenzi [A steelyard]." *Taiwan minpō* [Taiwan people's news] 92 (February 4), 93 (February 21).

Long Yingzong. 1937. "Papaya no aru machi [The little town with papaya trees]." *Kaizō* [Tokyo] 19.4.

Lu Heruo. 1935. "Gyūshya [Oxcart]." *Bungaku hyōron* [Review of literature] 2.1.

———. 1936. "Ona no baai [The fate of woman]." *Taiwan bungei* 3.7–8:11–36.

———. 1942. "Jai ko jyū [Wealth, sons, and longevity]." *Taiwan bungaku* [Taiwan literature] 2.2:2–37.

———. 1943. "Jakuro [Pomegranate]." *Taiwan bungaku* 3.3:169–188.

Lukes, Steven. 1974. *Power: A Radical View*. London: MacMillan.

Masuda Fukutaro. 1939. *Taiwan no shukyo: Noson o chushin to suru shukyo kenkyu* [Religions in Taiwan: A religious study centered on villages]. Tokyo: Yokendo.

Nakanishi Ushio. 1914. *Dōkaron* [On assimilation]. Taihoku.

Ricoeur, Paul. 1992. *Oneself as Another*. Chicago: University of Chicago Press.

Shibata Sunao. 1923. *Taiwan dōkasaku ron* [On the assimilative strategy in Taiwan]. Taihoku: Kobunkan.

Somers, Margaret. 1994. "The Narrative Constitution of Identity: A Relational and Network Approach." *Theory and Society* 23.5:605–649.

TSKE =*Taiwan sōtokufu keisatsu enkakushi* [Chronicle of the police affairs of the Government-General in Taiwan], 1933–1941, 6 vols. Vol. 2: subtitled *Ryōtai igo no chian jōkyō (jō-kan)* [The situation of the public order after Taiwan's occupation, first volume], 1938; and vol. 3: subtitled *Ryōtai igo no chian jōkyō (chū-kan): shakai undōshi* [The situation of the public order after Taiwan's occupation, middle volume: The history of social movement], 1939. Taihoku: Taiwan Sōtokufu.

Tsurumi Yūsuke. 1944 (1937). *Gotō Shimpei den Taiwan tōchihen* [The biography of Gotō Shimpei: Taiwan governance]). 2 vols. Tokyo: Taiheyo kyokai.

TY = *Tai oan chheng lian* [Taiwan youth], July 16, 1920–February 15, 1922 (18 issues). Tokyo: Taiwan seinensha. The magazine was entitled *Taiwan* from April 1922 to April 1924.

Uesuki Mitsuhiko. 1987. "Taiwan ni okeru kominka seisaku no tenkai—kaiseimei undō wo chūshin to shite [On the Japanese *kōminka* policy in Formosa in the 1930s]." In *Chūgoku kankei ronsetsu shiryō 29, daiyonbunsatsu (ue)* [Collected articles on China, part 4.1: History and social studies II], 143–170. Tokyo: Ronsetsu shiryō hōzenkai.

Wang Changxiong. 1943. "Kōryū [Torrent]." *Taiwan bungaku* 3.3:104–129.

Washizu Atsushiya. 1943. *Taiwan tōchi kaikō dan* [Reviewing the rule of Taiwan]. Taihoku: Taiwan Keisatsu Kyokai.

White, Hayden. 1987. *The Content of the Form: Narrative Discourse and Historical Representation*. Baltimore: Johns Hopkins University Press.

Williams, Raymond. 1977. *Marxism and Literature*. Oxford: Oxford University Press.

———. 1980. *Problems in Materialism and Culture*. London: Verso.

Wu Wen-Ceng. 1987. "Riju shiqi Taiwan zongdufu tuiguang Riyu yundong chutan [A preliminary study of Taiwan *sotōkufu*'s propagation of the Japanese language during Japanese rule]." *Taiwan fengwu* [Taiwan folklore] 37.1:1–31; 37.4:53–86.

Xie Chunmu. 1999. *Xie Nanguang zhuzuo xuan* [Selections from the works of Xie Cunmu]. Ed. Guo Pingtan. Taipei: Haixia xueshu chubanshe.

Yamakawa Hitoshi. 1966 (1926). "Shokumin seisakuka no Taiwan [Taiwan under colonial policy]." In *Yamakawa Hitoshi zenshu* [Collected works of Yamakawa Hitoshi], vol. 7, 258–291. Tokyo: Keiso shobo.

Yanaihara Tadao. 1984 (1934). *Teikokushugika no taiwan* [Taiwan under imperialism]. Trans. Zhou Xianwen. Taipei: Pamier.

Ye Rongzhong, et al. 1971. *Taiwan minzu yundongshi* [A history of the Taiwanese nationalist movements]. Taipei: Zili wanbaoshe.

Yokomori Kumi. 1982. "Taiwan ni okeru jinjia—kominka seisaku to kanren ni oite [Shinto shrines in Taiwan and their connection with the assimilation policy]." *Taiwan kingendaishi kenkyū* [Historical studies of Taiwan in modern times] 4:187–221.

Zhang Wenhuan. 1935. "Kajyū [Overload]." *Taiwan shinbungaku* [New Taiwan literature] 1.1:24–28.

———. 1941. "Geisha no uchi [The home of *geisha*]." *Taiwan bungaku* 1.1:48–89.

Zhou Jinbo. 1998. "Shiganhei [Voluntary soldiers]." In *Zhou Jinbo nihongo sakuhinshyū* [Zhou Jinbo's works in Japanese], 14–37. Ed. Nakajima Toshio and Huang Yingzhe. Tokyo: Ryokuin shobō.

PART 3

Visual Culture and Literary Expressions

[9]

CONFRONTATION AND COLLABORATION

Traditional Taiwanese Writers' Canonical Reflection and Cultural Thinking on the New-Old Literatures Debate During the Japanese Colonial Period

HUANG MEI-ER

In the history of cultural development, massive changes in language have often occurred, especially in times of ideological transition and cultural upheaval. These changes can for instance be seen in the Renaissance and the Japanese Meiji period. Similar occurrences have also been noted in China. The vernacular (*baihua* 白話) movement initiated by Hu Shih 胡適 (1891–1962)[1] in 1917 proposed the adoption of spoken Chinese in formal writing, in place of the traditional, archaic form (*wenyan* 文言). This later triggered confrontation and debate among proponents of the new and old literary schools. Due to then-prevailing educational policies adopted by the Chinese government, the propagation of vernacular Chinese writing quickly gained the upper hand, so that between 1920 and 1921, vernacular writing was officially adopted as standard for the Chinese national language (*guoyu* 國語).

In contrast, the Taiwanese experience in this regard was more arduous, the island being still under Japanese rule in this period. It was not until the Kuomintang 國民黨 government took power in Taiwan that vernacular Chinese finally gained the absolute upper hand. Major reasons for this include the fact that Japanese was then the official lingua franca, a situation that prevented both vernacular and archaic Chinese from becoming the mainstream written form in Taiwan. This scenario, different from that of China, made the Taiwanese experience in regard to the competition between vernacular and archaic Chinese, as well as the debate between proponents of the New and Old Literatures, take a different turn, compared to what transpired in China. In fact, the Taiwanese experience was far more complicated than the Chinese.

This confrontation between vernacular and archaic writing, and between New and Old Literatures, is termed the "New-Old Literatures Debate," which took place between 1924 and 1942. Because of this prolonged time period, the author has divided it into three phases for greater ease of observation of the events and conditions related to the controversy. These phases roughly coincide with ten-year periods of the 1920s, 1930s, and 1940s. This controversy is historically significant, for it brought new opportunities for the emergence of Taiwanese New Literature (*Taiwan xinwenxue* 台灣新文學), and its later development, as a third force after the New and Old Literatures mentioned above.

Although this issue has been well studied, scholars had two blind spots in their approach to it. One was that they started from the vantage point of New Literature, and for this reason often gave negative views of the old school, notably its adopted methods and conclusions. They failed to make correct assessments of the mentalities of old school proponents, and the situation they were in at that time. The second blind spot was their failure to make a wider, comprehensive observation of the controversy from 1924 to 1942. Instead, the focus was usually only on the period of the 1920s. As a consequence, scholars omitted the introspections and reflections of the two sides made after more than ten years had passed since the controversy first erupted.

Having taken note of this mistake, I started from the perspective of the old school. In addition to probing the various bones of contention related to the controversy, the author has also taken into consideration how proponents of the old school reacted, as well as their thinking after the dust of the controversy had settled. The author has tried to delve into the interactions between literature and culture, in the context of the debate. Furthermore, because the Taiwan New Literature movement has often been viewed as an anti-Japanese cultural endeavor, the author has also tried to emphasize the movement's cultural significance. For this reason, as relevant issues centering on the debate are studied, attention is likewise placed on their cultural implications. Only when this is done can it be possible to direct the spotlight onto the opposing viewpoints and the underlying motivations.

The controversy mainly centered on the literary canon. For this reason, the author has utilized the old school's canonical reflections and the cultural thinking behind them as a foundation on which to reconstruct the complex relationships that existed between the two camps in the repressive politico-cultural atmosphere created by the Japanese colonial government. The author has tried to probe into the issue of whether there existed any collaboration between the opposing sides during the confrontation. Furthermore, the author has also reexamined the positions and roles of proponents of both the old and the new schools in Taiwan literature during the colonial period.

PRE-CONTROVERSY LITERATURE REFORM AMONG
TRADITIONAL WRITERS

The period between the launching of *Taiwan Youth* (*Tai oan chheng lian* 台灣青年) in July 1920 and the publication of Zhang Wojun 張我軍's (1902–1955) "A Letter to Taiwan's Youth" in April 1924 marked the eve of the birth of the Taiwan New Literature movement. Many expressed their opinions through publications like *Taiwan Youth, Taiwan,* and *Taiwan People's Daily* (*Taiwan minpō* 台灣民報), in which they voiced support for vernacular Chinese literature, especially its role in social reform.

In his "Literature and Duties," published in *Taiwan Youth* on July 12, 1920, Chen Xin 陳炘 (1893–1947) discussed literature from the perspective of society and culture. This was the earliest published work advocating New Literature. Another work, "The Past, Present, and Future of Chinese New Literature," by Xiu Chao 秀潮 and published on July 15, 1923, in *Taiwan People's News*, criticized conservatism in Taiwanese society and culture, and called it a threat to the rise of New Literature. On December 21, 1923, Runhui sheng 潤徽生's article "On Literature" appeared in the *Taiwan People's News*. He pointed out that Old Literature represented the mainstream in Taiwan at that time, and that any attempt to promote literature in the vernacular was bound to meet obstacles. In the same work he predicted a clash between the old and the new schools. A mere four months later, this came true when fierce debate erupted between the two camps, following Zhang Wojun's article that appeared in *Taiwan People's Daily.*

When he initiated the debate in 1924, Zhang, like many contemporary Taiwan intellectuals, linked literature with culture. Many of his writings, including "A Letter for Taiwan's Youth," "Awful Taiwanese Literary Circles," and "Let's Clean Up the Temple Ruins Lying in the Wild," Zhang basically wrote from the perspective of culture in lambasting Old Literature and its advocates, which he branded as backward. He portrayed Old Literature proponents as decadent citizens who enjoyed special privileges. He attacked them for clandestinely collaborating with the colonial government, and, in so doing, touched on the sensitive issue of national identification.

During both the Pre- and Post-Controversy periods, New Literature intellectuals always viewed the old school and its advocates in a dually opposed way. A question then arose as to how the traditionalists viewed the cultural impact they had jointly created with the modernists, and the everyday modernizing society. Were they oblivious to the emergence of a new society? And were they so insensitive that they failed to think about the functional significance and the roles of Old Literature in the new era?

In fact, even before the controversy erupted, calls for reform had been heard in the Old Literature circles. Lian Heng 連橫 (1878–1936) proposed reform in the poetry circles. He offered his criticisms against Jiboyin 擊缽吟 poetry reading societies and berated poets for reading far too little and for their personal character. In his writings, Lian urged introspection. Similar opinions have been observed in "Taiwan Poetry Collection" (*Taiwan shihui* 台灣詩薈). Other writers, like Wei Qingde 魏清德 (1888–1964), who was director of the Chinese department of the *Taiwan Daily News* (*Taiwan nichinichi shinpō* 台灣日日新報) for many years and an important member of the Taipei Ying Society (*Yingshe* 瀛社), also offered his views on instituting reforms in Taiwan's Chinese literary circles.

On April 5, 1915, Wei delivered a speech entitled "Poetry and Citizen's Character" (Wei), in which he spoke about what poetry could accomplish in the effort to reform a citizen's character. He urged poets to take on the duty of emphasizing the building of citizen's character in their writings, in ways that could nurture them as better citizens. This bestowing of a reforming role to traditional poetry is, to some extent, similar to New Literature advocates' goal of using their writings to educate the masses in the face of a rapidly modernizing society. Having said this, it is easy to see why the fierce debate took place between proponents of both camps on literary canon. For the traditional writers, Old Literature already had a reformative function and assigning such a role to New Literature was therefore unnecessary.

In addition to these views from traditional writers, there were two important publications that advocated reforms in Taiwan's poetry circles on the eve of the controversy period. They include Lian Heng's *Taiwan Poetry Collection* (February 1924 to October 1925) and *Taiwan Poetry News* (*Taiwan shinpo* 台灣詩報, February 1924 to April 1925), which was jointly edited by Huang Chunchao 黃春潮 (1884–1959) of the Taipei Star Society (*Xingshe* 星社), Zhang Chunfu 張純甫(1888–1941), and others.

In the preface of the first issue of *Taiwan Poetry Collection*, Lian Heng touched on the increasing influence of the West and the relative decline in Chinese studies. He urged poets to give up their self-mandated embellishing roles and instead take concrete steps to help in nation building. Calls for introspection also appeared in another poetry publication, the *Taiwan Poetry News*. In one of its prefaces, Lin Shiyai 林石崖 cited China's *Book of Songs* (*Shijing* 詩經), and the works of Leo Tolstoy and Rabindranath Tagore to illustrate his view that noble works of literature are always inseparable from society, and are written with the goals of educating people's minds and reforming then-existing conditions, not merely nitpicking about words and phrases. Lin's views and his aspirations for *Taiwan Poetry News* reveal his familiarity with foreign literature, which he believed the Taiwanese could learn from. He suggested that Taiwanese Old Literature works must seek to showcase "social character."

In view of the above, it is easy to see that even before the controversy started, Taiwan's old writers had already realized the need to adjust to the challenges brought by the advent of the new society. The views expressed by Wei, Lian, and Lin share a common point: Writers must not take as their goals the mere writing of beautiful words and phrases. Instead, reform must be accomplished through what they wrote about. They all proposed that this type of poetry should be given priority in publication.

The question of how the writing of prose and poetry can be made to follow world trends and reach the goal of nurturing citizens arose next. The challenge of infusing new spirit into their works by imbibing world civilization was also crucial. Today, scholars usually praise new writers for adopting Western ideas and artistic theories to promote the New Literature movement. However, before and after the controversy erupted, proponents of the old school had also studied Western ideas. By the time the trailblazing *Taiwan Youth* was launched in 1920, old writers were already familiar with the vicissitudes of Western civilization. Clearly, Zhang Wojun's criticism of the Taiwanese literary circles as otherworldly, ignorant, cold, and conservative in his article "Awful Taiwanese Literary Circles," published on April 26, 1924, finds no substantial basis.

In 1920, Chen Xin, in his "Literature and Duties," wrote:

> Present conditions compel us to exercise self-awareness and to fulfill our duties, to uproot bad practices and awaken the lazy and the dormant. Let us realize that today's civilized thoughts must serve as our guide toward widespread reforms. On this, Taiwan's literary society, already with a shining record just more than year after its establishment, has to make great contributions.

These words reveal that Chen never totally denied the significance of the old school. He even looked to the "Taiwan literature society" to exercise its leading role in the tasks of instilling self-awareness in the literary circles, the assimilation of new ideas, and the institution of reforms.

In fact, other poetry societies—such as the Taiwan Literature Association (*Taiwan wenshe* 台灣文社), which was founded by twelve members of the Oak Club (*Lishe* 櫟社), one of the three largest poetry societies in Taiwan's colonial history, including Lin Youchun 林幼春 (1880–1939), Cai Huiru 蔡惠如 (1881–1929), Chen Cangyu 陳滄玉 (1875–1922), Lin Xiantang 林獻堂 (1881–1956), and others—set as their foundational objective greater assimilation of ideas from both East and West without being limited by geographical boundaries. The association's publication *Taiwan Literature Collective Journals* (*Taiwan wenyi congzhi* 台灣文藝叢誌), thus included foreign topics, such as introductions to Western civilization and works by foreign literary figures. For instance, the first issue included the British author John Finnemore's work on the history of Germany, translated by Lin Shaoying 林少英 (1878–?). Another of Lin's translations, Lucy Cazalet's "History of Russia," was published later, in the fourth issue. In the following year, Xu Sanlang 許三郎's Chinese rendition of Monty Python's "Meaning of Life" appeared in the fourth issue. All these helped opened the vista of the Taiwanese reading public at that time, making them aware of what was happening in the rest of the world. It is interesting to note that this publication was launched on

January 1, 1919, by a group of traditional writers. Using a quaint blend of the old and the new, this magazine was ahead of *Taiwan Youth* in carrying out the task of educating the Taiwanese people at that time.

———— ∞∞∞ ————

In the above paragraphs, the author has illustrated how writers of the old school started a reflection on the literary canon long before the Old-New controversy broke out. These writers sensed the changes occurring abroad and for this reason worked to familiarize themselves with the civilization of the West, as well as its artistic-literary creations, which they later dipped into for inspiration. Furthermore, they proposed reform in prose and poetry by way of a change in content. It is therefore certain that old writers believed that with the advent of the new age, Old Literature did have a role to play, with or without the initiation of a vernacular literature movement. It was precisely for this reason that the more influential old writers at that time, such as Lin Youchun, Fu Xiqi 傅錫祺 (1876–1946), Xie Xueyu 謝雪漁 (1871–1953), and others, did not participate in the debate. Most of those who expressed views were members of local poetry societies and avid followers of Jiboyin. In fact, even more prominent writers who were involved in the controversy, such as Lian Heng and Wei Qingde, wrote on the issue only on a limited scale.

Zhang Wojun was noted for having commented that old writers had never reacted to his critical writings.[2] Again, this reveals the fact that old writers were fully confident in the canon of the Old Literature. They believed that the educative goals outlined by proponents of New Literature were all achievable by using Old Literature methods. This being said, it is easy to understand why both sides remained adamant about their views and why the controversy raged on for a protracted period of time. In fact, the fires of controversy repeatedly died out and rekindled during the period lasting from 1924 to 1942.

THE FIRST PHASE OF THE DEBATE:
TRADITIONAL WRITERS' INSISTENCE ON THEIR CANON
AND THEIR CULTURAL THOUGHTS

From the above, we see that even before the controversy began, traditional writers had already thought of how they could adjust to the changing conditions, besides the issue of how reform could be instituted, in view of the different malaise of Old Literature accumulated over a long period of time. Despite the similarity of their ideas, both sides failed to jointly tackle issues of reform. Instead, they clashed with Zhang Wojun and others in a long unsolved confrontation. The critical reason is no other than the debate on canon.

Here, the term "canon" refers to "a generally accepted standard in literary creation and reading."[3] The Old-New Literatures Controversy was a debate on literary canon. While new writers proposed the adoption of vernacular literature in place of the original archaic or classical form, traditional writers protected the orthodoxy of Old Literature. For the proponents of traditional literature, the outcome of the debate would influence conditions then existing in Taiwan's literary world, including their right of control and their voice. In fact, the literary laurels monopolized by traditional writers at that time were at stake. The final outcome of the debate would decide the way in which resources—both literary and cultural—then in the hands of the traditionalists would be reallocated. It is understandable that with all this hanging in the balance, traditional writers chose not to remain passive.

Besides the risks of changes in the literary world, traditional writers also had reservations on the use of vernacular Chinese, especially its capability to replace Old Literature. To cite an example, Men Hulu Sheng 悶葫蘆生 writes in "Deliberation on New Literature": "Taiwan's so-called vernacular literature merely uses ordinary Chinese characters, with the insertion here and there of active words one cannot find in the dictionary" (Men). By this, he took "vernacular Chinese literature" as a mere play on words. In his "A Letter to Zhang Yilang," Zheng Kunwu 鄭坤五, a writer from Kaoxiong, wrote: "The so-called vernacular Chinese advocated by Zhang Wojun is actually based on the Peking dialect. Taiwan already has a common form of writing understandable throughout China. It is the language in which the *Annals of the Three Kingdoms* (三國演義), *Journey to the West* (西遊記), *Rouge Chamber* (*Fenzhuang Lou* 粉粧樓), and other classics were written. It is enough for a language" (Zheng).

The views cited above all considered the Peking dialect to have nothing special to offer; Taiwan's common language was closely similar to it, and therefore a change was not all that necessary. In his "Letter to Luo Hequan," Zhang Chunfu, a member of both the Taiwan Ying Society and the Star Society, also wrote to voice his doubts about the vernacular form. His opinions can be summarized as follows: (1) Proponents of vernacular language find it easier to express, but archaic form can likewise be used to achieve goals in communication. (2) Different dialects are spoken in China's many provinces. Vernacular Chinese, being just one of them, would not have a unifying role. Besides, archaic Chinese had once been the vernacular in ancient China. (3) Although vernacular Chinese is easy to learn, it is not succinct, and tends to be wordy. For this reason, readers have to spend longer amounts of time to read, straining the eyes ever further. It is far from being economical. Traditional writing had been in use for a long time, with the depth or shallowness of the linguistic register differing from writer to writer.

As such, it is more "commonplace." From his words, we see that Zhang Chunfu identified more with the traditional than with the vernacular, while also taking into consideration the vernacular form's suitability for Taiwan.

Regarding poetry, both sides held differing views on its canon, and therefore insisted on their own choices. The most contentious issue was the necessity of rhythm. Most poets considered "traditional literature to use rhythm in poetry ... while New Literature been freed from the use of meter, which serves as its distinct feature" (Yi, "Comparison"). To illustrate this, Lian Heng cited classical Chinese poetry, pointing its tradition of using rhythm. He stated further that even the relatively vernacular folk poetry also employed meter, and he thus expressed disfavor with the new poetry's lack of rhythmic character (Lian, "Remnant"). For him, the lack of rhythm was a challenge to the orthodoxy of poetry. As heated debate took place even on an issue like rhythm, it is easy to see that traditional writers were far from ready to accept the composition methods favored by advocates of new poetry.

Despite their insistence, followers of the old school had to make some adjustments as New Literature gradually became more common. In his "Refined Words" (*Ya Yan* 雅言), published in the 1930s, Lian Heng showed a stance different from what he had taken in the 1920s. His thoughts on oral and written forms were rich and varied. He believed that simple Chinese was more appropriate for the transmission of academic and philosophical ideas, an attitude that revealed his insistence on the traditional canon. He likewise concluded that easier words must be used in materials designed for education of the masses. Evidently, this was an adjustment intended to address criticisms from the New Literature camp. He also believed during that period of debate that the Taiwanese people had to conserve their native language while also learning languages from foreign lands, which were necessary to keep them well informed. He proposed that except novels and letters, which he said could be written in the vernacular, other works must be in standard Chinese, Japanese, or other languages, and even in some romanized form of vernacular Chinese. These views attest Lian Heng's flexibility on the use of language at a time of changing trends.

After the 1930s, old writers began a shift toward more vernacular, common language in poetry writing. They picked up previously neglected composition methods while at the same time injecting a more ethnic Taiwanese character into their works. This will be further discussed later.

In addition to the issue of canon, the controversy also featured both camps' insistence and interpretation of cultural issues in the context of the changing times. Much effort was devoted to debates on this issue. Before we begin a discussion of these debates, let us recall the origins of Taiwan's New Literature movement. Basically, it emerged because traditional Chinese was deemed unable to meet the challenges of the changing society and culture. As such, right from the very start, proponents of New Literature advocated a reform of the citizen's spirit and the assimilation of the emerging new world culture, as discussed above. Traditional literature and its supporters were branded as conservative and inflexible, and were compared to tomb-guarding hounds oblivious to the necessity of reform (Zhang 5–6).

The old writers' firm stand on tradition and the new writers' pursuit of modern, world civilization together made the Old-New Literatures Debate appear like a clash between modern and traditional cultures. One point that must receive our attention is the reason behind people's perception that the traditionalists rejected modern world culture and held on stubbornly to tradition.

The debate between Lian Heng and Zhang Wojun in 1924 allows us a glimpse into how the controversy transformed itself from the field of literature into the realm of culture. When the controversy erupted, traditional writers chose not to quickly adopt a defensive attitude, although they were much blamed at that time. It was not until Lin Xiaomei 林小眉 (1893–1940), descendant of the prominent Lin clan of Banqiao 板橋林家, published poetry distinct from the conventional that Lian made his critical comment. He writes:

> Lin is well grounded in classical Chinese culture, besides his excellent grasp of the English language. For this reason, Lin is not swayed by the ongoing trend. His sincere words, "when it comes to literature, Chinese is the most beautiful, no one gets tired of it," spring forth from his heart. The scholars of today call for "abolishing classical Chinese" even before they have read the six classics. They propose New Literature, and promote new poetry ... As for the so-called new, they refer to Western novels and drama, although they actually know so little about them. They feel elated, unknowing that they resemble toads inside a water well, oblivious to the vastness of this world. (Lian, *Taiwan Poetry Collection*, no. 10)

These accusing words were meant for someone else, for not long after their publication, Zhang Wojun wrote in response his "Shedding Tears for the Taiwanese Literary World":

> Reading this fine article makes us realize right away that this great poet, although not knowing what it is, disfavors New Literature. I'm least happy when he identifies "abolition of classical Chinese" with "advocating New Literature." ... Let me ask this great poet what made him conclude that those advocating New Literature and promoting new poetry also meant the abolition of classical Chinese.

From these excerpts, we can see that Lian Heng considered New Literature to be leftover crumbs of Western literature and classical Chinese poetry to be linked with classical Chinese culture. Lian believed that because new writers wanted to replace old poetry with new poetry, they considered classical Chinese and culture as things that can be abandoned. The question here is to define the relationship existing between new writers and classical Chinese, as well as Chinese culture. From Zhang's rebuttal, we realize that his advocacy of New Literature was not tantamount to the abandonment of classical Chinese. Although Zhang's cultural thinking was founded on world trends, he also identified with Chinese tradition, its culture, and its spirit. To him, however, Taiwan could learn from the experience of Chinese new culture and literature (Chen 1996:149–150) after the Chinese Republic was founded, in establishing a culture of its own. This differed from the view of Taiwan's old writers, who looked up to tradition.

At this point, we must examine why old writers held the misconception that new writers wanted to abandon classical Chinese, a grim situation about which they expressed great anxiety. The main reason was classical Chinese's feeble influence in that period in history. When he wrote "Congratulations to the Taiwan Literature Society on Its First Issue" in 1919, the Tainan writer Lin Xiangyuan 林湘沅 (1870–1923) stated that the arrival of the new era had made the Taiwanese people aspire for modernity, and this had led to a gradual decline in the popularity of classical studies. A year earlier, in 1918, Tainan's Xu Ziwen 許子文 wrote an article entitled "Maintaining Policies on Classical Studies" in which he observed that during the early Japanese colonial period, Taiwan had been faced with a scenario in which there was a clamor for new studies, usually equated with Western culture. The rise of new studies meant Westernization and thus the dislocation of colonial Japanese culture (Xu 32). He expressed concern about the repercussions of this trend. In 1927, a writer from Jiayi, Huang Maosheng 黃茂盛, wrote the preface to the one hundredth issue of the Congwen Literary Society, in which pointed out that the very nature of new studies and Western culture clashed with the morality and ethics enshrined in classical studies and Japanese culture. The rise of new studies meant a decline in classical Chinese philosophical and ethical teachings. In the long run he wrote, the Chinese traditional culture handed down from their forebears would vanish. This possibility made old writers feel threatened by the rise of new studies and Western culture.

Furthermore, old writers' recognition of Japanese culture clashed with new writer's penchant for Western culture. This clash is best illustrated by Zhang Wojun's "A Send Off to Prof. Gu," published on November 23, 1924. He writes:

He [Gu Hongming 辜鴻銘] traveled to Taiwan and Japan with a new sense of mission: That of advocating Japanese civilization and promoting the Japanese spirit in Taiwan and in Japan … in other words, a rejection of Western spirit and civilization. This is what we are not happy about. … After all, the Japanese civilization shows a lot of defects as seen from today's society, and is therefore not suitable for modernday life. This is a widely accepted fact that saddens everyone. … Already, there is too much Japanese spirit and civilization in Taiwan today!

Again, the above excerpt tells us that Zhang favored Western culture. It is therefore easy to understand why an uneasy, confrontational relationship existed between the two camps.

The confrontation between proponents of Western civilization and of Japanese civilization, and between classical Chinese studies and new studies, created much anxiety among those who strongly favored keeping classical Chinese as the language of the mainstream. This anxiety was exacerbated by the Japanese colonial government's attitude of favoring a gradual phase out of classical Chinese. In 1918, when the Japanese amended existing regulations governing public schools, only two hours per week were allotted for classical Chinese classes. In 1922, when the "Taiwan New Education Decree" was promulgated, classical Chinese classes became mere elective courses. Some schools abolished classical Chinese studies from their curricula altogether, a move that drew much anger and great anxiety. Some Taiwanese started a protest movement, although to a certain extent they were swayed by anti-Japanization sentiments (Wu 1995:335–336).

Under high-handed colonial policies on education, the Taiwanese were forced to study the "national language." If they could not perfect their command of the "national language" over the course of their lives, how could they find time to study classical Chinese ("Objectives")? With classical Chinese facing the threat of abolition, some Taiwanese failed to realize that they should resist Japanization. They instead felt that classical Chinese was something unnecessary. In the eyes of traditional writers, therefore, keeping classical Chinese was no longer just an issue of maintaining traditional norms on morality and ethics—it further symbolized the conservation of traditional culture and the Han Chinese spirit.

From the above, we see that the Old-New Literatures Debate occurred at a time of competition between new and classical studies, of confrontation between the cultures of the East and the West, of a struggle between the Japanese and Chinese spirit, and of a clash between the Japanese and Chinese languages. In such a complex cultural milieu, the debate attained a wider social repercussion. What was once a purely literary issue was given an expanded cultural connotation.

For old writers, New Literature was synonymous with Western literature and culture. One reporter made a comparison between Old and New Literature in an article that appeared in the *Taiwan Daily News.* He cited various differences: In linguistic expression, Old Literature used various classical phrase endings while New Literature adopted more colloquial replacements, with the added adoption of Western quotation marks. While Old Literature was printed in vertical lines, New Literature adopted Western horizontal printing. In structure, Old Literature kept the flow and tonal qualities of classical Chinese, while New Literature brimmed with Western linguistic characteristics, and read like translations from a Western-language original (Yi 1926).

A writer with the pseudonym of Laosheng Changtan 老生常談 ("Lengthy Discourse of the Old One") also wrote similar comments in his "On the So-Called

New Poetry." He wrote about how "new poets, unwilling to learn, were oblivious to the exquisite points of Old Literature. They curse classical Chinese culture, wishing for its early demise. ... They say Old Literature is like a spittoon, as though unknowing that this spittoon is an heirloom from their ancestors, which is much better than the Western spittoon that is their New Literature" (Laosheng 1926). If one were to accept this, then advocating New Literature would be allowing the demise of classical culture, something old writers would never do. This led Lian Heng into writing in "Taiwan Poetry Collection" (no. 17) that in their works new writers had abandoned a beautiful national treasure, unknowingly becoming foreigners in so doing. The struggle between the Chinese and the foreign, and the competition between the old and the new, had made this literary debate no longer a mere controversy on literary canon—it had now overflowed into the realms of culture and ethnicity.

In such a situation, the differences grew as the days went on. Lai Ho 賴和 (1894–1943) observed:

> The New Literature movement was born as a result of the influence of Western studies, which explains why it has an undeniably Western character. ... Although Taiwan's new literature is not creative, it is openly imported, not stolen. Let the glory be shared by old writers, who, by their hard work, have created this rotten Taiwanese culture, and nurtured people who are condescending. (Lai 1926)

As he argued in favor of New Literature and Western culture, Lai insinuated that Old Literature was to blame for the "rotten culture" at that time. His writings not only highlighted the clash between the two sides' values on contemporary and traditional cultures, but also convinced old writers to associate New Literature with Western culture and to believe that new writers were exploiting the idea of modernity to overcome tradition.

Even if one were to narrow the focus and direct attention only to attacks on "poetry-society culture," much reviled by the new writers as boring, pleasure-seeking, and currying to the Japanese, it is easy to discern the prejudice with which new writers viewed their opponents. According to research by the author, Taiwan had as many as 370 poetry societies during the Japanese colonial period. The reasons for this flowering—auguring well with accusations made by new writers—included both poets' boredom and their quest for fame. Some old writers also believed that poetry societies worked to propagate classical Chinese culture and spirit. The popularity of *jiboyin* was also swayed by people's belief that it played a role in improving literacy. Thus, despite the negative impressions of poetry societies and jiboyin in the colonial period, they were worthy of preservation in the eyes of proponents of traditional literature. Evidently, the two sides also held opposite views on the cultural "positioning" of poetry societies and jiboyin.

THE SECOND PHASE OF THE DEBATE: TRADITIONAL WRITERS' INVOLVEMENT IN THE NATIVIST LITERATURE MOVEMENT

During the debates of the 1920s, new writers also criticized old poets' work, in addition to branding them as backward. In 1926 Chen Xugu 陳虛谷 (1896–1965) published an article entitled "Crying for Taiwan's Poetry" in which he insulted Taiwanese poets for welcoming the newly installed Japanese governor-general of Taiwan. In 1929 Ye Rongzhong 葉榮鐘 (1900–1978) wrote an article entitled "Decadent Poets" for the 242nd issue of *Taiwan People's News* in which he mocked old writers for their decadent ways.

At this point in time, under the influence of socialist ideas, people identified aristocracy as the culprit behind Old Literature's lack of synchrony with the times (Yi 1927). These critical views led old writers to examine the issue of Old Literature's dissociation from society, and to find ways to give Old Literature a more popular appeal, in a manner that could benefit society at large. These introspections stimulated old writers to work toward this goal in the decade that immediately followed.

The debates overflowed into the 1930s. In 1934 the *wenyan* classical Chinese revivalist Jiang Kanghu 江亢虎 (1883–1954) arrived in Taiwan to promote a cultural renaissance movement. He found enthusiastic support from many old writers, and his arrival further fanned the flames of the debate. At this point in time, although old writers insisted on their literary canon, some of them were already pondering the question of how reforms could be started.

Through *Taiwan Arts Garden* (*Taiwan yiyuan* 台灣藝苑), a publication he had founded, Zheng Kunwu introduced the term "Taiwan national style" (*Taiwan guofeng* 台灣國風) in 1927. He collected Taiwan folk songs, such as "Spring for All Seasons." This move inspired Xiao Yongdong 蕭永東 (1897–1964), Chan Hong 懺紅 (Hong Tietao 洪鐵濤, 1892–1947), and others to serialize folk songs in the *369 Journal* (三六九小報) during the 1930s. These songs were popular vernacular pieces that had mass appeal, and that met the new writers' criteria for vernacular poetry. These folk songs in the Taiwanese dialect, different from the Chinese vernacular proposed by Zhang Wojun, better reflected the culture and psyche of the Taiwanese at that time. Besides, they were "traditional" in the sense understood by proponents of Old Literature. Zheng's approach was an adjustment to Zhang Wojun's objective, which stressed the idea of viewing Taiwanese literature from the perspectives of the Chinese. Zheng's work of arranging and collecting folk songs was praised by Huang Shihui 黃石輝 (1900–1945), who is commonly mistaken as the originator of nativist Taiwan literature, as a pioneer work. Huang commented that Zheng was not motivated by the idea of class difference (Huang 1930). The new trend of emphasizing Taiwan folk literature later fused with the nativist literature movement and new writers' efforts to use the Taiwan vernacular in creating a theme on Taiwan culture. Interestingly, this phenomenon marked a rare collaboration between proponents of Old and New Literature.

In August 1930, Huang Shihui, an old writer who enjoyed a friendly relationship with Zheng Kunwu, initiated the topic of nativist literature in his article "How Not to Advocate Nativist Literature." In July of the following year, he, together with Guo Qiusheng 郭秋生 (1904–1980), launched the Taiwan vernacular movement. This literary movement, focused on Taiwan, gained the immediate support of old writers like Zheng Kunwu, Huang Chunqing 黃純青, Lian Heng, and others.

Soon after the nativist literature and Taiwan vernacular movements started, Zheng Kunwu published an article entitled "A Few Words on Nativist Literature" on February 4, 1931. He cited the good points of nativist literature. The following excerpt shows his reasons for favoring nativist literature, as well as his recommendations:

How should we promote nativist literature at a time when people are emphasizing international language? ... Everything goes on a cycle. ... Nobody can make a claim on the benefits of a unified language, or whether the fragmentary nativist literature is superior. ... The nativist literature I favor is narrow in scope. Confucius' Book of Poetry and the poet Qu Yuan's 屈原 Lisao 離騷 too were once nativist literature. Nobody has dared to deny their value. If we in Taiwan advocate our nativist literature, one day it will attain the level of the Chinese classics. It would be even better if we create phonetic symbols that can supplement what Chinese characters are found to be inadequate in terms of transcribing the Taiwanese dialect. The creation of these phonetic characters (or what I call "auxiliary characters") has repercussions on the future of Taiwan nativist literature. ... In the future, Taiwan's distinct vernacular poems and melodious folk songs can no longer be looked down upon as it has been for hundreds of years. By then, it will join the ranks of the world literatures, to the fulfillment of our dreams. (Zheng 1931)

In this article, Zheng outlined the value of nativist literature as he discussed problems in transcribing the Taiwanese dialect. He even suggested the adoption of the 50 Japanese sounds for this purpose, the latter in consideration of Taiwan's status as a Japanese colony and the growing usage of the Japanese language on the island. From Zheng's later writings on this issue, it is evident that he had linked theory with creation, especially in his attempt to create his *"zailai"* 在來 Chinese, which embraced both vernacular Chinese and Taiwanese, as well as the infusion of Japanese words. Works using this language combination were published in *Poetry News* (*Shibao* 詩報), *Wind and Moon News* (*Fengguebao* 風月報) and *Southern* (*Nanfang* 南方).

In addition to Zheng, another who identified with the nativist and Taiwan vernacular movement was Huang Chunqing (1875–1956). Huang's article on the vernacular literature movement, "Theories on Reform of the Taiwan Dialect," appeared in *Taiwan News*. He expressed agreement with Guo Qiusheng on the latter's advocacy of unity between written and spoken language, and the adoption of the Amoy (Xiamen 廈門) tone as standard for pronunciation and the use of simple Chinese for the Taiwanese dialect.[4] Huang favored the "bamboo branch" (*zhuzhi ci* 竹枝詞) structure for writing nativist literature. On this, he writes:

> Taiwan's scenery and flora differ from those on the mainland. Since the Qing dynasty, officials visiting Taiwan have so marveled at the foreign scenery that they wrote in the *zhuzhi* structure. … Things are changing: political reforms, changes in customs, and the advent of new things and events. … We are born in these times and all around us are materials for *zhuzhi*. In other words, *zhuzhi* has a unique literary value, for poetry, for mass literature, and for the so-called nativist literature. I strongly believe so. (Huang, "Theories" 35)

The article emphasized the idea that Taiwan's local color made an ideal topic for bamboo-branch writing. He thought that this form of writing was close to local conditions and the general populace and might thus be lumped together with nativist and mass literature. Huang was convinced that *zhuzhi* writing had a traditional character while also possessing folk appeal, and thus was worth the support of old writers as the ideal best literary form for nativist and mass literature.

Among old writers, Lian Heng too was one of those who voiced support for nativist literature and the Taiwan vernacular movement. This is shown in his "Refined Words" (*Ya Yan*), serialized in the 369 *Journal* from January 1931 onward. On the reasons for writing, he says:

> In recent years there have been proposals calling for a nativist literature and for reforming the Taiwanese dialect. I have the same ideas in mind. But they are better said than done for reasons that those who speak may not necessarily be capable and those capable may not always be willing. In fact, this is the reason for the decline in Taiwan literature. For one to call for nativist literature, he must first act on the native language. … I'm a Taiwanese and therefore know how difficult this task is. But I have not dared to dwell too much on how difficult the task at hand is. I have therefore worked on a "Taiwanese Dictionary" since my return. Once completed, this book will help conserve the Taiwanese dialect, besides contributing considerably to the propagation of Taiwan literature. (Lian 1992:1)

Lian's words reveal his support for nativist literature. He even believed that Taiwan's native dialect should form the basis for a nativist literature, and that for this reason, arranging a system for the dialect was necessary. In fact, before Huang Shihui and Guo Qiusheng proposed the Taiwan vernacular movement, Lian had already started work on systematizing the Taiwanese native language. In November and December of 1929, Lian published two articles in *Taiwan People's News*, "Outlines on Arranging the Taiwanese Dialect" and "The Duty of Arranging the

Taiwanese Dialect." It is clear that Lian Heng was motivated by his desire to keep the national spirit at a time when the Japanese language was making inroads and the native tongue on a steady decline in importance.

It is interesting to note that during the 1920s debate between Lian and Zhang Wojun, the latter criticized the Taiwanese dialect for its lack of sophistication. Much later, Lian made the following statement in the preface of his dictionary: "The Taiwanese tongue possesses an elegance that escapes the eyes of the undiscerning." This reveals that the compilation of the dictionary was partly a reaction to Zhang's derogatory remarks on the Taiwanese dialect. To further rationalize the use of the Taiwanese dialect in nativist literature, Lian adopted the title "Refined Words" (*Ya Yan*) as a way to defend the language's reputation. Lian cited Chinese historical examples of the infusion of dialects into tradition. He expanded interpretation of the word "dialect" beyond the Taiwanese tongue to include foreign dialects, just like the way European words were transliterated, a practice sometimes adopted around that time (Lian 1992 4). Lian urged the preservation of native tongues and the learning of foreign languages as the world became a global village and as academic ideas increasingly became borderless. This reflects his practice of not limiting his vision to the Taiwan dialect alone.

Compared to the Taiwan vernacular movement, nativist literature received far more recognition and support from traditional literary writers. In 1935 Lai Ziqing 賴子清 adopted as criteria for publication a literary piece's geographical value, historicity, and vision in portraying Taiwan and its native character (Lai 1935). Evidently, nativism had become a standard for poetry collections in that period in history. The growth of nativist literature influenced the works of traditional writers. In his critique of Zhang Chunfu's poetry collection, Huang Chunchao writes: "His works shifted from the superficial to the realistic, to the Foukienese, then to the nativist and finally, the classical" (Huang 1941). With these adopted as the aesthetic and structural standards of poetry, we can see how deep the nativist literature movement has influenced traditional Taiwanese literature.

As mentioned above, several old writers participated in the collection of folk literature and in the creation of native poetry, while others voiced support for the Taiwan vernacular. All these reveal a collaborative relationship with new writers in this period in the development of Taiwan's literature.

THE THIRD PHASE OF THE DEBATE: CONFRONTATION AND COLLABORATION UNDER GREATER EAST ASIAN LITERARY POLICIES

After April of 1937, several newspapers and magazines removed their classical Chinese columns, a move that greatly affected publication of classical literature and reduced their discussion forums. However, several publications continued to allot space for articles in classical Chinese, such as *Poetry News (Shipō)*, *Confucius' Teachings (Kongjiao bao* 孔教報), *Wind and Moon News*, and the Chinese-Japanese bilingual *Taiwan Arts (Taiwan yishu* 台灣藝術). *Wind and Moon News* was renamed *Southern (Nanfang)* in July 1941. The third phase of the debate was centered on *Wind and Moon* and later *Southern*.

In 1941, a writer from Taipei's Wanhua district, Huang Wenhu 黃文虎, using the pen name "Yuan Garden Promenader" (Yuanyuan ke 元園客), published "The Seven Maladies of Taiwan's Poets." This piece was well received by Lan Ying 嵐映 (or Lin Jingnan 林荊南, 1915–1998), Yi Zu 醫卒, Pangguan Sheng 傍觀生, and others. But another group, consisting of Xiao Jingyun 小鏡雲, Rui Feng 銳鋒, Kaoshi Houren 高適後人, and Zheng Kunwu had an opposite reaction. They believed that Huang's seven maladies, such as plagiarism and imitation, were unavoidable, in consideration of then-prevailing conditions. They further said that at a time when classical studies were experiencing a decline, Taiwan writers should join hands to preserve Old Literature instead of staging attacks on each other. Opinions differed and a debate ensued. Between 1941 and 1942, groups separately led by Lin Jingnan and Zheng Kunwu attacked and blamed each other, using *Wind and Moon* and *Southern* as their forum. This marked the start of the third phase of the debate between proponents of Old and New Literature.

This phase can further be divided into two stages. The first stage started with the publication of Huang's "Seven Maladies" on July 1, 1941, in the 131st issue of *Wind and Moon*. The second stage began when Huang Shihui's article "Reviewing Old Records: Taiwan Poets' Maladies" appeared in the 150th issue of *Southern* on April 15, 1942. The debate drew the participation of Zhu Dianren 朱點人 (1903–1949), Lin Kefu 林克夫, and Liao Hanchen 廖漢臣 (1912–1980), who had had encounters with Huang in the 1930s debate. As many as one hundred twenty relevant articles were published during these two stages.

The quarrel in this period of debate was centered on the new writers' insistence that only New Literature could meet the demands of the times, a stance they had adopted following ideas derived from Darwin's theory of evolution, which was popular around that time. They emphasized contact with the rest of the world, giving importance to the future and keeping up with the times. Old writers paid attention to self-initiated changes within Taiwanese literature and cherished historical tradition, while taking note of the realism demanded by the times. On the issue of the decreased importance of classical studies in postwar Taiwan, new writers blamed long-term irregularities in classical poetry circles for the phenomenon. They advocated reform through the adoption of a new literary canon to replace the old. Old writers believed that because decline was already the case in classical studies, leniency must be exercised despite imitative and plagiaristic acts. They thought that only in this way could classical Chinese studies be conserved. As conservatism and reformism exchanged fire, old and new writers juggled with idealism and realism. As the two sides differed on how the classical studies crisis should be defused, the gap between the two grew wider and more unbridgeable.

Old writers launched a defensive attack against reform by insisting that the "new" in "New Literature" should refer to reform in content, not in literary format. Old writers believed that they too could institute such a reform. The question of which side would win this war between literary canons was to be decided by historical events around that time. After the end of the Pacific War, which side could conform to literary policies adopted for the Greater East Asia Co-Prosperity Sphere (大東亞共榮圈) would be deemed the most appropriate canon. Thus, those who fully understand the scenario were quick to express their opinion. Huang Chunqing, though he didn't participate in the debate, published the foundational goals of the "Society for Research in Classical Chinese Poetry" early after the debate erupted. He writes:

> Loyalty and filial piety are the virtues treasured most in the Orient. Thus, classical poets can dwell on these virtues even more. ... Since the Marco Polo Bridge Incident, poetry recitation meetings have been growing in popularity. What better way can the virtues of loyalty and filial piety be propagated? ... I have lately read *Southern* magazine and came to know the ongoing discussion on poetry studies. ... Why don't we take advantage of this opportunity to recruit more members and organize classical poetry associations through which we can promote these virtues? Isn't that a chance for poets to fulfill their duty of writing as a service to the nation? (Huang 1943:2)

Huang believed that although academic discussion helped propagate poetry studies, it would have been better to use the opportunity for promoting unity and doing great service to the country. On the one hand, Huang's idea appeared to be an attempt to reconcile the opposing sides, and on the other it looked like a suggestion to solve problems besetting Taiwan at that time. His idea was thus well received. In his "Reflections on the Foundation of Classical Poetry Societies," Lin Demo 林得模 elaborated on Huang's idea. He writes:

> I have read your 143rd issue, which included the article written by Mr. Huang Chunqing. His calls for the establishment of classical poetry societies as a means for poets to serve the nation are most timely. ... The island is a crucial center point of the Greater East Asia Co-prosperity Sphere. If the men of letters of Taiwan heed the calls of Mr. Huang to set up loyalty–filial piety poetry societies, which would focus on fomenting these virtues, then poets can fulfill their responsibilities as subjects of the empire. (Lin 1942)

The emphasis on loyalty and filial piety, be it in the form of classical poetry or loyalty–filial piety poetry, thus became the sole standard for ultimate literary creation. This reveals the fact that the aesthetic standard of being "politically correct" had by then overtaken the content-form controversy between the old and the new schools, and had become the highest literary canon. Finding themselves in such a situation, both sides of the debate realized the importance of being in conformity with official policies. Proponents of New Literature attempted to stress that New Literature was far more capable of fulfilling the new goals than classical literature. On this, Lin Kefu writes in his "Our Mission in the Literary Debate":

> Old poets are so obsessed with classical literature that they reject calls for reform. Any suggestion toward that is alienated. It comes as no surprise that Taiwan literature, the so-called vernacular literature, cannot develop with the times. After the war in Greater East Asia broke out, we expect impacts on culture, the economy, science and society. ... How then can we fulfill our mission once the East Asia Co-prosperity Sphere becomes a reality? (Lin 1942)

Lin noticed the close proximity between literature and the times, and called for attention to the role of literature in building the Co-prosperity Sphere.

An article by Lin Jingnan, "For Mr. Kunwu," further outlines the mission of New Literature. He writes:

> The Japanese empire is currently building the Greater East Asia Co-prosperity Sphere. We have no idea how many new writers are participating in this task, both here and abroad. How many old poets are involved in this task? In Taiwan, we use New Literature to write articles beneficial to the Co-Prosperity Theory through creation, translation, introduction, and stage performance. How much contribution are you making with your old poetry and literature? Local newspapers are allocating space for you. And what have been the benefits of doing so? From now on, stop writing those irrelevant works and instead focus your writing on issues with literary value. For it will benefit the building of the Co-Prosperity Sphere and the reading public alike. (Lin 1942)

In this article, Lin extolled fellow new writers to make contributions to the Co-Prosperity Sphere, and he took advantage of this opportunity to question the value of Old Literature.

Another article, Liao Hanchen's "Responsibilities of Taiwan's Writers," which was the last of its kind published in 1942, voiced similar opinions. Liao writes:

> Since the war broke out in China, the idea of a Greater East Asia Co-prosperity Sphere ... has gradually become a reality. For the sake of cultural communication between China and Japan, the importance of the Chinese language needs no further elaboration. The government is deeply aware of this. At this point in time, local writers must work toward the mission ... of promoting cooperation from the

people for the sake of the Co-prosperity Sphere. This is the only path for Taiwan writers in the near future. A task so great as that cannot be accomplished by just one person. How could we be talking about who advocates New Literature and who insists on the old? (Liao 1942)

Before this article was published, the editors of *Southern* had announced that they would not print a word on the topic of the debate again after the publication of Huang Xizhi 黃習之's "Preface to the Collection of Discussion on the Maladies of Taiwan's Poets." Yet a month later the ban was lifted for Liao's article. This was a confirmation of Liao's ideas on the sole mission of writing being for the benefit of the Co-Prosperity Sphere.

In view of the above, we see that under totalitarian government policies, political interference in matters of culture is inevitable. It is interesting to note that Huang Chunqing's opinions augured well with old writers' goal of writing to attain Nationalistic goals, but could not avoid the common accusation that old writers enjoyed especially cordial relationships with the colonial government. The positions of Lin Jingnan, Lin Kefu, and Liao Hanchen, who had always been branded as new writers, had changed to conform with official policies as seen through articles they separately published in *Southern*. In contrast with the debate in the 1920s, during which new writers advocated anti-Japanese goals, this was an evident shift in opinion.

CONCLUSIONS

The study of the history of Taiwanese literature is biased in favor of New Literature. This is the case both in Taiwan and in China, where little attention has been given to Old Literature and its writers. The harsh criticisms made by new writers in the 1920s are often repeated, and old writers are rarely viewed and assessed with objectivity. In fact, Taiwan's old writers and literati played important roles in the history of Taiwan literature. The author has made this observation by taking the Old-New Literatures Debate as focal point. Using the perspective of the old writers, the author had here carried out an analysis of the debates with the use of relevant records, which help in better understanding the psyche of old writers and the situation they were in at that time.

In this article, the author has made a chronological and synchronized analysis of relevant events during the period of the debate from 1924 to 1942. Findings show that the debate during the Japanese colonial period, though apparently related to literary canon, had deep cultural underpinnings. Both sides had differing interpretations and evaluations of issues like traditional and modern, Western and Japanese, and classical and new studies, and thus the resulting confrontation worsened as time went by. However, if we look at the debate in its various phases, we realize that from the 1920s to the 1930s, both sides had similar views on the use of literature to counteract Japanization and to preserve Chinese culture. In the final analysis, then, they held almost overlapping views when it came to national identity. In the 1940s, practical considerations made the debate using *Southern* as a forum acquire a more adaptive stance vis-à-vis official policies.[5] This was more evident among new writers like Lin Jingnan and marked a change in attitude from their anti-Japanese stance in the early stage of the debate in the 1920s.

The issues of "being universal" and "being Taiwanese" triggered much debate in the 1930s. Old writers, including Lian Heng, Zheng Kunwu, Huang Chunqing, and Zhang Chunfu, tried to shed the image of nobility for which they had been much criticized by new writers since the 1920s. Like the new writers, they too participated in promoting the Taiwan vernacular and nativist literature. They were involved in the collection of folk literature and in literary creation using the bamboo branch structure as well as other works rich in native color. This collaboration illustrates the fact that there were opportunities for cooperation for the two sides despite the confrontation.

In view of the above, although the Old-New Literatures Debate that had dragged on from 1924 to 1942 appeared as a confrontation, there were in reality opportunities for cooperation and actual collaboration between the opponents. The wide scope of the debate—ranging from literary canon to the Taiwanese vernacular and nativist literature movements, as well as the relationship between literature and national identity—contributed to the great complexity of the issues. Understanding the confrontation and collaboration between the opposing sides is necessary for a reevaluation of the history of Taiwanese literature, as well as of the roles and contributions of new and old writers of that period.

NOTES

1. Authors' years of birth and death will follow their names when they appear for the first time in this paper. This will be omitted if the information is unavailable, especially in the case of those using pen names.

2. In response to challenge from old writers, Zhang Wojun wrote an article entitled "Solving the Riddle" (*Jiepo menhulu* 揭破悶葫蘆). He writes: "It's been two months since the publication of my article 'Awful Taiwan Literary Circles.' ... I have not received any response so far and I sometimes think I lobbed a grenade into a mud pit."

3. The usage of the word "canon" is expanding in both its object and scope. It may now refer to legal or church decrees, biblical chapters recognized by the Protestant Church, and even literature teaching materials used in schools. In this paper, the word is used following David Wang Der-wei's definition, i.e., canon is "a generally accepted standard in literary creation and reading." Please see "The Birth of Canons" (*Dianlu de shengcheng*) in the book "How To Be Modern and Literature?" published by Wheatfield Publications (*Maitian chubanshe*) (Taipei, 1998), 30.

4. There are no extant copies of this writing by Huang Chunqing. For more on Huang's views on the Taiwan vernacular, see Yang 1931.

5. It is worth noting that the pro-Japanese opinion expressed in *Southern* by new writers did not represent the views of all new writers at that time. Some new writers with strong anti-Japanese sentiments, like Yang Lu, Lu Heruo, and others, did not participate in this phase of the debate.

REFERENCES

Chen Mingrou 陳明柔. 1996. "Old and New: Transformation in the Meaning of the Term 'Motherland.'" In *Collection of Papers on the Fortieth Anniversary of the Death of Zhang Wojun* 張我軍. Taipei: Council for Cultural Affairs.

Chen Xin 陳炘. 1920. "Literature and Duties." *Taiwan Youth* (台灣青年), July 12.

Huang Chunchao 黃春潮. 1941. "Mourning the Poet Zhang Chunfu." *Poetry News* (詩報), February 28.

Huang Chunqing 黃純青. 1941. "Society for Research in Classical Chinese Poetry." *Southern (Nanfang* 南方) 143.

———. 1934. "Theories on Reform of the Taiwan Dialect." *Lead Troops (Xianfa budui* 先鋒部隊) 1.

Huang Mei-Er 黃美娥, ed. 1998. *Complete Collection of Zhang Chunfu's Works (Zhang Chunfu quanji* 張純甫全集). Xinzhu: Xinzhu Cultural Center.

Huang Shihui 黃石輝. 1930. "How Not to Advocate Nativist Literature." *Our News* (吾報), 16 August 16–September 1.

———. 1942. "Reviewing Old Records: Taiwan Poets' Maladies." *Southern*, April 15.

Lai Ho 賴和. 1926. "Reflections Upon Reading 'Comparison Between Old and New Literatures.'" *Taiwan People's News*, January 24.

Lai Ziqing 賴子清. 1935. "Preface to Taiwan Poetry." *Taiwan Mellow Wine Poetry (Taiwan shichun* 台灣詩醇).

Laosheng Changtan. 1926. "On the So-Called New Poetry (Part 1)." *Taiwan Daily News* (台灣日日新報), February 25.

Lian Heng 連橫. 1992. *Refined Words: The Complete Collection of Lian Yatang.* Nantou: Taiwan Province Literature Reference Commission.

———. "Remnant Ink." *Taiwan Poetry Collection (Taiwan shihui)* 170.

Liao Hanchen 廖漢臣. 1942. "Responsibilities of Taiwan's Writers." *Southern*, November 1.

Lin Demo 林得模. 1942. "Reflections on the Foundation of Classical Poetry Societies." *Southern*, January 15.

Lin Jingnan 林荊南. 1942. "For Mr. Kunwu." *Southern*, September 1.

Lin Kefu 林克夫. 1942. "Our Mission in the Literary Debate." *Southern*, August 15.

Men Hulu Sheng 悶葫蘆生. 1925. "Deliberations on New Literature." *Taiwan Daily News*, January 5.

"Objectives on the Establishment of Taiwan Literary Societies." *Taiwan Literary Magazine (Taiwan wenyi congzhi)* 1.

Runhui sheng 潤徽生. 1923. "On Literature." *Taiwan People's News*, December 21.

Wang Der-wei David 王德威. *How To Be Modern? and What Literature? (Ruhe xiandai? Zenyang wenxue?)*. Taipei: Wheatfield Publications, 1998.

Wei Qingde 魏清德. 1915. "Poetry and Citizens' Character." *Taiwan Daily News*, July 8.

Wu Wenxing 吳文星. 1995. *A Study of Taiwan's Leading Class During the Japanese Colonial Period*. Taipei: Zhengzhong.

Xiu Chao 秀潮. 1923. "The Past, Present, and Future of Chinese New Literature." *Taiwan People's News*, July 15.

Xu Ziwen 許子文. 1927. "Maintaining Policies on Classical Studies." *Collection of the Congwen Literary Society* 1:32.

Yang Shuopeng 楊碩鵬. 1931. "Problems on Taiwan Dialect Reform." *Poetry News (Shipō)* 24 (November 15).

Yi Jizhe 一記者. 1926. "Comparison Between Old and New Literatures (Part 1)." *Taiwan Daily News*, January 3.

———. 1927. "Random Notes on My Casual Thoughts." *Taiwan People's News*, April 10.

Zhang Guangzheng 張光正. *Complete Works of Zhang Wojun (Zhang Wojun quanji)*. Beijing: Taihai Publications, 2000.

Zhang Wojun 張我軍. "Awful Taiwan Literary Circles." *Taiwan People's News*, February 24.

———. "Shedding Tears for the Taiwanese Literary World." *Taiwan People's News*, February 26.

Zheng Kunwu 鄭坤五. 1925. "A Letter to Zhang Yilang." *New Tainan News* (台南新報), January 29.

———. 1932. "A Few Words on Nativist Literature." *Southern Voice (Nanyin* 南音) 1:2.

[10]

COLONIALISM AND THE
PREDICAMENT OF IDENTITY

Liu Na'ou and Yang Kui as Men of the World

PENG HSIAO-YEN

On May 5, 1927, Liu Na'ou 劉吶鷗 (1905–1940), watching his younger brother leave for Tokyo from their home in Tainan 臺南, wrote in his diary, "Bon Voyage! O! frère!"[1] (Happy voyage! O, brother!; Liu's French). He himself, though thirsting to return to Shanghai, had to remain in Tainan until his grandmother's funeral. Inspired by Baudelaire,[2] Liu's seafaring feeling sounds a mumbo jumbo of cultural blending and affectation.

Born into a landlord's household and having lost his father when he was twelve, Liu Na'ou always had a problem with his mother, who represented the "feudal system" to him. Fortunately enough, his mother, though uneducated herself, did what most wealthy Taiwanese parents were doing at the time, sending her two sons and one daughter to Japan and China to study while generously providing for them. At the age of twenty-two Liu Na'ou was already an experienced traveler, constantly journeying between Taiwan, Japan, and China. Like the language in his diary, written in awkward Chinese studded with English, French, Japanese, German, and Taiwanese expressions, he was very much "a man of the world," a phrase concocted by one of his closest friends after his much-disputed murder in 1940.[3] This phrase was intended to connote an artist who aspires to artistic freedom and perfection while transcending national boundaries.

Indeed, his everyday life was by no means free from limitations. Born in colonial Taiwan in 1905 and a Japanese by nationality, in 1920 he transferred from the Presbyterian School in Tainan to the high school division of Aoyama College in

Tokyo, because there were limited opportunities for a colonized citizen to continue higher learning in the colony.[4] He continued his studies at the Kōtō gakubu 高等学部 (advanced learning division) of Aoyama College 青山学院 in 1923 and graduated with honors from the English Department in March 1926.[5] In the summer of 1926 he entered the special French program at L'Université L'Aurore in Shanghai and became Dai Wangshu 戴望舒's classmate; Shi Zhecun 施蟄存 and Du Heng 杜衡 entered the program the following year.[6] Liu's diary relates how in January of 1927 these students, who would later make a name for Shanghai neosensationism, dreamed together about an aborted plan of establishing a journal called *Jindai xin* 近代心 (Modern heart), which, incorporating illustrations and lighted-hearted vignettes, was intended to bridge the chasm between elitism and popular tastes.[7] Such a dream would not come true until December 1932, when *Furen huabao* 婦人畫報 (Women's pictorial) was established by the cartoonist Guo Jianying 郭建英 with Liu's coterie's support.

During the time Liu Na'ou was in Shanghai he pretended to be Fukienese, mainly because in the semicolonized metropolis in China a Taiwanese was likely to be suspected of being a Japanese spy.[8] There were contemporaries, such as Ye Lingfeng 葉靈鳳, who thought he was half-Japanese.[9] A man with multiple identities imposed on him, he eventually chose to be a self-styled modernist, an identity that accorded well with his personality and lifestyle as a dandy.

Liu was not alone in his experiences of diaspora and in resorting to art to defy the predicament of identity during the Japanese occupation. Yang Kui 楊逵, also born in Tainan in 1905, was the son of a laborer who made tin utensils such as candlesticks and plates for a living.[10] In 1915 as a youth he witnessed Japanese cannons and armed forces marching in front of his house on the way to suppress a local revolt.[11] Realizing how the Japanese distorted history and law to rule the colony, he decided to resort to the power of literature to reestablish the truth about the events of the time. In a 1982 interview saying that the Japanese colonial rulers had treated the Taiwanese fighters against colonialism as hooligans and rebels, he stated that it had been his intention to point out that injustice in his works.[12] In 1924 he dropped out of Tainan Second High School and went to Tokyo. The following year he entered the night school of Japan University to study literature and arts, supporting himself by working part-time during the day. While in Tokyo he participated in demonstrations against colonialism and was once jailed for three days, together with thirty-six Koreans.

Sensing the urgency of the socialist movement in Taiwan, Yang gave up his study and returned home in 1927 to join the Cultural Association Movement.[13] In no time he became the foremost of the proletarian writers on the island, undertaking to propagate European and Japanese proletarianism while urging his fellow proletarianists to be "writers of the world" (see discussion below). Throughout his life he was in and out of prison because of his socialist beliefs, which, because they demanded allegiance to the international proletariat instead of the nation, were not welcomed by either the Japanese colonial government or the postwar Nationalist regime in Taiwan. Unsurprisingly, as an activist and writer during the most turbulent years in Taiwan's socio-political history, he ended up in jail twelve times, ten times during the Japanese occupation and twice under the Nationalist government. The last time kept him incarcerated for twelve years, from 1949 to 1961.

Liu Na'ou and Yang Kui were born in the same city in the same year, but into two distinct classes. Although both chose literature to be their vocation, their aesthetic preferences form an intriguing juxtaposition: modernism and proletarianism. During the 1920s and the 1930s, these two dominant cultural trends exerted such an impact globally that it is hard to imagine that these two young men from Taiwan, in their quest for intellectual enlightenment in such metropolitan cities as Tokyo and Shanghai, would not have been influenced by them. Liu began his literary career in Shanghai with a few mediocre stories written in the proletarian vein, while the bookstore he established in 1929 with his own funds was a rendezvous for leftist intellectuals before it was eventually closed down by the Nationalist government.[14] He switched to modernism almost immediately, because he was tired of the proletarian emphasis on content at the expense of form.[15] On the other hand, Yang Kui found the modernists "indulging in petty skills"[16] and "groaning without being ill."[17] Yang's relentless support of "*kuso* realism" (feces realism), a phrase used by Japanese proletarian leaders to highlight the propensity of realist literature for disclosing the dark side of reality, bespeaks Yang's lifetime commitment to proletarianism.[18] The distinction of taste manifested here is closely connected to, if not determined by, the social classes in which they were born and brought up.

Class consciousness, a complex psychological state that involves identity and value judgment, is not easy to clarify. The observation Bourdieu makes in *La distinction* may provide us with a point of departure for our investigation here: distinct lifestyles and distinct tastes for culture form a system of evaluations, securely institutionalized by the education system, which operates both to identify and to maintain social difference.[19] A profoundly political discourse, taste functions as a legitimizer of social difference as well as a marker of class. Modernism and proletarianism maintain a strict distinction of lifestyles and tastes, which Liu Na'ou and Yang Kui found congenial to the classes they belonged to. The aesthetic choice each made is the result of the "system of evaluations" that each was acculturated to and trained to sustain.

For Liu Na'ou and Yang Kui, acquiring the class values of modernism or proletarianism required a complex process of acculturation, which is "a process of intercultural borrowing marked by the continuous transmission of traits and elements between diverse peoples and resulting in new and blended patterns."[20] While it was a prerequisite for each to imitate and show allegiance to international modernism or proletarianism, at the same time the modernist or proletarian traits and elements manifested in each were inevitably blended with the characteristics of their own cultural traditions and personal histories. Liu, disguised as a Fukienese in Shanghai with Baudelaire as his mentor, or Yang, always following the teachings of his Japanese and European counterparts such as Abramovich Lapidus and Funahashi Seiichi, remained Taiwanese at heart, though certainly transformed. The "new and blended patterns" manifested in Liu's modernism and Yang's proletarianism were no longer the original patterns found in Baudelaire or Funehashi, while our two writers, acculturated in these international trends through the experiences of diaspora, were in a sense emancipated from the limited visions of insulated islanders.

Denouncing the injustice of the colonial policy and the loss caused by exile, forced or self-willed, does not prevent one from recognizing the modernization brought about by colonialism, which benefits the colonized as well as the colonizer. Nor does it prevent one from appreciating the liberating capacity resulting from the experiences of diaspora. The question is, if for writers such as Yang Kui and Liu Na'ou the aesthetics of universal literary laws created the possibility of liberating the self, how did they come to terms with the particulars? Terry Eagleton, dealing with a similar situation confronting Irish writers, points out that the contradictions are not so irresolvable that "Particularity is either suppressed in the totality of universal Reason, the concrete Irish subject sublated to a citizen of the world, or celebrated as a unique, irreducible state of being impenetrable to all alien Enlightenment rationality."[21] Indeed, while governed by a universal aesthetic law, the work of art manifested in each artist is inscribed with individual emotions, sensations, and impulses as well as local, regional, and national particularities.

For 1930s Taiwan there was no totalizing vision that could easily reconcile the radical view of individual enlightenment and the regionalist particularity of twentieth-century Taiwanese Nationalist consciousness, especially when that consciousness was divided among Japan the colonial sovereignty, China the motherland, and Taiwan the native land. As Seamus Deane puts it when he refers to the Irish condition, it is not oppositions to be erased or a theoretical paradox to be resolved, "it is a condition to be passionately lived."[22]

Liu Na'ou and Yang Kui did live passionately through the contradictions facing their artistic lives during the Japanese occupation. Liu, as a dandy philandering in Shanghai, and Yang, earning his living as a gardener in Taiwan, infused their personal tastes and lives into their literary beliefs. Their respective literary practices, inseparable from the literary or socialist activities that implicated them in the semicolonial politics in Shanghai or colonial politics in Taiwan, eventually brought dangers to their lives. Liu's death by assassination and Yang's constant imprisonment bespeak the insurmountable laws of semicolonial or colonial politics that entangled individual identities while leaving universal aesthetic laws powerless.

As far apart as they seem, modernism and proletarianism have something basic in common: both ideologies originate from class identity. That proletarianism is a class ideology is a given. That modernism is a class ideology, on the other hand, needs justification. We can tackle the problem by examining the fact that Liu Na'ou's modernism is most effectively manifested in his dandyism.

A dandy by definition is a man with means and leisure, who pays meticulous attention to his dress and appearance. Liu had particular tastes about his clothes, as can be seen in his 1927 diary. It was his habit to go to specific stores for different styles of clothes, all tailor-made. For instance, on April 5 he writes: "Had a suit and two summer outfits made at Wang Qingchang 王慶昌's"; on December 8 he writes: "Had a tuxedo made at Wang Shunchang 王順昌's"; and on December 12: "Tried on the clothes at Wang Shunchang's."[23] In a family film, "The Man Who Has the Camera," probably taken in the mid-1930s in Shanghai, Liu is seen in different scenes wearing a white suit and a white hat, apparently his favorite outfit.[24] In addition, he is a devout dancer with the nickname "The Dancing King," regularly frequenting dance halls and exercising dance steps with his friends as well as studying dance manuals to perfect his skill. For instance, on February 3 Liu writes, "Returned to his home and taught him fox-trot."[25] Here "him" refers to his childhood friend from Tainan, Lin Chengshui 林澄水, who was at the time studying in Shanghai. On Liu's August reading list there is a dancing manual with an English title "Dancing do's and don'ts."[26]

Dandyism in Liu is a lifestyle and a matter of taste; it is the taste of the affluent class in metropolitan Shanghai, and the new aristocracy in democratic China. As much as Liu exhibits a fine specimen of a Shanghai dandy in the 1930s, however, we should not forget that the lineage of the dandy can be easily traced to Baudelaire in Paris or Oscar Wilde in London in the latter half of the nineteenth century. Baudelaire, though not exactly a dandy himself, wrote the single treatise on dandyism that defined the dandy as a species. The dandy as a species has crossed the boundaries of nations and time.

The thing to be noted is that the performance of the dandy, no less than a task, needs constant practice in order to achieve perfection. As Foucault argues in "What Is Enlightenment," the dandy is the quintessence of modernity, while to be a dandy requires an "ascetic elaboration of the self"[27] (pp. 41–42). For Foucault, modernity is an attitude, or an *ethos*. It is a "mode of relating to contemporary reality; a voluntary choice made by certain people ... a way of thinking and feeling; a way of acting and behaving that at one and the same time marks a relation of belonging and presents itself as a task." Diction such as "ascetic elaboration" and "task" denotes the idea that being a dandy requires a kind of rigorous discipline similar to that of a religion. If we check the passages titled "La modernité" and

"Le dandy" in Baudelaire's *Le peintre de la vie moderne* (The painter of modern life), we realize that Foucault's interpretation of modernity comes mainly from Baudelaire, while the meaning of the "ascetic elaboration of the self," which is in fact the central idea in Foucault's *History of Sexuality*, becomes much clearer.

In "Le dandy" the dandy is defined as "l'homme rich, oisif" (the rich, idle man), whose only occupation is "l'élégance," and who is raised in luxury and, from youth on, accustomed to the obedience of other people. He enjoys at all times "une physionomie distincte" (a distinct appearance), with a love for "distinction." In addition, dandyism is "une institution vague," meaning it is an institution without written laws. According to Baudelaire, dandyism as an institution is "en dehors des lois" (outside of laws), but has its own rigorous laws to which all its subjects strictly submit themselves, in spite of the fieriness and independence of their characters. For the adepts in the unwritten doctrines of this institution the main driving force is "le besoin ardent de se faire une originalité" (the ardent need to make oneself an original; p. 710).

Besides the idea that dandyism is an "institution," Baudelaire also points out that dandyism verges on "spiritualisme et ... stoicisme." In his mind, all the extravagant taste and material elegance a dandy subjects himself to are only a symbol of the "supériorité aristocratique de son esprit" (aristocratic superiority of his spirit). Baudelaire claims that dandyism is a sort of religion, with the most rigorous doctrine of all religions, namely that of elegance and originality. According to him, dandyism appears mostly in transitory periods, when democracy is not yet fully in force and aristocracy is partially faltering, with a view to engaging in "le projet de fonder une espèce d'aristocratie" (the project of founding a new species of aristocracy). Hence Foucault's claim that the dandy is a new aristocrat in democracy.[28] Thus dandyism, an institution with the unwritten doctrine of elegance and originality, is a class marked by the distinction of taste that separates itself from the mediocre and the trivial. (For Baudelaire, being trivial is an irreparable dishonor.) One can also easily see that Bourdieu shares with Baudelaire the idea of the distinction of taste.

In addition, dandyism embodies a particular attitude toward woman, as one can tell from the passage titled "La femme" (Woman) in *The Painter of Modern Life*. A dandy like Liu Na'ou is a woman lover and a relentless misogynist at the same time, in whose mind only man is capable of intellectual thinking and performance, while woman, a creature indulging in lust and using men to gratify her sexual desire, is totally alien to the realm of intellect. On the other hand, ironically enough, a dandy like Liu, a frequenter of dance halls and brothels, is always involved in carnal relationships with women. As Baudelaire puts it, "Si je parle de l'amour à propos du dandysme, c'est que l'amour est l'occupation naturelle des oisifs. Mais le dandy ne vise pas à l'amour comme but spécial" (If I speak of love in regard to dandyism, it is that love is the natural occupation of the idle. But the dandy does not aim at love as a special goal; p. 710).

From Liu Na'ou's 1927 diary one can tell that the image of woman as *femme fatale*, alluring but destructive at the same time, is deeply rooted in his psyche. That in his diary he should call his wife a "vampire" sapping his energy and blood is illuminating. She was one year older than he was and his first cousin, their mothers being sisters. They were married in 1922, when Liu was only seventeen years old. Right from the beginning he was dissatisfied with the marriage, the reason being partly that it was an arranged marriage, a "feudal remnant" in his eye, and partly that the two were incompatible in education and personality. Like most women of her time, his wife was educated at home by private tutors. The fact that the two did not get along can be told from his wife's scarce appearances in his 1927 diary. In January of that year, having finished his French courses at L'Université L'Aurore in Shanghai, he was living the leisurely life of a dandy there, idling and philandering, without doing anything specific. She is first mentioned in the diary entry of January 17, in which Liu complains that her letter in Japanese is so poorly written that he can hardly understand what she intends to say. On April 17 he returned from Shanghai to Tainan for his grandmother's funeral, but he does not mention his wife in the diary until May 18. This is also the second time she appears in the diary.

In the entry of that day and the next one his description gradually takes her as a representative of "woman," or even *femme fatale*, in general. In the May 18 entry he says, "Ah! Marriage is truly the gate to hell. ... Woman is dumb, good for nothing. ... Ah! that I should have been raped by her, the insatiable man-beast, the goblin-like vampire, knowing nothing except indulgence in sexual desire!" [29] In the following entry he says,

Women, whatever types they are, may be said to be the emblem of sex. Their life and existence depend entirely on the gratification of sexual desire. At the time of ... compared with what men can feel, how much more powerful is their orgasm! The center of their thought, behavior, and act is sex. Therefore besides sex they are completely devoid of intellectual knowledge. They don't like to learn things and they are incapable of learning. You see, aren't most women idiots and stupid jerks? Her stupidity really makes me mad. [30]

One can compare this passage with the description of *femmes fatales* in Baudelaire's "Spleen et idéal" and see the similarity:

Et vous, femmes, hélas! pâles comme des cierges,
Que ronge et que nourrit la débauche, et vous, vierges,
Du vice maternel traînant l'hérédité
Et toutes les hideurs de la fécondité! [31]
(And you, women, alas! pale like the candles,
gnawed and nourished by debauchery, and you, virgins,

From maternal vice dragging along heredity
and all the hideousness of fecundity!)

In Liu's mind woman, incapable of true feelings or love, wants nothing but sex, while her sexual drive more often than not causes man's downfall. In the vocabulary of the dandy, man is the emblem of intellect and ruler of the spiritual, and woman is a sex symbol and physical creature. To him a woman has only two functions, all tied to her body: to bear children and to make love.

Yet the dandy is also a keen observer of woman's physical form, which to him has a deeper meaning. In Liu's diary we can see that he is constantly strolling the street, looking for images of women that would meet his taste. Like Baudelaire's "À une passante," these women are passersby, or chance encounters in a café or a brothel, unknown to him, but all of them reveal the same quality: an intensity of desire that draws out their beholder's passions more than their own. Observing a woman, he is not concerned with what she thinks or feels, since to the dandy a woman is an unthinking and unfeeling creature; rather, he is concerned with her physical form with all its adornments and refinery adding to her allurement, which is the quintessence of "the 'heroic' aspect of the present moment," in Foucault's words.[32] Once in a brothel, looking at a young prostitute who awaits his patronage, Liu sighs, "Ah, My hungry heart! Ah, the translucent eyes that I can hardly devour, the face of *Modernité!*"[33] As Foucault's interpretation of Baudelaire's *flâneur*, he "has an aim loftier than that of a mere *flâneur*," who is "the idle, strolling spectator ... satisfied to keep his eyes open, to pay attention and to build up a storehouse of memories." In contrast, he is "looking for that quality which [is called] 'modernity.'"[34]

If we compare Foucault's words with Baudelaire's definition of *le flâneur* in "La modernité," we can see that he nearly quotes the latter verbatim. Baudelaire equates the modernist to a loner:

> [C]e solitaire doué d'une imagination active, toujours voyageant à travers *le grand désert d'hommes*, a un but plus élevé que celui d'un pur flâneur, un but plus général, autre que le plaisir fugitif de la circonstance. Il cherche ce quelque chose qu'on nous permettra d'appeler *la modernité*. (p. 694)[35]
>
> (This loner endowed with an active imagination, always voyaging across the great desert of men, has an aim more elevated than that of a pure *flâneur*, an aim more general than the fugitive pleasure of the moment. He is looking for the thing that we might call modernity.)

From the point of view of the laboring class, the *flâneur* seems idle and unproductive, but in fact it is his vocation to stroll the city, to *flâner*. His idleness is his labor.[36] As *l'observateur*, his imagination transforms the physical form he sees into something spiritual. Woman as a real-life being is not what attracts him; it is the woman in his imagination, seen through the dandy's eye. Thus to the dandy the complex image of woman is bewildering. No words are more telling than Baudelaire's own in "La femme": "C'est une espèce d'idol, stupide peut-être, mais éblouissante, enchanteresse, qui tient les destinées et les volontés suspendues à ses regards" (She is a kind of idol, stupid perhaps, but dazzling and bewitching, who holds wills and destinies suspended on her glance) (pp. 713–714).

One more passage from Liu's 1927 diary will suffice to illustrate how women's images are transformed through the aesthetics of the dandy. On November 10, when he was visiting Beijing, he went to see the performance of Jin Youqin 金友琴, a renowned Peking opera singer. Even though he meant to see the performance of a particular actress, in his description of her it is clear that he looked upon her as the representative of the collective noun "Peking women." In other words, Jin Youqin in his imagination was not a woman endowed with personal thoughts, emotions, or life history, but a representative of Peking women. His association of ideas with this particular Peking woman's voice and body discloses his prejudices against women in general. First, according to him, the idea that Peking women are good at speaking is probably wrong, because speech belongs to the realm of the intellect, and one needs to be well educated in order to be good at speech. In his view, since Peking women are totally uneducated, they cannot possibly be good at speech; they are talkative. Second, even though Peking women are talkative, their beautiful voices are a pleasure to listen to for men. Third, this particular Peking woman's voice reminds him of the reality of the panegyric "talking like swallows and singing like nightingales." But, according to him, this voice only reaches the realm of reality. In other words, in his mind's eye Peking women (or any other women) are incapable of being associated with spiritual beauty and sublimation.[37]

Liu's prejudices against women as shown in the aesthetics of a dandy certainly mold the images of women constructed in his work. This is true of the images of woman in the stories written by Shanghai neosensationists in general, as amply illustrated by Mu Shiying 穆時英's "Craven 'A,'" in which the features and body of the woman gazed at by the male narrator are turned into a sight-seeing spot fit for men's short visits.

The male narrator of "Craven 'A'" uses the trope of "a map of a country" to describe the woman he gazes at. As she sits and smokes alone in a café, the eyes of the woman are in his view "two lakes" that sometimes get icy cold, sometimes hot beyond boiling point. Her mouth is a "volcano" that spews forth the smoke and odor of "Craven 'A,'" the foreign cigarette she is smoking. Inside the volcano the milky larva (teeth) and the flame in the middle (tongue) can be seen. "The people here are still quite primitive, using men as sacrifice at their volcano festival. For travelers this country is by no means a safe place," says the narrator. Then he describes the landscape under the "thin clouds" of a black-and-white checkered design, apparently a blouse made of semitransparent material. As a result the "purple peaks" (nipples) of the "two hills ostensibly juxtaposing each other on the plain" seem to "protrude from the clouds."

Then the lower part of the map, blocked from view by the table the woman sits at, is likened to the landscape of the "South," which is even more enchanting than that of the "North." The narrator imagines how the "two breakwaters" (legs) under the table join to form a "triangular alluvial plain," and how the "important harbor" with "the majestic entrance of the giant steam boat" arouses "billows and splashes on the prow." When the narrator finds out the woman's name from an acquaintance, he says, "I know many of her stories. Almost all of my friends have traveled in that country. Since the traffic there is convenient, almost all of them manage to visit the whole country in one or two days. … Experienced ones are able to land on the harbor right from the start. … Some sojourn for one or two days, while others stay on for a week. When they return they boast to me about the alluring landscape of that country, and all look upon it as a wonderful sightseeing spot for short visits." [38]

Here we have a description of the "New Woman" typical to 1930s Shanghai, in a literary mode unique to the neosensationists. The story describes the kind of man-and-woman relationship typical of metropolitan Shanghai, in which no love is involved. It is mainly a one-night stand, purely for fun on both sides. There is no psychological stress or ethical judgment, unlike the stories of erotic love by Creation writers such as Yu Dafu 郁達夫 or Zhang Ziping 張資平. For instance, the male protagonist in Yu Dafu's "Lost Lamb," tormented by his love for the fickle actress who walked out on him, ends up in an asylum. The new women in Zhang Ziping's stories, though aspiring for sexual liberation, always lament and complain about the inability to be really free in a society still bound by traditional ethics. In contrast the light-hearted theme of neosensationist stories is marked by a playful tempo, as if the scenes were flickering with the male narrator's salacious eye seeing through the camera. A woman under his scrutiny becomes a mere object of desire, with all the parts of her body serving to provide men with pleasure. Always viewed from the outside, it is no wonder that her heart and mind are a mystery to the reader as well as the narrator.

In contrast to realistic stories such as those written by Creation writers, which often resort to the technique of psycho-narration to render the characters' psychology transparent,[39] the characters in neosensationist stories as a rule are a-psychological. We are told their looks, behavior patterns, and words, but their psychology remains opaque. As a result these characters are almost like actants in the stories, often without names. Even with names they are interchangeable. It makes no difference at all if one character is moved from one story to another, since all the characters are endowed with the same single character trait: seductiveness. Thus a woman in the aesthetics of dandyism is not a real woman who has heart and feelings, but a collective noun with a symbolic meaning beyond the real woman herself. Looked at from another perspective, these characters share the nameless characteristic of the masses that were becoming the central subject matter of proletarian literature at the time. The main difference is that the characters in neosensationist stories are members of the bourgeois class enjoying cosmopolitan life, whereas those in proletarian literature are either lower-class people described as victims of social injustice or the bourgeois meant to be targets of attack.

With outer looks becoming the one most important element to describe, it does not come as a surprise that fashion and material elegance turn out to be the focus of attention in neosensationist stories. The dandy is a species of man who believes in artifice rather than nature, as Baudelaire states in "Éloge du maquillage (Eulogy on make-up)," "la nature n'enseigne rien, ou presque rien. ... La nature ne peut conseiller que le crime. ... La vertu, au contraire, est *artificielle* (Nature doesn't teach anything, or almost nothing. ... Nature can advise nothing but the crime. ... Virtue, on the other hand, is artifice)."[40] Hence the dandy's heavy dependence on materiality. Fashion, the quintessence of materiality, reinforces woman's beauty, of course. Yet fashion is by no means an end in itself; it is the symptom of taste, which is the manifestation of the ideal in human mind to surpass and reform nature, where the unrefined, the terrestrial, and the squalid are accumulated. For Baudelaire, fashion is "une déformation sublime de la nature" (sublime deformation of nature). Fashion should not be considered in itself; it should be imagined when vitalized and vivified by the women who wear it (p. 716).

The new women in neosensationist stories are exactly like mannequins that display fashion and make it alive. They usually wear modernized *qipao* 旗袍 (Chinese gowns) or Western dresses, which were *à la mode* in 1930s Shanghai. Yet fashion in these stories is certainly more than an end in itself: it is a marker of class. The hooligan in Mu Shiying's story "Shouzhi 手指" (Fingers), with an envious eye for new women, describes in fitful ejaculation their fashionable outfit: "Today they crave Western products, tomorrow National goods. Their *qipao*, either long or short, in soft silk, satin, American chiffon, or Indian rayon ... fashion shows, exhibitions ... silk stockings, high-heeled satin shoes, tea-time dresses, party dresses, wedding gowns, salacious dresses, casual wear, short wear ..."[41] Fashion, an inseparable part of the new woman, adds to her dazzle and enchantment, while marking her off as belonging to a class that the hooligan both envies and hates. Not only does the class distinction here involve the differences of taste between the high and the low, and the bourgeois and the proletariat, but it involves the native and the foreign. It is the conflict between nationalism and colonialism that is at work here.

Shanghai with its many foreign concessions was a semicolony where foreign infiltration was felt everywhere. In Liu Na'ou's 1927 diary we see an ordinary citizen's daily life in Shanghai inconvenienced by English or Japanese soldiers who set up road blocks or check people's identifications.[42] There are entries in which he expresses the fascination he felt for the enchanting hybridity of the semicolonial human landscape there, as the January 12 entry, where he engages in a eulogy of Shanghai:

> Shanghai, o! Shanghai the enchanteresse!
> ….
> O what a golden pit you are! O Land of beauties! Red, white, yellow,
> dark, a shaft of light in the night, from the hands of narrow waists!
> A smile with floating gaze, the hybridity of short hair and bare knees.[43]

In contrast, there are also passages that show his aversion to foreign presences. For instance in the January 19 entry, after mentioning an unhappy episode with a Caucasian woman in the tram, he says, "An eye for an eye, the fire of hatred, you devil-like Caucasian women! Stand steady, or the oriental man burning with indescribable fire would rush you to the tramway hell!"[44] While Liu does not seem to sympathize with Caucasians, he does not feel akin to the Japanese way of life, either. In June of 1927 before he returned from Taiwan to Shanghai, he visited Tokyo and studied French and Latin briefly at the Athena-Francais Language School there, but was bored and missed Shanghai tremendously. He writes in the June 17 entry, "In these few days I feel suffocated. There is nothing serious, but I simply don't like the Japanese way!"[45]

Reading through Liu's diary one senses that on the one hand the diarist feels genuine resentment toward foreign exploitation and colonial expansion, while on the other he undeniably enjoys the cosmopolitan atmosphere and luxurious foreign products. The new women in neosensationist stories in fact share with him a fascination for things foreign. As if to highlight their colonial connotations, these women as a rule have foreign looks, with "a small square face in Parisian style," as the woman in "Craven 'A,'" or "a slender, straight Greek nose," as the one in Liu Na'ou's "Youxi 遊戲" (Game).[46] Coupled with Westernized fashion and their foreign looks, their love of foreign cars, cigarettes, and outdoor Western sports culminates in their image as the consummation of the modern in 1930s metropolitan Shanghai.

———— ∞∞∞ ————

Dandyism as a matter of taste is also manifested in Liu Na'ou's preferences for friends and associates. The year 1927, when Liu wrote the diary extant today, was also the year the Nationalist regime started the Northern Expedition and Party Purge. In the 1920s and the 1930s flocks of writers immigrated to Shanghai either to take shelter from the war in the north or to seek opportunities for artistic development there, since, with big publishing companies continually moving from Beijing to Shanghai starting in the early 1920s, it had become the new cultural center in China. Famous literary men such as Lu Xun 魯, who came to Shanghai in September 1927, and Shen Congwen 沈從文, who moved there in early 1928, gathered in the metropolis and fought for their livelihood. Teaching and writing were the main sources for them to earn a living, as writing gradually emerged as a full-time profession during that period.

Liu Na'ou, who came in 1926 and lived the life of a dandy there, did not get along with writers like Lu Xun or Shen Congwen. Or one should say more exactly, he did not bother to associate with them at all. He was intimate with friends from Taiwan, frolicking with them together and often letting them stay in his apartment. They included schoolmates from the Presbyterian School of Tainan and the renowned advocate of the vernacular literature movement in Taiwan, Huang Chaoqin, who had studied in Tokyo and Illinois and had written in 1923 one of the earliest important treatises on that subject.[47] He was at that time looking for a position in Shanghai and from 1928 on would work for the Overseas Chinese Bureau of the Ministry of Foreign Affairs of the Nationalist government.

In addition, Liu was closely involved with friends he had met at L'Aurore. They worked as a team in his bookstore, and after work they would frequent dance halls and brothels, ogling women together. In the dance halls he was always marveled at when he tangoed; people would stop dancing, spread out, and leave room for him to perform. He taught his L'Aurore friends Japanese whenever there was time in between work and play. Even during a trip to Beijing with Dai Wangshu from September 28 to December 3, they still continued their Japanese lessons.[48] They were held together by ties of common interests and taste.

Of the leaders of the many literary coteries in Shanghai, Liu and his companions chose to befriend Shao Xunmei 邵洵美, who, also from a wealthy family, was a dandy of great renown like Liu. Shao's residence in Shanghai, a palace-like marble building and a legend in itself,[49] became a salon where literary men and artists gathered for meals and conversation.[50] Among the distinguished guests constantly invited were people like Xu Zhimo 徐志摩, Zeng Jinke 曾今可, Zhang Ruogu 張若谷, and Xu Beihong 徐悲鴻, besides Liu and his friends.[51]

In contrast, Liu's coterie and Lu Xun's never hit it off. There could have been, in fact, a great many opportunities for these two parties to meet and associate with each other. When Liu was experimenting with proletarian literature during the late 1920s, *Wugui lieche* 無軌列車 (Trackless train), the journal he established with Dai and Shi Zhicun, often published Feng Xuefeng 馮雪峰's articles. Feng belonged to Lu Xun's coterie, but Liu and his friends never had direct contact with Lu. Shi did write Lu some letters concerning matters of the bookstore, but thought he was a "narrow-minded man."[52] As a matter of fact, Shi was living two blocks from Lu Xun's house at the time, but they somehow or other missed the chance to get to know each other, or they never intended to, since the two parties lived such distinct lives and developed gradually diametrically opposed literary beliefs.[53]

When the *haipai* 海派 (Shanghai types) controversy broke out in the early 1930s, Lu Xun and Shen Congwen, though they never befriended each other, both became fervent enemies of Shanghai types. From the language they used in the debate, one senses that the contention lay as much, if not more, in taste as in literary convictions. As a matter of fact, during the time of the controversy, there were no such literary schools as the Shanghai School or the Beijing School; the formation of these two schools of writers was a later invention. The controversy concerned mainly the incorporation of popular taste into literary works and the commercialization of literature in Shanghai, as opposed to the "serious" May Fourth literary tradition represented by the north, which Shen embraced so dearly even while he was living in Shanghai and had to conform to the popular taste there one way or other.[54]

Shen connected Creation writers such as Yu Dafu and Zhang Ziping and neo-sensationist writers such as Mu Shiying with the Saturday School writers by calling the latter the "Shanghai types" and their followers the "New Shanghai types." Shen said that Zhang Ziping, like the Saturday School writers, was a master of "low, vulgar taste," or "popular taste." He adds, "The most suitable place of appreciating Zhang Ziping's works is at the desk of those college students who, while looking at the beauty queens of Girls' Colleges in *Liangyou* 良友 (The young companion), talk about ways of kissing in the movies."[55] As for Mu Shiying, Shen says, "His works are almost like romance (with man-and-woman relationships as the subject matter, romance in Shanghai, so to speak). It is suitable for him to write works for pictorials or design magazines, or write for women, movies, and playful magazines. The city has made this writer, and yet limited him at the same time."[56] One is instantly reminded of *Women's pictorial*, to which Liu and his coterie constantly contributed articles.

The ridicule, and even contempt, in Shen's attitude toward the Shanghai types is unmistakable. Lu Xun, who did not have any thing nice to say about either of the two contending parties, on the other hand, pointed out the stereotypical views connected with regional prejudices, stating that "the literati in Beijing is akin to officials, those in Shanghai to merchants. ... In a word, the 'Beijing types' are the protégés of officials, while the 'Shanghai types "are the protégés of businessmen."[57]

If the neosensationists were despised for their metropolitan taste, Shen showed remarkable perception in singling out their fetishizing of the "New Woman," who in their stories represented the spirit of modernity in Shanghai. It was the spirit of an affluent society marked by the aesthetics of commodities, a cult of things Euro-American, light-hearted entertainment, and the fanfare of *la bourgeoisie*. It was the popular taste promoted by pictorials such as *Companion* and *Women's Pictorial*, a taste shared by college girl students, call girls, taxi dancers, and gentlemen's and merchants' wives, concubines, and daughters. In fact, we see the representations of these women not only in neosensationist stories, but in contemporary writers' works such as Mao Dun's *Ziye* 子夜 (Midnight, 1933), in which the call girl Xu Manli 徐曼麗, personifying the *carpe diem* spirit of the age, pursues sexual pleasures till the end of the story despite the ravages of civil war and the financial crises that destroy people's lives.

In such stories the women become enemies of the proletariat; they exist simply to highlight the necessity of proletarian revolution. In 1935 the leftist movie "Xin nuxing 新女性" (The new woman), featuring the famous actress Ruan Lingyu 阮玲玉, depicts a decadent woman writer who commits suicide in the end. In the movie the hard-working women laborers who are always in the background throw into relief the decay and decline of the woman intellectual who indulges in sensual pleasures and pursues her own destruction. The fact that the star Ruan Lingyu did commit suicide shortly after the movie was released[58] seemed to point to the apocalyptic vision of art and its inevitable unification with life.

After Liu Na'ou reverted from proletarianism to modernism during the late 1920s and the early 1930s, the collision between his coterie and the proletarianists eventually erupted in the "hard films/soft films" debate. In 1933 Liu, together with Huang Jiamo 黃嘉謨, a friend from Taiwan, and others, established the journal *Xiandai dianying* 現代電影 (*Modern Screen*; the editors' own English title). In the mission statement of the journal Huang states that with the importation of foreign movies into the Chinese market, the editors of the journal hope that Chinese will "produce movies that represent the Chinese spirit and taste," so that Chinese movies can be exported to the world and compete with foreign movies.[59] One article in the same issue points out that Chinese enterprises, especially the movie industry, were facing bankruptcy because of "the infiltration of foreign capital and the penetration of imperial culture. ... This explains the bankruptcy of our national capital in a semicolony."[60] In 1933 and 1934 there was in China a general movement to promote national products and enterprises in order to boycott Euro-American products and prevent further draining of the agricultural population, which would eventually deplete the rural areas.

Besides answering the call to promote national enterprises, Huang makes it clear that *Modern Screen* is completely free from the control of any ideology or the demand of propaganda, implying the existence of unwanted ideological domination by revolutionary literature and nationalist literature at the time. He points out that the movie is more than a kind of entertainment; it is "the highest class entertainment in modern times." It is in the second issue of the journal that Liu Na'ou further spells out the entertainment function of the movie. He says that it functions "like sleeping pills that help people escape reality. ... If we eliminated from current movies the sleeping pills like sentimentalism, irrationalism, fashionableness, intellectual fun, and romanticism and fantasy, would not this favorite of modern man become a great desert?"[61]

For Liu the success of a movie depends not on its content, but on the way the subject matter is handled and adapted into the movie. In other words, it is the form and autonomy of art that matters.[62] From the fifth issue on, he wrote a series of articles on movie techniques, for instance, "Dianying jiezou jianlun 電影節奏簡論" (A brief essay on the rhythm of the camera), "Kaimaila jigou—weizhi jiaodu jineng lun 開麥拉機構—位置角度機能論" (On the mechanism of the camera—the function of angle and position),[63] as a way to demonstrate his thesis that technique and form were everything for the movie. The article that directly triggered the debate with the leftist camp, though, was Huang Jiamou's "Yingxing yingpian yu ruanxing yingpian 硬性影片與軟性影片" (Hard films and soft films) in December 1933, in which he complained that the leftist "revolutionary movies" had "hardened" the soft films of the movie, and as a result meaningless slogans and didacticism were driving away audiences who used to throng to the movies. He emphasized the entertainment function of the movie by saying, "Movies are the ice-cream for the eye, and the sofa for the soul."[64]

Liu's coterie's theories met with severe opposition from the leftist writer Tang Na, who published in 1934 a series of articles in *Chen Bao* 晨報 (Morning post) rebutting their emphasis of form over content. In the article "Qingsuan ruanxing dianying lun—ruanxing lunzhe de quwei zhuyi 清算軟性電影論—軟性論者的趣味主義" (Purging the soft-film theory—the entertainment theory of soft-film theorists), which was serialized from June 19 to 27, Tang states that "art expresses not only emotions, but also thoughts. ... These emotions and thoughts are derived from the world of reality, and should be aroused from the inside of a person. Therefore on the one hand there is the reality that exists objectively, while on the other, there is the subjectivity of the writer in society." He emphasizes the social function of art and its didactic value, as opposed to Liu's coteries' entertainment theory. Tang says that since Liu and his coterie "fail to understand the unification of content and form," they criticize the leftists for "overemphasizing content," and thus insist on "the superiority of form over content in a work of art."[65]

Liu's coterie's modernist stance, which valorized the autonomy of art, their literary practice manifested in the aesthetics of the dandy, and their entertainment theory were poles apart from the politicized aesthetics of proletarian literature. A controversy of this nature was inevitable.

As much as modernism is a celebration of the metropolitan mode of life and an unthinking embrace of capitalism, proletarianism condemns the city and capitalist evil. The modernist dandy belongs to an affluent class that is ignorant of poverty and suffering, while the proletarianist takes it as his mission to fight head on against social injustice. A dandy such as Liu Na'ou, though marked by an aestheticism defying bourgeois mediocrity, is undeniably a product of bourgeois culture and capitalist expansion. A dandy like him seems to be a stark contrast to a proletarianist like Yang Kui, who looks upon the bourgeois and colonialism as his mortal enemies. Yet it is exactly in this sense that both can be considered the products of the amalgamation of the bourgeoisie, capitalism, and colonialism.

Besides belonging to two distinct classes, modernism and proletarianism certainly embrace different aesthetic values. If we can say that the modernism of Liu Na'ou is manifested in the neosensationist mode, which emphasizes the pleasures of the senses and thus highlights the metaphysical void of modern society, then Yang Kui's proletarianism resorts to the persuasive mode instead, which, like the discursive method used by the most stringent religions history has known, aims to convert the readers to the proletarian ideology. If we agree with Foucault that "the deliberate attitude of modernity is tied to an indispensable asceticism," it is no less true that the proletarianist executes his task with an asceticism equal to an angry prophet.

While the modernist experimentation with representation and narrative point of view throws into relief the flimsy demarcation between reality and fiction, the proletarianist insists that the nature and function of literature is to "tell the truth."[66] Hence Yang Kui's revulsion toward the modernist idea of the autonomy of art and his promotion of reportage, or documentary literature. We can say that in contrast to modernism, which is "the ironic heroization of the present," in Foucault's words, proletarianism is the urge for the reform of present society with a view to effecting a utopian future. The modernist seeks the "ascetic elaboration of the self," whereas the proletarianist subsumes the self into the cause of the masses.

The condition of the masses is the main subject matter in the work of Yang Kui, who all his life prided himself as being one of them. Readers remember him as "the old gardener," due to the well-known stories of how he supported his family by growing and selling flowers both before and after the war. The image of a lean old man with a hammer in his hand has become a perennial symbol in the public mind.[67] It is the image of a worker close to the land and the people, who survives ordeals by his strong will and persistence.

During his life Yang established two gardens. Shouyang Garden was built in 1937, a few months after the outbreak of the Sino-Japanese War, and Donghai Garden was built in 1962, a year after he was released from his twelve-year imprisonment on Green Island. The name "Shouyang 首陽" is an allusion to two Chinese intellectuals of the tenth century B.C. who refused to be subjects under the enemy and hid in the Shouyang Mountain until they starved to death. This allusion is of course a strong suggestion of Yang's own refusal to live under the Japanese, who were at war with China. Because these two gardens were built at such crucial moments in his life, the pieces of prose he wrote concerning them are invested with symbolic meanings hard for the reader to overlook.

These pieces, using the garden as a metaphor of literature as well as life, include "Shūyōen zakkan 首陽園雜感" (Random notes on Shouyang Garden; 1937), "Yuanding riji 園丁日記" (The gardener's diary; 1956), and "Momo de yuanding 默默的園丁" (The silent gardener; manuscript, circa 1966). In "Random Notes on Shouyang Garden" the narrator states that, while people are actively answering the call for talent at such a crucial moment — implying the Sino-Japanese War — he chooses to grow vegetables and flowers in the garden and manages to avoid starvation because of what he grows. He says, "Not all who hide in the Shouyang Mountain will die of starvation. It all depends on the psychological state of the hermit."[68] For the narrator, the garden represents a small world that he can control. While he may not be able to make the outside world right, where weeds grow at will and prevent the growth of flowers, in the garden, with diligence and care, he can get rid of the weeds so as to ensure the flowers' growth. Yet on the other hand, the weeds, though unwanted in the garden, represent to the narrator the persevering spirit of the lowly bred, since they are endowed with the ability to grow profusely all of a sudden if unattended to.

In "The Gardener's Diary," written and published while Yang was imprisoned on Green Island, the narrator tells how the inmates cooperate to build a garden in the prison compound. The green patch that is gradually coming into being becomes a source of hope for them, "the way travelers in a desert look upon an oasis as heaven."[69] Their dream is to grow in the middle of the garden a banyan tree that would provide shade for all in the years to come. Banyan trees in the narrator's mind represent fond memories: the photographs sent him of the archway formed by two banyan trees planted by his children at home; under the hundred-year-old banyan tree in his hometown, villagers, passengers, and workers in the field take shelter in hot summer, with children playing and old men telling stories or singing popular tunes accompanied by a folk string instrument. During the typhoon season the prison garden faces a series of setbacks. With typhoons coming one after another, the trees are repeatedly blown down and then replaced, but the inmates never lose heart. According to the narrator, if one wants to make contributions in life one will certainly face and overcome similar setbacks: "All careers good to the people are inherited, expanded, and fulfilled in a like manner."

"The Silent Gardener," not published during Yang's lifetime, was probably written five years after he was released from Green Island.[70] Like most of his prose works, this piece again aims to give the reader some wisdom. In the beginning the narrator states that his aim in cultivating the garden is to fulfill an ideal: to secure an independent life so that he does not have to work for others and thus will be able to write as he likes. For him the garden represents a "paradise" that he can create and monitor, and he compares it to the reality outside: "Silently he weeded the garden and drove away the malicious worms, while at the same time he cannot overlook the weeds and malicious worms in life and society. Whenever he heard of a moving story, he would think of his pen that has been left idle and getting rusty."[71] Literature for Yang Kui has the function of righting the wrong; it should not be looked upon as an end in itself. He soon discovers, however, that this dream of an independent life through gardening seems impossible, since out of good will his children's families have moved in, thinking such a family reunion would compensate him for his long absence from home. Yet the output of a small garden, though sufficient to feed an old couple, is not enough to feed more than a dozen people. In addition to the debt he has gone into to establish the garden, he is forced to borrow more money to expand it and buy necessary equipment. As a result the interest he has to pay accumulates to such an exorbitant amount that he is afraid that he may have to sell the garden eventually.

For Yang Kui, being a writer is equivalent to being a gardener. He says in the article "Wo you yikuai zhuan 我有一塊磚" (I have a brick):

> Right now I am the gardener of Donghai Garden. More than thirty years ago, when *Taiwan xinwenxue* (Taiwan new literature) was banned by the Japanese government for its anti-Japanese stance, I became the gardener of "Shouyang Garden." … More than twenty years ago, I was again the gardener of *Taiwan wenxue* 台灣 文學 (Taiwan literature).[72]

Taiwan New Literature and *Taiwan Literature* were the two journals that he founded in 1935 and 1948. The effort of establishing a garden, including tilling the land, sowing, irrigating, fertilizing, worming, and weeding, is likened to establishing a literary career, the purpose of both being to create a *taoyuanxiang* 桃源鄉, a paradise or a utopian world.[73] It is from this trope of looking toward a better future that the politicized aesthetics of his proletarianism derives its vitality and meaning: the writer should expose the evil of the present society while envisioning in his literary works a better society so that the masses will cherish hope and follow the right path to that better world. His article "Ya bubian de meiguihua 壓不扁的 玫瑰花" (The indomitable rose), written in 1957 when he was still serving time on Green Island, tells about a rose that manages to grow out of the rocks it has been buried under. The article, originally titled "Chunguang guan buzhu 春光關不住" (The uncontainable splendor of the spring), was first published in *Xinsheng yuekan* 新生月刊 (New life monthly), a journal for inmates on Green Island. In 1976 it was included in a junior high school textbook with the new title that is better known today. "The indomitable rose" has become in the public mind the symbol of the writer who overcame hardships and emerged triumphant in the end.[74]

———— ∞ ————

According to Yang Kui, a writer should live, think, and labor like the masses; he should look upon the interest of the people as his own, with a full understanding of the sources of the people's joy, anger, sorrow, and happiness. Yet, given all this, it is most important that a writer's wisdom and vision be above those of the masses; he should be able to see the tendency of the times and have a keen eye for the corruption and customs that thwart progress. In other words, a writer should aim at the reform of society, while this reform should be based on a thorough understanding of reality.[75]

Throughout his career Yang was highly concerned about the role of the writer in society. In "Sakka, seikatsu, shakai 作家, 生活, 社会" (Writers, life, and society; 1934) he makes "those who maintain art for art's sake" the target of attack:

> They are those who maintain art for art's sake, cut off from social reality because of one reason or another. They might be dandies from rich families, loose girls, or those who, due to some sort of bewilderment, are unconcerned about reality and remain onlookers, or they might be bohemians who have lost their feelings.[76]

Yang's criticism of "art for art's sake" can be seen in many of his articles. He thinks "pure literature" such as the "I-novel," which looks inward and is negligent of the outside world, is the product of "decadent literary men, whose will power to live is weak."[77] In "Geijutsu wa daishu no mono de aru 藝術は大衆のものである"(Art belongs to the people) he states that the writers of "pure literature" have escaped into the small world of "literature on the desk," caring for nothing but their own feelings, while completely neglecting the reader. They intend to hide in an ivory tower, writing only for people of like mind. In contrast, those who write popular literature, with a view to catering to the reader's taste, resort to erotic, eccentric, and melodramatic means. In his opinion both these two kinds of writers have departed from the path of real art. Instead, he advocates proletarian literature, which appeals to the masses, i.e., laborers, farmers, and the petty bourgeois. Although the main subject matter should be their lives, it is by no means restricted to these. One should, from the worldview of laborers, write about their enemies, such as the intelligentsia and the bourgeois, as well as their comrades. However, such a worldview must be not just an empty idea, but something concretely described in the kind of writing that will "touch our hearts, make our blood boil, and point to the correct road for us."[78]

For Yang Kui, the main value of literature lies in its content and subject matter. Writers of "pure literature," lacking theoretical thinking and enthusiasm, spend their whole lives pursuing "petty skills" and thereby fall to the level of vulgar craftsmen. To point out the complexity of the war between form and content, he comments on the *kōdō shugi* 行動主義 (activism) proposed by Japanese writers such as Komatsu Kiyoshi and Funehashi Seiichi, who introduced the works of French writers André Malraux and André Gide into Japan from 1934 to 1936 and maintained that the autonomy of art and the theoretical thinking of proletarian literature should be fused together, so that writers could exert their activism in society and art, while literature could reach a higher level. In an article titled "Kōdō shugi kentō 行動主義檢討" (Examining activism), Yang Kui states that the nature of art is to express the praxis of life and the active will power of the masses, and the reason why those who advocate *kōdō shugi* in Japan are opposed by leftists is that they have not been able to pinpoint a definite direction. Yang thinks that the dilemma they face is shared by all writers. He agrees with Funehashi that, although the autonomy of art is a must, the pitfall of *shuji shugi* 修辭主義 (rhetoric-ism, or the overemphasis on artifice and virtuosity) is a great loss for literature. According to him, the prevalent opposition between activism and *shuji shugi* is totally unorthodox. Yang thinks that the advocacy of *kōdō shugi* is an inevitable result of this dilemma. Yet while admitting that it is a good tendency, he makes it clear that these writers of *kōdō shugi* have yet to find their right direction, that they will face a series of difficult choices on the way, and that the efforts they make are to be approved of even if they fail in the end.[79]

In "Bungei hihyō no hyōjun 文藝批評の標準" (The criteria of art criticism) Yang further expounds on the idea of art for the masses. He insists that the most important aspect of writing is to convey the writer's emotions, thoughts, and ideas to the reader. Of those who think that the aim of art is self-fulfillment, while the reader's or the viewer's reaction is not their concern, Yang says, "It is like speaking Japanese to foreigners who do not know it." He thinks that the field of modern art criticism likewise shows this tendency. Most critics would put literary works on the anatomy table, analyzing in detail the specific descriptions of certain scenes and the virtuosity of certain passages, forgetting completely the overall impact of the works on people. To Yang, this is similar to the case of a doctor who takes the patient's pulses and listens to his heartbeat with a stethoscope, but feels nothing for the dying patient or his heartbroken family. He says,

> Among literary men today this kind of people seem to be the majority. They indulge in petty skills, but feel nothing for the essence of art that moves people's hearts. It is like some doctors who treat patients simply by taking their pulses and detecting their breathing but feel nothing for their lives and deaths. These writers, valuing rhetoric over art's nature to move people ... have lost sight of the holistic feeling of literary works, which is what gives them life.[80]

Yang then points out that in fact literary criticism should exist for literary works the way doctors exist for their patients. But when a school of critics, highly applauded by the media, becomes an overwhelming presence in journals and newspapers, almost all writers exert their every power simply to meet with the criteria set by these critics. He thinks that this phenomenon has veered off the right path. He proposes to use the "scientific method" to observe reality, since it is the only method that can create verisimilitudes to move the reader. He points out that the first priority of proletarian literature is to instigate the reader to move toward the right direction. If this is too difficult, one can then resort to "fiction." "Fiction" for Yang Kui means to "tell lies," and to write novels one needs the skills of telling lies while making the reader believe that the lies told are "truth." Truth for Yang Kui has an unsurpassable value in literary criticism, and this can be seen in his advocacy of reportage literature.

Yang thinks of realism as the genre that can best convey the truth of reality, however ugly that reality may seem. At the outbreak of the "*kuso* riarizumu 糞リアリ" (feces realism) debate in Taiwan in 1943, he defended its position, challenging the notion maintained by Nishikawa Mitsuru 西川満, a Japanese writer living in Taiwan, that it was only Taiwanese writers' poor imitation of Western realism. *Kuso* realism was in fact a key term invented during the Nihon rōmanha/Jinmin-bunko 日本浪漫派/人民文庫 (Japanese Romanticists/People's Literature) debate around 1935 to criticize the style advocated by the leaders of the journal *People's Literature*.[81] In a column titled "Bungei jihyō" 文芸時評 (Contemporary literary criticism) in the journal *Bungei Taiwan* 文藝臺灣 (Literary Taiwan), Nishikawa pointed out that the mainstream of Taiwanese literature had recently been *kuso* realism, a Euro-American literary trend that entered Japan during the Meiji period. To Nishikawa, the Japanese literary tradition was represented by romantic writers and works (distinct from Western Romanticism) such as Izumi Kyōka 泉鏡花 (1873–1939) and *Genji monogatari* 源氏物語 (The tale of the Genji), and he urged contemporary writers to learn from this tradition while contributing works called for by the prospect of establishing the "Kōkoku bungaku" 皇國文學 (Imperial literature) under the Great East Asian War. He labels *kuso* realism a "fragment of cheap humanism," which describes the vulgarity of worthless life.[82]

Nishikawa's article in fact criticizes writers in the journal *Taiwan Literature* such as Lu Heruo 呂赫若 and Zhang Wenhuan 張文環, while disclosing his own superiority as an imperial subject over the colonized. Two months later Yang Kui's article titled "Kuso riarizumu no yōgo 糞リアリズムの擁護" (In defense of *kuso* realism) appeared in *Taiwan Literature*, jokingly taking up the theme "*kuso* realism" by expounding on the function of feces: helping vegetables and rice grow so that people can be fed. If one, like Nishikawa, who puts a lid on a can of rotting organic matter, refuses to look at reality, one is covering up one's own nose and eyes instead of reality, which always exists. To rebut Nishikawa's praise of imperial literature at the expense of realist literature, Yang cites the 1943 story "Tomoshibi 灯" (Lamp) published in *Taiwan Literature* by Sakaguchi Reiko 坂口子, another Japanese writer living in Taiwan. The story describes a merchant's wife who sees her husband off to war. The wife, though complying with the emperor's command to unflinchingly support the holy war, cannot help worrying about her husband's safety.[83] Yang praises this story as a model work of realism, saying:

> In this way her mind is tossed by this and that thought, while savoring at the same time every worry and distress. The joy and ease that eventually grow out of this

state of mind would be real feelings. Since they are family, it is impossible for either the husband or the wife to feel nothing about the family. If it is possible, it would be disgraceful. The Japan that complies with the emperor's commandment is a big family of one hundred million people. If one does not feel the responsibility for the small family, how does one take action to fulfill one's responsibility for the big family? Thus, this work, though based on reality, does not indulge in reality, while it is able to create a romantic story to move us. ... "To propagate the Japanese spirit, how moving is such a beautiful short story compared with rhetorical outcries and lengthy theories!" said Mr. Wu Xinrong in *Kōnan shinbun* [Southern reconstruction daily], and I tend to agree with him. ... We understand that the Japanese spirit has a twenty-six hundred year tradition. Exactly because of that, if one thinks that it is like a hat that once put on can fit immediately, it would be tremendously ridiculous.[84]

In this passage the attitude shown by Yang toward the so-called Imperial Literature, or *Kōmin bungaku* 皇民文學 (Imperialization Literature), as it is more usually known, is ambivalent. One senses his contradictory emotional and psychological reactions to this new genre, established during the Sino-Japanese War, which demands allegiance of all subjects of Japan, colonizer or colonized. What is not expressed is probably louder than what is directly stated: as colonized, the couple about to be separated for the holy war find it hard to reconcile themselves to the imperial command. Yang says, "Even if one can understand the emperor's will and has the same patriotic feelings, distinct ways of life and specific environment control people's way of thinking."

For many critics of Yang Kui and contemporary writers, the most embarrassing aspect of their writing careers is that most of them wrote works in the spirit of imperialization literature at the time of the imperialization movement during the war.[85] Yang, proclaimed an anticolonialist writer by Taiwanese critics in the postwar era, in fact wrote quite a few pieces supporting the Great East Asian War. But if we examine these pieces carefully, we find that the pro–imperialization movement rhetoric found in them often shows a heightened ambivalence between tongue-in-cheek exaggeration and supportive rhetoric, which is difficult to take at face value. For instance, in "Ari ippiki no shigoto 蟻一匹の仕事" (Ant's work), which he wrote for the column "Omoide no shojosaku 思ひ出の處女作" (Memories of my first literary work) in *Southern Reconstruction Daily* in 1943, he talks about the personal experiences incorporated in his first literary work, "Jiyū rōdōsha no seikatsu danmen 自由勞動者の生活斷面" (Profile of a free laborer's life).[86] This piece tells his own story of working as a part-time construction worker while studying in Japan. It is a dangerous job, with the workers shouldering cement bags as they climb up and down stairs made of wooden planks. One time he has to walk over a plank placed on top of the two walls of a tall building. He trembles all over, with the wind blowing and the sand getting into his eyes. When he hears a big bang, he thinks he is dying. But in fact it is the cement bag that has fallen to the ground, while he is lying flat on the wooden plank. A few years later, six years before he writes "Ari ippiki no shigoto," he visits Tokyo again and admires in awe the building he helped to build. It has become the magnificent Imperial Parliament Building. The concluding part of the story then takes a surprising turn, eulogizing great jobs accomplished by many a little ant like himself. He says, "In the great construction job of building the Great East Asia, I would like to be the little ant that I used to be."[87]

Such contrived incorporation of the imperialization spirit can be found in similar stories by Yang. Another example will suffice. In a short piece titled "Wude kurabe 腕くらべ" (A wrist wrestling) the opening sentences are as follows:

> Someone asked me to write pro-war stories. To conceive an idea, I smoked three cigarettes. Great people's brave contribution should, of course, be the subject matter that one writes incessantly about. But I lack such knowledge, therefore I would like to write about citizens who diligently labor like ants, and the lives of those citizens who have sacrificed themselves and turned themselves into pawns, silently working as the foundations of the files and ranks of war.

This is a direct statement of why and how he wrote imperialization stories. But the piece ends with an event that has little or nothing to do with the beginning statement. His second son, scared by a dog that jumps at him while he is playing games with a friend, bursts into tears. His friend teases him and says that a crying baby cannot be a soldier. So the two engage in a wrist-wrestling match to see who is stronger.[88]

During the war the *jōhōka* 情報科 (information section) of the Japanese colonial government in Taiwan demanded that Taiwanese writers write literary works with a view to supporting Japan's all-out mobilizing effort for the war. Yang Kui and others certainly responded to that demand, yet somehow or other, while managing to convey the sense of the ambivalent situation they found themselves in, these works are also imbued with the authors' oscillation between irony and straightforward conformity. To write such works was clearly not a matter of choice. Whether they really felt for the rhetoric and to what extent they were sincere are questions in history that even the testimony of these writers themselves would find hard to answer.

Connected with the ambivalence of Yang Kui's writing of imperialization literature is the problem of the editions and revisions of his works, the study of which is an industry in itself. Most of his works, originally written in Japanese, were revised when translated into Chinese after the war, often translated and revised by himself or by another translator, sometimes revised by editors of newspapers, journals, or publishing companies intending to republish his works. There is also evidence of revisions made in his own handwriting in the manuscripts he left behind.[89] Some critics point out that the patriotic rhetoric and anti-Japanese slogans were added to the revised editions after the war, and thus question his position as an anticolonialist writer.[90]

Many writers during the Japanese occupation, such as Zhang Wenhuan and Long Yingzong, abruptly stopped publishing after the war, partly because of their inability to write in vernacular Chinese, which had replaced Japanese and become the official language on the island, and partly because of the unstable sociopolitical situation during the postwar years, which were marked by such horrific events such as the February 28 Incident[91] in 1947 and the so-called White Terror, which lasted for two or even three decades after the war.

Yang kept on writing as well as publishing during this period. He certainly paid dearly for his relentless effort to "tell the truth," with twelve years spent in prison for an article of less than seven hundred characters titled "Heping xuanyan 和平宣言" (Manifesto of peace), written in 1949. Advocating a general effort to build Taiwan as a "model country of peaceful construction," he urges the government to guarantee freedom of speech, gathering, publication, philosophical thinking, and religious beliefs for the people, and to enforce the autonomy of local administrations. Finally, he hopes that Taiwanese people of both mainland and native origins will give up their prejudices against each other and live in peace together so that Taiwan can be a "paradise."[92] This "manifesto," originally meant to be circulated among friends, was incidentally seen by a journalist from the Shanghai-based *Dagongbao* (Grand justice daily), and eventually saw publication on January 21, 1949. On April 6 Yang was arrested.

In fact Yang did not stop his socialist activities after the war. Before the war he was an active member of Nōmin Kumiai 農民組合 (Farmers' union), but he deliberately kept at a distance from the communists who infiltrated it, mainly because, with a literary career in view, he did not want to work "underground." The night before his wedding in February 1929 to Ye Tao, a Farmer's Union comrade in charge of the women's movement division, they were both arrested for the speeches they had been invited to give that day at the union's Tainan headquarters. After the war he did not see eye to eye with Xie Xuehong, the famous female leader of Renmin xiehui (People's association), a communist organization in Taiwan,[93] and seldom visited its headquarters, Dahua jioujia 大華酒家 (Grand China Restaurant), in Taichung. He was nevertheless still active in the cause of the Farmers' Union. Immediately after the February 28 Incident in 1947, he and several friends designed, printed, and distributed cards containing a poll to find out people's reaction and an announcement of a protest meeting on March 3. It failed to convene because of police intervention, while Yang and his wife disguised themselves as a farmer couple and went on a tour in neighboring villages to encourage young people to join the "27th division" of the Farmers' Union. The mission having failed, they escaped from home, hid in the mountains for a dozen days and then in a barn, and finally tried to escape by sea, but to no avail. They were arrested in mid-April and released in September.[94]

During his twelve-year term on Green Island resulting from his second arrest after the war, Yang wrote stories of how he and his wife learned to speak mandarin Chinese with one of their daughters, stories that have endeared themselves to the public. "Wo de xiao xiansheng 我的小先生" (My little teacher) was first published in January 1956 in *Xin shenghuo bibao* 新生活壁報 (New life bulletin), a newsletter posted on the wall for inmates to read. It tells his memory of how after the war, the little girl, a first grader at elementary school then, took every opportunity at home to teach her parents to speak simple phrases such as "wash hands before meals" and "eat lunch." But their lessons were interrupted by the uninvited visitors who barged into the house to arrest her parents. When the visitors came, she had just been back from school and was eating lunch. The image of her tears silently dropping into the bowl of rice in front of her had been imprinted on the father's memory since then. At the time he writes the story, he has been separated for seven years from his family, while the little girl, having finished elementary school and junior high school, is now studying at Taichung Normal College, looking forward to being an elementary school teacher someday and finding her lost childhood among innocent children.[95]

For decades before the publication of his *Complete Works* (1998–2001), the general impression was that Yang Kui had never written in Chinese before the war. In fact in 1935 he published a story, "Si 死" (Death), in Chinese in *Taiwan Xinminbao* 台灣新民報 (Taiwan new people daily). There is an unpublished version of the same story written in the Taiwanese dialect, "Pinnong de biansi 貧農的變死" (The unfortunate death of a poor farmer), in a manuscript discovered after his death. Compared with his writings in Chinese during the Green Island period and afterward, the language in "Death" is awkward, and full of grammatical and syntactical errors, disclosing the author's unfamiliarity with the language. The Taiwanese version of the story is in a like state, or even more unreadable, since there are words invented or borrowed from Chinese to imitate the Taiwanese sounds with no characters to match. One senses that these two versions of the same story might have been an experiment carried out by Yang Kui, since "Death" was published during the height of the famous Beijing huawen/Taiwan huawen 北京話文/臺灣話文 (Beijing vernacular/Taiwanese vernacular) controversy on the island.

The controversy started in the early 1920s, before the Chinese vernacular literature movement was systematically introduced in Taiwan in 1924 by Zhang Wojun 張我軍, a Taiwanese who had studied in Beijing. With Taiwan starting its own vernacular literature movement, Taiwanese intellectuals began to question the meaning of "vernacular" in the Taiwanese context: is the Beijing dialect the synonym of "vernacular," or is it possible to use the Taiwanese dialect to write vernacular literature on the island? In his 1923 article Huang Chengcong 黃呈聰 resorts to Hu Shih 胡適's rhetoric on the superiority of vernacular literature over classical literature. He does not think the Taiwanese dialect a suitable medium for vernacular literature, since it is used in limited areas, while Taiwan, unlike an independent country with a written language, will soon find its culture wiped out by another country backed up by the supremacy of its language, meaning Japan. Therefore he urges Taiwanese people to learn the Chinese vernacular so that they can expand their vision and sphere of movement to China.[96] Shi Wenqi 施文杞 in his 1924 article points out the deficiency of the Taiwanese in writing the vernacular; they tend to stud their articles with Minnan and Japanese expressions and thus make laughingstocks of themselves.[97]

On the other hand, there were also scholars who supported the idea of using Taiwanese in writing in the vernacular. For instance, Lian Wenqing 連溫卿, the famous historian who published *Taiwan tongshi* 臺灣通史 (General history of Taiwan) in 1921, maintained that the Taiwanese dialect should be improved in order to cope with the times. He proposed the establishment of standard pronunciation and grammatical rules for Taiwanese through a sound phonology.[98] Zhang Wuojun agrees with him in this regard, saying, "Our New Literature movement has the mission of reforming the Taiwanese dialect. We should change our dialect into a rational language suitable for the written form. We should reform the Taiwanese dialect with the Chinese vernacular as a model."[99]

During the 1930s when the *xiangtu wenxue* 鄉土文學 (native literature) debate broke out, the Taiwanese vernacular became an issue that attracted much attention again. In the special column titled "The Taiwanese Vernacular Forum" in the inaugural issue of the bimonthly *Nanyin* (Southern sound) established in 1932, someone with the pen name of "Jing 敬" uses the *katakana* of Japanese to illustrate the correct pronunciation of the Taiwanese dialect.[100] Guo Qiusheng 郭秋生, on the other hand, maintains that the "basic work" of establishing the Taiwanese vernacular is "creating new words."[101] In the third issue, Lai Ho 賴和, Yang Kui's mentor and close friend, continues the discussion of the same topic:

> I think to some extent it is necessary to create new words, but by all means it should be done when there is no choice, when in existing characters we are unable to find words that can match the sounds and meanings of what we need to express. If there are existing characters that match the meaning but do not match the sound, I think it would be easier for more people to understand by using the existing words with notes on the side.

Guo Qiusheng in response agrees with Lai's view, but points out that it is essential to try out the theories, and hopes that at this time of establishing the Taiwanese vernacular, more people will devote themselves to transcribing popular songs and ballads in the Taiwanese vernacular, so that by trial and error they can discover the "right method."[102]

Lai Ho certainly tried to influence Yang Kui with his view about the Taiwanese vernacular, as can be evidenced by the handwriting attributed to Lai changing into Chinese characters some of the new words Yang had created to match the Taiwanese sounds in the manuscript of "The Unfortunate Death of a Poor Farmer." It was in fact common for writers during the 1930s to create new words for the Taiwanese vernacular. These writers, including Lai Ho and Yang Shouyu 楊守愚, were eager to put into practice the theories discussed during the controversy.[103] But as Lai had predicted, since each writer had his own way of inventing words, it was hard to arrive at a unified system accepted for general usage. As a result mutual understanding became a problem, and the experiments did not last long. But Yang Kui continued incorporating phrases of the Taiwanese and Chinese vernaculars in his works written in Japanese, while he made an effort to transcribe popular Taiwanese songs and ballads, including those of Minnan, Hakka, and aboriginal origins, even during the Green Island period.

Whatever their contrasting ideologies, both modernism and proletarianism need to resolve the contradictions between the metropolitan and the native, the universal and the particular. In his article "Hōkoku bungaku ni tsuite 報告文學について" (On Reportage), Yang Kui, urging his fellow Taiwanese writers to be *sekai no sakka* 世界の作家 (writers of the world) and produce works such as Lu Xun's *The Story of A Q*, realizes that it is essential to base the universal on native experiences:

> The reason that we are advocating colonial literature is because we need to write about the Taiwanese society in which we were born and brought up, not because we intend to isolate ourselves on Taiwan. We sincerely hope that everyone of our writers is equipped with the broad perspective of a *sekaijin* (a man of the world), and looks at Taiwan and writes about it with such a perspective.[104]

In his theoretical works he constantly alludes to Japanese proletarian writers such as Tokunaga Sunao 徳永直 (1899–1958) and Funahashi Seiichi (1904–1976). Among his posthumously published works can be found the remaining segment of the translation of Russian writers Iosif Abramovich Lapidus' and Konstantin Ostrovitianov's 1929 book *Politicheskaia ekonomiia* (An outline of political economy: Political economy and Soviet economics).[105] In "Hōkoku bungaku mondō 報告文學問答" (Reportage: Questions and answers) Yang Kui draws on Komatsu Kiyoshi 小松清's introduction of Russian, French, and German reportage writers like Il'ya Grigorevich Erenburg, André Malraux, Egon Erwin Kisch, and so on.[106]

Yang is familiar with the international lineage of the proletarianist, and he spares no effort in drawing his reader's attention to the global condition of the proletarian movement. Yet within the broad view of the universality of the proletarian condition, how does one manage not to lose sight of one's native self? Does identifying with class compromise or further complicate one's identity quest? Yang Kui is, of course, keenly aware of the contradictions and repeatedly discusses the issue, as can be witnessed in his article "Geijutsu ni okeru 'Taiwan rashii mono' ni tsuite 藝術における"台灣らしいもの"について" (On the Taiwanese flavor in art), in which he states that it does not matter at all in what form a literary work is written. As far as literary form is concerned, it certainly transcends the boundaries of nation, people, and native land. But when one is talking about the content of literature, it is another matter. Yang unflinchingly emphasizes that Taiwanese writers should strive to describe the reality of Taiwan through a Taiwanese point of view.[107]

In 1920s Taiwan, young men aspiring to literary careers, like Yang Kui and Liu Na'ou, did not lack international models to emulate. Yet if Yang Kui followed the footsteps of Japanese proletarian writers, he would be imitating the colonizers of his native land. Identifying with the proletariat did not ease the colonizer-colonized tension for him. Liu Na'ou, practicing Baudelaire's theory of the dandy in life as well as in writing, found himself in a similar predicament. As much as he aspired to the universal aesthetic values of modernism, the laws of national boundaries still cornered him in the end. Perhaps due to his lack of territorial or national allegiance as a Taiwanese in semicolonial Shanghai, during his literary and film careers he did not hesitate to associate with the various contending political forces there: the leftists, the Nationalist government, the Wang Jingwei puppet regime, and the Japanese.

The cause of Liu's murder on September 3, 1940, by an unidentified gunman, who ambushed him from the staircase of a restaurant and shot him three times,[108] has been a mystery in literary history. The murder took place right after a lunch party held in his honor, celebrating his succession to the directorship of *Guomin xinwenshe* 國民新聞社 (National subjects' daily) after Mu Shiying 穆時英, a fellow neosensationist writer and filmmaker. *National Subjects' Daily* was a news agency run by the Wang Jingwei 汪精衛 puppet regime. On June 28 of the same year while functioning as its director Mu had likewise been shot to death.[109] No one knew if these two murders were connected or instigated by the same agency. There were rumors that Liu's murder was committed by the Japanese secret agency because they thought he was a double agent for the Nationalist government. Some, on the other hand, believed that the Nationalist Party secret agency had him killed because he was thought to collaborate with the Japanese.[110] Shi Zhecun even suspected that Liu's killer was sent by Du Yuesheng 杜

月笙's gang because of outstanding gambling debts.[111] Whatever the real cause was, Liu's tragic death points to the danger inherent in the semicolonial society in Shanghai, where no single government enforced its laws and protection was not guaranteed to subjects of any nationality; Liu's ambiguous identity certainly did not assist him in this regard.

As much as the language of creative writing became an issue for Yang Kui's generation of Taiwanese writers, Liu, living and writing in Shanghai, was also highly concerned about his own Taiwanese origin and the inadequacy of his Chinese proficiency. In his 1927 diary we can see his self-consciousness at being a nonnative speaker of mandarin Chinese and the efforts he made to improve his mandarin proficiency. For instance, on January 3 he wrote, "Practiced mandarin Chinese conversation tonight." On January 5, when he was reading a Japanese translation of the Russian writer Alexandre Kuprin's (1873–1938) novel *Yama: The Pit* (1901–1915) he wrote, "The author has really a great ability to tell stories. … I keenly feel that my ability to tell stories is limited. Perhaps because Fukienese has a limited vocabulary, I often fail to come up with the right expression to express what I have in mind." But even though he was highly conscious of his Minnan origin, Minnan expressions pop up from time to time in the diary, probably without himself being aware of them. For example, in the April 6 entry where he writes, "The trains to Jiangning 江寧 were all full of soldiers," the Minnan expression "bingmuanmuan 兵滿滿" is used instead of "full of soldiers."[112] In the July 14 entry where he writes, "This telegraph awakened my nightmare of five or six years," the Minnan expression "meimeng 迷夢" is used instead of "nightmare."[113]

As a Taiwanese during the Japanese occupation who became famous and was murdered in Shanghai, it took more than half a century for Liu Na'ou to be reestablished in Taiwan as a literary man. In the summer of 1997 when Liu's family entrusted his 1927 diary to me, they were still uncertain whether it was "safe" or appropriate to have its content meet the public eye. Even though it was already ten years after the lifting of martial law on Taiwan, his second daughter, the fourth of his five children, was still uneasy when talking about her father's murder. It had been a subject of taboo since her return to Taiwan from Shanghai with her mother and siblings shortly after the violent event. A child of seven at the time, she keenly felt the shock and horror that would persist for decades to come, over the years of the postwar handing over of Taiwan to the Nationalist government, the February 28 Incident, and the White Terror. In the summer of 1997 she still vaguely remembered her mother's description of her father having been active in Shanghai literary circles and film industry during the 1930s, but she would not know of his stature and significance as a literary man until the publication of his five-volume *Complete Works* in 2001.

For Yang Kui's family, the fourteen volumes of his *Complete Works* published consecutively from 1998 to 2001 was also an impossible dream come true. Compiling his works involved translating the untranslated prewar works into Chinese, comparing the various Japanese versions with the postwar Chinese versions, checking previous translations and correcting them wherever inaccuracies were found, and retranslating the original text if the previous translations differed from it too much to be simply "corrected," a more laborious task than one could have imagined.

If anyone questions the definition of "Taiwanese literature" and doubts that works written in Japanese could be considered a part of it, I would attempt only one argument in response: Although Taiwan to some extent shares in the global colonial and postcolonial experience, the specific case of Taiwan, which forced its educated population, versed in classical Chinese, to adopt Japanese as an official language for fifty years before the war, and then to abruptly switch to vernacular Chinese after the war for another fifty years, is hard to match. For many postmartial law critics, in the past century Taiwan had been twice colonized by outside regimes before the Democratic Progressive Party took over the government in 2000.

In the past decade the dynamic energy of scholars as well as the efforts of government cultural agencies to create a literary tradition for Taiwan is clearly shown in the canon formation process, as can be witnessed by the considerable number of complete works of Taiwanese writers already compiled and now being compiled. Should Taiwanese literature be considered a literature in its own right, or is it part of Chinese literature? What is the relationship between Japanese literature and prewar works written in Japanese by Taiwanese authors? How does one create "nationalism" without being provincial? We need a new discourse for a new relationship between colonial cultural hegemony and the burgeoning native consciousness evident in the invention of a "national" tradition.

NOTES

1. Liu Na'ou's diary, written in 1927, was found in the mid-1990s in a closet at his home in Tainan. It was published in two volumes in 2001. For the French quotation, see Liu Na'ou, *Rijiji* 日記集 [Diary], ed. and trans. Peng Hsiao-yen 彭小妍 and Huang Yingzhe 黃英哲, part I, in *Liu Na'ou Quanji* 劉吶鷗全集 [Complete works of Liu Na'ou], ed. Kang Laixin 康來新 and Xu Qinzhen 許秦蓁 (Tainan: Tainanxian Wenhuaju, 2001), 296. For Liu's family background and education in Taiwan and Japan, see Peng Hsiao-yen, "Langdang tianya: Liu Na'ou 1927 nian riji 浪蕩天涯: 劉吶鷗一九二七日記 [Flâneur of the world: Liu Na'ou's 1927 diary]," in *Haishang shuo qingyu* 海上說情慾: 從張資平到劉吶鷗 [Discourse of desire in Shanghai: From Zhang Ziping to Liu Na'ou] (Taipei: Institute of Chinese Literature and Philosophy, Academia Sinica, 2001), 106–144. Unless otherwise indicated, the translations of Chinese and French passages into English in this article are my own.

2. In Baudelaire's *Les fleurs du mal*, sea voyage always connotes freedom of spirit and elevation of mind as opposed to the mediocrity of the world. See especially verse XIV, titled "L'homme et la mer," in "Spleen et idéal," collected in *Les fleurs du mal*. Praising man and

the sea as two eternal fighters, the poem ends with the line "O lutteurs éternels, ô frères implacable!," meaning "O eternal fighters, o implacable brothers!" See Baudelaire, *Les fleurs du mal* (Paris: Gilbert Lély, 1934), 29.

3. Huang Tianzuo 黃天佐, alias Suichu 隨初, "Wo suo renshi de liu na'ou xiansheng 我所認識的劉吶鷗先生 [The Mr. Liu Na'ou I knew]," in *Osaka mainichi* 大阪每日 [Osaka daily], Chinese edition, 5.9 (Nov. 1, 1940). I will discuss Liu's murder later in this article.

4. Under the Japanese colonial policy Taiwanese were not entitled to the same education system as the Japanese. See Qin Xianci 秦賢次, "Zhang Wojun ji qi tongshidai de Beijing Taiwan liuxuesheng 張我軍及其同時代的臺灣留學生 [Zhang Wojun and contemporary Taiwanese studying in Beijing]," in Peng Hsiao-yen ed., *Piaobo yu xiangtu: Zhang Wojun shishi sishi zhounian jinian lunwenji* 漂泊與鄉土: 張我軍逝世四十週年紀念論文集 [Diaspora and nativism: Proceedings of the conference on the fortieth anniversary of Zhang Wojun's death] (Taipei: Xingzhengyuan wenhua jianshe weiyuanhui, 1996), 57–81.

5. See the list of Taiwanese who graduated in March 1926 from schools in Tokyo recorded in "Liujing zuyesheng songbiehui 留京卒業生送別會 [Farewell party for Taiwanese students graduating from schools in Tokyo]," in *Taiwan minpō* 台灣民報 [Taiwan people's daily] 99 (April 4, 1926), 8.

6. Shi Zhicun, *Zhendan ernian* 震旦二年 [Two years at L'Aurore] (Shanghai: Wenyi chubanshe, 1996), 289–290.

7. See especially diary entries of Jan. 18 and Jan. 19.

8. Huang Tianzuo, "The Mr. Liu Na'ou I knew."

9. See Shi Shumei, "Gender, Race, and Semicolonialism: Liu Na'ou's Urban Shanghai Landscape," in *The Lure of the Modern: Writing Modernism in Semicolonial China, 1917–1937* (California: University of California Press, 2001), 276.

10. In an interview with Dai Guohui 戴國輝 and Uchimura Gōsuke 內村剛介, Yang talks about his family background and childhood experiences. See Ye Shitao 葉石濤, trans., "Yige Taiwan zuojia de qishiqinian 一個臺灣作家的七十年 [The seventy-seven years of a Taiwanese writer]," in Peng Hsiao-yen, ed., *Yang Kui quanji* 楊逵全集 [Complete works of Yang Kui] (Tainan: Guoli wenhua zichan baocun yanjiou zhongxin, 1998–2001), 14:242–65. Originally published in *Taiwan shinpō* 臺灣時報 [Taiwan times], March 2, 1983. *Complete Works of Yang Kui* will abbreviated as CWOYK from now on.

11. Yang Kui, "Riben zhimin tongzhi xia de haizi 日本殖民統治下的孩子 [The child under Japanese colonial rule]," in CWOYK 14:20–30. Originally a speech at Furen University on May 7, 1982. Later published in *Lienhe bao* 聯合報 [United daily], August 10, 1982.

12. In an interview Yang Kui says that his motivation for writing was to "restore truth to the distorted history." See Tan Jia 譚嘉, "Fang laozuojia Yang Kui 訪老作家楊逵 [Interview with the senior writer Yang Kui]," in CWOYK 14:226–233. Originally published in *70 niandai* [The 70s], no. 154 (Nov. 1982).

13. Yang Kui, "The child under Japanese colonial rule."

14. Huang Tianzuo, "The Mr. Liu Na'ou I knew."

15. Huang Tianzuo, "The Mr. Liu Na'ou I knew."

16. See the discussion below on "petty skills."

17. Yang Kui, "Shōsetsu, hishōsetsu 小說, 非小說 [Fiction, anti-fiction]," in CWOYK 13: 535–538. Original in manuscript form (June 18, 1934).

18. See discussion of "*kuso*-realism" below.

19. Pierre Bourdieu, *La distinction: Critique sociale du jugement* (Paris: Editions de minuit, 1979).

20. I quote the definition of "acculturation" from *Webster's Third International Dictionary*.

21. See Terry Eagleton, "Nationalism: Irony and Commitment," in Seamus Deane, ed., *Nationalism, Colonialism, and Literature* (Minneapolis: University of Minnesota Press, 1990), 23–42.

22. Seamus Deane, "Introduction," in *Nationalism, Colonialism, and Literature*, 3–19.

23. See Liu Na'ou, *Diary*, I.232; II.762, 770.

24. The movie has another title, "The Man with a Hat." Judging by the approximate age of his children at the time of the movie, I presume that it was made in the mid-1930s. Around 1934 Liu's family, including his wife, two sons, and a daughter, moved to Shanghai. One daughter was born in Shanghai in 1936, and one son in 1938.

25. See Liu Na'ou, *Diary*, I.102.

26. In Liu's 1927 diary there is a reading list at the end of each month. See Liu Na'ou, *Diary*, II.553.

27. Michel Foucault, "What Is Enlightenment?" in *The Foucault Reader*, ed. Paul Rabinow (New York: Pantheon Books, 1984), 32–50.

28. Michel Foucault, "What Is Enlightenment?"

29. See Liu Na'ou, May 18, in *Diary*, I.322.

30. See Liu Na'ou, May 19, in *Diary*, I.324.

31. Baudelaire, verse V, "Spleen et idéal," in *Les fleurs du mal* 18.

32. Michel Foucault, "What Is Enlightenment?" 40.

33. Liu Na'ou, October 17, in *Diary*, II.716.

34. Michel Foucault, "What Is Enlightenment?" 40.

35. Charles Baudelaire, *Le peintre de la vie moderne* [The painter of modern life], in *Oeuvres complètes* (Paris: Edition Gallimard, 1976), 683–724.

36. See Water Benjamin, *Charles Baudelaire: A Lyric Poet in the Era of High Capitalism*, trans. Harry Zohn (London: Biddles Lts., Guildford and King's Lynn, 1989), 11–66.

37. Liu Na'ou, *Diary*, II.702.

38. Mu Shiying 穆時英, "Craven 'A,'" in *Gongmu* 公墓 [Public cemetery] (Shanghai: Xiandai Shuju, 1933), 107–138.

39. For the theory of psycho-narration, see Dorrit Cohn, *Transparent Minds: Narrative Modes for Presenting Consciousness in Fiction* (New Jersey: Princeton University Press, 1983).

40. See Charles Baudelaire, "Éloge du maquillage [Eulogy on make-up]," in *The Painter of Modern Life*, 714–718.

41. Mu Shiying, "Shouzhi 手指 [Fingers]," in *Nanbeiji* 南北極 [Poles apart] (Shanghai: Hufeng Shuju, 1932), 49–55.

42. See entries of March 21, April 3, April 6, and April 9, in Liu Na'ou, *Diary*.

43. Liu Na'ou, *Diary*, I.52.

44. Liu Na'ou, *Diary*, I.66.

45. Liu Na'ou, *Diary*, I.386.

46. Liu Na'ou, "Youxi [Game]," in *Dushi fengjingxian* 都市風景線 [Scène] (Shanghai: Shuimo Shudian, 1930), 1–17.

47. Huang Chaoqin 黄朝琴, "Hanwen gaige lun 漢文改革論 [On the reform of classical Chinese]," in Classical Chinese Section, *Taiwan* (January and February 1923), 25–31, 21–28.

48. See the entries written from September to December in Liu Na'ou's 1927 diary.

49. Cf. Heinrich Freuhauf, "Urban Exoticism in Modern and Contemporary Chinese Literature," in *From May Fourth to June Fourth: Fiction and Film in Twentieth-Century China*, Ellen Widmer and David Der-wei Wang, eds., (Cambridge, Mass: Harvard Contemporary China Series, 1998), 147.

50. For an account of Shao as a literary dandy and the literary salon he formed in his home, see Leo Lee, *Shanghai Modern* (Cambridge: Harvard University Press, 1999), 241–250.

51. "Wentan xiaoxi 文壇消息 [News of the literary circle]," in *Xin shidai* 新時代 [New age] 1.1 (August 1, 1931), 7.

52. This is Shi Zhicun's opinion as expressed during an interview with me in October 1998.

53. Cf. Peng Hsiao-yen, "Wusi wenren zai Shanghai: Linglei de Liu Na'ou 五四文人在上海: 另類的劉吶鷗 [May Fourth literary men in Shanghai: The unclassifiable Liu Na'ou]," in *Discourse of Desire in Shanghai*, 145–188.

54. Cf. Peng Hsiao-yen, *Discourse of Desire in Shanghai*, 95–103.

55. Shen Congwen 沈從文 (alias Jiachen 甲辰), "Yu Dafu, Zhang Ziping ji qi yingxiang 郁達夫, 張資平及其影響 [Yu Dafu, Zhang Ziping, and their influences]," in *Xinyue* 新月 [Crescent moon] 3.1 (March 1930), 1–8.

56. Shen Congwen, "Lun Mu Shiying 論穆時英 [On Mu Shiying]," in *Shen Congwen wenji* 沈從文全集 [Works of Shen Congwen] 11, 203–205. Originally published in 1934.

57. The translation is quoted from Yingjin Zhang, *The City in Modern Chinese Literature and Film: Configurations of Space, Time, and Gender* (Stanford: Stanford University Press), 23–24. See Lu Xun 魯迅 (alias Luan Tingshi 欒廷石), "Jingpai yu haipai 京派與海派 [Beijing types and Shanghai types]," in *Shen bao* 申報 [Shanghai post], February 3, 1934, 17. For an account of the *Haipai* controversy per se, the emergence of the "Beijing School," and the redefinition of the "Shanghai School," see Yingjin Zhang, 21–27.

58. See Katherine Huiling Chou, "Representing 'New Woman': Actresses and the *Xin Nuxing* Movement in Chinese Spoken Drama and Films, 1918–1949" (Ph.D. diss., New York: New York University, 1996), 132–133.

59. Huang Jiamo 黃嘉謨, "'Xiandai dianying' yu Zhongguo dianyingjie—benkan de chuangli yu jinhou de zeren—yubei geiyu duzhe de jidian gongxian 現代電影與中國電影節—本刊的創立與今後的責任—預備給與讀者的幾點貢獻 [*Modern Screen* and Chinese movies—the establishment of this journal and its responsibility from now on—a few contributions intended for the reader]," in *Xiandai dianying* 現代電影 [Modern screen], inaugural issue (March 1, 1933), 1.

60. Shen Xiling 沈西苓, "1932 nian Zhongguo dianying de zong jiezhang yu 1933 nian de xin qiwang 一九三二年中國電影界的總結帳與一九三三年的期望 [A summing up of the Chinese movie industry in 1932 and the new hopes for the year 1933]," in *Modern Screen*, inaugural issue (March 1, 1933), 7–9.

61. Liu Na'ou, "Ecranesque [About the screen]" [Liu's own French title], in *Modern Screen* 2 (April 1, 1933), 1.

62. Liu Na'ou, "Lun ticai 論題材 [On subject matter]," in *Modern Screen* 4 (July 1, 1933), 2–3.

63. Liu Na'ou, "Dianying jiezou jianlun 電影節奏簡論 [A brief essay on the rhythm of the camera]," in *Modern Screen* 6 (December 1, 1933), 1–2; "Kaimaila jigou—weizhi jiaodu

jineng lun 開麥拉機構一位置角度機能論 [On the mechanism of the camera—the function of angle and position]," in *Modern Screen* 7 (June 1, 1934), 1–5.

64. Huang Jiamo, "Yingxing yingpian yu ruanxing yingpian 硬性影片與軟性影片 [Hard films and soft films]," in *Modern Screen* 6 (December 1, 1933), 3.

65. Tang Na 唐納, "Qingsuan ruanxing dianying lun—ruanxing lunzhe de quwei zhuyi 清算軟性電影論一軟性論者的趣味主義 [Purging the soft-film theory—the entertainment theory of soft-film theorists]," in *Chen Bao* 晨報 [Morning post], June 19–27.

66. Barbara Foley, *Telling the Truth: The Theory and Practice of Documentary Fiction* (Ithaca: Cornell University Press, 1989).

67. See one picture of Yang Kui taken in Donghai Garden 晨報 in 1979 and reprinted in *CWOYK* 12.

68. Yang Kui, "Shuyōen zakkan [Random notes on Shouyang Garden]," in *CWOYK*, pp. 478–485. Originally published in *Taiwan shinbun* 臺灣新聞 [Taiwan news], March 30–April 2, 1937.

69. Yang Kui, "Yuanding riji 園丁日記 [A gardener's diary]," in *CWOYK* 10:337–345. Originally published in *Xinsheng yuekan* 新生月刊 [New life monthly], November 1956). *New Life Monthly* was a journal published by the inmates of the prison on Green Island.

70. Since the narrator mentions that he has worked in the garden for four years, and since Donghai Garden was established one year after he was released from Green Island, I presume the piece was written in 1966, five years after he was set free.

71. Yang Kui, "Momo de yuanding 默默的園丁 [The silent gardener]," in *CWOYK* 13: 727–732.

72. Yang Kui, "Wuo you yikuai zhuan 我有一塊磚 [I have a brick]," in *CWOYK* 10:398–420. Originally published in *Zhongyang ribao* 中央日報 [Central news daily], October 21, 1976.

73. Yang Kui, "I have a brick."

74. Yang Kui, "Ya bubian de meiguihua 壓不扁的玫瑰 [The indomitable rose]," in *CWOYK* 8:398–420. Originally published as "Chunguang guan buzhu 春光關不住 [The uncontainable splendor of the spring]," in *New Life Monthly* (1957).

75. Yang Kui, "Zuozhe yu duzhe 作者與讀者 [The writer and the reader]," in *CWOYK* 13:676–679. Originally a manuscript piece in *Xinsheng biji* 新生壁報 [New life notebook], which Yang kept during his imprisonment on Green Island.

76. Yang Kui, "Sakka, seikatsu, shakai 作家, 生活, 社会 [Writers, life, and society]," in *CWOYK* 13:543–547. Originally an unpublished manuscript.

77. Yang Kui, "Bungaku zakkan 文學雜感 [Random notes on literature]," in *CWOYK* 13:571–576. Originally an unpublished manuscript.

78. Yang Kui, "Geijutsu wa daishū no mono de aru 藝術は大眾のものである [Art belongs to the people]," in *CWOYK* 9:127–134. Originally published in *Taiwan bungei* 臺灣文藝 [Taiwan arts] 2.2 (February 1935).

79. Yang Kui, "Kōdō shugi kentō 行動主義檢討 [Examining activism]," in *CWOYK* 9: 143–146. Originally published in *Taiwan Arts* 2.3 (March 1935).

80. Yang Kui, "Bungei hihyō no hyōjun 文藝批評の標準 [The criteria of art criticism]," in *CWOYK* 9:154–162. Originally published in *Taiwan Arts* 2.4 (April 1935).

81. Cf. Chie Tarumi's article "An Author Listening to Sounds of the Netherworld: Lu Heruo and the *Kuso*-Realism Debate" in this volume.

82. Nishikawa Mitsuru, "Bungei jihyō 文芸時評 [Contemporary literary criticism]," in *Bungei Taiwan* 文藝臺灣 [Literary Taiwan] 6.1 (May 1943).

83. Sakaguchi Reiko, "Tomoshibi 灯 [Lamp]," in *Taiwan Arts* 3.2 (April 28, 1943), 2–25.

84. Yang Kui, "Kuso riarizumu no yōgo 糞リアリズムの擁護 [In defense of *kuso* realism]," in *CWOYK* 10:110–118. Originally published in *Taiwan Arts* 3.3 (July 1943).

85. See, for instance, Zhang Liangze 張良澤, "Zhengshi Taiwan wenxueshi shang de nanti —guanyu 'huangmin wenxue' zuopin shiyi 正視臺灣文學上的難題—關於台灣「皇民文學」作品拾遺 [Facing a difficult problem in the history of Taiwanese literature—about the resuscitated works of "imperialization literature"], in *Lianhe bao fukan* 聯合報副刊 [United daily literary supplement] (February 10, 1998), 41. Zhang's article triggered a series of debate on the nature of imperialization literature, involving famous writers such as Chen Yingzhen 陳映真 and Peng Ge 彭歌. For a discussion of the debate, see Peng Hsiao-yen, *Lishi henduo loudong: Cong Zhang Wojun dao Li Ang* 歷史很多漏洞: 從張我軍到李昂 [There are many loopholes in history: From Zhang Wojun to Li Ang] (Taipei: Institute of Chinese Literature and Philosophy, Academia Sinica, 2000), 42–45.

86. This work was published in a Tokyo-based journal, *Gōgai* 號外 [Exclusive] 1.3 (September 1927).

87. Yang Kui, "Ari ippiki no shigoto 蟻一匹の仕事 [An ant's work]," collected in *CWOYK* 10:127–130. Originally published in *Kōnan shinbun* 興南新聞 [Southern reconstruction daily], August 30, 1943.

88. Yang Kui, "Wude kurabe 腕くらべ [A wrist wrestling]," collected in *CWOYK* 10:134. Originally published in *Southern Reconstruction Daily* (December 9, 1943).

89. See my discussion in "Yang Kui zuopin de banben, lishi yu 'guojia' 楊逵作品的版本 歷史與「國家」 [Edition, history, and "nation/state" in Yang Kui's works]," in *There Are Many Loopholes in History: From Zhang Wuojun to Li Ang*, 27–50.

90. See, for instance, Tsukamoto Terukazu 塚本照和, "Yōki no 'Denen shōkei' to 'Mōhan mura' no koto 楊逵の「田園小景」と「模範村」 [On Yang Kui's "A Sketch of the countryside" and "Model village"], in *Yomigaeru Taiwan bungaku—Nihon tōtsiki no Taiwan sakka to sakuhin* よみがえる台湾文学—日本統治期の作家と作品 [Taiwanese literature revived: Taiwanese writers and their works during the Japanese occupation], ed. Shimomura Sakujirō, Fujii Shōzō, and Huang Yingzhe (Tokyo: Tōhō shoten, 1995), 313–344.

91. On February 27, 1947, in Taipei, policemen accidentally shot an onlooker in a crowd watching a cigarette vendeuse being beaten up by investigators of the Monopoly Bureau. The incident deepened popular discontent against the Nationalist government, and on February 28 large-scale strikes in the markets, factories, and schools in the city started. At noon when a crowd demonstrated in front of the office of the Taiwan governor, guards used machine guns to shoot at civilians. This triggered the series of resistance movements popularly known as the February 28 Incident. For documentary evidence of this incident, see Lan Bozhou 藍博洲, *Huangmache zhi ge* 幌馬車之歌 [The song of the swaggering horse wagon] (Shibao Publishing Co., 1991), 118; Lan Bozhou, *Chenshi, Liuwang, 2–28* 沉屍 · 流亡 · 二二八 [Buried bodies, exile, and February 28] (Taipei: Shibao Publishing Co., 1991). See also *2–28 shijian ziliao xuanji* 二二八事件資料選輯 [The February 28 Incident: A documentary collection] (Taipei: Institute of Modern History, Academia Sinica, 1992), four volumes. For short stories based on the incident, see Lin Shuangbu, *2–28 Taiwan xiaoshuo xuan* [Collections of Taiwan short stories on the February 28 Incident] (Taipei: Zili Wanbao Pub. Co., 1989).

92. Yang Kui, "Heping xuanyan 和平宣言 [Manifesto of peace]," in CWOYK 14:315–317. Originally printed in the Shanghai-based *Dagongbao* 大公報 [Grand justice daily], January 21, 1949.

93. See Chen Fangming 陳芳明, *Xie Xuehong pingzhuan* 謝雪紅評傳 [Xie Xuehong: A critical biography] (Taipei: Qianwei chubanshe, 1988), 260–280.

94. Wang Lihua, ed., "Guanyu Yang Kui huiyilu biji 關於楊逵回憶錄筆記 [About notes on Yang Kui's mémoir]," in CWOYK 14:70–88. Originally published in *Wenxuejie* 文學界 [Literary field] 14 (May 1985). See also Ho Xun 何眴, ed., "2–28 shijian qianhou [Around the February 28 Incident]," in CWOYK 14:89–98. Originally published in *Taiwan yu shijie* 臺灣與世界 [Taiwan and the world] 21 (May 1985).

95. Yang Kui, "Wo de xiao xiansheng 我的小先生 [My little teacher]," in CWOYK 10: 301–306. Originally published in *Xinshenghuo bibao* 新生壁報 [New life bulletin], January 1956.

96. Huang Chengcong 黃呈聰, "Lun puji baihuawen de xin shiming 論普及白話文的新使命 [On the new mission of propagating the vernacular]," in *Taiwan* (January 1923).

97. Shi Wenqi 施文杞, "Duiyu Taiwanren zuo de baihuawen de wojian 對於臺灣人作的白話文的我見 [My opinion on the vernacular writing of Taiwanese]," in *Taiwan People's Daily* 2.4 (March 11, 1924).

98. Lien Wenqing 連溫卿, "Jianglai zhi Taiwan yu 將來之臺灣語 [The future Taiwanese dialect]," in *Taiwan People's Daily* 2.20–21; 3.4 (October 11 and 21, 1924; February 1, 1925).

99. Zhang Wojun 張我軍, "Xin wenxue yundong de yiyi 新文學運動的意義 [The significance of the New Literature movement]," in *Taiwan People's Daily* 67 (Aug. 26, 1925).

100. Jing 敬, "Taiwan huawen taolun lan 臺灣話文討論欄 [The Taiwanese vernacular forum]," in *Nanyin* (Southern sound), inaugural issue (January 1932), 9.

101. Guo Qiusheng 郭秋生, "Shuo jitiao Taiwan huawen de jichu gongzuo gei dajia cankao 說幾條臺灣話文的基礎工作給大家參考 [On a few items of basic work of the Taiwanese vernacular for everyone's references]," in *Southern Sound*, inaugural issue (January 1932), 14.

102. Lai Ho 賴和 and Guo Qiusheng, "Taiwan huawen de xinzi wenti 臺灣話文的新字問題 [The problem of new words in the Taiwanese vernacular]," in *Southern Sound* 1.3 (February 1, 1932), 14.

103. See Xu Junya 許俊雅, "Yang Shouyu xiaoshuo de fengmao ji qi xiangguan wenti 楊守愚小說的風貌及其相關問題 [The style of Yang Shouyu's fiction and related issues]," in Peng Hsiao-yen, ed., *Minzu guojia lunshu—cong wanqing, wusi dao riju shidai Taiwan xinwenxue* 民族國家論述—從晚清，五四到日據時代臺灣新文學 [Discourse of nation/state—from late-Qing, May Fourth to Taiwanese New Literature during the Japanese occupation] (Taipei: Institute of Chinese Literature and Philosophy, Academia Sinica, 1995).

104. "Hōkoku bungaku ni tsuite 報告文學について [On reportage]," in CWOYK 9:466–468. Originally published in *Osaka asahi shinbun* 大阪朝日新聞 (Osaka morning sun daily), Taiwan edition (February 5, 1937).

105. Yang Kui, trans., "Makesi zhuyi jingjixue 馬克司主義經濟學 [Marxist economics]," in CWOYK 14:326–368. Originally published by Gongnong wenku 工農文庫 [Library of workers and farmers] in 1931. The original Russian book was written by Iosif Abramovich Lapidus and Konstantin Ostrovitianov: *Politicheskaia ekonomiia* [An outline of political economy: Political economy and Soviet economics], 1929.

106. Yang Kui, "Hōkoku bungaku mondō 報告文學問答 [Reportage: Questions and an-

swers]," in *CWOYK* 9:512–532. Originally published in *Taiwan New Literature* 2.5 (June 1937).

107. Yang Kui, "Geijutsu ni okeru 'Taiwan rashii mono' ni tsuite 藝術における"臺灣らしい"ものについて [On the Taiwanese flavor in art]," in *CWOYK* 9:471–474. Originally published in *Osaka Morning Sun Daily*, Taiwan edition (February 21, 1937).

108. See *Shanghai Post* (September 4, 1940), 9.

109. See *Shanghai Post* (June 29, 1940), 9. For news coverage of the murders of Mu Shi-ying and Liu Na'ou, see *Guomin xinwen* 國民新聞 [National subjects' daily], from June 29 to September 30, 1940.

110. Yan Jiayan, *Zhongguo xiandai xiaoshuo liupai shi* 中國現代小說流變史 [Schools of modern Chinese fiction] (Beijing: Renmin wenxue chubanshe, 1989), 131–141.

111. Shi Zhicun told me this during an interview in Shanghai in October 1998.

112. Liu Na'ou, *Diary*, I.234.

113. Liu Na'ou, *Diary*, II.450.

[11]

COLONIAL TAIWAN AND THE CONSTRUCTION
OF LANDSCAPE PAINTING

YEN CHUAN-YING

FROM JAPAN TO TAIWAN: DOCUMENTARY ART HISTORY

In modern times appreciation of the Taiwanese landscape, or the "construction" of landscape painting, gradually began taking shape after Japan established the colonial government, which then provided subjective and institutional guidance. The leading figure in the early phase of this process, and the person whose perceptions were most important, was Ishikawa Kinichirō 石川欽一郎 (1871–1945), who continuously used his watercolors and essays to report on what he observed in Taiwan, starting from the time of his first arrival in 1907.

Ishikawa was a multitalented individual, gifted as both a watercolorist and a writer. His loyal followers in Taiwan praised him for being a modest, self-disciplined gentleman, a poet, and an artist. His painting skills "combined the character of Western painting with that of Nanga [南畫]. His style was simultaneously that of naturalism, *pleinairism*, and Impressionism. He could be called Japan's Corot (1796–1875), Turner (1775–1851), or Millet (1814–1875)."[1]

In his 1926 essay, "Appreciating the Landscape of the Taiwan Region," written after he had lived in Taiwan almost ten years, Ishikawa wrote, "To appreciate Taiwan's landscape, one must first make a contrast and consider it from the perspective of the Japanese landscape."[2] Whenever this initiator of modern Taiwanese art looked at Taiwan's landscape and, indeed, any scene of natural or human interest, he was always reflecting on his homeland, Japan. He would view the "virgin territory" of Taiwan through the filter of a traditional understanding of Japan's natural and manmade scenery. Like many other cultural figures of the Meiji period, Ishikawa was especially talented as a writer of travel literature. Only three months after he retired and returned to Japan in April 1932, he published an essay, "Taiwan's Landscape,"[3] in which he provided a composite evaluation of the various characteristics of Taiwan's landscape. He strongly emphasized general first impressions. For instance, "When one first arrives in Taiwan and gazes afar at the scene of Kheelung from the deck of one's ship, the most enjoyable aspects are the fullness of natural color and the powerful contours of the mountains." In 1935, when he once again reviewed his Taiwan experiences, he repeated that he would never forget his first impressions of Taiwan. He used general, strongly contrastive language: "According to legend, the place is hell, but once one sees it, it becomes heaven. This was my first impression of Taiwan. It is an island of very beautiful forms and colors, and it is pleasing."[4]

In his early years, when Ishikawa worked for the Bureau of Engraving and Printing (*seiheikyoku* 製幣局) in the Finance Ministry, he was a member of the Meiji Fine Arts Society (*meiji bijutsukai* 明治美術會) and a well-known painter of tourist sites in Yokohama.[5] Watercolor paintings were then at the leading edge of the introduction of Western-style painting to Japan, and Japanese artists used watercolors to introduce Japanese scenes and local customs to foreign tourists. The functional aspect of watercolor matched Ishikawa's fondness for travel, his erudition, and his powerful memory, but he also considered watercolor to be a Western medium that could fully express the flavor of Japan.[6]

In 1900, when Japan joined the eight allied powers to put down the Boxer Rebellion in China, Ishikawa used his English and painting skills to serve as a translator at the Japanese army headquarters. He once received orders to sketch a battle in progress for presentation to the Meiji emperor.[7] In 1907, when he came to Taipei again as an army translator, he was already a well-known Tokyo watercolorist and an important contributor of essays to *Mizue* (*Watercolor*, a monthly journal established in 1905). During his first sojourn in Taiwan, from 1907 to 1916, his main outlets remained the Japanese art circles and magazines. Each year, like a migrating bird, he traveled back and forth between Taiwan and Japan.[8]

From his writings, one can readily deduce that he wished to report on Taiwan's landscape, and that his anticipated reading audience consisted of Japanese people who had never visited Taiwan or who had not stayed in Taiwan very long. His first essay published after arriving in Taiwan, "Watercolor Painting and Taiwan's Scenery," encouraged Japanese amateur painters who lived in Taiwan to make use of watercolor's convenience, and introduce Taiwan's beautiful scenery to friends in Japan.

In his early reports, he expressed the thought that the colors of Taipei's old street scenes were more beautiful than their counterparts in Japan. "The red eaves and yellow walls, matched with the green of the bamboo groves, create an effect of thorough intensity. The green of the acacia trees presents a deep majesty never seen before in Japan, and under the blue of the sky it becomes even more exqui-site."[9] The images that created his initial impressions, such as houses, bamboo, acacias, and so on, became the main subject matter of Ishikawa's Taiwanese land-scapes, such as *Little Stream* (fig. 11.1). Depicting an arched stone bridge on one of Taipei's old streets, the painting was admitted to the Bunten (文展; Ministry of Education art exhibition) in 1908. It would be no exaggeration to say that this was his interpretation of what was to him exotic about Taiwan's special qualities or an equivalent of southern China's rich colors.

FIGURE 11.1 Ishikawa Kinichirō, *Little Stream*, 1908.

PAINTINGS OF MOUNTAINS AND THE POLICY OF "CIVILIZING BARBARIANS"

The early development of Taiwanese landscape painting paralleled the opening and exploitation of the aboriginal lands in the mountains. The complex relation-ship between these developments involves many issues deserving of attention. The first concerns the subjugation of the aboriginal peoples.

Ishikawa's first arrival as an army translator coincided with the campaign led by Army General and Governor-General Sakuma Samata 佐久間左馬太 (1844–1915) to militarily subjugate "untamed barbarians" in the mountains so that the forest resources could be exploited. The bloody battles in the mountains lasted ten years.[10] In the early period of Ishikawa's stay in Taiwan, he produced many paintings of the historic battles undertaken to subjugate Taiwan. One of his monumental battleground pictures was hung up in the main hall of the new Taiwan Governor Museum in 1909.[11]

That same year Ishikawa was ordered to enter the central mountain range from Puli and draw topological maps of barbarian territories. He was accompanied and guarded by twenty soldiers, and the entire party, including policemen, translators, and porters, formed a line more than one hundred meters long. Along the guarded perimeter of their encampments, Ishikawa set up tables and chairs to paint large watercolors. Occasionally the guards next to him fired off warning shots toward the mountains, setting off wave after wave of echoes. Ishikawa recalled how he had had to conceal his sketching work on the Tianjin battleground in China, and how this time the work was different: "This time I could spend long periods of time in the open on the perimeter painting the scenery. It was a happy experience that I will never forget."[12] These sketches were sent personally from the governor-general to Tokyo, where they were presented to the Meiji emperor to promote his success in "civilizing barbarians." It was reported that the emperor "was extremely satisfied" with the work.[13]

During this period, when the Japanese army was subjugating aboriginal tribes in the mountains, many Japanese artists like Ishikawa followed the army deep into the mountains to explore and discover new subject matter. These early artists maintained good relations with the military, and after they finished their paintings they would always present the works to the governor-general and other officials. For its part, the colonial government never tired of using art to promote its grand accomplishments.

However, the first persons to enter the mountain territories after Japan took control of Taiwan in 1895 and to study the aborigines had in fact been anthropologists from Tokyo University, such as Torii Ryūzō 鳥居龍藏 (1870–1953).[14] The explorer Mori Ushinosuke 森丑之助 (1877–1926) became acquainted with Torii in Taiwan in 1895 and became his loyal assistant and correspondent in Taiwan. Mori, who studied the aborigines for more than twenty years, not only published descriptive articles under the heading "Correspondence from Taiwan" in the *Tokyo Anthropology Magazine* (*Tōkyō jinruigaku zasshi* 東京人類學雜誌) but also wrote large numbers of expedition reports for the Taiwanese newspaper *Taiwan nichinichi shinpō* 台灣日日新報 and the monthly *Taiwan jihō* 台灣時報 (Taiwan times). Sponsored by the colonial government, he also published *Illustrated Guide to Taiwan's Barbarian Tribes* (*Taiwan banzoku zufu* 台灣蕃族圖譜, 1915; 2 vols.) and *Record of Taiwan's Barbarian Tribes*, vol. 1 (*Taiwan banzoku shi dai-ikkan* 台灣蕃族誌第一卷, 1917). These were used as handbooks for learning about Taiwan's aboriginal peoples, and they were widely read.[15]

The anthropologists' exploratory activities took place primarily during the first ten years of Japan's rule of Taiwan, when the mountain regions were still basically at peace. They were able to gather a wealth of material in a very short period of time. The anthropologists' detailed, lively reports not only became the artists' guidebooks in the mountains and inside their studios—they also became a primary resource for the colonial government as it exploited and oppressed the aborigines under its "civilizing barbarians" policy. If we consider events from this perspective, might it be that while Ishikawa was happily sitting among soldiers at his table in the mountains, depicting the scenery of the central mountain range, he was thinking about the role played by artists under the colonial government?

SUBJECTIVITY AND OBJECTIVITY IN CULTURAL AND ARTISTIC VIEWS

In 1924, one year after he experienced the Great Tokyo Earthquake, Ishikawa was offered a position as art instructor at Taipei Normal School. By this time, Taiwan was being administered by civil, not military, officials, and Ishikawa considered the job offer to be a great opportunity to promote watercolor painting, which had been steadily losing importance in Japan's Western painting circles. Meanwhile, in Taiwan, where art education was just beginning its development, Ishikawa could fully devote himself to spreading his knowledge and techniques.

Ishikawa took seriously his role as a disseminator of culture. For instance, in 1925, he published a painting or an essay almost every other day in the newspaper *Taiwan nichinichi shinpō*. He also published numerous articles on painting techniques and basic appreciation in the monthly journal *Taiwan kyōiku* 台灣教育 (Taiwan education), which was read by teachers and students. He was the most important art educator in Taiwan at that time. In the July 1929 issue of the *Taiwan jihō* he published a long essay on art and culture, "Kumpūta 薫風榻" (The south chair), that centered mainly on the theme of mild nostalgia that develops out of patriotic sentiment. He expressed the thought that Taiwan's natural and human environments lacked an intrinsic flavor and had no distinguished, lingering charm—there was only a bright, hard, coarse quality, no feeling of mysterious loneliness.[16] In contrast to Japan's delicate, stylish culture, Taiwan's culture was coarse, monotonous, and naïve; contrasted with Japan's subdued, gentle landscape, Taiwan's landscape was bright, majestic, and hard.

Because Ishikawa's role changed during his second Taiwan sojourn to that of an art teacher, he dealt with students who were extremely eager to learn, and he was warmly welcomed and revered by them. However, his knowledge of Taiwan seemed to remain stuck at the level of drawing superficial, impressionistic comparisons, especially with regard to light and color. In fact, because he usually did not date the large quantity of Taiwanese landscapes that he finished during the seventeen years he stayed in Taiwan, we always have to rely on changes in his signature or the appearance of newly constructed buildings in his pictures to arrive at approximate dates for his paintings. It is not easy to judge the dates based on his stylistic development or his interpretation of the landscape.

As we re-read Ishikawa's "The South Chair," we see that Japan is always the subjective reference point for his cultural perspective, and that Taiwan functions only occasionally as an objective contrast. He begins his essay:

> As a balmy breeze blows, I sit on my chair, meditating on stylistic perspectives, which is also very much a cooling pleasure. The first question I think about is, does Taiwan really have that kind of stylistic perspective we think of? Thus, it's necessary to first study and examine the so-called Japanese stylistic perspective.

He then introduces in some detail the formation of Higashiyama culture during the Muromachi period (1333–1568), including the tea ceremony, *nō* drama, literature, and art. He infers that Taiwan has no similar stylistic perspective. Although his essay is subtitled "Taiwan's stylistic perspective," he discusses Japanese styles or attitudes toward artistic appreciation only from the Muromachi period to the Edo period. We can well imagine that searching for signs of Muromachi aristocratic culture in Taiwan during the early colonial period was no different than searching for fish in a tree. However, this prompts us to consider a more worthwhile question: what is the deeper meaning to what he considered was the stylish, elegant cultural perspective of the Japanese people?

THE LANDSCAPE OF JAPAN AND TAIWAN

In 1931, another famous watercolorist, Maruyama Banka 丸山晩霞 (1867–1942), Ishikawa's friend, spent nearly two months traveling in Taiwan. He exhibited the works that he painted at the sites he visited and lectured in Taipei on what he had seen and heard.[17] Like Ishikawa, Maruyama was fond of categorizing landscapes, and he also thought that the acacia was Taiwan's most noble tree.

His impressionistic categorizations of Taiwan's rural and natural scenes not only follow Ishikawa's but can also be traced further back to an 1894 work that influenced the aesthetic views of both artists, *The Landscape of Japan* (*Nihon fūkeiron* 日本風景論) by Shiga Shigetaka 志賀重昂 (1863–1927).[18] A cultural-geographical treatise, the book presents a lively description of Japan's landscape. By describing the landscape as a heaven on earth, it promoted a highly patriotic viewpoint. Shiga identified three particular characteristics of the Japanese landscape: elegance, beauty, and boldness. This emphasis on literary elegance is echoed in Ishikawa's "The South Chair" when he extols the stylistic elegance of Japan's Muromachi period. Even though Ishikawa's argument might not come directly from Shiga Shigetaka, the two probably have a common source, and Shiga's theories had circulated widely in Japanese intellectual circles for many years.

Shiga encouraged Japan's geographers to go out and research the geography of all continental Asia. He wrote:

> Japan is a "forerunner country" for Asia, and Asian cultural development is a natural occupation for the Japanese. Therefore, while Europe's geographers have not yet fully researched the geography of continental Asia, Japan's geographers should work to do so. ... This will help establish a lasting reputation for Japan's natural sciences.[19]

Under this "Great Japan" mindset, Mount Fuji became the standard for famous mountains. Shiga suggested that Taiwan's highest mountain, Mount Jade, be renamed "Taiwan's Fuji." Likewise, Mount Tai in Shandong province could be renamed "Shandong's Fuji."[20]

While Shiga elevated Japan's pine trees, Ishikawa chose Taiwan's acacias as a conventional representative of the landscape.[21] *Landscape of Japan* also encouraged an enthusiasm for mountain climbing among Japan's watercolorists, which accounts for the appearance of "mountain painters" (*sangaku gaka* 山岳畫家). They formed groups to study Japan's landscape and local folkways. Thus, when the elderly Maruyama Banka went to Taiwan, he headed directly to Alishan, where he investigated the climate and flora. Based on this first impression of Taiwan's landscape, he categorized Taiwan as a sweet potato–shaped island with a north–south central mountain range that looks like the background of a painting when viewed from the western shore: "In the foreground [of the painting] is an acacia grove, or just one or two acacias, or perhaps a small hill covered with acacias. Matching this in the background is the central mountain range. Water buffaloes function to decorate the scene."[22] This kind of simple, formulaic view-finding, coupled with a poetic vision, is similar to the aesthetic structuring methods used by Shiga Shigetaka to categorize the Japanese landscape.[23] Despite the brevity of such descriptions, they are full of romanticism and nostalgia.

This kind of nostalgic sentiment may be said to represent Ishikawa's main theme in his depictions of Taiwanese landscapes. Among his Taiwanese landscape paintings, we find many that depict acacia trees (fig. 11.2: *Taiwan Street*), and many others that seek to express a nostalgic mood through the depiction of old buildings, such as *Old City*, painted around 1910. The pavilion-like structure in this painting is Taipei's Little South Gate (Hsiao-nan-men), which remains from the Ch'ing dynasty city wall. Later in his career Ishikawa repeatedly depicted Little South Gate from memory, even though the scene had long since changed, as in 1932's *South Gate Street* (fig. 11.3). In his earlier *Old City*, the detail in the clouds, the broad, low horizon, and the majestic height of the trees clearly reflect the influence of nineteenth-century English landscape painting.

FIGURE 11.2 Ishikawa Kinichirō, *Taiwan Street*, undated.

FIGURE 11.3 Ishikawa Kinichirō, *South Gate Street*, 1932.

With all this as background, we can better understand how Ishikawa came to define Japanese stylistic elegance via a blend of Muromachi period literature and artistic tradition. Meanwhile, under the rising influence of patriotism from the beginning of the Meiji era, he considered Japanese aesthetics as the highest expression of East Asian civilization. Due to the impact of Shiga's *Landscape of Japan*, Ishikawa could not avoid using "Japan's three most beautiful sights" as standards for all other landscapes, or for considering the coast of the Seto Inland Sea as the most beautiful in the world.[24] Perhaps the same kind of Meiji era nationalism that led him to join the eight allied forces in China also accompanied him after he went to Taiwan's mountains and portrayed the governor-general's invasions there.

We cannot overlook the lasting influence that the rural landscapes promoted by Ishikawa and other watercolorists had on the first phase of modern Taiwanese art. The influence was not limited to the students who studied directly under him but extended to all who formed their earliest artistic perspectives by reading his many articles. We cannot help but recall that Huang T'u-shui 黃土水, the first-generation Taiwanese sculptor active during the 1920s, also understood the Taiwanese landscape through the filter of a kind of rural romanticism (fig. 11.4).[25]

If we look at the list of works shown in the first three Taiwan Art Exhibitions (*Taiwan bijutsu teurankai* 台灣美術展覽會; 1927–1929), we find that acacia trees were a very popular subject, especially in rural scenes, where their gently curving branches often appear at the foot of mountains or along roadsides. In the Oriental painting (*Tōyō ga* 東洋画) category of the exhibitions, artists like Lin Yü-shan 林玉山 (b. 1907; *Large Southern Gate*, 1927, fig. 11.5) and Kishita Seigai 木下靜涯 (1887–1988; *Wind and Rain*, 1927, fig. 11.6) paid very close attention to the forms of acacia trees. As for the Western painting (*Seiyō ga* 西洋画) category,

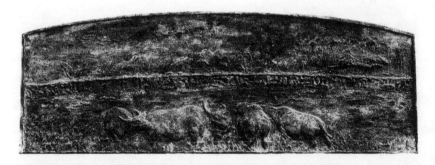

FIGURE 11.4 Huang T'u-shui, *Landscape of the South*, relief, 1927.

FIGURE 11.5 Lin Yü-shan, *Large Southern Gate*, 1927.

FIGURE 11.6 Kishita Seigai,
Wind and Rain, 1927.

FIGURE 11.7 Su Hsin-I,
To the Three Gorges, 1928.

many paintings by Ishikawa's students were admitted, such as Su Hsin-i's *To the Three Gorges* (1928; fig. 11.7).

WATERCOLOR PAINTING AND TRENDS IN
CONTEMPORARY ART

Ishikawa's promotion of watercolor painting in Taiwan was an extension of the early-twentieth-century popularity of modern Western art in Japan, and Taiwan in the 1920s was an excellent place for him to establish watercolor painting.[26] Of course, he succeeded in cultivating many amateur artists. As for Ishikawa himself, though, he gradually lost touch with the mainstream trends of Western-style art in Japan, including the academic school, after he spent so many years in Taiwan — not due to the geographic distance so much as the rapidity of change in Japanese artistic trends. More important, with the opening of the Taiwan Art Exhibition in 1927, more and more professionally trained artists appeared. These included Taiwanese and Japanese students who had received training in the Tokyo School of Fine Art and eminent Japanese artists who had been invited to come to Taiwan as judges for the art exhibitions. As these artists enriched the Taiwanese art scene, watercolor painting gradually faded from the mainstream, and Ishikawa's influence waned quickly.

Furthermore, the other Japanese judge of Western-style exhibition painting, Shiotsuki Tōhō 鹽月桃甫 (1885–1954), specially addressed the issue of watercolor painting in his brief judge's statement after the exhibition in 1927:

> Watercolor painting, which is more prone to technical constraints than oil paint-ing, can easily fall into the old pattern of following prior masters' methods. I hope that watercolorists deeply reflect on this. If they forget to explore their own unique realm, then their painting stops at the level of mere work.[27]

Shiotsuki's brief warning cut deep. By the 1930s, his distinctive style and in-fluence had formed a counterbalance to that of Ishikawa, replaced it, and be-come another force—which will be the subject of another essay. In short, at the sixth Taiwan Art Exhibition in October 1932, only one watercolor painting was included, Lan Ying-ting 藍蔭鼎's *Commercial Lane* (fig. 11.8). Lan was consid-ered Ishikawa's handpicked successor, but after this year he withdrew from the competition.

FIGURE 11.8 Lan Ying-ting, *Commercial Lane*, 1932.

As for the Taiwan Watercolor Society, founded under the guidance of Ishikawa in 1926, it faced a serious trial in 1931, due to the storm caused by the exhibition in Taipei of Fauvist and surrealist paintings by artists of the Dokuritsu Bijutsu-kyōkai 獨立美術協會 (Association of Independent Artists) from Tokyo: one after another member abandoned watercolor and joined the new schools of painting. At the summer art seminars of the Dokuritsu Bijutsukyōkai in Taipei, more and more younger Taiwanese and Japanese artists who had been born in Taiwan were in attendance.[28] From this time onward, watercolor painting was no longer part of the Taiwanese artistic mainstream, just as rural cowherd romanticism had also faded. The artists of the younger generations would have a much broader subject matter and much brighter prospects to confront in their individual works.

NOTES

1. "Onshi Ishikawa Kinichirō sensei [Our beloved teacher, Mr. Ishikawa Kinichirō]," *Taiwan kyōiku* 台灣教育 [Taiwan education] 412 (Nov. 1936), 71–74.

2. Ishikawa Kinichirō, "Taiwan hōmen no fūkei kanshō ni tsuite," *Taiwan jihō* 台灣時報 [Taiwan review] (March 1926), 53.

3. Ishikawa Kinichirō, "Taiwan no sansui," *Taiwan jihō* (July 1932), 110–116.

4. Ishikawa Kinichirō, "Taiwan fūkō no kaisō [Recollections of Taiwan's scenery]," *Taiwan jihō* (June 1935), 53.

5. Tachibana Gishō, "Ishikawa Kinichirō—aru Meiji seishin no dansei to sono shūen [Ishikawa Kinichirō: The birth of a certain Meiji spirit and its final moment]," in *Shizuoka no bijutsu V—Ishikawa Kinichirō ten* 静岡的美術五—石川欽一郎展 [Fine Arts of Shizuoka V —Exhibition of Ishikawa Kinichirō] (Shizuoka: Shizuoka Prefectural Museum of Fine Art, 1992), 10.

6. Ishikawa, "Suisaiga to Taiwan fūkō [Watercolor painting and Taiwan's scenery]," *Taiwan nichinichi shinpō* 台灣日日新報 [Taiwan daily news], Jan. 23, 1908.

7. Ishikawa, "Tattaka no omode [Recollections of Tattaka]," *Taiwan jihō* (November 1929), 124.

8. "Ishikawa Kinichirō nempu [Chronology of Ishikawa Kinichirō]," in *Shizuoka no bijutsu V—Ishikawa Kinichirō ten*, 168–169; Lin Ju-wei, "Shih-ch'uan Ch'in-i-lang ti-i-tz'u tsai T'ai-wan te huo-tung [Ishikawa Kinichirō's activities during his first sojourn in Taiwan]," *I-shu-chai* [The artist], June 1995, 350–360.

9. Ishikawa, "Suisaiga to Taiwan fūkō."

10. Fujii Shitsue, *Li fan—Jih-pen chih-li T'ai-wan te chi-ts'e* [Civilizing the barbarians: Japan's policy in governing Taiwan] (Taipei: Wen-ying-t'ang, 1997), 209.

11. "Hakubutsukan no itsu isai (Kitashirakawa go dassen no hengaku) [A conspicuous addition to the museum (Prince Kitashirakawa's battleground picture)]," *Taiwan nichinichi shinpō*, March 8, 1909, 5; Ishikawa, "Nōkyū shinnō tenshita Hakkeyama sensō yuga kinsaku ni tsuite [Regarding the respectfully composed oil painting of His Majesty Prince Nōkyū at the Mount Pakua Battle]," in Taiwan Hakubutsukan kyōkai, *Sōritsu sanjū nen kinen ronbun-*

shū [Essays on the thirtieth anniversary of the Taipei museum's founding] (Taipei: Haku-butsukan, 1939).

12. Ishikawa, "Tatsutaka no omode."

13. "Nantō bankai shaseiga no kenjō [Presentation of paintings of the barbarian regions]," *Taiwan nichinichi shinpō*, July 24, 1909, 2; "Eikan no seiban shasaiga (Ishikawa Kin'ichirō shi no kōei) [Imperial approval of the paintings of untamed barbarians (Mr. Ishikawa Kin'ichirō's honor)]," *Taiwan nichinichi shinpō*, Aug. 29, 1909, 6.

14. Nakasono Hidesuke, *Niao-chu Lung-tsang—ts'ung-heng T'ai-wan yü Tung-ya te jen-lei-hsüeh hsien-ch'ü* [Torii Ryūzō: Pioneering anthropologist who covered Taiwan and East Asia], trans. Yang Nan-ch'ün (Taichung: Hsing-chen, 1998).

15. See Miyaoka Maoko, "Yajin no bunka jinruigaku [Rustics' cultural anthropology]," in *Nanpō bunka* 24 (Nov. 1997), 123–137; Mori Ushinosuke, *T'ai-wan hsing-chiao—Sen Ch'ou-chih-chu te T'ai-wan t'an-hsien* [Taiwan tracks: Mori Ushinosuke's Taiwanese expeditions], trans. Yang Nan-ch'ün (Taipei: Yuan-liu, 2000), 26.

16. Ishikawa, "Kumpūta [The south chair]," *Taiwan jihō* (July 1929), 50–55.

17. Maruyama Banka, "Watashi no moku ni Taiwan fūkei [Taiwanese landscapes I have seen]," *Taiwan jihō* (August 1931), 32–42.

18. This book was so widely read that by June 1903 it was already in its fifteenth printing, and had been expanded with each reprinting.

19. Shige, *Nihon fūkeiron*, 326.

20. Shige, *Nihon fūkeiron*, 320, 329.

21. Ishikawa, "Suisaiga to Taiwan fūkō."

22. Maruyama, "Watashi no moku ni Taiwan fūkei"; Yen Chuan-ying, *T'ai-wan chin-tai mei-shu ta-shih nien-piao*, 115–116.

23. Shiga, *Nihon fūkeiron*, 17.

24. The "Three Famous Scenes" in Japan are Matsushima 松島, Amanohashidate 天橋, and Itsukushima 嚴島, all of which are famous for their pine trees. For descriptions of these three places and the Seto Inland Sea, see Maruyama, "Watashi no moku ni Taiwan fūkei," and Ishikawa, "Kumpūta."

25. For a discussion of Huang T'u-shui's rural style, see Yen Chuan-ying, "P'ai-huai tsai hsien-tai i-shu yü min-tsu i-shih chih chien—T'ai-wan chin-tai mei-shu-shih hsien-ch'ü Huang T'u-shui [Wandering between modern art and ethnic consciousness: Huang T'u-shui, a forerunner of Taiwan's modern art history]," in Yen, ed., *T'ai-wan chin-tai mei-shu ta-shih nien-piao*, xvii–xxiii.

26. Nakamura Giichi, "Nihon kindai bijutsushi ni okeru Taiwan—Ishikawa Kinichirō to Shiotsuki Tōhō [Taiwan in modern Japanese art history: Ishikawa Kinichirō and Shiotsuki Tōhō]," in *Shizuoka no bijutsu V—Ishikawa Kinichirō ten*, 24.

27. Shiotsuki Tōhō, "T'ai-chan yang-hua kai-p'ing," trans. Wang Shu-chin, in *Taiwan jihō* (November 1927), 21–22.

28. About the activities of Taiwan's newly developed arts groups, see Yen Chuan-ying, "Jih-chih shih-tai mei-shu hou-ch'i te fen-lieh yü chieh-shu [Divisions and endings in art during the late period of Japanese rule]," in *Ho wei T'ai-wan*, 17–18.

12

AN AUTHOR LISTENING TO VOICES FROM THE NETHERWORLD

Lu Heruo and the *Kuso* Realism Debate

TARUMI CHIE*

Lu Heruo 呂赫若[1] (1914–1950) is one of the Taiwanese authors who best represents prewar Taiwanese literature. In January 1935 Lu made his debut in the Japanese proletarian magazine *Bungaku hyōron* 文学评论 with "Gyūsha 牛車," a tragedy set in colonial Taiwan and indicting modernization. Further, Lu enthusiastically helped lead the 1930s Taiwan New Literature movement as an influential writer and during the 1940s he was active as a singer in the Tōhō performance troop, which gained popular favor with their enterprising combination of Greater East Asian Co-Prosperity Sphere ideology and orientalism. When he returned to Taiwan, Lu played a leading role in local theatrical and musical movements and also stood as one of the emblematic authors of the magazine *Taiwan bungaku* 台湾文学—a publication that cannot be overlooked in any consideration of Taiwanese literature. Finally, shortly after the war, Lu lost his life in the Luku incident 鹿窟事件, when he and others led by the Chinese Communist Party attempted to liberate Taiwan. In opening, then, the rise and fall of the proletarian literature movement as well as the conversion-literature phenomenon, the influence of Greater East Asian Co-Prosperity Sphere ideology, and the effects of wartime cultural regulation, wartime cooperation, and postwar decolonization on the question of the essential colonial Taiwanese self all have a direct bearing on our attempt to understand the traces left behind by Lu Heruo.

Certainly any study of Lu Heruo must raise a number of questions, but I want to narrow the focus of this essay to the attack on Lu in May of 1943 by one of

the Japanese authors who best represents colonial Taiwanese literature, Nishikawa Mitsuru 西川满. By first providing a comparative analysis of Nishikawa's
"Ryūmyakuki 龙脉记" and Lu's "Fūsui 风水," which both take fengshui as a
theme, and then continuing with a similar comparative analysis of the coterie
magazines *Bungei Taiwan* 文艺台湾 and *Taiwan bungaku* in which each played
a leading role, I consider the line stretching across both time and space that con-
nects the 1940s Taiwanese *bundan* 文坛 and the 1930s Japanese *bundan*. In conclusion I discuss the nature of the connection between colonial Taiwanese literature and the Japanese proletariat literature movement and the limits of the
latter.

First, I wish to make explicit the form of Nishikawa's attack on Lu. In the "Contemporary Criticism" section of the May 1943 issue of *Bungei Taiwan*, Nishikawa,
as directing editor, wrote: "this '*kuso* realism' that has become the mainstream in
Taiwanese literature is entirely the style of writing which has been coming into
Japan from America and Europe since the Meiji [era]. For we Japanese, ... who
love the cherry blossoms, this sort of thing elicits no resonance." He adds, "Among
the unchanging narration of the ever poorly treated stepchild, family struggles,
and other such matters as well as important events and local customs, this island's
next generation is faithfully reporting and volunteering to duty. [You] authors of
kuso realism, [are] turning [your] backs on and [are] unconscious of the times.
What an irony it is!"

That unnamed *Taiwan bungaku* authors, especially Lu Heruo and Zhang
Wenhuan 张文环, were the object of Nishikawa's attack was readily self-evident.
Further, *Taiwan bungaku* authors, including Yang Kui 杨逵, published responses
to the attack.[2] The discussion that developed from this exchange came to be
known and simply referred to as the *kuso* realism debate.[3]

Together *Bungei Taiwan* and *Taiwan bungaku* were a driving force in the 1940s
Taiwanese literary field. With its inaugural issue published in January 1940 and
Nishikawa Mitsuru as a core member, *Bungei Taiwan* served as the bulletin for
the Taiwan Literatus Association (Taiwan bungeika kyōkai 台湾文艺家协会).
This is the same group that was originally founded by Yano Hōjin 矢野峰人, a Taihoku Imperial University professor, and was largely composed of Japanese people
living in Taiwan. The magazine changed direction from its original strongly artistic focus and began actively participating in national policy vis-à-vis its editorial
posture and viewpoint. It is well known that Zhou Jinbo 周金波's "Shiganhei 志愿
兵," Chen Huoquan 陈火泉's "Michi 道," and other so-called *kōminka* literature
appeared in its pages. In May 1941 *Taiwan bungaku* splintered off from *Bungei
Taiwan* with its inaugural issue. Members of *Taiwan bungaku* made use of the
slogans supporting promotion of local culture issued by the cultural department
of the Taisei Yokusan Kai 大政翼赞会 inasmuch as they claimed to have the Taiwanese people at heart and espoused literature of a realistic spirit with Taiwanese
life as its root (*gen/kon*).[4] Lu enthusiastically adopted Taiwanese folk customs and

traditions as subject matter for his works and best embodied the direction of the magazine.

Still, what in general were the literary tendencies and inclinations in Lu's works that Nishikawa critiqued in his disavowal of Lu's texts as *kuso* realism? In fact, Lu and Nishikawa had both published works on the theme of fengshui ("Fūsui" and "Ryūmyakuki") in the year, more or less, prior to the eruption of the debate; though the narratives both take the theme of fengshui, in the end the two works appeal to completely different tastes. Perhaps the differences are what the *kuso* realism debate itself represented, and this in turn is emblematic of the divergences between the two authors and the dissimilarities between *Taiwan bungaku* and *Bungei Taiwan*. As such, I begin this evaluation with a comparative reading of the two narratives.

LU HERUO, "FŪSUI"

Lu Heruo's "Fūsui" was published in the October 1942 issue of *Taiwan bungaku*. The story follows the Zhou brothers and their families, and as the narrative begins the elder brother is on the verge of a nervous breakdown because of his younger brother's opposition to the performance of a bone-cleaning for their father, who died fifteen years earlier. The younger brother argues that that the family's prosperity stems from the location, that is to say the fengshui, of their father's grave; and, predicating his argument on the advice provided by a geomancer, the younger brother demonstrates that a bone-cleaning would unnecessarily disturb tomb fengshui.

Now, however, the younger brother's family is running into misfortune, and he claims that the poor fengshui of their mother's five-year-old grave is to blame; therefore, he asks his elder brother to surreptitiously perform the mother's bone-cleaning ritual earlier than prescribed. When the coffin is exhumed the horrific stench of the still-putrefying corpse is overpowering and, in a manner suiting his character, the younger brother abandons his plan to clean their mother's bones. In the past, the family had respected its ancestors and had placed a great deal of importance on rites and rituals and their accompanying decorum as had always been done, but now they were using the rites and fengshui for personal gain and profit, which in turn was leading to family discord. The elder Zhou brother weeps as he realizes what has happened to his family and their respect for fengshui as the story closes.

A close examination of the broad range of fengshui customs in Taiwan and East Asia is beyond the scope of this paper, but I would like to paraphrase Watanabe Yoshio 渡边欣雄, who explains that the fortunes and ills that humanity encounters can all be traced back to fengshui. Simply stated, there are two kinds of fengshui: *yin* 阴 fengshui, which attends to graves, and *yang* 阳 fengshui, which concerns cities, settlements, and homes.⁵ The fengshui addressed in "Fūsui" then is necessarily *yin*, or grave, fengshui. Moreover, Kataoka Iwao 片岡巖's *Taiwan fūzokushi* 台湾风俗志 includes these explanatory notes on the customs and traditions surrounding fengshui in Taiwan:

> After a prescribed period of time has passed the grave is excavated and the bones picked out, cleaned, and inserted into a pot, which is then placed in a structure as per fengshui. This (practice), which is nothing more or less than superstition, is supported by belief in the words of geomancers, Daoist priests, prophets, and others. A bad tomb placement will lead to misfortune for the family, or prevent success for future generations and for this reason there are numerous cases of bone-cleaning and re-burials for the purpose of tomb relocation.⁶

But why did Lu choose fengshui as the theme for a story? Perhaps one of the reasons for the choice was the fact that while he was writing "Fūsui" Lu himself faced the problem of an ancestral bone-cleaning and tomb relocation.⁷ His interest in fengshui did not arise from his personal experiences alone, however. Ever since the publication of "Zaishiju 財子寿" in March 1943, each of his *Taiwan bungaku*–era stories had been characterized by narrations of traditional Taiwanese lives and customs; in other words, Lu was profoundly concerned with ethnological story material.

For example, the appearance of a mansion named Fukujūdō 福寿堂 in "Zaishiju" is described with precise attention to architectural detail; this description creates an immutable stage to the complex human relations which therein develop. Other examples of minute spatial descriptions affecting interlaced settings and human relationships from Lu's fiction include "Gōka heian 合家平安" and "Rinkyō 隣居." Furthermore, foregrounded in these architectural and spatial depictions are descriptions of religious customs. In "Fūsui" Lu writes very concrete descriptions, from the explanation of bone-cleaning and the time it takes for bones to ossify—which is in turn linked to the method of examining the color of paint on the coffin (as an indicator of decomposition)—to the manner in which the geomancer uses a *luojia pan* 羅針盤 to determine proper tomb site location. Further, in "Gōka heian" and "Zakuro 拓榴" the various Taiwanese customs surrounding marriage and adoptive marriage, such as *zhaofu* 招夫 and *pinjin* 聘金, are narrated in a manner deeply connected to the theme.

The rich descriptions of the situations and events that constitute the customs and traditions of Taiwanese life along with Lu's narration of his ethnological concerns as he constructed universes within his works suggest we consider that he consciously adopted a methodology predicated on these same ethnological concerns. We postulate three reasons for Lu's reaching such a methodology. The first is that he published in *Taiwan bungaku*. As noted above, *Taiwan bungaku* claimed to have the Taiwanese people at its heart and to espouse literature of a realistic nature with Taiwanese life as its root. The second factor we can point to is the November 1940 publication and ensuing stage performances of Shōzi Sōichi 庄司總一's novel *Chin fujin* 陳夫人. The work, which includes a Tainan capital-ist, Chen Qingwen 陳清文, and his Japanese wife, Yasuko 安子, as protagonists, stirred public response; and the following year Shōzi's novel was dramatized by Bungakuza 文学座 in May and by Shinsei shinpa 新生新派 in August.[8] More-over, because it "offered a pragmatic resolution to the unification of Taiwan and Japan proper in a literary work," the novel was awarded the East Asian Literary Award; in a sense it was a work of national policy literature.[9]

After watching the Bungakuza performance of *Chin fujin*, Lu published a six-part critique, "The Performance of *Chin fujin*," in *Kōnan shinbun* (May 20–25, 1941), and obtained a copy of the original text, which he spent a sleepless night reading. Lu revealed in the critique that he was moved by Shōzi's "wonderful expression of [Taiwanese] anguish and character personality within the Chen family," and further wrote about Yasuko that she was "a character with completely different customs who served as a benchmark against which [one could] clearly pick up numerous Taiwanese customs and institutions." However, he added that "the narrative grasp of natives [Taiwanese] who have received a modern edu-cation" would be successful, but that "comparatively speaking more traditional natives, or those further distanced from modern education and current native trends, are probably in a difficult position to describe the so-called native." In the end, envious of the successful performance of *Chin fujin* Lu wondered, "What would happen if this sort of drama was presented on the Taiwan stage?" and, burning with ambition, concluded, "it's regrettable that Tokyo seized the initia-tive and brought it first to the stage."

Not long after seeing the performance, in August of the same year Lu wrote "Zaishiju," stirring from the literary stagnation he had been in since 1937 and ini-tiating his most productive period with *Taiwan bungaku*.[10] Characteristic of Lu's texts from this era is the already noted meticulous narration of traditions and cus-toms as well as descriptions of traditional Taiwan. In his critique of *Chin fujin* he argued that the successes and failures of the novel were layered in the narra-tion of the traditional. In brief, Lu was conscious of the fact that the success of *Chin fujin* was due to the attraction and satisfaction of the Japanese gaze by, to, and with ethnic Taiwan. For Lu this realization stirred a new ambition—a desire to record and document more clearly than Shōzi the "Taiwan" that the Japanese colonizer couldn't see. In a manner of speaking, rivalry with the colonizer Shōzi made Lu aware of "traditional" Taiwan. Still it must be further added that a pas-sion for documenting and recording the Taiwan that the Japanese gaze couldn't find was not limited only to Lu. The July 1941 publication of *Minzoku Taiwan* 民俗台湾's inaugural issue remains the third issue key to understanding the ori-gin of Lu's methodology.

Minzoku Taiwan, a monthly magazine dedicated to the research and presen-tation of Taiwanese customs and traditions, was published by the Taipei branch

(Taipeishiten 台北支店) of Tokyo *Shoseki kabushikikaisha* (東京書籍株式会社). A total of forty-three issues were published during its run from July 1941 to January 1945.[11] Each issue carried records and collections of ethnological data, ethnological studies, essays connected to ethnology, and other such writing, focusing on the main island of Taiwan. Serving as the authorial and editorial core of the magazine were Ikeda Toshio 池田敏雄 and Kanaseki Takeo 金關丈夫. Kanaseki, a professor of anatomy at Taihoku Imperial Medical College, also acted as editor. Lu published two articles in the magazine; "*Laqing* and *baguashi*—a history of marriage customs 拉青と八卦篩—結婚習俗の故事" (2.1, January 1942) and "The circumstances surrounding adopted daughters-in-law 媳婦仔の場合" (3.11, November 1943). Furthermore, Ikeda and Kanaseki's names repeatedly appear in Lu's journal, suggesting that he maintained a strong connection with *Minzoku Taiwan*.

Prior to publication the magazine would distribute a multifaceted prospectus entitled "*Minzoku Taiwan*—at the presses." This was a *kōminka* employing charmlike (*jūmon* 呪文) text used to avoid the authorities; but, if read as something other than a charm, the prospectus reveals traditional Taiwanese culture as on the brink of eradication by *kōminka*. It was a sad voice crying out that if things continued as they were traditional culture's extinction was inevitable. This feeling of crisis was the true reason for the creation of *Minzoku Taiwan*. Even more clearly expressing the sense of crisis is Kanaseki Takeo's editor's note in the inaugural issue, wherein he transparently implied Taiwan as he wrote of the destruction of Carthage.

Lu Heruo felt this sense of crisis with Kanaseki. The fear of cultural extinction and his self-imposed mission to record Taiwanese culture for posterity led Lu to depict with cameralike realism in his literary works various human relationships, architectural structures, and clothing, as well as traditions and customs. This passion for recording did not lead to dull transformations of reality, but rather linked complex transformations of reality to textual creation. "Fūsui" thus stands prominently as an example of Lu's concern with ethnic Taiwan, as driven by his participation in *Taiwan bungaku*, his response to *Chin fujin*, and his association with *Minzoku Taiwan*.

NISHIKAWA MITSURU, "RYŪMYAKUKI"

What were Nishikawa Mitsuru's intentions when he wrote "Ryūmyakuki" and first published it in the September 1942 issue (4.6) of *Bungei Taiwan*?

Becker, the protagonist, is a German engineer who under the direction of Liu Mingchuan 劉銘傳 strives to establish a railway system. However, in order to build the railroad he must break a fengshui "dragon's back" by boring a tunnel. However, building the tunnel in these negative conditions meets resistance from the Qing laborers, which eventually brings construction to a standstill. With Liu's support Becker devotedly proceeds with the railway and in the end completes the tunnel. Regardless of fate and misfortune or cause and effect the tunnel is bored through the middle of the dragon's head.

As Nakajima Toshio 中島利郎 has correctly pointed out, beginning with the June publication of "Taiwan no kisha 台湾の汽車" Liu Mingchuan and the German engineers Becker and Piteran appear as characters in the related works "Futari no doitsujin gishi 二人の独逸技師," "Ryūmyakuki," and "Tōen'no kyaku 桃園の客" and are linked with Nishikawa's most important work, *Taiwan jyūkantetsudō* 台湾縦貫鉄道.[12] That Nishikawa's father, Jun 純, came along with his uncle Akiyama Giichi 秋山義一 to help manage the Akiyama 秋山 coal mines in Jilong and later became the president of Shōwa Coal is well known;[13] and Nishikawa, because he came from a colonizing family, possessed intense self-confidence. Consequently, his motivation to choose *Taiwan jyūkantetsudō* for a string of linked stories is not difficult to imagine. In the afterword to the 1979 reprint of *Taiwan jyūkantetsudō*, Nishikawa writes that his interest in presenting the untold story of the Taiwan railroad from the time of Liu Mingchuan forward stemmed from a strong attachment to his father, and a desire to "describe the Taiwan of the pioneering days before any Japanese had set to work."[14] Becker's attitude as he struggles with the superstitions of his Chinese laborers reveals colonizer Nishikawa's position. Simply stated, Nishikawa constructed a narrative of nation-building around fengshui.[15]

Returning to Lu: Nishikawa's ridicule of his *Taiwan bungaku*–era work as stories about the "ever poorly treated stepchild, and family struggle" is not excessive, because the works did continually depict the tragedy of traditional Taiwanese households. Through the contrasting attitudes between the two brothers in "Fūsui" Lu shows the collapse of the traditional family unit based on ancestor worship. The older Zhou brother's ideal is "a family which like so many others followed the orders of a long-bearded, queue-wearing grandfather—a family valorizing the rights of and venerating ancestors."[16] For the elder Zhou fengshui is the symbol that binds such a family together, but as the story concludes he is forced to recognize that such prosperity has already been destroyed. Furthermore, as sugar factory smokestacks are reflected in the elder brother's eyes while he is returning home from the graveyard, the younger brother, whose avarice led to the collapse of the traditional family, thinks, "There is no reason for [my] son and daughter to enter medical school." The sugar factory and medical school, which are emblematic of the modernity that has come to Taiwan with the colonial government, are for the younger Zhou the reason for the collapse of tradition.

Here we see the contrasting attitudes of these authors toward modernization. "Ryūmyakuki" glorifies modernization as it chronicles a chapter in a nation-building saga; and "Fūsui," by positing the brothers' argument as a microcosm, depicts the collapse of tradition in the face of modernization. The difference between the two stories also reflects the manner of taking up fengshui. Lu treats *yin* fengshui (tombs) in "Fūsui" and Nishikawa treats *yang* fengshui (cities, settlements, and homes) in "Ryūmyakuki." The Japanese colonizer Nishikawa depicts the modernization of living space. The colonized Taiwanese Lu looks to the domain of the dead. Lu attains what the colonizer cannot: he listens to the voices of the netherworld.

BACKGROUND TO THE *KUSO*
REALISM CONTROVERSY

It seems that the contrast between "Fūsui" and "Ryūmyakuki" can be understood as a classic example of the dichotomy between colonizer and colonized. Although these authors were endowed with completely different gifts, the notion that their confrontation stemmed from the *kuso* realism debate is not inconceivable. But if this is the case, does comparing the authors and discussing the *kuso* realism debate then do nothing more than reinforce a confirmation of the diametricism of the colonizer and the colonized? I now wish to draw out the supplementary and connecting line between Japanese proletariat literature and colonized writers. The critical term "*kuso* realism" must first be attended to.

Actually, "*kuso* realism" was not coined by Nishikawa—in 1935 (Shōwa 10) it was well known and on the lips of all the members of the Japanese *bundan* in describing *Jinminbunko* 人民文庫. The term evolved from the search for literary direction following the collapse of the proletariat literature movement, and the ensuing *Nihonrōmanha* debate. In 1932, following the Manchurian incident, suppression of the Japanese proletariat literature movement markedly increased. In February 1933, Koabayashi Takiji 小林多喜二, the defining author of the movement, died in prison as he was being interrogated. In June 1933 two of the central Japanese Communist Party leaders, Sano Manabu 佐野学 and Nabeyama Sadachika 鍋山貞親, issued a joint statement of conversion. Thereafter renouncements of communism followed one after another, and in March 1933 the Japanese Proletariat Writers' League (NALP) was dissolved.

Against this background and arising from the January 1934 publication of the "Nihonrōmanha kōkoku 日本浪漫派広告," another literary debate developed and evolved into two camps, *Nihonrōmanha* and *Jinminbunko*; both groups were firmly entrenched by the March 1936 publication of *Jinminbunko*'s inaugural issue. At this time Hayashi Fusao 林房雄 used the term "*kuso* realism" in a criticism of the *Jinminbunko*.[17]

Originally Hayashi Fusao had been a member of the central committee of the Japanese Proletariat Writers' League, but around 1935 he announced he was a romanticist, and as he drew closer to *Japanism* (*nihonshugi* 日本主義) he announced his withdrawal from proletariat literature in 1936. Thereafter, he joined the radical right and affirmed the war; moreover, even in the postwar GHQ purge he did not change his stance.[18] In 1963, moved by Hayashi's ideas, Mishima Yukio wrote *Hayashi Fusao ron* 林房雄論. The period in which Hayashi began his shift to the radical right overlaps with the start of his attack on the realism so important to Takeda Rintarō 五田麟太郎, the leading *Jinminbunko* author, and other members of the collective.[19]

Jinminbunko replies to Hayashi's critique include those by Hirabayashi Hyogo 平林彪吾, who wrote "Hayashi Fusao e'no Tegami 林房雄への手紙," and Shibukawa Takashi 渋川驍; both are authors of critical pieces defending realism. Moreover, there were also literary roundtables, such as "Nihon no romanha wo tadasu 日本の浪漫派を訊す."[20] These *Jinminbunko* activities had the tripartite goal of (1) challenging any government-establishment literary movement; (2) establishing an orthodox developmental trajectory for realism with a prose spirit; and (3) the creation of fiction for the masses.[21] Years later the following summary remains accurate: "Despite accompanying various weak points, at what is clearly a turning point in modern literature *Jinminbunko* chose the path of resistance literature, and from that position accomplished various experiments with (their) works."[22] Former proletarian literature writers employed *kuso* realism as their last seawall before literary fascism.

This realism was quite removed from the social realism that had originally been employed toward political goals, because with the passage of time it had expanded to encompass depictions of the common and everyday. Consequently, the *Jinminbunko* authors, especially Takeda Rintarō, were charged with writing *fūzoku* 風俗 fiction. Years later, in Shōwa 10, when *fūzoku* fiction was popular, the critique came that, "realism as a technique has 'withered' away to the level of professional technicians."[23]

JAPANESE *BUNDAN* AND TAIWANESE *BUNDAN* CONNECTIONS

The *kuso* realism debate in Taiwan was preceded in Japan by seven years by another *kuso* realism debate (the *Rōmanha* debate), but did Nishikawa and others related to him open their Taiwan debate by grounding their argument in this context? Based on the statements issued by the persons involved in these two arguments a direct connection cannot be proven; however, from connections among *Bungei Taiwan*'s Nishikawa and Hamada, and Hayashi Fusao, as well as *Taiwan bungaku*'s Zhang Wenhuan and the writers of the *Jinminbunko*, it is natural to consider that they were conscious of each other.

Hayashi Fusao published the poem "Renpai ni yosu 連盃に寄す" in the November 1941 *Bungei Taiwan*. Not only did he write in the preface to the poem "a Paiwan *renpai* that [my] Taipei friend Hamada Hayao 濱田隼雄 gave me," but the tone of the preface also reveals and implies an intimate connection between Hamada and Hayashi.[24] When and where Hamada and Hayashi became friends is something that requires further investigation; for now, however, we can only follow the threads that these two have in common. Both writers changed their philosophical orientation by leaving the left-wing movement to participate in the creation of extremist national policy literature.[25]

Similarly, there exists no direct proof that Nishikawa and Hayashi had any association prior to 1943.[26] Only the fact that Hayashi's "Renpai niyoseru" and Nishikawa's short fictional narrative titled "Rōman 浪漫" appeared in the same issue of *Bungei Taiwan* suggests a connection. "Rōman," along with Nishikawa's style, shows a close affinity with the *Rōmanha* and what they advocated. Taking into account the publication of "Renpai niyoseru" and Nishikawa's implied approval of publishing the work as well as the expectation that Nishikawa looked over Hayashi's other works, it emerges that the critical pen that wrote "this *kuso* realism that has become the mainstream in Taiwanese literature" and "deeply vulgar, indiscriminate depiction of life" in *Bungei Taiwan* was probably reflecting Hayashi's ideas.

But what sort of connections might have existed among the targets of Nishikawa's attacks: Zhang Wenhuan, Lu Heruo, and members of *Jinminbunko*?[27] The friendship between Japanese-era Zhang Wenhuan and the *Jinminbunko* members Hirabayashi Hyogo and Takeda Rintarō has only recently been elucidated, in Liu Shuqing's *A Thorny Road—the Literary Movements and Cultural Thinking of Youth in Japan: The Formosa Coterie*.[28] Further, what cannot be overlooked with regard to Zhang and his possible connection to *Jinminbunko* was that he too was criticized as a *fūzoku* writer.[29] It has been elsewhere demonstrated that at the time the critical term *fūzoku* fiction was regularly used by all the *Jinminbunko* writers, especially Takeda Rintaro. By using the term "*kuso* realism" as he criticized Takeda's style as *fūzoku* Hayashi stylistically links Takeda to Zhang; and certainly it is interesting that Zhang was criticized by Nishikawa as a *kuso* realist.

In addition to the connections among Zhang, Hirabayashi, and Takeda, the connection between Lu and Takami Jun cannot be overlooked. It is well known that Takami highly praised Lu's "Gōka heian" in ""Shōsetsusōhyo—shōwa jyū-hachinen jōhanki Taiwanbungakukai 小說總評＝昭和十八年上半期台湾文学界."[30] This is the very Takami who along with Takeda Rintaro formed the core of *Jinminbunko*. Takami also published "Rōmantekiseishin to Rōmantekidōkō 浪漫的精神と浪漫的動向" before the formation of *Jinminbunko*; in this piece he criticized Hayashi Fusao and other members of the *Rōmanha*.[31] In the same critique Takami acknowledged the "flavor of *kuso* realism" in his own work for which Hayashi had criticized him. He pointed out that it was a "dark realism unable to narrate an ideal," and added that because of such dark realism he could not "brightly sing a romantic song." Takami clearly expressed his conviction: "[I] continue to hurl myself against reality and grapple [with it] … and so I can only fall and fail." He concluded, "for the realist, there is misery and there is honesty in wrestling with reality."

Nishikawa concludes that Lu and Zhang ignore the reality that "this island's next generation is faithfully reporting and volunteering to duty" as they (i.e., the *kuso*-realists) depict family troubles and folk customs. But, as I believe the comparison of "Ryūmyakuki" and "Fūsui" has clearly revealed, Lu vis-à-vis the realistic portrayal of a family's collapse manages to illuminate the destruction of Taiwanese culture.

When he was publicly confronted by Nishikawa, Lu penned no official response; however, the response that never appeared now remains in his personal journal, where he developed a discussion of himself: "I don't simply write down one example after another of reality. My viewpoint is contained [in my work]. There are many who do not see this" (unpublished journal entry, May 20, 1943). And yet he wrote "Zakuro," an even darker piece with an undercurrent of heavy gloom and melancholy. Of the strong death image that governs "Zakuro"—dispersal, mental disorder, and separation by death—he later wrote, "I wrote about the dark aspect, well, and from that wrote a beautiful thing" (unpublished journal entry, June 1, 1943).

Lu appears to embody Takami's thinking when his remarks are put alongside Takami's ideas of "facing dark reality," "[the] inability to sing a romantic song," and "[the] realists' struggle with reality." In short, in 1943 Lu had reached Takami's ideal that "the flavor of *kuso* realism" was the same as "[a] realist grappling with reality." Here then is the probable reason that Takami, who had "only read two of [Lu's] works," had such high praise for him.

A SETTLING

By employing the key term *kuso* realism here I have elucidated the connections between Hayashi Fusao and *Bungei Taiwan* as well as those among Lu Heruo, Zhang Wenhuan, and *Jinminbunko*. While the "dark reality" that Lu exposed in "Fūsui" was the destruction of Taiwanese culture in colonial Taiwan, Nishikawa's "reality," in which "this island's next generation is faithfully reporting and volunteering to duty," is bound up with his narration of nation-building and the settlement of Taiwan. Lu apprehends as "reality" the collapse of traditional structures and institutions as well as the destruction of Taiwanese culture. It is for this reason that he continued to turn his ear to the voices of the dead, or the sound of the netherworld. And as the tide of the proletariat literature movement swept through the two Asian entities of Taiwan and Japan, a "tradition" was reborn.

Finally, perhaps best exposing Lu's talent was the July 1943 (in the heat of the *kuso* realism debate) appearance in *Taiwan bungaku* of "Zakuro." Briefly, the story depicts three brothers who, because their mother and father died while they were still young children, are in due time adopted, separated, and raised by different families. With the passage of time the youngest brother is lost, is imprisoned, and finally weakens and dies due to mental infirmity. Still alone and living in an adopted home, the eldest brother, feeling pity for the younger brother from whom he was separated, sets out to place his brother's mortuary tablet alongside those of their ancestors and make offerings. As he attends to these tasks he also searches for his second brother. In his journal, Lu writes of the story, which combines the themes of separation, madness, and death: "For my part I'm quite happy with the work" (July 2, 1943).

Is what makes "Zakuro" so appropriate the fact that this story in every sense breaks away from orthodoxy, and thus becomes increasingly cut off from a Taiwan identity?[32] But in the conclusion to "Zakuro" the brother is adopted anew through the erection of the tablet. Can we say that this image is an example of Lu listening to the netherworld and at the same time returning from the netherworld with a seed to plant in the world of the living? Is it possible that Lu at this time was looking to Taiwan's future and its struggle against colonialism?

In February 1944, having emerged from the Japanese proletariat literature movement, Kubokawa Tsurujirō wrote of Lu's "Zakuro":

> From this work, though it is not easy to touch the spirit of the story for us, in the weird light it throws out, I think we can see an aspect of the true posture of the farmers from this island. ... Because the work is harmoniously true, it all the better shows the deep roots of the island's traditional world, but as for what sort of connection it makes with the island's agrarian life-style development—I was not less than a little dumfounded. But, I was most impressed with the depth of the work.[33]

That the Japanese writers who understood Lu's work, Takami Jun and Kubokawa Tsurujirō, had both previously participated in the proletarian literature movement is not coincidence. Japanese *kuso* realism authors certainly reacted to the message from Taiwanese *kuso* realists. As Kubokawa wrote, "though it is not easy to touch the spirit of the story for us," the former Japanese, forced to stand on the side of the colonizer, slowly and painfully reacted.[34]

Jinminbunko, which had striven against the movements of the *Rōmanha*, stopped publishing in January 1938. But in 1943, during the Taiwanese *kuso* realism debate, "Zakuro," a work which perhaps no Japanese writer at the time could have produced, was published. In discussing and understanding the connection between 1930s Japanese *bundan* and the 1940s Taiwanese *bundan* we must also put to question the reason that Japanese authors who had resisted imperialism before Taiwanese authors also first retreated from the resistance. I myself as a Japanese person must return to this stumbling block and consider the layers of ideas implicit and explicit.

Lu Heruo, gazing where the colonizer could not, went deeper and deeper into the spirit of the Taiwanese people, and listened to the sounds of the netherworld. The beauty of the black and dark world of Lu's writing still continues to shine out over time and space and sheds light on the position of Taiwan in the colonial era. The beauty of his works also provide us hope and obligation as we again confront the difficult colonial era.

NOTES

*Translation by Bert Scruggs, University of Pennsylvania.

1. *Translator's note:* As per the author's wishes, Taiwanese names are rendered according to their standard *putonghua/guoyu* pronunciation and Japanese names are rendered according to their Japanese pronunciation.

2. Nishikawa Mitsuru, "Bungeijihyō 文艺时评," *Bungei Taiwan* 6.1 (May 1943), 38. The *Taiwan bungaku* response: Wu Xinrong 吴新荣, "Yoki bunshō, ashiki bunshō 良き文章、悪しき文章," *Kyōnan shinbun* 兴南新闻 (May 24, 1943), sec. 面 4, and Yun Ling 云岭, "Hihyōka ni yosete 批评家に寄せで," *Kyōnan shinbun* (May 24, 1943), sec. 面 4; and Yitō Ryō 伊東亮 (Yang Gui 杨贵 [Yang Kui 杨逵]), "*Kuso* riarizumu no yō 糞リアリズムの拥护," in *Taiwan bungaku* 3.3 (July 1943): 17–21, among others. However, this literary debate can be traced back to Kudo Yoshimi 工藤好美, "Taiwanbungakushō to taiwanbungaku—tokuni Hamada, Nishikawa, Chō Bunkan no sanshimei nitsuite 台湾文学赏と台湾文学—特に滨田、西川、张文环," in *Taiwan jihō* 台湾时报 279 (March 1943): 98–110, and Hamada Hayao 滨田隼雄, "Hibungakuteki'na kansō 非文学な的感想," in *Taiwan jihō* 280 (April 1943): 74–79. For more details see Chuishui Qianhui (Tarumi Chie) 垂水千惠, "Fen realism zhi beijing—糞 Realism 之背景," in Zheng Jiongming 郑炯明, ed., *Ye Shitao ji qi tongshidai zuojia wenxue guoji xueshu yantaohui lunwenji* 葉石濤及其同時代作家文學國際學術研討會論文集 (Gaoxiong, Taiwan: Chunhui, 2002), 31–50.

3. All articles published in this debate are collected in: Zeng Jianmin 曾建民, "Pingjie 'Goushi xianshizhuyi' lunzheng—guanyu riju moqi de yichang wenxue douzheng 评介「狗屎现实主义」争论—关于日据末期的一场文学斗争," in *Jinya de lunzheng* 噤哑的争论 (Taipei: Renjian chubanshe, 1999), 109–123. However, Ye Shitao 叶石涛 has recently explained that the "Open Letter to Mr. Se, Seshi e no kōkaijyō 世氏への公开状" originally published under his name in the *Kyōnan shinbun* (May 17, 1942) was in fact penned by Nishikawa Mitsuru. See also "'Fen xieshizhuyi shijian' jiemi: fang Ye Shitao xiansheng tan 'gei Shi shi de gongkaixin' 「糞写实主义事件」解密—访叶石涛先生谈＜给世氏的公开信＞," *Wenxue Taiwan* 文学台湾 42 (summer 2002), 22–36.

4. Kawahara Isao 河原功, "Chūgoku zasshi kaidai 'Bungei Taiwan' 中国杂志解题『文艺台湾』," in *Ajia keizai shiryō geppō* アジア经济资料月报 186 (February 1975), 1–18. Liu Shuqin 柳書琴, *Zhanzheng yu Wentan* 战争与文坛 (M.A. thesis, Taipei: Taiwan University, 1994). For a consideration of *Bungei Taiwan's* attack on its participation in national policy discussion from *Taiwan bungaku's* side of the debate, see Tarumi Chie, *Ro Kakujyaku kenkyū* 吕赫若研究 (Tokyo: Kazama shobō, 2002), 193–206.

5. Watanabe Yoshio, *Fōsui ki no keikanchirigaku* 风水气の景观地理学 (Tokyo: Jinbunshoin, 1994), 193.

6. Kataoka Iwao, *Taiwan fūkuzokushi* (Taipei: Taiwanhibishinbunsha, 1921), 41, 851.

7. Lü's personal journal, entry dated October 5, 1942. Unpublished.

8. Bungakuza's performance of *Chin fujin* was originally slated to run for a total of fourteen performances from April 23 to May 4, 1941; good reviews led to the addition of three performances, on May 5, 6, and 7. Members of the cast were paid thirty yen (*Bungakuza gojyū'nenshi* 文学座五十年史 [Tokyo: Bungakuza, 1987], 187).

9. Togawa Sadao 戸川貞男, "Jyushō no nisakuhin 受賞の二作品," *Bungakuhōkoku* 文学報国 2 (September 1943), 3.

10. In 1937 the New Taiwanese Literature movement slipped into a period of stagnation. For more details see Tarumi, *Ro Kakujyaku kenkyū*, 127–132.

11. For information about *Minzoku Taiwan* see *Minzoku Taiwan* 5 (Taipei: Nan tian shuju, 1998). Included are: Ikeda Toshio's "Shokuminchika Taiwan no Minzokuzasshi 植民地下台湾の民俗雑誌," Ikeda Mana's 池田麻奈 "Shokuminchika Taiwan no Minzokuzasshi kaidai 植民地下の台湾民俗雑誌" (originally published in *Taiwan kingendaishi kenkyū* 台湾近現代研究 4 [October 1982]), and Ikeda Hōshi's 池田鳳姿 "'Minzokutaiwan' no jidai 『民俗台湾』の時代."

12. Nakajima Toshio, "Nishikawa Mitsuru sakuhin kaisetsu 西川満作品解説," in *Nippontōchiki Taiwanbungaku nihonsakka sakuhinshū niken Nishikawa Mitsuru II* 日本統治期台湾文学日本作家作品集二巻西川満 *II* (Tokyo: Ryokuin Shobō, 1999), 407–414.

13. See Chen Zaoxiang 陳藻香, *Nihonlyōtaijidai 'no'nihonjinsakka—Nishikawa Mitsuru wo chūshintoshite* 日本領台時代の日本人作家西川満を中として (Ph.D. diss., Taipei: Soochow University, 1995).

14. Nishikawa Mitsuru, "Atogaki あとがき," in *Taiwan jyūkantetsudō* (Tokyo: Ningen'no-teisha, 1978), 401–416.

15. Moreover, that the tunnel is in the end bored through the head of the dragon forces us to consider Nishikawa as a mystic or occultist.

16. Lū Heruo, "Fūsui," *Taiwan b ungaku* 24 (October 1942), 56.

17. See Hasegawa Izumi 長谷川泉, *Kindaibungaku ronsō jiten* 近代文学論争辞典 (Tokyo: Shibundō, 1962), 242–245; Hirano Ken 平野謙, "Bungaku Shōwa jyunen zengo 文學・昭和十年前後," in *Hirano Ken zenshū* 平野謙全集 4 (Tokyo: Shinchō, 1975; 1st ed. 1972), 451–459; Takami Jun 高見順, "Shōwa bungaku seisuiki 昭和文学盛衰記 [esp. article 19: "Fuashizumu no nami フアシズムの波")," in *Takami Jun zenshū* 15 (Tokyo: Keisōshobō, 1972; 1st ed. 1956), 249–267; and Moriyama Kei 森山啟 et al., "Bungakukai dōjin zadankai (dai san kai) 文学界同人座談会(第三回)," in *Bungakukai* (文学界) 3.3 (August 1936): 152–169.

18. Hayashi Fusao, "Hayashi Fusao ryaku nenpu 林房雄略年譜," in *Daitōasen kōteiron* 大東亞戰肯定論 (Tokyo: Natsume shobō, 2001), 480–487.

19. Hayashi Fusao, *Rōmanshugi no tameni* 浪漫主義のために (Bungakukai shuppanbu, 1936), 41–51, 171–193.

20. Hirabayashi Hyogo, "Hayashi Fusao he'no Tegami [A Letter to Hayashi Fusao]," in *Jinminbunko* 1.4 (June 1936): 140–142; Shibukawa Takashi, "Genjitsusei he'no michi 現実への道," in *Jinminbunko* 1.6 (August 1936): 125–127, "Shiseishin to sanbunseishin 詩精神と散文精神," in *Jinminbunko* 2.8 (July 1937): 89–94, and "Nihon'no romanha wo tadasu 日本の浪漫派を訊す," in *Jinminbunko* 2.5 (April 1937): 124–143. Prior to the March 1936 establishment of *Jinminbunko*, Takami Jun responded to Hayashi's "Riarizumudansō リアリズム断想" in the December 1934 *Bunka shūdan* 文化集団 with "Rōmantekiseishin to rōmantekidōkō 浪漫的精神と浪漫的動向" (reprinted in *Gendai nihon bungaku ronsōshi (chū現代日本文学論争史(中))*, ed. Hirano Ken et al. [Tokyo: 1957], 306–312).

21. Tsujihashi Saburō (辻橋三郎), "Jinminbunko," in Nihonkindai bungaku daijiten 5 日本近代文学大辞典 5 (Tokyo: Kōdansha, 1977), 211–212.

22. Odagiri Hideo (小田切秀雄), "Kaidai to kaisetsu 'Jinminbunko'—Gendaibungaku-shi'no bunkitende 解題と解説"人民文庫"-現代文学史分歧点," in "Jinminbunko"—kaisetsu, sōmokuji, sōsakuin "人民文庫"解說,總目次,總索引 (Tokyo: Funishuppan, 1996), 5–17.

23. Sugiyama Heisuke 杉山平助, Bungei gojyūnenshi 文芸五十年史 (Tokyo: Masu shobō, 1942), 416; Nakamura Mitsuo 中村光夫, Fūzoku shōsetsuron 風俗小說論 (Tokyo: Kawade shobō, 1950), 180–191.

24. Hayashi Fusao, "Renpai'niyoseru," in Bungei Taiwan 3.2 (November 1941): 54–57.

25. On Hamada's left-wing activities see Matsuo Naota 松尾直太, Bintian Zhunxiong yan-jiu—Riben tongzhiqi Taiwan 1940 niandaide Bintian wenxue 濱田隼雄研究-日本統治期台灣1940年代的濱田文學 (M.A. thesis, Tainan: Chenggong Daxue, 2001).

26. During the Ye Shitao conference in Gaoxiong, Taiwan (December 8–9, 2001), Qiu Ruoshan 邱若山 pointed out that Satō Haruo 佐藤春夫 was caught in between Nishikawa and Hayashi; and Chen Mingtai 陳明台 pointed out the postwar connection between Nishi-kawa and Hayashi.

27. Regarding the response to the Bungei Taiwan attack written by Yang Kui under the pen name of Itō Ryō and the connection to Jinminbunko, see the aforementioned Tarumi, "Fen Realism."

28. Liu Shuqing 柳書琴, Jingji zhi dao—liuri qingnian de wenxue huodong yu wenhua gouxiang—yi "fuermosha" xitong zuojia wei zhongxin 荊棘之道—留日青年的文學活動與文化構想—以福爾摩沙作家系統為中心 (Ph.D. diss., Xinzhu, Taiwan: National Tsinghua (Qinghua) University, 2001), 262–266.

29. Fujino Yusuji/藤野雄士, "Yosaru sonota zatsudan 夜猿その他, 雜談," in Taiwan bun-gaku 2.2 (March 1942): 98–101. Zhang Wenxun has been extremely helpful in elucidating this connection.

30. Takami Jun, "Shōsetsusōhyō—Shōwajyūhachinen kamihanki Taiwanbungakukai," in Taiwankōron 台湾公論 (August 1943), 86–92.

31. Hirano Ken et al., "Rōmantekiseisen to romantekidōkō."

32. For an examination of Lü, adoption, and national identity see Tarumi Chie, "Hou Xiaoxian Gekiyumejinsei: Sairon 侯孝賢劇夢人生:再論," in Chūgoku 中国 21 11 (March 2001): 81–92.

33. Kubokawa Tsurujirō, "Taiwanbungaku hankkenen (1)—Shōwa jyūhachinen shita-hanki shōsetsu sōhyō 台湾文学半ケ年1-昭和十八年下半期小說總評," in Taiwan kōron (February 1942): 104–111.

34. "Conversion literature" and its relation to Taiwan literature is currently a point of dis-cussion. For one view, see Tarumi Chie, "Lü Heruo ni okeru Fūtōsuibi no ichi 呂赫若における風頭水尾の位置," in Nihon Taiwangakkai daisankai gakujyutsudaikai hōkokusha ron-bunshū 日本台湾学会第三回学術大会報告者論文集, 2001.

PART 4

From Colonial to Postcolonial

REDEEMING OR RECRUITING THE OTHER?

13

REVERSE EXPORTATION FROM JAPAN OF THE
TALE OF "THE BELL OF SAYON"

The Central Drama Group's Taiwanese Performance
and Wu Man-sha's *The Bell of Sayon* *

SHIMOMURA SAKUJIRŌ

The story of the "The Bell of Sayon 莎秧" is based on the true tragic accident of
a girl from the Atayal tribe. The accident occurred on September 27, 1938, when
this young girl, carrying the luggage of her respected teacher, who was on his way
to war, slipped off a log bridge near the stream of Nanao (present day region of
Nanao and Suao of Yilan prefecture) and disappeared after being swept away by
the raging river. The name of this story originates from "The Bell of the Patriotic
Maiden Sayon," which is engraved on a hanging bell that was presented to the
eighteenth governor-general of Taiwan, Hasegawa Kiyoshi 長谷川清, in order to
commemorate Sayon (real name, Sayon Hayon, born on January 18, 1922).

The governor-general of Taiwan was moved by the story of Sayon, and after he
sent "The Bell of the Patriotic Maiden Sayon" to the Liyohen community, the
narrative of "The Bell of Sayon" was retold in various artistic mediums. First, it
was sung as a song, then it appeared as a painting and a picture-card show, and
later it became a minstrel song, an epic song, a play, a novel, and a movie. Eventually it even became a part of the teaching content of textbooks. The following
chronological list assembles the various versions of "The Bell of Sayon" tale produced during the 1940s.[1]

> Murakami Genzō 村上元三, producer, playscript *Sayon no kane* サヨンの鐘
> [The bell of Sayon] (one act), *Kokumin engeki* 国民演劇 [National drama] 1.10,
> December 1941.
> Wu Man-sha, *Shayang de zhong: Ai guo xiao shuo* 莎秧的鐘: 愛國小説 [The

bell of Sayon: A tale of patriotism] (*Nan fang za zhi she* 南方雜誌社 [Nanfang Magazine Company]), March 1943.

Movie script, *Sayon no kane* [The bell of Sayon], *Taiwan jihō* 台湾時報 [Taiwan bulletin], May 1943.

Wu Man-sha, author, Chun Guang-yuan 春光淵, translator, *Sayon no kane* [The bell of Sayon] (Tōa shuppansha [East Asian Publishers]), July 1943.

Nagao Kazuo 長尾和男, author, *Junjō monogatari aikoku otome: Sayon no kane* 純情物語愛国乙女：サヨンの鐘 [Pure-hearted story of the patriotic maiden: The bell of Sayon] (Kōdō seishin kenkyū fukyūkai [Association for research on the propagation of imperial spirituality]), July 1943. (Shimizu Hiroshi, producer, premier screening of *Sayon no kane* [The bell of Sayon], July 1943.)

Kokumin gakkō kyōkasho 国民学校教科書 [national school textbook], *Sayon no kane* [The bell of Sayon], 1944.

Murakami Genzō's playscript was the earliest production of the "Bell of Sayon" tale. In this paper, I will explain the background against which Murakami Genzō's playscript was produced and its relation to Wu Man-sha's *The Bell of Sayon*. I intend to discuss the other works in another paper.[2]

I will look first at the historical background that produced the "Bell of Sayon" tale, which was born during the time when the Japanese imperialization movement (*kōminka*) was in full swing in Taiwan. It can be said that the "Bell of Sayon" tale was a child of this imperialization movement and that it emerged as a product of the movement. Many argue that the Japanese imperial movement began after the Marco Polo Bridge incident of July 7, 1937. This is basically true. However, when examined in more detail, the following facts become clear. Two years after the occurrence of the July 7 North China incident, also known as the Marco Polo Bridge incident, Asayoshi Hakusei 朝吉白井 and Ema Tsunekichi 江間常吉's *Japanese Imperialization Movement* (publishers: Takahara Hiroshi; book agents: *Higashi Taiwan shinpōsha, Taipei shikyoku* [East Taiwan Publishing Company, Taipei branch]) was published (October 1939). Although much about the two writers is unknown, the book was published relatively early in the period following the Marco Polo Bridge incident, and is thus useful in understanding the origins of the imperialization movement.

According to the authors, at that time it was already unclear when the imperialization movement had started, as the following passage indicates.

We do not have clear knowledge of whether or not they used the word "imperialization" from earlier times. Therefore, we initially examined the book, *Taiwan no shakai kyōiku* 台湾の社会教育 [The social education of Taiwan], annually published by the Ministry of Education (*Bunkyōkyoku shakaika* 文教局社会科). However, the term "Japanese imperialization movement" (*kōminka* 皇民化) did not appear until after 1937. Next, upon searching through the government records from the beginning of the colonization period, instructions in a speech given at the Education Consultation Association (*Gakuji shimon kai*) by the chief of the Civil Administration Association, Viceroy Gotō Shimpei 後藤新平, on November 10, 1903, were discovered and are as follows.

> *Although assimilating people of different dispositions through a national language is difficult, in the future, in assimilating this kind of Taiwan there is no one who would object to making them citizens of our Emperor and washing them in this Imperial blessing.* ... (page 10)

According to the above quote, "the term 'Japanese imperialization movement' did not appear ... until after 1937." And since it is out of the question that the instructions of Gotō Shimpei of 1903 could be given as the source of the Japanese imperialization movement, it would not be a mistake to say that the beginnings of the so-called imperialization movement came about after the 1937 Marco Polo Bridge incident.

Again, after the July 7 Marco Polo Bridge incident, a pamphlet entitled *Current Affairs Pamphlet (Volume One): The Facts About the China Incident and Taiwan's Position* was published (Taiwan Jihōsha, September 1937). According to this publication, "The development of this situation involves our Taiwan becoming transformed into a 'state of war' starting from this past August 14" (p. 60). In other words, shortly after the Marco Polo Bridge incident, Taiwan became entangled in the Japanese "state of war." The pamphlet goes on to tell us that on the following day, August 15, the Taiwanese army commander, Furushō Mikio 古庄幹郎, announced in a speech, "Once again, 'Alert the Taiwanese officials and civilians'!" And in that speech he urged the Taiwanese "to display honor as imperial subjects and to show the truth of [their] patriotism with a sincere heart" and to increase their self-awareness as "imperial subjects." Of course, this encouragement was directed toward all residents of Taiwan, focusing mainly on the Taiwanese (*hontōjin* 本島人).

On August 16 a warning was put forth by Governor-General Kobayashi 小林. And again, the term "Japanese imperialization (*kōminka*)" was used:

> All you Taiwanese (*hontōjin*) are also definitely equal to the Japanese (*naichijin* 内地人). Those Taiwanese who do not have the opportunity to stand on the war front and perform courageous acts should not avoid their equivalent obligations and responsibilities on the home front. In this way, you can obtain valuable honor as a citizen of this true empire. ... If there are people with weak convictions, they will absolutely not become imperial subjects. Those who do not become imperial citizens, or those people who do not participate in the Japanese imperialization movement fundamentally cannot be true citizens of Japan. ... Foremost, you must be true loyal subjects of the empire. ... In particular, for the Taiwanese, it is enough to just completely rely on the empire. (pp. 57–59)

As one can see from the above quotation, Taiwan was quickly drawn into the military establishment, and the Taiwanese were persuaded to assume "obligations on the home front." From this point on it was stressed that Taiwanese (*hontōjin*) were "citizens of the empire" or "imperial citizens," and the need for them to participate in the "imperialization movement" was emphasized. It was declared that "foremost, they must be true loyal subjects to the empire" and "rely entirely on the empire."

This is one theory regarding the imperialization movement. Although nowhere in the pamphlet are the words "imperialization movement" used, it is an important source in that it proves that the so-called "imperialization movement" began as an emotional campaign encouraging a kind of "absolute reliance" on the "empire."

At this point, I would like to present one proposal. That is, I would like to place the literature written during the imperialization movement period, such as what appeared after the July 7 Marco Polo Bridge incident, into its own category in the history of Taiwanese literature, which will be known as "Literature of the Imperialization Movement Period."[3] In other words, I designate as "imperialization movement period literature" what was written in Taiwan during the period of the "state of war," when the "imperialization movement" was spreading throughout Taiwan. The time period consists of the eight years from when Taiwan was drawn into a "state of war" on August 14, 1937, until Japan's surrender on August 15, 1945. From this perspective, "The Bell of Sayon" can be regarded as a representative work of imperialization movement period literature. In addition, it was created on an extremely popular and common level and holds a special position as an entertainment story.

The imperialization movement had its start as related above. However, as we saw from the previous quotation, with the exception of the spiritual encouragement of self-awareness "as imperial citizens," the initiation of the movement itself was a slow process. Following the above events, with the enactment of such policies as Japanese language assimilation (*kokugo katei* 国語家庭) (1937), temple/shrine reorganization (*jibyō seiri* 寺廟整理) (1938), and the Japanization of Taiwanese names (*kaiseimei* 改姓名) (1940), the imperialization movement picked up speed and spread throughout the entire island after the Imperial Service Association (*kōmin hōkōkai* 皇民奉公会) was established in Taiwan on April 19, 1941. According to the book edited by Ōsawa Sadakichi 大澤貞吉, *An Easy Guide to the Imperial Service Association* (published by the Imperial Service Association Publicity Department, July 1941), the government assistance movement, fostered by the Government Assistance Association formed in Japan by the cabinet of Konoe

Fumimaro on October 12, 1940, was the model for the imperial assistance movement promoted by the Imperial Service Association in Taiwan and "the Government Assistance Movement in Japan was a spiritual womb, and the assistance
movement which was born through the special conditions in Taiwan was the imperial assistance movement" (pp. 10–11).

Governor-General Hasegawa of Taiwan took on the position of president of
the Imperial Service Association, and he explained the causes and the motives
for the foundation of the Imperial Service Association movement in his speech
for the opening ceremony":

> The role that Taiwan, as the key national defense for the southern gate of the em-
> pire, should take in the defense of the empire, in economics and in cultural factors
> has increased more and more in importance. All citizens of Taiwan should hold
> fast as imperial citizens and strive to establish a national organization in order to
> fulfill the national policy with complete devotion. At this time there is nothing
> more important than for the Taiwanese to fulfill the achievement of the impor-
> tant mission that has been imposed on them. In other words, that is the reason for
> the birth of this Imperial Service Association.
>
> Today, the establishment of this Imperial Service Association Movement is a
> movement for the preservation of practical morality as loyal subjects throughout
> the island. The Imperial Service Association is nothing more than an island-wide
> citizens' organization by which all Taiwanese must gather their strength in unity
> to conform to the nation's objectives and in this way, unify together six million
> into one heart and push forward in the direction that Japan faces. (p. 15)

In this way, the Imperial Service Association was established as an "island-wide
citizens' organization" and evolved into the Imperial Assistance Association
movement, by which "all island citizens gather[ed] their strength in unity to conform to the nation's objectives in order to unite together six million into one heart
and push forward in the direction that Japan faces."

In the broad view, this Imperial Service Association movement can be regarded
as one part of the imperialization movement. Accordingly, literature produced
during this time may be said to belong to the genre of imperialization movement
period literature. The "Bell of Sayon," then, was created precisely during the time
of the imperialization movement, and with the development of the movement,
its contents were embellished and further misconstrued, and it changed rapidly
at the time of the inauguration of the Imperial Service Association movement.
What spurred this rapid transformation was Murakami Genzō's play, *The Bell of
Sayon.* I shall explain its significance below.

To be frank, many similarities can be pointed out between Murakami Genzō's
play, *The Bell of Sayon* (hereafter, "Murakami's book"), and Wu Man-sha's *The
Bell of Sayon* (hereafter, "Wu's book"). First, the character development is very

similar. For example, both authors have established the presence of Sayon's lover
—in Murakami's book identified as *Patsusai Naui* and in Wu's book as *Patsusai*.
Although Sayon's "teacher's" real name is "Takita Masaki 田北正記" and he was
single, in Murakami's book—his name is changed to Kitada Naoki 北田直記 and
he is married to a woman named Kitada Akiko 北田あき子. Like Murakami's
book, Wu's book also described him as a married man, although The "teacher's"
true name, Takita, is used, and the wife's name was also "Akiko."

One can notice similarities in other characters of both writers. In Murakami's
book supporting character roles are given to Shirase Shigeo 白瀬繁夫, the Taiwan
government-general mining, part-time engineer and his wife, Miyako 宮子, the
Taiwanese guard Kō 黄, and Shirase's subordinate Saito 斎藤. In Wu's book, the
name of the mining engineer, Shirase Shigeo and his wife, Miyako, are the same.
As for the rest, although their roles differ slightly, the same characters, such as the
assistant Kō Koku-ryo, and the old man, Saito, and people with the same names
also make appearances. Since these are all fictitious characters, it can clearly be
seen that Wu's book was modeled after Murakami's book.

Furthermore, there are many similar features, such as the description of the
Liyohen community 利有亨社 (Murakami's book: "A peaceful village of 46
houses"; Wu's book: "A peaceful community of less than 50 houses") and the explanation of the summons scene (in both books it is written that a telephone call
was received notifying the arrival of draft papers from the country office calling
for enlistment in the military in Taipei by the following day).

In addition, what is very interesting is that as a whole Wu's book further embellished fictitious aspects of Murakami's book and developed it into a tale emphasizing Sayon's role as a patriotic maiden. For example, in Wu's book, upon
her teacher's departure, Sayon carries two pieces of his luggage and, in addition,
carries Police Officer Takita's Japanese sword. Although this kind of fictitious portrayal is not apparent in Murakami's book, during the scene of Sayon's tragic accident, the Japanese sword is used as a symbol for further illustrating Sayon's role
as a patriotic maiden and the spirit of the Japanese people. In Murakami's book,
Sayon's tragic accident portrays her as a patriotic maiden by her sacrifice. Prior
to her demise, Sayon signed the flag of the Rising Sun that was to be brought to
the battlefield by her teacher. To her fiancé, Patsusai, she handed a shirt she had
made for him. In this scene, Wu's book does follow the portrayal of Murakami's
book, except for the Japanese sword.

Reflecting the situation of the times, Murakami's book relates that in Taiwan's
near future a voluntary enlistment system will be implemented and that Patsusai and others would become "fine Japanese soldiers." This is because in 1938,
when Sayon's tragic accident occurred, the enlistment system had not yet been
implemented in Taiwan, but by the time his scenario was written (June 1941),
the enforcement of a voluntary enlistment system had been announced. In addition, patriotic marching tunes and the Taiwan military anthem and other songs

were inserted to further enhance the tale's military spirit. Furthermore, Sayon's death is glorified in the grandest manner: "From within Sayon Hayon's death, we can hear the pulse of a very strong spirited Japanese woman. Sayon is no longer just a young aborigine girl. As a brave, robust 'graceful Japanese woman' (*Yamato nadeshiko* 大和撫子) she faced a very noble death." "She is truly a brave, praiseworthy graceful Japanese woman."

Of the five versions of *The Bell of Sayon* listed at the beginning of this paper, Wu's book exhibits the most militaristic atmosphere. Various devices are employed, such as the raising of the national flag on New Year's Day, the worship of the emperor from a distance, the performance of a drama on Japanese imperialization, a report on production increases, and Patsusai's volunteering to become a military porter; in a dream, Sayon serves as a nurse in the military.

The above has shown both the similarities between Murakami and Wu's books and some unique characteristics of each. Clearly, Wu's book follows the content as well as the story of Murakami's book. The question arises as to why the stories are so similar to each other. As mentioned above, Wu Man-sha did not understand Japanese. Consequently, he could not have read Murakami Genzō's play in Japanese. How then did Wu Man-sha come to understand the content of Murakami's book? As I will relate below, Murakami Genzō's play, *The Bell of Sayon*, was performed in Taipei. It was during this time that Wu Man-sha saw the play in Taipei and used it as a basis for his script of *The Bell of Sayon*.[4] This is the source for the creation of Wu's book, and the reason for the similarities in both writers' tales.

Until now, no research has addressed the above facts concerning *The Bell of Sayon*. In addition, it was relatively unknown until recently that Murakami Genzō's play *The Bell of Sayon* was performed in Taiwan. I will now describe how Murakami Genzō's play *The Bell of Sayon* came to be performed in Taiwan.

The particulars of Wu Man-sha having observed the performance of Murakami Genzō's *The Bell of Sayon* are described in note 4 above. Another useful source is "Saikin mita jikyokugeki shokan 最近見た時局劇所感 [Reflections on recently observed plays]," in *Minzoku Taiwan* 民俗台湾 [Folklore Taiwan], March 1942) by Takita Sadaharu 瀧田貞治, who was a professor at Taipei Imperial University at that time. He relates the following:

> Actually it can be said that the performances of *Raccoon* and of the Central Theater Group's (*Chūō butai* 中央部隊) *The Bell of Sayon* are quite skillful presentations. By this type of drama group coming to Taiwan, there have been many types of discussions in Taiwan, and much stimulus and suggestions have been provided by the transition to the actual performance, and by the large number of performers, actors, stage equipment, lighting, etc., and it can be thought that quite a large number of facets of Taiwanese drama have also been enlightened. ... We continually pray that through the thorough studying and researching by leaders of drama in Taiwan, there will be a birth in this land of performance groups that can

manage well performances at least on the level of *Raccoon* and *The Bell of Sayon*, and in the near future there will appear productions to the level of *Raccoon* which will receive the support of delighted cultured persons. (January 22, 1941)

Takita Sadaharu is quoted in Hamada Hidesaburō 濱田秀三郎's "Taiwan engeki no tame ni 台湾演劇の為に [For the sake of Taiwan's drama]" (Hamada Hidesaburō, ed., *Taiwan engeki no genjō* 台湾演劇の現状 [The state of Taiwanese drama], Tanseishobō, May 1943), and it is through this book that I first came to know of this very interesting article.

In the above quote, the phrase *"The Bell of Sayon* of the Central Theater Group" refers to the performance of Murakami Genzō's production of *The Bell of Sayon* presented by the imperial capital's Central Stage Drama Group.[5] Takita Sadaharu, through an invitation from the governor-general's Information Bureau, observed performances held in 1941 (from November to December) of the *Nihon shojo kageki* [Japanese Maidens' Review], the *Kurogane idō butai* [Kurogane Traveling Stage], and the *Chūō butai* [Central Stage Group]. Takita relates his impression of *The Bell of Sayon* performed by the Central Stage Group:

> The Central Stage Group has performed the two pieces, Murakami Genzō's *Sayon no kane* [The bell of Sayon] and Ōbayashi Kiyoshi 大林清's *Shiganhei* [Volunteer soldier 志願兵]. The first piece has 5 parts and when the curtains open the location is a police substation in Liyohen that has a backdrop of high green mountains. The lifestyle created by Police Officer Kitada and his wife Akiko living deep in the mountains together with the Taiwanese aborigines, is presented as a lifestyle of bright happiness. Observers receive a good first impression, and the play takes the winning mark on this point. In this way we are drawn into the tension of Police Officer Kitada's orders to go to the war front. Next, the tragedy of the maiden Sayon appears. However, the arrival of the climax of this play, which is the tragedy of Sayon, comes too disappointingly easily, and the reasons and explanations for the great heroism of the tragedy and the internal reasons for the tragedy are vague. Also, the tragic scenes of Sayon, who shed blood, are too long to the degree of tediousness. This is the responsibility of the playscript and the directors. However, the typhoon passes, and the sound of the so-called bell of Sayon hanging peacefully near the quiet police station providing unlimited deep emotions is quite effective. Police Officer Kitada played by Mitsui, and Asako played by Hamura lend strength to the performance. On a side note, it needs to be additionally noted that using the fruit of the Chinese quince on a palm tree on the set is something that would not be permitted in actual Taiwan.

What we can see from the above review of the play, the performance of *The Bell of Sayon* by the Central Stage Group was for the most part generally successful. Wu Man-sha also observed the Central Stage Group's *The Bell of Sayon* as it is depicted in this review. His viewing of the drama of this period was later incorporated in his novel, *The Bell of Sayon*.

Next, I wish to examine the details of this Central Stage Drama Group. According to Hamada Hidesaburō 濱田秀三郎's "Idō engeki kōen hōkoku: Gunmaken-ka engeki ryokō 移動演劇公演報告: 群馬県か演劇旅行 [Report on the performances of the traveling group's trip to Gunma prefecture]" carried in *Kokumin engeki* [National performance] (December 1941, nos. 1–10), the Drama Group/Central Stage was formed in August 1941 in Tokyo. And then "as the playscript of the flagship public performance, Murakami Genzō's *The Bell of Sayon* was first completed." Below I cite some recorded details written before the Central Stage Drama Group was completely formed.

> Plans among members to finish construction of the Drama Group/Central Stage were for early summer of this year [1941]. In this situation, those referred to as members are the group of young authors (novels, plays) who embrace a great passion for performance, including the five: Murakami Genzō, Ōbayashi Kiyoshi, Muneta Hiroshi 棟田博, Mori Kenji 森健二, Hamada Hidesaburō, and the many others whose names are not provided, but who have participated in contributing in various capacities. … Entering July the group slowly started to materialize as a drama association. Searching for performers and others while placing importance on the spiritual union, eventually the association was completed in the middle of August and as the playscript of the flagship performance, Murakami Genzō's *The Bell of Sayon*, was first completed. Progressing further, Yata Yahachi's *Yashi no shima* 椰子の島 [Palm tree island], Ōbayashi Kiyoshi's *Shiganhei* [Volunteer soldier], Kikuoka Hisatoshi 菊岡久利's *Yaji Kita bōchō dōchūki* 彌次北防諜道中記 [The travel diaries of Mr. Yaji 彌次 and Mr. Kita 北's prevention of espionage] were all completed, and after finishing an examination of all these works, they started practicing in late August. …
>
> In this way, in the beginning of November, the time was ripe and the group started a travel performance in Gunma prefecture, and took the first steps of their Drama Group's activities. …
>
> As the program of their performance, the group prepared the following repertoire of three pieces:
>
> 1) Murakami Genzō, producer, Hamada Hidesaburō, director, (modern performance) *Kinnō Urakaidō* [The dark side of the loyalists] (3 scenes)
>
> 2) Murakami Genzō, producer, Ōbayashi Kiyoshi, director, *Sayon no kane* [The bell of Sayon] (4 scenes)
>
> 3) Kikuoka Hisatoshi, producer and director, (variety) *Yaji Kita bōchō dōchūki* [The travel diaries of Mr. Yaji and Mr. Kita's prevention of espionage] (14 acts)

The group was formed in this manner and the Drama Group/Central Stage in the first part of November, 1941 "started a travel performance in Gunma prefecture, and took the first steps of their drama group's activities" inside Japan. Then in December, as mentioned above, the group held performances in Taiwan. Murakami Genzō's *The Bell of Sayon* that was written as the "flagship performance playscript" of the Central Stage Drama Group is contained as one act in the same issue of *Kokumin engeki* [National performance] that is quoted above.[6]

Here, the new question arises as to why Murakami Genzō wrote the playscript [The bell of Sayon], and in this regard, attached to the same playscript as "notes of the author" the following is written:

> This summer [of 1941], at the time that I accompanied Mr. Hasegawa Shin 長谷
> 川伸 and Ōbayashi Kiyoshi and traveled to Taiwan, I heard the facts of the story
> *The Bell of Sayon* from Governor-General Hasegawa and I used it as material for a
> dramatization. And because a good part of the author's creative work is contained
> in the play, I have to request the consent of the Taiwanese people.

In this way, *The Bell of Sayon* as created by Murakami Genzō, as is related above, was the "flagship performance playscript" "performed as the first traveling performance by the *Central Stage Group* in various localities and received favorable acclaim." ("Henshū o oete [Finishing the editing]") in (*Kokumin engeki* [National performance] nos. 1–10) and unintentionally, in Taiwan, the place where it was born as a story, it became a part of traveling stage performances.

The performance of the Central Stage Group in Taiwan, while forming the tale of "The Bell of Sayon," achieved two ends. The first of these, as I related above, was that the "The Bell of Sayon" tale that was born in Japan was came back to Taiwan and gave rise to Wu Man-sha's *The Bell of Sayon*. The other is that the story became connected with the birth of the Taiwanese traveling theater (*Taiwan idō engeki* 台湾移動演劇). Below I will examine circumstances connected to the birth of the Taiwanese traveling theater.

According to Hamada Hidesaburō's "Taiwan engeki no tame ni [For the sake of Taiwanese drama]," quoted above, while "taking the Central Stage Group and traveling throughout Taiwan giving performances" in January of 1942 "under orders of the Imperial Service Association, [Hamada] took responsibility as one member of a volunteer group of leaders, and, temporarily entrusting the Central Stage Group to other managers, he gladly stepped into the Taiwan theater practice arena and assumed leadership of the 'First Volunteer Drama Troupe' (*Dai ikki engeki teishintai* 第一期演劇挺身隊) which had just recently been created at that time."

The "First Volunteer Drama Troupe" was the so-called executive organization of the Taiwan traveling theater that had recently been created in January of 1942 and for which two groups consisting of thirty males and females had been selected as "Taiwanese performers." Hamada had been requested by the Imperial Service Association to be the theater leader of this group of people. Below, I summarize the activities of this Volunteer Drama Troupe, using as my sources Hamada Hidesaburō's "Taiwan engeki no tame ni [For the sake of Taiwanese drama]" and Takeuchi Osamu 竹内治's "Taiwan engeki shi [Records of Taiwanese drama]," which are both published in *Taiwan engeki no genjō* [The present state of Taiwanese theater] (quoted above).

1942

January: The Taiwanese traveling theater was formed. Two preexisting drama troupes, the Nanshin-za Troupe and the Takasago Theater Group, designated by the Imperial Service Association as volunteer drama groups and managed by representative "Japanese" (*naichijin*), were formed.

January 12th: The First Volunteer Drama Group ("Taiwanese" [*hontōjin*]—two groups, 30 people), in addition to performing a solemn initiation ceremony in front of the deities at a Taiwanese Shinto shrine, immediately thereafter entered into the Taipei Dazhi National Spiritual Training Center in order to receive enculturation and education as volunteer troupe members, and held a training session there for ten days. Hamada Hidesaburō, while traveling together with the Central Stage Group making performances throughout Taiwan, was requested to become a volunteer drama troupe leader in order to provide guidance on drama.

January 29th: At the Sakaeza 栄座 Theater in Taipei the volunteer drama troupes "Nanshin-za 南進座 Troupe" (directed by Togawa Hayao 十河隼雄) and "Takasago Theater Group" (directed by Minami Yasunobu 南保信) held a joint trial performance. Hasegawa Kiyoshi, Taiwan's governor-general, observed this performance.

(Program)

The Nanshin-za Troupe: Presented by the Taiwan Government-General Information Bureau. *Shiganhei* [Volunteer soldier] (4 scenes); Takeuchi Osamu's *Tanki doko e iku* 童乩何処へ行く [Where are you going shaman?] (2 scenes); picture-card show *Sayon no kane* [The bell of Sayon].

The Takasago Theater Group: Presented by the Taiwan Government-General Information Bureau. *Shiganhei* [Volunteer soldier] (4 scenes); Takizawa Chieko 瀧澤千絵子's *Nisshōki no moto ni* 日章旗の下に [Beneath the Japanese flag] (1 act); vocal solo *Sayon no kane* [The bell of Sayon]; picture card show *Sayon no kane* [The bell of Sayon]; dance *Kensetsu no fū* 建設の賦 [An ode to establishment].

February 1st: Departure for the first performance of the volunteer drama troupe.

Hamada has the following to say about the formation of the troupe:

From February 1942 the two volunteer drama troupes born in this way—formed as one organization of the Imperial Service Association, which was one wing of the "imperial building movement" (*kōmin rensei undō* 皇民練成運動)—advanced the Japanese imperialist movement in Taiwan another step. ("Taiwan engeki no tame ni 台湾演劇のために [For the sake of Taiwanese drama]," p. 19)

Shortly later, in April of the same year [1942], the Taiwan Traveling Drama Troupe evolved into the Taiwan Drama Society (*Taiwan engeki kyōkai*). The president was the Imperial Service Association central headquarters general section head, Yamamoto Shimpei 山本真平, and the vice president was the Imperial Service Association central headquarters public relations head, Ōsawa Sadakichi 大澤貞吉, and Hayashi Teiroku 林貞六 also served as the Imperial Service Association central headquarters cultural head. "The island-wide drama groups became a unified leadership system under the direction of the Imperial Service Association" (Takeuchi Osamu, "Taiwan engeki shi [Records of Taiwanese drama]," p. 99).

I have tried to clarify above the connection between Murakami Genzō's *The Bell of Sayon* and Wu Man-sha's *The Bell of Sayon*, and I have further demonstrated the connection between the Central Drama Group's Taiwan performance and the Taiwan traveling theater. Finally, I want to touch upon a broader objective of the imperialist movement, the problem of the military conscription of the Taiwanese (*hontōjin*) and the Takasago aborigines (*Takasago zoku* 高砂族).[7]

In another paper (see note 1 above), when I quoted the article "The Governor-General Sends an Offering Bell: The Story of the Patriotic Maiden, Pure-Hearted Sayon," which was carried in the April 13, 1941, issue of the *Asahi Shinbun* 朝日新聞 (Taiwan version), I related how there was clearly an intent to beautify Sayon's tragic accident by placing it within the context of the war. Furthermore, the same article also describes how military porters and attached civilians of the "Takasago" aborigines were sent to war following the Marco Polo Bridge incident. I quote that section here:

> Since the [Marco Polo Bridge] incident members of the Takasago tribes throughout the island are absolutely inspired by the heroic and peerless activities of the imperial army, and many of them, writing their entreaties in blood, are saying "Please hire me as a military porter," "Use me as an attached civilian" and in particular, in response to the summons from the local area police stations the villagers are holding emotional send off and farewell parties, where they are sending off conscripts with the words, "Fight bravely."

The resulting military conscription imposed on those people from the "Taiwanese" (*hontōjin*) and "Takasago aborigine" populations originated in the military porter system after the Marco Polo Bridge incident, and was gradually followed first by the implementation of a Takasago Volunteer Corps, then by volunteer enlistment, and finally by a compulsory draft system.

In this way, as I showed in the first part of this paper, Taiwan was incorporated into the "state of war." In what can be hailed as a complete imperialization, the "home front responsibilities" were explained to the "Taiwanese" (*hontōjin*) as "All Taiwanese, as loyal subjects, are equal to the Japanese. And for you Taiwanese who do not have the chance to stand on the war front and perform brave and daring actions, you should not shirk all the equivalent domestic responsibilities," of which "the first is to become a true loyal subject of the empire." The military conscription in Taiwan was implemented according to the following schedule within the imperialization movement, and was in the end a forced conscription.

> June 20, 1941: announcement of the implementation of a voluntary conscription (implemented the following year).
> March 1942: enlistment into the "Takasago Volunteer Patriotic Corps" and "Takasago Volunteer Corps" begins.
> April 1, 1942: implementation of the army special volunteer conscription.
> May 12, 1943: implementation of the navy special volunteer conscription.
> September 1944: partial implementation of the compulsory draft system.
> April 1945: total implementation of the Taiwanese compulsory draft system.

As listed in the "flagship performance playscript" of the Central Stage Group seen above, three scripts had been prepared in addition to *The Bell of Sayon*, one of which was Ōbayashi Kiyoshi's *Shiganhei* [Volunteer soldier]. In the context of Taiwanese literary history, the version of *Shiganhei* by Zhou Jinpo 周金波 published in the September 1941 issue of *Bungei Taiwan* [Taiwan literary works] is well known; Ōbayashi Kiyoshi's *Shiganhei* was written about the same time. The implementation of the voluntary conscription system was announced on June 20, 1941, and both pieces were written in direct concert with that announcement. However, one author was a Taiwanese and the other a Japanese and their viewpoints were completely opposite—one corresponded to the volunteering soldier and the other represented the summoner of volunteers, and their literary styles were naturally quite different.

Ōbayashi Kiyoshi's *Shiganhei* was staged "in the area near Tainan Anping," and in the playscript the scene of the young Taiwanese submitting their "entreaties in blood" is depicted through the eyes of the Japanese. As indicated above, the first performance of the Drama Volunteer Corps, which was presented by the Taiwan government-general Information Bureau, took place "in every area of Taiwan under recommendation of the Taiwan government-general" ("Afterword" in *Kokumin engeki* [National drama], nos. 2–3, March 1942), prior to the implementation of the army special volunteer conscription system on April 1, 1942. It was thus helpful to the imperialization movement in terms of volunteer conscription enlistment.

Next, as I stated previously, the performance of *Shiganhei* by the Central Stage Group preceded the performance by the Drama Volunteer Corps. In Takita Sada-haru's article mentioned above, after his review of *The Bell of Sayon*, he relates his reflections concerning his impressions of *Shiganhei*, and overall he criticizes it as "having no attraction for viewers, and no emotional scenes."

However, through the Central Stage Group's performance of Murakami Genzō's *The Bell of Sayon* and Ōbayashi Kiyoshi's *Volunteer Soldier* they contributed to the enhancement of the war consciousness of the Takasago aborigines and Taiwanese in Taiwan, and they performed a useful role as a wing of the government assistance movement in Japan and as a drama group connected to the imperialization movement deep within Taiwan.

NOTES

* *Translator's note*: Transliterated forms of both Japanese and Chinese names in this article follow the traditional East Asian method of order, family name first, and then first name. In addition, the Pinyin transliteration system was used to romanize the Chinese names.

The author wishes to extend his appreciation to Matthew J. Eynon, Department of Japanese Studies, Tenri University, for translating this article from the original Japanese.

1. In an earlier paper, "Substantiating Research Concerning the Process of the Birth and Circulation of *Sayon no kane*, Part 1," I discuss the historical facts concerning the tragedy of Sayon, which occurred on September 27, 1938, and the presentation by Taiwan Governor-General Hasegawa of "The Bell of the Patriotic Maiden Sayon" on April 14, 1941, to the Liyohen community. See *Tenri-Taiwan gakkai nempō* 10 (March 2001).

2. "Substantiating Research Concerning the Process of the Birth and Circulation of *Sayon no kane*, Part 3," unpublished.

3. among other scholars who accept the literature of this period as "imperialization movement literature" are Li Yu-hui and Hoshina Hironobu.

4. When I asked Mr. Wu Man-sha if "before he had written *Sayon no Kane*, he had read Murakami Genzô's *Sayon no kane* (*Kokumin engeki* 1.10, December 1941) or any other works by that name," he quickly provided the following answer. I include only the relevant parts here: "Thank you for asking about my book *The Bell of Sayon*. I have never read Murakami's book, and I just saw the play that the Japan New Drama Troupe presented in Taipei. I felt the story is lovely, therefore, I wrote a story based on its summary and structure. It became popular among the readers after it was published and so I asked Zhang Yuan-fu (Chun Guang-yuan) to translate it into Japanese. I have not seen Mr. Zhang for years, however, I heard that he has passed away" (August 3, 1998).

Nothing further is known about the translator he mentions.

5. In the *Fuyō ni Haneutsu* 扶揺に羽搏つ: *Taipei Prefecture, Taipei No. 3, Middle School,*

Records (June 1998) it is written in "No. 1, History Viewed Through a Chronological Table" that around December 27, 1941, there was a "viewing of *Sayon no kane*." Most likely *Sayon no kane* was performed during the year-end closing ceremonies of the second semester. I received this data from the research student Zhao Xun-da of the Taiwan Literature Graduate School of National Cheng Gong University.

6. Like Murakami Genzô's *Sayon no kane*, Yata Yahara's *Yashi no shima* [Palm tree island] and Ōbayashi Kiyoshi's *Shiganhei* [Volunteer soldier] were also included in the *Kokumin engeki* 国民演劇 [National performance], the former in the January issue of 1942, and the latter in the March issue of 1942.

7. *Translator's note*: The distinction is being drawn here between the original Taiwanese aborigines consisting of nine tribes (a tenth one added in 2001) who were called *Takasago-zoku* 高砂族 by the Japanese and who live mainly on the eastern side of the island, and the mainlander Han Chinese (*hontōjin*) who arrived to Taiwan in great numbers after the seventeenth century and who came to populate the main centers on the western side of the island.

[14]

GENDER, ETHNOGRAPHY, AND COLONIAL CULTURAL PRODUCTION

Nishikawa Mitsuru's Discourse on Taiwan

FAYE YUAN KLEEMAN

Colonial enterprises and colonial encounters generate the need to produce and possess the knowledge of other(s). There is an urgent need for the colonizing subject to acquire information on the colonized people, in order to aid in the management of its newly acquired territory, and it is equally pressing for the colonized to gain knowledge of their overlord. This transculturation, or the exchange of colonial knowledge, is nevertheless a reluctant liaison fraught with asymmetrical, nonreciprocal, and at times dangerous misreadings. As Said so clearly demonstrated in his *Orientalism*, the production of the Orient created a writing subject and a narrated object that was often translated into a relationship characterized by a dominant, omnipotent image of imperial masculinity (i.e., the West) on the one hand, and a subservient, silenced, and often feminized East on the other.

In *Orientalism* Said does not examine gender as a category constitutive of colonialism; sexuality appears almost as if it were just a metaphor for other. In a sense, he sees the sexualization of the Orient mainly as a symptom of empire's hermeneutical difficulties. As Revathi Krishnaswamy and many others have pointed out, Said's emphasis on the metaphor of gender tends to "dehistoricize the semantics of sexuality, disconnecting it from the varied yet specific contexts in which Orientalism developed and deployed a whole array of sexual stereotypes."[1]

As the only Asian colonial power during the period from the late nineteenth century until the end of the World War II, Japan could not avoid casting its own oriental gaze toward its colonial subjects and landscapes. Fujimori Kiyoshi 藤森

清's study of tourism and its impact on the formation of a modern identity for Japanese intellectuals around the turn of the nineteenth century illustrates two fundamental shifts in Japanese perceptions of their own environment.[2] The nascent practice of tourism (a privilege reserved for high-level bureaucrats and the elite), which mirrored the British "grand tour" tradition of (re)discovering Greece and Italy, was a nostalgic awakening for the Japanese, leading them to look at their own geographical and cultural landscape anew from the point of view of a foreigner, much like the very successful "Discover Japan" campaign of the 1970s, which mobilized the mass consumption of the leisure time that was being afforded to the middle class for the first time in Japan's history. Fujimori's discussion focuses primarily on domestic travel, but he does mention frequent organized group tours to the colonies (Manchuria, Korea, and Taiwan) and their implications for the formation of a modern national consciousness. Fujimori effectively demonstrates, through literary works by Tayama Katai and Nagai Kafū, how tourism at the turn of the century fostered various cultural dichotomies, such as urban/rural, nature/human, and most of all, center/periphery.[3]

This process of internal self-exoticization was later extended outward to the colonies, especially by people such as the art historian and theorist Yanagi Muneyoshi 柳宗悦 (1889–1961), who, through his "discovery" of the simple, austere everyday folk objects of Korean peasant culture, sought to reclaim the authentic cultural and aesthetic prototype that he deemed lost in Japan due to the onslaught of modernization and urbanization. Yanagi and his predecessor, the father of Japanese folklore study, Yanagita Kunio 柳田国男 (1875–1962), have come under fire recently in regard to their brand of Orientalism and constructed authenticity. Their naïve celebration of a constructed past has been subject to new scrutiny inspired by recent discourses in postcolonialism and cultural studies. These critics seek to free the object/subject (op)positions from a single, unified, predetermined trajectory and transform it into a multidirectional process of transculturational interchange that sheds light on issues such as appropriation and agency, as well as intercultural subject positioning.[4]

This essay examines the interstices of colonial cultural production and various discursive spaces (such as historiography, ethnography, and gender) in the Japanese writer Nishikawa Mitsuru 西川満's discourse on Taiwan. Yanagi Muneyoshi was fascinated with locating the origin of the Japanese past in the rustic colonized Korean countryside; Nishikawa Mitsuru's passionate search for authenticity in Taiwanese folk art and popular belief is the southern counterpart of this same impulse. In many ways, this southbound imagination complemented the northbound imaginaries fashioned by Yanagi and completed the full cycle of Japanese Orientalism.[5] By far the most prolific and outspoken colonial intellectual on the subject of Taiwanese culture, Nishikawa spent the first half of his life navigating through multiple cultural influences and repeated identity crises. In this paper I will first trace the journey of this colonial intellectual, examining his identity poli-

tics and the many twists and turns in his literary affiliations and aesthetic align-
ments. Specifically, I hope to bring back a material reality grounded in a colonial
context to avoid the Foucauldian-Saidian model of treating colonialism as a predominantly discursive phenomenon that is autonomous and dehistoricized. I will
also examine the role of the colonial collector and the amateur ethnographer in
the context of Nishikawa's project on Taiwanese folk arts. Finally, I will provide
a close reading of one of the fruits of this project, *Taiwan kenpūroku* 台湾顕風
録 (The prominent folk customs of Taiwan, 1998), and pay special attention to
Nishikawa's appropriation of gender as the main trope of the text.

A STRANGER AT HOME:
NISHIKAWA MITSURU (1908–1999)

To understand the fascination with native Taiwanese cultural artifacts and practices that constitutes the core of Nishikawa's literary production, one needs to
understand the personal journey he had traversed, culturally and geographically,
between his motherland Japan and the only place he knew as home, colonial
Taiwan. Nishikawa Mitsuru was one of the most prominent members of the cultural elite in Taiwan at the time. His first name, *Mitsuru* or *Man* 満, was said to
have been given him by his father to commemorate his own adventurous youth
in Manchuria. With his birth in 1908 and death in 1999, Nishikawa's life parallels
the tumultuous course of twentieth-century Japan, moving from modernization
and imperial expansion to retreat in the postwar era.

His family moved to Taiwan when he was two to run a coal mine in the northern part of the island. Other than the five years (from 1928 to 1933) he spent
at Waseda University in Tokyo for his college education, Nishikawa spent the
first four decades of his life in colonial Taiwan, relentlessly writing about its cultural and natural topographies. Throughout his prewar career, the ever-prolific
Nishikawa published ten poetry collections, funded and edited eighteen different
poetry and literary magazines,[6] penned numerous critical essays, and published
several novels and many short stories.[7] As editor for the cultural section of the
Taiwan nichinichi shinpō 台湾日日新報 (Taiwan daily news), publisher at several publishing houses, and creator and editor of the influential journal *Bungei
Taiwan* 文芸台湾 (Literary Taiwan), Nishikawa was put in an authoritative position that allowed him to mediate the native and colonial cultural discourses.
Bungei Taiwan and its rival journal *Taiwan bungaku* 台湾文学 (Taiwanese literature), edited by Zhang Wenhuan 張文環 (1909–1978), are considered the two
catalysts that fostered a literary golden age in colonial Taiwan during the early
forties.[8]

Starting out as a poet and a student of French romanticism, Nishikawa nevertheless transformed himself into a cultural and historical arbiter for colonial Tai-

wan. He wrote an epic-length novel on the trans-island railway, detailing the technological advances accomplished through the multiple colonizations of this tiny island since the fifteenth century by the Spanish, the Portuguese, the Dutch, the remnants of Ming rule by Zheng Chenggong 鄭成功, the continental Qing dynasty, and finally the Japanese colonial government.[9] His (self-appointed) charge as a historian of Taiwan prompted him to write the short story "Tale of Fort Orange (赤嵌記)," a fictionalized *rekishi shōsetsu* 歴史小説 (historical tale) centering on Zheng Chenggong 鄭成功 (or Koxinga 國姓爺, as the Japanese refer to him) and the history of managing and cultivating Taiwan. The turning point in his development from a Romantic poet to a journalist and amateur historian, in my opinion, came after his return from an extended stay in the metropolis. While pondering whether to stay on in Japan for his writing career or to return to the colony, he took his mentor Yoshie Takamatsu's advice to return. Later, Nishikawa recalled that Yoshie had encouraged him to "devote my whole life to [creating] a regional literature that rivals French provincial literature"; advice which "convinced me to return to Taiwan."[10] Yoshie composed a poem for Nishikawa upon his return to the island:

> The South,　　　　　　　　　　南方は光の源
> Source of the light.　　　　　　　我々に秩序と
> Gives us order, joy, and splendor.　歓喜と華麗とを与える[11]

The mission assigned him by his teacher was certainly daunting, yet Nishikawa was determined to live up to this ambitious role. Taking his teacher's words to heart, he sought to cultivate the island's barren cultural scene and to establish a distinct brand of *nanpō bungaku* 南方文学 (Southern literature) as part of the greater genre of *gaichi bungaku* 外地文学 (colonial literature) that might counter the *naichi bungaku* 内地文学 (metropolitan literature).[12] Part of his mission involved rediscovering Taiwan, the island he had inhabited since age two but had never really gotten to know. Taiwanese history, poetic and oral traditions, folk art, and customs all became subjects for this eager student to study.

In his now-famous essay "Rekishi no aru Taiwan 歴史のある台湾" ("The Taiwan with a history"),[13] written not long after his return to the colony, he lamented the failure of a colonial education in which native history was not taught at all, and he talked about a new "awareness" and "conversion" to Taiwanese history that had seized him upon his return.

> I was fifteen when I first set foot in Japan (*naichi* 内地) and was embraced by its mountains and rivers. It was then, for the first time, that I was able to understand the indescribable sadness I have always felt toward the place called Taiwan. That is a sadness that came from—perhaps I am using the wrong words—not having had a history. ... For several years after I came back to Taiwan, I was obsessed with dis-

covering the history of Taiwan. … I came to understand the absurdity of my child-like opinion that Taiwan has no history; I could not help but be angry with myself. But then on further reflection, I realized that the situation is not my fault alone. When we were young, how much were we taught about the history of Taiwan before it came into our possession? Only about Hamada Yahei, Zheng Chenggong, and Wu Feng. After that, it was nothing but Japanese history.[14]

What is the significance of Nishikawa's conversion experience and his subsequent obsession with recovering Taiwan's history? Why does he turn his eyes to "the Taiwan with no history" after being "embraced by the mountains and rivers of Japan?" The years in Tokyo were the first time since infancy that Nishikawa had experienced Japan. Having realized that he had no part in the history of Japan, where his roots were supposedly located, he returned to Taiwan, only to discover that he was ignorant of the history of the island where he had been raised. The subsequent impulse to learn about Taiwan—to recapture, to represent, and to record it in words and images—was a reaction, either conscious or unconscious, to compensate for his lost Japaneseness.

It is ironic that Nishikawa's rediscovery of Taiwan had to be mediated by the alienation he experienced while living in Japan. The estrangement he felt in the "motherland," and his realization that he did not really know the place where he had grown up underscored his "in-betweenness." Unfulfilled desire for the lost (or that which is about to be lost) is at the core of romanticism. Nishikawa's constant longing for the lost (both Japanese and Taiwanese) formed the basis of his writing and gave shape to a brand of colonial romanticism that is uniquely his own. The young man who started out as a modernist poet turned to the ruined buildings of the past, the artless folk objects and paintings of Taiwanese peasants, and the native history ignored by the colonial educational institution. The anxiety of loosing his grip on a metropolitan identity, to which Nishikawa had heretofore clung, was being mapped onto the angst of the colony with its old (precolonial) past that was about to lost to the onslaught of modernization.

Much as Yanagi Muneyoshi's excursions into colonial folk art were grounded in his involvement with the humanist literary group White Birch School (*Shirakaba-ha* 白樺派) and most of his early expositions on folk crafts were published in literary journals such as *Kaizō* and *Humanism*, Nishikawa Mitsuru's work on Taiwanese folk traditions also had its literary base.[15] His newspaper columns, his own literary journal, and his own publishing houses provided Nishikawa with venues through which to espouse his views on poetics, French literature, and aestheticism in general. Though *Literary Taiwan* started out as a purely literary journal, it evolved into a general cultural magazine (*sōgo bunkashi* 綜合文化誌) that served as a nexus for productive dialogues between culture, art, and literary and ethnographic writings. Articles on European, Japanese, and the local art scene regularly shared pages with reproductions of woodblock prints, etchings, sketches, and paintings that featured local and foreign artists of the past and present.[16]

Nishikawa's romanticist tendency reached its peak with the collective effort of *Bungei Taiwan*. In his reading of Nishikawa's historical tale "The Chronicle of the Red Fort" (*Sekikan ki* 赤嵌記), Fujii Shōzō, cautioning against an overemphasis on Nishikawa's romantic bent, points out the collusive nature of Nishikawa's romanticism and political ideology.[17] The fact that by the very end of *Bungei Taiwan*'s lifespan, when the Pacific War had intensified considerably, the magazine promoted the war effort and the imperial subject literature (*kōmin bungaku* 皇民文学) should always be kept in mind when reading works written by Nishikawa during this period.[18] However, I would like to present a slightly different interpretation of Nishikawa's romanticization of Taiwan. That is, Nishikawa's oriental gaze was not necessarily directed to the objectified code of "Taiwan" but rather to the Japanese homeland.

Having taken his mentor Yoshie Takamatsu's proposal to heart, Nishikawa devoted himself to cultivating the "barren cultural scene on the island" with the goal of establishing "a distinct brand of Southern literature." Though this proceeded well locally, it garnered no notice from Japan. Nishikawa's conception of this "Southern literature" is best defined in his article "Prospects for the Taiwanese Literary Scene" (*Taiwan bungeikai no tenbō*).[19] In this article Nishikawa outlines the literary developments, significant poets, and new native writers worthy of note since the early occupation period. He concludes:

> When I examined these accomplishments, I came to realize that Taiwanese literature is now blossoming and it should be left to develop in its own way. It should never become a sub-trend of metropolitan literature, nor should it be relegated to a secondary position. Frédéric Mistral, from an impoverished village in the south of France, produced exquisite poems written in Provencal dialect to counter the metropolitan literature of Paris. Eventually he built up his glorious palace of Provencal. At the same time that we raise our voices in praise of his extraordinary determination, we shall push for a literature that lives up to the name of our beautiful island in the South Seas and that occupies *a unique place* in Japanese literary history. ...
>
> South is south and north is north. What good will it do to yearn for the endlessly gloomy snowy sky while one is under the forever clear, bright blue sky? Taiwan will soon become the center for Japan's southern advancement. For those of us engaging in literary endeavors, how are we to face our offspring if we do not have a deep awareness of our duty? It is our mandate to create a Taiwanese literature that stands tall like the highest mountain in the South Sea.

Nishikawa's conceptualization of an independent Taiwanese literature distinct from Japanese literature did not gain much notice in Japan, however. His ambitions frustrated, Nishikawa sought a different strategy to gain the attention of readers back in the Japanese homeland, as seen in many of his later essays. For example, in an article titled "Colonial Literature Under the New System" (*Shintaiseika no gaichi bungaku* 新体制下の外地文学)[20] he compared the difference in scale of supported cultural activities in Taiwan and Manchuria, and expressed his hope that the newly appointed minister of culture, Kiahida Kunio, would right the imbalance in the central government's treatment of the two colonies.

Nishikawa was careful to cultivate his connections with metropolitan writers. He regularly sent them publications, including his own artfully produced books and magazines, and was proud of the fact that his reputation for bookmaking had spread to Japan. His magazine *Bungei Taiwan* actively solicited endorsements and contributions from well-known Japanese writers.[21] Nishikawa himself became known as a local intellectual leader in Taiwan, to whom most Japanese writers visiting the island paid courtesy calls. However, his view of the metropolitan literary establishment and writers in Japan was often contradictory and ambivalent. In "Encouraging Colonial Literature" he defended the unique and difficult conditions of the newly emerging Taiwanese literature to the metropolitan writers visiting Taiwan:[22]

> Here in this far-flung place, we have the utmost yearning for the central literary establishment. We have been through a lot of hardship in pioneering [the local literature] with only a very limited number of literary magazines sent here monthly as our sole consolation. Now we are on the threshold of the blossoming of colonial literature. ... In order to know the colonies as well as those who live there, one needs at least to spend a significant amount of time there. It is dangerous to assume one knows the true colonies only by what one sees on a short trip to the area. We have seen more than a few cases of this kind. In this sense, even if metropolitan writers write about the colonies on the basis of an actual information-gathering trip, their works still cannot be called "colonial literature," and certainly should not be given awards for colonial literature. ... Colonial literary awards should be given only to unknown writers who live in the colonies.

Nishikawa's conflicting attitudes toward the metropolitan literary establishment are evident here. While his admiration for their accomplishments was great, he also felt threatened by the impromptu visitors from the Japanese homeland. Positioning himself as the authoritative connoisseur of authentic Taiwanese aesthetics, he revealed his displeasure with the tourist/writer who wrote about Taiwan from a limited experience. His exoticization objectifies the other while simultaneously reaffirming one's own subjectivity. Nishikawa's long-time obsession with Taiwan can thus also be read as an active attempt on his part to distinguish himself from Taiwan and to reinforce his Japaneseness. While his exotic, Orientalist gaze may have been directed toward the objects of Taiwan, it was also a signal of his authentic knowledge of the other that would merit his acceptance back into the Japanese fold.

Herein lies the precariousness of this balancing act for Nishikawa. On the one hand, he promoted the ideology of "Japanese homeland extensionism" (*naichi enchō shugi* 内地延長主義), as advocated by the central government in Japan; this viewed the Taiwan colony as a mere extension of the Japanese homeland and emphasized the continuity of its literary affiliation. On the other hand, Nishikawa jealously guarded the territorial boundaries of his authority from writers based in Japan. It is within this constant tension, the tension that would attract the gaze of the Japanese homeland and yet keep sufficient distance to maintain an aura of authenticity, that Nishikawa's brand of exoticism is situated.

There is a similar balance evident in Nishikawa's divided loyalties to Taiwan and Japan. Some interpret Nishikawa's passion for Taiwan as a colonizing desire on his part to merge with the native culture, but there is little evidence to that effect. Others accuse him of perpetuating the controlling mechanism of imperial authority. Although Nishikawa's role in the colonial enterprise is ambiguous, in his own way he attempted to distinguish himself from the totalizing imperial discourse. Nishikawa's lineage was from Aizu, which often saw itself in an antagonistic relationship with the Tokyo government. Through his advocacy of an aesthetic he considered unique to Taiwan, he sought to deal with the dominance of the metropolitan discourse on his own terms. The Taiwanese aesthetics he carved out is the evidence of this aesthetic and identity distinction. The passionate images of Taiwanese culture that are captured frozen on page after page of his books and periodicals became a part of the standard lexicon employed in discourse on the landscape and material culture of the colony well into the postcolonial era.[23]

DOMESTICATING AND GENDERIZING
THE EXOTIC

Nishikawa's generic turn from poetry to journalism and narrative, like his transformation from romanticism to historicism, was influenced by one of the dominant intellectual trends of the time, the birth of folklore studies (*minzokugaku* 民俗学). Promoted by scholars like Yanagita Kunio and Origuchi Shinobu in Japan, and Gu Jiegang in China, folklore studies was capturing the imagination of both intellectuals and the public.

Yanagita had dabbled in romantic new-style poetry in his youth, and was known for his participation, along with Tayama Katai and Shimazaki Tōson, in the preeminent romantic literary journal *Bungakkai* 文学界. While Tayama and Shimazaki later became major writers of the naturalist school, Yanagita pursued a career in agriculture and became a top bureaucrat, heavily involved in land reform policy in colonial Korea.[24] Yanagita turned to folklore studies after resigning from a prestigious position as chief secretary of the House of Peers (*Kizokuin shoki kanchō* 貴族院書記官長) in 1919. Through tireless fieldwork, collecting folktales and recording local customs, editing journals, and founding research groups and associations devoted to local history, Yanagita was able to establish *minzokugaku* as a legitimate academic discipline and even to suggest that the discipline might one day achieve the status of a "new national learning" (*shinkokugaku* 新国学).[25] Despite his close ties to Korea (he participated in the annexation of Korea and served as a colonial bureaucrat involved in agrarian policy) and his involvement with the south in both a personal and an official capacity (as Japanese representative to the League of Nations, he served as a commissioner to the Trust Territory of the Pacific Islands Committee stationed in Geneva, the headquarters of the League of Nations), his research rarely extended to either of these regions. For Yanagita, the southern frontier of Japan stopped at Okinawa. He resolutely resisted a comparative approach, arguing that it was still premature.

This inward-looking tendency prompted scholars to label Yanagita's brand of *minzokugaku* a "one-nation ethnology" (*ikkoku minzokuron* 一国民族論) or sometimes an "insular-nation ethnology" (*shimaguni minzokuron* 島国民族論). Despite Yanagita's reluctance to reach beyond the boundaries of the Japanese archipelago in his own research, ethnological research and fieldwork were flourishing in many parts of the colonies, often carried on by Yanagita's own disciples and followers. In an interview (*taidan*) in *Minzoku Taiwan* 民俗台湾 entitled "The Establishment of a Great East Asia Ethnology and the mission of *Minzoku Taiwan*" ("Daitōa minzokugaku no kensetsu to *Minzoku Taiwan* no shimei 大東亜民俗学と民俗台湾の使命"), Yanagita pointed out that Taiwan was an ideal laboratory (*keikōba* 稽古場) for the development of a Greater East Asian ethnology that would encompass Japan's colonial empire:

> In Korea we have Akiba-kun (Akiba Takashi 秋葉隆), and I think he will agree with the idea. In Manchuria, Ōmachi-kun (Ōmachi Tokuzō 大間知篤三) is there, and I am sure he most likely would wish the same thing.[26]

The construction of a Greater East Asian ethnology, a concept that paralleled the political ideology of that time, was thus conceptualized and carried out with the tacit encouragement, albeit without any direct involvement, of the father of Japanese native ethnology.[27]

Taiwan was an inviting object of study for the Japanese ethnographers. Geographically situated at the eastern edge of East Asia and at northern end (excluding the "Japanese" Ryūkyū Islands) of an archipelago stretching through the Philippines to Southeast Asia, it was the gateway to Japan's new ambitions in the South Pacific. Culturally, it was a mixture of continental Han culture and the primitive aboriginal inhabitants, who were, despite significant internal cultural and linguistic differences, collectively referred to as "Takasago-zoku 高砂

族" by the Japanese ethnographers. The Han culture of Taiwan shared with Korea and traditional Japan a settled, rice-based agriculture and a continental culture defined by the use of Chinese characters and the canonical status of the Chinese classics. The aboriginal culture of Taiwan was predominantly Austronesian, sharing characteristics with the native cultures of the Philippines, the South Pacific, and the Malaysian-Indonesian archipelago. This was the closest example to Japan of the Southern culture that Yanagita came to see as the ultimate origin of the Japanese people.

The confluence of the continental culture and imaginations of the South, coupled with a multilayered colonial past, made the island fertile ground for exploration and anthropological fieldwork. This is attested by the fact that two of the most famous prewar Japanese anthropologists, Inō Kanori 伊能嘉矩 (1867–1925) and Torii Ryūzō 鳥居龍蔵 (1870–1953),[28] for example, arrived in Taiwan the first year the colony had been acquired by Japan. Paul Barclay notes that Inō's classical education predisposed him to work in areas of Taiwan that had come under Qing administrative control while Torii, on the other hand, investigated a more "authentic" Malayan Taiwan, a Taiwan "unspoiled" by Chinese contact.[29] These two distinct "master narratives," as Barclay called them, produced the discursive space on Taiwan.

Nishikawa's ethnographic work is not in any way comparable to that of Inō and Torii's. Inō and Torii were academically trained anthropologists with institutional backing who employed the tropes and methods then current in Victorian colonial ethnography.[30] Nishikawa remained an avid amateur armchair enthusiast and a colonial collector who practiced a brand of orientalized romantic ethnography that is somewhat closer to the spirit of Inō than Torii. His Taiwan project must be placed within the context of the Greater East Asian ethnology that was being promoted in Japan and throughout the colonies. Perhaps Nishikawa understood his personal mission to be, in part, to write against the rigidly evolutionary scientific discourse espoused by the two experts in an attempt to recapture a certain ephemeral aesthetic essence that had been lost in the austere language of academia.

Unlike most Japanese visitors to the colony at the time, who were fascinated with the exotic savages and wrote numerous accounts of them, Nishikawa showed very little interest in the aboriginal populations and their culture. He was more interested in the folk arts and crafts of the island's Chinese cultural milieu rather than the high culture of the continental Chinese culture. He was, for example, not particularly interested in *kanshi* 漢詩 (Chinese poems), which had delighted many of his predecessors of the previous generation, but opted instead for free-style modern poetry and the artifacts of a rustic, artless, South China regional culture. Unlike other expatriate Japanese writers in the colony, Nishikawa rarely wrote about the Japanese community, nostalgia for the metropolis, or the exotic barbarism of the indigenous Takasago-zoku; his gaze and obsession were directed solely toward the native Taiwanese culture. As an amateur art critic, colonial collector, and a fine bookbinder who created elaborate and artistic special editions of books, using mundane everyday materials to record mundane, everyday practices, Nishikawa's passion yielded voluminous records of local daily life, religious practice, customs, folk art, and architecture.

Nishikawa's discourse on Taiwan, as manifested in works such as *Masosai* 媽祖祭 (The Mazu festival, 1935), *Ahen* 阿片 (Opium, 1938), *Ressenden* 列仙伝 (Biographies of immortals, 1939), *Taiwan fudoki* 台湾風土記(ふどき) (A Record of Taiwanese customs and lands, 1940), *Kareitō shōka* 華麗島頌歌 (A paean to the beautiful isle, 1940), *Kareitō minwashū* 華麗島民話集 (Folktales of the beautiful isle, 1942), *Kareitō kenpūroku* 華麗島顕風録 (A record of prominent customs of the beautiful isle, 1935–1936, 1981) and *Taiwan ehon* 台湾絵本 (Taiwan pictorial, 1943) were part of a colonial ethnographical intervention being carried out at that time throughout the colonies. Nishikawa's engagement in cultural production can be roughly categorized into three overlapping areas: landscape and material culture; ethnographical accounts; and historical reappropriations.

Taiwan Pictorial (*Taiwan ehon* 台湾絵本) is a collection of images of the subtropical island accompanied by short essays that explain each image. One assumes that the book is intended not merely as a tourist guide but as an informational work directed to both natives and a metropolitan audience. This collage of images of the flora, fauna, material cultural, architecture, and customs of Taiwan fostered the formation of a visualized consciousness of the colony and provide a codified vocabulary for a discourse on Taiwan. Moreover, this discourse of otherness became transfigured, reproduced, and productively fused with postcolonial discourses of selfhood, local identity, and self-determinism.

While the images of *Taiwan Pictorial* appear benign and neutral, Nishikawa's interpretative intervention in the more ethnographically specific works is somewhat problematic and therefore warrants closer scrutiny. How does gender intersect with Nishikawa's ethnographical and cultural production in the *Taiwan kenpūroku* 台湾顕風録? *Taiwan kenpūroku*, (literally, "distinctive customs of Taiwan") was a series of essays serialized in *Taiwan jihō* 台湾時報 from 1935 to 1936. They covered topics such as local religious sites ("Jōkōbyō 城隍廟," "Masobyō 媽祖廟"), Taoist ritual ("Kaka 過火," "Tōya 燈爺," "Fuhōshi 符法師"), festivals ("Fudo 普渡," "Sōshin 送神," "Jinen 辭年," "Shichijōmasei 七娘媽生," "Chūshūsetsu 中秋節"), folk practices, customs, rites of passage ("Saika kandō 栽花換斗," "Dōhō kasoku 洞房花燭," "Mangetsu 満月," "Dosai 度歳"), and local attractions ("Hanayome 花娘," "Kōzanrō fukin 江山樓付近," "Rin Hongen teien 林本源庭園").

At first look, the collection seems to constitute an objective ethnographical account of the native cultural life. The texts are accompanied by photographs, drawings, precise quotations of native texts (songs, ditties etc), and painstakingly meticulous and detailed notes. But on closer scrutiny, one notes that the texts are framed in a fictionalized poetic (at times even fantastic) prose with a third-person narrative voice often set in the pleasure quarters. Take, for example, the chapter on Pudu 普渡, or the Rite of Universal Salvation. The photography and annotation lends an authoritative air to the piece, but the highly ornate text is interspersed with decidedly genderized, if not erotic, descriptive passages. The essay supposedly documents the Middle Prime Festival at the Mazu Temple in Jilong 基隆媽祖廟中元祭. Following intense, colorful descriptions of the sights and sounds, the smells of the food and the rituals performed by Daoist priests, the following passage takes the reader by surprise:

> The silver paper (銀紙), robes (経衣), and money (白高銭) for the dead began to flame and drift upward in a spiral. The decorative flowers sewn with golden thread shone brightly, bathed in the sparks of the fire. Some sexy *geidua* 芸姐, with incense sticks in hand, narrowed their eyes, praying for the bliss of their lovers and shaking the full breasts that swelled up out of their *cheongsam*. (Nakajima and Kawahara 1998:56)

> 死者のための銀紙、経衣、白高銭がうなりを生じて燃え上がり、金糸で縫ひ取った結彩 は火の粉を浴びて益奕奕と照り輝いた。手に手に線香を持った妖冶たる芸姐たちは眼を細くとじ、あらはに長衫の上まで盛り上がった乳房をふるわせて、情人の平安を祈ってゐる。

Another example is in the entry on the Temple of the City God 城隍廟. Nishikawa created a persona to carry the narrative movement along, a sixteen-year-old girl (called *Xiaomei* 小妹) who had been sold to a famous establishment in the entertainment quarter (Hall of Rivers and Mountains 江山楼) and had come to the temple to divine the future of her love affair with a young man (Nakajima and Kawahara 1998:92–96). Examples like this, where representatives of the female gender have been placed in the center of the discursive space of the "folk," occur throughout the work. Female goddesses, in particular Mazu, the patron goddess of the seafarers, assume a prominent position within Nishikawa's pantheon of deities, surpassing such male deities as Guandi 關帝 (Lord Guan) and Baosheng dadi 保生大帝 (the Great Lord who Preserves Life) who were at least as important in the daily religious practice of the Taiwan natives.

Although such essays are peppered with highly charged romantic imagery, one also finds interspersed throughout the text ethnographically precise native terms for rituals, food, material cultures, and the life of prostitutes. Nishikawa's modus operandi was to create a highly poetic narrative context while entrusting the burden of the ethnographic information to the notes and photographs. He was thus able to transmit colonial knowledge with scholastic accuracy while remaining true to the romantic poetic tradition in which he was immersed.

Nishikawa's injection of eroticism into the depiction of somber rituals has its counterpart on the macrotextual level of the collection as a whole in its sexualizatiōn of religious practice. Nishikawa's interest in local deities seems limited to female goddesses. The collection devotes the most space to two regional female deities popular not only in Taiwan but also in the southeastern coastal area: namely Mazu (j. Maso; Nakajima and Kawahara 1998:119–124),[31] the most wide-spread cult on the island and the patron goddess of all seafarers, and the Seventh Mother (c. Qiniang masheng, j. Shichijō masei 七娘媽生; 97–101), the patron deity of feminine beauty and talents. Other chapters depict highly genderized practices by women, but as incantations for changing the sex of fetuses in the womb ("Saika kandō 栽花換斗"; 86–91) or initiating conjugal bliss ("Dōhō kasoku 洞房花燭"; 79–85).

How should we, as readers-in-decolonization, interpret the gender implication of Nishikawa's discourse on Taiwan? What does this intersection of the exotic and the erotic reveal about the economy of colonial desire? This conflation of exotic knowledge concerning ethnological space into a feminized discursive space operates at various levels. Such texts fulfilled the artist/writer Nishikawa's personal aesthetic aspirations at the same time that they countered realism, the dominant literary discourse of the day. The representation of cultural encounters was, and still is, a tricky business. Nishikawa's obsessive recording, inscribing, and appropriating of the ethnic attested to his extraordinary appetite for knowledge of the native culture but, at the same time, exposed its limited ability to grapple with the true cultural significance of folk practices. The erasure of the colonial male presence or the effeminization of the colonial subject inevitably transformed the subject into the ultimate object of desire and pleasure.

CONCLUSION (EPILOGUE)

The interface of the visual and narrative texts and the interplay of the exotic and the erotic, as shown in the images in his book, demonstrate Nishikawa's agility in moving into different phases of his interest. He is shedding his sensibility as a romantic poet of the French impressionist school and gradually tilting toward a more objective historical and ethnographical representation of the colony. The literary inscription of colonial femininity and masculine desire as presented in *Kareitō kenpūroku* 華麗島顕風録 (A record of prominent customs of the beautiful isle) sheds light on Nishikawa Mitsuru's interpretation of the erotic, ethnographic, and historic.

By embedding Nishikawa's orientalist enterprise within concrete contexts—texts (lived experience and literary texts) and visual texts—I hope I have helped in explicating the specific and particular ways in which colonial power operates. The Japanese colonial empire was not founded upon the subjugation of one race by another, and the rhetoric of the Greater East Asian Co-Prosperity Sphere highlighted the common racial bonds that linked the people of the region; for this reason, the sexualized view of race relations delineated in recent research on European colonialism is not strictly applicable. Nevertheless, we see in Nishikawa's writings a decided sexualization of the colonized by the colonizer that affirms the significance of a genderized asymmetry in the colonial environment. As Fredric Jameson proposed, "the aesthetic act is itself ideological, and the production of aesthetic or narrative form is to be seen as an ideological act in its own right, with the function of inventing imaginary or formal 'solution' to irresolvable social contradictions" (Jameson 1981:79).

My purpose here is not to reproduce Said's monolithic, omnipotent image of imperial masculinity. Instead, as my reading of Nishikawa Mitsuru's cultural production suggests, the eroticization of the exotic, or the exoticization of the erotic, came at the expense of yielding the real power of representation to ideologies.

As an interesting final note, in 1999 both the *Kareitō minwashū* 華麗島民話集 (1942, 1999) and the *Kareitō kenpūroku* 華麗島顕風録(1935–1936, 1981, 1999) were translated into Chinese and recirculated among a new reading public. Translated by a group of college students who were studying the Japanese language, the project had as its goal, as stated in the preface by the editor Chen Zaoxiang, the recovery of the long-forgotten customs of their ancestors, which had been concealed by the Japanese colonial government and crushed by the Nationalist regime. Nishikawa's texts are thus transfigured into practical pedagogical tools that can both aid in acquiring Japanese language skills (the Japanese original is provided on the facing page with a vocabulary list for self-study) and promote the younger generation's knowledge of their own (lost) cultural and material history. One must point out the irony of reclaiming a collective agency and one's own past through the mediation of colonialism.

NOTES

1. Krishnaswamy 1998:2.
2. Fujimori 1998.
3. Fujimori 1998:53–68.
4. See Oguma 1995:205–234, 1997, 1998. Also, Murai 1992 and Takenaka 1999.
5. For the difference in the development of southbound imagination and northbound imagination in modern Japanese poetics, see Sugawara 2002:86, 94–99. Sugawara argues that the southbound imagination of Japanese expatriate poets, such as Irako Seihaku and Nishikawa Mitsuru, who wrote about exotic Taiwan drew its inspiration directly from both the romanticized *nanban* southern barbarian tradition that had existed in Japan since the late sixteenth century and the early Meiji translation of European-style poems (*shintaishi*), and

is not necessarily a direct result of Japanese colonialism. Nevertheless, I contend that both Irako's and Nishikawa's poetry on Taiwan could not have existed but for the Japanese acquisition of the colony of Taiwan.

6. See appendix 1, "List of magazines edited by Nishikawa Mitsuru" (*Nishikawa Mitsuru henshū zasshirui ichiran*) in Nakajima and Kawahara 1998.2:485–490.

7. Eight novels, including *Madame Rika* (*Rika fujin*), *The Chronicle of the Red Fort* (*Sekikan ki*) and *Taiwan Cross-Island Railway* (*Taiwan sōkan tetsudō*), were published when Nishikawa was in Taiwan. Most of his short stories appeared in *Bungei Taiwan*. Some of these works were reissued after the war by the publisher Nigen no hoshi sha.

8. Fujii 1998:25–67.

9. Nishikawa's treatment of the railway, both a real life and metaphoric representation of technological triumph of modernity and coloniality, can be seen in the novel *Cross-Island Railway* (*Taiwan sōkan tetsudō* 台湾縦貫鉄道) and in short stories such as "Trains in Taiwan" ("Taiwan no kasha 台湾の汽車"), "Two German Technicians" ("Futari no doitsujin gishi 二人の独逸人技師"), and "Story of the Dragon Mountain" ("Ryūmyakuki 龍脈記"). See Nakajima and Kawahara 1997.2:25–384.

10. See "The Abridged Biography of Nishikawa Mitsuru" (*Nishikawa Mitsuru ryakureki*) in appendix 3 of Nakajima and Kawahara 1998.2:509–512.

11. Fujii 1998:105.

12. However, Nishikawa's attitude regarding whether Taiwanese literature should be part of the metropolitan literature—as an extension of the *naichi*, the so-called *naichi enchōshugi* 内地延長主義—remained ambiguous at times. On the one hand, he saw the urgent need for Japan to have access to and to develop appreciation for literature produced locally; on the other hand, he was concerned that the *naichi* writers might get too close to the colony and chip away at his authoritative hold on Taiwan. These conflicting positions can be seen in articles such as "Shitaiseika no gaichi bunka 新体制下の外地文化" (*Taiwan jihō* 258 (December 1, 1940): 112–113), in which he compared the discrepancy in cultural support from the central government between Manchuria and Taiwan, and called for more understanding and material support from *naichi*. In "Gaichi bungaku no shōrei 外地文学の奨励" (*Shinchō*, July 1942, 46–48), he complained bitterly that the *gaichi* (colonial) literary awards should not be given to tourist-writers from Japan but should be awarded only to those who lived and wrote in the colonies.

13. *Taiwan jihō* (February 1938), 65–67, reprinted in Nakajima and Kawahara 1998.1:449–451.

14. Nakajima and Kawahara 1998.1:449–451.

15. For Nishikawa Mitsuru's Taiwan project within the context of prewar and postwar Japanese folklore studies, see Kleeman 2001a.

16. Artists such as Ikeda Yasaburō and Tatsuishi Tesshin were frequent contributors, providing illustrations and other works of art for the journal. On the art scene and salons in colonial Taiwan, see Wang Shujin 1996 and 1997.

17. Fujii 1998:104–126.

18. For example, see Nishikawa Mitsuru's poetry collection *One Determination* (*Hitotsu no ketsui* [Taipei: Bungei Taiwan sha, 1943]).

19. *Taiwan jihō* (January 1939), 78–85; reprinted in Nakajima and Kawahara 1998.1:461–468.

20. Nakajima and Kawahara 1998.1:469–470.

21. *Bungei Taiwan* periodically featured a column called "Belle Lettres from Various Famous Writers" (*Shoka hīshin*), which published letters from famous Japanese poets and writers of the day, such as Fukao Sumako, Irako Seihaku, Horiguchi Daigaku, and Kawamori Kōzō. See *Bungei Taiwan* for March 1941 and Ito 1993:54–56.

22. Nakajima and Kawahara 1998.2:471–473.

23. For Nishikawa's colonial appropriation of Taiwanese culture and its postcolonial implication, see Kleeman 2001b.

24. For the relationship between colonialism and Yanagita's brand of Japanese folklore studies, see Kawamura 1996, 1997; Oguma 1997.

25. Koyasu 1996:51–52.

26. *Minzoku Taiwan* (December 1943).

27. For a discussion of other aspects of wartime Japanese ethnology and figures such as Takata Yasuma, see Kevin Doak's recent article (2002), which discusses the conceptual foundation and institutionalization of ethnology in and after wartime. Also, see Barclay 2001.

28. For Torii's work on Taiwan, see for example Torii 1996.

29. Barclay 2001:117.

30. Barclay 2001:117.

31. Though Nishikawa's interest in Mazu can be traced back to the poetic journal of this title that he edited in the 1930s, Japanese fascination with the goddess did not begin with him —for instance, the poet Irako Seihaku (1877–1946) composed on this subject; see Sugawara Katsuya 2002 on the connection between Irako Seihaku and Nishikawa Mitsuru's poems on Mazu and their connections to the Japanese *nanban* (southern barbarian) poetic tradition. Also see Lin 2002 on Japanese poets' appropriation of Mazu cult during the colonial period. For Nishikawa, however, the interest was impassioned and long-lasting, from his first published poetry collection titled *Masosai* (A festival to Mazu) to his many essays and poems on the subject, which spanned the entire course of his life, culminating in his establishment of a Mazu temple in Tokyo. For a complete list of Nishikawa's writings on Mazu, see Chen 2002:33–36.

REFERENCES

Barclay, Paul D. 2001. "An Historian Among the Anthropologists: The Inō Kanori Revival and the Legacy of Japanese Colonial Ethnography in Taiwan." *Japanese Studies* 21.2 (September): 117–136.

Chen Zaoxiang 陳藻香. 2002. "Xichuang Man yu Mazu." In Chen Mingzi 陳明姿, ed., *Houzhiminzhuyi Taiwan yu riben lunwenji* 後植民主義－台湾與日本 論文集 (Taipei: Taiwan daxue riben yuwen xuexi, 2002), 15–36.

Doak, Kevin M. 2001. "Building National Identity Through Ethnicity: Ethnology in Wartime Japan and After." *Journal of Japanese Studies* 27.1 (winter): 1–40.

Fujii Shōzō 藤井省三. 1998. *Taiwan bungaku kono hyakunen* 台湾文学この百年. Tokyo: Tōhō shoten.

Fujimori Kiyoshi 藤森 清. 1998. "Meiji sanjūgone tsūrizumu no sōzōryoku 明治三十五年・ツーリズムの想像力." In Komori Yōichi 小森陽一 et al., eds., *Media hyōshō ideorogii:*

Meiji sanjūnendai no bunka kenkyū メディア・表象・イデオロギー―明治三十年代
の文化研究 (Tokyo: Ozawa shoten, 1998), 50–71.

Hirakawa Hirosuke 平川祐弘. 2002. "Xiaoquan Bayun de zuopin 'Xuenu' yu Xichuang Man
de 'Hedien guniang'chongfan guli: Zai Globalization yu Creolization zhijian 小泉八雲
的作品『雪女』與西川滿的『河蜆姑娘』重返故里―在Globalization與Creolization
之間." In Chen Mingzi 陳明姿, ed. *Houzhiminzhuyi Taiwan yu riben lunwenji* (Taipei:
Taiwan daxue riben yuwen xuexi, 2002), 1–14.

Kawamura Minato 川村湊. 1996.「*Daitōa minzokugaku*」 *no kyojitsu*「大東亜民俗学」
の虚実. Tokyo: Kōdansha.

———. 1997. "Shokuminchishugi to minzokugaku/minzokugaku: Yanagita minzokugaku
no mienai shokuminchishugi wo toinaosu 植民地主義と民俗学・民族学：柳田民俗学
の見えない植民地主義を問い直す." In Ōmori Chiaki 大森千明, ed., *Minzokugaku ga
wakaru* 民俗学がわかる (Tokyo: Asahi shinpōsha, 1997), 136–140.

Kleeman, Faye Yuan. 2001a. "Colonial Ethnography and the Writing of the Exotic: Nishikawa Mitsuru in the Tropics." In Rebecca Copeland, Elizabeth Oyler, and Marvin Marcus, eds., *Proceedings of the Association for Japanese Literary Studies* 2 (summer 2001):
355–377.

———. 2001b. "Minzuxue yu zhiminzhuyi: Xichuang Man zai Taiwan 民俗学与植民地
主义：西川満在台湾 [Ethnography and colonialism: Nishikawa Mitsuru in Taiwan]."
Zhongguo wenzhe yanjiu tongxun 中國文哲研究通訊 11.1 (March 2001): 135–145.

Komori Yōichi 小森陽一. 1998. "'Hogo' to iu na no shihai: shokuminichi shugi no bokyabu-
rarii「保護」という名の支配―植民地主義のボキャブラリー." In Komori Yōichi 小
森陽一, et al., eds., *Media hyōshō ideorogii: Meiji sanjūnendai no bunka kenkyū* メディ
ア・表象・イデオロギー―明治三十年代の文化研究 (Tokyo: Ozawa shoten), 319–334.

Koyasu Nobukuni 子安宣邦. 1996. *Kindai chi no arukeorojii: kokka to sensô to chishikijin* 近
代知のアルケオロジー 国家と戦争と知識人. Tokyo: Iwanami shoten.

Krishnaswamy, Revathi. 1999. *Effeminism: The Economy of Colonial Desire.* Ann Arbor: University of Michigan Press.

Lin Lianxiang 林連祥. 2002. "'Shengmiao chunge' Riben shiren chaobai Mazu zhi ge『聖
廟春歌』―日本詩人朝拝媽祖之歌." In Chen Mingzi 陳明姿, ed., *Houzhiminzhuyi Taiwan yu Riben lunwenji* 後植民主義―台湾與日本 論文集 (Taipei: Taiwan daxue riben
yuwen xuexi, 2002), 101–112.

Murai Osamu 村井紀 . 1992. *Nantō ideorogi no hassei: Yanagita Kunio to shokuminchi shugi*
南島イデオロギ の発生：柳田國男と植民地主義. Tokyo: Fukutake shoten.

———. 1998. *Taiwan kenpūroku* 台湾顕風録. In Nakajima and Kawahara 1998:55–124.

Oguma Eiji 小熊英二. 1995. *Tan'itsu minzoku no kigen* 単一民族の起源. Tokyo: Shinyōsha.

———. 1997. "Yanagita Kunio to 「ikkoku minzokugaku」「 sōzō no kyōdōtai」 Nihon
wo kanseisaseta gakumon" 柳田國男と「一国民俗学」「想像の共同体」日本の完成
させた学問. In Ōmori Chiaki 大森千明, ed., *Minzokugaku ga wakaru* 民俗学がわかる
(Tokyo: Asahi shinpōsha, 1997), 146–150.

Said, Edward. 1978. *Orientalism.* New York: Vintage Books.

Sugawara Katsuya 菅原克也. 2002. "Cong 'nanman' dao 'hualidao' Riben jindai shi zhong de
iguo fengqu" 從 '南蛮' 到 '華麗島' 日本近代詩中的異国風趣. In Chen Mingzi, ed. *Houzhiminzhuyi Taiwan yu riben lunwenji* (Taipei: Taiwan daxue riben yuwen xuexi), 83–100.

Torii Ryūzō 鳥居龍蔵. 1996. Trans. and ed. Yang Nanjun 楊南郡. *Tanxian Taiwan Niaoju longzang de Taiwan renleixuezhilü* 探險臺灣 鳥居 龍藏的臺灣人類學之旅. Taipei: Yuan-liu chuban gonxi.

Yamane Yūzō 山根 勇藏. 1989. *Taiwan minsu fengwu zaji* 臺灣民俗風物雜記. Taipei: Wu-ling chubanshe.

Wang Shujin 王淑津. 1996. "Images of the aboriginals: Shiotsuki Tōhō's painting on the theme of Taiwanese aboriginals" (Gausha tuxiang—Yanyue Taofu de Taiwan yuanzhu-min ticai huazuo 高砂圖像—鹽月桃甫的臺灣原住民題材畫作). In *What Is Taiwan: Taiwanese Modern Art and Cultural Identity: A Collection of Critical Essays (Hewei Tai-wan? Jindai Taiwan meishu yu wenhua rentong: lunwenji* 何謂臺灣？近代臺灣美術與文化認同語文集) (Taipei: Taiwan meishu yantaohui), 116–144.

———. 1997. "The art of 'local color' and its cultural implications during the colonial period: A case of 'Images on Taiwan' by Japanese artists in Taiwan" (Zhiminshiqi 'difangsecai' de meishu yu wenhuayihan: yi zaitai rirenhuajia de 'Taiwan tuxiang' weili 殖民時期「地方色彩」的美術與文化意涵—以在台日人畫家的「臺灣圖像」為 例). A conference paper presented at the Conference for Social History of Taiwanese Modernization (Tai-wan chongdie yashuoxing jindaihua de shehuishi yanjiu yantaohuiyi 臺灣重疊.壓縮型近代化的社會史研究研討會議), July 5–6, 1997, at National Taiwan University, Taipei, Taiwan.

[15]

WERE TAIWANESE BEING "ENSLAVED"?

The Entanglement of Sinicization, Japanization, and Westernization

HUANG YING-CHE[*]

The end of World War II resulted in the defeat of Japan and the end of Japanese colonial rule in Taiwan. The government of the Republic of China (henceforth, the Nationalist government) took over Taiwan from Japan.[1] During the half-century of colonial rule, the Japanese colonial government aggressively promoted assimilation policies, employing state coercion to transfer Japanese culture to Taiwan in order to make Japanese culture dominant in the colony. Japanese nationalism was introduced through educational institutions on various levels. The assimilation policy was further intensified after the outbreak of the Sino-Japanese War in 1937; the imperial subjugation movement banned Chinese newspapers, and imperial subject training centers were established throughout the island to mold the Taiwanese into true imperial subjects. Under such conditions, it is no wonder that the Taiwanese came to identify with Japan, and in fact, by the end of the occupation, the Taiwanese had indeed become to a certain degree japanized.[2] Writer and literary historian Ye Shitao 葉石濤, commenting on the japanization of the Taiwanese, proclaimed that two-thirds of the population had been japanized by the end of the war.[3] In 1944, the year before Japan's defeat, 71.30 percent of school-age children were enrolled in school, with the total for boys reaching 80.86 percent and girls 60.94 percent.[4] Most of these schoolchildren had become "military youth." The degree of japanization can be noted both from the personal experience of Ye Shitao and from statistics in historical documents.

The formation of modern nation-states in Asia, especially in previously colonized countries, is different from that of Western European states. Ex-colonies that moved from decolonization to independence faced a difficult situation in that they established central governments first, and then had to move quickly to nationalize the various ethnicities that lived within their boundaries. Unlike static nation-states, they were state-nations undertaking a nation-building process that moved from the top down.[5] Taiwan immediately after the war faced exactly this predicament.

To the Nationalist government, the first priority was the task of incorporating noncitizens, i.e., the japanized Taiwanese, into the society of the Republic of China. In order to reconstruct the national consciousness of the Taiwanese people to speed up their sinicization, the Nationalist government pursued thorough sinicization cultural policies and embarked on a series of cultural reconfigurations that were top-down in their orientation.[6]

This article explores a controversial keyword, "enslaved," as it could be applied to the 1947 Nationalist government's cultural reconstruction on the eve of the February 28 Incident. It is through the examination of the term and its surrounding issues that I hope to present what intellectuals at the time thought about the colonial culture and their attempt to find a cultural path for themselves in the postcolonial era.[7]

NATIONALIST GOVERNMENT POLICY FOR RECONFIGURATION OF TAIWANESE CULTURE

The "Cairo Declaration," announced on December 2, 1943, proclaimed that after the defeat of Japan, Taiwan, Penghu, and Manchuria should be returned to China. After the Cairo conference (November 22 to 26), the highest-ranking Chinese official, Chiang Kaishek 蔣介石, returned to China and immediately ordered the Central Planning Bureau, which was an affiliation of the National Defense Primary Committee (the organization in charge of the Nationalist government's administration and military affairs), to create a committee to investigate conditions on the island in preparation for Taiwan's takeover. The chair of this new committee was Chen Yi 陳儀, who later became the first head of the Taiwan Provincial Administrative Bureau, the organization that ruled Taiwan in the immediate postwar era.

The first task given to the Taiwan Investigation Committee was to draft "Guidelines for Receiving Taiwan." The guidelines were formally announced on March 23, 1945. The guidelines included sixteen sections and served as the blueprint for the receivership and administration in Taiwan during the immediate postwar era. They consisted of: section 1: general principles; section 2: domestic affairs; section 3: diplomacy; section 4: military; section 5: monetary policy; section 6: finance; section 7: industry, mining, and commerce; section 8: education and culture; section 9: transportation; section 10: agriculture; section 11: society; section 12: food supply; section 13: legal system; section 14: irrigation; section 15:

health; section 16: land.[8] Directly concerned with postwar Taiwanese cultural reconfiguration were section 1, item (4) in the general principles and section 8 (education and culture), items (40)–(51), which drafted the basic principles for the concrete reconfiguration of Taiwanese culture.[9] What particularly warrants our attention is item (4) of the general principles:

(4) The cultural facilities after taking over Taiwan should emphasize their functions in reinforcing national identity, eradication of thoughts of slavery, popularizing opportunities for education, and raising the level of culture.[10]

The passage indicates that the Nationalist government considered the Taiwanese to have a weak national identity that had been completely enslaved by Japan. There was therefore a need to expunge Japanese culture and strengthen national identity.

JAPANIZATION AND ENSLAVEMENT

The basic guiding principles held by the Nationalist government in reconfiguring Taiwanese culture, as stated in the previous section, were to reinforce national consciousness, eradicate thoughts of enslavement, promote educational opportunities, and raise the level of culture. The Nationalist government categorized all Japanese culture that pervaded the colonial period as "thoughts of enslavement," and colonial education as "slavery education" that thus needed eradication.

While serving on the Taiwanese Investigative Committee in Chongqing, Chen Yi wrote a private letter to then–Minister of Education Chen Li-fu 陳立夫:

Taiwan is different from other provinces after being occupied by the enemy for forty-nine years. During the forty-nine years, the enemy employed all sorts of treacherous schemes to constantly carry out his enslaving education. Besides the slavery mentality, our national language is banned in order to popularize Japanese language and education. There are more than seven thousand Japanese language schools and more than half of the population is educated in Japanese. As a consequence, those who are under the age of fifty have had no chance to learn about Chinese culture and the Three Principles of the People, so naturally they are ignorant. This is indeed dangerous. It is most important, after the restoration, to get rid of the old enslaved mentality from its roots and to establish the revolutionary mentality. And this will mainly be done through education.[11]

Later, after taking over as head of the Taiwan Provincial Administrative Bureau, Chen listed the "eradication of poisonous thoughts"[12] as one of the main educational goals. The official newspaper of the Provincial Administrative Bureau, *Taiwan xinshengbao* 台灣新生報, spoke openly in its editorials of the need to "purge poisonous elements from our thoughts":

> Taiwan has been under the oppressive rule of Japanese imperialism. ... The Japanese spread numerous poisonous elements to numb and to captivate the Taiwanese people so that they will have no clear idea of the motherland and will gradually distance themselves in order to achieve the goals of japanization and imperialization. ... We think it is an urgent task for us to eradicate the poisonous elements of thoughts that Japan has been creating in Taiwan for the past fifty years; and it should be done immediately![13]

For the officials of the Nationalist government, japanization in Taiwan was equated with imperialism, enslavement, and poisoning. All culture, thoughts, customs, and habits were targets for eradication.

However, amid this trend, an editorial in *Taiwan xinshengbao*, "Constructing New Culture in Taiwan," also advocated the following:

> If we judge Taiwanese culture by Chinese standards, certainly there are many deficiencies. After all, Taiwan has been away from China for half a century and there is nothing we can do about it. However, if we judge Taiwan from a world perspective, then we must conclude that there are a lot of good things about it. During the fifty years of Japanese rule, Taiwanese people did learn something. To put it bluntly, though the national culture of Taiwan is not up to that of the motherland, its level in world culture is by no means low. ...We should retain international academic studies, and not only retain them but also further develop them.[14]

Another editorial, "To Know the Mainland and to Know Taiwan" further proposed:

> In order to profit from and to rule Taiwan, Japan had conducted various investigations, published numerous books during the past fifty years. Almost any object, any issue, as large as Taiwanese history, geography, politics, economy, and customs and as small as spiders, in Taiwan has been studied and written about. ... We think that future building and research in Taiwan should first start with the translation of various reports done by scientific and technological institutions of the Japanese colonial era to be used by the experts of the administration in their planning of construction projects.[15]

The official newspaper of the bureau presented a view slightly different from the official stance. Xu Shoushang 許壽裳,[16] who was the chief of the National Editorial and Translation Bureau and who played an important role in the reconfiguration of Taiwanese culture, wrote:

Academic culture in Taiwan has had a good foundation and can serve as a model for other provinces. ... Surely we should be rid of the militarism of Japanese rule, but at the same time, we should not deny the value of pure academic achievement. We should inherit it and improve upon it. If we should sort through and translate the accomplishments of the Japanese scholars' research on Taiwan, and publish a series of books on Taiwanese studies, I am sure it would reach a hundred volumes.[17]

From the editorials in *Xinshengbao* and Xu Shousheng's opinions, then, we can see that during the process of cultural configuration, there were those who proposed to incorporate the colonial academic cultural heritage into this process.

As for slavery education, Chen Yi pointed out at a conference for provincial middle school principals that "the Taiwanese people were educated by the Japanese slavery educational system, which made a point of fooling the people, to keep them from understanding politics correctly."[18] But at the same time, he commented:

I feel that there are two good habits that Taiwanese people possess which make me optimistic [about the future]: one is that they have a tradition of self-governance. This is perhaps a benefit from Japanese rule, since the Japanese emphasized self-governance. ... The second good habit is that they have an insatiable desire for knowledge. This may also be the influence of Japanese education. ... Self-governance and the desire for knowledge are two basic conditions for modern politics. In this respect, Taiwan is far superior to other provinces.[19]

Chen Yi's comments are somewhat self-contradictory. On one hand, he indicated that the Taiwanese lack of a correct understanding of politics was due to "Japanese enslaving education," but on the other hand, he praised their ability for self-governance and desire for knowledge. He pointed out that two basic elements of modern politics had resulted from the Japanese educational system. He was therefore positive about the contributions of Japanese education.

The basic premise of the Nationalist government in its cultural reconfiguration was to negate and eradicate the prewar influence of Japanese education. However, after seeing the educational level Japan had achieved in Taiwan during the prewar period, and after comparing it with that of the mainland, they realized that they could not completely deny the positive effects of Japanese education. At least a school of thought like this existed within the administrative bureau.

On the other hand, what was the common view of "enslavement" among Taiwanese intellectuals? To the equation of japanization with enslavement, the privately run Taiwanese local newspaper *Minbao* 民報 asserted editorially, "Taiwan was not 'enslaved'":

Taiwanese people never embraced the Japanese enslaving education. Other than a small number of people who possessed a slave mentality and were willing to lower themselves to serve as slave, nobody else was willing to submit themselves. ... Taiwanese people, though economically oppressed, were absolutely not slaves. It is only after the restoration that we see the term "enslavement" used so often.[20]

Taiwanese critic and poet Wang Baiyuan 王白淵 also commented the newspaper *Taiwan xinshengbao* in an article entitled, "The so-called 'enslavement' issue":

When we were under Japanese rule there was a term, "imperial subjectification" (*kōminka* 皇民化), which put much pressure on the Taiwanese people. After the war, the word that constant threatens us is "enslavement." The current leadership of Taiwan uses the word whenever they speak, political enslavement, economical enslavement, language enslavement, even our names were enslaved. It is as though if they do not speak of Taiwanese people being enslaved, they are not qualified to be leaders of this people.[21]

In another article, "For gentlemen from outer provinces," in *Zhenjingbao* 政經報, he continued:

Taiwan was originally an orderly society. ... It is equipped with various preconditions of a modern democratic society. Many from outside provinces like to say that the Taiwanese were under fifty years of Japanese enslavement, their thoughts distorted and thus not fit for holding political power. This is pure nonsense. It is completely incorrect unless they have another motivation in saying so. If that's the case, how about the Chinese people under the enslaving Manchu rule for three hundred years, and women who still wear Manchu costume? Why is it that after the fall of the Manchu, Han ethnics can reign? The Taiwanese people, though under Japanese rule for half a century, were not enslaved at all. We can firmly state that ninety-nine in a hundred were absolutely not enslaved. It is shallow, insulting, and self-deceiving to label someone as being "enslaved" only because they cannot speak fluently or write competently in Mandarin Chinese. ... There is a need to distinguish between substance and phenomenal conditions. One cannot claim the Taiwanese had been transformed or imply that they are useless because of superficial phenomena such as speaking the Japanese language or possessing a temperament that is similar to the Japanese, or because they do not speak or write beautiful Mandarin. ... Taiwanese people, though under oppressive Japanese rule, had nevertheless been baptized by a high level of capitalism; there are very few feudalistic vestiges left among the people. This is something we can be proud of.[22]

Wang Baiyuan's articles pointed out the main reasons for which the Taiwanese were accused of having been "enslaved": they neither spoke nor wrote Mandarin Chinese, and they practiced certain Japanese customs and habits—in other words, they had been japanized. However, to the Taiwanese, these elements of japanization were precisely the necessary conditions for constructing "a modern democratic society" and achieving a "high level of capitalism."

Another Taiwanese intellectual and journalist, Wu Zhuoliu 吳濁流, also expressed his opinion:

> After the restoration there were all sorts of people discussing Japanese education in Taiwan. Some are experts on education while others know nothing about education. Though there was a lot of noise, they all arrived at the simplistic conclusion of enslaving education or poisonous education. It is a shame that most of them were subjective and emotional in their assessment and were not able to see the true essence of Japanese education in Taiwan.
>
> Japanese education paid attention to spiritual education in teaching the concept of national polity (*kokutai* 國體), ethics, and history in order for its subjects to blindly follow the so-called "enslavement education." However, in the field of science, there was no such effort at enslavement. As I have mentioned previously, the spiritual education Japan carried out in Taiwan — the so-called "enslavement education" — was not successful. Rather, it was often at the point of bankruptcy. Taiwanese people openly and secretly resisted it. There were many who went back to the motherland to join the resistance to defeat the Japanese empire.
>
> On the other hand, science education was successful. Taiwanese youth are not only not inferior to youth from other provinces, but in general they are in fact superior to them.[23]

Wu Zhuoliu also did not think that being educated in the Japanese way would inevitably lead to being enslaved. On the contrary, by accepting Japanese education the Taiwanese could enjoy modern scientific education and develop scientific thought. He was somewhat positive about Japanese education during the colonial period.

During the immediate postwar period, the Taiwanese continued to use the Japanese language, which was viewed by the Nationalist government as an enslavement phenomenon. Japanese language had come to symbolize "enslavement." According to one estimate, at the end of the war approximately four million two hundred thousand people — 70 percent of Taiwan's roughly six million people — used Japanese.[24] Faced with this reality, the Nationalist government permitted Japanese sections in newspapers and magazines that were published locally right after the war. In June 1946, a "National Language Promotion Committee" was set up to promote Mandarin Chinese. However, those who came from China to teach Mandarin did not necessarily speak standard Mandarin, and this added to the confusion of the Taiwanese. Some even mistakenly thought that there were six different kinds of Mandarin. The campaign did not go well.[25]

In September of the same year, the Nationalist government issued an order that forbade middle schools to use Japanese. On October 25, asserting that since "the province had been restored for one year, the national language should be promoted in order that national policy can be carried out,"[26] and a proclamation banning Japanese in newspapers and magazines was issued. The "national policy" refers to the sinicization of Taiwan. The Nationalist government attempted to use linguistic enforcement to ensure and to hasten the sinicization of Taiwan. Banning the use of Japanese language in middle schools and getting rid of the Japanese sections of newspapers and magazines was a major event in cultural reconfiguration in the immediate postwar period. The Taiwanese reacted vociferously. Privately owned newspapers and magazines in Taiwan all came out against the measure. The monthly magazine *Xinxin* 新新, for example, argued openly:

> The banning of Japanese in newspapers and magazines will start this coming October twenty-fifth. This will in effect seal the eyes and ears of the Taiwanese people. Young people and the middle-age generation all express their resentment and reproach toward this overreaching, ineffective act.
>
> Japanese colonial rule employed high-pressure tactics when they ruled Taiwan, but even they did not ban the use of Chinese until long into the second year of the Sino-Japanese War. Other than that, a certain degree of freedom was allowed, and no restrictions were put on education or literary activities. "Banning Chinese" was something that happened only eight years ago, a sweeping and radical policy change that occurred at the very end of a lengthy Japanese rule. In a sense, this fact reveals that the Japanese were rather respectful of public sentiment.
>
> We hope the authorities can reconsider the policy and listen to the wishes of common folks.[27]

Xinxin opined on the banning of Japanese and at the same time criticized the Nationalist government's intolerance that was worse than that of the Japanese. Wu Zhuoliu also expressed his dissatisfaction:

> What's wrong with Japanese? It is a language that was once armed, however, now it has already been disarmed. Japanese has returned to its original state and it is not a bad thing. ... The disarmed Japanese is carrying out an important mission of introducing culture. Most of the culture of the world has already been translated into Japanese. One can come into contact with all sorts of world cultures as long as one knows Japanese. Before the Sino-Japanese War, many students were dispatched to Japan by our state, using taxpayer money. Now, all of a sudden six and a half million students who study abroad have to return to the motherland. They follow world trends by speaking Japanese, reading newspapers and magazines in the Japanese language. There is nothing strange about it; in fact, it is something to be delighted about. We really cannot understand why the authorities are so foolish in banning Japanese. They not only do not appreciate those who brought back precious cultural information, but irrationally trample it. How would future histo-

rians judge this affair? ... There were various factors involved in banning Japanese. Unfortunately, it has caused acrimony between the Taiwanese and the mainlanders. In the current hostile environment, all theories are empty and nothing works even if it is rational. But for the sake of culture, we should reexamine the whole issue in a balanced way to see whether preserving Japanese would hinder Chinese culture. In my opinion, only governmental publications should abolish Japanese language versions. On the other hand, Japanese language newspapers and magazines, no matter whether they are during the transitional period or not, should be allowed to continue to publish permanently.[28]

Right after the war, for Taiwanese who did continue to speak their mother tongues (which included Fukienese, Hakka, and aboriginal dialects), Japanese seemed the only intellectual language. Therefore, a total ban on Japanese and a vehement denial of Japanese culture would contribute to a loss of self-identity. The Taiwanese were appalled by the discriminatory treatment and oppression of colonial rule, but they had also been introduced to modernity and had come into contact with the outside world through Japanese education. Taiwanese intellectuals, after reflecting on Japan's cultural influence, reacted strongly to the word "enslavement." They tried to overcome the issue of "enslavement" and a narrow sense of right or wrong in the argument over "japanization," and tried to rethink Taiwan's postwar cultural path through the lens of "Westernization."

SEARCHING FOR A CULTURAL PATH
FOR POSTWAR TAIWAN

Immediately after the end of the war, after the debate on "enslavement," it was natural for Taiwanese intellectuals to ascertain their own cultural path. An editorial in the local newspaper, *Minbao*, titled, "The true spirit of sinicization," commented on the official policy:

It is a matter of course that various organizations are currently involved in promoting Chinese culture. In principal, we have no qualm about the idea. However, in reality there are several issues that need to be carefully thought through.

What is sinicization? Many think that by getting rid of customs and habits developed during the Japanese rule and by transplanting everyday customs from China they will achieve the purposes of sinicization. On the whole, we agree with this direction, but we need to clearly articulate the guiding principles so that mistakes will not be made. First, the way of thinking and customs in China are not necessarily all suitable for our emulation. Some wise men have pointed out that modern life in China is full of filth, laziness, and decadence, and itself needs to be improved with notions of order, cleanliness, simplicity, and artlessness. ... Second, though the ways and customs under Japanese rule did not follow the Three Principles of the People advocated by Dr. Sun Yat-sen and need to be completely purged, there are, nevertheless, some concepts that are necessary in a law-abiding society. Ideas such as obeying the law and social morality cannot be ignored if we are to maintain a basic civil society. ...We are absolutely against the outright rejection of these conceptions simply because they do not exist in China, and they have been categorized as being the result of Japanese enslavement. In this respect, we not only do not want sinicization, we ask those who came from outside provinces to join us in Taiwanization. ... Whether they were born here in this province or came from other provinces, our goal should be to improve everyone's life, to make a rich and prosperous life for the nation and its people.[29]

Xinxin, which was a private, nongovernmental magazine, gathered local Taiwanese intellectuals for a dialogue on the future of Taiwanese culture. Huang De-shi 黃得時, an assistant professor at Taiwan University at the time, commented:

There are two aspects in considering the direction of Taiwanese culture after the restoration. One is the fact that Taiwanese culture has been under the strong influence of Japanese culture, and thus has been able to reach world standards. The other is that, comparing current cultural conditions in Taiwan to those in China, we can see that many areas still have not been sinicized.

In the future, how does one promote, simultaneously, Westernization and sinicization? Those aspects that have reached world standards should be expanded and promoted. Areas compared with China's own culture that are not suitable or not up to its standards should also be improved to push for positive sinicization.[30]

Taiwanese writer Wu Ying-tao 吳瀛濤 also published an essay, "The road for Taiwanese culture." When he published the piece, the Japanese language had already been banned in all newspapers and magazines.

The recent decline in culture and increase in suffering have not resulted merely from the sudden shift of language. Although it might be possible to attribute this decline to the past fifty year's ailment and symbolic castration of ethnic identity, if we reflect carefully we will realize that we cannot ignore the level of culture Taiwan has achieved under the influence of Japanese culture, which is up to world standards.

World cultural standards, in a broad sense, do not exclude spiritual education and the moral environment of everyday life. Taiwan not only maintains the best national spirit, but also provides a glorious, solid cultural foundation to serve as a model province for China.

However, several decades' estrangement has resulted in a small part of Taiwanese culture that does not fit into Chinese culture. For this, we need to carefully consider the appropriate path to resolve recent confusions and to follow the grand route of Chinese culture.[31]

The above opinions share belief in both future sinicization and also internationalization. There is a consensus among Taiwan's intellectuals on the path its culture should take. They all agree that the future of Taiwanese culture should seek a balance between top-down sinicization and the Westernization Taiwan inherited from the Japanese colonial rule.

But during the postwar era, the Taiwanese were fooled not only by the Nationalist government's cultural policy but also by its economic policy. "How does one look at Taiwan?" an editorial in another nonofficial magazine, *Renmin daobao* 人民導報 (People's report), painstakingly pointed out: "We agree with the need for sinicization in Taiwan. However, sinicization in Taiwan does not mean the corruption of Taiwan; neither does it mean the impoverishment of Taiwan."[32] Taiwanese intellectuals were well aware of the great difference between Taiwanese society and that of mainland Chinese.

Wang Baiyuan made this awareness explicit in his "The struggle of Taiwanese history,"

> Though Taiwan was under oppressive Japanese imperialism, it has lived through half a century in a highly developed industrial capitalism. Its consciousness, social institutions, and political inspiration all came out of an industrial society. ... During its eight-year resistant war with Japan, China has become very progressive in many areas. However, it has still not completely risen from the hyper-colonial state that entails many of the defects of an agricultural society. This takeover clearly demonstrates the advantages and disadvantages of an agricultural society and an industrial society. Taking over Taiwan in a sense is taking over Japan. It is certainly not an easy task for an underdeveloped society to take over a highly developed society.[33]

Leaving aside a discussion of whether Wang Baiyuan's understanding of historical conditions is correct, it is evident that Taiwanese intellectuals sensed the difference between the two societies of Taiwan and the mainland. They not only asserted the superiority of Taiwanese society, but they also indisputably recognized the cultural advantages and disadvantages of the two.

Taiwanese poet and historian Yang Yunping 楊雲萍 also stated in his "Cultural exchange":

> After the restoration, one of the most talked about issues is the "cultural exchange" between this province and that of other provinces [in China]. I have talked about it, the people in this province have talked about it, and friends from other provinces have talked about it too. Unfortunately, after a year, there are not many concrete accomplishments.

To begin with, there is a set pattern for cultural flow, which is like that of water flowing from a high to a low place. The flow is rapid. However, the current situation in this province is somewhat different from this pattern. Cultural levels in this province and other provinces are not uniform, so it is not a simple matter of one side flowing to the other. This is the main reason that cultural exchanges have not progressed. If we want to talk about cultural interaction, we need to face up to this reality.

Cultural interaction has not moved forward as expected because there is a certain psychological division separating the people of this province and other provinces. If they do not respect or trust each other, how will it be possible to have cultural exchanges? It takes effort to break this barrier when we talk about cultural exchange.

Another important phenomenon that interferes with cultural exchange is the continuing civil wars all over China. With the unceasing warfare, there is no way to deal with exporting to or bringing in other cultures.

We pointed out several factors as to why the cultural exchange between Taiwan and the mainland is being held back. There is nothing we can do about the first reason. However, the second and third reasons are manmade circumstances and can be improved or eliminated. Those of us, comrades from both sides, who care about culture, should work toward that goal![34]

From these remarks by Taiwanese intellectuals, one can see the predicament the Nationalist government faced in the first year of its takeover of Taiwan, and their struggle to accept this cruel reality. The result of more than a year of the cultural reconfiguration campaign was that many local intellectuals did not agree with the sinicization process. It not only failed to bridge the distance between the two peoples but also, on the contrary, further separated the two. One sign of the detrimental animosity that had grown between the Taiwanese and Chinese was the February 28 Incident, which took place one month after Yan Yunping published his "Cultural exchange."

CONCLUSION

In summary, the postwar Nationalist government's cultural reconfiguration and its "rebuilding of the national citizen" in Taiwan moved from outside to inside, from top to bottom. It was a process of reincorporating the japanized, nonnational subject Taiwanese back into the fold of the republic.

The Taiwanese did not react well to this cultural reorganization. The deeply rooted Japanese customs and ways, and the lack of the ability to either speak or write Mandarin Chinese led the Nationalist government to equate japanization with slavery. Nevertheless, Taiwanese intellectuals and journalists vehemently

denied that japanization had resulted in their enslavement and their dehuman-
ization; rather, they argued that the other side of japanization was modernization/
Westernization. They maintained that the future for postwar Taiwanese culture
would have to lie in the balancing of sinicization and Westernization.

Taiwanese intellectuals and the Nationalist government differed in their outlook on the effects of Japanese culture. Certainly, though rash in its conclusions,
the Nationalist government's objections were understandable in that it felt it urgent to quickly incorporate Taiwan back into China. But on the other hand, the
perspective of the Taiwanese intellectuals perhaps explains, or even attests, the
depth of the trauma and the difficulty of a decolonized people moving into
the postcolonial period.

NOTES

*Translated by Faye Yuan Kleeman.

1. The Nationalist government used the term "restoration" to define the takeover as "re-
possession" or "returning to the motherland." However, many Asian and African colonized
states that established independent nations after the war tended to use terms such as "independent" or "liberated" to describe their decolonized status. The historical factors are different in each case, but the connotations of "restoration" and "independent" or "liberation"
are obviously different. For details, see Wu Mi-cha 吳密察, "Taiwanese Dream and the 2–28
Incident: The Decolonization of Taiwan," in *Kindai nihon to shokuminchi* [Modern Japan
and its colonies], vol. 8 (Tokyo: Iwanami shoten, 1993): 39–70. In this paper I will avoid such
value-laden terms and instead refer to this period as "postwar." However, quotations or reference material using terms such as "restoration" will maintain original usage.

2. Huang Chao-tang 黃昭堂, "Taiwan no minzoku to kokka—sono rekishiteki kōsatsu,"
Kokusai seiji 84 (1987): 73–76.

3. Hsu Hsueh-chi 許雪姬, "Taiwan guangfu zhuqi de yuwen wenti—yi er er ba shijien
qianhou weili," *Si yu yan* 思與言 29.4 (1991): 158.

4. E. P. Tsurumi, *Japanese Colonial Education in Taiwan, 1895–1945* (Cambridge, Mass:
Harvard University Press, 1977), 148.

5. Okabe Tatsumi, "Ajia no minzoku to kokka," *Kokusai seiji* 84 (1987): 3.

6. The Nationalist government's cultural reconstruction in the immediate postwar era included the establishment of new cultural institutions through the following four organizations focusing on education, media, and culture: Taiwanshen bienyiguan (Taiwan Provincial
Editorial and Translation Bureau), Taiwanshen xingzheng zhangguan gongshu xuenchuang
weiyuanhue (Taiwan Provincial Administrator Bureau Propaganda Committee), Taiwanshen
guoyu tuixing weiyuanhue (Taiwan Provincial National Language Promotion Committee),
and Taiwan wenhua xiejinghue (Taiwan Cultural Association). See Huang Ying-che 黃英哲,
"The Light and Shadow of the Reconfiguration of Taiwanese Culture (1945–1947)" (Tokyo:
Sōtosha, 1999). Also, "The Development of the 'National Language' Movement in Postwar
Taiwan," *Faxue yenjiu* 75.1 (2002).

7. Some assert that Taiwan, decolonized from Japan, was immediately recolonized by the

Republic of China, and thus differs from other newly independent nations in the appropriate application of postcolonial theory to its condition. However, this paper deals with intellectuals on the eve of the February 28 Incident. At that time, neither the intellectuals nor the common people felt that the island had been recolonized.

8. "Outlines for Receiving Plan in Taiwan—1945.3.14 no. 15493," ed. Chinese Secondary Historical Resource Center, *Taiwan ererba shijien danganshiliau* 1 (Nankin: Dangan chubanshe, 1991), 20–31.

9. "Outlines for Receiving Plan in Taiwan," 21, 25–27.

10. "Outlines for Receiving Plan in Taiwan," 21.

11. "Chen Yi's private correspondence to Chen Li-fu on education after the Taiwan restoration" (May 10, 1944), in Chen Mingzhong and Chen Xingtang, eds., *Taiwan guangfu he guangguhou wunien shengqing* 1 (Nanjing: Nanjing chubanshe, 1989), 58.

12. "This year in Taiwan's education," edited by the Taiwan Provincial Administrator Bureau Education Office (Taipei: 1946): 96.

13. "Suqing sixiang dushu," editorial, *Taiwan xinshengbao*, December 17, 1945.

14. "Jienshe Taiwan xinwenhua," editorial, *Taiwan xinshengbao*, November 6, 1945.

15. "To Know the Mainland and to Know Taiwan," editorial, *Taiwan xinshengbao*, December 13, 1945.

16. For the role that the Taiwan Provincial Editorial and Translation Bureau played in the reconfiguration of Taiwanese culture, see my article "Sengo shoki Taiwan ni okeru bunka saikochiku—Taiwansho henyakukan o megutte," *Ritsumeikan bungaku* 537 (December 1994): 342–372.

17. Xu Shoushang, "Draft of press conference: Task and goals of the Provincial Editorial and Translation Bureau" (August 10, 1946).

18. *Renmin daobao* (February 10, 1946).

19. Chen Yi, "My thoughts on arriving in Taiwan for three months," *Chen zhangguan zhitai yenlunji* 1 (Taipei: Taiwan Provincial Administrator Bureau Propaganda Committee, 1946), 48–49.

20. "Taiwan was not 'enslaved'," editorial, *Minbao*, April 7, 1946.

21. Wang Baiyuan, "The so-called 'enslavement' issue," *Taiwan xinshengbao*, January 8, 1946.

22. Wang Baiyuan, "For gentlemen from outside provinces," *Zhenjingba* 2.2 (Janaury 25, 1946), 1–2.

23. Wu Zhuoliu, *Taiwan before dawn* (Taipei: Xyeyou shuju, 1947), 15–18.

24. Zhang Liangze, "Taiwan ni ikinokotta nihongo—'kokugo' kyoiku yori ronzuru," *Chugoku gengo kenkyu* 22 (June 1983): 17.

25. Xu, "Taiwan guangfu zhuqi de yuwen wenti," 182.

26. Taiwan Provincial Administrator Bureau Propaganda Committee, "Propagandas in Taiwan in the past year," *Xin Taiwan jienshe conshu* [New Taiwan construction series] 20 (Taipei, 1946), 34.

27. "It's still too early to ban Japanese," *Xinxin* 7 (August 1946): 16.

28. Wu Zhouliu, "My opinion on banning Japanese," *Xinxin* 7 (October 1946): 12.

29. "True spirit of sinicization," editorial, *Minbao*, September 11, 1946.

30. "On the future of Taiwanese culture," *Xinxin* 7 (October 1946): 5–6.

31. Wu Yin-tao, "The road for Taiwanese culture," *Xinxin* 2 (January 1947): 20–21.

32. "How does one look at Taiwan? A question for Mr. Zhou Xian wen," editorial, *Renmin daobao* (June 13, 1946).

33. Wang Bai-yuan, "The struggle of Taiwanese history," *Zhengjingbao* 2.3 (February 10, 1946): 7.

34. "Cultural exchange," *Xinxin* 2 (January 1947): 1.

[16]

READING THE NUMBERS

Ethnicity, Violence, and Wartime Mobilization in Colonial Taiwan

DOUGLAS L. FIX

In the fall of 1945—after the announcement of Japan's surrender to the Allied Forces but prior to the formal takeover of Taiwan—some two or three hundred incidents of assault and theft in Taiwan were reported by the colonial police bureau.[1] Although contemporary newspapers, as well as latter-day memoirs and oral histories, briefly mention these incidents, few historians have given them much attention.

Contemporary and historical accounts provide various explanations for this unlawful activity. A leaflet distributed in September 1945 in mid-Taiwan (with the intent of curtailing this activity) stated:

> Ignorant and stupid brothers, watching for the chance to commit wrongs and taking advantage of circumstances to act like brutes, have disrupted social order, encroached upon personal liberty, and damaged public construction materiel.[2]

In contrast, a November 1945 police bureau report that targeted areas for immediate attention inferred that postsurrender violence and plunder had been instigated by suppressed bandits who had reemerged in 1945 to incite the culturally deprived populace to commit crimes against the state.[3] More recent explanations, on the other hand, tend to favor circumstantial (e.g., a political vacuum) or Nationalistic (e.g., anti-Japanese sentiment) explanations.[4] This essay offers an alternative theory.

In this version of my analysis of this postsurrender behavior, I am concerned with the following issues. First, should we agree with the pundits and some post-colonialists that historians have no direct access to the motives and explanations of these acts of violence and incidents of plunder? Second, for those who recall the colonial period and its "lawful society" with nostalgia, how can these incidents of assault and theft, numbering in the hundreds, be understood? Will this evidence suggest that colonial-era law and order was but a myth? Or can we better understand this modernist rhetoric through a rigorous analysis of irregular data? Finally, how does one assess the state's evidence without internalizing (or adopting temporarily) the state's discourse and perspective? Are these immediate postsurrender actions really "crimes against the state"? Will this official data reveal what is powerful about the myth of political vacuums?

CONFLICT AND THEFTS: THE STATISTICS

The data on "violence" and "plunder" cited here was presented in quantitative form when it was first reported by the Taiwanese colonial police authorities in the fall of 1945, and it was the quantitative aspect of the documents that first caught my interest.[5] Since 1993, when I first encountered this data on postsurrender violence and theft, I have analyzed the police reports (with supplementary tables and maps) intensively on two occasions, and in both instances the quantitative data obtained from these sources has been the primary focus of my effort and attention. I suspect there is something soothing about the knowledge that comes to us (from a source such as the police bureau) in the form of numbers. Like other "facts" (such as dates), numerical data may invite our interpretation, but we often expect that the analytical process will be relatively transparent, unlike our readings of textual information. Even the best of us question this assumption very seldom.

Thus, I begin my analysis here by looking at the quantitative data and my first-level manipulation of it. In fact, not much manipulation was really required. The brief tabular data of violence against police officers, and against public officials (excepting police officers), and incidents of mass plunder required more translation—then to now, Japanese to English—than manipulation. Dates, place-names, numbers of perpetrators, etc., were already distinguished from one another and arranged in chronological fashion in the tables. The visual presentation of violent action and thefts on the map required a "symbol-to-text" translation that was also rather straightforward.[6] Even the narrative description and analysis of "hotspots" in the November 1945 police report had more information presented in tabular form than one expects to find in most documents.[7]

I also suspect that my first-level manipulation was governed by general disciplinary training—social history or maybe social science. Along with the police investigator, I expected that distinguishing the ethnicity of the victim, the locations of the violent (or plundering) incidents over time, or the relative numbers of perpetrators might explain these acts of human violence and theft. In addition to these correlations, I hoped to learn something from a basic chronological analysis (for example, whether events can be seen to occur in clumps, in peaks, or according to some sort of rhythm). And from the supplementary data in the tables—more interpretative in nature—I could at least compile a general listing of stated causes and police responses or compare the types and numbers of public officials involved in these conflicts. I was hoping that these first-hand annotations and speculations were as accurate as any that we latecomers could imagine. I have completed each of these manipulations more than once and discuss my results immediately below.

Finally, like any trained historian, I also expected that careful attention to mistaken calculations or conflicting figures would provide some critical distance from the numbers, whatever their reliability quotient might be. Thus, when I found three different sets of regional analyses, I compared them, though without obtaining any immediate revelations.

INITIAL INSIGHT FROM STATISTICAL ANALYSES

Regional Analysis

The three sources of regional information (i.e., tabular data, "critical areas," and map) provide different data, perhaps because they are the results of three different "snapshots" of social (dis)order (see tables 16.1 and 16.2). Tainan prefecture rates high (in absolute numbers of incidents of violence and theft) in all three data sets, while Taipei and Kaohsiung prefectures score highest on the tabular and map data sets, respectively. With respect to incidents of disorder in single districts, Wunshan district (in Taipei prefecture) rated high in all three data sets. Dajia (in Taichung prefecture), Sinhua (in Tainan prefecture), and Gangshan (in Kaohsiung prefecture) registered high numbers of incidents in at least two of the data samples. One might conclude, then, that these areas revealed a relatively greater amount of social disorder in these months immediately after surrender.

If these statistics are reliable, then one might ask what is unusual about these particular areas of the island. This question occupied the police bureau analyst who compiled the report entitled "Information on critical areas of activities," which I'll discuss below.[8] On the other hand, after exploring the disorder recorded in the tabular data,[9] I find it clear that in some instances the reporting authority gave "incident" status to (what seem to be) individual segments of a larger "event." Although a reconstitution and subsequent recalculation of the data may lower the scores of certain districts, I don't suspect that this will change the overall re-

TABLE 16.1 Total Incidents of Violence and Plunder, Regional Analysis:
Comparison of Three Sources of Information

	Tabular Data	"Critical Areas" Data	Map Data
Taipei 臺北 *prefecture*			
Danshuei 淡水 district	5	—	5
Keelung City	3	3	6
Keelung 基隆 district	9	—	6
Cising 七星 district	8	1	6
Taipei City	6	27	7
Sinjhuang 新莊 district	—	9	2
Wunshan 文山 district	17	14	23
Haishan 海山 district	9	13	9
Yilan 宜蘭 district	3	2	4
Luodong 羅東 district	1	—	4
Other	2	—	—
Totals	63	69	73
Hsinchu 新竹 *prefecture*			
Taoyuan 桃園 district	6	7	6
Jhongli 中壢 district	2	4	3
Dasi 大溪 district	3	4	4
Hsinchu 新竹 district	5	6	10
Hsinchu City	1	1	1
Jhudong 竹東 district	7	7	7
Jhunan 竹南 district	3	3	6
Miaoli 苗栗 district	3	5	3
Dahu 大湖 district	—	2	—
Other	2	—	—
Totals	32	39	4

TABLE 16.1 (*continued*)

	Tabular Data	"Critical Areas" Data	Map Data
Hualien 花蓮港 *administrative area*			
Hualien City	1	—	1
Totals	1	0	1
Taichung 臺中 *prefecture*			
Dongshih4 東勢 district	—	1	—
Fongyuan 豐原 district	2	1	2
Dajia 大甲 district	12	5	14
Nenggao 能高 district	—	3	1
Datun 大屯 district	2	1	2
Taichung City	1	3	2
Changhua 彰化 district	3	9	5
Nantou 南投 district	4	—	4
Yuanlin 員林 district	5	—	2
Beidou 北斗 district	4	8	5
Jhushan 竹山 district	—	1	1
Other	4	—	—
Totals	37	32	3
Tainan 臺南 *prefecture*			
Douliou 斗六 district	—	1	—
Huwei 虎尾 district	1	5	2
Chiayi 嘉義 district	6	7	9
Beigang 北港 district	8	14	8
Sinying 新營 district	5	6	6
Chiayi City	—	2	1
Dongshih2 東石 district	3	9	5

TABLE 16.1 (*continued*)

	Tabular Data	"Critical Areas" Data	Map Data
Zengwun 曾文 district	8	10	10
Beimen 北門 district	3	8	3
Sinhua 新化 district	10	1	14
Sinfong 新豐 district	8	5	12
Tainan City	4	5	3
Other	2	—	—
Totals	58	73	73
Taitung 臺東 administrative area			
Taitung district	1	—	2
Totals	1	0	2
Kaohsiung 高雄 prefecture			
Cishan 旗山 district	9	1	9
Pingtung 屏東 district	1	2	2
Gangshan 岡山 district	6	—	13
Yuan[Gang?]-shan district	—	12	—
Kaohsiung City	6	7	17
Pingtung City	3	—	4
Fongshan 鳳山 district	7	6	18
Chaojhou 潮州 district	2	1	4
Donggang 東港 prefecture	4	—	9
Hengchun 恆春 district	4	—	9
Other	2	—	—
Totals	44	29	85
Penghu 澎湖 administrative area			
Penghu district	4	—	6
Totals	4	0	6

TABLE 16.1 (*continued*)

	Tabular Data	"Critical Areas" Data	Map Data
All Prefectures/Areas			
TOTALS	240	242	318

Sources:
Tabular data: [Taiwan Kempeitai Shireibu], "Funjō boppatsu o yosō shieru chi-iki ni okeru jōhō," [October 1945].
"Critical areas": Taiwan Sōtokufu, Keimukyoku, "Sōjō boppatsu no kanōsei aru chi-iki ni kan suru jōhō," November 1945.
Map: [Taiwan Kempeitai Shireibu], "Kiō no hassei jiken yori nitaru funjō boppatsu kanōsei chi-iki gaikenzu," [October 1945].

TABLE 16.2 Incidents of Violence and Plunder, Regional Analysis:
Comparison of Three Sources of Information

	Tabular Data		"Critical Areas" Data		Map Data	
	Plunder	Violence	Plunder	Violence	Plunder	Violence
Taipei prefecture						
Danshuei	—	5	—	—	—	5
Keelung City	1	2	—	3	1	5
Keelung	3	6	—	—	3	3
Cising	2	6	—	1	2	4
Taipei City	3	3	—	27	4	3
Sinjhuang	—	—	3	6	1	1
Wunshan	8	9	11	3	12	11
Haishan	4	5	4	9	4	6
Yilan	1	2	1	1	1	3
Luodong	1	—	—	—	2	2
Other	2	—	—	—	—	—
Subtotals	25	38	19	50	30	43
Combined Totals	63		69		73	

TABLE 16.2 (*continued*)

	Tabular Data		"Critical Areas" Data		Map Data	
	Plunder	Violence	Plunder	Violence	Plunder	Violence
Hsinchu prefecture						
Taoyuan	1	5	—	7	2	4
Jhongli	1	1	—	4	1	2
Dasi	1	2	—	4	2	2
Hsinchu	3	2	—	6	4	6
Hsinchu City	1	—	—	1	1	—
Jhudong	5	2	2	5	5	2
Jhunan	—	3	—	3	—	6
Miaoli	—	3	—	5	—	3
Dahu	—	—	—	2	—	—
Other	2	—	—	—	—	—
Subtotals	14	18	2	37	15	25
Combined Totals	32		39		40	
Hualien administrative area						
Hualien City	—	1	—	—	—	1
Subtotals	—	1	—	—	—	1
Combined Totals	1		0		1	
Taichung prefecture						
Dongshih4	—	—	—	1	—	—
Fongyuan	—	2	—	1	—	2
Dajia	—	12	—	5	—	14
Nenggao	—	—	1	2	—	1
Datun	—	2	—	1	—	2
Taichung City	1	—	—	3	2	—
Changhua	—	3	—	9	—	5
Nantou	2	2	—	—	2	2

TABLE 16.2 (*continued*)

	Tabular Data		"Critical Areas" Data		Map Data	
	Plunder	Violence	Plunder	Violence	Plunder	Violence
Yuanlin	—	5	—	—	—	2
Beidou	1	3	—	8	1	4
Jhushan	—	—	—	1	—	1
Other	2	2	—	—	—	—
Subtotals	6	31	1	31	5	33
Combined Totals	37		32		38	
Tainan prefecture						
Douliou	—	—	—	1	—	—
Huwei	—	1	3	2	—	2
Chiayi	4	2	4	3	4	5
Beigang	—	8	4	10	—	8
Sinying	—	5	5	1	—	6
Chiayi City	—	—	2	—	—	1 [?]
Dongshih2	—	3	2	7	—	5
Zengwun	—	8	5	5	—	10
Beimen	—	3	—	8	—	3
Sinhua	4	6	1	—	5	9
Sinfong	2	6	4	1	4	8
Tainan City	2	2	4	1	1	2
Other	1	1	—	—	—	—
Subtotals	13	45	34	39	14	59
Combined Totals	58		73		73	
Taitung administrative area						
Taitung	—	1	—	—	1	1
Subtotals	—	1	—	—	1	1
Combined Totals	1		0		2	

TABLE 16.2 (continued)

	Tabular Data		"Critical Areas" Data		Map Data	
	Plunder	Violence	Plunder	Violence	Plunder	Violence
Kaohsiung prefecture						
Cishan	8	1	1	—	7	2
Pingtung	—	1	—	2	—	2
Gangshan	4	2	—	—	4	9
Yuan[Gang?]shan	—	—	—	12	—	—
Kaohsiung City	6	—	—	7	9	8
Pingtung City	2	1	—	—	2	2
Fongshan	5	2	—	6	6	12
Chaojhou	2	—	—	1	2	2
Donggong	2	2	—	—	5	4
Hengchun	4	—	—	—	7	2
Other	2	—	—	—	—	—
Subtotals	35	9	1	28	42	43
Combined Totals	**44**		**29**		**85**	
Penghu administrative area						
Penghu	3	1	—	—	3	3
Subtotal	3	1	—	—	3	3
Combined Totals	**4**		**0**		**6**	
All Prefectures/Areas						
Combined Totals	**240**		**242**		**318**	

Sources:
Tabular data: [Taiwan Kempeitai Shireibu], "Funjō boppatsu o yosō shieru chi-iki ni okeru jōhō," [October 1945]. "Critical areas": Taiwan Sōtokufu, Keimukyoku, "Sōjō boppatsu no kanōsei aru chi-iki ni kan suru jōhō," November 1945.

Map: [Taiwan Kempeitai Shireibu], "Kiō no hassei jiken yori nitaru funjō boppatsu kanōsei chi-iki gaikenzu," [October 1945].

sults significantly. The question stands: "Why did more incidents of violence and theft occur in some areas than in others?"

There are also some startling numbers in each of the data sets that require some explanation. For instance, in the "critical areas" data (see table 16.2), the authorities recorded twenty-five incidents of violence against public officials in Taipei City north.[10] That number exceeds the total amount of disorder for any other city or district in the data samples (see table 16.1). Although this figure is not consistent with the map data for Taipei City (which may reflect more complete regional reporting) or the tabular data, I can find no reason to discard it without some explanation (though I do want to register some tentative suspicion). However, even if this figure for Taipei City north in the "critical areas" report is a clerical error, the same cannot be said for Tainan prefecture. In all three data samples, Tainan ranks first (or second in the "critical areas" data if Taipei City north figures are accurate) in incidents of violence committed against officials and police officers. Why would either region be so prone to violence against public officials? The statistics themselves provide us with no immediate answer; for that we will have to turn to other sources.

Finally, another figure that requires some explanation is the number recorded for collective plunder in Kaohsiung prefecture in two data sets (see table 16.2). I suspect that these unusual numbers of incidents (35 and 42) may simply reflect the concentration of military facilities in this southern prefecture rather than any "southern Taiwanese" predilection for collective plunder.

Chronological Analysis

Unfortunately, my efforts to discover some pattern in the temporal arrangement of the incidents of disorder provided me with very few insights (see table 16.3). In part, the data for violent attacks begins later than the information on thefts. In addition, the fluctuation in number of incidents from day to day during the peaks of social disorder are quite difficult to interpret. One overall impression is clear: mid-September was a difficult period of time for those in law enforcement. On September 15, nineteen incidents of mass plunder and assaults upon police and public officials were reported by the colonial law enforcement authorities, and figures for September 17 and 18 are also unusually high. A second peak was experienced about ten days later (on the 24th and 25th), and the early days of October were relatively unstable. All other periods pale in comparison.

However, I suggest that we treat these numbers with some caution. The total number of nineteen incidents recorded on September 15 is not, in retrospect, surprising to me (though I wish I had data on the incidence of social conflicts for tense periods during 1941–1945 with which to compare these late 1945 figures). Ten attempts to steal military provisions, together with seven attacks on

TABLE 16.3 Chronological Analysis of Incidents of Violence and Plunder

Date	Mass Plunder	Violence Against Officials	Violence Against Police Officers	Total
August 1945				
27th	1	—	—	1
28th	1	—	—	1
September 1945				
4th	1	—	—	1
5th	1	—	—	1
6th	2	—	—	2
7th	1	—	1	2
8th	3	—	—	3
9th	1	—	1	2
10th	6	—	1	7
11th	2	—	3	5
12th	5	—	3	8
13th	7	—	1	8
14th	—	2	1	3
15th	10	7	2	19
16th	—	—	5	5
17th	13	1	1	15
18th	6	3	4	13
19th	5	1	—	6
20th	—	5	5	10
21st	1	4	1	6
22nd	1	3	—	4
23rd	1	3	3	7
24th	1	5	5	11

TABLE 16.3 *(continued)*

Date	Mass Plunder	Violence Against Officials	Violence Against Police Officers	Total
25th	2	7	3	12
26th	5	1	1	7
27th	1	2	5	8
28th	1	3	5	9
29th	2	1	1	4
30th	—	1	2	3
October 1945				
1st	2	—	2	4
2nd	2	2	1	5
3rd	2	3	5	10
4th	1	3	1	5
5th	4	2	4	10
6th	—	—	1	1
7th	—	1	—	1
8th	—	1	—	1
9th	1	—	1	2
10th	1	1	1	3
11th	2	2	2	6
12th	1	—	3	4
13th	—	1	4	5
14th	—	1	—	1

Source: [Taiwan Kempeitai Shireibu], "Funjō boppatsu o yosō shieru chi-iki ni okeru jōhō," [October 1945].

public officials and two incidents of violence against patrolmen, do not comprise an island-wide movement to overthrow the colonial government. Furthermore, although total incidents for September 17 and 18 are comparatively high, (attempted) thefts of military provisions seem to account for these peaks; violence against officials and the police rose later in the month (on the 20th, 24th, and 25th). In all honesty, I suspect that the chronological analysis merely tells us that it took about a month for the authority of the colonial police force to wear thin. However, these figures also support my contention that as late as the middle of October (before any of Chen Yi's troops had arrived), the colonial government was still in control.

Having made those very general claims, though, I want to register some skepticism with these explanations. All data is limited, and this chronological data is no exception. One hopes that limited data can still tell us something about change over time. While change in this case may merely be that associated with administrative stability and control capabilities (i.e., the degree to which local police stations are able to record and respond to acts of civil disorder), change might also be found in the incidence of civilian resistance against the colonial regime. Similar events, or shifts in civilian (or official) attitudes, may have had an impact on both types of change. However, at this point in my research I cannot yet pinpoint the specific (potential) events in the mid- and late September history of immediate postsurrender Taiwan that would give me a clearer explanation for the trends I see in this chronological analysis of civilian disorder.[11]

Perpetrator Numbers

Most of my in-depth quantitative analysis in this paper is based on the textual record of immediate postsurrender conflict compiled by the military police in mid-October—what I have called the data set in tabular form, or "tabular data."[12] Although this source is relatively precise when recording the ethnicity and number of victims, it is less accurate in regard to incident perpetrators. For example, fewer than one-third of the ninety-six incidents of collective theft (or "mass plunder") give precise information on the number of perpetrators (see table 16.4). The term "villagers" is employed for fifty-two of these incidents, and no information is given for an additional seventeen cases.[13] Reports on violent attacks are relatively more useful in this regard, but a substantial number of these records employ the term "several" or "many" rather than specifying the exact number of people involved. One can hardly blame the compiler for this flaw in the data. I mention it here merely to call attention to the uneven quality of the information being analyzed.

What do we learn from the statistics on perpetrators? First of all, it appears that a substantial number of the violent encounters were initiated by individuals or small groups. More than one-half of the violent attacks on public officials were

TABLE 16.4 Analysis of Numbers of Perpetrators

Number/Types of Perpetrators	Incidents of Mass Plunder of Military Materiel	Incidents of Violence Toward Officials	Incidents of Violence Toward Police Officers
"Villagers"	52	—	—
1	—	20	14
2–5	3	14	13
6–10	1	2	7
"Several"	7	11	19
"Many"	1	—	5
11–19	1	2	7
20–49	2	3	3
"Several 10s"	1	—	2
50–99	2	4	2
100–150	7	4	1
200	1	4	3
500	1	—	—
600–700	—	—	1
"Several hundreds"	—	1	—
1,500–1,600	—	—	1
Unknown	17	—	1
Total	96	65	79

Source: [Taiwan Kempeitai Shireibu], "Funjō boppatsu o yosō shieru chi-iki ni okeru jōhō," [October 1945].

committed by single individuals or groups of individuals fewer than five. If "several" refers to more than three and fewer than ten individuals, then attacks on policemen reveal the same type of pattern. I suspect that this is also true for the thefts of military provisions. However, one cannot end discussion here. The tabular data clearly states that twenty-four of these events (nine cases of mass plunder, nine instances of violence against public officials, and six attacks on police officers) involved a crowd of more than one hundred people. Within the history of social grievance in Taiwan, whether colonial or postwar periods, this level of large-scale action is astounding.

In order to understand these large-scale incidents as an extraordinary type of collective theft or violent attack, I looked for patterns among the twenty-four instances of crowd behavior. First of all, regional concentration was readily apparent: nine cases occurred in Kaohsiung prefecture, while ten others erupted in Tainan prefecture. On the other hand, I found no significant temporal bunching, in part because of the small total number of events for any single date. Recorded causes were more useful than date of occurrence in understanding who had been involved in these large-scale incidents. Police authorities provided causal arguments for none of the incidents of large-scale plunder, but of the remaining sixteen incidents of large-scale disorder, five involved conflicts over goods provisioning. In addition, information on thirteen of the large-scale incidents is sufficient to trace the "development" of an event. (In other words, the original recorder envisioned a violent event developing over time.) Though no "pattern" of protest or rioting emerges, it is significant that in ten of these incidents, specific conflicts, protests, or demands concentrated the crowd together and focused their attention on a particular (group of) victim(s). Banners articulating demands (or "requests") were associated with two of these incidents.

Victim Ethnicity Analysis

At least one-third (and probably far more) of the officials and two-thirds of the police officers cited as victims in these incidents of violence were labeled "Islander" or "Taiwanese" by the compiler of the report (see table 16.5). Although we will want to consider the complex meaning of the term "Taiwanese" in this late colonial context, the phenomenon it attempts to distinguish in the report is especially interesting, and suggests several types of questions: Is this unlawful behavior grass-roots condemnation of the Taiwanese collaboration with the colonial state? Would an organizational analysis of local police forces and local government offices prove, on the contrary, that these acts only represent dislike for colonial rule per se at an important transition period in the political history of the island? In other words, is it more likely that lower levels of the police and governmental bureaucracies were manned by "Islander" or "Taiwanese," and therefore any post-surrender violent encounters that occurred would necessarily involve a greater percentage of "Islanders"/"Taiwanese"? Do the labels (and the actions that they attempt to record) challenge the goals and the stated claims of the kōminka movement in a fundamental way? These and other questions are addressed below.

Analysis of Victims' Official Positions

Nearly all of the victims in attacks on police officers were patrolmen in direct contact with the local populace, though in some of the large-scale group protests that took place at the local police station, the police officer in charge was

TABLE 16.5 Victim Ethnicity Analysis

Victim Ethnicity	Incidents of Violence Toward Officials	Incidents of Violence Toward Police Officers
"Islander" or "Taiwanese"	26	53
"Japanese"	2	17
"Japanese and Taiwanese, one each"	—	2
Unknown	37	7
Total	65	79

Source: [Taiwan Kempeitai Shireibu], "Funjō boppatsu o yosō shieru chi-iki ni okeru jōhō," [October 1945].

occasionally the target of attack. In contrast, violence toward public officials targeted a broader spectrum of local authorities, so a statistical analysis of this data presents additional information about these encounters (see table 16.6).

Three types of government services involve the majority of official victims: a) the staff of local government offices; b) officials involved in labor mobilization work (whether for air defense, general mobilization, or specific labor provisioning); and c) officials affiliated with agricultural affairs or the local agricultural association. In local areas these three entities (all interrelated) initiated and managed many of the demands made by the colonial government on the rural populace. Therefore, their presence on the roster of victims is not surprising. However, it does raise (for me) some more specific questions about late wartime governance and postsurrender assessment of colonial control: Do these acts of violence prove that late wartime mobilization of goods and labor at the local level was unreasonably harsh? (And can this proof of harsh rule be projected back earlier than 1945 or 1944?) In the execution of local governance, did town and village officials play a larger role in the active requisitioning of labor and goods than local patrolmen? Were these demands on rural resources *the* most important act of colonial government and therefore far more likely to cause enmity than other aspects of colonialism?

Stated Explanations for Incidents of Violence

Some tentative answers to the above questions can be found in the next set of figures (table 16.7). This list of motives for attacks upon officials and patrolmen corroborates some of my conclusions—namely, the wartime provisioning of labor and goods, as well as inequities in the requisition and assessment of these provisions and services, was a matter of contention between local communities and colonial authorities, and resulted in violent retribution in the fall of 1945. More

TABLE 16.6 Victims' Official Position Analysis

Victim's Official Position/Role	Number of Incidents Against
Government office staff	20
General affairs	1
Police station	1
Mobilization	8
Provisioning of labor	2
Air defense	4
Provisioning of goods	1
Rationing of goods	1
Agricultural affairs	10
Industrial affairs	6
Animal husbandry affairs	1
Education related	2
Railway	2
Unknown or uncertain	6
Total	65

Source: [Taiwan Kempeitai Shireibu], "Funjō boppatsu o yosō shieru chi-iki ni okeru jōhō," [October 1945].

than half of the military police report's explanations for violent behavior directed toward public officials are related to this type of disagreement. Immediate conflicts, personal enmity, or revenge for prior arrests comprise a much smaller percentage of the explanations cited by military police intelligence.

Violence against police officers is not so easily explained. "Immediate conflicts" [my term; see note to table 16.7] comprise a larger number of the stated explanations here, and revenge for prior arrests or confiscation of gambling monies is as prominent a motive in this listing as the discontent over the requisitioning of goods. Although the large number of unknown or unstated causes precludes a stronger argument at this point, the list of stated causes suggests that postsurrender violence against the police was motivated differently from assaults on public officials.

Finally, let me say a word about police responses, based on the information found in the tabular data set, which is limited primarily to thefts (see table 16.8).[14] First, it is important to remember that more than half of the thefts were still

TABLE 16.7 Stated Causes for Incidents of Violence

Stated Source of Discontent Leading to Violence	Resulting Number of Incidents
Against officials	
Conflicts over the provisioning of labor	7
Conflicts over labor mobilization	4
Demanding labor wages	1
Conflicts over air defense duties	1
Quota inequities (goods, labor, etc.)	6
Conflicts over provisioning of grains and goods	8
Demanding return of provisions (rice, eggs, etc.)	5
Demanding rice	1
Taxes and fees	3
Rationing inequities	2
Fertilizer distribution	1
Iron recycling	1
Previous arrests (or reporting leading to arrest)	4
Personal emnity	4
Improper official attitude	2
Official wrongdoing	2
Unknown or not specific	13
Total number of incidents	65
Against police officers	
Immediate conflict(*)	16
Previous arrest (or reporting leading to arrest)	6
Previous confiscation of goods or money	3
[Excessive] control of provisioning (grain, etc.)	8
Improper officer behavior	2
Fertilizer problem	1

TABLE 16.7 (continued)

Stated Source of Discontent Leading to Violence	Resulting Number of Incidents
Wages inappropriate for labor given	1
General discontent with officer's regular duties	4
Unknown or not specific	38
Total number of incidents	79

* Note: "Immediate conflicts" include: collecting information (2); arresting illegal slaughter (2); arresting illegal fishing (2); arresting illegal business transactions (2); arresting theft (1); arresting illegal gambling (1); arresting illegal tree cutting (1); interrupt fighting (1); labor pressing (1); over foodstuff (1); other (2).

Source: [Taiwan Kempeitai Shireibu], "Funjō boppatsu o yosō shieru chi-iki ni okeru jōhō" [October 1945].

under investigation when the report was compiled. This suggests that either the authorities (police, military police, and local base security forces) were reluctant to pursue any vigorous investigation of these thefts of military property or their ability to investigate had been severely hampered—for any number of reasons. Nevertheless, the data in this table does indicate that sentries were still protecting military supplies at some facilities and that different types of policing forces were working together in order to minimize the loss of goods to "mass plunder."

OFFICIAL INTERPRETATIONS

A report on "critical areas" where trouble was most likely to occur, compiled in November 1945 by the police bureau, singled out twelve districts and provided the relevant statistics for assaults, organized plundering, and other disturbances in each (see table 16.9).

A comparison of these results with the three data sources cited in the first section of this essay reveals some interesting discrepancies. Table 16.10 lists, based on *total disturbances alone,* the top ten areas where trouble was most likely to occur. It's surprising that there is so *little* overlap between this set of three rankings and the "critical areas" in the November report (table 16.9).

Furthermore, it is important to note that in the descriptive analysis of "critical areas" in the November report the investigator did not cite quantitative data to support his list of twelve hotspots. Instead, he presented a historical argument: chronicles of early-20th-century resistance to Japanese rule had provided him with answers to the present dilemma. In the November report, the descriptions of each region and its "characteristic disorder" follow the same general narrative

TABLE 16.8 Police or Military Responses to Plunder Incidents

Response	Plunder Incidents
Sentry discovered perpetrators, challenged them; they fled	2
Sentry fired weapon, and perpetrators fled	1
Sentry fired weapon, and some perpetrators were arrested	1
Criminals discovered/confirmed (and arrested), and materials recovered	5
Some criminals arrested and some materials recovered; rest being investigated	5
[Criminals] questioned, reprimanded, (forced to write an apology), released; goods returned	3
Criminals reported (and arrested) and matter under investigation	1
Criminals reported (and/or arrested) by military police; under investigation by the police	2
All goods recovered	1
Most goods recovered	1
Military detachment ordered to be more vigilant	1
Being investigated	58
Being investigated by military police with assistance from police	1
Being investigated with assistance from military police	3
Being investigated with assistance from military detachment	6
Response unknown	3
Total number of incidents	**96**

Source: [Taiwan Kempeitai Shireibu], "Funjō boppatsu o yosō shieru chi-iki ni okeru jōhō" [October 1945].

structure: Early colonial–era banditry (which included attacks on government offices and seizures of army materials) was suppressed by the Japanese military and police, without completely destroying anti-Japanese sentiment. For various reasons, cultural development in the region did not keep pace with other areas of the island, and lawless elements continued to exist. Consequently, in 1945, when the political situation began to change, local villagers believed the anti-Japanese propaganda of former bandits, who incited their followers to resist the colonial government. The author of the report literally took the history of region-specific social unrest in the early years of the colonial period as a mirror for predicting which areas would experience anti-Japanese disturbances in the fall of 1945.

TABLE 16.9 Police Bureau Summary of "Critical Areas" (November 1945)

District	Incidents of Violence Against State and Officials	Organized Plundering	Other Disturbances	Total
Beigang	10	4	—	14
Sinchuang	6	3	—	9
Dongshih2	7	2	—	9
Beidou	6	—	2	8
Jhudong	5	2	—	7
Fongshan	6	—	—	6
Miaoli	4	—	1	5
Keelung	2	—	1	3
Sinhua	—	1	—	1
Dajia	—	"Many"	yes	"Many"
Cishan	—	"Many"	—	"Many"
Jhushan	—	—	—	—

There were also other interpretations in 1945. Three interim police reports[15] and contemporary elite observers[16] explained these popular acts of violence and plunder differently. Most describe (or assume) a foundational Taiwanese hatred for Japanese rule, though official accounts are ambivalent about the truth or power of these islander emotions. In the August and September police bureau reports, "Han Chinese nationalism" served as an equivalent term to classify one type of islander motive. However, careful attention to context and underlying assumptions reveals an important shade of difference among these various explanations. Police spokesmen inferred that news from China (or from Nationalist Chinese representatives in Taiwan in early September) drove a wedge between the Taiwanese and the Japanese; the changing situation and elite islander activism facilitated this distancing action. In contrast, elite Taiwanese observers, in particular those from the more conservative Nationalist camp, tended to describe this action as more of an awakening, in response to new circumstances and new potentialities. However, all contemporary observers agreed that popular characteristics were essential to the understanding of postsurrender developments. Police analysts depicted a Taiwanese propensity to look out for themselves, while

TABLE 16.10 Likely Troublespots Identified by Data Sets

Tabular Data	"Critical Areas" Data	Map Data
Wunshan district (17)	Taipei City north (25)	Wunshan district (23)
Dajia district (12)*	Wunshan district (14)	Fongshan district (18)
Sinhua district (10)*	Beigang district (14)*	Kaohsiung City (17)
Keelung district (9)	Haishan district (13)	Dajia district (14)*
Haishan district (9)	Yuan[Gang?]shan (12)	Sinhua district (14)*
Cishan district (9)*	Zengwun district (10)	Gangshan district (13)
Cising district (8)	Sinhuang district (9)*	Sinfong district (12)
Beigang district (8)*	Changhua district (9)	Hsinchu district (10)
Zengwun district (8)	Dongshih2 district (9)*	Zengwun district (10)
Sinfong district (8)	Beidou district (8)*	Haishan district (9)
	Beimen district (8)	Chiayi district (9)
		Cishan district (9)*
		Donggang district (9)
		Hengchun district (9)

* Areas included in November 1945 predictions (table 16.9).

elite Taiwanese observers across the political spectrum cited cultural and social backwardness of their lower-class brethren to explain acts of popular violence and plunder. Finally, whenever nationalism and cultural (or class) traits were necessary but insufficient explanations for disorder, official reporters tended to rely on the explanatory power of a rapidly changing situation: With each incidence of assault or theft, a spiraling circle of popular doubt in police abilities and the consequent decline in police effectiveness ensured the ultimate inability of a formerly powerful police force to control popular violence and plunder.

MY ALTERNATIVE INTERPRETATION: CONCLUSIONS IN BRIEF

In the following two sections, I wish to present an alternative set of explanations for the tens and hundreds of conflicts from late August to mid-October 1945 that are recorded in postsurrender police reports. In brief, my argument consists of the following points:

1. Beginning in 1944, the colonial authorities made increasing demands upon local goods, possessions, and labor to meet the needs of the Japanese imperial military as it began to lose the Pacific War. By late 1945, these demands had taken a serious toll on the resources and personal well-being of the average Taiwanese.

2. A rapidly changing situation immediately following the announcement of Japan's surrender in August provided a fertile context for innovative actions in citizen-police-official encounters. Stable parameters in these relationships were very difficult to gauge—by all parties.

3. Despite variations in practices and differences of effectiveness, police officers and local government officials continued their attempts to maintain social order and (where possible) to carry out many of their official duties. The data presented in the October 1945 military police report documents those official actions.

4. I do not consider elite Taiwanese activism to be the dominant storyline of this postsurrender drama. The record of elite activities tells us that their political maneuvering and competition during the months of August, September, and October resembled the activism of the pre-1937 period.

5. Finally, subaltern voices (and behavior) suggest that the postsurrender civilian actions documented in the police bureau's "crime report" were a direct response to the wartime demands of the colonial state. From this perspective, these demands for various kinds of restitution and reimbursement were not crimes; and most were not motivated by the nationalism promoted by elite activists.

PROBING CONTEXTUAL KNOWLEDGE

Although I am unable to provide a comprehensive summary of late wartime demands for Taiwanese goods and labor, and the means by which those demands were met, perhaps I can suggest an outline of that rather complex and (to most of us) unclear history.

Increased Demands

All official sources indicate that local police and officials mobilized more provisions and labor in the last two years of the war than they had previously. To organize this increased exploitation, the colonial authorities made several changes in their hierarchy. In December 1943 the government-general established citizens mobilization departments and sections in prefectural, administrative-area, and district levels of government. In all towns and settlements, the authorities created a new specialized position to manage these mobilization affairs.[17]

After April 1944 there was a much greater need for local labor resources to construct additional military facilities (e.g., airfields, military roads). New government-general directives (first in July 1944 and then again in February 1945) mandated greater mobilization of local labor and established new organizations at all levels of government to control and manage these new resources efficiently.[18] Most of this mobilizing was organized by local police and the officials of town government offices.[19]

In most (but not all) areas of the colony, the Japanese surrender in August 1945 brought an end to much of this wartime construction work. Mobilized work units were disbanded and returned home. Although colonial officials recognized the need for immediate reconstruction work, they were hesitant to organize this activity.[20] The tabular data in the October military police report does suggest, however, that labor mobilization did continue in a few outlying towns and settlements.

The memoirs of one colonial official, Morita Shunsuke, remind us that one of the more important matters facing the colonial state in August 1945 was reimbursing these mobilized laborers for unpaid wartime wages.[21] Morita sought to resolve the issue of unpaid wages before the Chinese authorities arrived. However, his attempt to obtain workers' confirmation of the daily wage for this wartime work backfired when his selected workers' representatives refused to accept the figure of 80 *cash* per day, which was the amount specified in the original state budget. Morita tells us why: Although (he contends, but I doubt, that) local governments had paid for the daily meals of laborers during the war, the black market rate for labor substitutes was as high as 2 yen per day. Thus, even Morita knew that 80 *cash* per day was an improper reimbursement in the minds of those who had loaned their labor to the state.

Greater Control

Most research on the wartime years has focused on the *kōminka* movement or the training of Taiwanese youth (both men and women) for service in the military.[22] We know very little about the actual work of *kōmin hōkōkai* activities in local areas, in particular during the last two years of the war. Without more detailed research on this activity, it's impossible for me to elaborate on the impact of these institutions and their activities on civilians in the postsurrender drama that I'm narrating.

Likewise, we also need more detailed studies of the day-to-day disciplining of local police forces as they attempted to mobilize increasingly more goods and labor to meet the needs of the Japanese military in 1945. The economic police force was a product of the war, initiated in 1938 and then institutionalized in 1940 when economic police divisions and departments were established in all prefectures and administrative areas. One indication of their duties would be the statistics on "economic crimes" committed in 1944.[23] This source also gives us an indication of the major areas of conflict between populace and police. The highest number of crimes in this listing is for violations of the price-control regulations, but the next three or four major types of crimes on this list are all directly related to the postsurrender activities I've been discussing: violations of the regulations on pork rationing and hide rationing (related to illegal slaughter of livestock); and violations of regulations controlling the storage of unhulled rice and the rationing of rice and other grains (related to conflicts over provisioning, quota inequities, and grain rationing).

Japanese Officials and Elite Taiwanese as Participants

According to the August 1945 police reports, policing strategies were revised in that month on order to shift their primary focus to the maintenance of law and order; chaos prevention and maintaining basic living conditions were given the highest priorities. The central police bureau strengthened the work of special policing corps even as it encouraged the efforts of local police stations and ordered more frequent patrols. Local police chiefs were required to collect more intelligence on potential ideological and economic problems and report such information more rapidly to police headquarters. Police officers were instructed to avoid actions that might induce conflicts between Taiwanese and Japanese. It is likely that these changes in policy and practice had some impact on subsequent encounters between police officers and local islanders.

The story that I and others have previously told of these interactions between colonial officials and civilians has focused primarily upon the activities of a small group of well-known cultural and political elites, though several businessmen and a few professionals have played significant roles in some of our tales.[24] Depending on the particular subject of research, historians have highlighted the machinations of pro-independence forces, the meetings of welcoming committees and their chairman, or the public rallies in late September and October that brought elite activists directly in contact with a broader segment of the (primarily) urban populace. Students and youth play a strong supporting role in these historical dramas. In some accounts they take responsibility for social control, garbage collection, and cultural censorship as early as late September. Yet youth deference to welcoming committee chairmen or the newly designated leaders of the "Three Peoples Principles Youth Corps" is repeated in many a memoir and biography.

More recent accounts help us understand the political maneuvering and competitive rivalries of all these groups and individuals, as well as the high stakes that such political battles involved. However, as I am attempting to argue in this essay, our histories have not explained the data on violent assaults and the plundering of military goods.

INTERPRETING SUBALTERN STATEMENTS

More than half the incidents of violence against local officials mentioned in this data involve some type of conflict over wartime provisioning, rationing, or the taxing of goods and services (see table 16.7). The statistics on violence committed against police officers are more difficult to interpret. Stated causes are not recorded for nearly half of these "crimes." Of the remainder (41 incidents), only 13 incidents are specifically related to conflicts over provisioning, while 16 of the incidents involve more immediate conflicts between civilians and policemen. However, I wish to suggest that these numbers are also significant. The relatively higher incidence of immediate conflicts between police and civilians demonstrates that colonial police continued to perform their official duties, a strategy that may have placed them right in harm's way.

Multiple Cases in One Area

New insight may also be found by exploring the multiple instances of crime in a single town or settlement. Only nine such multiple-incident sites can be detected in the tabular data. (Surprisingly, the map data is much less precise in this regard.) Three incidents of theft in Yuehmei village, Cishan district, suggest that the military was dispersing its stored provisions away from military bases in the latter months of the war, and this may have confused the issue of ownership in villagers' minds. In addition, thefts of building materials near Hu-hsi-chuang in Penghu involved coastal encampments already abandoned by the Japanese navy in mid-September. And the so-called thefts at Man-chou settlement in Heng-chun district were in fact only attempts; vigilant military guards prevented any loss of property, but we might also note that villagers attempted more than once to pilfer military supplies.

Multiple cases of violent assaults are not especially revealing. On September 24, in Hua-X settlement, Changhua district, the same thirty villagers apparently beat up more than ten officials in two separate incidents. Here the stated cause for the violence was declared to be civilian discontent with the high-handed attitude and behavior of local officials. The record of the late September and early October assaults in Dongshih settlement, Sinhua district, is decidedly more helpful because it shows an escalation of violence over the period of a week, as well as a strong degree of discontent. Approximately thirty Taiwanese assaulted an on-duty Taiwanese policeman on September 30. The same day, several Taiwanese injured a Taiwanese policeman who was attempting to check the household registry data in the settlement. Whether the same policeman was involved in both conflicts is impossible to determine, but it's important to note that both assaults occurred away from government offices.

In contrast, on October 4 approximately two hundred villagers surrounded the police station in Dongshih settlement and demanded that the police chief return the fines and money that he had confiscated when he arrested suspected gamblers. This incident either was unresolved on that day or stimulated other recollections. The following day, several tens of villagers surrounded the station again in an attempt to force the police chief to apologize for his excessive zeal in the control of commercial transactions in the past. That the military police was called in to deal with the latter incident suggests to me that local authorities had to admit their weaknesses in the face of repeated villager demands.

Subaltern Demands or Threats

Finally, I turn to subaltern demands themselves. Like the rumors embedded in newspaper reports, the occasional demands, threats, or challenges that have been recorded in Japanese police reports can assist us in comprehending the complexities of subaltern motives. In this instance, the statements are few and the messages cannot be taken as verbatim or complete quotes. Nevertheless, I employ them to reiterate claims made by subaltern actions.

A single statement in a police report articulated a Nationalist claim, and would seem to confirm all the myths about postsurrender civilian-official conflict we have read in other accounts of the period. On September 9, when a solitary Japanese patrolman tried to curtail the work of five Taiwanese who were cutting trees from a windbreak (in Anting settlement, Sinhua district), the accused responded: "Taiwan is not Japan's land. Why are you stopping us?" This is the only statement in the report that articulates this fundamental Taiwan vs. Japan difference.

Three of the eleven quotes demonstrate the utility of shouting a threat in a conflict situation. For example, pressing Donggang residents to join an announced work corps must have been dangerous business for the patrolman that five men threatened to destroy in early October. However, the swift dispersal of the five islanders, without any violent action taking place, attests the power of police authority even at this late date. On the other hand, the threat "I will kill this pitiful policeman who is all alone" (October 13, Chi-lung) reminds us of the insecurity of patrolmen and the increasing likelihood that they would abandon their out-of-office duties.

The rest of these recorded statements confirm the story that I have been trying to tell in this essay. Representing assaults or public protests that occurred between September 16 and October 11, these seven statements register a) vehement protests against the scale and inequity of wartime provisioning assessments;

b) demands for the reimbursement of agricultural goods that were requisitioned by the imperial army; c) criticism of repeated attempts at tax collection in the postsurrender period; and d) denials of the legitimacy of police attempts to define "crimes" (e.g., gambling and illegal slaughter).

In short, the subaltern message that I have read in police reports and police crime statistics does not confirm the Nationalist tale previously told in our histories, but rather articulates a far more compelling story of late wartime exploitation and injustice, one that requires our further attention.

NOTES

1. I thank the many friends and colleagues who provided me with valuable feedback on earlier versions of this analysis. In December 1996, I first presented some of these findings to students in Wu Micha's graduate symposium at National Taiwan University. Later the next year, I discussed revised analyses of this data in two settings: at one of the regular symposia of the Institute of Taiwan History at Academia Sinica, and for a group of graduate students at Chi Nan University. Several scholars at each of these gatherings suggested additional sources to me. In the summer of 2001, I also received much substantive input from scholars gathered for the "Symposium for Exchange Between Japanese and Taiwanese Historians of Taiwan," at Ilan, Taiwan. In addition, I'm especially indebted to Wu Micha (for providing copies of Gaimushoo reports and police reports that were "companion volumes" to the reports, maps, and tabular data that I found in the U.S. National Archives) and Kondo Masami (for sharing reports from the thought-control police). Marc Schneiberg, a sociologist at Reed College, also gave my statistical analysis a careful specialist's critique. For all of this assistance and feedback, I am truly grateful.

2. Yeh Jung-chung 1985: 283.

3. Taiwan Sōtokufu, Keimukyoku, November 1945.

4. For example, Chen Tsui-lien 1994, 1995.

5. See Taiwan Sōtokufu, Keimukyoku, November 1945; and Taiwan Kempeitai Shireibu, [Tabular data], October 1945.

6. Taiwan Kempeitai Shireibu, October 1945.

7. Taiwan Sōtokufu, Keimukyoku, November 1945.

8. Taiwan Sōtokufu, Keimukyoku, November 1945.

9. Taiwan Kempeitai Shireibu, October 1945.

10. The figure of twenty-seven violent incidents for Taipei City in table 16.2 includes two incidents for Taipei City south and twenty-five incidents for Taipei City north.

11. Marc Schneiberg has even suggested that this evidence provides a "powerful rebuttal of the alternative hypotheses for all of [my] data: that these patterns reflect business as usual." For example, the tabular data associates the theft of building materials in Kaohsiung City on September 15 with the "dissolution of the commissariat for the headquarters of the Kaohsiung strategic area."

12. Source: Taiwan Kempeitai Shireibu, October 1945.

13. Based on the presentation of information in the data as a whole, I do think this refer-

ence to "villagers" represents a rather small number of people involved in each case of collective theft or plunder.

14. The information on responses to assaults in the tabular data set was brief and unitary, giving me very little insight into this type of conflict.

15. Taiwan Sōtokufu, Keimukyoku, August and September 1945.

16. Yeh 1967; Chen Yi-sung 1994; Wu 1981.

17. See Taiwan tōchi gaiyō and Tsai 1994, 1995. For example, one of Tsai Hui-yü's informants told her that clerks in charge of mobilizing local labor resources were established within the local public office in towns and settlements in the Kaohsiung in late wartime.

18. Taiwan tōchi gaiyō.

19. Tsai 1994, 1995.

20. Taiwan tōchi gaiyō.

21. Morita 1979.

22. For example, Kondō 1996; Li 1997.

23. Taiwan tōchi gaiyō, pp. 111–115.

24. For example, Chen Tsui-lien 1995; He 1998; Kondō 1996.

REFERENCES

Chen Tsui-lien 陳翠蓮. 1994. "228 shih-chien yen-chiu 二二八事件研究." Ph.D. diss., Graduate Institute of Political Science, National Taiwan University.

———. 1995. P'ai-hsi tou-cheng ch'uan-mou cheng-chih 派系鬥爭與權謀政治. Taipei: Shih Pao.

Chen Yisong 陳逸松. 1994. Ch'en Yi-sung hui-yi-lu 陳逸松回憶錄. Wu Chun-ying and Lin Chung-sheng, compilers. Taipei: Ch'ien Wei.

Fix, Douglas. "Taiwanese Nationalism and Its Late Colonial Context." Ph.D. diss., University of California, Berkeley

Gaimushō, Kanrikyoku, Sōmubu, Nampōka 外務省管理局総務部南方課. 1946. "Taiwan no genkyō 台湾の現況." February 10.

———. 1946. "Taiwan kankei 台湾関係." March 10.

He Yi-lin 何義麟. 1998. "Taiwanjin no seiji shakai to 228 jiken 台湾の政治社会と２２８事件." Ph.D. diss., University of Tokyo.

Ikeda Toshio 池田敏雄. 1982. "Haisen nikki 敗戦日記." Taiwan Kin Gendaishi Kenkyuu 4:55–108.

Kondō Masami 近藤正己. 1996. Sōryokusen to Taiwan: Nihon shokuminchi hōkai no kenkyū 総力戦と台湾: 日本植民地崩壊の研究. Tokyo: Tōsui Shobo.

Li Kuo-sheng 李國生. 1997. "Chan-cheng yü T'ai-wan-jen: Chih-min cheng-fu tui T'ai-wan te chun-shih jen-li tung-yuan 戰爭與臺灣人: 殖民政府對臺灣的軍事人力動員 (1937–1945)." M.A. thesis, Graduate Institute of History, National Taiwan University.

Morita Shunsuke 森田俊介. 1979. Nai Tai gojūnen mokuji: Kaisō to zuihitsu 内台五十年もくじ: 回想と随筆. [Tokyo].

Mukōyama Hiroo 向山寛夫. 1987. Nihon tōchika ni okeru Taiwan minzoku undōshi 日本統治下における台湾民族運動し. Tokyo: Chuuō Keizai Kenkyuujo.

Shiomi Shunji 塩見俊二. 1979. *Hiroku: Shūsen chokugo no Taiwan: Watakushi no shūsen nikki* 秘録—終戦直後の台湾：私の終戦日記. Kochi: Kochi Shinbunsha.

Strategic Services Unit, Canary Mission. 1945. "Cables (outgoing)." September–November.

[Taiwan Kempeitai Shireibu 台湾憲兵隊司令部.] 1945. "Funjō boppatsu o ŷosō shieru chiiki ni okeru jōhō 紛擾勃発お予想し得る地域における情報." [Tabular data.] [October].

[———.] 1945. "Kiō no hassei jiken yori mitaru funjō boppatsu kanōsei chiiki gaikenzu 既往の発生事件より観たる紛擾勃発可能性地域概見圖." Map. [October 1945].

Taiwan Sōtokufu 台湾総督府警務局. 1945. *(Shōwa nijūnen) Taiwan tōchi gaiyō* (昭和二十年) 台湾統治概要. Taihoku, [1945].

Taiwan Sōtokufu, Keimukyoku. 1945. "Taishō kampatsu ato ni okeru tōnai chian jyōkyō nara[bi ni] keisatsu sochi (dai-ichi hō) 大詔渙発後における島内治安状況並びに警察措置 (第一報)." August 1945.

———. 1945. "Taishō kampatsu ato ni okeru tōnai chian jyōkyō nara[bi ni] keisatsu sochi (dai-ni hō) 大詔渙発後における島内治安状況並びに警察措置 (第二報)." August 1945.

———. 1945. "Shūsen ato ni okeru tōnai chian jyōkyō nara[bi ni] keisatsu sochi (dai-san hō) 終戦後における島内治安状況並びに警察措置 (第三報)." September 1945.

———. 1945. "Sōjō boppatsu no kanōsei aru chi-iki ni kan suru jōhō 騒擾勃発の可能性ある地域に関する情報." ["Critical areas of activity".] November 1945.

Ts'ai Hui-yu 蔡慧玉. "Pao-cheng, pao-chia shu-chi, chieh chuang yi-ch'ang 保正, 保甲書記, 街庄役場—口述歷史." *Shih Lien* 23 (1993): 23–40; *Taiwan Fengwu* 44.2 (1994): 69–111; *Taiwan Fengwu* 45.4 (1995): 83–106.

———. 1995. "Pao-cheng, pao-chia shu-chi, chieh chuang yi-ch'ang—K'ou-shu li-shih 保正, 保甲書記, 街庄役場—口述歷史." *Taiwanshih Yenchiu* 2.2:187–214.

Wu Hsin-jung 吳新榮. 1981. *Wu Hsin-jung rih-chi (chan-hou)* 吳新榮日記 (戰後). Chang Liang-tse, editor. Taipei: Yuan Ching.

———. 1989. *Wu Hsin-jung hui-yi-lu* 吳新榮回憶錄. Lin Heng-che, et al., editors. Taipei: Ch'ien Wei.

Yeh Jung-chung 葉榮鐘. 1985. "T'ai-wan-sheng kuang-fu ch'ien-hou te hui-yi 臺灣省光復前後的回憶." *Taiwan jen-wu ch'ün-hsiang*. Taipei: Po-mi-erh. Reprinted from *Hsiao-wu ta-ch'e chi* (Taipei: Chung-yang Shu-chu, 1967).

[17]

THE NATURE OF *MINZOKU TAIWAN* AND THE CONTEXT IN WHICH IT WAS PUBLISHED

WU MICHA*

Minzoku Taiwan 民俗台湾, a journal in ethnology published during the war, has always enjoyed a positive response in both Taiwan and Japan. However, in July 1996, with the publication of *The Fiction and Fact of "Greater East Asian Ethnology"*『大東亞民俗學』の虛實, the Japanese literary critic Kawamura Minato 川村湊 contradicted this accepted opinion, generating controversy.

Kawamura picked up the term "Greater East Asian ethnology" for his book title from the transcript of a symposium published in the December 1943 issue of *Minzoku Taiwan* entitled "The construction of Greater East Asian ethnology and the mission of *Minzoku Taiwan*." In his book Kawamura attempts a retrospective survey of prewar ethnological investigation and research conducted by the Japanese in the "Greater East Asia region," which included Korea 朝鮮, Taiwan, the South Pacific, and Manchuria 滿州.

Kawamura's focus was the written transcript of a symposium convened on October 17, 1943, in Tokyo at the residence of Yanagita Kunio 柳田國男, a leading scholar in the field of Japanese ethnology at the time. The symposium centered on Yanagita Kunio, and the other participants were central figures associated with the journal *Minzoku Taiwan* (Kanaseki Takeo 金關丈夫, Nakamura Akira 中村哲, and Okada Yuzuru 岡田謙) and Yanagita Kunio's disciple, Hashiura Yasuo 橋浦泰雄, the editor of the journal *Minkan denshō* 民間傳承. Kawamura borrowed the term "Greater East Asian ethnology" from this symposium transcript; he also pointed out what Yanagita Kunio was intending with that wartime symposium:

To create, in the Greater East Asian region, a "discipline of ethnology" that employs the Japanese language to collect, categorize, and analyze [phenomena], which shall become the analytical target for comparison and contrast with "Japanese ethnology." In other words, what Yanagita Kunio conceptualized was *not* an "ethnology" established in each of these areas that possessed its own autonomous set of topics and problematiques. On the contrary, it was a vision of a mode of ethnological research that radiated or expanded outward from the center, which was Japan. Or better yet, it resembled the organizational chart of a "Japanese ethnology" with a core–periphery network composed of local researchers, teachers, and interested amateurs in all of Japan's districts, organized around Yanagita Kunio's ethnological research center situated in Tokyo.[1]

Kawamura argued that the role played by transregional ethnology (i.e., the study of ethnology in each region) within the "Greater East Asia Co-Prosperity Sphere" as conceived by Yanagita was that of being the hands and feet of "Japanese ethnology." None of these regional ethnologies had its own autonomous "head." If one did *not* adopt a friendly reading of Yanagita's comments at the symposium, he could say that Yanagita hoped [local] ethnologies would play a supplementary role. Yanagita did not intend to offer the Taiwanese, Koreans, or Manchurians the means for comprehending the self with regard to Japan (i.e., the meanings of self-affirmation and self-realization that were manifest in Japanese ethnological theories). On the contrary, the ultimate goal of these regional ethnologies was merely to measure "how much (ethnological) distance existed between them and us Japanese," and thus Yanagita lacked the perspective of a comparative ethnology that would relativize Japanese ethnology.[2]

Using the phrase "Greater East Asian ethnology" appearing in the symposium proceedings as a lead-in, Kawamura Minato looked back (from a critical and self-reflexive position) on the prewar ethnological investigation and documentation carried out by the Japanese in Korea, Taiwan, the South Seas, and Manchuria, and sketched for us what can be called a "Greater East Asian Co-Prosperity Sphere 大東亞共榮圈" in the realm of ethnological study. One might regard Kawamura's perspective as but one in a series of critical reassessments of Yanagita Kunio's ethnology that have recently appeared in Japan. His view also reflects a recent fashionable trend of reconsidering the colonial element in prewar academic investigations.[3]

Kawamura's critical perspective and analytical context have resulted in an assessment of *Minzoku Taiwan* that pays particular attention to the tendencies of colonialism and exoticism associated with that journal. Kawamura's way of interpreting *Minzoku Taiwan*, which is contrary to previous assessments, attracted the attention of those originally affiliated with *Minzoku Taiwan*. Professor Kokubu Naoichi 國分直一,[4] one of the chief contributors to that journal, immediately published a rebuttal as a book review, despite his age of more than ninety years.[5]

Kokubu Naoichi's critical review made three main claims: the first concerned the leader of *Minzoku Taiwan*, Kanaseki Takeo; the second dealt with the nature of the journal; and the third addressed postwar Taiwanese assessments of the journal. Kokubu cited the postwar respect that Taiwanese had for Kanaseki Takeo, as well as Kanaseki's involvement in international academic circles and his academic legacy, to prove that Kanaseki was absolutely *not* a racist. Kokubu made it clear that the reason he and his colleagues from *Minzoku Taiwan* had conceived of the plan to document and investigate Taiwanese folklore in the early 1940s was because they had observed that older Taiwanese customs and folklore were soon to be destroyed. *Minzoku Taiwan* did not stoop to the level of becoming an exoticizing, colonialist journal. Furthermore, the fact that postwar Taiwanese assessments of both *Minzoku Taiwan* and Kanaseki Takeo have been very positive readily demonstrates that there was no racial or ethnic prejudice associated with the *Minzoku Taiwan* movement.

Kokubu Naoichi's view is consistent with that found in the postwar memoirs of those formerly related to *Minzoku Taiwan* (no matter whether they are Taiwanese or Japanese) as well as with the image of *Minzoku Taiwan* depicted by most postwar scholars of Taiwan's history. A brief review of that genealogy of postwar Taiwanese judgments concerning *Minzoku Taiwan* follows below. It begins with the 1960s.

In December 1960, when Professor Kanaseki Takeo visited Taiwan to attend a medical conference, he accepted an invitation to give a lecture for the Department of Archaeology and Anthropology at Taiwan University.[6] During his visit, Kanaseki reminisced about *Minzoku Taiwan* in rather general terms at the "Symposium Welcoming Dr. Kanaseki Takeo," which had been convened for former contributors to *Minzoku Taiwan*. During the last round of comments made at that gathering, one of the originators of *Minzoku Taiwan*, Huang Deshi 黃得時 (in 1960 a professor at Taiwan University), had this to say:

> Now as I look back on those earlier years, I note that among the Japanese expatriates living in Taipei there were two types of people: One was composed of isolated, self-protecting Japanese, who sought a living only among the Japanese community and who did not wish to develop any connections with the outside world. The other kind had personal interactions with Taiwanese; they entered into the daily lives of the Taiwanese and tried very hard to comprehend that community. Of course, Mr. Kanaseki belonged to that second type.[7]

In 1966 the journal *Taiwan fengwu* 台灣風物 (which modeled itself on *Minzoku Taiwan*, with the English title "Taiwan Folkways") convened the symposium "Research trends in the contemporary study of local Taiwan" at its tenth anniversary celebration. Nearly all the participants at that event praised the legacy of *Minzoku Taiwan* and hoped that *Taiwan fengwu* would grow like *Minzoku*

Taiwan had. Some speakers also suggested the publication of Chinese-language translations of *Minzoku Taiwan* in future issues of *Taiwan fengwu*. Summarizing the specific characteristics of *Minzoku Taiwan*, Huang Deshi made the following remarks:

> Perhaps some suspect that because *Minzoku Taiwan* was edited by Japanese, it might therefore have manifested a style of racial prejudice or racial condescension. However, as one of the original organizers, I can say (without any reservation whatsoever) that "This kind of tendency absolutely did not exist." As noted earlier in the symposium, when the journal first appeared, it was subject to severe repression and white-eyed attention on the part of the colonial authorities. Furthermore, the fact that there were more local Taiwanese than Japanese among Professor Kanaseki Takeo's friends provides additional evidence of my claim. One can get a general sense of this phenomena from Kanaseki's loving and protective attitude toward his Taiwanese friends, or from Ikeda Toshio 池田敏雄's (general editor for the journal) preference for wearing native clothing, living in Taiwanese-style housing and later marrying a local woman, Ms. Huang Fengzi 黃鳳姿.[8]

During the war, Yang Yunping 楊雲萍, a literary critic, had taken an attitude of disbelief towards *Minzoku Taiwan* when it was first published. He wrote an essay demanding that those affiliated with *Minzoku Taiwan* must possess love for Taiwan, in addition to their scientific attitude, as they began to research Taiwanese folklore and conduct local investigations. However, after the war, Yang (having become a professor at Taiwan University) admitted that he had accused his colleagues at *Minzoku Taiwan* unfairly, owing to his youthful hotheadedness. Yang wrote that there was evidence to demonstrate that *Minzoku Taiwan* did indeed address Taiwanese folklore and old customs in a sincere fashion.[9]

In 1982 an article by Ikeda Toshio was published posthumously, nearly forty years after the appearance of *Minzoku Taiwan*. As a key member of the *Minzoku Taiwan* circle, Ikeda had taken charge of editing the journal from beginning to end. His article, "A folklore journal of Taiwan under colonial rule," was a kind of "Master's own way" piece, and it is now frequently cited by those who analyze *Minzoku Taiwan*.[10] Immediately following the death of this major figure from the *Minzoku Taiwan* group in 1981, *Taiwan fengwu* published a "Special issue commemorating the death of Mr. Ikeda Toshio." In that publication, Yang Yunping expressed the following words of respect for *Minzoku Taiwan* and Ikeda Toshio in his eulogy, "Words of grief for the death of Mr. Ikeda Toshio":

> The very existence of the monthly journal *Minzoku Taiwan* represented the Japanese conscience. Though shameful aspects of Japanese colonial rule are numerous, Japanese people can cite the existence of this publication as something to be proud of. And of those colleagues who planned, edited, and published this jour-

nal, the one who devoted the most effort to these affairs was Ikeda Toshio. "Sir, you loved Taiwan and you researched her customs and recorded her folk practices. ... The history of Taiwan will give you an evaluation with great care and respect. Rest very peacefully, Mr. Ikeda Toshio."[11]

Wang Shilang 王詩琅, who interacted with Ikeda Toshio only after the war, made the following historical assessment of Ikeda Toshio and *Minzoku Taiwan*:

> In Taiwan, the emergence of ethnology as an academic discipline occurred only recently. Or more simply stated, ethnology was one of those things established only at the end of the colonial period. Furthermore, when one is considering that history, *Minzoku Taiwan* should be cited first as making the greatest contribution. As for *Minzoku Taiwan* the journal, ... the person actually responsible for that publication was the late Ikeda Toshio. ... In those times he dared to brave the danger of "opposing the trend of the times," as well as the military's displeasure, to carry through the unprecedented act of openly managing this kind of journal. For those acts, we have great respect for Ikeda. Fortunately, his efforts were not in vain; this journal has become a classic. All who research Taiwan must now cite it as a reference. For this alone, the deceased can certainly be very proud. From the perspective of Taiwan ethnology, this is a milestone worthy of commemoration.[12]

These commemorative articles written by intellectuals who were at the center of *Minzoku Taiwan* established the foundation for the postwar evaluation of *Minzoku Taiwan*. Beginning in the 1990s, the judgments of the postwar generation of scholars with no personal relationship to the journal also appear to adhere completely to the perspectives of those affiliated with the journal.[13] Thus, it's no surprise that Kawamura Minato's new view of *Minzoku Taiwan* appeared quite "strange"; it also engendered serious debate.[14]

This opposition between the view of Kawamura, on the one hand, and those of Kokubu Naoichi and Ikeda Toshio on the other can be interpreted in several ways. Of the two sides, one acts as researcher, while the other has now become the object of research. From the perspective of an unadorned empiricism, the self-descriptions of those being researched (i.e., Kokubu Naoichi and Ikeda Toshio) have considerable persuasive power. Furthermore, if one recognizes the near unanimous postwar Taiwanese affirmation of *Minzoku Taiwan* (including the views of those who participated in the activities of *Minzoku Taiwan* during the war as well as the postwar assessments of a younger generation of scholars), then the perspective of Kokubu Naoichi and Ikeda Toshio could not possibly be false. However, why is it that Kawamura Minato has adopted such a different point of view? Might Kawamura Minato have engaged in a mis-reading of the journal and the historical context in which it was published?

WARTIME CONSCIENCE OR
SUPPORTERS OF WAR?

Minzoku Taiwan was a monthly magazine whose front cover made a clear reference to the journal's goal of "researching and introducing folklore and customs." It first appeared in July 1941, and despite the scarcity of materials during the war, the journal continued to be published until January 1945, printing forty-three issues all together. (Recently the reprint edition of the journal included the February 1945 issue, which had been readied for publication but not ultimately released; it would have been the 44th issue.[15]) The central figures affiliated with the journal were Kanaseki Takeo, a professor of anatomy in the Medical School at Taihoku Imperial University 台北帝國大學醫學部 (also known as Taipei Imperial University), and Ikeda Toshio, from the Taiwan government-general's Information Office. Those who wrote for the journal included scholars teaching at Taihoku Imperial University, such as political scientist Nakamura Akira and sociologist Okada Yuzuru; members of the Japanese cultural circle in Taiwan, such as woodblock printer Tateishi Tetsuomi 立石鐵臣 and photographer Mishima Itaru 三島格; and several Taiwanese intellectuals.

Prior to the establishment of the journal, Okada Yuzuru, Sudō Toshiichi 須藤利一, and Kanaseki Takeo (all professors at Taihoku Imperial University), along with Chen Shaoxin 陳紹馨 (a Taiwanese research assistant in the Office of Folklore and Anthropology at Taihoku Imperial University), Huang Deshi (a literary critic and Taiwanese graduate from Taihoku Imperial University), and Manzōji Ryu 萬照寺龍, drafted and released to the public a signed statement of collective intent. The most important part of that public statement is included below:

> The imperial subjectification (*kōminka* 皇民化) of the islanders (*hontōjin* 本島人) must be actively promoted. We must note that when compared with an earlier situation where there were no policies and no results, the recent forceful promotion [of *kōminka*] is cause for special excitement. One should welcome the rapid destruction of crude customs and corrupt practices of the islanders and be thankful for the grace of modern culture that the islanders will now receive. However, at the same time, old customs devoid of any harm will not escape the fate of being sacrificed and destroyed. Though not perhaps the victim of an active man-made policy, they cannot possibly avoid the fate of being naturally destroyed in the distant months and years to come.
>
> However, civilized citizens who possess the ability to document and study [such customs] have the duty to record and investigate all phenomena. Not only is it the duty of our nation's citizens to document and research the mean customs as mean customs and the corrupt practices as corrupt practices. Since our citizens will expand the nation's power toward the south—no matter whether it's toward south

China or toward the South Pacific—the most necessary group and the one with the greatest opportunity for promotion is none other than the Chinese race [*Shina minzoku* 支那民族]. In order to comprehend them, it is essential that we first understand the islanders of Taiwan. Furthermore, our nation's absolute superiority over any other country comes from the fact that it possesses this convenience.[16]

From this statement of intent, as printed in the inaugural issue of the journal, one can ascertain that when *Minzoku Taiwan* was first published, colleagues affiliated with the journal perceived an impending crisis with regard to the destruction about to be wrought upon Taiwanese folklore and old customs, and for that reason they hoped to investigate and document it. In the discussions recorded in the December 1943 issue of *Minzoku Taiwan* (i.e., the article specifically cited by Kawamura Minato: "The network surrounding Yanagita Kunio: The construction of the Greater East Asian ethnology and the mission of *Minzoku Taiwan*"), Kanaseki Takeo provided examples to explain the immediate importance of investigating the old customs of Taiwan:

> As for the problem of ancestor worship, originally only a plaque used for sacrifice was placed on the altar in the main hall, but now the plaque has been placed to the side, and in the exact center of the altar are placed the Shinto paper offerings from the Grand Shrine of Ise 伊勢神宮. Consequently, the former ancestor worship will gradually be diluted and forgotten. Therefore, if we don't undertake this kind of investigation right now, in no time at all there will be no traces of the practice. With the continual and rapid imperial subjectification of the island, one might say that the investigation of Taiwan folklore is a very pressing matter.[17]

This sense of crisis regarding the imminent destruction of Taiwanese folk customs was caused by the imperial subjectification movement (*kōminka undō* 皇民化運動) being promoted by the government-general of Taiwan. The imperial subjectification movement was an aggressive assimilation movement forcefully promoted during the years in which Kobayashi Seizō 小林躋造 served as governor-general (from September 1936 to November 1940). In particular, after the outbreak of the Marco Polo Bridge Incident on July 7, 1937, as the situation between China and Japan became increasingly confrontational, the Taiwan government-general initiated a movement for the "general spiritual mobilization of the nation's citizens" similar to that being promoted in Japan proper. In addition, because the Taiwanese were still considered to be of the same race as that of Japan's opponent, the Chinese, the government actively carried out a vigorous mobilization of the Taiwanese to wipe away the Chinese cultural and lifestyle tendencies of the Taiwanese and to encourage or force them to learn Japanese culture and practice a Japanese lifestyle. In Ikeda Toshio's memoirs, he gives this description of the period:

The colonial government was working hard to destroy (or to cause the Taiwanese to forget) everything that might have aided the development of a Taiwanese ethnic identity [such as] the nostalgic emotions of popular religion, the activities associated with the festival year, as well as life course rituals such as cappings, weddings, and funerals. Amaterasu 天照 was substituted for Matsu 媽祖; Taiwanese clothing was exchanged for Japanese dress; the flat beds [peculiar to Taiwanese housing] were given over to *tatami* 畳; those surnamed Chen 陳 or Huang 黄 changed their names to Satō 佐藤 or Kobayashi 小林, along with given names such as Tarō 太郎 or Hanako 花子—Japanese-style names. Forcefully carrying out this kind of formalistic imperial subjectification, in the midst of B-24 and B-25 air raids, was none other than forcing "instant" imperial subjectification.[18]

Facing such a situation, Kanaseki Takeo and key members of the *Minzoku Taiwan* circle felt a sense of crisis and collective mission: they ought to document Taiwanese folklore before it disappeared. In the transcript of another roundtable discussion that was printed in the September 1944 issue of the journal, Kanaseki Takeo remarked:

> These are some data that will disappear forever if not recorded now. In particular, at a time like the present during what is called the success of *kōminka*, in a period when this kind of [assimilation] is continually brought to fruition, one becomes very concerned. Being a scholar who documents it for posterity is a [special] type of responsibility for the residents of Taiwan [to accept]. This is hard to comprehend for those who normally don't rely on data for their academic research. "Data" refers to what I just mentioned. Now for some of it we can know its historical significance, while for other data, its importance is not yet clear. And if we don't yet understand [its meaning], then in the future perhaps it will become apparent. Furthermore, if we don't keep [a record] of it, it may disappear. That is what data is.[19]

From the statements of contemporaries cited above (whether postwar recollections or wartime opinions printed in the journal), one should be able to confirm that one of the factors that explains the publication of *Minzoku Taiwan* was the hope of documenting Taiwanese folklore that was about to disappear as a consequence of the *kōminka* policy. It was this kind of thinking that brought on the criticism of Yang Yunping, the Taiwanese critic. Yang Yunping specifically emphasized his belief that with regard to Taiwanese folklore, one could not be content with mere objective and scientific documentation; one had to love the material. This kind of criticism must have come from Yang's being uncertain whether Kanaseki Takeo and his colleagues at *Minzoku Taiwan* were merely interested in strange customs, or whether they possessed a sincere respect for Taiwanese folklore. However, once we recognize that Yang Yunping not only wrote for *Minzoku Taiwan* but also later admitted the rashness of his earlier criticism, we realize that *Minzoku Taiwan*, as well as Kanaseki Takeo and his colleagues, did receive the strongest affirmation from this Taiwanese critic famous for his harshness.

Nevertheless, in the statement of intent published in *Minzoku Taiwan*, and cited above, as well as in some of the published articles, it's not difficult to detect traces of an imperialist policy within the journal or at least a move toward following some wartime trends. In his posthumous article, Ikeda Toshio said that these words and opinions, whose tone was similar to imperialist policies, had been employed only to protect the journal.

> It was simply that because *Minzoku Taiwan* was not in harmony with the drift of the authorities, it could not have avoided being shut down if it did not occasionally chant this type of incantation.
>
> Today I still recall that to defend *Minzoku Taiwan* we would occasionally quote in the editor's comments at the end of an issue the instructions of the governor-general or the head of the Civil Administration, or perhaps quote from their prefaces to published monographs and the like. Or we would collect together some appropriate old customs and show that people from an earlier era did indeed say that these practices were of an elevated style.[20]

It's not difficult to imagine that during the war, editors and writers for the journal had to write texts appropriate to the current situation, in a manner in which their hearts and mouths revealed a substantial degree of inconsistency. Ikeda Toshio used a considerable amount of space in his postwar memoirs to explain the censorship that *Minzoku Taiwan* experienced. The pressure coming from unbending promoters of *kōminka* that was experienced by *Minzoku Taiwan* during the time it remained in existence was evidently quite heavy. One can get a general picture from the transcript of a discussion of "public sacrifice and the study of Taiwanese folklore" that was written up in the September 1944 issue. In this discussion, Kanaseki Takeo pointed out that some circles had expressed a lack of confidence in *Minzoku Taiwan*.

> Particularly in Taiwan, this kind of research has been considered to manifest some sort of "nationalistic political odor," or at least the danger of this kind of result. It seems as though there really are those good-for-nothings who for some strange reason want to prevent us [from doing our work]. As for the inane misunderstanding of these people and their uninteresting motives, we hope to express a bit more clearly our real support of the current situation.[21]

Without doubt, the goal of that September 1944 discussion was to respond to the doubts coming from the hard-liners and to be quite frank about the matter by clearly showing that *Minzoku Taiwan*'s activities were not in violation of any *kōminka* policies—on the contrary, this work embodied the meaning of public service. Furthermore, at this roundtable the participants discussed how popular folklore investigations could make an even greater concrete contribution to the national policy of *kōminka*. Granted, the very nature of this type of discussion allows for the possibility of a number of different (or even directly opposing) interpretations. However, if one carefully digests the statements made during the roundtable discussion, it's not difficult to see just how strong the pressure placed on *Minzoku Taiwan* really was. During that session, Kanaseki Takeo reviewed the objectives and achievements of the journal and pointed out that given the present situation and the difficult conditions associated with it, if *Minzoku Taiwan* had to be discontinued, then they would just have to accept that decision. However, if the journal could remain in circulation, then they would do their best to complete their original mission and respond as much as they could to the demands of the current situation and contribute to national policy. Kanaseki Takeo's statement reveals that he and his colleagues from *Minzoku Taiwan* were already mentally prepared for the journal to be discontinued at any moment, even though they still hoped to stubbornly continue their work if at all possible. The opinions of Nakai Tadashi 中井淳, professor at Taihoku Imperial University, as given in this roundtable discussion, permit one to see even more clearly how *Minzoku Taiwan* struggled to survive despite being accused of being "incompatible with the times":

> Although I'm not very clear on this matter, I certainly have heard rumors to the effect that the work of *Minzoku Taiwan* needs to be altered. But I have also heard Tateishi and Ikeda say that what the authorities actually notice is not the fundamentals or the basics, but the superficial or the trivial; besides this, there's not really anything [to be worried about]. For someone like myself (who knows little about the field), I don't believe there's anything that needs to be changed. If there is, then it's only that [authors] haven't clearly stated whether some phrase is still being used [in daily speech]. Besides that, when [authors] have mentioned traditional practices, perhaps they haven't explained how such practices would be changed, what their present situation was, or how they ought to be changed. As for suggestions for revising the content of the journal, I suppose that a bit more concrete evidence of the public service movement might be good. However, I remind you that an ethnologist is surely not a politician. Those who are involved in the promotion of the imperial subjectification and public sacrifice movements should make better use of the journal. If this can be done, then that's probably enough.[22]

These statements made by Nakai indicate that Kanaseki Takeo had arranged for him, situated as he was in a position on the outside, to provide camouflage against surprise attacks on *Minzoku Taiwan*. From Nakai's discussion, one can see just what doubts were being expressed concerning *Minzoku Taiwan*: This kind of journal, whose stated purpose was the investigation and documentation of Taiwanese folklore, not only made no contribution to the *kōminka* national policy being demanded by the current situation, but was actually harmful to the *kōminka* movement. This type of doubt and accusation had certainly always come from the outside, especially from the hard-liners in the colonial bureaucracy.

These various sources—Kanaseki Takeo's remarks at a roundtable discussion while *Minzoku Taiwan* was still being published, or Ikeda Toshio's postwar memoirs, or the like—help us apprehend that the central figures affiliated with *Minzoku Taiwan*, such as Kanaseki Takeo, Ikeda Toshio, and Kokubu Naoichi, without a doubt constantly felt a sense of imminent crisis regarding the likelihood that traditional Taiwanese customs and folklore would disappear as a result of the *kōminka* policies. Furthermore, each of them possessed a sense of mission concerning the need to generate documentation of this Taiwanese folklore before it disappeared. Second, during the period in which *Minzoku Taiwan* remained in circulation, it continued to be the target of accusations that it not only provided little support for official *kōminka* policies but actually ran in opposition to those policies. One could say this, then, of the central members of the *Minzoku Taiwan* group: During that period when they experienced formidable pressures from enemies on all sides, they still maintained the existence of the journal despite untold hardships. Consequently, it is not surprising that even though these events happened fifty years ago, as soon as Kawamura Minato's criticism was published, the ninety-year-old Kokubu Naoichi had to step up and defend himself or, better yet, defend Kanaseki Takeo.

THE PERIOD IN WHICH *MINZOKU TAIWAN* WAS DISCONTINUED

During the war, Kanaseki Takeo and Ikeda Toshio faced pressure from the colonial state's radical *kōminka* policies. Fifty years later, however, the accusations and questioning that they face comes from the opposite direction: the anticolonialism camp. How do we ultimately interpret the *Minzoku Taiwan* movement of Kanaseki Takeo and his colleagues? I believe that we must return to the historical context to answer this question.

Most scholars believe that the active promotion of the *kōminka* movement by the colonial government in Taiwan began in 1936 when Kobayashi Seizo was governor-general. The *kōminka* movement that Governor-General Kobayashi promoted was a program of social mobilization under the general name of the "movement for national spiritual mobilization." The specific content of this movement included banning Chinese-language newspaper columns, promoting the daily use of the "national language" (i.e., Japanese), enforcing worship at

Shinto shrines, "rearranging" local monasteries and temples, promoting the re-designing of central rooms in residential homes, banning Chinese-style customs and practices, enacting Japanese-style living, and changing personal and family names into accepted Japanese formats.[23] However, similar to the "national spiritual mobilization (國民精神總動員)" in Japan proper, this social mobilization movement had few concrete results, and the reactions of citizens in the colony was not as expected. In Taiwan in particular, where the authorities demanded that Taiwanese give up or at least alter their traditional beliefs, customs, lifestyle, and culture, it was highly unlikely that the movement would be accepted by the islanders. Although Taiwanese may have responded superficially when pressured by the police or local officials, such responses are not to be confused with any real or effective results of the campaigns.[24]

In 1941 the radical *kōminka* policies of Governor-General Kobayashi's administration were altered. Konoe Fumimaro 近衛文麿 organized his second cabinet in July 1940, and under the name "New structure" (*shin taisei* 新體制), his government promoted the slogan "national unity" (*kyokoku-itchi* 舉國一致) and implemented the adjustment of all types of government policies. In particular, with the formation of the "Association for the Support of Imperial Rule" (*Taisei yoku-sankai* 大政翼贊會) in October of that year, the Konoe administration possessed a nationwide mobilization system alongside the extant national-provincial government. Complementing this personnel reorganization and policy adjustment at the central government level in Tokyo, Hasegawa Kiyoshi 長谷川清 took over as governor-general of Taiwan in November 1940.

Those in control of policy in Konoe Fumimaro's "New structure" in 1940 came primarily from Konoe's private national policy think tank, the *Shōwa Kenkyūkai* 昭和研究會, or from the national mobilization organization "Association for the Support of Imperial Rule." The cultural policy designed by the *Shōwa Kenkyūkai* during this period was articulated in the "Outline of cultural policy" that was drafted by the Cultural Research Association lead by Miki Kiyoshi 三木清, the famous literary figure. This policy outline revealed the liberal tendencies of those intellectuals affiliated with the *Shōwa Kenkyūkai*:

> Although previously the emphasis has been placed solely on prohibitionary policies, in the future it won't be limited to this. Instead we intend to put more effort into active guidance. We will try hard to encourage the creative energies of the citizenry toward the direction of cultural creativity. Even though the concept of *kokutai* 國體 has been strengthened, it should not just be conceptual in nature; rather, it is necessary to thoroughly implement this concept via the popular experience of cooperative living. As for ideological issues, we will not dwell on them as abstract ideological problems but rather relate them to the new organization of the citizenry and solve them in that manner.[25]

More directly relevant to the topic at hand, though, are the suggestions detailed in the policy outline for enriching local culture, highlighting nonurban areas, and revising the mode of propagation. Let me cite a few relevant quotes.

> Reform the undesirable flaws of the urban-centeredness of culture, and put all efforts into achieving the balanced development of local culture in each region. For example, change the current situation whereby higher educational institutions are concentrated in large cities. In order to strengthen and uplift local culture, we should make a careful study of ways to ensure the dispersed development of schools, libraries, art museums, research institutes, meeting centers, and entertainment facilities. In addition, we need to make a careful study of the means for encouraging talented specialists and leaders of all kinds to remain in local areas. ... In order to cultivate clear and bright popular lives and healthy spirits, we should strengthen healthy and bright entertainment facilities, in addition to prohibiting low-class or mean forms of entertainment. Improve the content of radio, motion picture, and drama programs. In particular, we need to increase and improve the entertainment facilities in farming and fishing villages. This will result in the spread of superior cultural resources to localities, as well as the revival of traditional festivals that manifest local flavor.
>
> An extremely important foundation of the new governmental structure consists of stimulating the citizenry and propagandizing in their midst. Aware that all previous official or official-civilian collaborative publications have been dull and boring, we should employ those in cultural circles who are especially able to carry out this propaganda and stimulation work. Furthermore, we need to integrate and reorganize all propaganda institutions, strengthen and enrich the mid-level institutions, while inducing nongovernmental cultural organizations to support official propaganda efforts from a perspective derived from their own special characteristics. We oppose propaganda that seeks culture only for the purposes of propaganda. Instead we should make a careful study of appropriate ways to ensure that propaganda is at the same time a means of enhancing the culture of the citizenry.[26]

These views of the *Shōwa Kenkyūkai* were generally accepted and continued by the "Association for the Support of Imperial Rule" (*Taisei yokusankai*). For example, in order to generate enthusiasm for local cultural activities, Sakai Saburo 酒井三郎, the central member of both the *Shōwa Kenkyūkai* and the *Taisei yokusankai*, along with his colleagues in the *Taisei yokusankai*, made a tour of numerous localities throughout the nation, inciting much enthusiasm. In a small booklet that Sakai distributed throughout Japan, *The strategies for and significance of reviving local culture*, he had this to say:

> Central culture has consuming and entertainment tendencies, and is increasingly distant from our individual lives. Local culture is healthy, and it possesses

qualities of being directly related to our lives as well as connected to production. The traditions of Japanese culture are rooted in everyday lives in this way; they thrive amidst healthy local culture. We must trace out these traditions to use them as a fertilizer for the cultural resources of the front lines at the center. Mutually interacting with each other is the only way that we can construct a new culture.[27]

During this period, the director of the cultural department of the "Association for the Support of Imperial Rule" was the famous playwright and specialist of French literature, Kishida Kunio 岸田國士, and the assistant director was Kamii-zumi Hidenobu 上泉秀信, a writer of peasant literature. In January 1941 the cultural department released its first policy statement, "Ideals and current directions for the new construction of local culture." In that document, the cultural department emphasized the notion that the cultural construction of the "New structure" meant the creation of new culture that would stand firmly upon the foundation of the entire nation and be integrated with production needs. For this reason, its key goal was the revitalization of local culture in order to produce national culture anew. The department's immediate tasks included the following:

1) Respect native traditions as well as the particular characteristics of local areas, in order that local culture can manifest its unique essence to the greatest possible extent. At all times take the new creative development of the entire nation as our goal in order to avoid repeating the former situation of being satisfied with the expansion of metropolitan culture into peripheral areas.
2) Reform the old culture of individualism. Continue to maintain and increase the intensity of the interrelationships among social groups, which is the unique trademark of agricultural villages. Promote love for the homeland and increase the sense of public spirit; affirm the living cooperative community in local areas, which is [the source of] the basic unity of our national family.
3) Correct regional imbalances in culture, production, politics, and administration. Promote the healthy development of central culture as well as the enrichment of local culture, and attain a balanced cultural development from the close interaction of the two.[28]

Kishida Kunio emphasized the "cultural nature of politics"; he argued, in other words, that politics should promote a society that reflected the actual nature of culture. Therefore, he criticized the earlier "movement for the total mobilization of the national spirit" for lacking any cultural content:

As is the case with the language of all propaganda, it is unrealistic to expect that the revitalization of morality can actually adjust and improve the daily lives of the populace. ... Customs themselves are the root of morality. To use the force of morality to improve customs is to mistake the root for the branch.

Kishida felt that the original character of culture was expressed in the daily lives of the nation's citizens and that therefore the culture of daily life had to be emphasized. However, Kishida did not reaffirm all extant popular culture across the board. He argued that there were three standards for assessing the value of culture: a) its scientific nature (or efficiency); b) its moral quality (or being healthy); and c) its artistic value. These three had to be harmonized. Likewise, a commodity's cultural value depended upon its reasonableness (scientific nature) or utilitarian value, its unadorned nature (moral quality), and the beauty of its form (or artistic value). Kishida's views are similar in some respects to the critical assessment of industrial crafts found in the folk art movement of Yanagi Muneyoshi 柳宗悦.[29]

While the "Association for the Support of Imperial Rule" trumpeted this promotion of culture, cultural activists from all areas of the nation were organizing their own cultural organizations. In November 1941 there were 120 cultural organizations nationwide; by June of 1943 they numbered 250; and in January 1944 the total had reached 407. Although these local cultural associations were established in response to a campaign organized by the cultural department of the association, and although each such organization had had to obtain official permission to establish itself, these entities did not resemble other national movement organizations with an identical and unified organization all across the nation. Consequently, in this instance, the force of a strong system emerging from within government was comparatively less; there was also no financial support from the state for these local organizations. Local leaders had to establish the organization themselves, which meant gaining support from interested persons from their native areas.

Although the activities of the movements organized by these local cultural associations were therefore quite different from each other, in terms of the overall structure, the revival of traditional culture was their most salient characteristic. This work included the observation of local festivals; the collection and documentation of local legends, dialects, and popular songs; the study of folk and local art, historical markers, and famous sights; the exhibition of folk art and native materials; the organization of local folk dances, folk song fests, and native drama presentations; the compilation of local histories; and the formal recognition of local heroes. Because of these cultural activities, local nativism reached a high level for a brief period.[30]

Once we become aware of the nationwide situation in Japan proper, we can have a better understanding of the moment when *Minzoku Taiwan* came into being. Although there were no immediate changes of personnel in the Taiwan government-general's office when the Konoe government was established, after the "Association for the Support of Imperial Government" was created in Japan proper, authorities in Taiwan did prepare to establish a local equivalent of that association.[31] Then, in November 1940, Hasegawa Kiyoshi took over the position of governor-general of Taiwan, replacing Kobayashi Seizo. After Governor-General

Hasegawa took office, he signaled a clear intent to adjust the radical *kōminka* policies of Governor-General Kobayashi Seizo's era. This can be seen through an examination of the contents of a special issue of the government-general's official publication, *Taiwan jihō* 台灣時報, published in January 1941: "Special issue on the guiding principles of *kōminka*."[32] This issue began with the "New Year's greetings" of the governor-general and the director of the civil administration and was followed by an introductory article by Nakamura Akira entitled *"Kōminka* issues as cultural policies." There were articles by others discussing several *kōminka* programs: name-changing, economical lifestyles, language, family residences, monasteries and temples, agricultural villages and peasants' problems. The majority of the contributors to the special issue were professors at Taihoku Imperial University; all were considered experts in their own fields.

Nakamura Akira's introductory article, *"Kōminka* issues as cultural policies," especially caught the attention of readers. If one carefully examines the content of this article, he can see not only that Nakamura criticized the previous radical *kōminka* policies for not taking into consideration the special conditions of Taiwan—his article was, in essence, a promotion piece for the Taiwan equivalent of the local cultural movement of the "Cultural Department of the Association for the Support of Imperial Government" in Japan proper. Let me give some sample quotes from Nakamura's article:

> There is a natural connection between politics and culture. ... There is a natural connection between politics and the cultural world of the daily realm of activities. ... Cultural policies do not infer that politics guide culture, but rather that a culture will guide other cultures in moving toward a political direction. ... That element of politics that guides culture is not politics per se, but rather it should be a politics that possesses a cultural nature and a politics that manifests cultural content. ... The problem of *kōminka* in Taiwan is a problem of cultural policies; it's a question of how the culture of one country can guide a different culture via politics. ... Amidst the new politics of the "New structure," there is an opportunity to reconsider the cultural policies of our country, and of course, we must reassess the problems of *kōminka*. ... Broadly speaking, for a policy to manifest the significance of a policy, it must be able to get results. Therefore, an ineffective policy is necessarily meaningless. ... In order for the *kōminka* problem as a cultural policy to be effective, officials must pay particular attention to responses toward *kōminka* policies at all times, and use this knowledge to consider methods for the next stage of *kōminka* policy-making. ... The key issue for *kōminka* in Taiwan is changing Han Chinese culture into Japanese-style [culture], so that the islanders are incorporated into the Japanese national community. ... The *kōminka* problem entails acknowledging that in actuality Han Chinese culture exists in a part of Japanese national territory, as well as determining how to incorporate it. ... The nature of an *ethnos* is determined by its history. Thus, the assimilation of an *ethnos* is a long-

term historical process; there is no alternative. The essence of an *ethnos* will be found in its personality and its ambition, as well as in the style of its actions, ideology, and feelings. Consequently, it is very difficult to alter an *ethnos* overnight. ... Even if an ethnic cultural assimilation policy were capable of changing the cultural content of an *ethnos*, it would still be difficult to change the mode of thinking and feeling of the culture of that *ethnos*. ... If one wishes to get rid of shrines and temples, then you must first determine which previous religio-psychological needs of the islanders were met by shrines and temples, and then provide a substitute that can compensate for these psychological needs. ... If one does not provide a substitute to compensate but merely bans extant religious rituals, he will not be able to satisfy the psychological needs of the islanders, and that can only result in empty policies. ... If you are determined to destroy even that type of dispersed local deities, then the policy has become too extreme. To preserve in an appropriate fashion the unique songs, dances, and music of the islanders is a necessary step in relieving and calming the daily lives of the islanders. Otherwise, if politics interferes to such a degree, then all tendencies toward intimacy will be lost from politics. ...

An *ethnos* is a religious and linguistic collectivity, and therefore the next problem after the religious problem is a linguistic one. ... One must first implement compulsory education for the islanders before he can realize the expansion of the national language in Taiwan. ... The implementation of compulsory education is one point that must be given even more attention. ... If there is a need to employ the national language in one's daily life, then the frequent use of the national language will be attained in a natural fashion. On the contrary, if it is not necessary to use the national language in one's daily life, it will not be easy to implement the policy promoting the frequent use of the national language. Therefore, the first step toward solving this problem is to cause them to feel the need of the national language. If this language is necessary, as well as convenient, then naturally they will be inclined toward that direction. If it is inconvenient, then even if you enforce a national language policy, in the end there naturally will be no concrete results. ... The matter of clothing is the same. Even if you reward the wearing of the kimono, it will not be easy to induce people to give up clothing worn by the islanders that is convenient for wearing during daily activities. ... Convenient things are naturally used. Even if you force them under the name of the *kōminka* policy to use inconvenient things from ancient Japan, these policies will have no results. Therefore, *kōminka* as a cultural policy requires the popularization of a Japanese lifestyle, and this lifestyle must at least be more convenient and reasonable than the islanders' own counterpart.[33]

Although the above quote is quite long, this material is too important to be omitted here. Nakamura's article not only criticized previous *kōminka* policy, it also expressed the notion that in the future the principle for implementing *kō-*

minka policies was the necessity of paying careful attention to Taiwanese responses and to policy results in order to provide convenient and reasonable policy content to induce the Taiwanese to change, while avoiding the one-sided tactic of forcing Taiwanese to practice Japanese lifestyle and culture. When he wrote this article, Nakamura Akira was an assistant professor at Taihoku Imperial University, and he was responsible for the lectureship in constitutional law at that institution. Even more critical to our story is the fact that he was the student of Tokyo Imperial University professor Yabe Teiji 矢部貞治, who was an important member of the Shōwa Research Association, the think tank for Prime Minister Konoe Fumimaro.[34] We are reminded again that Nakamura Akira had personal connections to central government figures in Japan while holding a lectureship in the colony. This article of his was positioned as the centerpiece for the "Special issue to reconsider *kōminka* policies" of the government-general's official journal. And the new governor-general of Taiwan wrote a preface for that issue not long after taking his new position. Given all of this, we have reason to believe that Nakamura's article was the announcement of the new governor-general's change in the *kōminka* policies applicable to Taiwan. Furthermore, this adjustment was a response to the cultural policies of the central government in Japan proper.

THE LOCAL CULTURE MOVEMENT IN COLONIAL TAIWAN

Another article appearing in this special issue of *Taiwan Jihō*, one written by Kanaseki Takeo, on the other hand, did not stray far from his academic specialty—he was a professor of anatomy in the School of Medicine at Taihoku Imperial University. Kanaseki's article was entitled "*Kōminka* and racial questions."[35] Though Kanaseki discussed the topics of eugenics and the offspring of interracial marriages from the perspective of his own field of study, he was very careful to express the opinion that these issues of research would require much time to fully apprehend. As for the other articles in the special issue, with the exception of Nakamura Akira's piece that clearly expressed his critical views toward previous radical *kōminka* policies, none of the other writers expressed particularly clear opinions. Perhaps this is explained by the fact that of the contributors to the special issue, Nakamura was the most knowledgeable concerning changes in colonial government policy; perhaps he was the very person in charge of making this change!

However, because of the government-general's policy adjustments, in May 1941, Kanaseki Takeo and his colleagues released their signed statement of intent to publish *Minzoku Taiwan*. In comparison with the colonial government's new policies, their statement of intent appeared rather conservative, as it only emphasized the point that Taiwanese traditional customs and practices were about to be destroyed, and that before they were destroyed it was necessary to quickly document them. It seems quite natural that such an ambition concerned only with "documenting" Taiwanese customs about to be destroyed would stimulate the dissatisfaction of a critically-minded and self-aware Taiwanese intellectual like Yang Yunping. In particular, although the published statement of intent did contain language that called for the documentation of Taiwanese customs, the authors of the text were careful to include remarks that appeared not to oppose the destruction of Taiwanese practices, such as this sentence: "We are not anxious about the destruction of Taiwanese traditional customs, but documenting and researching these customs is our duty." Consequently, Yang Yunping published his critical response, "Research and love," in *Taiwan nichinichi shinpō* 台灣日日新報, from which I quote:

> "Taiwan studies," until now generally shunned or treated with a cold shoulder, has quite recently experienced a new bit of luck—take for example [the new interest in] "literature" and "folklore." That's not to say I don't feel secretly pleased by this. However, it's hard to avoid feeling a little uneasy, for while they are getting their hands dirty in this new research, they still maintain that cold and high-level, even mechanical, attitude and method. Though they don't even understand "vernacular texts" or the "Taiwanese language," they still [have the audacity to] claim that "vernacular" works are "mostly imitations"! Or when they say they plan to study "Taiwanese traditional practices" in the future yet already note they are "not worried if they get destroyed." ... I hope that in the years to come these "scholars" and "researchers" will have just a little more warm understanding and love [for their subject], as well as a bit more modesty.[36]

In this critical piece, Yang Yunping expressed confidence in his own learning and his dissatisfaction with those who took the position of "documenting" Taiwanese customs and folklore. And it seems that he was also expressing his resistance toward any radical *kōminka* policy that seldom undertook any actual investigation of Taiwanese folklore[37] while contributing to its destruction. Although Kanaseki Takeo did publish a response to Yang Yunping's criticism, creating a very small debate between them, this battle gradually became but a debate over words. However, not long after *Minzoku Taiwan* appeared in print, Yang Yunping also became a contributor to that journal, despite originally having expressed some doubt about its mission.

In July 1941 *Minzoku Taiwan* officially came out in print. The preface to the inaugural issue, which was written by Kanaseki Takeo, was a short piece but pitched at a high level. In content, it still emphasized documenting ethnic memorabilia that would soon be destroyed, but in the column on miscellaneous topics, "Noisy notes," two of the journal's most important members chastised the radical *kōminka* movement with a clear and shrill voice:

"Imperial subjectification," "imperial subjectification," but without love can you really transform others? From ancient times till the present, I'm afraid there's not an example of such a thing. The success of love is probably the most common whether in ancient times or the present, and it will forever be a central issue in life and in literature. If artists and writers in Taiwan who have a self awareness of the duty of their profession chant [the need for] "Imperial subjectification!" shouldn't they need to call up their feelings for the islanders? A strategy that is satisfied with merely shouting out slogans and considering one's work finished is useless. (Kanaseki Takeo)[38]

Whether considering *kōminka* programs such as the frequent usage of the national language or the redesigning of central dining rooms in private residences, relying only on statistical figures to judge a program's success or failure is especially dangerous. It's terribly disappointing to see those who don't know where they should worship stuff the paper offerings from the sacred shrine into a flower vase that's full of ashes, or even those who keep the paper offerings in a desk drawer. [Or those who] in the evening place the Shinto god shelf inside a filthy bird cage, or the [unbelievable case] of a bare-footed man using a carrying pole to carry them around for others to see, shouting all the way. Who is responsible for these mistakes? ... Those people who stand in the front lines of the *kōminka* movement should deeply reflect on this kind of phenomenon. (Ikeda Toshio)[39]

There was hardly any issue after the first that did not carry this kind of spicy-hot criticism of the implementation of *kōminka*. Thus we can confirm that despite the fact that the initial issue of *Minzoku Taiwan* took a rather careful stance — calling only for documenting Taiwanese customs that were soon to disappear — those involved with the journal were in fact quite dissatisfied with the policies of the aggressive *kōminka* movement. The public expression of this dissatisfaction apparently had to wait until the colonial government had clearly expressed the readjustment of its policies before it could emerge from hiding and come out into the open.

If one can argue that *Minzoku Taiwan* was itself a type of local cultural movement in Taiwan, then exactly what kind of movement (in terms of content) did it implement there? First, with the publication of the inaugural issue, *Minzoku Taiwan* declared that it was not the kind of research journal common in the academic world, but that it rather hoped to be an ethnology journal that incorporated reports and records of interviews carried out in all areas. For example, in the first issue, under the "editors' afterthoughts" column, they had this to say:

As for research magazines, or in other words academic folklore journals, the island already has *Nampō minzoku* 南方民俗. Our journal will not attempt to become that kind of magazine. Rather we intend that ours is the product of a different type of mission. And that's the hope that it has emerged from an atmosphere of more easygoing, intimate discussions on the evening porch or verandah, and that these conversations unconsciously increase people's concern for islander folklore. We welcome manuscripts with this kind of easygoing character. Perhaps the kind of articles in the present issue that are the best pieces may not, on the contrary, be able to fully reveal our interests. ... We have special expectations for [the future contributions of] those with ambitions who still are hiding out in local areas; we hope you will stand up and say, "We have this in our area!" and then follow through to submit a manuscript that documents that phenomenon. ... With the journal's unique mission in mind, we certainly do hope to see those from all areas with such ambitions contribute manuscripts to our journal. We hope that there will be people from every part of the island—no matter whether it be agricultural towns or fishing villages—who will present their such reports for publication.[40]

Those affiliated with *Minzoku Taiwan* also held folklore discussions and workshops throughout the island, and in 1942 they organized a series of ten folklore-collection meetings. In general, this type of data-gathering meeting was limited to visits to famous scenic or historical sites in a single area, supplemented by a simple discussion afterward. The process and accomplishments of these collecting meetings were printed up and reported in subsequent issues of the journal. Furthermore, as a result of these local activities, a group of participants with a strong interest in such activities was formed. These individuals, along with local folklore reporters and historians throughout the island, formed a cultural network that included both Japanese and Taiwanese (with the journal serving as the main organ of communication).

At this point, let me cite another example of the cultural development promoted by *Minzoku Taiwan* that was perhaps even more regional in nature. The December 1941 issue (volume 1, issue 6) of *Minzoku Taiwan* was a "Special issue devoted to Shirin." Shirin [Shilin 士林] was a small town on the outskirts of Tai-hoku [Taipei]; in northern Taiwan, people took pride in the strong literary atmosphere associated with Shirin that had existed for a very long time. (It was also the hometown of Yang Yunping.) In August 1941 a group of young people in their twenties in Shirin organized (under the direction of a Christian minister who had studied in Tokyo) a cultural organization called the "Association of like-minded Shirinites 士林協志會." The association came together as a reading and discussion group, inviting famous individuals to attend their meetings and introduce (in workshop fashion) new world trends in literature and philosophy or to spread common knowledge from the fields of medicine and hygiene. They also organized a choir.

For August 23–25, 1941, however, this Shirin Association of Like-minded Shirinites organized a comparatively bigger activity: a "culture exhibition," which included an "exhibition of local materials," a "photography exhibition," a "hygiene

exhibition," and a choral concert. Cao Yonghe 曹永和, who was employed in the
Shirin cooperative, was responsible for the history component of the "exhibition
of local materials," while Pan Naizhen 潘迺禎, a student in the medical school
at Taihoku Imperial University, was in charge of the folklore and traditional customs section of the exhibition.[41] Using this exhibition as a foundation, *Minzoku
Taiwan* editors invited Yang Yunping to design a "special issue on Shirin" as the
December issue of the journal for that year. For this special issue, Yang Yunping,
Cao Yonghe, and Pan Naizhen individually conducted the planning and the collection of materials on Shirin's historical heroes, historical writings, shrines, yearly
festivals, legends, and stela, while Kanaseki Takeo, Tateishi Tetsuomi, Mishima
Itaru, and Matsuyama Kenzō 松山虔三, the Japanese contributors to *Minzoku
Taiwan*, wrote articles that introduced the folk art and interesting phenomena of
the city of Shirin that they were acquainted with. The special issue mobilized the
cultured intellectuals of the locality—Yang Yunping, Cao Yonghe, and Pan Naizhen all came from well-known lineages in the area—and assisted in the compilation and documentation (in a substantive form) of local history and popular customs. In addition, it assisted substantively in establishing a sense of pride in local
culture. To cite but one piece of evidence to support this claim, an important
member of *Minzoku Taiwan*, the woodblock printer Tateishi Tetsuomi, noted in
his article that the editor and designer for this special issue, Yang Yunping, used
the phrase "rivers and mountains extremely beautiful—that is my hometown" to
describe his hometown of Shirin.[42]

Historical market towns like Tainan 台南, Rokukō 鹿港, Manka 艋舺, and
Shirin were naturally important cites for initiating the collection of data on local
popular customs. However, it is important to note here that in the journal *Minzoku Taiwan* there were a lot of reports concerning a place called Hokumon [Bei-
men 北門]. Hokumon was a very poor coastal area on the southwestern part of the
island of Taiwan, a place where the residents farmed, fished, or manufactured salt
to make ends meet. In this area in the mid-1930s, a group of younger-generation
intellectuals, who had received new-style colonial education or who had experienced study abroad in Japan, just happened to join together. In their midst was
a medical doctor who had studied in Japan, Wu Xinrong 吳新榮, who was especially active. Though he was a practicing physician, when studying in Japan he
had had some contact with contemporary trends in literature and the arts, as well
as the new social thought being propagated at the time. In 1932, when he returned
to Taiwan, he set up a clinic in his hometown while also undertaking some creative writing. Not long after establishing his professional office in his hometown,
Wu became one of the new local men with a high social visibility. Surrounding
him were a group of new youth of about the same age, and all of these people
were capable of writing. Thus, in the mid-1930s they joined the Taiwan new literature movement in the form of a local corps of writers, and in Taiwan literary
circles of the time, they were rather special. Not only did they participate in lit-

erary activities, they were also an active force in this local area in the *kōminka* movement instigated by the colonial government in the late 1930s. In fact, some of the individuals in this group stepped up to take on the role of local assembly members.[43] The July and August issues of *Minzoku Taiwan* for the year 1942 were written by some of the members of this group: Wu Xinrong, Wang Bijiao 王碧蕉, Guo Shuitan 郭水潭, and Kokubu Naoichi. The content of the two issues included articles on historical geography, legends, and historical relics. Of these articles, the ethnological investigation of an "ethnic group that worshiped vases," which was written by Kokubu Naoichi and Wu Xinrong, left the most striking impression. After this, both Wu Xinrong and Wu Xiuqi 吳修齊, who was also from Hokumon, continued to write articles on local folklore for *Minzoku Taiwan*.

RETURN TO THE INITIAL QUESTION

At this point in our discussion, let us return to the question with which we began: Can *Minzoku Taiwan* be considered a component of the so-called Greater East Asia ethnology? Although Kawamura Minato picked up the term "Greater East Asian ethnology" from a roundtable discussion that centered around Yanagita Kunio, had he carefully read and analyzed the transcript of that discussion, he still might have seen that the Yanagita Kunio, who proposed a "national ethnology," had a rather hesitant attitude toward comparative ethnology across such an expansive region as "Greater East Asia"; this was a Yanagita Kunio who finally only reluctantly agreed that perhaps scholars could use the medium of a shared Japanese language to accomplish some comparison. In contrast to the reluctant attitude of Yanagita Kunio, however, Kanaseki Takeo appears to have been more enthusiastic.

If *Minzoku Taiwan* did take advantage of the adjustments made to the national policies of the Japanese imperial government in the early 1940s to begin publication, and if it manipulated the loopholes in these policies to criticize national policy, then its fate could certainly be tied to further revisions in policy or changes in wartime conditions. It's impossible for us to completely deny the possibility, as Ikeda Toshio noted after the war, that the rhetoric in the journal that followed closely the demands of the wartime situation served as a defensive shield. For example, with regard to the following quote from *Minzoku Taiwan*, though a completely different interpretation is possible, it may not hurt to interpret this passage as Ikeda Toshio suggested:

> With the outbreak of war with Great Britain and America, the anxious situation on the home front became even more intense. Those of us who edited the journal doubled our efforts with the renewed sense of purpose of sacrificing for the nation. We also believed that this publishing was by no means a leisurely activity. From

the perspective of the raw breadth of the victories obtained by the imperial army—more territories than the eye could see—it was impossible not to imagine that the day was not far off when this new region of greater southeast Asia would be brought under the sphere of Japanese influence. Of course, the social and economic center of this new region was the overseas Chinese born in southern China, and therefore, our interaction and collaboration with the overseas Chinese was already a fate that could not be avoided. In order to make this cooperation smooth and intimate, it was necessary to understand the overseas Chinese. In order to comprehend the overseas Chinese, understanding the islanders in Taiwan was the shortest route. ... Studying and understanding the Taiwanese ethnic group was a very important factor in explaining why Taiwan became the base for southern expansion and development. To not use Taiwan in any attempt to investigate the southern areas would without any doubt be seen as proof that our nation was incapable of expanding southward. With regard to this point, investigating and comprehending the Taiwanese ethnic group was the most immediate work for the moment. We colleagues hoped to grasp the significance of this fact as a means of contributing to the wartime situation.[44]

On the other hand, we can also find opinions that more clearly and concretely emphasized the necessity of an East Asian ethnology. Those were the words of Kanaseki Takeo. In the July 1942 issue of the journal, when reviewing Yanagita Kunio's book, *Notes on Dialects* 方言覺書, Kanaseki made the following remarks:

I have full respect for Yanagita Kunio's position of [implementing] a national ethnology. However, in addition to this, might it be possible to establish the perspective of an East Asian ethnology? In the present wartime situation, I feel even more strongly that it is essential. Even those as simple as myself also believe that the time for this perspective has arrived. Taiwan will surely make its contribution to this East Asian ethnology that is soon to emerge.[45]

In order to complement the establishment of the "Greater East Asia Ministry," the title on the front cover of the October 1942 issue of *Minzoku Taiwan* was changed from "Introducing and investigating customs and practices" to the phrase "Introducing and investigating the customs of the South." An individual with the initials T.K.—surely this was Kanaseki Takeo—left the following quote in the editors' notes at the end of the journal:

Hearing the news of the establishment of the Ministry for Greater East Asia causes one to feel that our faith in the notion that "Greater East Asia is but one body" has already become a stable thing. ... As of today it is no longer necessary to explain the fact that researching the ethnology of Taiwan is definitely not limited to questions specific to Taiwan. Investigating the ethnology of Taiwan has provided us with material with which to contribute to completing a Greater East Asian ethnology. Previously it was not the case that there were none who thought that studying the ethnology of the island conflicted somewhat with the imperial subjectification of the islanders. However, as the leader of the Greater East Asian alliance, we Japanese must elucidate not only Taiwan ethnology. We must—and we have the duty to—elucidate the folklore of China, the South Pacific, India, and Australia, i.e., all the areas within the Co-prosperity Sphere. Taking the research on Taiwan ethnology as one essential aspect of this greater whole, to complete one component of this important duty is the task for us residents of the island of Taiwan.[46]

This kind of rhetoric was not unique to Kanaseki Takeo; Mori Oto 森於菟 (son of the famous modern Japanese author Mori Ōgai 森鷗外 and also professor in the medical school at Taihoku Imperial University), Utsushikawa Nenozo 移川子之藏 (professor of ethnology and anthropology at Taihoku Imperial University), and Nakamura Akira all published articles with a similar tone in the pages of *Minzoku Taiwan*.

The proposal of an "East Asian ethnology" that emerged in closer step with the changing wartime situation was, in fact, manifested in a conceptualization with clearer content and strategy at the roundtable discussion that centered around Yanagita Kunio in October 1943. That proposal consisted of the enumeration of specific items necessary to ethnological investigation, the preparations for separate data collection in areas of East Asia, and then the comparative analysis of these investigation results. And during the meeting, Yanagita Kunio proposed three potential topics for investigation: a) the treatment of different surroundings, b) concepts toward ancestors, and c) marriage ethics. Of course, these three topics proposed by Yanagita Kunio contained aspects that would meet the needs of the wartime situation. In January 1944 at the nation-wide "Festschrift for Mr. Yanagita Kunio," where Kanaseki Takeo was also one of the participants, the "International cooperative research topics proposal" was finally made public, and the specific content of that proposal was but an enumeration of sixteen research items within the scope of the three major topics that Yanagita Kunio had originally proposed in 1943.[47]

Thus we can say that the appearance of *Minzoku Taiwan* was related to the changes in politics, in particular the "local culture movement," that accompanied the establishment of the second Konoe cabinet. For example, the director of the Cultural Department of the Association to Support Imperial Rule, Kishida Kunio, expressed in definite terms the view that the problem of the culture of outlying territories [*gaichi* 外地] was also part of the problem of local culture. Furthermore, he said that with regard to this problem of the culture of outlying territories, Japan proper and the outlying territories would be grasped without any difference whatsoever. "Use this principle: let Taiwan stand in Taiwan's own special character, and let Korea stand in Korea's own special essence." [48] In the colony of Taiwan, it was manifested concretely when Governor-General Hasegawa Kiyoshi made adjustments to the radical *kōminka* policies implemented by Kobayashi Seizo, by "allowing Taiwanese traditional religion, worship, customs, local popular entertainment, and lifestyle to exist as long as they do not conflict with the goals of colonial rule." [49]

Minzoku Taiwan did, in fact, appear at just that opportune moment when the extreme *kōminka* policies were being adjusted. And it was not only the ethnological research of Kanaseki Takeo and his colleagues that came into being in the historical context that produced the second Konoe cabinet and the governor-generalship of Hasegawa Kiyoshi. Even in the realm of literature and drama, ambiguous phenomena were also quite evident. [50] *Minzoku Taiwan* did indeed develop the concept of "East Asian ethnology," and of the major figures responsible for the journal, Kanaseki Takeo's promotion of this idea was most clear and certain. Furthermore, this concept of "East Asian ethnology" had its own particular national policy and wartime context.

If *Minzoku Taiwan* was able to publish by taking advantage of policy changes, then it was also possible that it would move in accordance with the changes made to those policies. In another of his articles, Kawamura Minato has articulated even further criticisms of this inherent nature of *Minzoku Taiwan*, whereby it "came all together with the birth," and would ultimately float or sink in accordance with the wartime situation. In essence, then, all Japanese scholars who taught in imperial universities in outlying territories before the end of the war manifest some "colonialist" tendencies. Therefore, that these ethnologists and anthropologists follow "colonial policies" is not just related to a scholar's own inherent qualities or personality but rather is caused by the "original sin" of "colonialism" that is necessarily manifested in these kinds of "modern knowledge" such as ethnology or folklore studies. [51] Since Kawamura Minato has taken such a superior position, then according to *his* terms, *Minzoku Taiwan* must therefore be reassessed as a component of "Great East Asian ethnology."

NOTES

*Translated by Douglas Fix, Reed College.

1. Kawamura Minato 川村湊, *"Dai Toa minzokugaku" no kyojitsu* 「大東亜民俗学」の虚実 (Tokyo: Kodansha, 1996), 9–10.

2. Kawamura, *"Dai Tōa minzokugaku" no kyojitsu*, 10.

3. In recent years, the more important work in the field of Yanagita Kunio ethnological studies is the following: Murai Osamu 村井紀, *Nantō ideorogi no hassei: Yanagita Kunio to shokuminchi shugi* 南島イデオロギーの発生 (Tokyo: Ota Shuppan, 1995).

4. Before the war Kokubu 國分 had taught at Tainan Girls Middle School 台南女子中學 and at Taihoku Normal School 台北師範學校. In the years immediately following the end

of the war, Kokubu was retained as a professor at Taiwan University. He has conducted important pioneering research in the fields of Taiwanese ethnology and archaeology.

5. Kokubu Naoichi 國分直一, "*Minzoku Taiwan* no undō wa nande atta ka 民俗台灣 の 運動はなんであったか?" *Sinica* 8.2 (February 1997): 122–127.

6. Kokubu Naoichi, a younger scholar with a lectureship in native ethnology in the History Department at Taihoku Imperial University and a very close associate of Professor Kanaseki Takeo before the war—also an important writer for *Minzoku Taiwan*—had remained for a short period of time, specifically as a retained professor, at this university after the end of World War II.

7. "Taiwan minsu yanjiu de huigu (Kanaseki Takeo boshi huanying zuotanhui) 台灣民俗 研究的回顧 (金關丈夫博士歡迎座談會)," *Taipei Wenwu* 10.1 (March 1963): 60.

8. "Dangqian Taiwan xiangtu yanjiu de fangxiang 當前台灣鄉土研究的方向," *Taiwan Fengwu* 17.1 (February 1967): 10–11.

9. Yang Yunping, "Kanaseki Takeo sensei no omoide 金關丈夫先生の思い出," *Esunosu* 21 (July 1983).

10. Ikeda Toshio, "Shokuminchika to minzoku zasshi 植民地時期の民俗雜誌," *Taiwan Kin Gendaishi Kenkyū* 4 (1982): 109–145.

11. Yang Yunping, "Ikeda Toshio xiansheng zhuidao ci 池田敏雄先生追悼辭," *Taiwan Fengwu* 31.2 (June 1981): 1.

12. Wang Shilang 王詩琅, "Taiwan minsuxue de kaituozhe Ikeda Toshio 台灣民俗學的 開拓者池田敏雄兄," *Taiwan Fengwu* 31.2 (June 1981): 6.

13. For example, Wang Zhaowen 王昭文, in his M.A. thesis, "Rizhi moqi Taiwan de zhishi shequn 日治末期台灣的知識社群 (1940–1945)—*Bungei Taiwan, Taiwan bungaku* ji *Minzoku Taiwan* san zazhi de lishi yanjiu 文藝台灣, 台灣文學, 民俗台灣 三雜誌的歷史 研究" (Qinghua University [Taiwan], 1991), argues that the topics of ethnology and history became issues of concern for Taiwanese intellectuals because they had wanted to avoid the fascist coercion and depression of war. At the same time, since discussion of history and ethnology was quite distant from reality, one could avoid the contemporary situation. Furthermore, they were worried that with the deepening of the wartime imperial subjectification movement, the folk customs and older traditions of Taiwan were threatened with extinction and thus they needed to document them for posterity. In contrast, Dai Wenfeng 戴文鋒, in his 1999 Ph.D. dissertation, "Taiwan ethnology and the issue of late colonial period folklore, with an analytical focus on *Minzoku Taiwan* 日治晚期的民俗議題與臺灣民俗學: 以 民俗 臺灣 為分析場域" (Chungcheng University, Graduate Institute of History), seems to replicate the views of those directly related with *Minzoku Taiwan*, i.e., that Kanaseki Takeo and Ikeda Toshio risked the dangers of wartime and its limited resources in order to hasten the delivery of an infant Taiwan ethnology. According to this view, Dr. Kanaseki created anthropology, archaeology, and historiography to give life to Taiwanese ethnology, while Ikeda was the "Manka 艋舺 authority" who took Taiwan as his new homeland; he paid particular attention to grassroots Taiwanese culture; he wore Taiwanese clothing, spoke Taiwanese, learned to sing Taiwan folk songs; and he even married a Taiwanese woman. This sufficiently demonstrated his deep love for the native life of Taiwan. In addition, Chen Yanhong 陳豔紅's "Japan and Taiwanese culture during the colonial period: Centering on *Minzoku Taiwan* 領 台時代的臺灣文化與日本—以 民俗臺灣 為中心" (Ph.D. dissertation, Graduate Institute of Japan Studies, Soochow University, 1997) provides the same type of assessment.

14. Kawamura Minato's harshest critic is probably Suzuki Mitsuo 鈴木満男; see Suzuki Mitsuo, *"Teikoku no chi" no soshitsu: Sengo Nihon saiko—Higashi Ajia no genchi kara* 帝國 の知 の喪失 (Tokyo: Tentensha, 1999), 317–323.

15. The reprint edition published by Nantian Shuju 南天書局 (SMC Publishing) in 1998 included issue 44, which was not able to be published during the war.

16. This "statement of intent" was only a single sheet, and at the time it was distributed everywhere. After being criticized by Yang Yunping at the end of May, Kanaseki Takeo compiled this "statement of intent" and the articles from both sides in the pen war and published them in volume 1, numbers 2 and 3 of *Minzoku Taiwan* (August and September 1941).

17. "Zadankai: Yanagita Kunio o kakomite: Dai Tōa minzokugaku no kenssetsu to *Minzoku Taiwan* no shimei 座談會 柳田國男を圍みて－大東亞民俗學の建設と民俗台灣の使命," *Minzoku Taiwan* 3.12 (December 1943): 9–10.

18. Ikeda, "Shokuminchika no minzoku zasshi," 122.

19. "Zadankai: Hōkō undō to Taiwan no minzoku Kenkyū 座談會 奉公運動と台灣の民俗研究," *Minzoku Taiwan* 4.9 (September 1944): 18.

20. Ikeda, "Shokuminchika no minzoku zasshi," 141–142.

21. "Zadankai," 9.

22. "Zadankai," 11.

23. For a clear and concise description of the content of the *kōminka* movement, see Washinosu Atsuya, *Taiwan Hōkō kōminka tokuhon* (Taihoku: Taiwan Keisatsu Kyokai, 1941).

24. Assessments of the effects of the *kōminka* movement seem to vary with each individual author. Currently, research that has paid particular attention to the ways in which Taiwanese responded to the policies of the colonial government include: Chou Wan-yao 周婉窈, "Cong bijiao de guandian kan Taiwan yu Hanguo de huangminhua yundong 從比較的觀點看台灣與韓國的皇民化運動 (1937–1945)," *Xin shixue* 5.2 (June 1944) and Cai Jintang 蔡錦堂, "Riju moqi Taiwanren zongjiao xinyang zhi bianqian: Yi 'zhengting gaishan yundong' wei zhongxin 日據末期台灣人宗教信仰之變遷－以 正廳改善運動 為中心," *Si Yu Yan* 29.2 (December 1991).

25. Sakai Saburo 酒井三郎, *Shōwa Kenkyūkai: Aru chishikijin shūdan no kiseki* 昭和研究會－ある知識人集團の軌跡 (Tokyo: Kodansha, 1985), 155–156.

26. Sakai, *Shōwa Kenkyûkai*, 156–158.

27. Sakai, *Shōwa Kenkyûkai*, 220.

28. "Chihō bunka shin kensetsu no kompon rinen oyobi tōmen no kadai 地方文化新建設 の根本理念及び當面の課題," in *Shiryō Nihon gendaishi* 13: *Taiheiyō Sensō ka no kokumin seikatsu*, ed. Akazawa Shiro, Kitagawa Kenzo, Yui Masaomi (Tokyo: Otsuki Shoten, 1985), 248–250.

29. Kitagawa Kenzo, "Senjika no chihō bunka undō: Hoppō bunka renmei o chūshin to shite 戰時下の地方文化運動－北方文化聯盟を中心に," in *Bunka to fashizumu: Senjiki Nihon ni okeru bunka no kobo*, ed. Akazawa Shiro, Kitagawa Kenzo (Tokyo: Nihon Keizai Hyoronsha, 1993), 210–211.

30. Kitagawa Kenzo, "Senjika no bunga undō 戰時下の文化運動," *Rekishi horon* (January 1989): 57.

31. Later it was given the formal name of "Association to Promote the Public Service of Imperial Subjects" (*Kōmin hōkōkai* 皇民奉公會).

32. Though the table of contents for this issue gave the title "Special issue to reconsider

kōminka," the title given at the beginning of the main article was "The guiding spirit for *kōminka*."

33. Nakamura Akira 中村哲, "Bunka seisaku to shite no kōminka mondai 文化政策とし ての皇民化問題," *Taiwan jihō* (January 1941), 6–12.

34. For a concise description of Nakamura Akira's activities during his years at Taihoku Teikoku Daigaku 台北帝國大學, see "Nakamura sensei o kakomite," *Okinawa bunka kenkyû* 16 (1990). In addition, in 1997, accompanied by Professor Hika Minoru 比嘉實 (Okinawa Research Center, Hosei University), I visited Professor Nakamura at his home, and at that time, Professor Nakamura said that during the war he frequently had to travel between Taihoku and Tokyo because he was helping Professor Yabe 矢部 with his work.

35. *Taiwan jihō* (January 1941), 24–29.

36. Yang Yunping, "Kenkyū to ai 研究と愛," *Taiwan nichinichi shinpō* (May 29, 1941). Kanaseki Takeo later included this article and his own written response together in *Minzoku Taiwan* 1.2 (August 1941).

37. In "Taida to Taiwan Kenkyū 台大と台灣研究," published in *Taiwan nichinichi shinpō* (February 15–17, 1939), Yang Yunping criticized Taihoku Teikoku Daigaku for not conducting research on Taiwan; he strongly promoted establishing a chair in "Taiwan history," "Taiwan literature," and "Xiamen language 廈門語" at the colony's imperial university.

38. "Randan 亂彈," *Minzoku Taiwan* 1.1 (July 1941): 32.

39. "Randan," 33.

40. "Henshū kōki 編輯後記," *Minzoku Taiwan* 1.1 (July 1941): 48.

41. Cao Mingzong 曹銘宗, *Zixue dianfan: Taiwanshi yanjiu xianqu Cao Yonghe* 自學典 範一臺灣史研究先驅曹永和 (Taipei: Lianjing, 1999), 53–56.

42. Tateishi Tetsuomi 立石鐵臣, "Shirin no getsu 士林の月," *Minzoku Taiwan* 1.6 (December 1941): 26–27.

43. For information on Wu Xinrong 吳新榮 and the local politics of the Beimen 北門 and Jiali 佳里 area, see Wu Xinrong, *Wu Xinrong huiyilu* 吳新榮回憶錄, ed. Lin Hengzhe et al. (Taipei: Qianwei, 1989) or Kondo Masami 近藤正己, *Soryokusen to Taiwan: Nihon shokuminchi hōkai no Kenkyū* 總力戰と台灣一日本植民地崩壞の研究 (Tokyo: Tosui Shobo, 1996).

44. See the editor's comments for issue 2.7.

45. *Minzoku Taiwan* 2.7 (July 1942): 46.

46. T.K., "Henshu koki," *Minzoku Taiwan* 2.10 (October 1942): 48.

47. The international collective investigation designed under the auspices of celebrating Yanagita Kunio 柳田國男's seventieth birthday had begun to be planned in 1943. The introductory comments in volume 4, issue 4 (April 1944) of *Minzoku Taiwan* included an article entitled "Making plans for the construction of the items for folklore collection and investigation," and the fifth issue of that volume listed the specific items that were to be collectively investigated.

48. "Gaichi bunka no shomondai, Yokusankai Bunkabucho Kishida shi: to no Ichimon itto 外地文化の諸問題一翼贊會文化部長岸田氏との一問一答," *Taiwan nichinichi shinpō* (August 28, 1941).

49. *Hasegawa Kiyoshi den* 長谷川清傳, compiled by Hasegawa Kiyoshiden Kankokai (Tokyo: Hasegawa Kiyoshiden Kankokai, 1972), 128.

50. For information on the vibrant activities of drama and literary circles in Taiwan dur-

ing this period, see the following: Liu Shuqin 柳書琴, "Zhanzheng yu wentan: Riju moqi Taiwan de wenxue huodong 戰爭與文壇—日據末期台灣的文學活動" (M.A. thesis, Graduate Institute of History, Taiwan University, 1994); Liu Shuqin, "Sensō to bundan: Rokokyō jihen go no Taiwan bungaku katsudō no fukkō 戰爭と文壇—蘆溝橋事變後の台灣文學活動の 復興," in *Yomigaeru Taiwan bungaku: Nihon tochiki no sakka to sakuhin*, ed. Shimomura Sakujiro et al. (Tokyo: Toho Shoten, 1995); and Shi Wanshun 石婉舜, "1943-nian Taiwan 'Housheng Yanju Yanjiuhui' yanjiu 九四三年台灣厚生演劇研究會 研究" (M.A. thesis, Drama Department, Taiwan University, 2002).

51. Kawamura Minato, "Shokuminchi shugi to minzokugaku / minzokugaku 植民地主義と民俗學/民族學," in *Minzokugaku ga wakaru*, AERA Mook 32 (Tokyo: Asahi Shinbunsha, 1997), 139.

NOTES ON CONTRIBUTORS

Douglas L. Fix is professor of history and humanities at Reed College.

Fong Shiaw-Chian is professor of sociology in the Department of Journalism, National Chengchi University, and author of *The Search for Identity in Colonial Taiwan: A Narrative Analysis* (in Chinese).

Fujii Shōzō is professor of modern Chinese literature in the Department of Chinese Language and Literature at Tokyo University. His areas of specialization include Japanese literature in Taiwan under Japanese rule, and modern Chinese literature.

Huang Ying-che is professor of modern Chinese studies at Aichi University. His areas of specialization include modern Taiwanese history and Taiwanese literature.

Huang Mei-er is associate professor of Taiwanese literature in the Department of Chinese Literature, Chengchi University. Her areas of specialization include traditional Taiwanese literature under the Ching dynasty and Japanese rule in Taiwan.

Kawahara Isao is one of the editors of the *Taiwanese Literature Anthology* (in Japanese); his research involved Taiwanese literature and censorship in the Japanese period.

Faye Yuan Kleeman is associate professor of East Asian languages and civilizations at the University of Colorado, and author of *Under an Imperial Sun: Japanese Colonial Literature of Taiwan and the South*. Her areas of specialization include Japanese colonial literature, comparative literature, and the culture of Taiwan and Japan.

Komagome Takeshi is assistant professor in the Faculty of Education, Kyoto University, and author of *The Cultural Unification of the Japanese Colonial Empire*.

Liao Ping-hui is professor of general literature at National Tsing Hua University and author of *Guanjianzi 200* (Keywords in Literary and Critical Studies).

Peng Hsiao-yen is research fellow at the Institute of Chinese Literature and Philosophy, Academia Sinica, Taiwan, and author of *Haishang Shuo Qingyu: cong Zhang Ziping dao Liu Na'ou* [Desire in Shanghai: From Zhang Ziping to Liu Na'ou].

Shimomura Sakujirō is professor at Tenri University. His areas of specialization include Taiwanese literature.

Tarumi Chie is professor of Japanese at the International Student Center, Yokohama National University, and author of *Japanese Literature in Taiwan*.

Ts'ai Hui-yu Caroline is associate research fellow at the Institute of Taiwanese History, Academia Sinica, Taiwan. Her areas of specialization include Taiwanese history under Japanese colonization and modern Chinese social and economic history.

Wakabayashi Masahiro is professor of Asian-Pacific area studies in the Department of Area Studies at Tokyo University. His areas of specialization include the political history of Taiwan in modern times and the contemporary politics of Taiwan.

Wu Mi-cha is professor of history at National Taiwan University, and author of *A History of Taiwan in Comics of Ancient Times: Austronesian Origins*.

Yao Jen-to is an assistant professor in the Graduate Institute of Sociology at National Tsing Hua University in Taiwan, where he teaches political sociology, historical sociology, and Foucault studies.

Yen Chuan-ying is research fellow at the Institute of History and Philology, Academia Sinica, Taiwan, and author of *Landscape Moods: Selected Readings in Modern Taiwanese Art*.

INDEX

Abe Shigetaka, 152–56

aborigines, Taiwanese (*Takasago zoku*), 7, 13, 64, 290–92, 293n7; education of, 82; folklore of, 237, 302–3; land rights of, 51, 66; languages of, 4, 83, 320; military conscription of, 290–91; and missionaries, 83; Musha uprising by, 9–10; studies of, 57, 79, 251–52, 303; subjugation of, 4–5, 26, 27, 250–52; and Taiwanese identity, 170. See also *The Bell of Sayon*

acculturation. *See* assimilation

activism (*kōdō shugi*), 229–30

Africa, 38

agriculture, 9, 45, 303, 322; and folklore studies, 301–2; Japanese, 110; and KMT takeover, 313; and local administration, 112; modernization of, 166–67, 180n7; and postsurrender violence, 343, 344, 345, 355

Agriculture and Forest, Ministry of (Japan), 110

Ahen (Opium; Nishikawa Mitsuru), 304

Akashi Motojirō, 8, 92

Akiba Takashi, 302

Akiyama coal mines, 268

Akiyama Giichi, 268

Alliance for the Acculturation of Taiwan (*Taiwan kyōka rengōkai*), 133

Allied Occupation, 111

Amaterasu (sun goddess), 173–74, 177, 179, 365

The Ambassadors (painting; Holbein), 88

anamorphosis, 88, 90, 91–93

ancestor worship, 167, 171, 273, 382; *vs.* assimilation, 169, 176, 364; and fengshui, 264, 268

Anderson, Benedict, 2, 11, 55, 63, 71, 78; on media, 88, 90, 92

Annals of the Three Kingdoms, 193

anthropology. *See* ethnology

anti-Japanese sentiment, 83, 211–12, 213, 234; and Lim Bo-seng, 144, 148; in literature, 73, 188; and New-Old Literatures Debate, 206, 207, 208n5; and postsurrender violence, 347, 348. *See also* resistance

"Ant's work" (*Ari ippiki no shigoto*; Yang Kui), 232–33
Aoyama College (Tokyo), 210–11
Appadurai, Arjun, 38–39, 44–45, 51
"Appreciating the Landscape of the Taiwan Region" (Ishikawa Kinichirō), 248
architecture, 265, 267, 304
arts, 5–6, 8, 11, 12–13; associations for, 9, 249; and colonial government, 248, 251; exhibitions of, 250, 256, 258–59; folk, 296, 372; and journals, 137, 138, 199, 203, 298–99; and politics, 225
Asahi Shinbun, 290
Asayoshi Hakusei, 280
Asia, 1, 254, 256. *See also* Greater East Asia Co-Prosperity Sphere; *particular countries*
assimilation, 2, 8, 11, 181n15; and class, 175–78; cultural, 12, 148–51, 167, 169, 363–68; economic, 70, 322; and education, 71, 148–51, 154–55, 156, 157; and emperor, 168–69, 177; and identity, 63, 75, 212–13, 365; intentional, 62–64; limited, 178; linguistic (*kokugo katei*), 70, 81, 126, 132, 134, 168, 173–75, 177, 179, 180n10, 281, 282; and literature, 70–71, 266; and mobilization, 109, 369; and nationalism, 154, 166–73, 178–79; and newspapers, 12, 14, 81, 122–40, 202, 312, 314–15, 368; religious, 168, 169, 173–74, 176, 177, 178, 179, 364, 365; *vs.* tradition, 167–68, 197. *See also* Chinese language; Japanese language; Japanization; *kōmin bungaku*; *kōminka*
Australia, 382
Avicenna, S., 78

Baber, Zaheer, 57
"bamboo branch" (*zhuzhi ci*) structure, 201, 207
bandits, 163–64, 165, 178, 179n2, 180n3. *See also* crime; violence
Barclay, George W., 41, 52–53, 54
Barclay, Paul, 303
Barclay, Thomas, 143
Baudelaire, Charles, 210, 213, 214–17, 218, 220, 238

Beijing huawen/Taiwan huawen (Beijing vernacular/Taiwanese vernacular) debate, 235–37
Beijing School, 223
The Bell of Sayon (*Shayang de zhong*; Wu Man-sha), 137, 279–93; and Murakami's play, 283–85, 286–87, 288, 290
Benjamin, Walter, 78, 82
Bhabha, Homi, 56
Bible, 83
Book of Songs (*Shijing*), 190, 200
The Book of the Alert Heart (*Jingxinpian*), 166
botany, 57, 78–79
Bourdieu, Pierre, 212, 215
bourgeoisie, 220, 229, 295; and dandyism, 225–26; and popular taste, 223–24; Taiwanese native landed, 23–30
Boxer Rebellion (China; 1900), 249
Braibanti, Ralph, 118n27
Brown, Melissa, 2, 10
Buddhism, 165–66, 169
Budget Committee (Japanese Lower House), 123–26, 128
Bunten (Ministry of Education art exhibition), 250
bundan (literary circles), 263, 269, 270–72, 273
Bungakkai (journal), 301
Bungaku hyōron (journal), 262
Bungakuza (theater group), 266
"Bungei hihyō no hyōjun" (The criteria of art criticism; Yang Kui), 230
Bungei Taiwan (Literary Taiwan; journal), 139, 231, 267, 270–72, 291, 298; and Nishikawa Mitsuru, 296, 299, 300, 308n7; and *Taiwan bungaku*, 263, 264
buraku (hamlets, natural villages), 105, 106–7, 108, 109, 110, 111, 115, 117n19
buraku shinkōkai (sub-village revival associations), 111–12
burakumin (hamlet people), 102, 104
bureaucracy, 12, 40, 97–118, 131, 160, 165, 351; and banning of Chinese, 126; civil *vs.* military, 22–23, 91, 92, 99, 129, 252; education, 126, 127, 181n15; extra-, 98–

312; newspapers published in, 84, 85, 91;
and Nishikawa Mitsuru, 296, 297, 298,
299; and Okinawa, 91; politics in, 20–23,
88, 91–92, 123–26, 129–30, 375; public
opinion in, 133; religion of, 130, 173–74,
177, 178, 179, 289, 364, 365, 377; rural revival movement in, 108, 109; students in,
5, 211, 212; Taiwan studies in, 11; Taiwanese attitudes towards, 2–3; and Taiwanese
identity, 2, 5, 10, 178, 213; Taiwanese
students in, 144, 147, 148, 178, 210–11,
319, 379; theater in, 288; tourism in, 295;
Western-style painting in, 258; women
in, 110. *See also* emperor, Japanese; government, Japanese central; government,
Japanese colonial; Sino-Japanese War

Japanese language: and assimilation, 62, 109,
130, 168, 173–75, 177, 179, 281; banning
of, 74, 318–21; and banning of Chinese,
124–25, 138; and *The Bell of Sayon*, 285;
and Chinese, 187, 197, 200, 236; in education, 67, 70–74, 139n1, 146, 147, 149; and
enslavement, 314, 317–20; and ethnology,
359, 377, 380; everyday use of, 127, 128,
133; Japanese national system of, 11; and
kōminka, 368, 373, 374; literacy in, 70,
71, 72, 90, 123, 139n1; literature in, 222;
and name-changing movement, 175; in
newspapers, 73, 83, 90, 319–20; official,
63; as official language, 63, 75, 82; reading
market for, 63, 70; in schools, 318–19; and
Taiwanese, 2; and Taiwanese culture, 307,
320; and Taiwanese dialect, 202; Taiwanese literature in, 73, 139, 240; and Yang
Kui, 233–34, 237, 240

Japanese language families (*kokugo jōyō
katei*), 133, 178

Japanese people: ethnographers, 360–61;
intellectuals, 10, 295; and local culture
movement, 378; and national identity, 172–73; and new culture, 146–47;
postsurrender violence against, 343;
in schools, 82; and Taiwanese people,
360–61

Japanese Proletariat Writers' League
(NALP), 269

Japanese Romanticists/People's Literature
(Nihon rōmanha/Jinminbunko) debate,
231, 269, 270, 271, 273

Japanism (*nihonshugi*), 269

Japanization, 2, 15n2, 312–26; as enslavement, 314–20, 321, 323–24; and language,
197, 317–20; and New-Old Literatures
Debate, 206, 207; *vs.* re-sinification,
13–14, 314–20; and Sino-Japanese War
(1937), 312, 319, 364; of Taiwanese elites,
12, 176–78; and Westernization, 320,
322, 324. *See also* assimilation; *kōminka*
(imperial subjectification) movement

Jiang Kanghu, 199

Jiang Weishui, 169–71, 172, 173

Jiboyin poetry reading societies, 189–90, 192,
198

Jinminbunko, 269, 270, 271, 272, 273

Jitsugyo no Taiwan (newspaper), 84

"Jiyū rōdōsha no seikatsu danmen" (Profile
of a free laborer's life; Yang Kui), 232–33

journals, literary, 70, 71–72, 91, 263; and the
arts, 137, 138, 199, 203, 298–99; banning
of Chinese in, 135–36; censorship of, 135,
137–38; Chinese language in, 72, 135;
and modernization, 93; and New-Old
Literatures Debate, 203; and Nishikawa
Mitsuru, 296, 300; popular, 211; and reading market, 63. See also *Bungei Taiwan*;
Minzoku Taiwan; *Taiwan bungaku*

Journey to the West (*Xiyouji*), 193

*Junjō monogatari aikoku otome: Sayon no
kane* (Nagao Kazuo), 280

Kaizō (journal), 70, 298

Kamiizumi Hidenobu, 371

Kanaseki Takeo, 267, 358, 360–68, 375,
376–77, 379; and Greater East Asian
ethnology, 380, 381, 382, 383

Kanbun Taiwan nichinichi shinpō (Taiwan
daily news; Chinese language newspaper), 84, 87. See also *Taiwan nichinichi
shinpō*

Kandel, I.L., 152, 154–55, 156, 157

Kangxi, Emperor (China), 4

Kaohsiung prefecture, 85, 103, 112, 128; post-